HEBREW-ENGLISH
LEXICON

COMPANION TEXTS FOR
OLD TESTAMENT STUDIES

A Concordance of the Septuagint (Morrish)
A Grammar of Septuagint Greek (Conybeare and Stock)
A Hebrew-English Lexicon (Osburn)
A Reader's Hebrew-English Lexicon of the Old Testament (Armstrong, Busby, and Carr)
Do It Yourself Hebrew and Greek (Goodrick)
The Analytical Hebrew-Chaldee Lexicon (Davidson)
The Englishman's Hebrew and Chaldee Concordance of the Old Testament (Wigram)
The Hebrew-English Old Testament (Lee)
The Hebrew Old Testament Slidaverb Conjugation Chart (Peterson and Barker)
The Interlineary Hebrew-English Psalter
The NIV Interlinear Hebrew-English Old Testament (Kohlenberger)
The NIV Triglot Old Testament (Kohlenberger)
The Septuagint: Greek and English (Brenton)
The Septuagint With Apocrypha: Greek and English (Brenton)

HEBREW-ENGLISH LEXICON

CONTAINING

ALL THE HEBREW AND CHALDEE WORDS
IN THE OLD TESTAMENT SCRIPTURES,
WITH THEIR MEANINGS IN ENGLISH

by
William Osburn, Jr.

ZONDERVAN
PUBLISHING HOUSE
OF THE ZONDERVAN CORPORATION
GRAND RAPIDS, MICHIGAN 49506

Originally published by
SAMUEL BAGSTER & SONS, LONDON, 1844;
another edition, 1882

This edition 1981

Library of Congress Catalog Card Number: 72-106438
ISBN 0-310-20361-9

Printed in the United States of America

PREFACE

THE best modern authorities have been consulted in the preparation of the present work; and we have endeavoured to give the results of their researches in as condensed and convenient a form for reference as possible.

The arrangement is that of Leopold's "Lexicon Manuale," which is itself taken altogether from the larger lexicons of Gesenius and Winer.

The valuable analytical Index which Leopold, from the same authorities, prints separately as an appendix, we have incorporated with the lexicon itself, in alphabetical order; thus making, it is hoped, a useful addition to his already copious collection of references.

To economise the student's time as far as possible, the meaning in English accompanies the reference wherever it has been found practicable to express it by a single word; in the hope of combining, in some degree, the advantages of the alphabetical with those of the radical arrangement, upon which the lexicon of Leopold is formed.

All fictitious roots have been discarded: i. e. words

occurring in no language, but which ought to be the roots whence certain Hebrew nouns have been derived, according to the analogy of the Hebrew grammar.

We are well aware of the advantage which these invented words afford to the arrangement under roots; but it is obvious, nevertheless, that nothing of this nature can compensate for the evil which arises from the presentation of a falsity to the mind of a beginner. The only words not occurring in the Bible which will be found in this lexicon are roots from the cognate languages, bearing a fair similarity of meaning to the Hebrew compounds which are arranged with them. In the many cases in which no such resemblance is to be found, the simplest form of the Hebrew compound has been printed in the larger character by which radical words are denoted.

The proper names are arranged as Leopold has given them, under the roots whence, according to the analogy of the Hebrew grammar, they would appear to be derived. This, however, is merely for the convenience of finding them in the lexicon. The derivations which he has added have been all but invariably discarded. A high authority in Hebrew lexicography having questioned the necessity, or even propriety, of inserting the proper names in the lexicon at all, it is right to explain that they have been retained in order to relieve the beginner in Hebrew from the necessity of resorting to the very expedient whereby that author proposes to dispense with them, namely, by referring him to an approved version. The compiler of the present work has found a frequent appeal to translations to interfere so fatally with his own progress in the acquisition of a language, that he has felt it his duty to bestow much care and pains upon them, making many additions to Leopold, so as to put the student in possession of the whole of the proper names that occur in the Hebrew Bible, even though in so many instances no better account of them can be given, than that they are names of persons or places.

As to the meanings (which form of course the really important part of the work), but very little use has been made of the Latin renderings of Leopold, which are only of any value when they repeat those of the authors upon whose labours his lexicon is founded. Leopold's authorities themselves, as well as others, to whose works he had probably no access, have been consulted upon every word. The concordance of Noldius and Fürst have also been appealed to in all cases of difficulty arising from variations of opinion among the authorities consulted; and thus from the passages themselves it has been endeavoured to form a judgment of the words which best expressed the sense of the sacred text. For this purpose, the racy idiomatic English of Professor Lee's renderings has been freely taken advantage of; this obligation to him is thankfully acknowledged.

The lexicon is specially designed to put into the hands of the English student, in a compressed and compendious form, the contributions of modern philology to the interpretation of the Hebrew Scriptures. There are many words the meaning of which the researches of the learned have not succeeded hitherto in elucidating. In such cases it has been deemed the best course to give the rendering in the Authorised English Version only. The speculations which may have been indulged in by interpreters, ancient or modern, as to their meaning, are of little value in themselves, while to the beginner they are worse than worthless; they are moreover known to the proficient, and the student will readily find them in the larger lexicons. We give a single instance. The word אַבְרֵךְ Gen. 41:43 is rendered by our translators "bow the knee," assuming it to be an anomalous Hiphil form of the denominative from בֶּרֶךְ "knee." This, though somewhat forced, is at any rate more feasible than the modern interpretation, which, assuming with considerable probability that it is an Egyptian word or phrase, declares that it is equivalent to ⲁⲡⲉⲣⲉⲕ, which is to be translated "bow the head." Such however is by no means the case. The general meaning of the word ⲁⲡⲉ or ⲁⲫⲉ is "the top or summit of a thing." It does not appear to be used of the head at all in the Coptic Bible, but rather of the crown or scalp. The Egyptian word for the head, as a member of the body, is ϫⲱ. The word ⲣⲉⲕ means "to bow," but the construction of the supposed phrase is althogether foreign to the idiom of the language. Nor does it appear in any degree probable from the remains of it, which are very copious, that ⲁⲡⲉⲣⲉⲕ or ⲁⲫⲉⲣⲉⲕ would be a more intelligible direction to an Egyptian to bow the head than "crown bow" would be to an Englishman. The phrase repeatedly occurs in the Coptic Bible, and is written **ⲡⲉⲕϫⲱ.** It is to be regretted that biblical difficulties are too often dealt with in this loose unsatisfactory manner.

In the English meanings throughout, it has been endeavoured to counteract the blasphemous attempt of one of the great modern schools of sacred hermeneutics to vulgarise and debase the word of God by quaint and burlesque interpretations. On the other hand, it has been deemed expedient to avoid the equally fallacious principle of another class of interpreters, who elevate into authoritative glosses the renderings of writers confessedly ignorant of Hebrew, for no better reason than that they wrote some twelve or fifteen centuries ago.

We have striven to give the student the benefit of the labours of both schools, without leading him into the errors of either.

It is only needful further to explain that wherever a word or meaning is accompanied by one, or in some instances by two references, it is denoted that such word or meaning occurs in those places only in the Hebrew Bible.

ABBREVIATIONS OF GRAMMATICAL TERMS
USED IN THE LEXICON

m.	masculine	Niph.	Niphal form of verb
f.	feminine	Hiph.	Hiphil form of verb
s.	substantive	Hith.	Hithpael form of verb
pa.	particle		
part.	participle	Pi.	Piel form of verb
denom.	denominative; that is, a verb derived immediately from a noun (*de nomine*)	Pu.	Pual form of verb
		Po.	Poel *or* Polel form of verb
patron.	patronymic: a proper name derived from that of the father of the individual	Hoth.	Hothpael form of verb
		Ith.	Ithpael form of verb
		imp.	imperative mood
sing.	singular	const.	construct state of noun
pl.	plural	emph.	emphatic state of noun

HEBREW-ENGLISH
LEXICON

LEXICON.

אב

אָב m (const. אֲבִי and אַב, Gen. 17:4, 5; with suff אָבִי, אָבִיךָ, אֲבִיכֶם; pl. אָבוֹת).—I. *a father.*—II. *a progenitor, ancestor;* used generally for any senior male relative.—III. *an originator, inventor,* Gen. 10:21, &c.—IV. *a head, chief,* or *ruler;* applied to kings, prophets, priests, &c.; אָב לְפַרְעֹה *a father,* that is, *a counsellor* to Pharaoh, Gen. 45:8.

אַב m. Ch. (with suff. אֲבוּךְ, אֲבִי, אֲבוּהִי, pl. אֲבָהָן), *a father.*

אָבַב not used.

אֵב m., *greenness, freshness,* אִבִּים *green herbs.*

אֵב m., Ch. *fruit;* אִנְבֵּהּ for אִבָּהּ, *his fruit.*

אָבִיב m.—I. *a green ear of corn,* Lev. 2:14.—II. *shooting into the ear,* spoken of barley, Ex. 9:31. Hence חֹדֶשׁ הָאָבִיב *the month Abib,* the name of the month in which the barley shoots into ear, corresponding partly with our March, partly with April, otherwise called נִיסָן.

אֲבַגְתָא p.n., one of the chamberlains of King Ahasuerus, Est. 1:10.

אבה

אָבַד (inf. אֲבֹד, אָבַד, fut. יֹאבַד and יֹאבֵד).=—I. *strayed, lost.*—II. *was ruined, perished* (const. with לְ or מִן); part. אֹבֵד *one about to perish, a wretch;* Pi. אִבַּד, and Hiph. הֶאֱבִיד *made to stray, dispersed, laid waste, ruined, destroyed.*

אֲבַד Ch. (fut. יֵאבַד), *perished;* Aph. הוֹבַד *destroyed;* Hoph. הוּבַד *was destroyed.*

אֹבֵד m., *perishing, ruin.*

אֲבֵדָה f., *something lost, the grave·* see following word.

אֲבַדּוֹן *extermination, destruction, the grave,* the place where the body decays after death, opposed to שְׁאוֹל the place of the soul after death, Pro. 15:11, &c.; see the word.

וָאֲבַדְךָ (וַאֲאַבֶּדְךָ, אַבֶּדְךָ for אֲאַבֶּדְךָ), Pi. fut. with suff.

אַבְדָן m., *extermination, ruin,* Est. 9:5; אָבְדָן the same, Est. 8:6.

אָבָה (fut. יֹאבֶה), in Kal only, *desirous, willing;* const. mostly with the neg. לֹא and with or without לְ.

אֵבֶה m., *a reed, rush;* אֳנִיּוֹת אֵבֶה *vessels made of reeds,* Job 9:26

אבו

2

אבי

אָבוּא for אָבוּ pret. pl.

אֶבְיוֹן m., *wishing, desiring*; hence, *destitute, poor, miserable*.

אֲבִיּוֹנָה f., *desire*, Eccl. 12:5.

אֲבוֹי (lit. *misery*), *alas!* Pro. 23:29.

אָבוֹשׁ fut.; see בּוֹשׁ.

אַבְחַת חֶרֶב ; .f אֲבָחָה ,אֶבַח, *the resting, descent of the sword*; according to others, *the threatening of the sword*, or, *the drawn sword*. Ezek. 21:20.

אֲבַטִּחִים m. pl., *melons*, Nu. 11:5; see מבח.

אָבִי for אָבִיא Hiph. fut. 1 pers.; see בּוֹא, 1 Ki. 21:29; Mic. 1:15.

אֲבִי (*my father*), p. n., the mother of King Hezekiah, 2 Kings 18:2.

אֲבִידָה for אֲאַבִּידָה Hiph. fut. 1 pers.; see אבד.

אֲבִיאֵל (*the divine Father*), p. n.—I. the grandfather of Saul, 1 Sa. 9:1.—II. one of David's generals.

אֲבִיאָסָף ,אֶבְיָסָף (*father of gathering, collector*), p. n., one of the Korahites.

אֲבִינֹעַל ,אֲבִיגַיִל (*she whose father rejoiceth*, or, *the dancer*), p. n.—I. the wife of Nabal, afterwards of David.—II. the sister of David, 1 Chron. 2:16.

אֲבִידָן (*the father of judgment, the judge*) p. n., one of the princes of Benjamin, Nu. 1:11, &c.

אֲבִיָּהוּ ,אֲבִיָּה (*he whose father is Jehovah*), see אָבִים ; p. n.—I. of a man. —II. of a woman

אֲבִיהוּא p. n., a son of Aaron.

אֲבִיהוּד (*the father of glory*, πατροκλος), p. n. of a man

אֲבִיחַיִל (*the father of artifices, he who is skilful*), p. n. of a man.

אֲבִיחַיִל (the same), p. n. of a woman.

אֲבִיטוּב (*father of goodness*), p. n. of a man.

אֲבִיטַל (*father of dew, vigorous*), p. n., a wife of David.

אֲבִיָּם (*the sailor*), p. n. of a man; the same as אֲבִיָּהוּ, and probably an error of some transcriber.

אֲבִימָאֵל p. n. of a man.

אֲבִימֶלֶךְ (*father of a king*), p. n.—I. a king of the Philistines, Gen. c. 20, perhaps the common name of the kings of that country.—II. name of a man, Jud. 8:31, &c.

אֲבִינָדָב (*father of willingness*), p. n. of a man.

אֲבִינֹעַם (*father of pleasantness*), p. n. of a man.

אֲבִינֵר ,אַבְנֵר (*father of light*), p. n., one of Saul's generals.

אֲבִיעֶזֶר (*father of help*), p. n. of a man.

אֲבִי־עַלְבוֹן m. (*violator*), p. n. of a man.

אַבִּיר ,אָבִיר *mighty*; see אבר.

אֲבִירָם m. (*father of pride, a proud one*), p. n. of a man.

אֲבִישַׁג f. p. n., one of David's concubines, 1 Kings 1:15, &c.

אֲבִישׁוּעַ (*father of salvation*), p. n. of a man.

אֲבִישׁוּר (*father of song, singer*), p. n. of a man, 1 Chron. 2:28.

אֲבִישַׁי ,אַבְשַׁי (*father of gifts, generous*), p. n. of a man.

אֲבִישָׁלוֹם (*father of peace*), the grandfather of Abijam king of Judah, 1 Kings 15:2.

אֶבְיָתָר (*a father of excellence, he who excels*), Abiathar, the son of Ahimelech, a high priest in David's time, 1 Sa. 22:20.

אָבַך Hith. only. יִתְאַבְּכוּ "they swell with a rolling motion like volumes of smoke," Isa. 9 : 17.

I. אָבַל (fut. יֶאֱבַל), *mourned, lamented;* const. with עַל; Hiph. הֶאֱבִיל *made* or *caused to mourn;* Hith. הִתְאַבֵּל *grieved, betook himself to mourn;* const. with אֶל or עַל.

אָבֵל m. (const. אֲבֶל-, אֲבֶל־; pl. אֲבֵלִים), אֲבֵלָה f. *mourning;* אֵבֶל m. (with suff. אֶבְלוֹ) the same, *grief, howling.* אֵבֶל מִצְרַיִם (the mourning of Egypt), p. n., a place beyond Jordan, where the children of Israel mourned for their father when they carried him forth to his burial, Gen. 50 : 11.

II. אָבֵל not used (Arab. *fresh, green, grass*).

אָבֵל *a grassy place, field;* hence the following names of places.—I. א' הַגְּדוֹלָה *the greater Abel,* a district of the Philistines, 1 Sa. 6 : 18.—II. א' בֵּית־מַעֲכָה a large city in the land of the tribe of Manasseh, called א' מַיִם, 2 Chron. 16 : 4.—III. א' הַשִּׁטִּים a place in the land of Moab. —IV. א' כְּרָמִים a village of the Ammonites.—V. א' מְחוֹלָה. a village in the land of Issachar; hence the appellation מְחֹלָתִי; see the word.

III. אֲבָל adv., *certainly, but, indeed.* אוּבָל, אֻבָל see יבל.

אֶבֶן f., I. *a stone, rock* (pl. אֲבָנִים, אַבְנֵי); לְאֶבֶן יָד like *a stone;* אֶבֶן יָד a stone which may be thrown with the hand; אַבְנֵי בָרָד (אֲבָנִים גְּדֹלוֹת) hail stones.—II. *precious stones, jewels;* אַבְנֵי־אֵשׁ *shining stones.*

—III. *a weight;* אֶבֶן וָאֶבֶן *divers weights.*—IV. *a plummet.*

אֶבֶן הָעֵזֶר (*stone of help*), p. n. of a place, 1 Sa. 7 : 12.

אֶבֶן הָאָזֶל (*stone of departure*), p. n. of a place.

אַבְנָא f. Ch. emph. state; *a stone.*

אֹבֶן m., dual אָבְנָיִם—I. "potter's wheel," Jer. 18 : 3.—II. "upon the stools," Ex. 1 : 16; Eng. Ver. The true meaning is uncertain.

אֲבָנָה p. n., a river of Damascus, 2 Ki. 5 : 12.

אַבְנֵט see בנט.

אַבְנֵר p. n. of a man; see אֲבִינֵר.

אָבָס, part. אָבוּס *fattened.*

אֵבוּס m. (pl. אֵבוּסִים) *a crib* or *stall* in which animals are fed; מַאֲבוּס m., *barn, granary,* Jer. 50 : 26.

אֲבַעְבֻּעוֹת *ulcers;* see בּוּעַ.

אָבֵץ p. n. of a city in the tribe of Issachar.

אִבְצָן (*he who is shining, famous*), p. n., a judge of Israel.

אָבָק m., *fine dust, powder;* אֲבָקָה f., אַבְקַת רוֹכֵל *aromatic dust, powdered perfume;* "powder of the merchant," Cant. 3 : 6, Eng. Ver.; נֶאֱבָק Niph. *wrestled* (because the ancient wrestlers covered their bodies with dust before they began to wrestle).

אָבַר Kal, not used, *was strong;* Hiph הֶאֱבִיר *flew, soared.*

אֵבֶר m., *quill, wing-feather.*

אֶבְרָה f., the same.

אַבִּיר, אָבִיר m.—I. *mighty* (an epithet of God).—II. *strong, valiant, noble,* אַבִּירִים *strong bulls,* or *horses;* אַבִּיר הָרֹעִים *the prince of the shepherds.*

אַבְרָם (*exalted father*), p. n., *Abram*;
אַבְרָהָם (*father of a multitude*), p. n., the patriarch *Abraham*.

אַבְרֵךְ Gen. 41:43, "bow the knee," Eng. Ver. The true meaning is uncertain.

אַבְרְכָה Pi. fut. with suff.; see ברך.

אֲבִשַׁי p.n., see אבישי.

אֲבִשָׁלוֹם (*father of peace*), p. n., *Absalom*, the son of David.

אֲגָא (*fugitive*), p. n. of a man.

הִנְאַלְתִּי Hith. pret. 1.pers. for אֶנְאַלְתִּי; see גאל.

אֲגַג p.n., a king of the Amalekites.

אֲגָגִי *Agagite*, a title of Haman, Est. 3:1.

אָגַד not used (Ch. and Arab. *bound in a mass*).

אֲגֻדָּה f.—I. *a bunch* or *bundle* (*of hyssop*).—II. *a band* or *body of men*; אֲגֻדָּתוֹ *his church, people*, Am. 9:6.—III. *knots, bindings*, Isa. 58:6.

אֱגוֹז m., *a nut*, Cant. 6:11.

אָגוּר (*companion*), p. n. of a woman.

אֲגוֹרָה *wages*; see אגר.

אָגַל not used (Arab. *gathered together, collected*).

אֶגֶל m., אֶגְלֵי טַל *drops of dew*, Job 38:28.

אֶגְלַיִם (*two fountains*), p. n., a village of the Moabites, Isa. 15:8.

אָגַם not used (Arab. *was hot*).

אֲגַם Ch., *was stagnant* (of water); see אגן.

אֲגַם m. (pl. אֲגַמִּים, אֲגַמֵּי).—I. *a pool, pond, marsh*.—II. *flags, reeds*.

אָגֵם m., *sorrowful*.

אַגְמוֹן m.—I. *a reed, rush.*—II. *a rope of rushes.*—III. *a cauldron, kettle,*

Job 41:12, this is however doubtful. See Lee in loco.

אַגָּן (Arab. *a bason*); אַגָּן m., אֲגָנָה f., (pl. אֲגָנוֹת), *a bason* or *bowl.*

אֲגַף or אָגָף m., pl. אֲגַפִּים *hosts, armies*; see גף.

אָגַר (fut. יֶאֱגֹר), *he laid up provision.*

אֲגוֹרָה f., *a small coin*; ὀβολός, 1 Sa. 2:36; see גרה.

אִגְּרָא f. Ch. emph. state אִגַּרְתָּא; same as the following word.

אִגֶּרֶת f. (pl. אִגְּרוֹת), *letter, edict.*

אֲגַרְטָל *a dish* or *bason*, Ezr. 1.9.

אֶגְרוֹף *the fist*; see גרף.

אֵד *mist, vapour*; see אוד.

אָדַב Kal, not used, Hiph. *he languished, was fatigued*; לְהַאֲדִיב for לַאֲדִיב inf.).

אַדְבְּאֵל (*the finger of God*), p.n. of a man

אֶדְרָה for אֶתְדַּדָּה Hith. fut.; with suff. אֲדַדֵּם; see דדה.

אַדַּר (*long-lived*), p. n. of a man.

אַדוֹ p. n. of a man.

אָדוֹן, אֲדֹנָי *Lord*; see אדן.

אֲדוֹרַיִם (*two hills*), p. n., a city of Judah.

אֲדוֹרָם p. n. of a man.

אֱדַיִן Ch. adv., *then*; בֵּאדַיִן *at that very time*; מִן אֱדַיִן *from that time.*

אַדְרִיקֵם Hiph. fut. with suff. for אַדְרִיק; see דקק.

אַדִּיר *great*; see אדר.

אֲדַלְיָה (*Jehovah's righteousness*), p. n. of a man.

אָדַם *was red, reddish brown*; Pu. part מְאָדָּם *growing, turning red*; Hiph *be red*; Hith. *grow red.*

דָּם m.(const.דָּם; with suff.דָּמוֹ, pl דָּמִים (דְּמֵי).—I. *blood*;

innocent blood; אִישׁ דָּמִים *a man of bloods*, i.e. *cruel.*— II. *slaughter, murder*; גֹּאֵל הַדָּם *avenger of blood*; אֵין לוֹ דָּם *blood is not on him*, i.e. *he has done no murder*; בֵּית הַדָּמִים *a bloody house.*—III. דַּם עֲנָבִים *blood of grapes, wine*; see דמה.

אָדָם m., *man* (in general); כָּל־אָדָם *all men*; אָדָם *a man*, as distinguished from a woman; בֶּן־אָדָם *mortal man.*

אָדָם p.n.—I. *Adam*, the first man.— II. *a city on Jordan*, Jos. 3:16.

אָדֹם, אֲדַמָּה m., אֲדֻמָּה f., *red, reddish brown.*

אֱדֹם (*red*), p.n., one of the names of Esau.

אֱדֹם p.n., *the land of Edom*; אֲדֹמִי *an Edomite.*

אֹדֶם m., *a ruby*, or *carnelion.*

וָאֱדָם, אָדֹם Kal fut.; see דמם.

אֲדַמְדָּמֶת m.;f. אֲדַמְדֹּמֶת pl. אֲדַמְדַּמּוֹת *very red, glowing.*

אֲדָמָה f.—I. *ground, soil*; אֹהֵב אֲדָמָה *given to agriculture*, lit. *loving the ground.* —II. *fruit, produce.*—III. *region, country, the whole earth.*—IV. p.n., *a city of the tribe of Naphtali.*

אֲדָמָה p.n., one of the cities of the plain.

אֲדָמָה for אֶתְדַּמֶּה Hith. fut. 1. pers.; see דמה.

אֲדָמִים p.n. of a place.

אַדְמוֹנִי *red haired*, πυῤῥάκης.

אַדְמִי p.n., a city of the tribe of Naphtali.

אַדְמָתָא (*land*), p. n. of a man.

אֶדֶן m. (pl. אֲדָנִים)—I. *the base of a column.*—II *any foundation.*

אֲדוֹן, אָדֹן p. n. of a man.

אָדוֹן m. (from אדן, pl. אֲדֹנִים), *proprietor, master, lord.*

אֲדֹנָי m., *the Lord*, exclusively applied to God.

אֲדֹנִי בֶזֶק (*lord of Bezek*), p. n., a king of the Canaanites, Jud. 1:5.

אֲדֹנִי צֶדֶק (*righteous lord*), Canaanitish king of Jerusalem, Jos. 10:1.

אֲדֹנִיָּה (*the Lord is my Lord*),p.n.of a m. אֲדֹנִיָּהוּ p. n. of a man.

אֲדֹנִיקָם (*the Lord confirmeth*), p.n.of a m.

אֲדֹנִירָם (*the Lord exalteth*), p. n. of a man, 1 Ki. 4:6.

אָדַר does not occur in Kal; Niph. part. נֶאְדָּר, with Jod parag. נֶאְדָּרִי, *it hath become glorious*; Hiph. (fut. יַאְדִּיר) *he made glorious.*

אַדִּיר *great, powerful, glorious, majestic.*

אַדִּיר m., *a prince*

אֶדֶר m.—I. *a cloak*; see אַדֶּרֶת—II. *amplitude, splendour.*

אַדֶּרֶת f. (with suff. אַדַּרְתּוֹ).—I. *a cloak*; אַ' שֵׂעָר *a Babylonish garment*; אַ' שֵׂעָר *a hair cloak.*—II. *magnificence.*

אֲדַרְגָּזְרִין Ch. pl., *officers of the court at Babylon*, Dan. 3:2, 3, the nature of their office unknown.

אַדָּר p n.—I. *a place in the tribe of Judah.*—II. *of a man.*

אַדָּר *threshing-floor*; see נדר.

אֲדָר m., *the twelfth month of the Hebrew year, corresponding with our February and March.*

אַדְרַזְדָּא Ch., *quickly, diligently.*

דַּרְכְּמוֹן, אֲדַרְכֹּן, δαρεικὸς, a Persian gold coin

אַדְרַמֶּלֶךְ (*the exalted Moloch*), p. n.—I.
an idol of the Sepharvites, 2 Ki.
17:31.—II. a son of Sennacherib,
Isa. 37:38, &c.

אֶדְרָע *arm*; see דרע.

אֶדְרֶעִי (*planting*), p. n.—I. the city of
Og, Deu. 1:4.—II. a city of the
tribe of Naphtali.

אִדָּרֵשׁ for הִדָּרֵשׁ Niph. inf. abs.; see
דרש.

אָדוּשׁ (inf. אָדוֹשׁ the same as דּוּשׁ),
threshing, beating out corn with the
wheel, Isa. 28:28.

אָהַב, אָהֵב (inf. const. אֲהֹב, אַהֲבָה;
imp. אֱהַב; fut. יֶאֱהַב; p. 1. אָהַב
and אָהֵב (אֹהֵב), *loved, desired, delighted
in*; part. אֹהֵב (pl. אֹהֲבִים, f.
אֹהֶבֶת) *a friend*; Niph. part. pl.
נֶאֱהָבִים *loved, amiable*; Pi. part.
מְאַהֵב *lover*.

אֲהַב Kal fut. 1. pers.

אַהֲבָה f., *love, beloved*.

אֲהָבִים m. pl. (sing. אַהַב), *amours,
loves, love-gifts*.

אֳהָבִים m. pl. (sing. אֹהַב), the same.

אֹהַד (*strength*), p. n., one of the sons of
Simeon.

אֲהָהּ *ah! alas!* an exclamation of
sorrow.

אַהֲוָא p. n.—I. of a country.—II. of a
river.

אֵהוּד (*he who is powerful*), p. n. of a
man.

אוֹהִירֶנּוּ(אֲהוֹרֶנּוּ for)Hiph. fut. 1. pers. with
suff.; see ירה.

אֱחִי the same as אַי *where?*

אֱחִי probably for אַיֵּה *where?* which
see: Hos. 13:10.

אֱחִי fut. apoc. 1. pers.; see חיה.

אָהַל (fut. יֶאֱהַל,יַאֲהִל), *pitched a tent, lived
in tents*; Pi. fut. יַהֵל for
the same; יַאֲהִיל *shone*, Job 25:5;
see הלל *to shine*.

אֹהֶל m. (with ה parag. אֹהֱלָה; with
suff. אָהֳלִי, אָהֳלֶךָ; Syr. אֹהְלִי;
pl. אֹהָלִים; Syr. אֹהָלִים,אֹהֳלֵי).—
I. *tabernacle, tent, habitation*.—II.
p. n. of a man, 1 Chron. 3:20.

אָהֳלָה (*her tent*), p.n., allegorical name
of Samaria, Eze. 23:4.

אָהֳלִיאָב (*tent of her father*), p.n. of a m.

אָהֳלִיבָה (*my tent with her*), p.n., allegorical name of Jerusalem, Eze.
23:4.

אָהֳלִיבָמָה (*my tent a high place*), p.n
of a wife of Esau.

אֲהָלִים m. pl., אֲהָלוֹת f., ξυλαλόη,
ἀγάλλοχον, *lign-aloes*, a perfumed
wood.

אֲחַמֶּה fut. with ה parag. for אֲחַמָה,
see המה.

אַהֲרֹן p. n., Aaron, the brother of
Moses; בֵּית א', בְּנֵי א' *Aaronites*.

אוֹ conj.—I. *or, either*; יָמִים אוֹ עָשׂוֹר
ten days at least.—II. *for*; אוֹ כִּי
but if.—III. אוֹ....אוֹ, *whether....or*.

אַו *desire*; see אוה.

אוּאֵל p. n. of a man.

אוֹב not used.

אוֹב m. (pl. אוֹבוֹת).—I. *a spirit of divination*, or *necromancy*.—II. νεκρό-
μαντις, *a necromancer*, one who
calls up spirits from the abyss to
foretel future events.—III. *th. art
of necromancy*.

אוֹבוֹת I. *skins used as bottles for
wine*, Job 32:19.— II. p. n. of a
place in the wilderness.

אוֹבִיל (he that causeth joy), p. n. of a man, 1 Chron. 27:30.

אוּבָל; see יבל.

אוּד not used (Arab. bent, crooked; also wood); etymology doubtful.

אֵד m., smoke, mist.

אוּד m., smoking firebrand.

אֹדוֹת f. pl., projects, means, cause; עַל אֹדוֹת (and אֶל אֹדוֹת) for because of; עַל אֹדוֹתִי on my account; עַל אֹדוֹתֶיךָ because of thee.

אוֹדְךָ, with נ epenth. אוֹדֶךָ Hiph. fut. 1. pers. with suff.; see ידה.

אֵיד m., calamity, destruction.

מְאֹד m.—I. power, might, excess; בְּכָל מְאֹדְךָ with all thy might; בִּמְאֹד מְאֹד in great excess; עַד מְאֹד עַד לִמְאֹד even to excess, exceedingly.—II. adv. exceedingly.

אוה not used (Arab. desired); Pi. אִוָּה (fut. יְאַוֶּה), desired, longed for, const. with ב and ל; Hith. הִתְאַוָּה (fut. apoc. יִתְאָו), desired, coveted, claimed; וְהִתְאַוִּיתֶם לָכֶם and claim for yourselves, Nu.34:10.

אָו or אָיו m., desire, Pro. 31:4.

אַוָּה f.—I. natural desire for food.—II. lust.

מַאֲוַי m. (pl. מַאֲוַיִּים), desires, Ps. 140:9.

תַּאֲוָה f.—I. desire, lust.—II. an object of desire; see תאה.

אוֹחִילָה Kri אֲחִילָה, אוֹחִלָה Hiph.fut. 1.pers.; see חול.

אוֹי, אוֹיָה I. alas! expression of grief.—II. ho! expressing anger.

אוֹת com. (pl. אֹתוֹת).—I. mark, memorial, warning.—II. sign, portent, miracle.

אָת Ch. (pl. אָתִין), the same.

אִי m. (pl. אִיִּים).—I. habitable land, continent, island.—II. shore, coast, countries on the coast; אִיֵּי הַגּוֹיִם and אִיֵּי הַיָּם isles of the Gentiles, isles of the West, countries little known to the Hebrews.—III. אִיִּים savage land animals, Is. 13:22, hence:—IV. interj. woe! horror! see אוֹי.

אוֹיֵב enemy; see איב.

אוּנִי p. n. of a man.

אוּזָל p. n. of a city in Arabia; probably Senaar, the capital of Arabia Felix, Gen. 10:27.

אֱוִי p. n. of a king of Midian.

אוֹבִיל Hiph. fut. 1. pers.; see אכל.

אוֹכַל Kal fut. 1. pers.; see אכל.

אוּל root not used; same as איל.

אֱוִיל a fool, an impious person.

אֱוִיל־מְרֹדַךְ p. n., a king of Babylon, descendant of Nebuchadnezzar, 2 Ki. 25:27.

אֱוִילִי same as אֱוִיל.

אִוֶּלֶת f. (with suff. אִוַּלְתִּי), folly, sin.

I. אוּל (Arab. to dispose, govern aright); root not used.

אוּל m.—I. a prince.—II. administration.—III. body, Ps. 73:4.

אוּלַי adv.—I. perhaps, unless.—II. p.n. of a river, Dan. 8:2.

אוּלָם, אֻלָם (pl. אֻלַמִּים).—I. m., an entrance hall, vestibule.—II. pa. but, nevertheless.—III. p. n. of a man.

II. אוּל (Arab. grew thick, of fluids); root not used.

אַיִל m. (const. אֵיל; pl. אֵילִים).—I. a ram.—II. lintel, arch over a door or window.

אֱיָל m., *strength, force.*

אֱיָלוּת f., the same.

אַיִל com., *an antelope, gazelle.*

אַיָּלָה אַיֶּלֶת f. (pl. אַיָּלוֹת ; const. אַיְּלוֹת),
female antelope.

אַיֶּלֶת f., the same; אַיֶּלֶת הַשַּׁחַר the
name of the tune to which the
Psalm is to be sung, Ps. 22.

אַיִל m. (pl. אֵילִים, אֵלִים).—I. *hero,
mighty man.*—II. *the pine or terebinth* (a tall thick tree).

אֵלִים p.n. of one of the stations of the
Israelites in the wilderness, Ex. c. 15.

אֵל (with suff. אֵלִי ; pl. אֵלִם, אֵלִים).—
I. *hero, man of might.*—II. *power* ;
יֶשׁ־לְאֵל יָדִי *it is in the power of
my hand*, i. e. I am able.—III. *God*
(the true God); בְּנֵי אֵלִים *the
sons of God*, i. e. *the angels.*—IV.
an epithet denoting excellence;
אַרְזֵי אֵל *cedars of God*, i. e. lofty,
well grown.—V. *an idol, false god.*

אֵלָה f., *terebinth;* see אַיִל, אַלָּה, &c.

אַלּוֹן m.—I. *oak, lofty tree;* compare
preceding word.—II. p.n. of a man.
—III. bf a city.

אֵלָם אֵילָם m., *a lintel;* see אוּלָם I.

אִילָן m. Ch., *a tree.*

וָאֹלֶךְ אוֹלִיךְ Hiph. fut. 1. pers. ; see
הָלַךְ, יָלַךְ.

אוֹמָר p.n. of a man.

אוֹן or אַיִן root not used; (Arab. *time,
a fit time*).

אָוֶן m. (with suff. אוֹנִי, אוֹנְךָ; pl.
אוֹנִים).—I. *vanity, falseness, that
which is nothing,* hence:—II. an
idol; בֵּית אָוֶן *house of idols;*
בִּקְעַת אָוֶן *valley of idols* (a valley
near Damascus, now *Un,* Am. 1:5).
—III. *sin, wickedness.*—IV. *sorrow,*

distress; בֶּן־אוֹנִי *the son of my sorrow;* לֶחֶם אוֹנִים *bread of affliction;* see אָנַן.

אוֹן m. (ע th suff. like אָוֶן).—I. *power.*
—II *manhood;* רֵאשִׁית הָאוֹן *first-
born.*—III. *wealth, riches.*

אַיִן const. אֵין I. *non-existence;* אֵין
בַּבּוֹר *he was not in the pit.*
אֵין יֹצֵא וְאֵין בָּא *there was neither
going out nor coming in;* אֵין לִי *I
have not,* lit. *there is nothing to me;*
אֵין לָבוֹא *"none might enter,"* Eng.
Ver., Est. 4:2 ; אֵין דָּבָר, מְאוּמָה
nothing; אֵין כֹּל *absolutely nothing;*
אֵינֶנּוּ *it is not.*—II. with persona
pronoun אֵינֶנִּי, אֵינְךָ, אֵינֵךְ
אֵינֶנָּה, אֵינְכֶם, אֵינָם and אֵינֵימוֹ
*am, was, not, shall not be, thou art
not,* &c.—III. with prepositions,
בְּאֵין *in not being, before, without,*
כְּאֵין *like not being, nearly,* Ps. 73:2 ;
לְאֵין *to him who has not,* Is. 40:29 ;
מֵאֵין (poetic only), *not, absolute
negation;* מֵאֵין יוֹשֵׁב *no inhabitant,* Jer. 33:10.

אֵין same as אַיִן, 1 Sa. 21:9.

אִי (perhaps from אַיִן), *not,* Job c. 22 ;
אִי־כָבוֹד (*ignoble*), p.n. of a man.

תְּאֵנָה f. (pl. תְּאֵנִים), *fig* (tree and fruit);
יֵשֵׁב תַּחַת תְּאֵנָתוֹ *he sat under
his fig-tree,* i. e. *he lived peace-
fully and prosperously.*

תַּאֲנִים m. pl., *vexation, vanity, falsehood,* Eze. 24:12.

אוֹן I. (*strength*), p.n. of a man.—II.
אֹן, אוֹן *Heliopolis,* a city of Lower
Egypt.

אוֹנוֹ (*strong*), p.n. of a city in the tribe
of Benjamin.

אוֹנָם (the same), p.n. of a man.

אוֹנָן (*vigorous*), p. n., one of the sons of Judah.

אוּפָז p. n., a country where gold was found (perhaps the same as the following word).

אוֹפִיר, אוֹפֵר p. n., a country abounding in gold, gems, and perfumed wood.

אוֹפָן a wheel; see אפן.

אוּץ *pressed, was urgent upon*; const. with בְּ, לְ, מְ; Hiph. *pressed, hastened*; const. with בְּ, לְ.

אוֹצָר *treasure*; see אצר.

אוֹצְרָה Hiph. fut. 1. pers. with ה parag.; see רצא.

אוֹר I. *became light, shone, enlightened.* —II. *prospered*; imperat. אוֹרִי f. *shine thou*, Isa. 60:1. Niph. נָאוֹר (fut. יֵאוֹר), *become bright*; part. נָאוֹר *illustrious.* Hiph. הֵאִיר (fut. apoc. יָאֵר).—I. *enlighten, illuminate, kindle.*—II. פ' עֵינֵי, פְּנֵי ה' *cheer up, exhilarate*, lit. *enlighten the eyes*, or *face*; פָּנָיו ה' (const. with עַל, לְ, בְּ, אֶת, אֶל).—III. *instruct, inform* (illuminate the mind), Ps. 119:130.

אוֹר m. (f. Job 36:32).—I. *light, brightness, lightning, luminary*; אוֹר חַיִּים *the light of life*; א' פָּנִים *light of the face*, i. e. cheerfulness, good will; pl. אוֹרִים *stars*, i. e. *luminaries*, Ps. 136:7.—II. metaph. *prosperity.*—III. *knowledge.*

אוּר I. *fire, the light of fire.*—II. p. n. of a man.—III. (אוּרִים וְתֻמִּים) LXX. δήλωσις καὶ ἀλήθεια, "Urim and Thummim," Eng. Ver., a part of the high-priest's breast-plate; meaning uncertain.—IV. אוּרִים

(*lights*), p. n. of a country.—V. אוּר כַּשְׂדִּים p n., *Ur of the Chaldeans*, a place in Mesopotamia.

אוֹרָה f. (pl. אוֹרוֹת).—I. *light*, Ps. 139: 12.—II. *prosperity, joy*, Est. 8:16.—III. טַל אוֹרוֹת *light reflecting dew*, Isa. 26:19; אוֹרוֹת *herbs*, 2 Kings 4:39.

אוֹרוּ imp. pl.; see ארר.

מָאוֹר m.—I. *light*; מְאוֹרוֹת *stars; luminaries.*—II. *candlestick*; מְנוֹרַת הַמָּאוֹר *the candlestick in the tabernacle*, lit. *place of light.*

מְאוּרָה f., *den, hole, of a serpent*, Isa. 11:8.

אֲוֵרוֹת *stables*; see ארה.

אוּרִי (*fiery*), p. n. of a man.

אוּרִיאֵל (*fire of God*), p. n. of a man.

אוּרִיָּה (the same), p. n.—I. the husband of Bathsheba.—II. a priest in the reign of Ahaz.

אוֹת *sign*; see אוה.

אוֹת or אָאת; Niph. (fut. pl. p. 1. נֵאוֹת, p. 3. יֵאוֹתוּ), *consenting to, agreeing.*

אוֹתִיּוֹת part. f. pl.; see אתה.

אָז adv., *then, at that time* (used with either tense); (מָאָז‎,מִן־אָז).—I. *from that time, of old, before.*—II. *whence*; מֵאָן אַפֶּךָ *whence thine anger* (was kindled); מֵאָן בָּאתִי *whence I came*; with infin. מ' דַּבֶּרְךָ *where-of thou hast spoken.*

אֲזַי *then*, Ps. 124: 3,4,5.

אָזָא or אֲזָה Ch., *he kindled.*

אָזַב, root not used; Arab. the same meaning.

אֵזוֹב m., *hyssop.*

אֶזְבִּי p. n. of a man.

אֲזַד Ch., *went forth, departed*

אֵזוֹר belt; see אזר.

אָזִין for אַאֲזִין Hiph. fut. 1. pers.; see אזן.

אַזְכָּרָה memorial; see זכר.

אָזַל he went away, departed; מֵאוּזָל from אוּזָל Uzal (see the word), Ez. 27:19, taken by mistake for Pu. part. of this verb. See Rosenmüller on the passage.

אֲזַל Ch., the same.

אָזֵל m., departure, 1 Sa. 20:19, (some call it a p. n.).

אֲזַל Ch. imp. for אֱזַל, Syr. for אָזַל; see אזל.

אָזַן, Pi. אִזֵּן attended to and investigated, Ecc. 12:9. Hiph. הֶאֱזִין heard, attended; const. with לְ, אֶל, עַד, עַל: of God, he hearkened, heard prayer; of man, he obeyed.

מֹאזְנַיִם dual, the balance, lit. having two dishes, bilanx.

מֹאזְנַיִן Ch., the same.

אֹזֶן f. (with suff. אָזְנִי; dual אָזְנַיִם), the ear; בְּאָזְנֵי פ׳ in the ears (that is, the hearing), of any one.

אַזְנוֹת־תָּבוֹר p. n. of a city in the tribe of Naphtali.

אָזְנִי (he who hearkens), p. n. of a man, Nu. 26:16.

אֲזַנְיָה (whom the Lord hears), p. n. of a man.

אֶזֶן שְׁאֵרָה p. n. of a place.

אֵזֵן m. (pl. אֲזֵנִים), "weapons," Deu. 23: 14, Eng. Ver.; meaning uncertain.

אֲזִקִּים chains; see זקק.

אָזַר (imp. אֲזֹר; fut. יֶאְזָר; with suff. יַאַזְרֵנִי), bound, girt, clothed himself; trop. אָזְרוּ חַיִל they clothed themselves with strength; const. with

בְּ. Niph. part. נֶאְזָר girded: const. with בְּ. Pi. sense as Kal. Hith. became bound, armed himself.

אֵזוֹר m.—I. a belt, girdle.—II. fetters.

אֶזְרֹעַ arm, same as זְרֹעַ; see זרע.

אֶזְרָחִי, אֶזְרָח native; see זרח.

אָח m., (const. אֲחִי; with suff. אָחִי, אֲחִיכֶם, אָחִינוּ; pl. אַחִים, אַחֶיךָ; with suff. אֲחִיגוֹ, אֶחָיו, אַחֶיךָ, (אֲחִיכֶם)—I. a brother.—II. a relative.—III. a fellow countryman. —IV. a friend.—V. any person or thing like another.—VI. a term of affection; אִישׁ מֵעַל אָחִיו one from the other; אִישׁ אֶל אָחִיו one from the other.

אָח Ch., a brother.

אַחֲוָה f., fraternity.

אָחוֹת f. (with suff. אֲחוֹתִי; pl. אֲחָיוֹת with suff. אַחְוֹתֵיךָ, אַחְיוֹתַי).—I. sister.—II. used as אָח V., which see; אִשָּׁה אֶל אֲחוֹתָהּ one from the other (of persons or things fem.).

אָח interj., alas! exclamation of grief.

אָחַח not used; οἰμώζειν, to howl; whence is derived:—

אֹחִים m. pl., howlings, or howling animals (it is uncertain which), Isa. 13:21.

אָח f., a pot filled with hot coals to warm rooms in winter, Jer. 36: 22; 23.

אַחְאָב (brother of the father), p.n., Ahab king of Israel.

אַחָב p. n. of the same king.

אֲחְבָּן p. n. of a man.

אֶחָד const. אַחַד m., אַחַת with the pause, אֶחָת f.—I one.—II. the first

(used with days of the month);
בְּאֶחָד לַחֹדֶשׁ *on the first day of the month;* שְׁנַת אַחַת *the first year.*—
III. *alone, a single one;* אֵין, לֹא
אֶחָד *not a single one, no one.*—IV.
a certain one (τις); it has the power of the ind. article *a, an;* אֶחָד *one of* הָעָם *one of the people, a person;* נָבִיא אֶחָד, προφήτης τις, *a certain prophet.*—
V. *the same one, the same;* אַחַת
בְּאַחַת (פַּעַם), *at the same time, together;* כְּאֶחָד *as one man, together;* pl. אֲחָדִים *the same, united into one, a few.*

אָחַד Hith., *take hold of, unite thyself;* see יָחַד.

חַד Ch., *one, first, any one,* same as אֶחָד.

אָחוּ m., *the bulrush, reed,* an Egyptian word; Copt. ἄχι.

אֶחְגֻּד (*union*), p. n. of a man.

אַחֲוָה and אָחוֹת; see אָח.

אַחֲוָה; see חוה.

אַחְיָה, אֲחוֹת p. n. of a man; patr.
אֲחוֹחִי.

אַחֻוָּד, with נ epenth. אַחֻוָּךְ, Pi. fut. 1.
pers. with suff.; see חוה.

אֲחוּמַי p. n. of a man.

אָחוֹר *after;* see אחר.

אָחַז (inf. c. אֲחֹז, אֱחֹז; with pref. בֶּאֱחֹז,
imper. אֱחֹז; fut. יֹאחֵז and יֹאחֵז
(יֶאֱחֹז).—
I. *seized* (fear, terror); const. with
בְּ.—II. *caught* (i.e. in hunting).
—III. *took hold of, seized;* const.
with בְּ of the part seized.—IV.
held, kept.—V. *joined, united.*—VI.
locked up, Neh. 7:3.—VII. *covered,
overlaid, veneered,* 1 Ki. 6:10.—
VIII. *drew by lot.* Niph.—I. *was*

caught, Ecc. 9:12.—II. *was held,*
Gen. 22:13. Pi. מֵאַחֵז *shut up*
(same as Kal VI.), Job 26·9. Hoph.
מֵאָחֵז *joined, united* (same as Kal
V.), 2 Chron. 9:18.

אָחָז p.n.—I. *Ahaz,* king of Judah.—
II. of a man.

אֱחָז fut. apoc. in pause for אֶחֱזֶה, אַחַז;
see חזה.

אֲחֻזָּה f., *possession, tenure.*

אַחְזַי p. n. of a man.

אֲחַזְיָהוּ and אֲחַזְיָה p.n.—I. of the son
of Ahab king of Israel.—II. of the
son of Joram king of Judah.

אֲחֻזָּם p. n. of a man.

אֲחֻזַּת p. n. of a man.

אַחְטֶנָּה Pi. fut. 1. pers. with suff. for
אַחְטְאֶנָּה; see חטא.

אֲחִי p. n. of a man.

אֲחִידָה; see חוד.

אֲחִיָּה (*friend of God*), p. n. of a man.

אֲחִיהוּד (*friend of the Jews*), p.n. of a m.

אֲחִיו p. n. of a man.

אֲחָיוֹת *sisters;* see אָחוֹת, in אָח.

אֲחִיהוּד and אֲחִיחֻד p. n. of a man.

אֲחִיטוּב (*loving good*), p. n. of a man.

אֲחִילוּד (*brother's son*), p. n. of a man.

אֲחִימוֹת (*brother of death*), p.n. of a m.

אֲחִימֶלֶךְ (*brother of a king*), p.n. of a m.

אֲחִימָן (*brother of gifts*), p. n. of a man.

אֲחִימַעַץ (*brother of anger*), p.n. of a m.

אֲחִיָן (*brotherly*) p. n. of a man.

אֲחִינָדָב (*brother of good will*), p. n. of
a man.

אֲחִינֹעַם (*brother of delight*), p.n. of a w.

אֲחִיסָמָךְ (*brother of defence*), p.n. of a m.

אֲחִיעֶזֶר (*brother of help*), p. n. of a man.

אֲחִיקָם (*brother of enmity*), p. n. of a m.

אֲחִירָם (*exalted brother*), p. n. of a m.

אֲחִירַע (*evil brother*), p. n. of a man.

אֲחִישַׁחַר (brother of the morning), p. n. of a man.

אֲחִישָׁר (brother of song), p. n. of a man.

אֲחִיתֹפֶל (foolish brother), p.n. of a m.

אָחֵל Hiph. fut. 1. pers., אָחֵל with dag. forte imp.; see חלל.

אָחְלָב (fecundity), p. n. of a place in the tribe of Asher.

אַחְלַי (would that!) p.n.—I. of a man.— II. of a woman.

אַחֲלַי, אַחֲלֵי would that! I wish! see חלה.

אַחְלָמָה amethyst; see חלם.

אֲחַסְבַּי p. n. of a man.

אַחְמְתָא p. n., Ecbatana, a city of Media, Ezr. 6:2.

אָחַר root not used; fut. 1. pers. pl. אֵחַר, Gen. 32:5. Pi. אִחַר (fut. יְאַחֵר), delayed, waited, deferred (Arab. the same); see יחר.

אָחוֹר m. (pl. אֲחוֹרִים).—I. the but-end of a spear, 2 Sa. 2:23.—II. the west, westward. Adv. behind, after; מֵאָחוֹר, לְאָחוֹר, בְּאָחוֹר behind; לְאָחוֹר hereafter, Isa. 41:23.

אַחֵר m., אַחֶרֶת f. (pl. אֲחֵרִים, אֲחֵרוֹת).—I. another; אֱלֹהִים אֲ' other gods, idols.—II. p. n. of a man.

אַחַר the hinder part. Adv. of time and place, behind, afterwards. Prep. behind, after; הָלַךְ אַ' follow; אַ' הַדְּבָרִים הָאֵלֶּה after these things, afterwards; אַ' דִּבֶּר פּ' after he had spoken; ... cnst. אַחֲרֵי (with suff. אַחֲרַי, אַחֲרֶיךָ, אַחֲרָיו), behind, after; אַחַר כֵּן אֲ' after; אַ' אֲשֶׁר כֵּן afterwards; with prefixes מֵאַחֲרֵי after something past, after that; מֵאַ' כֵּן afterwards; מֵאַ' behind him; אֶל אַחֲרֵי after; עַל אַחֲרֵי behind.

אָחֲרוּ Pi. pret. pl. for אִחֲרוּ; see אחר.

אַחֲרוֹן m., אַחֲרוֹנָה f.—I. the hinder part, the back part.—II. the latter day, or time.—III. the west; הַיָּם הָא' the Mediterranean sea.—IV. posterity; דּוֹר א' the generation to come; אַחֲרֹנִים successors; לָאַחֲרֹנָה, בָּאַחֲרֹנָה afterwards.

אָחֳרִי Ch. adj. f., another.

עַד אָחֳרֵין Ch., at last, at length.

אַחֲרִית f.—I. the last, the latter time; אַחֲרִית הַיָּמִים the latter days.—II. the end; אַ' הַשָּׁנָה end of the year.— III. posterity.

אָחֳרָן Ch. m., another.

אֲחֹרַנִּית adv., backwards.

אֲחַרַח (after his brother?) p.n. of a man.

אֲחַרְחֵל (behind a wall), p. n. of a man.

אֲחַשְׁדַּרְפְּנִים m. pl., chief satraps, or doorkeepers, officers of the Persian court. יןֿ— Ch., the same.

אֲחַשְׁוֵרוֹשׁ a title common to all the kings of Persia. It is spelt Chosroes by the later Greek and Latin historians.

אֲחַשְׁרֹשׁ the same.

אֲחַשְׁתָּרִי p. n. of a man; see next word.

אֲחַשְׁתְּרָנִים m. pl., mules.

אַחַת f., one; see אֶחָד.

אֲחֵת Ch. Aph. imp.; see נחת.

אֶחְתָּה Niph. fut. 1. pers. with ה parag.; see חתת.

אַט Hiph. fut. apoc. 1. pers. for אַטֶּה; see נטה.

אָטָד m., black thorn; rhamnus paliurus (Linn.).

אָטָד p.n., a place beyond Jordan, where was a threshing-floor; afterwards Abel-mizraim, Gen. 50:10, 11.

אֵטוּן m., *linen* (of Egypt) ὀθόνιον, probably an Egyptian word, Pro. 7:16.

אָטַם *not used;* (Arab. *uttered a low sound*).

אַט m. (pl. אִטִּים).—I. *necromancers, enchanters.*—II. *gentle, soft.* Adv. לְאַט, לָאַט, אַט *softly, slowly;* לְאִטִּי *at my convenience.*

אָטַם *shut up, closed.* Hiph. the same; יַאֲטֵם אָזֶן *he closes* (his) *ear.*

אָטַר with עַל *shut;* fut. יֶאְטַר, Ps. 69:16.

אִטֵּר *maimed;* אִ׳ יַד יְמִינוֹ lit. *having his right hand bound* (left-handed).

(he that halteth), p. n. of a man.

אִי; see אֵוֶה and אִין

אֵי *where?* with suff. אַיֶּכָּה *where art thou?* אַיּוֹ *where is he?* אַיָּם *where are they?* also with pronouns and adverbs, אֵי זֶה *who? what? where?* אֵי מִזֶּה *whence?* אֵי לְזֹאת *wherefore? why?* with ה demonst. אַיֵּה *where?*

אֵיכָה *where? how?*

אֵיךְ (apoc.) *how?*

אֵיכֹה (Kri) (אֵיכוֹ) *where?* 2 K. 6:13.

אֵיכָכָה *how?*

אַיִן *always in comp.;* מֵאַיִן *whence?* (for another meaning see אֵין).

אֵיפֹה *where? how?*

אָן (contract. from אַיִן), *where? whither?* מֵאָן *whence?* עַד־אָן *until;* with the paragogic ה, אָנָה *whither? whereunto? where?* עַד־אָנָה *how long?* וָאָנָה *hither and thither,* 1 K. 2:36, 42.

אָיַב *hated, was an enemy,* Ex. 23:22.

אֹיֵב m., *enemy;* אֹוֶיבֶת f., the same.

אֵיבָה f.. *enmity.*

אֵיד *calamity;* see אוד.

אַיֵּה *where?* see אֵי.

אַיָּה f.—I. name of a bird of prey; "vulture, kite," Eng. Ver.; LXX. ἰκτῖν; Vulg. vultur.—II. p. n. of a man.

אִיּוֹב (miserable), p.n., *Job,* the patriarch.

אִיזֶבֶל p. n., *Jezebel,* the wife of Ahab.

אַיֶּכָה, אֵיךְ; see אֵי.

אִי־כָבוֹד (where is the glory? i.e. without glory); p. n. of a man.

אַיֶּכָּה *where art thou?* אֵי with suff. and נ epenth.

אַיִל, אֵיל, אֵל, &c.; see אול.

אֵילוֹן (oak), p. n.—I. of a city.—II. of a man.

אַיָּלוֹן (place of hinds), p. n. of a city.

אֵילְכָה for אֵלְכָה Kal fut. 1. pers. with ה parag.; see הלך, ילך.

אֵילִם (grove of oaks), p. n. of a place.

אֵילַת (tree), אֵילוֹת (trees), p.n., *Elath,* a city on the eastern gulf of the Red Sea, now Akabah.

אַיֶּלֶת *a gazelle;* see אול.

אָיַם root not used, *was terrible;* Ch Pa. *frightened.*

אָיֹם, אָיֵם m., *terrible,* Hab. 1:7.

אֵימָה f. (pl. אֵימוֹת; with ה parag אֵימָתָה) *terror;* pl. אֵמִים, אֵימִים.—I. *terrible things.*—II. *idols,* Jer. 50:38.—III. p.n. of one of the tribes of the Moabites.

אַיִן; see אֵון and אֵי.

אֵינֵימוֹ *they are not;* see אַיִן with suff.

אִיעֶזֶר (helpless), p.n. of a man.

אֵיפָה, אֵפָה f., *Ephah,* a corn measure, capacity unknown; אֵיפָה וְאֵיפָה *divers measures;* אֵי שְׁלֵמָה *just measure.*

אֵיפֹה ;see אֵי.

אֵיפֹוא same as אֵפֹוא.

אִישׁ m. (pl. אֲנָשִׁים, see אֱנוֹשׁ; three times אִישִׁים).—I. *a man*, as distinguished from a woman.—II. *a husband.*—III. *a male.*—IV. used collectively for the inhabitants of a country; אִישׁ יִשְׂרָאֵל *the Israelites.*—V. used to denote the qualifications of men; אִישׁ מִלְחָמָה *a warrior;* אִישׁ אֱמֶת *a faithful man;* אִישׁ שָׂדֶה *a husbandman.*—VI. any one; אִישׁ...אִישׁ *one...another.*—VII. *every man;* opposed to אָח, וַיֵּלְכוּ אִישׁ לִמְקֹמוֹ *they went every one to his place;* כָּל־אִישׁ *every one.*—VIII. *every thing,* Ex. 25:20.—IX. impers., כֹּה אָמַר הָאִישׁ *thus it was said.*

אִישׁ, Hith. הִתְאֹשֵׁשׁ (ἀνδρίζεσθαι, 1 Cor. 16:13); pl. הִתְאֹשֵׁשׁ *become ye men,* i. e. be courageous, Isa. 46:8.

אִישׁוֹן m., lit. *little man,* i. e. the small image of one's self seen in the eye of another.—I. אִישׁוֹן עַיִן, אִי בַּת עַיִן *pupil of the eye;* hence:—II. אִישׁוֹן לַיְלָה, אִי חֹשֶׁךְ lit. *pupil,* i. e. *middle, of the night, midnight.*

אִשָּׁה or אֵשֶׁת f. (with suff. אִשְׁתִּי, אֶשְׁתְּךָ and אִשְׁתֶּךָ), I.—*woman.*—II. *wife.*—III. *concubine.*—IV. opposed to אָחוֹת and רֵעוּת, like אִישׁ.—V. *any one, every one.*—VI. applied to men by way of reproach.

אִישׁ־בֹּשֶׁת p. n. of a son of Saul.

אִישׁהוֹד (*man of vigour*), p.n. of a man.

אִישַׁי (*manly*), p. n. of a man.

אִיתַי Ch., same as יֵשׁ *he is;* אִיתֶיךָ

אִיתָךְ *thou art;* אִיתוֹהִי *he is;* אִיתָנָא *we are;* אִיתֵיכוֹן *ye are.*

אִיתַי p.n. of a man.

אִיתִיאֵל (*God with me*), p.n. of a man.

אֵיתָם for אֶתָּם Kal fut. 1. pers.; see תמם.

אֵיתָמָר (*place of palm trees*), p.n. of one of the sons of Aaron.

אֵיתָן p.n. of a man; see יתן.

אַךְ adv., *only, alone, except;* אַךְ שָׂמֵחַ *only* (i.e. nothing else but) *rejoicing,* Deu. 16:15; אַךְ חֹשֶׁךְ *only* (nothing but) *darkness,* Ps. 139:11; אַךְ טָרֹף טֹרָף *he is only torn in pieces,* i.e. nothing else has happened to him, Gen. 44:28.

אַכָּד (*fortress*), p. n. of a city built by Nimrod, Gen. 10:10.

אָכֹּות Kal fut. 1. pers., see כתת.

אַכְזִיב p.n.—I. of a city in the tribe of Asher, Greek ἔκδιππα, now *Zib.*—II. of a city in the tribe of Judah.

אַכְזָר, אַכְזָרִיּוּת see כזר.

אָכִישׁ (*Ethiopian*), p. n. of a king of the Philistines.

אָכַל (inf. אָכֹול; const. אֲכֹל; with pref. לֶאֱכֹל; with suff. אָכְלְךָ, אָכְלוֹ; imper. אֱכֹל; with ה parag. אָכְלָה; fut. יֹאכַל and יֹאכֵל).—I. *ate.*—II. *devoured,* spoken of men or things; joined to the accusative with בְּ, אָכַל לֶחֶם מִן *feasted;* בְּלֶחֶם and אָכַל לֶחֶם פ׳ אִי לֶחֶם עַל שֻׁלְחָן פ׳ *to be the guest inmate, of any one;* אָכַל לִפְנֵי יְהֹוָה *ate that which was offered in sacrifice;* אָכַל בְּשַׂר פ׳ *ate his flesh,* i.e. *injured him,* Ps. 27:2; Niph נֶאֱכַל, part. f. נֶאֱכֶלֶת *is, may be, eaten.* **Pu.** אֻכַּל *devoured, consumed.* **Hiph.** הֶאֱכִיל (fut. יַאֲכִיל; inf. הַאֲכִיל) *gave, made, caused, to eat, devour.*

אֲכַל **Ch.,** the same.

אֹכֶל m., *food;* with suff. אָכְלִי.

אָכְלָה f., *meat, food,* Gen. 1:29, 30.

אֲכִילָה f., *meat, feast,* 1 K. 19:8.

מַאֲכָל m., *food, that which may be eaten;* עֵץ מ' *fruit tree;* צֹאן מ' *cattle to be slaughtered for the table.*

מַאֲכֹלֶת, מַאֲכֶלֶת f., *food.*

מַאֲכֶלֶת f., *slaughtering knife,* lit. *devourer;* pl. מַאֲכָלוֹת.

אֻכָל (*eaten, consumed*), p. n. of a man.

וָאֵכֵל Pi. fut. apoc. 1. pers.; see כלה.

אֲכַלְךָ Ex. 33:3, Pi. fut. 1. pers. with suff. for אֲכָלְךָ; see כלה.

אָכֵן *truly;* see כון.

אַכֶּנּוּ Hiph. fut. 1. pers. with suff.; see נכה.

אָכַף *compel, bow down to,* Pro. 16:26.

אֶכֶף m. (with suff. אַכְפִּי), *palm of the hand,* Job 33:7.

אֶכֹּף for אֶכְפֹּף Niph. fut. 1. pers.; see כפף.

אָכַר root not used;(Arab. *digged*).

אִכָּר m., *ploughman, husbandman.*

אַכְשָׁף (*city of magicians*), p. n. of a city in the tribe of Asher.

אַל *not,* &c.; see אלל.

אֵל *God;* see אגל.

אֶל, אֵל prep. (with suff. אֵלַי, אֵלֶיךָ, אֵלֶיךָ, אֵלָיו, אֵלֶיהָ, אֵלֵינוּ, אֲלֵיכֶם; אֲלֵיהֶן, אֲלֵיהֶם; poet. אֵלֵימוֹ; pl. poet. אֱלֵי).—I. sign of the dative, like לְ.—II. *to, towards.*—III. *unto,*

at.—IV. *of, concerning.*—V. *in, into*—VI. *among.*—VII. *by, through.*—VIII. *for, on account of;* the original meaning is *to, towards,* variously modified by the context; אֶל־פִּי יְהֹוָה *according to the command (mouth) of God;* אֶל־אַמָּה *a cubit,* i. e. according to the measure of a cubit, Gen. 6:16; וַיֹּאמֶר אֶל־שָׂרָה *he said concerning* (relative to) *Sarah;* וַיֵּלֶךְ אֶל־נַפְשׁוֹ *he went, having regard to his life,* i. e. to save his life; אֶל־בְּאֵר הַמַּיִם *near* (i. e. *towards*) *the well;* יֵשֶׁב אֶל־הַשֻּׁלְחָן *he sat at* (i. e. *to*) *the table.* —IX. used with other particles; אֶל־אַחֲרֵי *behind me;* אֶל־מְחוּסַר לְ *without;* אֶל־תַּחַת *a pleonasm,* same as תַּחַת.

אֵל, הָאֵל, אֵלֶּה pron., *these, those;* אֵלֶּה־וְאֵלֶּה οἱ μὲν— οἱ δέ, *these—those;* **Ch.,** the same.

אֵלָא (*terebinth*), p.n. of a man; see אלה.

אֶלְגָּבִישׁ m., *hail;* see גבש.

אַלְמֻגִּים name of a tree; see אלמנים.

אֶלְדָּד (*beloved of God*), p. n. of a man.

אֶלְדָּעָה (*called of God*), p. n. of a man

אָלָה I. *lay under a curse, imprecate.* —II. *howl,* see אלל. **Hiph.** *swore, execrated, laid under a curse;* fut. apoc. וַיֹּאֶל.

אָלָה f.—I. *oath, imprecation;* בּוֹא בְאָלָה *come into the terms of the oath, agree by oath,* Neh. 10:30; הֵבִיא בְאָלָה *make one swear,* Eze. 17:13; נָשָׂא אָלָה בְּ *lay an oath upon any one.*—II. *curse, cursing;* הָיָה לְאָלָה *he was for a curse;* נָתַן לְאָלָה *he gave over unto cursing*

תַּאֲלָה f., *cursing.*

אֱלָהּ m. Ch., *God.*

אֱלוֹהַּ m., *God* (pl. אֱלֹהִים).—I. *God,
the true God.*—II. *false gods,* idols;
followed by the verb in the sing.,
very rarely in the pl.; אִישׁ אֱ' *a
man of God;* בְּנֵי אֱ' *sons of God,*
i. e. they that loved and served
God; with pref. בֵּאלֹהִים, כֵּאלֹהִים,
לֵאלֹהִים; const. אֱלֹהֵי.

אֵלָה *gazelle;* see אוּל.

אֵלָה *terebinth;* see אלל.

אֲלוּ Ch., *behold!* same as אֲרוּ.

אִלּוּ for אִם־לוּ, *otherwise, unless,*
Ecc. 6:6, Est. 7:4.

אֱלוּל m.—I. *vanity;* same as אֱלִיל;
see אלל.—II. *Elul,* the sixth month
of the Hebrew year, answering
nearly to our September, Neh. 6:15.

אֵלוֹן *oak;* see אוּל. אַלּוֹן the same; in
אלל.

אַלּוּף *friend;* see אלף.

אֶלְעוּשׁ (*lion's den*), p. n., one of the
encampments of the Israelites.

אֱלִיזָבָד (Θεοδῶρος), p. n. of a man.

אָלַח, Niph. נֶאֱלַח *was corrupt, base.*

אֶלְחָנָן (*gift of God*), p. n. of a man.

אֱלִיאָב (*who has God for his father*), p. n.
of a man.

אֱלִיאֵל (*strong in God*), p. n. of a man.

אֱלִיאָתָה or אֱלִיָּתָה (*to whom God
comes*), p. n. of a man.

אֶלְדָּד (*beloved of God*), p. n. of a prince
of the Benjamites.

אֶלְיָדָע (*known of God*), p. n. of a man.

אַלְיָה f. (Arab. the same), the fat tail
of the sheep in the East.

אֵלִיָּהוּ, אֵלִיָּה (*the Lord he is God*), p. n.,
Elijah ('Ηλίας), the prophet.

אֱלִיהוּא, אֱלִיהוּ (the same), p. n. of one
of Job's friends.

אֱלִיהוֹעֵינַי, אֶלְיוֹעֵינַי (*mine eyes are
unto the Lord*), p. n. of a man.

אֱלִיַּחְבָּא (*hidden of God*), p. n. of one of
David's generals.

אֱלִיַחְרֻף (*God is his avenger*), p. n. of a
man.

אֱלִיל *vanity;* see אלל.

אֱלִימֶלֶךְ (*God is king*), p. n. of a man.

אִלֵּן, אִלֵּין pron. pl. Ch., *these, those*

אֶלְיָסָף (*increased of God*), p. n. of a
prince of the Gadites.

אֱלִיעֶזֶר (*holpen of God*), p. n. of a man.

אֱלִיעֵינַי (*God is mine eye,* i. e. directs
me), p. n. of a man.

אֱלִיעָם (*people of God*), p. n. of a man.

אֱלִיפַז (*God is precious*), p. n.—I. of a
son of Esau.—II. of one of Job's
friends.

אֱלִיפָל (*my God is strong*), p. n. of a man.

אֱלִיפְלֵהוּ (*whom God makes famous*),
p. n. of a man.

אֱלִיפֶלֶט (*God is his help*), p. n. of a m.

אֱלִיצוּר (*God is his rock*), p. n. of a man.

אֶלְיָצָפָן or אֶלְצָפָן (*whom God protects*),
p. n. of a man.

אֱלִיקָא p. n. of a man.

אֶלְיָקִים (*whom God makes strong*), p. n.
—I. of the house-steward of Hezekiah.—II. of a king of Judah,
afterwards changed to יְהוֹיָקִים
(*Jehovah makes strong*).

אֱלִישֶׁבַע (*vowed to God*), p. n., *Elishe-
bah* ('Ελισάβετ), the wife of Aaron.

אֱלִישָׁה p. n. of a place on the shores
of the Mediterranean.

אֱלִישׁוּעַ (*whose salvation is God*), p. n. of
a son of David.

אֶלְיָשִׁיב (whom God pardons), p.n. of a man.

אֶלְיָשָׁמָע (whom God hears), p.n. of a m.

אֱלִישָׁע (whose salvation is God), p.n., Elisha (Ἐλισσαῖος), the prophet.

אֱלִישָׁפָט (God is the judge), p.n. of a m.

אֱלִיתָה p.n.; see אֶלְיָאתָה.

אֵלֶּךְ pron. m. pl. Ch.; same as Heb. אֵלֶּה those, Dan. 3:12, 13

אֵלֵךְ with ה parag. אֵלְכָה, וָאֵלֶךְ Kal fut. 1. pers.; see הלך, ילך.

אָלַל root not used (Arab. passed away quickly).

אַל s., nothing, Job 24:25.; adv. not; with the fut. אַל־תִּירָאוּ fear not; אַל־נָא do not (I beseech you), Gen. 19:18.

אֱלִיל vain things, vanity; אֱלִילִים idols, lit. vain things.

אֲלַי woe is me! see ילל.

אֵלָה f., terebinth, Jos. 24:26; see אוּל.

אַלּוֹן m.—I. oak.—II. p.n. of a man; see אוּל.

אָלַם not used in Kal either in Heb. or Arab. Niph. נֶאֱלַם was dumb, silent, lit. tongue-tied. Pi. bound, like sheaves of corn, Gen. 37:7.

אֵלֶם m., silence; אֵלֶם צֶדֶק is justice silent? Ps. 58:2; יוֹנַת אֵלֶם the dove of silence, title to Ps. 56.

אִלֵּם m., dumb person; pl. אִלְּמִים.

אֲלֻמָּה f. (pl. אֲלֻמִּים and (אֲלֻמּוֹת, a sheaf of corn.

אַלְמֹן m., widowhood, Isa. 47:29.

אַלְמָן m., a widower, Jer. 51:5.

אַלְמָנָה f., a widow.

אַלְמְנוֹת for אַרְמְנוֹת palaces, Isa. 13:22.

אַלְמָנוּת f., widowhood; pl. אַלְמְנֻתִים.

אַלְמֹנִי m., some one, a certain one, lit. one not to be named; always joined with פְּלֹנִי, which see.

אֵלָם and אֻלָם; see אוּל.

אַלְגֻּמִּים a resinous and odoriferous wood, not the produce of Canaan; perhaps the red sandal-wood, 1 Ki. 10:11, &c.; in 2 Chron. 2:7, it is transposed to אַלְמֻגִּים.

אַלְמוֹדָד p.n. of one of the descendants of Shem, Gen. 10:26.

אַלַּמֶּלֶךְ (the king's oak), p.n. of a place in the tribe of Asher.

אַלְמֹנִי, אַלְמָנוּת, אַלְמָנָה, אַלְמֹן, אַלְמָן; see אלם.

אֶלְנַעַם (God is his delight), p.n. of a man.

אֶלְנָתָן (given of God), p.n. of a man.

אֶלָּסָר p.n. of a city.

אֶלְעָד (God is his help), p.n. of a man.

אֶלְעָדָה (whom God adorns), p.n. of a m.

אֶלְעוּזַי (God my strength), p.n. of a m.

אֶלְעָזָר (God is HIS helper), p.n. of a m.

אֶלְעָלֵא, אֶלְעָלֵה p.n. of a town in the tribe of Reuben.

אֶלְעָשָׂה (made of God), p.n. of a man.

אָלַף learnt; fut. יֶאֱלַף. Pi. אִלֵּף taught. Hiph. part. f. מַאֲלִיפוֹת (from אֶלֶף), producing a thousand, Ps. 144:13.

אֶלֶף m., a thousand; dual אַלְפַּיִם two thousand; pl. אֲלָפִים thousands: שְׁלֹשֶׁת אֲלָפִים three thousand, אַרְבָּעִים אֶלֶף forty thousand, מֵאָה אֶלֶף a hundred thousand; אֶלֶף אֲלָפִים a thousand thousands, אַלְפֵי רִבְבָה 10,000,000; אֶלֶף s.— I. a chiliad (a troop of 1000 soldiers); שַׂר הָאֶלֶף, χιλίαρχος, commander of a chiliad.—II a nation tribe (i.e. *many persons*).—III. pl. אֲלָפִים *oxen*; see below.—IV. p.n. of a city in the tribe of Benjamin, Jos. 18:28.

אֱלַף Ch., *a thousand.*

אַלּוּף adj., *familiar, tame,* Jer. 11:19. s.—I. *a friend.*—II. *an ox (a tame animal).*—III. *head of a tribe or family,* φύλαρχος.

אֶלְפָּלֶט (*God the deliverer*), p.n. of a m.

אֶלְפַּעַל (*God who performeth*), p.n. of a man.

אֶלְצָפָן p.n. of a man; see אֱלִיצָפָן.

אָלַץ (Syr. *he urged*). Pi. אִלֵּץ *pressed, urged on,* Jud. 16:16.

מֶלֶךְ אַלְקוּם m., Prov. 30:31, עִמּוֹ *a king who is irresistible;* "against whom there is no rising up," Eng.Ver.; meaning uncertain.

אֶלְקָנָה (*for whom God cared*), p. n. of a man.

אֶלְקֹשִׁי p.n. of a people.

אֶלְתּוֹלַד p.n. of a city; same as תּוֹלָד.

אֶלְתְּקֵה, אֶלְתְּקָא p. n. of a city of the Levites in the tribe of Dan.

אֶלְתְּקֹן p.n. of a city in the tribe of Judah.

אֵם f. (with suff. אִמִּי; pl. אִמּוֹת).—I. *a mother.*—II. *a grand-mother.*—III. *a step-mother.*—IV. *metropolis, chief city;* אֵם הַדֶּרֶךְ *mother,* i.e. *head of two ways,* Ez. 21:26.—V *nation, entire people.*

אַמָּה f.—I. *fore arm,* hence:—II. *a cubit,* measure of 21.888 inches; dual אַמָּתַיִם *two cubits;* עֶשֶׂר אַמּוֹת *ten cubits;* שְׁלֹשׁ מֵאוֹת אַמָּה *three hundred cubits.*—III. *a basis or pedestal,* Isa. 6:4.—IV. p. n. of a hill, 2 Sa. 2:24.

אַמָּה f. Ch., *cubit.*

אֻמָּה f. (pl. אֻמּוֹת, אֻמִּים), *families, tribes.*

אֻמָּה f. Ch., *the same.*

אִם cond.pa.—I. *surely, truly,* this is its radical meaning, hence:—II. *if;* אִם...אִם *whether...or;* עַד־אִם *whilst, until.*—III. *if? whether?* הַ...אִם, וְאִם...אִם, הֲ...אִם *whether?...or?*—IV. used as an asseveration אִם has the power of denial, אִם־לֹא of affirmation; אִם־אֶעֱשֶׂה *let me be accursed if I do it,* i.e. I will not do it.—V. in comp. הַאִם same as הֲלֹא *is not?* אִם־לֹא *unless.*

אֶמְסְאַךְ Hos. 4:6; perhaps for אֶמְאָסְךָ i. e. אֶמְאָסְךָ Kal fut. 1. pers. with suff.; see מאס.

אָמָה f. (with suff. אֲמָתִי; pl. אֲמָהוֹת; const. אַמְהוֹת), *maid-servant;* בֶּן־אָמָה *servant.*

אֲמָהוֹת pl.; see אָמָה.

אִמָּה, אַמָּה; see אֵם.

אֲמֻנָה, אָמוֹן, אָמֹן; see אמן.

אָמוֹץ (*strong*), p.n. of the father of Isaiah, Isa. 1:1.

אָמִי p. n. of a man.

אֵמִים p.n. of one of the giant races in Canaan.

אַמִּיץ *strong;* see אמץ.

אָמִיר *top;* see אמר.

אָמַל root not used; *was sick.* Pul. אֻמְלַל *sick, wasting, declining.*

אֲמֵלָה f., *pained, sick,* Eze. 16:30.

אֻמְלַל m., *wasting with disease,* Ps. 6:3.

אֻמְלַל m. (pl. אֻמְלָלִים), *wasted, feeble men,* Neh. 3:34.

אָמָם p. n. of a city.

אָמַן I. *was true, faithful;* part. אֹמְנִים *the faithful.*—II. *nursed, brought up;* part. אֹמֵן *foster-father, nurse.* Niph. נֶאֱמַן—I. *was sure.*—II. *was enduring, durable;* בַּיִת נֶאֱמָן *an enduring house.*—III. *was faithful.*—IV. *was carried* (as a child), Isa. 60:4. Hiph. הֶאֱמִין *confided, entrusted, believed, relied on,* followed by בְּ, לְ with inf.

אֲמַן Ch. Aph. הֵימִן *entrusted.*

אֳמָן m., *artificer,* Cant. 7:2.

אֹמֶן m.—I. *a true thing, truth;* אֱלֹהֵי א' *the God of truth.*—II. *formula of acquiescence, Amen, so be it.*

אָמוֹן m.—I. *constant, unvarying,* Pro. 8:30.—II. same as הָמוֹן *the multitude,* Jer. 52:15.—III. p. n. of an Egyptian idol *Amoun* in נֹא אָמוֹן which see.—IV. p. n. of a king of Judah.

אֵמוּן m.—I. *a faithful, true, sincere one.*—II. *educated, brought up,* Lam. 4:5.

אֹמֶן m., *faith;* adv. *truly.*

אֹמְנָה f., *beam, lintel,* 2 Kings 18:16.

אֱמוּנָה I. f. of אָמוּן וַיְהִי יָדָיו אֱמוּנָה *his hands were made steady, true.*—II. *faithfulness.*—III. *truth.* Pl. אֱמוּנוֹת

אֲמָנָה f.—I. *covenant, contract,* Neh. 11:23.—II. p. n. of a river near Damascus.—III. of a region.

אָמְנָה I. adv., *truly, indeed.*—II. f., *education, nursing,* Est. 2:20.

אָמְנָם adv., *certainly, verily;* הַאֻמְנָם *indeed?* 1 Kings 8:27.

אֲמַת f. (with suff. אֲמָתוֹ).—I. *per-*

manency, durability.— II. *truth,* especially religious truth; used for truthfulness in God, and piety in man.

אֲמִינוֹן, אַמְנוֹן (*faithful*), p. n. of a son of David.

אָמֵץ (imp. אֱמַץ; fut. יֶאֱמַץ), *was powerful, courageous;* with מִן *prevailed, was mightier than.*—Pi. I. *strengthen,* Job 4:1.—II. *repair* (a house), 2 Chro. 24:13.—III. *fasten, secure,* Pro. 8:28.—IV. *encourage.* —V. א' לֵב פ' *harden the heart.* Hiph. *strengthen, confirm.* Hith. *acquired power, took courage.*

אַמִּיץ *strong, prevailing.*

אֹמֶץ m., *vigour,* Job 17:9.

אָמֹץ m., *powerful, vigorous* (of horses) pl. אֲמֻצִּים Zec. 6:3.

אַמְצָה f., *strength,* Zec. 12:5.

אָמְצִי (*strong*), p. n. of a man.

אֲמַצְיָהוּ, אֲמַצְיָה (*strengthened of God*), p. n., *Amaziah* king of Judah.

מַאֲמַצֵּי כֹּחַ m. pl.: *confirmers of power,* Job 36:19.

אָמַר I. *he said* (to any one, with אֶל, לְ; of any one, with לְ and accus.); sometimes same as דִּבֶּר *he spoke;* inf. לֵאמֹר *saying.*—II. *commanded* —III. *he thought,* lit. *he spake inwardly,* Gen. 44:28, Ex. 2:14, &c. &c. בְּלִבּוֹ, בִּלְבָבוֹ. Niph. *was said of or concerning any one* (with לְ); impers. יֵאָמֵר *it is said;* with לְ *it is said to some one.* Hiph. *made declared,* "avouched," Eng. Ver., Deu. 26:17, 18. Hith. *were declared, published, made famous*

אֲמַר Ch., *he said, commanded.*

אֵמֶר m.—I. same as דִּבֵּר *a discourse,*

speech; אֲמְרֵי אֵל *the words of God.*
—II. *an appointment, declaration,*
Job 20:29; with suff. אִמְרִי; pl.
אֲמָרִים.

אֹמֶר m., *enunciation, expression, saying*; same as דָּבָר *a thing, a
matter.*

אָמֹץ (*tall*), p. n. of a man.

אִמֵּר Ch., *a lamb*, Ezr. 6:9, 17, &c.

אִמְרָה f., *word, declaration, discourse*;
pl. אֲמָרוֹת.

אֶמְרָה f., the same.

אָמִיר m., *the pod which contains
the fruit of the palm tree*, Isa.
17:6.

מַאֲמָר m., *edict, command*, Ezr. 1:
15, &c.

מֵאמַר m. Ch., the same.

אִמְרִי (*eloquent*), p. n. of a man.

אֱמֹרִי *the Amorite*; LXX. Ἀμορραῖος.

אֲמַרְיָה and אֲמַרְיָהוּ p. n. of a man.

אַמְרָפֶל p. n. of the king of Shinar,
Gen. 14:1, 9.

אֶמֶשׁ *yesterday*, lit. the day before
last night.

אֱמֶת *truth*; see אמן.

אַמְתַּחַת *sack*; see מתח.

אֲמִתַּי (*truth-teller*), p. n. of the father
of the prophet Jonah, Jon. 1:1.

אָן, אָנָה, אֲנָה; see אי.

אֹן *Heliopolis*; see און.

אָנָא, אָנָה Ch., pers. pron. *I.*

אָנָּא interj., *gently, I pray*, &c.

אַנְבֶּה Ch., for אֵב; see אֵב in אבב.

אָנַדְּע; see ינדע.

אָנָה *he suffered*, Isa. 3:19. Pi. אִנָּה
he caused pain, Ex. 21:13. Pu.
was made to suffer, Pro. 12:21,
Ps. 91:10. Hith. part. מִתְאַנֵּה

*affecting irritation, seeming to be
irritated*, followed by לְ.

אֲנָחֲרָת p. n. of a city.

אֲנִיָּה f., *suffering, pain*, Isa. 29:2.

תַּאֲנִיָּה f., the same, Lam. 2:5.

אֳנִי com., *a ship*; collectively, *a fleet.*

אֳנִיָּה f., *a ship.*

תַּאֲנָה f., *sexual impulse*, Jer. 2:24.

תֹּאֲנָה f. *opportunity, revenge*, Jud.14:4.

אֲנוּ com., *we*, Jer. 42:6; see אָנֹכִי.

אִנּוּן m., אִנִּין f. pron. pl. Ch., *these,
those.*

אֱנָשׁ p. n.; see אנשׁ.

אָנַח. Niph. נֶאֱנַח *he sighed* (the things
sighed for preceded by עַל, מִן).

אֲנָחָה f., *sighing, sobbing.*

אֲנִי *I*; see אָנֹכִי.

אֲנִיָּה, אֲנִיָּה, אֲנִי; see אנה.

אַנְעָם (*mourning of the people*), p. n. of
a man.

אֲנָךְ m.—I. *lead.*—II. *a plummet*, Am.
7:7, 8.

אָנֹכִי (contr. אָנִי; with the pause אָנִי),
pers. pron. *I*; pl. אֲנַחְנוּ, sometimes
נַחְנוּ (אָנוּ) Jer. 42:6), *we.*

אָנַן. Hith. הִתְאוֹנֵן *he groaned*, Nu.
11:1, Lam. 3:39.

אָנַס *urge, force*, Est. 1:8.

אֲנַס Ch., the same; *trouble*, Dan. 4:6.

אָנַף (fut. יֶאֱנַף), *breathe through the
nose, snort*; hence *was irritated,
angry* (with בְּ). Hith. הִתְאַנַּף
became angry.

אַף m. (with suff. אַפִּי).—I. *nose*; נִבְּה
אַף *disdainful, haughty*, lit. *turned
up of nose*, Ps. 10:4.—II. *anger*;
dual אַפַּיִם I. *nostrils* by synecd.—
II. *face, countenance*; לְאַפֵּי same

לִפְנֵי as *in the sight of, before*; מָנָה אַחַת אַפַּיִם *one of two persons*, i. e. a double portion, 1 Sa. 1:5.— III. *anger*, אֶרֶךְ אַ׳ *slow to anger*; קְצַר אַ׳ *quick to anger, hasty*.

אַף *also*; see in its place.

אַנַף Ch., dual, *nostrils, face*.

אֲנָפָה f., name of an unclean bird, "heron," Eng. Ver.; LXX. χαραδριὸς; Lev. 11:19, Deu. 14:18.

אָנַק *cry out for pain*; inf. אֲנֹק; fut. יֶאֱנַק. Niph. נֶאֱנַק *lament*.

אֲנָקָה const. אֶנְקַת f.—I. *crying out for pain*.—II. name of a reptile so called from its cry, Lev. 11:30.

אָנַשׁ root not used. (אֲנַס Ch., *compress, compel*). Part. אָנוּשׁ m., אֲנוּשָׁה f. *incurable* (of a wound), *grievous, mortal, unlucky* (of a day), *malignant* (of a disposition); Niph. he *became mortally sick*, 2 Sa. 12:15.

אֱנוֹשׁ m.—I. *man* (as mortal and miserable). — II. *mankind*. — III. *plebeian, low person*; pl. אֲנָשִׁים (const. אַנְשֵׁי; with suff. אֲנָשֶׁיךָ, אַנְשֵׁיהֶם), *man, men*; see אִישׁ.— IV. אֱנוֹשׁ p.n. of a son of Seth.

אֱנָשׁ, אֲנַשׁ Ch., *man*.

אַנְתָּה Ch., pers. pron. m., *thou*.

אָסָא (*healing*), p.n. of a king of Judah.

אָסוּךְ *cup*; see סוּךְ.

אָסוּר, אָסִיר *bound*; see אסר.

אָסִיף *harvest*; see אסף.

אָסָם m., pl. אֲסָמִים *store-houses, granaries*; LXX. ταμεῖα.

אָסַן root not used; (Arab. *death, destruction*).

אָסוֹן m., *injury, death by accident*.

אָסְנָה p. n. of a man.

אָסְנַפַּר p.n. of an Assyrian general

אָסְנַת (*belonging to Neith*), p.n. of the wife of Joseph.

אֶסְעָרֵם Syr. for אֶסְעָרֵם Pi. fut. 1.pers. with suff.; see סער.

אָסַף (inf. אֲסֹף; const. אֱסֹף; with suff. אָסְפְּךָ; fut. יֶאֱסֹף, with suff. יַאַסְפֵנִי; 1.pers. אֶאֱסֹף and אֹסֵף).— I. *collected, gathered* (with אֶל and עַל before the place in which). —II. *take away, take off, destroy* אָ׳ נַפְשׁוֹ *he deprived himself of life*. Niph. נֶאֱסַף I. *was gathered, received*.—II. *was taken away, ceased*. — III. *perished*, Hos. 4:3, (with עַל, לְ, אֶל) נ׳ אֶל־עַמּוֹ; עַמָּיו, אֲבוֹתָיו, *was gathered to his people, fathers*, i. e. was buried; used in this sense alone נֶאֱסַף Nu. 20:26.—Pi. I. *gather, receive*.— II. *close the rear of a march*, Nu. 10:25, Jos. 6:9, 13. Pu. *was gathered*. Hith. הִתְאַסֵּף *gather themselves together*, Deu. 33:5.

אָסָף (*collector*), p.n. of a man.

אֹסֶף m., *ingathering, harvest of fruits*.

אָסִיף m., *harvest of apples*.

אֲסֵפָה f., *collection, gathering*, Isa. 24:22.

אֲסֻפִּים m. pl., *collection of stores* or *money, storehouses*.

אֲסֵפוֹת f. pl., the same.

אֶסְפְּךָ Kal fut. 1.pers. with suff. 1 Sa. 15:6; Kal part. with suff. 2 Ki. 22:20; see אסף.

הָאסַפְסֻף m., with the article *mixed multitude*, Nu. 11:4.

אָסְפַּרְנָא Ch. adv., *exactly, carefully, quickly*.

אַסְפָּתָא p. n. of a son of Haman.

אָסַר (fut. יֶאְסֹר and יַאֲסֹר).—I. *he tied, bound,* followed by לְ; א׳ הַמֶּרְכָּבָה *yoking the horses to the chariot.*— II. מִלְחָמָה א׳ *he kept together the battle,* i. e. made his troops attack closely and continuously. — III., אָסַר אִסָּר עַל־נַפְשׁוֹ *he bound himself by an oath;* part. אָסוּר *captive, prisoner.* Niph. *becoming bound.* Pu. *taken, reduced to bondage.*

אֵסוּר m., *chain;* pl. אֲסוּרִים; בֵּית הָאֵסוּר *prison.*

אֱסוּר Ch., the same.

אָסִיר m., *a captive.*

אַסִּיר m.—I. *captive.*—II. p.n. of a man.

אֱסָר m., *an obligation.*

אֱסָר m. Ch., the same.

אִסָּר m., the same.

מוֹסֵר m.; see in its place.

אֵסַר־חַדֹּן p. n., *Esar-haddon* king of Assyria, the successor of Sennacherib; LXX. Ἀσορδάν.

אֲסֻפִּים Kal fut. 1. pers. with suff.; see יסף

אֶסְתֵּר (*star*), p. n., *Esther* queen of Persia; her name before was הֲדַסָּה Est. 2:7.

אָע m. Ch., same as Heb. עֵץ *wood.*

אַף *nose;* see אנף

אַף part., *also, moreover, nay, indeed;* אַף כִּי אָמַר *indeed, truly,* כִּי *hath* (God) *indeed said,* Gen. 3:1.

אַף Ch., the same.

אַפְאֵיהֶם Hiph. fut. 1. pers. with suff.; see פאה.

אָפַד *he put on the Ephod,* Ex. 29:5, Lev. 8:7 (with לְ of the person, and בְּ of the thing).

אֵפוֹד m.—I. *Ephod,* a garment worn

by the priesthood; א׳ נָשָׂא *he wore the ephod,* i. e. he fulfilled the priest's office.—II. perhaps the name of an idol, Jud. 8:27, &c.

אֲפֻדָּה f., *made like an ephod;* probably the dress of an idol.

אֵפֹד p. n. of a man.

אַפֶּדֶן *camp;* see פדן.

אָפָה *baking.* Niph. *baked.*

אֹפֶה m., *a baker;* pl. אֹפִים.

אֵפָה f., *the same;* pl. אֵפוֹת.

מַאֲפֶה m., *bakemeat.*

אֵפוּ Syr. for אֵפוֹ imp. pl. of the verb אפה.

אֵפוֹ, אֵפוֹא pa., οὖν, δή, *now, then;* אַיֵּה אֵ׳ *where then?* אִם כֵּן אֵ׳ *if then it be so;* מָה אֵ׳ *what then!* דְּעוּ אֵ׳ γινώσκετε οὖν! *know then!*

אֵפוֹד *ephod;* see אפד.

אַפִּיחַ p. n. of a man.

אַפַּיִם p. n. of a man.

אָפִיק *swelling;* see אפק.

אָפַל root not used (Arab. *set as the sun*).

אָפִיל m., אֲפִילָה f.—I. *concealed.*— II. *very dark.*

אֹפֶל m., *obscure.*

אֲפֵל m., *thick darkness;* more intense than חֹשֶׁךְ.

אֲפֵלָה f., *darkness;* חֹשֶׁךְ אֵ׳ *thick darkness.*

מַאְפֵּל m., *darkness.*

מַאְפֵּלְיָה f., *extreme darkness,* Jer 2:31.

אֲפַלָל (*judgment*), p. n. of a man.

אָפַן root not used; same as פָּנָה *turn, roll.*

אוֹפָן m., *wheel;* const. אֹפַן; pl אֹפַנִּים.

אֹפֶן *season* (περίοδος); דָּבָר עַל־אָפְנָיו *a word in season,* Pro. 25:11.

אֶפֶס m.—I. *termination, extremity;* אַפְסֵי אֶרֶץ *ends of the earth;* dual אֲפָסַיִם *two extremities,* i.e. of both feet; *the soles* or *ankles,* Eze. 47:3. —II. *deficiency, wanting;* בְּאֶפֶס *without,* lit. *in there not being,* followed by the genitive of the thing; עַד אֵי *until there is none;* אַפְסִי *besides me;* בְּאֶפֶס *without;* מֵאֶפֶס *of, from nothing;* אֶפֶס כִּי *except, unless.*

אֶפֶס דַּמִּים p. n. of a town in the tribe of Judah, 1 Sa. 17:1; see פַּס דַּמִּים.

אֶפְעַ m., *an adder,* Isa. 41:24; see פֵּעָה.

אֶפְעֶה *adder;* see פֵּעָה.

אָפַף *enclose, hem in;* pret. pl. אָפְפוּ; with suff. אֲפָפוּנִי.

אָפַק Kal, root not used; (Arab. *visited many countries*). Hith. הִתְאַפֵּק I. *went on, proceeded.*—II. *restrained himself from proceeding,* Gen. 45:1, &c.; LXX. ἀνέχομαι, ἐγκρατεύομαι.

אָפִיק m. adj.—I. *mighty, eminent man,* Job 12:21.—II. *river, torrent.*—III. *the bosses of a shield,* Job 41:7.—IV. *swellings of the sea.*—V. p. n. of a city in the tribe of Asher, Jud. 1:31, same as:—

אֲפֵק p.n.—I. of a city in the tribe of Asher.—II. of a city in the tribe of Issachar.

אֲפֵקָה p. n. of a town in the mountains of Judah, Jos. 15:53.

אָפַר root not used; (Arab. *casting away*).

אֵפֶר m.—I. *ashes.*—II. *any thing worthless.*

אוֹפִיר p. n. of a kingdom; see in its place.

אֲפֵר m. (transpos. of פְּאֵר), *a tiara, crown,* 1 Ki. 20:38, 41.

אֶפְרֹחַ *chicken;* see פרח.

אַפִּרְיוֹן m., LXX. φορεῖον, *car, sedan,* Cant. 3:9, 10.

אֶפְרַיִם p.n.—I. *Ephraim,* the younger son of Joseph.—II. the tribe that descended from him.—III. afterwards, the kingdom formed by the ten tribes that revolted from the house of David.

אֶפְרָתָה, אֶפְרָת p.n.—I. of a city in the tribe of Judah: called also בֵּית־לֶחֶם.—II. same as אֶפְרַיִם, Ps. 132:6.

אֶפְרָתִי I. *an Ephraimite.*—II. an inhabitant of Ephratah.

אֲפָרְסַיְא p. n. of an unknown people, Ezr. 4:9.

אֲפָרְסְכָיֵא p.n.,as above, Ezr. 5:6.

אֲפָרְסַתְכָיֵא p. n. of the inhabitants of a city in Assyria, Ezr. 4:9.

וָאֵפֶת, אֵפַת Niph. fut. apoc. 1. pers. for אֶפָּתָה; see פתה.

אַפְּתֹם pa., *thus then, then moreover,* Ezr. 4:13.

אֶצְבּוֹן p. n. of a man.

אֶצְבַּע *finger;* see צבע.

אַצִּיעָה Hiph. fut. 1. pers. with ה parag., see יצע.

אָצַל I. *holding back, withholding,* with מִן.—II. *laying up with one's self,* with לְ. Niph. *contracted,* Eze 42:6. Hiph. *withhold;* fut. וַיָּאֶצֶל Nu. 11:25.

אָצִיל m. (Arab. *rooted, firm*).—I. *nobleman*, Eze. 24:11.—II. *end, extremity*, Isa. 41:9.

אַצִּיל m. *joint, suture*; אַצִּילֵי יָדַיִם *the wrists*.

אָצֵל p. n.—I. of a man.—II. of a place near Jerusalem, Zec. 14:5. אֵצֶל prep., *near*; מֵאֶצְלוֹ *near him*.

אֲצַלְיָהוּ p. n. of a man.

אֹצֶם p. n. of a man.

אֶצְעָדָה *bracelet*; see צעד.

אֶצֹּק Kal fut. 1. pers. of the verb; see יצק.

אָצַר *treasured*. Niph. *laid up*, Isa. 23:1,18. Hiph. הוֹצֵר *appoint as treasurer*, Neh. 13:13, with עַל; fut. with ה parag. אוֹצְרָה.

אוֹצָר m. (pl. אוֹצָרוֹת).—I. *treasury*. —II. *treasure*; בֵּית הָאֹ׳ I. *treasure-house*.—II. *warehouse*.

אֶצֶר p. n. of a man.

אֶצֳּרְךָ Kri, Jer. 1:5, Kal fut. 1. pers. with suff.; see יצר.

אֶקְדָּח *carbuncle*; see קדח.

אַקּוֹ m., *gazelle*, Deu. 14:5.

אֶקַּח Kal fut. 1. pers. of the verb לקח.

אֶקָּחָה for אֶקְחָה Isa. 56:12, Kal fut. 1. pers. with ה parag., from לקח.

אֶקְרָאָה Kal fut. 1. pers. with ה parag., from קרא.

אֹר *light*; see יְאוֹר.

אֲרָא p. n. of a man.

אֵרָא, וָאֵרָא Niph. fut. apoc., from ראה.

אֲרִאֵל, אֲרִאֵלִי name of Jerusalem; see אריה.

אָרַב *lying in wait, ambush*; with לְ, עַל; fut. יֶאֱרֹב יֶאֱרֹב t. אוֹרֵב *ambus-*

cader. Pi. part. pl. מְאָרְבִים *lying in wait*. Hiph. *he places an ambush*, 1 Sa. 15 · 5.

אֲרָב p. n. of a town in the tribe of Judah.

אַרְבִּי a native of Arabia.

אֶרֶב m., *lying in wait, place of ambush*, Job 37:8, 38:40.

אֹרֶב m., *the same*; with suff. אׇרְבּוֹ.

אׇרְבָּה f., *the same*; pl. אׇרְבוֹת; const. אׇרְבוֹת.

אַרְבֶּה m., a species of *locust*, from רָבָה *was many*.

אֲרֻבָּה f.—I. *net* or *wicker work* to cover windows: hence,—II. *window*.—III. *pigeon-holes*, Isa. 60:8. IV. applied to the visible heavens, Gen. 7:11, 8:2.—V. a *chimney*, Hos. 13:3.

אֲרֻבּוֹת (*plots*), p. n. of a place in the tribe of Judah.

מַאֲרָב m., *ambush, ambuscade*.

אַרְבֵּאל p. n. of a place, Hos. 10:14; see בֵּית.

אַרְבַּע p. n. of a giant.

אַרְבַּע *four*; see רבע.

אָרַג I. *plaiting the hair*, Jud. 16:13. —II. *weaving*, Isa. 59:5; part. אֹרֵג a weaver, f. אֹרְגָה.

אֶרֶג m.—I. *texture, web*, Job 7:6.— II. *weaver's comb*, Jud. 16:14.

אַרְגֹּב p. n.—I. of the district of Og. —II. of a man.

אַרְגְּוָן Ch., *purple*, same as אַרְגָּמָן.

אַרְגָּז *bag*; see רגז.

אַרְגָּמָן m., *purple*.

אַרְדְּ p. n. *Ard*, a son of Benjamin; אַרְדִּי patronymic of Ard.

אַרְדּוֹן p. n. of a man.

אָרָה I. *pluck fruit*, Ps. 80:13.—II. *gather*.

אֱרֵה Nu. 22:6, imp. with ה parag.; see ארר.

אֲוֵרוֹת f. pl., *stables, stalls for beasts*, 2 Chron. 32:28.

אֲרָיוֹת f. pl., const. }
אֲרָווֹת f. pl., const. } —I. *stalls*. —II. *stable*.

אֲרִי m., *a lion*; pl. אֲרָיִים and אֲרָיוֹת אַרְיֵה m., *a lion*.

אַרְיֵה m. Ch., *a lion*; pl. אַרְיָוָן.

אֲרִיּוֹת Isa. 16:9, transpos. for אֲרַיֵּוֶךְ or אֲרַיְוֵךְ (same as רָיָה). Pi. fut. 1. pers. with suff.; see רוה.

אֲרִיאֵל, אֲרִאֵל (*lion of God*).—I. a name of the altar of burnt-offering.—II. a name for Jerusalem.—III. p. n. of a man.

אֲרְאֵל (the same), p. n. of a man.

אַרְאֵלִי (the same), p. n. of a man.

אֶרְאֶלָּם m., "their valiant ones," Isa. 33:7, Eng. Ver.; probably for אֶרְאֶה לָהֶם *I will appear unto them* (Lee).

אָרוֹן com.—I. *ark, chest*; אֲרוֹן הַבְּרִית, אֲרוֹן הָעֵדֻת, אֱלֹהִים, *the ark of the covenant*.—II. *coffin, mummy-case*, Gen. 50:26.

אֲרוּ Ch., *behold! see!*

אַרְוַד p. n., *Aradus*, a city and district on the coast of Phœnicia.

אַרְוֹדִי, אֲרוֹד p. n. of a man.

אֲרוּכָה *repairing*; see ארך.

אֲרוּמָה p. n. of a city.

אֲרוֹמִים *Syrians*; see אֲרָם, אֲרַמִּי.

אֲרוֹמַם for אֶתְרוֹמַם Hith. fut. 1. pers.; see רום

אָרַז *was firm, closely packed*; part אֲרוּזִים.

אֶרֶז m., *cedar*; pl. אֲרָזִים, const אַרְזֵי.

אַרְזָה f., *cedar wainscot*, Zep. 2:14.

אָרַח *he goeth to herd with*, Job 34:8; part. אֹרֵחַ *traveller*.

אָרַח (*wanderer*), p. n. of a man.

אֹרַח com. (with suff. אָרְחִי; pl. אֳרָחוֹת; const. אָרְחוֹת; with suff. אָרְחֹתָם and אָרְחֵי).—I. *way, road, path*.—II. *mode* or *manner*; אֹ יְהֹוָה *way of the Lord*, i. e. the way that pleases the Lord; אֹ חַיִּים *the way of life*, i. e. that leads to life; אֹ עוֹלָם *the old path*, i. e. the manners of ancient times.—III. *wayfaring man*.

אֹרַח m. Ch., *the same*; pl. אָרְחָן.

אָרְחָה f.—I. *step, progress*.—II. *travelling company, caravan*.

אֲרֻחָה f.—I. *fixed portion, ration*.—II. *portion generally*.

אֲרִיאֵל, אֲרָיוֹת, אַרְיֵה, אֲרִי; p. n.; see ארה.

אֲרִידַי p. n. of a son of Haman, Ἀριδαῖος.

אֲרִידָתָא (*strong*), p. n. of a man.

אַרְיוֹךְ p. n.—I. of a king of Ellasar, Gen. 14:1.—II. of a Chaldean.

אֲרִיסַי p. n. of a son of Haman.

אָרַךְ (fut. יֶאֱרַךְ; pl. יַאַרְכוּ), *was long, became* or *was made long*; אָרְכוּ לוֹ הַיָּמִים *he had tarried there many days*, Gen. 26:8. Hiph. הֶאֱרִיךְ trans. *make long, prolong*; הֶ יְמֵי פ׳ *lengthen his days, prolong life*; הֶ אַפּוֹ נַפְשׁוֹ *was long suffering, patient*.

אֲרֻכָה, אֲרֻכָּה f.—I. *lengthening out*.

—II. *repairing, restoring, healing;*
(Arab. the same).

אֲרַךְ Ch. (part. אָרִיךְ), *becoming,*
suitable.

אָרֵךְ (const. אֶרֶךְ), *long;* א הָאֵבָר *with*
long pinions, Ecc. 7:8; א אַפַּיִם
slow to anger; א רוּחַ μακρόθυμος,
long-suffering.

אֶרֶךְ p. n. of a city of Shinar, Gen.
10:10; hence אַרְכְּוָיֵא an inhabitant of Erech; אַרְכִּי the same.

אֹרֶךְ m., *length* (of time and space);
with suff. אָרְכּוֹ.

אֹרֶךְ m., אֲרֻכָּה f., *long, lasting long.*
אַרְכָה, אַרְכָא f. Ch., *time, duration.*

אַרְכֻּבָּה *the knee,* Dan. 5:6; see ברך.

אֲרָם f. (const. אֲרַם), p.n., *Aramea;* the
region of Damascus and Syria to
the Orontes and Mesopotamia; א
פַּדַּן אֲרָם נַהֲרַיִם *Mesopotamia;*
Padan Aram; א צוֹבָה part of
Syria; א דַּמֶּשֶׂק *Syria of Da-*
mascus; א מַעֲכָה the region beyond Jordan at the foot of Anti-
Libanus; א בֵּית־רְחוֹב part of
Syria; see רְחֹב.

אֲרַמִּי m., *Syrian* (f. אֲרַמִּיָּה; pl. אֲרַמִּים
and אֲרוֹמִים).

אֲרַמִית adv., *in Syriac, in the lan-*
guage of Syria.

אַרְמוֹן m. (pl. const. אַרְמְנוֹת), *palace.*
אַרְמֹנִי p.n. of one of the sons of Saul.

אֹרֶן m., *the mountain ash,* Isa. 44:14;
LXX. πίτυς; Vulg. *pinus.*

אֹרֶן p. n. of a man.

אֹרֶן p. n. of a man.

אַרְנֶבֶת f., *the hare,* Lev. 11:6, Deu.
14:17; (Arab. the same).

אַרְנֹן (*sounding,* see רָנַן), p.n., *Arnon,*

a river which bounded the land of
Israel to the east.

אַרְנָן p. n. of a man.

אֲרַנְיָה (אֲרַוְנָה 2 Sa. 24:15). p. n., *Arau-*
nah, the Jebusite.

אַרְעָא, אֲרַע m. Ch.—I. *the earth.*
—II. an epithet: *low, inferior* followed by מִן.

אַרְעִית f. Ch., *low, mean.*

אַרְפָּד p. n. of a city of Syria.

אַרְפַּכְשַׁד p.n. of a son of Shem.

אֶרֶץ f., sometimes m. (with art. הָאָרֶץ;
with suff. אַרְצוֹ; pl. אֲרָצוֹת).—I.
earth.—II. *the world.*—III. *the*
ground; אַרְצָה *on the ground.*—
IV. *region, province.* Pl. אֲרָצוֹת
I. *lands, countries.*—II. *heathen*
nations.

אַרְצָא p. n. of a man.

אֲרַק f. Ch., *the earth,* Jer. 10:11.

אָרַר (imp. אֹר; with ה parag. אָרָה;
pl. אֹרוּ; fut. יָאֹר), *denounce, curse.*
Niph. part. pl. נֶאָרִים *denounced,*
cursed. Pi. אֵרֵר *denounce, bring*
on a curse; part. pl. מְאָרְרִים. Hoph.
fut. יוּאָר *is made accursed.*

מְאֵרָה f., *cursing.*

אֲרָרָט p.n., *Ararat,* a mountain in
Armenia.

אֲרָרִי same as הֲרָרִי *Ararite.*

אָרַשׂ Pi. אֵרַשׂ, אֵרֵשׂ (with accusative
אִשָּׁה) *espouse a wife* by entering
into a contract under a fine; with
בְּ of the sum mulcted. Pu. pret. f.
אֹרָשָׂה *espoused;* part. f. מְאֹרָשָׂה.

אָרַשׁ root not used; (Arab. *he desired*)

אֲרֶשֶׁת f., *petition;* LXX. δέησις, Ps
21:3.

אַרְתַּחְשַׁשְׂתָּא, אַרְתַּחְשַׁסְתָּא, אַרְתַּחְשַׁשְׂתָּא } *Artaxerxes,* king of Persia.

אֲשַׂרְאֵל (same as אֲסַרְאֵל), p.n. of a m.

אֲשַׂרְאֵלָה p.n. of a man; '— patronymic of above.

אֵשׁ f., sometimes m. (with suff. אִשּׁוֹ (אֶשְׁכֶם, אִשָּׁם).—I. *fire.*—II. *lightning;* אֵשׁ אֱלֹהִים *lightning.*—III. *heat of the sun,* Joel 1:19, 20.—IV. *appearance of God.*—V. *God's fierce anger.*—VI. *ardour of mind.*—VII. *great tribulations.*

אֵשׁ com. Ch., emph. state אֶשָּׁא *fire.*

אִשֶּׁה m. (const. אִשֵּׁה; pl. אִשִּׁים, אִשַּׁי).—I. *burnt-offering.*—II. *incense-offering.*

אִשָּׁה f. (אֶשְׁתָּם Jer. 6:29), for אֵשׁ תָּם (by) *fire is consumed.*

אַשְׁבֵּל p.n. of a son of Benjamin, patronymic of the same.

אַשְׁבָּן p.n. of a man.

אֶשְׁבֹּעַ p.n. of a son of Saul.

אֶשְׁבַּעַל p.n. of a son of Saul.

אָשַׁר root not used; (Arab. *he rushed*).

אֶשֶׁד m., *bed of a river* or *brook;* אֶשֶׁד הַנְּחָלִים *bed of the torrents,* Nu. 21:15.

אַשְׁדָּה *foot, base of a mountain;* pl. אֲשֵׁדוֹת; const. אַשְׁדוֹת.

אַשְׁדּוֹד (from שָׁדַד), p.n. Ashdod (Ἄζωτος), a city of the Philistines; אַשְׁדּוֹדִי *an Ashdodite;* ית— I. *a woman of Ashdod.*—II. *in the language of Ashdod.*

אִשָּׁה *woman;* see אֱנֹשׁ.

אָשְׁיָה f., *foundation,* Jer. 50:15; from שׁוּת.

אַשּׁוּרִי, אַשּׁוּר, אַשּׁוּר *footstep;* see אָשַׁר.

אֲשְׁחוּר p.n. of a man.

אַשִׁימָא p.n. of a god of the Hamathites.

אֲשֵׁרָה *erection;* see אֲשֵׁרָה.

אָשִׁישׁ *foundation,* Isa. 16:7, see אֵשׁ, perhaps for אִישֵׁי *men,* as Jer 48:31.

אֲשִׁישִׁין, אֲשִׁישָׁה *food;* see אֵשׁ.

אֶשֶׁךְ m., *testicles,* Lev. 21:20.

אֶשְׁכֹּל *Eshcol;* from שָׁכַל.

אַשְׁכִּים Ch. Hiph. inf. abs.; from שָׁכַם.

אַשְׁכְּנַז p.n. of a people of North Asia

אֶשְׁכָּר *a rich gift,* Eze. 27:15, Ps. 72:14; from שָׁכַר.

אֵשֶׁל m., *the tamarisk,* a middle-sized thorny tree; tamarix orientali (Linn.).

אָשֵׁם and אָשַׁם (fut. יֶאְשַׁם).—I. *was guilty, sinned* (when against any one, with לְ; when in any thing, with בְּ and לְ).—II. *was conscious of guilt.*—III. *suffered for sin,* Ps. 34:22, &c. Niph. *suffered the consequences of sin,* Joel 1:18; Hiph. *bring on the consequences of guilt,* Ps. 5:11.

אָשֵׁם m., *guilty.*

אָשָׁם m.—I. *guilt,* i.e. the consequence of sin.—II. *a sacrifice to expiate it.*

אַשְׁמָה f.—I. (inf. of אָשַׁם), לְאַשְׁמָה בָהּ *to trespass therein,* Lev. 5:26; לְאַשְׁמַת הָעָם *so that the people trespass.*—II. *guilt, trespass.*—III. *a trespass-offering,* Lev. 6:5.

אַשְׁמַנִּים m., "*desolate places,*" Eng. Ver., Isa. 59:10; meaning uncertain.

אַשְׁמֻרָה f., *the three watches into which the night was divided;* root שָׁמַר

אֶשְׁנָב m., *a latticed window*, Jud. 5: 28, Pro. 7:6.

אַשְׁנָה p. n. of two cities in the tribe of Judah.

אֶשְׁעָן (*a prop*), p. n. of a city in the tribe of Judah.

אַשָּׁף m. Heb. and Ch. (pl. אַשָּׁפִים), an *enchanter*.

אַשְׁפָּה f., *quiver*; בְּנֵי א' *sons of the quiver, arrows*, Lam. 3:13.

אַשְׁפּוֹת f. pl., *dung, dung heap*.

אַשְׁפַּתּוֹת f. pl., the same.

אַשְׁפְּנַז p. n. of one of the eunuchs of Nebuchadnezzar.

אֶשְׁפָּר measure, cup, 2 Sa. 6:10, 1 Chron. 6:3.

אַשְׁקְלוֹן p. n. of a city of the Philistines.

אָשַׁר *went straight on, walked along*. —Pi. I. *guide, lead aright*.—II. consider, pronounce good, happy; Pu. אֻשַּׁר, אֹשַּׁר—I. was guided.—II. was esteemed happy.

אָשֵׁר p. n. of one of the sons of Jacob; אָשֵׁרִי I. *an Asherite*.—II. p. n. of a city near Sichem, Jos. 17:7.

אֹשֶׁר m., *happiness*; only in the const. pl. as אַשְׁרֵי הָאִישׁ *blessed is the man*, Ps. 1:1; אַשְׁרֶיךָ *blessed art thou*, Deu. 33:29.

אֹשֶׁר m., *happiness*, Gen. 30:13; with suff. אָשְׁרִי.

אֲשֻׁר f.—I. *a step*.—II. *wood of the box tree*, Eze. 27:6.

אַשּׁוּר f.—I. *step*, Job 31:7.—II. p. n. f., *Assyria*, kingdom of; m., *an Assyrian*; דֶּרֶךְ א' אַשּׁוּרָה *into Assyria; the way of Assyria*.—III. אַשּׁוּרִים *a race of Ishmaelites*, Gen. 25:3.

אֲשׁוּר p. n. of a man.

אַשַּׁרְנָא m.Ch., *wall, building*, Eze. 5:3.

תְּאַשּׁוּר m., *the box tree*, Isa. 41:19, 60:13.

אֲשֶׁר I. relat. pron. of every gender and number; *he who, she who, it which, &c.*—II. note of the relative when it comes before pronouns and adverbs; אֲשֶׁר הוּא חַי *he who lives*; א' אֶת־עָפָר *which is dust*; א' לוֹ, לָה, לָהֶם *to whom*, sing.; א' לָהֶן, to whom, which, pl.; א' אֹתוֹ אֹתָה, *whom, which*, sing; א' אֹתָם אֹתָן, *whom, which*, pl.; אֲשֶׁר־לְשֹׁנוֹ *whose tongue*; א' בּוֹ, בָּהּ *in whom, which*; א' בְּאַרְצָם *in whose land*; א' מִמֶּנּוּ *from whom*; שָׁם א' *where*; מִשָּׁם א' *whence*; שָׁמָּה א' *whither*; א' תַּחַת כְּנָפָיו *under whose wings*.—III. precedes pron. of the 1.and 2. pers.; א' מְכַרְתֶּם אֹתִי *(ye) who have sold me*; א' בְּחַרְתִּיךָ *thee whom I have chosen*.—IV. compounded with preps.; אֶת־אֲשֶׁר *him whom*; בַּאֲשֶׁר *where; according to, as if, because, when*;—V. מֵאֲשֶׁר *from thence, whence*.— preceded by adverbs; בַּעֲבוּר, אַחַר, תַּחַת, עַל, עַד, יַעַן connecting them with the following words.—VI. אֲשֶׁר לְ note of the genitive; הַצֹּאן לְאָבִיהָ *her father's cattle*; אֲשֶׁר conj. ὅτι, *because, that*; ἵνα with fut.; *since, when*, ὅτε; ὡς *as*, with כְּ.

שֶׁ with dag. forte (sometimes שְׁ) same as אֲשֶׁר relat. pron. and in its other significations; שֶׁשָּׁם *where*; שֶׁל *of, whose*; בְּשֶׁ *because*; כְּמְעַט שֶׁ *almost*; עַד־שֶׁ *until*. For שֶׁ and שְׁ; see Noldii Concordantiæ, and Prof. Lee's Grammar

בְּשֶׁל *because, on account of;* בִּשְׁלִי *for my sake;* בְּשַׁלְמִי *on whose account?* בְּשֶׁל אֲשֶׁר *whatever.*

אֲשַׂרְאֵלָה (from אֲשֶׁר and אֵל), p. n. of a man.

אֲשֵׁירָה, אֲשֵׁרָה (probably m. of עַשְׁתֹּרֶת), p. n. of a deity of the Syrians; pl. אֲשֵׁרִים and אֲשֵׁרוֹת images of this idol.

אַשַׁרְנָא *buildings;* see אָשֵׁר.

אָשֵׁשׁ root not used. Hith. הִתְאֹשֵׁשׁ *be men;* see אִישׁ.

אָשִׁישׁ m. pl., const. אֲשִׁישֵׁי *foundations;* see in its place.

אֲשִׁישָׁה f., *cake, pancake;* pl. ־ים and אֲשִׁישׁוֹת.

אֻשִּׁין m. pl. Ch., *foundations.*

אֵשֶׁת *woman;* see אֲנֹשׁ.

אֶשְׁתִּיו Ch. pret. pl. with א prosthet., from שָׁתָה.

אֶשְׁתָּאֹל p. n. of a town of the Danites.

אֶשְׁתַּדּוּר Hith. of שׁדר.

אֶשְׁתּוֹן p. n. of a man.

אֶשְׁתְּמֹה and אֶשְׁתְּמֹעַ p. n. of a town in the tribe of Judah.

אָת *sign;* see אוה.

אֵת m., *ploughshare;* pl. אִתִּים and אֵתִים 1 Sa. 13:21; with suff. אִתֵּיכֶם.

II אֵת־, אֶת־ note of:—I. the accus.—II. the nom. with verbs passive and neuter; יִקָּרֵא אֶת־שִׁמְךָ *thy name shall be called;* with suff. אוֹתְךָ, אֹתְךָ, אוֹתִי, אֹתִי *me* (with pause אֹתָךְ); with ה parag. (אוֹתְכָה) אֹתְךָ m., אֹתָכָה, אֹתָךְ f., *thee;* אֹתוֹ אֹתוֹ *him;* אֹתָהּ *her;* אֹתָנוּ *us;* אֶתְכֶם, אֹתָם, אוֹתָם *you,*

אוֹתָם, אֹתָם *them,* m.; אֹתָן with ה parag. אֶתְהֶן, אֹתָנָה *them,* f.

III. אֶת־, אֵת prep. *with, by, one; besides, towards;* אֶת־פְּנֵי *before some one;* with suff. אִתִּי *with me;* אִתְּךָ (with pause אִתָּךְ) m., אִתָּךְ, אִתָּךְ f., *with thee;* אִתּוֹ *with him;* אִתָּהּ *with her;* אִתָּנוּ *with us;* אִתְּכֶן, אִתְּכֶם *with you;* אִתָּם *with them* (sometimes אֹתִי, אֹתוֹ, &c.); מֵאֵת denotes separation, *from;* מֵאִתִּי, *from me;* מֵאוֹתָךְ, מֵאִתְּךָ *from thee,* &c.

אֶתְבַּעַל p. n. of a king of Sidon.

אַתָּה (sometimes אַתְּ m.; אָת, with pause אָתְּ, sometimes אַתִּי f.), pers. pron. *thou;* אַתֶּם m., אַתֵּן, אַתֶּנָה f., *ye.*

אֵתָה (אָתָא Isa. 21:12), *came;* pret. pl. אָתָנוּ; imper. pl. אֵתָיוּ; fut. וַיֵּאתֶה, תֶּאתֶה, וַיֵּאתָא; pl. יֶאְתָיוּ. Hiph. imper. pl. הֵתָיוּ *bring ye.*

אֲתָה Ch., *came.* Aph. הַיְתִי *brought.* Hoph. *was brought.*

אִיתוֹן m., *entrance,* Eze. 40:15.

אֶתְוַדַּע Hith. fut. 1. pers., from ידע.

אַתּוּן com. Ch., *furnace,* Dan. 3:6, 11, 15.

אַתִּיק, אַתּוּק m., *gallery,* Eze. 41:3, 15.

אֶתְנִי p. n. of a man.

אֵתָיוּ Syr. for אֱתָיוּ which is for אָתוּ imp. pl., from אתה.

אֵתָיוּ for אֶתְאָנוּ pret. pl. 1. pers., from אָתָה. אָתָא.

אַתֶּם you; אַתֵּן, אַתֶּם see אַתָּה.

אֵתָם p. n. of a place in the desert.

אִתְמוֹל ,אֶתְמוּל ,אֶתְמוֹל *yesterday;* same as תְּמוֹל.

אָתַן root not used (Arab. *stepping shortly, she-ass*).

אָתוֹן f., *she-ass.*

אֶתְנָן אֶתְנָה *gift;* see יתן.

אֶתְנִי *(gift),* p. n. of a man.

אֶתְקְנֶךָ Kal fut. 1. pers. with suff. and נ epenth., from נתק.

אֲתַר m. Ch., *place;* אֲתַר דִּי *in that place, where;* בָּאתַר *after;* בָּאתְרָךְ *after thee.*

אֲתָרִים m., *places;* or p. n. according to others Nu. 21:1.

ב

בְּ prep.—I. of place: *in, among, with, near, before;* never motion either to or in a place.—II. of time: *in, within.*—III. used of the means or instrument: *by, with.*—IV. of the cause: *for, because.*—V. of the rule: *according to.*—VI. *by* (in an oath).—VII. often prefixed to the inf. of verbs, translated by *in* or *when;* with suff. בִּי; בְּךָ m. (with the pause בָּךְ); בָּךְ f., בּוֹ, בָּהּ; בָּנוּ; בָּכֶם and בָּכֶם, בָּהֶן and בָּם, בָּהֶם בָּם.

בָּאָה imp. with ה parag.; בָּאִים, בָּא part. pl.; בְּאֵכָה inf. with suff.; בָּא and בָּאת pret. f. 2. pers., from בוא.

בָּאָה *entrance;* see בּוֹא.

בָּאִישׁ *wicked;* see באש.

בָּאַר Pi. בֵּאַר—I. *dig, cut upon or into, define well;* with עַל.—II. *make clear, publish,* Deu. 1:5.

בְּאֵר f. (pl. const. בְּאֵרוֹת).—I. *well, cistern.*—II. p. n. of one of the stations in the desert.—III. p. n. of

a town in the tribe of Judah. בְּאֵר אֵלִים (*the well of heroes*), p. n. of a well. בְּאֵר לַחַי רֹאִי (*the well of the living God that seeth me*), p. n. of a well in the desert. בְּאֵר שֶׁבַע (*well of the oath*), p. n. of a city in the tribe of Simeon. בְּאֵרוֹת p. n. of a city in the tribe of Benjamin; בְּרֹתִי בְּאֵרֹתִי, epithet of an inhabitant of Beeroth. בְּאֵרוֹת בְּנֵי יַעֲקָן (*wells of the sons of Iaachan*), p. n of a station in the desert.

בְּאֵר often, בּוֹר m.—I. *well of water; well of bitumen,* Gen. 14:10.—II. *pit* or *dungeon in which prisoners were kept;* בֵּית הַבּוֹר *prison house.*—III. *grave, sepulchre;* יוֹרְדֵי בוֹר *they that go down into the pit,* i. e. *the dead;* עַד בּוֹר *even to the grave;* with ה *den, place,* בֹּרָה, pl. בֹּרוֹת, בָּאֵרוֹת.

בְּאֵרָא p. n. of a man.

בְּאֵרָה p. n. of a man.

בְּאֵרִי p. n.—I. of the father of Hosea.—II. of the father-in-law of Esau.

בָּאַשׁ (fut. יִבְאַשׁ) *emitted an ill savour, stank.* Niph. *became fetid, in ill odour,* i. e. *hateful;* (with בְּ, אֶת). Hiph. הִבְאִישׁ *rendered, made bad,* i. e. *odious;* (with בְּ); int. *stank,* Ex. 16:24; *did wickedly, became bad;* (with עִם), 1 Chron. 19:6.

בְּאֵשׁ Ch., *was evil;* (with עַל), Dan. 6:15.

בְּאֹשׁ m.—I. *stench;* with suff. בָּאְשׁוֹ בָּאְשָׁם.—II. *evil, affliction.*

בָּאְשָׁה f., *poisonous herb,* probably hemlock, Job 31:40.

בְּאֻשִׁים m. pl., *wild, sour grapes,* Is. 5:2, 4.

בְּאֵשׁ m. Ch., *bad, wicked*; f. emph. בְּאִשְׁתָּא.

בָּאתַר *after*; see אָתַר.

בָּבָה *pupil of the eye*; see בּוּב.

בִּבַי p. n. of a man.

בָּבֶל p.n.f.—I. *Babylon*; with ה, signifying place, בָּבֶלָה.—II. *the kingdom of Babylon*.

בַּבְלִי Ch. *Babylonish*; pl. const. בַּבְלָיֵא.

בַּג m., לְבַג, Eze. 23:7, a wrong reading; Kri לָבַז "*for a spoil*," Eng. Ver.

בָּגַד (fut. יִבְגֹּד, יַבְגֹד; inf. בָּגוֹד; const. בְּגוֹד; with suff. בִּגְדוֹ), *dissembled, acted perfidiously, cheated*, with בְּ and מִן; part. בֹּגֵד *a perfidious person*.

בֶּגֶד m. (f. Lev. 6:20; with suff. בִּגְדִי, בִּגְדוֹ; pl. בְּגָדִים; const. בִּגְדֵי, בִּגְדוֹתָיו, Ps. 45:9).—I. *wrapper, coverlet*.—II. *cloak, garment*.—III. *dissimulation, perfidy*.—IV. *rapine, violence*.

בֹּגְדוֹת f. pl., *great perfidy*, Zep. 3:4.

בָּגוֹד m., בָּגוֹדָה f., *perfidious*, Jer. 3:7, 10.

בֻּנִּי p. n. of a man.

בִּגְלַל *because*; see גלל.

בִּגְתָא p. n. of a eunuch of Ahasuerus.

בִּגְתָן p.n. of a eunuch of Ahasuerus.

בַּד m., *fine linen*; בַּדִּים *linen garments*; see also בַּד under בדד.

בָּרָא *originated, innovated*; part. with suff. בֹּרְאָם Syr. for בֹּרְאָם.

בָּדַד part. בּוֹדֵד *separate, solitary person*.

בַּד m., *being alone, separate, apart*; pl בַּדִּים.—I. *shoots, branches*.—II.

staves of wood.—III. *limbs, members of the body*.—IV. *defences*, i.e. *princes*, Hos. 11:6, &c.—V. *lies*, Is. 16:6, &c.

לְבַד adv., *alone, separate, only*; אָנֹכִי לְבַדִּי *I alone*; אַתָּה לְבַדֶּךָ *thou alone*; לְבַדְּךָ *to thee alone*; לְבַדּוֹ *he alone*; וְלְבַד מִן and מִלְּבַד *besides*; מִלְּבַד אֲשֶׁר *beside that which*; לְבַד עַל *the same*.

בָּדָד m., *separate, alone, solitary* and בָּדָד adv. *apart, separate*.

בְּדַד p. n. of the father of Hadad king of Edom.

בְּדִי *same as* בְּ; see דַי.

בְּדְיָה p. n. of a man.

בָּדַל Niph. *was separated*; with לְ it signifies, *unto something*; with מִן, *from something*; with אֶל, *he separated himself unto one thing alone*. Hiph. הַבְדִּיל I. *made, caused division*, const. with מִן and מֵעַל.—II. *distinguished, divided*, with בֵּין...לְ, בֵּין, לְבֵין, בֵּין...וּבֵין.—III. *designed*, with לְ.

בָּדָל m., בְּדַל אֹזֶן *portion of the ear*, Amos 3:12.

בְּדִיל m., *tin*; אֶבֶן הַבְּדִיל *the weight at the plumb-line, the plummet*.

מִבְדָּלוֹת f. pl., *separations, separate places*, Jos. 16:9.

בְּדֹלַח m. *bdellium*, a translucent and odoriferous gum; according to Lee, a precious stone, either *the crystal* or *the beryl*, Gen. 2:12, Num. 11:7.

בְּדָן p. n.—I. of a judge, perhaps the same as בָּרָק, 1 Sam. 12:11.—II. of another man, 1 Chron. 7:17.

בָּדַק (Arab. *tear, rend*); inf. בְּדוֹק

repairing injury, decay, 2 Chron. 34:10.

בֶּדֶק *injury, decay in a building*; with suff. בִּדְקֵךְ.

בִּדְקַר p. n. of a man.

בְּדַר Ch. same as Heb. בָּזַר; Pa. imper. בַּדַּרוּ *sprinkle*.

בָּהָה (Arab. *void*).

בֹּהוּ m., *emptiness, destitution*.

בַּהַט m., *marble*, Est. 1:6.

בָּהַל Niph. נִבְהַל.—I. *was terrified, astonished*.—II. *cast down, ruined*, with לְ *at*, מ *from*. Pi. בִּהֵל.—I. *cause to hurry, hasten*.—II. *astonish, confound, ruin*; fut. יְבַהֵל. Pu. part. מְבֹהָל *hurried, gotten too speedily*. Hiph. הִבְהִיל same as Pihel.

בְּהַל Ch., Pa. *affrighted*. Ithp. part. *alarmed*.

בֶּהָלָה f., *fear, terror, ruin*; pl. בֶּהָלוֹת.

בְּהִילוּ f. Ch., *hurry, haste*, Ezr. 4:23.

הִתְבָּהָלָה f. Ch., *haste*.

בָּהַם root not used; (Arab. *was dumb*).

בְּהֵמָה f. (const. בֶּהֱמַת; with suff. בְּהֶמְתְּךָ).—I. *cattle.*—II. *wild beast*, בֶּהֱמַת יַעַר, הָאָרֶץ, הַשָּׂדֶה, *wild beasts*; pl. בְּהֵמוֹת; const. בַּהֲמוֹת, Job 40:15, name of some stupendous quadruped.

בֹּהֶן m.—I. *the thumb.*—II. *the great toe*; pl. בְּהֹנוֹת.

בֹּהַן (*thumb*), p. n. of a son of Reuben; אֶבֶן בֹּהַן p. n. of a place in the tribe of Judah.

בָּהַק root not used; (Arab. *was shining*).

בֹּהַק m., LXX. ἀλφός, *a white scurf, cicatrix on the skin*, Lev. 13:39.

בָּהַר root not used; Ch. *he shone*.

בָּהִיר m., *breaking through the clouds* (of light), Job 37:21.

בַּהֶרֶת f., the *white spot* covered with hair which was the sure symptom of leprosy; pl. בֶּהָרוֹת, Lev. *c*. 13

בְּהָרֵן for בְּהֵהָרֵג Niph. inf. with pref. בְּ from הרג.

בְּהָשַׁמָּה for בְּהַשְׁשַׁמָּה Hoph. inf. with suff. and pref. from שׁמם.

בּוֹא (fut. יָבוֹא, וַיָּבֹא; part. pl. בָּאִים, בָּאֵי), *entered, came* or *went in, to, for*, &c., with לְ, בְּ, אֶל, יָצָא וּבָא same as הָלַךְ, *he went in and out*, i. e. he lived familiarly; with בּוֹא לִפְנֵי הָעָם *to go before, lead the people*; בּוֹא בְרִית *he entered into covenant*; בּוֹא אֶל with עַל אִשָּׁה *had connection with a woman*; שֶׁמֶשׁ בָּאָה *the sun was setting*; const. also with אֶל, בְּ, לְ, עַד, עַל, בּוֹא בַיָּמִים *advanced in years*; with אֵת, עִם *went with, had intercourse with*, Ps. 26:4, Pro. 22:24. Hiph. הֵבִיא (with suff. הֱבִיאוֹ). imper. הָבִיא, הָבֵא, הָבִי; fut. יָבִיא, הָבֵא, הָבִיא, (וַיָּבֵא) *caused, made, induced to enter, come in*; with לְ, עַל, אֶל. Hoph. הוּבָא *brought in.*

בָּאָה f., *entrance*.

מָבוֹא m., *entrance, porch*; מְבוֹא הַשֶּׁמֶשׁ *place of sunset*. Pl. מְבוֹאִים, const. מְבוֹאֵי and מְבוֹאוֹת.

מוֹבָא m., *entrance*, 2 Sa. 3:25, Ez. 43:11.

תְּבוּאָה f.—I. *income.*—II. *store.*—III. *profit.*—IV. *produce*; pl. תְּבוּאוֹת

תְּבוּאָה f., Job 22:21; תְּבוּאָתְךָ from בּוֹא, fut. Kal with ה parag.

בּוּב Niph. part. נָבוּב.—I. *proud, insolent*, Job 11:12.—II. *hollow*.

בָּבָה f., *apple of the eye, pupil*; בָּבַת עַיִן *pupil*, Zec. 2:12.

בּוּז (fut. יָבוּז), *despised, neglected*; with comp. לְ בָּזָה.

בּוּז m.—I. *contempt.*—II. p. n. of a brother of Abraham, and of the nation he founded in Arabia Deserta; בּוּזִי *a Buzite.*—III. p. n. of a man, 1 Chron. 5:14.

בּוּזָה f., *contempt, contemptible thing.* בְּנִי p. n. of a man.

בּוּךְ Niph. נָבוֹךְ *confused, perplexed*, Ex. 14:3, Est. 3:15.

מְבוּכָה f., *confusion, perplexity*, Isa. 22:5; Mic. 7:4.

בּוֹכִיָּה Kal, part. from בכה.

בּוּל *increase*, same as יְבוּל; see יבל.

בּוּן and בִּין.—I. *distinguished, discerned.*—II. *perceived, understood*, with בְּ, לְ, אֶל, עַל; part. בָּנִים *prudent persons*; pret. בַּנְתָּ, בָּן and בִּין, בִּינוֹתִי; fut. יָבִין. Niph. נָבוֹן *became discerning*; part. נָבוֹן *wise*; נְבוֹן דָּבָר *wise in word, eloquent*. Pil. בּוֹנֵן *made him discerning*, Deu. 32:10. Hiph. הֵבִין.—I. *taught, explained*, with לְ, בְּ, אֶל.—II. *understood, was wise*; part. מֵבִין *skilful, learned*; imper. הָבֵן and הָבִין; with suff. הֲבִינֵנִי; fut. וַיָּבֶן, יָבִין. Hith. הִתְבּוֹנֵן *same as Niph.*; with עַד, בְּ, אֶל.

בַּיִן const. בֵּין s.—I. *interval, midst*; dual בֵּנַיִם בְּנַיִם *man of two intervals*, i. e. between the two armies,

1 Sam. 17:4.—II. prep. *between among, within*; בֵּין...לְ, בֵּין...וּבֵין, בֵּין...לְבֵין *between...and (whether... or*, Lev. 27:12); with suff. בֵּינְךָ, בֵּינִי; with pause בֵּינֶךָ; בֵּינוֹ; with suff. pl. בֵּינֵיכֶם, בֵּינֵינוּ and בֵּינֹתֵינוּ, בֵּינֵיךָ; בֵּינֵיהֶם; fem. בֵּינוֹת אֶל־בֵּין־בֵּינוֹת *among*; אֶל־בְּנוֹת לְ *the same*; מִבֵּין *from between*; מִבֵּינוֹת *the same*; עַל־בֵּין *up among*; לְ בְּבֵין *in the midst*.

בֵּין Ch., *among*; pl. with suff. בֵּינֵיהוֹן.

בִּינָה f., *intelligence, discernment, prudence*; Ch. the same.

תְּבוּנָה m., תָּבוּן f., *understanding, prudence*; pl. תְּבוּנוֹת.

בּוּנָה (*intelligence*), p. n. of a man.

בּוּנִי from בָּנָה, p. n. of a man.

בּוּס (fut. יָבוּס and יָבוּס; part. pl. בּוֹסִים) *trampled, trod upon, despised.* Pil. בּוֹסֵס *trod down* (profaned holy place). Hoph. part. מוּבָס *trodden down*. Hith. part. f. מִתְבּוֹסֶסֶת *become trodden down*, Eze. 16:6, 22.

מְבוּסָה f., *treading upon.*

תְּבוּסָה f., *destruction*, 2 Chron. 22:7.

בּוּע root not used; Ch. *was boiling.*

אֲבַעְבֻּעוֹת f. pl., *spots on the skin.*

בּוּץ root not used; (Arab. *fine linen*).

בּוּץ m., בֵּן בּוּץ *βύσσος, linen, fine linen* בֵּיץ m., or בֵּיצָה f., pl. בֵּיצִים *eggs.*

בּוֹצֵץ (*shining*), p. n. of a rock near Gibeah.

בּוּק root not used; (Arab. *heavy rain* see בקק).

בּוּקָה f., *emptiness, devastation*, Neh 2:11.

מְבוּקָה f., *emptiness*; the same.

בּוֹר *well*, same as בְּאֵר; see בָּאַר

בוּר (same as בָּרַר), *explored.*

בּוֹשׁ (pret. בּוֹשׁ, בֹּשֶׁת, בּוֹשְׁנוּ, בַּשְׁנוּ; fut. יֵבוֹשׁ (אֵבוֹשׁ) *ashamed, put to shame, blushed,* with מִן and לְ; עַד־בּוֹשׁ *until they were ashamed.* Pil. בֹּשֵׁשׁ *put to a stand, delayed,* Jud. 5.28, Ex. 32:30. Hiph. הֵבִישׁ and הוֹבִישׁ (from cognate יָבֵשׁ) *brought to shame, confusion;* part. מֵבִישׁ *bringing, causing shame, wicked.* Hith. הִתְבֹּשֵׁשׁ *become ashamed,* Gen. 2:25.

בּוּשָׁה f., *shame, ignominy.*

בָּשְׁנָה f., *the same,* Hos. 10:6.

בֹּשֶׁת f.—I. *shame, blushing.*—II. *ignominy.*—III. *an idol.*

מָבוּשׁ m., pl. מְבֻשִׁים *secret parts,* Deu. 25:11.

בְּשָׁסְכֶם Po. inf. with suff. from בשש

בּוּת Ch. בָּת *passed the night,* Dan. 6:19.

בַּיִת m. (const. בֵּית; with suff. בֵּיתְךָ, בֵּיתוֹ; pl. בָּתִּים, const. בָּתֵּי), *habitation.*—I. *temple* of God or idols.—II. *palace.*—III. *house, tent, cave;* אֲשֶׁר עַל בַּיִת *mayor of the palace,* or בֶּן יְלִיד בַּיִת *household-slave).*—IV. *sepulchre.*—V. *receptacle* of anything; בָּתֵּי נֶפֶשׁ *perfume boxes,* Isa. 3:20.—VI. *family, race.* With ה parag. בַּיְתָה, const. בֵּיתָה, adv. *inwards;* מִבַּיִת, מִבֵּית לְ, בֵּית לְ *within;* מִבֵּיתָה, לְמִבֵּית לְ *within.*

בַּיִת m. Ch., *house, palace, temple.*

בִּיתָן m., *great house, palace,* Est. 1: 5; 7:7,8.

The p.n. of many towns are compounds of בַּיִת; בֵּית אָוֶן in the tribe of Benjamin; בֵּית־אֵל between Jerusalem and Sichem; בֵּ' אֶצֶל הָאֵלִי a *Bethelite;* in Samaria; בֵּ' אַרְבֵּאל *Arbela* in Galilee; בַּעַל מְעוֹן, בֵּ' בַּעַל מְעוֹן and בֵּית מְעוֹן in the tribe of Reuben; בֵּ' בָּרָה (*ferry-house*) Βηθαβαρά, near Jordan; בֵּ' בִּרְאִי in the tribe of Simeon; בֵּ' גָּדֵר in the tribe of Judah; בֵּ' הַגִּלְגָּל same as גִּלְגָּל, see גָּלַל, בֵּ' גָּמוּל (see גָּמַל) in the land of Moab (see בֵּ' דָּגוֹן ; בֵּ' דִּבְלָתַיִם, see בֵּ' (*temple of Dagon*), in the tribe of Judah, also in the tribe of Asher; בֵּ' הָרָם and הָרָן in the tribe of Gad; בֵּ' חָגְלָה (*place of partridges*), town of the Benjamites in the tribe of Judah; בֵּ' חָנָן (*house of mercy*), in the tribe of Judah or Dan; בֵּ' חֹרוֹן two towns in the tribe of Ephraim; בֵּ' הַיְשִׁימוֹת town of the Reubenites on the shore of the Red Sea; בֵּ' כַּר a strong place of the Philistines in the tribe of Judah; בֵּ' הַכֶּרֶם (*house of vineyards*), in the tribe of Judah; בֵּ' לְבָאוֹת (*place of lionesses*), in the tribe of Simeon; בֵּ' לֶחֶם (*house of bread*) Βηθλεὲμ, in the tribe of Judah, see אֶפְרָתָה; another town in the tribe of Zebulun; בֵּ' הַלַּחְמִי a *Bethlehemite;* בֵּ' מְלוֹא, see עַפְרָה, בֵּ' לְעַפְרָה see מְלוֹא; בֵּ' מַעֲכָה a town at the foot of Hermon; בֵּ' הַמַּרְחָק (from רָחַק), on the banks of Kedron; בֵּ' הַמַּרְכָּבוֹת (*house of chariots*), in the tribe of Simeon; בֵּ' נִמְרָה (*place of pure water*) in the tribe of Gad; ב׳ עֶדֶן (*pleasant place*), a town near Damascus; ב׳ הָעֵמֶק see עַזְמָוֶת; ב׳ עַזְמָוֶת (*house of the valley*), in the tribe of Asher; ב׳ עֲנוֹת (*place of echo*), in the tribe of Judah; ב׳ עֲנָת (the same), in the tribe of Naphtali; ב׳ עֵקֶד הָרֹעִים (*place where shepherds bind their sheep*), near Samaria; ב׳ הָעֲרָבָה (*place in the desert*), on the confines of Judah and Benjamin; ב׳ פֶּלֶט (*place of flight*), in the tribe of Judah; ב׳ פְּעוֹר (see פְּעוֹר), in the land of Moab, not far from Jordan; ב׳ פַּצֵּץ (*place of dispersion*), in the tribe of Issachar; ב׳ צוּר (*house of the rock*), in the mountains of Judah; ב׳ רְחֹב (see רְחֹב), a city of Syria; ב׳ שָׁן, שֵׁן (אֲרָם), ב׳ שְׁאָן (*house of sleep*), in the tribe of Manasseh, beyond Jordan; ב׳ הַשִּׁטָּה (see שִׁטָּה), a town on Jordan; ב׳ שֶׁמֶשׁ (*house of the sun*), name of several towns: *a.* of the Levites in the tribe of Judah; בֵּירִת־הַשִּׁמְשִׁי *inhabitant of....*; *β.* in the tribe of Naphtali; *γ.* in the tribe of Issachar or Zebulon; *δ.* same as אוֹן in Egypt; ב׳ תַּפּוּחַ, תֻּלְרָמָה, see תֻּלְרָמָה (*place of apple trees*), in the tribe of Judah.

בַּז from בָּזַז for בָּז, Zec. 4:10; see בּוּז.
בָּזָה, בַּז *spoiled*; see בָּזַז.

בָּזָא בָּזָאוּ Isa. 18:2, *have spoiled*.

בָּזָה same as בּוּז *despised, spurned*; const. with לְ, עַל. Niph. part. נִבְזָה *despised*; pl. נִבְזִים. Hiph. inf. הַבְזוֹת *make despised*, Est. 1:17.

בָּזֹה inf., *despised*, Isa. 49:7.

בָּזָיוֹן m., *great contempt*, Est. 1:18.

בִּזְיוֹתְיָה (*despised of the Lord*), p. n. of a town in the tribe of Judah.

נִבְזָה *contemptible*, 1 Sa. 15:9.

בָּזַז *took the spoil or prey*; part. pl. בֹּזְזִים *spoilers*; pret. pl. בָּזַזְנוּ, בָּזְזוּ and בַּזּוֹנוּ; inf. בֹּז; fut. יָבֹז. Niph. נָבֹז, and Pu. בֻּזַּז *were spoiled*, Jer. 50:37.

בַּז m. (with suff. בִּזָּה), *spoil*; הָיָה לָבַז *was for a spoil*; נָתַן לָבַז *gave for a spoil*.

בִּזָּה f., *booty*.

בָּזָק m., *lightning*, Eze. 1:14.

בֶּזֶק p.n. of a town to the southward of Bethshan, Βεζέκ.

בָּזַר (fut. יִבְזֹר), *dispersed*, Dan. 11:24; Pi. בִּזַּר the same, Ps. 68:31.

בִּזְתָא p.n. of a eunuch of Ahasuerus.

בָּחַל *was greedy, niggard*; with בְּ, Zec. 11:8. Pu. part. f. מְבֹחֶלֶת *coveted, gotten by covetousness*, Pro. 20:21.

בָּחַן (imper. בְּחַן; with suff. בְּחָנֵנִי, בְּחָנוּנִי; fut. יִבְחַן).—I. *tried, tested* (metals with fire).—II. *tried* (men with affliction).—III. *tried* (God.... the heart). Niph. *be tried*.

בֹּחַן m., *examination, trial*, Isa. 28:16, Eze. 21:18.

בַּחַן m., *watch-tower*, Isa. 32:14.

בָּחוּן m., *mound, watch-tower*, Isa. 23:14.

בָּחוֹן m., *trial, experiment*.

בָּחַר (fut. יִבְחַר), *chose*; with בְּ, לְ, עַל; בָּחַר לוֹ *he chose for himself*; with מִן *preferred*; part. בָּחוּר

chosen, excellent. Niph. *chosen;* part. נִבְחָר *elect, excellent;* with מִן *better.*

בָּחִיר m., *elect;* (ἐκλεκτὸς τοῦ Θεοῦ *the elect of God*).

בָּחוּר m., *a youth;* pl. בַּחוּרִים *youths,* liable to be chosen (balloted) for military service.

בְּחוּרִים m. pl., *youth.*

בְּחוּרוֹת f. pl., the same.

בַּחֻרִים p. n. of a town in the tribe of Benjamin; בַּחֲרוּמִי and בַּרְחֻמִי an inhabitant of Bachurim.

מִבְחָר, מִבְחֹר m.—I. *the choice, the best.*—II. p. n. of a man.

מִבְחוֹר m., the same, 2 Ki. 3:19; 19:23.

בָּטָא and בָּטָה *speaks wrongfully, falsely,* Pro. 12:18; part. בּוֹטֶה. Pi. בִּטֵּא *spake falsely.*

מִבְטָא m., *rashness in speaking;* מ' שְׂפָתַיִם, Nu. 30:7,9.

בָּטַח (inf. בָּטוֹחַ; with suff. בְּטֶחֲךָ; imper. בְּטַח; fut. יִבְטַח; pl. f. תִּבְטַחְנוּ), *trusted in, to, on;* with בְּ, אֶל, עַל, לְ, Job 6:20; impers. *was for a confidence;* part. בָּטוּחַ *trusted, was confident, incautious;* part. בּוֹטֵחַ *secure, confiding.* Hiph. הִבְטִיחַ *made to confide, trust;* with עַל and אֶל.

בֶּטַח m., *confidence, security;* בֶּטַח and לָבֶטַח adv. *confidently, securely, safely.*

בֶּטַח p. n. of a town of Aram Zobah, 2 Sam. 8:8.

בִּטְחָה f., *confidence,* Isa. 30:15.

בִּטָּחוֹן m., the same, Isa. 36:4, Ecc. 9:4.

בַּטֻּחָה f., the same; pl. בַּטֻּחוֹת, Job 12:6.

מִבְטָח m. (with suff. מִבְטָחִי, מִבְטַחֶךָ; pl. מִבְטַחִים (מִבְטָחִים), *trust, confidence;* metonym. *he in whom trust is reposed.*

אֲבַטִּיחִים see אבטח.

בָּטֵל *cease, fail,* Ecc. 12:3.

בְּטֵל Ch., *ceased,* Ezr. 4:24. Pa. בַּטֵּל *caused to cease, hindered.*

בֶּטֶן f. (with suff. בִּטְנִי).—I. *belly.*—II. *womb;* פְּרִי בֶטֶן *fruit of the womb, offspring;* מִבֶּטֶן, מִן־הַבֶּטֶן, מִבֶּטֶן אִמִּי ἐκ γαστρὸς, the same.—III. ἡ κοιλία *the inner man, seat of thought, feelings.*—IV. the projecting part of the chapiter of a column, 1 Ki. 7:20.—V. p. n. of a town in the tribe of Asher.

בָּטְנִים m. pl., *nuts,* Gen. 43:11. Pistachia vera (Lin.), a tree abounding in Palestine, but unknown in Egypt.

בְּטֹנִים p. n. of a town in the tribe of Gad.

בִּי pa. of supplication, (always with אֲדֹנָי or אֲדֹנִי), *Lord, I pray thee; ah, Lord !*

בִּינָה, בֵּין, בִּין *understand;* see בּוּן.

בֵּיצִים *eggs,* see בּוּץ.

בִּיקְרוֹתָיִךְ f. pl., with suff., pref., and dag. euphon. see יְקַר.

בַּיִר *well;* same as בְּאֵר.

בִּירָה f.—I. *palace.*—II. *the temple.*

בִּירָה f. Ch., the same.

בִּירָנִיּוֹת f. pl., *palaces;* sing. never occurs.

בִּיתָן, בַּיִת, *house,* &c.; see בּוּת.

בָּכָה (fut. יִבְכֶּה, וַיֵּבְךְּ; inf. בְּכוֹ and בְּכֹה).—I. *wept.*—II. *mourned;*

with אֶת, בְּ, עַל, לְ, אֶל. Pi. *deplored*, with עַל.

בָּכָא m.—I. *the Baka shrub, Amyris Gileadensis* (Linn.); pl. בְּכָאִים —II. עֶמֶק הַבָּכָא (*valley of weeping*), p. n. of a valley in Palestine, Ps. 84:7.

בֶּכֶה m., *weeping*, Eze. 10:1.

בְּכֹה inf. abs. from בכה.

בְּכִית and בְּכִית f., *weeping*, Gen. 50:4.

בְּכִי m. (with pause בֶּכִי; with suff. בִּכְיִי).—I. *weeping*.—II. *dropping of water in wells*, Job. 28:11.

בֹּכִים p. n. of a town near Gilgal.

בָּכַר Kal, root not used; (Arab. *early*). Pi. בִּכֵּר.—I. *brought forth early fruits.*—II. *was the first-born*, Deu. 21:16. Pu. passive of Pi., Lev. 27:26. Hiph. *brought forth her first-born*, Jer. 4:13.

בְּכוֹר m., *first-born*, בְּכֹרוֹת pl., *the first-born of brutes*, Gen. 4:4, Deu. 12:17. Trop. בְּכוֹר מָוֶת *the worm*, Job 18:13; בְּכוֹרֵי דַלִּים *the first-born of the poor, the poorest.*

בְּכוֹרָה f., *primogeniture.*

בְּכוֹרַת p. n. of a man, 1 Sa. 9:1.

בְּכִירָה f., *eldest, first-born daughter.*

בֶּכֶר (same as בְּכֹר הוּא), p. n. of a man.

בִּכְרִי (*my first-born*), p. n. of a man.

בֶּכֶר m., *a young camel*, Isa. 60:6; f. בִּכְרָה *a young she-camel*, Jer. 2:23.

בַּכְרִי, בֶּכֶר p. n.—I. of a son of Ephraim.—II. of a son of Benjamin.

בִּכּוּר m., pl. בִּכֻּרִים and בִּכּוּרִים *first-fruits*; יוֹם הַבִּכּוּרִים *feast of first-fruits, Pentecost*, Nu. 28:26.

תְּאֵנֵי בַכֻּרָה f., *the early fig*; בַּכֻּרוֹת *early figs.*

בְּכוֹרַת p. n. of a man.

בֵּל; see בלה.

בֵּל *Bel*, same as בַּעַל.

בִּלָּא *destroy*; see בָּלָה.

בַּלְאֲדָן (*whose lord is Baal*), p. n. of a king of Babylon; see מְרֹדַךְ.

בָּלַג Kal, root not used (Arab. *opened, shone*).—Hiph. הִבְלִיג with עַל I. *made to rise*, Am. 5:9.—II. *made glad*, Ps. 39:14.

בִּלְגָּה (*joy*), p. n. of a priest.

מַבְלִיגִית f., *exhilaration*, Jer. 8:18.

בִּלְדַּד p. n. of one of Job's friends.

בָּלָה (fut. יִבְלֶה).—I. *grew old.*—II. *perished*; with מֵעַל *worn off*, spoken of clothes. Pi. בִּלָּה *made cold.*

בְּלָא Ch. form. Pa. *destroy, make to disappear*, Dan. 7:25; see בלה Pi.

בָּלֶה m., בָּלָה f., *old, effete, worn out*, Jos. 9:4,5, Eze. 23:43.

בָּלָה p. n. of a city.

בְּלוֹיִם and בְּלֹאִים m. pl., *old, worn*, Jer. 38:11,12.

בְּלוֹ m. Ch., *custom, tax.*

תַּבְלִית f., *destruction*, Isa. 10:26.

בָּל m. Ch., *the heart, mind*, Dan. 6:15.

בַּל (*wanting*); adv., *not, nothing.*

בְּלִי I. *loss, destruction*, Isa. 38:17.—II. *wanting, without* (written בִּבְלִי and בְּלִי); בְּ דַעַת *without knowledge*; לִבְלִי *without*; מִבְּלִי *from want of.*—III. adv., same as לֹא *not*; הֲמִבְּלִי אֵין *is it not because there is not?* מִבְּלִי אֲשֶׁר לֹא *excepting that not*, Ecc. 3:11; עַד בְּלִי *until the ceasing of*, Mal. 3:10; עַל בְּלִי *because not*, Gen. 31:20

בְּלִמָה (compounded of בְּלִי and מָה), nothing, Job 26:7.

בְּלִיַּעַל (compounded of בְּלִי and יַעַל).—I. uselessness. — II. wickedness, sin; אִישׁ בּ׳ a wicked man.—III. injury, destruction; נַחֲלֵי בּ׳ destructive torrents, i.e. overwhelming oppressions, Ps. 18:5.

בִּלְעֲדֵי and בַּלְעֲדֵי (compounded of בַּל and עֲדִי).—I. besides, without.—II. not concerning, nothing to; nothing to me מִבַּלְעֲדֵי the same.

בְּלָא consumption; used only with the parag. jod, בִּלְתִּי.—I. without.—II. besides, except.—III. adv., not; with suff. בִּלְתִּי besides me, בִּלְתֶּךָ besides thee; לְבִלְתִּי not, that it may not, with a verb; מִבַּלְתִּי with inf., because it is not; עַד־בִּלְתִּי until it is not.

בָּלָה. Pi. בִּלָּה same as בָּהַל, harassing, Ezr. 4:4.

בַּלָּהָה f.—I. terror.—II. calamity.

בִּלְהָה p.n.—I. of the handmaid of Rachel.—II. of a town in the tribe of Simeon.

בִּלְהָן p.n. of a man.

בְּלוֹ ;בְּלוֹאִים, see בָּלָה.

בֵּלְטְשַׁאצַּר p.n., Chaldee name of Daniel.

בֵּל ,בְּלִיַּעַל ,בְּלִמָה; see בָּלָה.

בָּלַל (fut. יָבֹל).—I. suffused, Ps. 92:3.—II. confounded, const. with בְּ. Hith. become confounded, Hos. 7:8, with בְּ.—III. from בְּלִיל gave fodder, Jud. 19:21.—IV. fade, wither, Isa. 64:5.

בְּלִיל m., fodder for cattle, lit. mixture.

תֶּבֶל m., unnatural intercourse, Lev. 18:23, 20:12.

תְּבַלֻּל m., a disease in the eye, Lev. 21:20; ת׳ בְּעֵינוֹ confused (i. e. indistinct for vision) in his eye.

בָּלַם bound, bridled, Ps. 32:8.

בָּלַס pluck figs, Am. 7:14.

בָּלַע I. swallowed. — II. destroyed עַד־בִּלְעִי רֻקִּי untii I have swallowed my spittle; i.e. in a moment, Job 7:19. Niph. be swallowed up, lost; with מִן הַיַּיִן immersed in wine, Isa. 28:7. Pi. as Kal; (כְּבַלַּע as in a moment), Pu. was swallowed up. Hith. as Niph., Ps. 107:27.

בֶּלַע m.—I. swallowing up.—II. destruction; with suff. בִּלְעוֹ.—III. p.n. of a town on the Dead Sea.—IV. of a man.—בַּלְעִי m., inhabitant of Bela.

בַּלְעֲדֵי ,בִּלְעֲדֵי besides; see בָּלָה (stranger).

בִּלְעָם—I. p. n. of the prophet Balaam.—II. same as יִבְלְעָם.

בָּלַק make waste, Isa. 24:1. Pu. part. f. מְבֻלָּקָה desolate, Nah. 2:11.

בָּלָק p.n. of a king of Moab.

בֵּלְשַׁאצַּר and בֵּלְאשַׁצַּר p.n. of the last king of the Chaldees (Nabonnedus or Labynetus).

בִּלְשָׁן p.n of a man.

בָּלְתִּי not; see בָּלָת under בָּלָה.

בָּמָה f. (pl. בָּמוֹת, const. בָּמֳתֵי [בָּמֳתִי Kri] with suff. בָּמוֹתֶיךָ.—I. high place for idolatrous worship; רָכַב עַל בָּמוֹתֵי אָרֶץ he rode upon the high places of the earth, i.e. he conquered. — II. places for true worship.—III. fortresses, places of strength; דָּרַךְ עַל בּ׳ he rode upon the high places, i. e. he subdued.—IV. *waves of the sea*, Job 9:8.—V. *clouds*, Isa. 14:14. בָּתֵּי הַבָּמוֹת same as בָּמוֹת *idol temples*; וְהֲגֵי הַבָּמוֹת *idolatrous priests*.

בָּמוֹת and בַּעַל בָּמוֹת p. n. of a town in Moab on the Arnon.

בְּמֶהָל (*son of circumcision*), p.n. of a m.

בְּמוֹ same as בְּ; see מוֹ, מָה.

בָּמֹתַי pl. const. from בָּמָה.

בָּנָה בָּנֹה (inf. בְּנֹה; const. בְּנוֹת; fut. יִבְנֶה, וַיִּבֶן).—I. *built*, really.—II. *built*, metaphorically, i. e. *raised*, *increased in family*; const. with בְּ; עַל, כְּ, לְ; אֶת־הָהָר he built upon the hill, 1 Ki. 16:24; בְּ בַּיִת לְ he raised up a house to.—Niph. I. *was built*.—II. *was raised up*, as a house, family.

בְּנָא בְּנָה Ch., *built*. Ithp. *was built*.

בֵּן m. (const. בֶּן, sometimes בֶּן); with suff. בְּנֶךָ, בְּנוֹ בְּנִי; pl. בָּנִים, בְּנֵי).—I. *son*; בְּנֵי בָנִים *grandsons, posterity*; בְּנֵי עַמּוֹן *Ammonites*; אִישׁ מִבְּנֵי יִשְׂרָאֵל *an Israelite*; בְּנֵי צִיּוֹן *inhabitants of Zion*; בְּנֵי נְבִיאִים *sons*, i.e. *disciples of the prophets*.—II. used metaphorically; בֶּן־עַוְלָה *son of perverseness*, i. e. *perverse person*; בֶּן־מָוֶת *son of death*, i.e. *a person guilty of a capital crime*; בֶּן־קֶשֶׁת *son of the bow*, i.e. *arrow*, Job 41:20.—III. used with numerals; בֶּן־שְׁמוֹנִים שָׁנָה *one eighty years old, octogenarian*; בֶּן־שָׁנָה *yearling*.—IV. *the young of brutes*; בֶּן־יוֹנָה *young dove*.—V. *young shoots of trees*; בֶּן־פֹּרָת *twig of a fruit tree*.

בֵּן p. n. of a Levite, 1 Chron. 15:18.

בֵּן m. Ch., *son*; pl. בְּנִין, בְּנֵי.

בֶּן־אוֹנִי (*son of my sorrow*), p.n. given to Benjamin by his mother.

בֶּן־הֲדַד p.n. of the kings of Damascus.

בֻּנִּי p. n. of a man.

בֶּן־חַיִל (*strong*), p. n. of a man.

בֶּן־חָנָן (*son of mercy*), p.n. of a man.

בָּנִי (*built up*), p. n. of a man.

בֻּנִּי (*built up*), p. n. of two men.

בְּנֵי בְרַק p. n. of a town in the tribe of Dan.

בְּנֵי יַעֲקָן p.n. of a place.

בִּנְיָה f., *building*, Eze. 41:13.

בְּנָיָה (*built up of God*), p.n. of a man.

בְּנָיָהוּ the same.

בִּנְיָמִין (*son of my right hand*), p. n., *Benjamin*, the son of Jacob; אִישׁ־יְמִינִי, בֶּן־הַיְמִינִי, בֶּן־יְמִינִי and *a Benjamite*; pl. בְּנֵי יְמִינִי; אֶרֶץ־יְמִינִי *land of the Benjamites*.

בֶּן־יָמִין I. same as בִּנְיָמִין.—II. p. n. of a man, 1 Sa. 9:1.

בִּנְיָן m., *building*, Eze. 40:5.

בְּנִינוּ (*our son*), p.n. of a man.

בָּאנוּ for בָּאנוּ Kal pret. pl. 1. pers., from בּוֹא.

בְּנֹתֶיךָ for בְּנוֹתֶךָ Kal inf. with suff., from בנה.

בַּת f. (with suff. בִּתִּי; pl. בָּנוֹת; const. בְּנוֹת).—I. *daughter*.—II. *niece*.—III. the female inhabitants of any place; בְּנוֹת צִיּוֹן *the daughters of Zion*, Isa. 3:17; בְּנוֹת יִשְׂרָאֵל *daughters of Israel*.—IV. used for the inhabitants of any place collectively; בַּת צֹר *the Tyrians*, Ps. 15:12; בַּת מִצְרַיִם *the Egyptians*.—V. בְּנוֹת הָעִיר *smaller cities* dependent upon larger ones. — VI. used with numerals in the age of women: בַּת תִּשְׁעִים שָׁנָה *a woman of ninety* (see בֶּן III.).—VII. used metaph.: בְּנוֹת הַשִּׁיר *daughters of song*, i.e. *singers*; בַּת עַיִן *pupil of the eye* (see בֶּן II.).—VIII. applied to the produce of animals, trees, or places: בַּת הַיַּעֲנָה *female ostrich, &c.*

בַּת f. Ch., the same; pl. בְּתִין.

בַּת־רַבִּים (*daughter of multitudes*), p. n. of the gate of Heshbon.

בַּת־שֶׁבַע (*daughter of an oath*), p. n. of the wife of Uriah.

בַּת־שׁוּעַ the same.

מִבְנֶה m., *building*, Eze. 40:2.

תַּבְנִית f.—I. *model*, πρωτότυπον.—II. *form, resemblance.*—III. *building.*

בֶּנֶט Pers. *bando*; Sansc. *bandha*; Eng. *band.*

אַבְנֵט m., *a girdle* (a foreign word).

בְּנַס Ch., *was angry*, Dan. 2:12.

בִּנְעָה, בִּנְעָא p. n. of a man.

בְּסוֹדְיָה (*in the council of the Lord*), p. n. of a man.

בֵּסִי p. n. of a man.

בֹּסֶר root not used; (Arab. *unripe date*).

בֹּסֶר m., *unripe, sour grape*, Job 15:33.

בֹּסֶר m., the same.

בְּעָא; see בעה.

בָּעַד root not used; (Arab. *after*).

בַּעַד prep., *after, behind*, as to time or place; with suff. בַּעֲדִי and בַּעֲדֵנִי, בַּעֲדְךָ, בַּעֲדֵנוּ and בַּעֲדִינוּ, מִבַּעַד לְ; בַּעַדְכֶם *behind*, Cant. 4:1, &c.

בָּעָה I. *pressed forward, ran over*, Isa. 64:1.—II. *requested, importuned*;

fut. pl. תִּבְעָיוּן; imp. pl. בְּעָיוּ. Niph —I. *become obtruded, swelled out* Isa. 30:13.—II. *being sought*, Obad v. 6.

בְּעָה and בְּעָא Ch., *requested, prayed* with מִן and קֳדָם. מִן קֳדָם.

בָּעוּ f. Ch., *petition*, Dan. 6:8, 14.

בְּעִי m., *prayer*, Job 30:24.

בָּעוֹן *habitation*; same as מָעוֹן.

בְּעוֹר p. n. of the father of Balaam.

בֹּעַז p. n.—I. the husband of Ruth.—II. name of one of the pillars in Solomon's temple.

בָּעַט I. *trample upon, kick at:* hence, —II. *despise, reject.*

בְּעִי *building*; see בָּעָה.

בְּעִיוּ Kal imper. pl. with pause, from בעה.

בְּעִיר *beast*; see בער.

בָּעַל I. *possess, govern.*—II. *marry a wife*; part. pl. majest. בְּעָלָיִךְ *thy husband*; בְּעֻלָה בַּעַל and בְּעוּלָה *married.* — III. (with בְּ) *despised*, Jer. 3:14; 31:32. Niph. *be married.*

בַּעַל m. (suff. בַּעֲלֵיהֶם, בַּעֲלָהּ, בַּעֲלִי) —I. *lord.*—II. *husband.*—III. *owner, possessor*, that wherein any one excels; בַּעַל הַחֲלֹמוֹת *dreamer*; שְׁכֶם *the Shechemites, &c.*; pl. בְּעָלִים (const. בַּעֲלֵי; with suff. בְּעָלָיו, בְּעָלֶיהָ) often used of one only.— IV. הַבַּעַל p. n., *Baal*, name of a Phenician god; הַבְּעָלִים *statues of Baal.*—V. p. n. of a man.—VI. compounded in the names of many towns: בַּעַל גָּד a town on the borders of Palestine, to the north; בַּעַל חֶרְמוֹן at the foot of Lebanon; בַּעַל חָצוֹר in the tribe of Ephraim

---

בְּ׳ חֶרְמוֹן one of the peaks of Mount Hermon; a town near it; בְּ׳ מְעוֹן and בֵּת מְעוֹן in the tribe of Reuben; בְּ׳ פְּרָצִים (place of slaughter) where the Philistines were routed by David; בְּ׳ צָפוֹן in Egypt; בְּ׳ שְׁלִשָׁה in Mount Ephraim; בְּ׳ תָּמָר (place of palms) not far from Gibeah; בַּעֲלֵי יְהוּדָה Jews.

בְּעֵל m. Ch., lord.

בַּעֲלָה f.—I. lady.—II. used collectively (like בַּת) a city.—III. p. n. of a city in the north of Judah; otherwise קִרְיַת־בַּעַל and קִרְיַת יְעָרִים.—IV. another city in Judah; otherwise בָּלָה and בִּלְהָה.

בַּעֲלָת p. n. of a city in the tribe of Dan.

בְּעָלוֹת p.n. of a city in the tribe of Judah.

בְּעֶלְיָדָע (whom Baal knows), same as אֶלְיָדָע.

בְּעַלְיָה (in whom the Lord rules), p.n. of a man.

בַּעַל חָנָן (the Lord of grace), p. n. of a king of Edom.

בַּעֲלִים p.n. of a king of the Ammonites.

בַּעֲנָא (son of misery), p. n. of a man.

בַּעֲנָה (the same), p.n. of a man.

בָּעַר injure, consume.—I. by fire.—II. with anger.—III. burn.—IV. that which injures, is brutish (from בְּעִיר); part. בֹּעֲרִים cattle, beasts. Niph. become brutish. Pi. בִּעֵר.——I. injured, destroyed.—II. consumed with fire, with בְּ, מִן and אַחֲרֵי. Pu. part. f. מְבֹעֶרֶת burnt. Hiph. same as Pi.

בְּעִיר m.—I. beast, cattle generally.—II. beast of burden.

בַּעַר m., stupid, brutish.

בְּעֵרָה f., burning, Ex. 22:5.

בַּעֲרָא p. n. of a man.

תַּבְעֵרָה p.n. of a place in the desert.

בַּעֲשֵׂיָה (work of God), p.n. of a man.

בַּעְשָׁא p. n. of a king of Israel, son of Ahijah.

בְּעֶשְׁתְּרָה an idol; see עַשְׁתֶּרֶת.

בָּעַת. Niph. נִבְעַת was terrified. Pi. בִּעֵת.——I. alarmed.—II. excited, came suddenly upon; fut. יְבַעֵת; part. f. with suff. מְבַעִתֶּךָ.

בְּעָתָה f., terror, Jer. 8:15; 14:19.

בִּעוּתִים m. pl., terrors, Ps. 88:17.

בֹּץ mud; see בצץ.

בְּצָאתִי for בְּצָאתִי pl. with suff. from בצץ or בֹּץ.

בְּצִי (same as בֶּסִי), p. n. of a man.

בָּצִיר vintage; see בצר.

בָּצָל m., onion, Nu. 11:5.

בַּצְלִית, בַּצְלוּת p.n. of a man.

בָּצַע I. cut off parts, pieces.—II. acquire gain. Pi. בִּצַע I. cutting off (as the weaver his web from the loom): hence,—II. finish, complete.—III. acquired filthy lucre, Eze. 22:12.

בֶּצַע m. (with suff. בִּצְעָם).—I. gain.—II. filthy lucre; מַה־בֶּצַע what gain?

בָּצַץ root not used; (Arab. run slowly).

בֹּץ m., mud, mire, Jer. 38:22.

בִּצָּה f., the same; pl. with suff. בִּצֹּאתָו for בִּצֹּתָיו.

בָּצֵק swelled (of the foot), Deu. 8:11, Neh. 9:21.

בָּצֵק m., *dough* (from its swelling in fermenting).

בָּצְקַת p. n. of a town in the tribe of Judah.

בָּצַר I. *cut, cropped off :* hence,—II. *pruned the vine.*— III. *gathered the vintage,* Ps. 76:13; part. בֹּצֵר *vintage-gatherer ;* trop. *remorseless enemy ;* part. בָּצוּר *inaccessible,* lit. *cut off from access;* בְּצֻרוֹת *hidden, incomprehensible,* Jer. 33:3. Niph. *cut off, prohibited,* with מִן. Pi. *fortified* (of cities).

בָּצִיר m., *vintage;* adj., same as בָּצוּר *fortified,* Zec. 11:2.

בֶּצֶר m., *gold;* perhaps *wealth,* Job 36:19.

בֶּצֶר m.—I. the same, Job 22:24,25. —II. p. n. of a city in the tribe of Reuben.—III. p. n. of a man.

בָּצְרָה f.—I. *fold for cattle,* Mic. 2: 12.—II. p. n. of a city of Edom, Βόστρα.—III. of a city of Moab.

בִּצָּרוֹן m., *fortified place,* Zec. 9:12.

בַּצֹּרֶת f., and pl. בַּצָּרוֹת *withholding of rain, drought,* Jer. 14:1; 17:8.

מִבְצָר m.—I. *fortification;* עִיר מ׳ *fortified town;* pl. מִבְצָרִים and מִבְצָרוֹת—II. p. n. of a chief of the Edomites.

בְּקִי, בַּקְבּוּק, &c.; see בקק.

בָּקַע with בְּ—I. *cut, cleft, divided.*— II. *laid open,* i. e. *subdued,* took (of fortified places).—III. *let go* (as young birds from eggs, or water from a dam).—Niph. I. *became cleft, destroyed.*— II. *laid open, subdued.*—III. *let go* (as young birds or water). Pi. same

as Kal. Pu. pass. of Pi. Hiph. I. *cause to be subdued* —II. *sent forth,* with אֶל. Hoph. *was broken up,* Jer. 39:2. Hith. as Niph. I., Jos. 9:13, Mic. 1:4.

בָּקִיעַ m., *fissure,* Isa. 22:9, Am. 6:11.

בֶּקַע m. (*cutting*), half a shekel, Gen. 24:22, Ex. 38:26.

בִּקְעָה f., *valley, plain;* pl. בְּקָעוֹת, בִּקְעַת הַלְּבָנוֹן *valley of Lebanon,* between Anti-Libanus and Hermon, κοίλη Συρία, Coele-Syria, Jos. 11:37, 12:7; בִּקְעַת אָוֶן, see אָוֶן.

בָּקַק I. *threw, cast off, out* (as fruit from a tree); with אֶת־עֵצָה *I will cast off* (*deprive of*) *counsel,* Jer. 19:7.—II. *make empty, void,* Isa. 24:1. Niph. נָבַק (inf. הִבּוֹק, fut. יִבּוֹק) *become void,* Isa. 19:3; 24:3. Pi. fut. יְבַקְקוּ *make empty, void,* Jer. 51:2.

בַּקְבּוּק I. *bottle, narrow-necked vase;* the word expresses the sound of a fluid issuing from it.—II. p. n. of a man.

בַּקְבֻּקְיָה p. n. of a man.

בַּקְבַּקַּר p.n. of a man.

בֻּקִּי p. n. of a man.

בֻּקִּיָּהוּ p. n. of a man.

בָּקַר *cut, laid open;* not in use: hence, Pi.—I. *look, inquire after.*—II. *observe.*— III *care for,* with לְ and בֵּין ... לְ.

בַּקַּר Pa. Ch., *inquired.* Ithpa. *was sought.*

בַּקָּרָה f., *inquiring after, seeking,* Eze. 34:12.

בִּקֹּרֶת f., *observation, chastisement,* Lev. 19·20.

בָּקָר (from the plough which *cleaves* the earth).—I. *oxen* used in ploughing, Job. 1:14.—II. *oxen* generally; בְּ' עֲלוֹת *milch cows*; בֶּן בָּקָר *steer*; seldom pl. בְּקָרִים *oxen*.

בּוֹקֵר m., *herdsman*, Am. 7:14.

בֹּקֶר m. (pl. בְּקָרִים).—I. *dawn, morning*; לַבֹּקֶר, בַּבֹּקֶר, בֹּקֶר *in the morning*; לַבְּקָרִים, בַּבֹּקֶר *every morning*; עַד הַבֹּקֶר *to-morrow morning*. — II. לַבֹּקֶר *early, soon*, Ps. 49:15, &c.

בָּקַשׁ. Pi. בִּקֵּשׁ *sought, sought out, after* or *into*, with לְ, מִן, עַל or אֶל *according to the sense*; בְּ' אֶת־יְהֹוָה or אֶת־פְּנֵי יְהֹוָה *he sought the Lord*; נֶפֶשׁ פּ' בְּ' *the soul, life of any one, to injure destroy it*; דָּם פּ' בְּ'...*his blood*.

בַּקָּשָׁה f., *petition*, Est. 5:3; 7:3, Esr. 7:6.

בַּר, בַּר, בֹּר *son, &c.*: see ברא and ברר.

בָּרָא (inf. בְּרֹא; with suff. בְּרַאֲךָ; imp. בְּרָא; fut. יִבְרָא).—I. *created, formed, made.*—II. same as בָּרָה *he ate.* Niph. *was created, born, produced.* Pi. בֵּרֵא — I. *cut*, as with a sword or axe.—II. *make, form.* Hiph. הַבְרִיא *fatten*, 1 Sa. 2:29.

בְּרִיאָה f., *a wonderful, new thing.*

בַּר m., *son*; with suff. בְּרִי; another meaning, see in ברר.

בַּר m. Ch.—I. *son.*—II. *grandson*; with suff. בְּרֵהּ.

בְּרָאיָה (*created of God*), p. n. of a m.

מְרֹאדַךְ; see בְּרֹאדַךְ.

בַּרְבֻּרִים *fed beasts*; see ברר.

בָּרַד *hailed*, Isa. 32:19.

בָּרָד m., *hail.*

בָּרֹד m. (pl. בְּרֻדִּים), *spotted, "grisled,"* Eng. Ver.

בֶּרֶד p. n.—I. of a place in the wilderness of Shur.—II. of a man.

בָּרָה I. *ate.*—II. same as בָּרַר *chose.* Pi. inf. בָּרוֹת *eating.* Hiph. *gives food.*

בָּרִיא m., בְּרִיאָה f., *fat*; see another meaning above.

בְּרִי m., בְּרִיָה f., *fat*, Eze. 34:20.

בִּרְיָה f., *food*, 2 Sa. 13:5, 7, 10.

בָּרוּת f. *food*, Ps. 69:22.

בְּרִית f.—I. *any agreement*; בַּעֲלֵי בְּ' *united in covenant*, Gen. 14:13.—II. the covenant made by God with the patriarchs, and ratified in the person of Jesus Christ.—III. the sign of that covenant (circumcision), Gen. 17·13; מַלְאַךְ הַבְּרִית μεσίτης, *the angel of the covenant, Messiah*; בַּעַל בְּרִית a name of Baal.

בָּרוּךְ *blessed*; see ברך.

בְּרוֹמִים *costly clothing*; see ברם.

בְּרוֹשׁ m.—I. *fir-tree*; עֲצֵי בְרֹשִׁים *instruments of fir-wood*, 2 Sa. 6:5.—II. *staves of lances made of fir-wood*, Nah. 2:4.

בְּרוֹת m. the same, Cant. 1:17.

בֵּרוֹתָה, בֵּרוֹתַי p. n. of a city in Syria of Zobah.

בָּרוּת *eating*; see ברה.

בְּרֻחִית p. n. of a woman.

בַּרְזֶל m. (with suff. בְּרִזְלוֹ).—I. *iron.*—II. *hard as iron.*—III. *instrument of iron.*

בַּרְזִלַּי p. n. of a man.

בָּרַח (fut. יִבְרַח; part. m. בֹּרֵחַ, f. בֹּרַחַת).—I. *pass on.*— II. *fly*, with מִן

בְּרַח לְךָ ;imper. אַחֲרֵי ,מִפְּנֵי ,מֵאֵת flee away.—IV. pass through, Ex. 36:33. Hiph. made to pass, fly.

בְּרִיחַ, בָּרַח m.—I. a fugitive.—II. p. n. of a man.

בְּרִיחַ m.—I. transverse bar.—II. bars or bolts for fastening the gates of a city; בְּרִיחֶהָ, Isa. 15:6, "her fugitives" as above, not "her princes" i. e. bars, defences.

מִבְרָח m., fugitive, Eze. 40:2.

בָּר ,בָּרִיא ,בִּרְיָה; see ברה.

בֵּר (same as בְּאֵרִי my well), p. n. of a man.

בְּרִיאָה; see ברא.

בְּרִיעָה p. n. of a man.

בְּרִית covenant; see ברה.

בֹּרִית soap; see ברר.

בֶּרֶךְ f., knee; dual בִּרְכַּיִם both knees.
בְּרַךְ ,בֶּרֶךְ f. Ch., the same.

בָּרַךְ (fut. יִבְרַךְ; inf. abs. בָּרוֹךְ).—I. knelt.—II. worshipped, blessed; בָּרוּךְ יְהֹוָה and בָּרוּךְ לַיהֹוָה blessed of the Lord; בָּרוּךְ יְהֹוָה blessed be the Lord. Niph. be blessed. Pi. בֵּרֵךְ ,בָּרַךְ pronounced, made, blessed, with לְ; בְּשֵׁם יְהֹוָה. Pu. בֹּרַךְ be or become blessed. Hiph. הִבְרִיךְ made kneel down, Gen. 24: 11. Hith. הִתְבָּרֵךְ be made blessed, Gen. 22:18, &c.; account oneself blessed, Deu. 29:18, &c.

בְּרַךְ Ch., knelt. Pa. blessed.

בָּרוּךְ p. n. of the friend of Jeremiah.
בֶּרֶכְאֵל (blessed of God), p.n. of a man.

בְּרָכָה f. (בְּרָכָה Gen. 27:38; const. בִּרְכַּת; pl. בְּרָכוֹת, const. בִּרְכוֹת).—I. blessing, ascription of praise to God.—II. the same received

from God.—III. favour, present—IV. p. n. of a man.

בְּרֵכָה f., pool, fish-pond.

בֶּרֶכְיָה and בֶּרֶכְיָהוּ (blessed of the Lord), p. n. of a man.

אַבְרֵךְ; see in its place.

אַרְכֻּבָה f. Ch., knee.

בָּרַם Ch. pa. of confirmation, but.

בָּרַם root not used; (Arab. garment adorned with gems).

בְּרוֹמִים m. pl., costly raiment, Eze. 27:24.

לִבְרָם, בָּרָם Kal inf. with pref. and suff. from ברר.

בַּרְנַע (fountain of delight), p. n. of a place in the wilderness, written קָדֵשׁ־בַּ׳, which see.

בֶּרַע p. n. of a king of Sodom.

בְּרִיעָה p. n. of a man.

בָּרַק lightened, Ps. 144:6.

בָּרָק m. (pl. בְּרָקִים).—I. lightning.—II. glitter of a sword.—III. p. n. of the captain who defeated the Canaanites, Jud. 4:6, &c.

בָּרֶקֶת f., carbuncle.

בַּרְקָנִים m. pl., threshing waggons, having sharp iron teeth, Jud. 8: 7, 16.

בַּרְקוֹס p. n. of a man.

בָּרַר I. examined, tested, Ecc. 3:18.—II. separated, selected, chose, Eze. 20:38, with מִן and לְ; part. בָּרוּר pure, chaste. Niph. נָבַר became pure; part. נָבָר pure Pi. purify, Dan. 11:35. Hiph. make clean, polish. Hith. become, appear pure.

בַּר m., בָּרָה f.—I. beloved, Cant. 6:9. —II. pure, clean.—III. empty void, Pro. 14:4.

בַּר m.—I. *corn*, purified from the chaff.—II. *growing corn;* see another meaning in בָּרָא.

בַּר m., *field, open plain*, Job 39:4.

בַּר m. Ch., the same.

בֹּר m.—I. *pureness.*—II. same as בֹּרִית.

בֹּרִית f., *soap*, Jer. 2:22, Mal. 3:2.

בַּרְבֻּרִים m., *stalled cattle*, 1 Ki. 5:3.

בִּרְשַׁע p. n. of king of Gomorrah.

בְּשׂוֹרָה, בְּשׂוֹר *good news;* see בשׂר.

בֶּשֶׂם m. (Anyrum opobalsamum), *the balsam tree*, an aromatic shrub.

בֹּשֶׂם and בֶּשֶׂם m. (pl. בְּשָׂמִים).—I. *the odour of perfumes.*—II. *the perfumes themselves.*

בָּשְׂמַת I. p. n. of the wife of Isaiah. —II. of the daughter of Solomon.

מִבְשָׂם p. n. of a man.

בָּשַׂר Pi. בִּשֵּׂר I. *announce, declare.* —II. *tell glad tidings.* Hith. *was, became informed*, 2 Sa. 18:31.

בְּשׂוֹרָה and בְּשׂרָה f.—I. *good tidings*, 2 Sa. 18:22, 27.—II. *the reward of good tidings*, 2 Sa. 4:10.

בְּשׂוֹר p. n. of a river near Gaza.

בָּשָׂר m.—I. *flesh.*—II. *body.*—III. כָּל־בָּשָׂר *all living creatures.*—IV. עַצְמִי וּבְשָׂרִי *my bone and flesh, kinsman;* also בְּשֵׂר *kinsman*, Lev. 15:2, &c.—V. *secret parts* (male).

בְּשַׂר m. Ch.—I. *flesh.*—II. *mankind.*

בָּשַׁל I. *ripened*, Joel 4:13.—II. *boiled, cooked*, Eze. 24:5. Pi. *boiled, cooked;* part. pl. מְבַשְּׁלִים *cooked*, Eze. 46:24. Pu. *was cooked*. Hiph. *matured, ripened*, Gen. 40:10.

בָּשֵׁל m., בְּשֵׁלָה f., *cooked.*

מְבַשְּׁלוֹת f. pl., *boilers*, Eze. 46:23.

בְּשֶׁלְמִי, בְּשֶׁלִי; see שֶׁל in אֲשֶׁר.

בִּשְׁלָם p. n. of a man.

בָּשָׁן p.n., *Batanea*, the region beyond Jordan, between Hermon and the brook of Jabbok.

בָּשְׁנָה *shame*; see בּוּשׁ.

בָּשַׁס Po. בּוֹשֵׁס same as בּוּסֵס *trampling on, injuring*, Am. 5:11.

בֹּשֶׁת *shame*; see בּוּשׁ.

בַּת *daughter*; see בנה.

בַּת *measure*; see בתת.

בָּתָה and בַּתָּה; see בתת.

בְּתוּאֵל p.n.—I. of the father of Laban. —II. same as בְּתוּל name of a place.

בְּתִיָה p. n. of a man.

בָּתִּים *houses*; see בַּיִת, בּוּת.

בָּתַל root not used; (Arab. *separated*).

בְּתוּלָה f. (pl. בְּתוּלוֹת).—I. *a virgin.*—II. used for *nation, city, people*, like בַּת, which see.

בְּתוּלִים m. pl., *tokens of virginity.*

בָּתַק Pi. בִּתֵּק *cut, pierce*, Eze. 16:40.

בָּתַר Pi. בִּתֵּר *dissect, cut in two*, Gen. 15:10.

בֶּתֶר m. (with suff. בִּתְרוֹ).—I. *part, piece.*—II. *separation*, Cant. 2:17.

בָּתַר Ch., same as בָּאתַר *after;* see אתר.

בִּתְרוֹן p.n. of a place on Jordan.

בָּתַת root not used; (Arab. *cut, cleft*).

בַּת m. (f. Isa. 5:10), *Bath;* a liquid measure, the tenth part of a Homer.

בַּת m. Ch., the same.

בָּתָה f., *desolation, excision*, Isa. 5:6.

בַּתָּה f. (pl. בַּתּוֹר), Isa. 7:19, *clefts, fissures.*

ג

גָּאָה (fut. יִגְאֶה).—I. *grew high* (as a plant), Job 8:11; (as water,) Exr. 47:5.—II. *becoming lofty, powerful, proud.*

גֵּא m., *proud,* Isa. 16:6.

גֵּאֶה m.—I. *elevated.*—II. *proud, arrogant;* pl. גֵּאִים.

גַּאֲוָה f., *pride, arrogance,* Pro. 8:13.

גַּאֲוָה f.—I. *excellency, majesty.*—II. *pride, arrogance.*

גְּאוּאֵל (*the divine majesty*), p. n. of a man.

גָּאוֹן m.—I. *excellency, glory.*—II. *pride;* pl. גְּאוֹנִים.

גַּאֲוּת f.—I. *ascent,* Isa. 9:17.—II. *sublimity, excellency.*—III. *pride, arrogance.*

גֵּאַיוֹן m., *proud,* Ps. 123:4.

גֵּוָה f. (for גַּאֲוָה).—I. *elevation, victory,* Job 22:29.—II. *pride,* Job 33:17.

גֵּוָה f. Ch., the same, Dan. 4:34.

גֵּאָיוֹת *valleys;* see גֵּוָה.

גָּאַל (fut. יִגְאַל).—I. *redeem by paying value for.*—II. *retribute, avenge.*—III. *pollute;* part. גֹּאֵל *redeemer, avenger, relative,* to whom the duty of avenging the death of any one was assigned; part. pass. גְּאוּלִים, גְּאוּלֵי *redeemed, set at liberty.* Niph. נִגְאַל *was redeemed, liberated, polluted.* Pi. גֵּאַל *polluted,* Mal. 1:7. Pu. *was polluted.* Hiph. אֶגְאָלְתִּי *contaminate,* Isa. 63:1. Hiph. *polluted himself,* Dan. 1:8.

גֹּאַל m., *pollution;* pl. const. גֹּאֲלֵי. Neh. 13:29.

גְּאֻלָּה f.—I. *relationship.*—II. *right, duty of redemption.*—III. *price of redemption.*—IV. *thing redeemed.*

מֹגְאָל m., *next of kin after the Goel.*

גֵּב *locust;* see גּוּב.

גָּבָא root not used; (Arab. *gathered together*).

גֶּבֶא m., *cistern, pit.*

גָּבַב root not used.

גַּב m. (with suff. גַּבִּי; pl. גַּבִּים, גַּבּוֹת).—I. *back.*—II. *defence, mound.*—III. *vaults.*—IV. *arch of the eyebrow,* Lev. 14:9; גַּב מָגֵן *the boss of a shield,* Job 15:26.

גַּב m. Ch., *back.*

גֹּב m. Ch., *well;* emph. גֻּבָּא.

גּוֹב m., *locust;* pl. גּוֹבַי.

גֵּב m. (pl. גֵּבִים), *locusts.*

גָּבַה (fut. יִגְבַּה; inf. גָּבְהָה).—I. *was high, lofty,* with עַל; when with מִן *was higher than.*—II. *exalted;* גָּבַהּ לִבּוֹ *his heart was lifted up;* or merely גָּבַהּ *lifted up.* Hiph. *raise, exalt.*

גָּבֹהַּ m. (const. גְּבֹהַּ; f. גְּבֹהָה).—I. *high, tall.*—II. *haughty, proud.* Subst. *height,* 1 Sa. 16:7.

גָּבֵהַּ; const. גְּבֵהַּ m.—I. *high.*—II. *arrogant, proud.*

גֹּבַהּ m. (with suff. גָּבְהוֹ; pl. const. גָּבְהֵי).—I. *height.*—II. *majesty,* Job 40:10.—III. *arrogance;* גֹּבַהּ אַף *insolence,* Ps. 10:4.

גַּבְהוּת m., *pride,* Isa. 2:11, 17.

גְּבוּל, גְּבוּלָה *border;* see גבל.

גִּבּוֹר, גְּבוּרָה *mighty;* see גבר.

גִּבֵּחַ m., *bald,* Lev. 13:41.

גַּבַּחַת f.—I. *baldness.*—II. *loss of knap* (in cloth), Lev. 13:55.

גַּב p. n. of a man.

גֵּבִים (see גֵּב), p. n. of a place not far from Jerusalem.

גְּבִינָה cheese; see גבן.

גָּבִיעַ cup; see גבע.

גְּבִירָה, גְּבִיר master; see גבר.

גָּבִישׁ see גבש.

גָּבַל limited; with בְּ and אֶת Hiph. set bounds to.

גְּבָל p. n. of a Phenician city; גִּבְלִי an inhabitant of Gebal.

גְּבָל p. n. of a mountainous district beyond Jordan, Ps. 83:8.

גְּבוּל, גְּבֻל m.—I. limit, boundary.—II. space or country limited.

גְּבוּלָה, גְּבֻלָה f., pl. גְּבוּלוֹת boundaries, lands.

נַבְלֻת f., artificial work, device, Ex. 28:22; 37:15.

מִגְבָּלָה f. (pl. מִגְבָּלוֹת), the same, Ex. 28:14.

גָּבֵן root not used; (Syr. curdled).

גְּבִינָה f., cheese, 2 Sa. 16:2.

גִּבֵּן m., hunchback, Lev. 21:20.

גַּבְנֻנִּים m. pl., risings, mounds, הַר גַּ׳ a hill of mounds, i. e. made up of other hills.

גָּבִיעַ m. (with suff. גְּבִיעִי; pl. גְּבִיעִים). —I. a cup or vase.—II. flower, the calix of an artificial flower.

גֶּבַע p. n. of a town in the tribe of Benjamin.

גִּבְעָא p. n. of a man.

גִּבְעָה f., a hill; pl. גְּבָעוֹת.

גִּבְעַת אֱלֹהִים p.n. of a place.

גִּבְעַת בְּנֵי בִנְיָמִן p.n. of a city in the tribe of Benjamin.

גִּבְעַת פִּינְחָס p. n. of a city.

גִּבְעַת שָׁאוּל p. n. of a hill.

גִּבְעָתִי inhabitant of Gibeah.

גִּבְעוֹן p.n. of a city in the tribe of Benjamin.

מִגְבָּעָה f. (pl. מִגְבָּעוֹת), the mitre or bonnet of the priests.

גִּבְעֹל flowering (of flax), Ex. 9:31

גָּבַר and גָּבֵר (fut. יִגְבַּר).—I. was powerful, mighty.—II. conquered, (prevailed), with מִן or עַל. Pi. made strong. Hiph. I.was powerful, Ps. 12:5.—II. confirm, Dan. 9:27. Hith. became powerful, victorious.

גֶּבֶר m.—I. man, husband, hero; pl. גְּבָרִים; לַגְבָרִים manfully.—II. p. n. of a man, 1 Ki. 4:19.

גְּבַר m., Ch. the same; pl. גֻּבְרִין.

גֶּבֶר m. (same as Ch:), man, Ps.18:26.

גְּבִיר m., lord, Gen. 27:29, 37.

גְּבִירָה f., lady, queen.

גְּבֶרֶת f. (with suff. גְּבִרְתִּי), the same.

גִּבּוֹר, גִּבֹּר m.—I. mighty, brave.—II. renowned; גִּבּוֹר חַיִל renowned for wealth, rich.

גְּבַּר m. Ch.—I. brave, strong, heroic. —II. p. n. same as גִּבְעוֹן, Ezr. 2:20.

גְּבוּרָה f.—I. power.—II. courage.— III. acts of courage, power; גְּבוּרוֹת יְהוָֹה acts of God, i. e. miracles.

גְּבוּרָה f. Ch. the same.

גַּבְרִיאֵל p.n. of an archangel.

גָּבֵשׁ root not used; (Arab. congelation).

גָּבִישׁ m., crystal (lit. ice), Job 28:18.

גִּבְּתוֹן p. n. of a town of the Philistines in the tribe of Dan.

גָּג m. (with suff. גַּגּוֹ; pl. גַּגּוֹת).—I. roof of a house.—II. covering, grate of the altar.

גַּד, גָּד; see נדד.

גִּדְבְרִין m. pl. Ch., *treasures*, Dan. 3: 2, 3; same as נִּזְבָּר.

גְּדוּדָה p. n. of a place in the Arabian desert.

גְּדוּד *assault, attack* (as an army). Hith. הִתְנּוֹדֵד I. *cutting, making incisions.*—II. *attacking, assembling to attack.*

גְּדַד Ch., *cut down* (of a tree), Dan. 4: 11, 20.

גְּדוּד m. (pl. גְּדוּדִים, גְּדוּדוֹת).—I. *cutting,* Jer. 48:37.—II. *furrow,* Ps. 65:11.—III. *section, detachment of an army.*

גַּד m., *coriander seed,* Ex. 16:31, Nu. 11:7.

גַּד m., *good fortune;* בְּגָד *prosperously,* Gen. 30:11.

גַּד nom., p.n. of an idol, Isa. 65:11.

גָּד p. n. Gad.—I. one of the sons of Jacob.—II. the tribe descended from him; גָּדִי *a Gadite.*

גַּדִּי p.n. of a man, Nu. 13:11.

גַּדִּיאֵל p. n. of a man.

גָּדָה root not used; (Syr. *leaping*).

גְּדִי m., *a kid;* pl. גְּדָיִים; const. גְּדָיֵי.

גְּדִיָּה f., pl. גְּדִיּוֹת *female kids,* Cant. 1:8.

גָּדָה f., const. pl. גְּדוֹת *banks of a river.*

גְּדִי, גְּדוּד; see נדד.

גְּדוּלִים, גְּדוּלָה, גָּדוֹל *great;* see גדל.

גְּדוּפָה, גִּדוּף *reproach;* see גדף.

גְּדִי, גְּדִיָּה; see גדה.

גָּדִישׁ *heap;* see גדש.

גָּדַל and גָּדֵל (fut. יִגְדַּל), *was or grew great* (in anything), with עַד, מִן, לְ, בְּ, אֶת. Pi. גִּדֵּל I. *made or pronounced great:* hence,

—II. *trained, educated.* Hiph. I. *became great.*—II. *made great high;* הִגְדִּיל אֶת פִּיו *he spake insolently.* Hith. *showed himself great.*

גָּדֵל m., pl. const. גִּדְלֵי, *great ones,* Eze. 16:26.

גָּדוֹל m. (const. גְּדוֹל and גְּדָל; f. גְּדוֹלָה), *great* (in anything); גְּדוֹלִים *nobles;* גְּדָל חֶסֶד *great in mercy;* עוֹד הַיּוֹם גָּדוֹל *it is yet high day,* i. e. early, Gen. 29:7; pl. גְּדוֹלוֹת *great* (i. e. proud) *things,* Ps. 12:4.

גֹּדֶל m. (with suff. גָּדְלוֹ, גָּדְלוֹ), *greatness, magnificence, pride.*

גְּדוּלָה, גְּדֻלָּה f.—I. *great* (act or deed). —II. *greatness;* pl. גְּדֻלוֹת *great things.*

גְּדִילִים m. pl., *platted chain-work,* 1 Ki. 7:17.

גִּדֵּל p. n. of a man.

גְּדַלְיָהוּ, גְּדַלְיָה Gedaliah, p.n. of a man.

גְּדַלְתִּי p. n. of a man, 1 Ch. 25:4, 29.

מִגְדָּל (pl. מִגְדָּלִים, מִגְדָּלוֹת).—I. *tower, castle.*—II. *pulpit,* Neh. 8:4.—III. artificial *mound,* in a garden covered with sweet flowers, Cant. 5:13.

מִגְדּוֹל, מִגְדָּל p. n. of a city in Egypt.

מִגְדַּל־אֵל p.n. of a fortress in the tribe of Naphtali.

מִגְדַּל־גָּד p. n. of a place in the tribe of Judah.

מִגְדַּל־עֵדֶר p. n. of a place near Bethlehem.

גָּדַע I. *cut off* or *down.*—II. *broke.* Niph. *became cut off, down.* Pi. *broke.* Pu. *was cut down,* Isa. 9:9.

גִּדְעֹם p. n. of a place in the tribe of Benjamin.

גִּדְעוֹן p. n. of a judge of Israel.

גִּדְעֹנִי p. n. of a man.

גָּדַף. Pi. גִּדֵּף blasphemed.

גִּדּוּף m., pl. גִּדּוּפִים, גִּדּוּפוֹת re-proaches, Isa. 43:28; 51:7.

גְּדוּפָה f., reproach, Zep. 2:8.

גָּדַר walled, fenced up; part. גֹּדֵר fencer.

גָּדֵר com. (const. גְּדֶר; with suff. גְּדֵרוֹ; pl. גְּדֵרִים).—I. wall, fence. —II. fenced place.

גְּדֵרָה f.—I. wall.—II. fence, hurdle.— III. same as בֵּית גָּדֵר p.n. of a town in the tribe of Judah; גְּדֵרָתִי a Ge-derite.—IV. גְּדֵרוֹת and גְּדֵרֹתַיִם p.n. of places in the tribe of Judah.

גְּדֶרֶת f., a fence, Eze. 42:12.

גֶּדֶר p.n. of a city of the Canaanites.

גְּדֹר p.n. of a town in the tribe of Judah.

גָּדְרִי an inhabitant of בֵּית גָּדֵר.

גָּרַשׁ root not used; Ch. heaped up.

גָּדִישׁ m.—I. sepulchral mound.—II. heap of corn.

גָּה for זֶה, Eze. 47:13.

גָּהָה raise up, Hos. 5:12.

גֵּהָה f., relief, healing, Pro. 17:22.

גָּהַר bowed, bent downwards.

גּוֹ, גֵּו, גַּו; see נוה.

גּוּב cut, cleft; part. גֹּבִים ploughers.

גַּב m.—I. board, plank.—II. well; see another meaning in גֵּבָה.

גּוֹב (cistern), p.n. of a place; see another meaning in גֵּבָה.

גּוֹג p.n. of the king of Magog; see מָגוֹג.

גּוּד, יְגוּדֶנּוּ, see גָּדַד; shall rush upon him, Gen. 49:19; Hab. 3:16.

גָּוָה root not used.

גּוּא, גַּו m. Ch., middle.

גַּו m. Ch.—I. middle; with suff. גַּוֵּהּ. —II. Heb. back; with suff. גֵּוִי.

גַּו m.—I. back.—II. middle; with suff. גֵּוִי.

גֵּוָה f., a body, Job 20:25; see another meaning under גֵּאָה.

גְּוִיָּה f.—I. body, person.—II. dead body, carcase of men or animals.

גּוֹי m. (with suff. גּוֹיִי; pl. גּוֹיִם, with suff. גּוֹיֶהָ (גּוֹיֵהֶם).—I. gene-rally people, Israelites as well as foreigners.—II. specially, foreign nations.—III. multitudes of locusts, Joel 1:6; of animals, Zep. 2:14.

גַּיְא com. (const. גֵּיְא; pl. גֵּיָאוֹת), valley.

גֵּיְא, גַּיְא the same.

גַּי m. (const. גֵּי), the same.

גֵּאָיוֹת f. pl., valleys.

גּוּז pass over, Ps. 90:10; fut. apoc. וַיָּגָז, Nu. 11:31.

גּוֹזָל young bird; see נזל.

גּוֹזָן p.n., a district in North Mesopo-tamia, between the rivers Chaboras and Saocoras, the Γαυζανίτις of Ptolemy.

גּוּחַ break forth; see גיח.

גּוֹיָה, גְּוִיָּה; see נוה.

גּוּל rejoice; see גיל.

גּוֹלָן, גּוֹלָה; see נלה.

גּוּפִיץ pit; see נמץ.

גּוּנִי p.n. of a man.

גָּוַע (fut. יִגְוַע; inf. גּוֹעַ; const. גְּוַע and גְּוַע), expire, die.

גּוּף Kal, root not used; (Arab. shut up). Hiph. fut. pl. יָגִיפוּ let (them) shut, Neh. 7:3.

גּוּפָה f., dead body; (Arab. the same).

גּוּר I. sojourned, dwelt, with בְּ, עִם,

אֶת; part. גָּר dwelling with; גָּרַת
בֵּיתָהּ her inmate.—II. avoided,
feared, with מִן מָן and מִפְּנֵי—III.
congregated, come together, with
עַל; see גָּרָה. Hith. הִתְגּוֹרֵר—I.
withdraw.—II. dwell, 1 Ki. 17:20.
—III. violent destroying, Jer. 30:23.

גּוּר (גֵּיר, 2. Ch. 2:16), m., sojourner,
stranger.

גֵּרוּת f., sojourning, residing, Jer. 41:
17.

גּוּר m.—I. גּוּר אַרְיֵה lion's whelp;
Gen. 49:9, &c.—II. jackall, 2 Sa.
4:3.

גֹּר m. the same; f. pl. גֹּרוֹת.

גּוּר בַּעַל (dwelling of Baal), p. n. of a
town in Arabia.

מָגוּר m.—I. sojourning.—II. residence,
habitation.—III. human life; so-
journ on earth.

מָגוֹר m., fear, terror; pl. מְגוּרִים.

מְגוֹרָה f., fear; pl. מְגוֹרוֹת.

מְגוּרָה f.—I. granary.—II. fear, terror; pl. מְגוּרוֹת.

מַמְּגֻרָה f. (pl. מַמְּגֻרוֹת), granaries,
Joel 1:17.

גּוֹרָל lot; see גרל.

גּוּשׁ m., clod, Job 7:5.

גִּישָׁן p. n. of a man.

גֵּז fleece; see גזז.

גִּזְבָּר treasurer, Ezr. 1:8; pl. גִּזְבְּרִין,
Ezr. 7:21, and גִּזְבְּרִין, Dan. 3:2, 3.

גֹּזֶה (Arab. bring forth); part. גֹּזִי,
lit. "he who brought me forth," Ps.
71:6.

גָּזִית f.—I. lit. cutting, hewing: hence,
—II. hewn stones.

גָּזַז (fut. יָגֹז, inf. גֹּז and גָּזֹז).—I. shear,
cut off hair, wool, &c.; part. גֹּזְזִים

shavers.—II. drive away (of quails),
Nu. 11:31. Niph. pret. pl. נָגֹזּוּ
were cut off.

גֵּז m. (pl. const. גִּזֵּי).—I. shearing of
sheep: hence,—II. the fleece.—III.
young grass after mowing.

גִּזָּה f., fleece, Jud. 6:39, 40.

גָּזֵז (barber), p. n. of a man.

גָּזַל I. cut off.—II. snatch away, injure.
Niph. was taken away, Pro. 4:16.

גָּזֵל m., const. גֵּזֶל rapine, plunder.

גְּזֵלָה f., the same.

גּוֹזָל m., young pigeon, Gen. 15:9;
Deu. 32:11.

גָּזַם root not used; (Arab. destruction)

גָּזָם m., a species of locust.

גַּזָּם p. n. of a man.

גִּזּוֹנִי m., an inhabitant of Gizon.

גָּזַע root not used. (Arab. cutting off)

גֶּזַע m. (with suff. גִּזְעָם), stock; trunk
of a tree.

גָּזַר I. cut off, down.—II. in two parts
divided.—III. decided, as judgment. Niph. was cut off, with
מִן; was decided, Est. 2:1.

גְּזַר Ch., decided, determined the fate
of others by astrology; part. pl.
גָּזְרִים soothsayers.

גֶּזֶר I. division, section; pl. גְּזָרִים—
II. p. n. of a city on the western
frontier of the tribe of Ephraim,
Γάζηρα.

גְּזֵרָה (גְּזֵירָה) f., place cut off, separated,
Lev. 16:22.

גְּזֵרָה f. Ch., decision. Dan. 4:14, 21.

גָּזְרָה f.—I. cut, polish (of precious
stones), Lam. 4:7.—II. insulated,
separated (of a certain enclosure
of the temple), Eze. 41:42.

מַגְזֵרָה f., axe, 2 Sa. 12:31.

גִּזְרִי inhabitant of Gezer.

גָּחוֹן belly; see גחן.

גֵּיחֲזִי, גֵּחֲזִי p. n. of a servant of the prophet Elisha.

גָּחַל root not used; (Arab. to burn).

גֶּחָל m. (pl. גֶּחָלִים).—I. burning coals.—II. thunderbolts.

גַּחֶלֶת f., the same; with suff. נַחַלְתִּי.

נַחַם p. n. of a man.

גָּחַן root not used; Ch. גְּחַן bowed down.

גָּחוֹן m., belly of a serpent, Lev. 11:42; with suff. גְּחֹנְךָ, Gen. 3:14.

גֵּי, גַּיְא, גַּי, גֵּי; see גוה.

נַחַר p. n. of a man.

גִּיד m., sinew, nerve.

גִּיחַ and גּוּחַ (fut. יָגִיחַ; part. גָּח).—I. drew out.—II. extended, elongated. Hiph. drew out.

גִּיחַ or גּוּחַ Ch. Aph. rushed forth.

גִּיחַ p. n. of a place near Gibeon, 2 Sa. 2:24.

גִּיחוֹן I. p. n. of a river of Paradise, Gen. 2:13.—II. of an aqueduct near Jerusalem; otherwise שִׁלֹחַ.

גִּיל and גּוּל (fut. יָגִיל) leap, exult, rejoice, with בְּ, עַל, לְמַעַן.

גִּיל m., exultation, rejoicing.

גִּיל m. Ch., equal in age, rank, &c., Dan. 1:10.

גִּילָה f., exultation.

גִּילֹנִי see גלה in נלה.

גִּינַת see גנן.

גִּיר, גֵּר m., burnt lime-stone, Isa. 27:9.

גִּיר m. Ch., plaster of lime, Dan. 5:5.

גֵּיר stranger, same as גֵּר; see גור.

גִּישׁ clod, same as גּוּשׁ.

גִּישָׁן p. n. of a man.

גַּל for גֹּל Kal imper. from גָּלַל Ps. 119: 12. Pi. imper. apoc. from גָּלָה, Ps. 119:18.

גְּלָא Ch., reveal; see גלה.

גָּלַב root not used; (Arab. drew, shaved).

גַּלָּב m., barber, Eze. 5:1.

גִּלְבֹּעַ p. n., Gilboa, hills in the tribe of Issachar.

גָּלֹת, גִּלְגָּל, גַּלְגַּל; see גלל.

גֶּלֶד m., skin; with suff. גְּלְדִּי my skin, Job 16:15.

גֻּלָּה bowl; see גלל.

גָּלָה (fut. גָּלֹת, יִגְלֶה; inf. גָּלֹה, גָּלוֹת).—I. laid bare, disclosed, opened.—II. depopulated a country, i. e. led into captivity, migrated; part. m. גּוֹלֶה, f. גּוֹלָה migrated, gone into captivity; גָּלוּי opened, proclaimed, published (of an edict). Niph. נִגְלָה (fut. יִגָּל, יִגָּלֶה; inf. abs. נִגְלֹה, נִגְלוֹת).—I. was uncovered, exposed, revealed.—II. migrated, went into captivity, Isa. 38:12; part. f. pl. נִגְלֹת revealed, Deu. 29:29. Pi. גִּלָּה (fut. יְגַל, יְגַלֶּה).—I. uncovered, made naked.—II. had carnal connexion with, with אֶל and עַל. Pu. גֻּלָּה was uncovered; part. f. מְגֻלָּה openly said. Hiph. הֶגְלָה, הִגְלָה led captive (fut. וַיֶּגֶל, וַיַּגְלֶה). Hoph. הָגְלָה was made captive. Hithp. הִתְגַּלָּה made himself naked; fut. apoc. וַיִּתְגַּל, Gen. 9:21.

גְּלָא Ch., revealed. Piel גַּלִּי גַּלָּא revealed. Aph. הַגְלִי carried captive, Ezr. 4:10, 12.

גָּלֹה p. n. of a city in the mountains

of Judah; its inhabitants were styled גִּילֹנִי.

גֹּלָה‎ גּוֹלָה f.—I. *captivity.*—II. *captive, troop of captives.*

גּוֹלָן p.n. of a city of Batanea, Γαυλών.

גָּלָת‎ גָּלוּת f., *captive;* as גּוֹלָה.

גָּלֻת f. Ch., the same.

גִּלָּיוֹן m., *tablet, book,* Isa. 8:1; pl. גִּלְיוֹנִים *mirrors,* Isa. 3:23. Writing tablets and mirrors were both, in ancient times, plates of metal.

גָּלְיָת p.n., *Goliath,* the giant whom David slew.

גַּלְגַּלִּים‎ גְּלִילָה‎ גָּלִיל‎ גָּלִים; see נלל.

גָּלוּם; see נלם.

גָּלַח. Pi. גִּלַּח.—I. *shaved head or beard.* II. *devastated by war,* Isa. 7:20. Pu. *was shaven,* Ju. 16:17, 22; Jer. 41:5. Hithp. *shave himself.*

גִּלֹה p.n. of a city.

גְּלִיָּת‎ גְּלִילָה; see נלה.

גָּלַל (sing. p. 1.גַּלּוֹתִי, pl. גָּלְלוּ; inf. גֹּל‎ גּוֹל; imp. גַּל‎ גֹּל).—I. *roll* (as a stone).—II. with מֵעַל *roll away,* used metaphorically of things morally heavy. — III. with אֶל‎ עַל, *commit to,* lit. *roll upon;* גּוֹל עַל יְיָ דַּרְכֶּךָ *commit thy way unto the Lord,* Ps. 37:5. Niph. נָגֹל *were rolled up,* Isa. 34:4; *rolled away,* Am. 5:24. Pil. גִּלְגֵּל *roll off,* Jer. 51:25. Hithpal. *roll, rush in violently,* Job 30:14. Hiph. הָגֵל *roll,* Gen. 29:10. Po. גּוֹלֵל *roll about in,* Isa. 9:4. Hithpo. הִתְגּוֹלֵל *rolled in, weltered in,* 2 Sa. 20:12.—II. *fall upon,* with עַל, Gen. 43:18.

גָּלָל m.—I. *dung.*—II. בִּגְלַל *because, for the sake of;* בִּגְלָלְךָ *for thy sake.*—III. p.n. of a man.

גְּלָל m. Ch., *great, heavy,* (of stones)

גֵּל m. (with suff. גֶּלְלוֹ; pl. גְּלָלִים; const. גֶּלְלֵי) *dung.*

גִּלֲלַי‎ גְּלָל p.n. of a man.

גִּלּוּלִים m. pl., *idols.*

גָּלִיל m.—I. *that which can be turned on hinges,* 1 Ki. 6:34.—II. *ring,* Cant. 5:14.—III. *circuit, tract of country;* הַגָּלִיל and הַגָּלִילָה p.n. of a region in the tribe of Naphtali, *Galilee.*

גְּלִילָה f. *circuit, region.*

גַּל m. (pl. גַּלִּים).—I. *a heap* (of stones, &c.).— II. *spring, fountain.*—III. pl. *waves, breakers.*

גַּלִּים p.n. of a town in the tribe of Benjamin; 1 Sa. c. 25; Jos. c. 10.

גֻּל m., *oil jar,* Zec. 4:2.

גֻּלָּה f.—I. same as גַּל (pl. גֻּלֹּת) *well,* Jos. 15:10; Jud. 1:15.—II. const. גֻּלַּת *oil jar* or *vessel.*— III. *vaselike ornaments,* or *flowers on the capitals of columns.*

גַּלְגַּל m.—I. *wheel;* pl. גַּלְגַּלִּים.—II. *whirlwind.*—III. *chaff* (as driven by the wind).

גַּלְגַּל m. Ch., *wheel,* Dan. 7:9.

גִּלְגָּל m.—I. *cart wheel,* Isa. 28:28. —II. p.n. of a city between Jericho and Jordan.

גֻּלְגֹּלֶת f.—I. *skull.*—II. used in numbering men, as we say, *head of cattle;* with suff. גֻּלְגָּלְתּוֹ; pl. with suff. גֻּלְגְּלֹתָם.

מְגִלָּה f., *volume, roll, book.*

מְגִלָּה f. Ch., the same.

גָּלַם *wrapped together* (as a mantle) 2 Ki. 2:8.

גְּלוֹם m., *cloak, mantle,* Eze. 27:24.

גֹּלֶם m., embryo, fœtus, Ps. 139:16.

גַּלְמוּד m., hard, barren, fruitless.

גָּלַע Hithp. הִתְגַּלַּע intermeddle, be impudent.

גִּלְעָד I. p.n., Gilead, the son of Machir, grandson of Manasseh: hence,— II. p.n. of a hill and town near Lebanon.—III. of a region beyond Jordan ; גִּלְעָדִי a Gileadite.

גַּלְעֵד (heap of witness), p.n. of the heap of stones erected by Laban and Jacob, Gen. 31:47, 48.

גָּלַשׁ "appear," Cant. 4:1; 6:5, Eng. Ver.; meaning uncertain.

גַּם; see גמם.

גָּמָא Pi. drink in, Job 29:24. Hiph. give to drink, Gen. 24:17.

גֹּמֶא m., the paper reed; תֵּבַת גֹּמֶא an ark of reeds, and כְּלִי גֹ׳ a boat of reeds.

גֹּמֶד m., pruning knife, short-sword, Ju. 3:16.

גַּמָּדִים m. pl., short-swordsmen, Eze. 27:11.

גִּמְזוֹ p. n. of a town in the tribe of Judah.

גָּמַל (fut. יִגְמֹל).— I. recompense, repay, with לְ and עַל.—II. mature, ripen. — III. wean as a child. Niph. was weaned.

גְּמוּל recompence, retribution, either of good or bad actions.

גְּמוּל p. n. of a man.

גְּמוּלָה f., recompence, retribution.

גְּמַלִיאֵל (God my restorer), p.n. of a man.

תִּגְמוּל m., retribution, kindness, Ps. 116:12.

גָּמָל com., camel; pl. גְּמַלִּים.

גְּמַלִּי p. n. of a man.

גָּמַם (Arab. filled up, desired).

גַּם moreover, also; הֲגַם is it not also! גַּם…גַּם and…also; גַּם כִּי out if, although.

מְנַמָּה f., desire, object, Hab. 1:9.

גֹּמֶץ (Syr. a well).

גּוּמָץ m., a well or pit, Ecc. 10:8.

גָּמַר (fut. יִגְמֹר).— I. bring to pass.— II. finish, fail.

גְּמַר Ch., complete, learned, Eze. 7:12.

גְּמַרְיָה and גְּמַרְיָהוּ p.n. of a man.

גֹּמֶר p n.—I. of a northern race of people, perhaps the Cymri.— II. of the wife of Hosea.

גַּן garden; see גנן.

גָּנַב he stole, with or without violence; with לֵב, Gen. 31:20, 26, 27, "stole away unawares." Niph. stolen. Pi. secretly, Ex. 22:11. Pu. steals, was stolen. Hith. stole themselves away.

גַּנָּב m., a thief.

גְּנֵבָה f., stolen thing, Ex. 22:2, 3.

גְּנֻבַת p. n. of a man.

גֻּנָּה, גַּנָּה; see גנן.

גָּנַז root not used; (Arab. covered).

גֶּנֶז m., pl. גְּנָזִים; const. גִּנְזֵי treasures.

גְּנַז or גֶּנֶז m. Ch., pl. גִּנְזִין treasures.

גִּנְזַךְ m., treasury, 2 Ch. 28:11.

גָּנַן guard, protect, with עַל, אֶל. Hiph. the same.

גַּן com. (with suff. גַּנִּי, pl. גַּנִּים) garden.

גַּנָּה f., a garden; pl. גַּנּוֹת.

גִּנָּה f., the same.

גִּינָח p. n. of a man.

גִּנְתוֹן, גִּנְתוֹי p. n. of a man.

מָגֵן m. (suff. מָגִנִּי, pl. מָגִנִּים) *shield*,
fig., *God the protector*, Gen. 15:10;
מָגִנֵּי־אֶרֶץ *shields of the earth*, i.e.
princes, Ps. 47:10., &c.

מְגִנָּה f., with לֵב *veiling, covering of
heart*, Lam. 3:65.

גָּעָה *lowed* (as oxen), Job 6:5.

גֹּעָה p. n. of a place near Jerusalem.

גָּעַל *loathed, abhorred.* Niph. *was
rejected, cast away*, 2 Sa. 1:21.
Hiph. *cast* (brought forth prema-
turely), Job 21:10.

גֹּעַל m., *loathing*, Eze. 16:5.

גַּעַל p. n. of a man.

גָּעַר (fut. יִגְעַר) *rebuked, reproved*,
with בְּ.

גְּעָרָה f., *chiding, reproof.*

מִגְעֶרֶת *rebuke, calamity*, Deu. 28:20.

גָּעַשׁ *shook, trembled*, Ps. 18:8. Pu.
גֹּעַשׁ *was shaken*, Job 34:20. Hithp.
was moved. Hithpo. the same,
Jer. 25:16.

גַּעַשׁ p. n. of a mountain in the tribe
of Ephraim.

גַּעַת Kal. inf. const. from נגע.

גַּעְתָּם p.n. of the son of Eliphaz.

גַּף *body*; see נפף.

גֶּפֶן com.—I. *climbing plant.*—II. *vine.*

גָּפַף *root not used*; (Arab. *troop of
men*).

גַּף m.—I. *person, self*; בְּגַפּוֹ *with himself only*, i.e. *alone*, Ex. 21:3,4.—
II. *back*, i.e. *hillock*, Pro. 9:3.

גַּף m. Ch., pl. גַּפִּין *wings.*

גֹּפֶר m., *name of a tree*; probably,
the pitch-pine, Gen 6·14.

גָּפְרִית f., *brimstone.*

גֵּר; see גָּרַר and גּוּר.

גֵּר, גַּר; see גּוּר.

גֵּרָא (same as גֵּרָה), p. n. of a man.

גָּרַב *root not used*; like *scratch, scurf*,
and many other words in all languages, an imitation of the noise
made in *scratching*, &c.

גָּרָב m., *scurf, scurvy.*

גָּרֵב p. n. of one of David's generals

גַּרְגַּר, גַּרְגְּרוֹת; see גרר.

גִּרְגָּשִׁי p. n. of a nation of Canaanites

גָּרַד Hithp.inf. הִתְגָּרֵד *scrape, scratch*,
Job 2:8; see גָּרַב.

גָּרָה Pi. גֵּרָה *produce, kindle strife.*
Hithp. *prepare to contend, contend
with*; const. with בְּ.

תִּגְרָה f., *attack, stroke*, Ps. 39:11.

גָּרוֹן m., *throat*; see גרר.

גֵּרוֹן, גֵּרָה; see גרר.

גֵּרוּת *sojourning*; see גּוּר.

גָּרַן same as גָּזַר. Niph. pret. נִגְרַזְתִּי
I am cut off, Ps. 31:23; 88:6.

גַּרְזֶן m., *axe.*

גִּרְזִי (גְּרִזִי) p.n. of a nation of Canaanites.

הַר גְּרִזִים p n. of a mountain, *Gerizim.*

גָּרַל *root not used*; (Arab. *was gravelly,
sandy*).

גּוֹרָל m. (pl. גּוֹרָלוֹת).—I. *lot*, lit. *the
pebble by which it was determined.*
—II. הִפִּיל, הִשְׁלִיךְ, יָדָה, יָרָה,
נָתַן הַגּוֹרָל *determined by lot*,
הָיָה לוֹ גוֹרָל, עָלָה עָלָיו גוֹרָל i.e.
יָצָא *the lot fell.*—III. *the thing
obtained by lot.*

גָּרַל (const. גְּרָל) Pro 19:19; keri
גָּדֹל *great.*

גֶּרֶם m. (pl. גְּרָמִים).—I. bone.—II. powerful, Gen. 49:14.—III. framework, pulpit, 2 Ki. 9:13.

גְּרַם m. Ch., bone.

גָּרַם cut, spoil, Zep. 3:3. Pi. fut. יְגָרֵם shall destroy.

גַּרְמִי p. n. of a man.

גֹּרֶן root not used; (Arab. place for drying dates).

גֹּרֶן f. (pl. גְּרָנוֹת; const. גָּרְנוֹת).—I. open place at the gate of a city, court of justice.—II. threshing-floor.—III. corn of the floor, Job 39:12. גֹּרֶן הָאָטָד p. n. of a place beyond Jordan; see אָטָד.

גָּרַס pained, overwhelmed, Ps. 119:20. Hiph. fut. וַיַּגְרֵם and brake, destroyed, Lam. 3:16.

גֶּרֶשׂ m. (with suff. גְּרִשׂה), thrashed; perhaps, ground corn, Lev. 2:14, 16.

גָּרַע I. took away.—II. shaved, took away the beard, Jer. 48:37. Niph. (fut. יִגָּרַע, יִגְרַע) was taken away. Pi. draws off; fut. יְגָרַע Job 36:27.

מִגְרָעוֹת f. pl., ledges, steps in buildings, 1 Ki. 6:6.

גָּרַף swept away (as a flood), Jud. 5:21. אֶגְרוֹף m., fist. מַגְרֵפָה f., furrow, Joel 1:17.

גָּרַר he drew, dragged; fut. יִגּוֹר. Niph. fut. יִגֹּר chew the cud. Po. sawed, 1 Ki. 7:9. Hithpo. swept away, Jer. 30:23.

גֵּרָה f.—I. the cud.—II. Gerah, a weight equal to the twentieth part of a shekel.

גַּרְגַּר m., berry, Isa. 17:6.

גַּרְגְּרָה f., throat, front of the neck.

גָּרוֹן m. (const. גְּרוֹן), throat.

מְגֵרָה f., saw.

גְּרָר p. n. of a city of the Philistines.

גֶּרֶשׂ flower; see גרם.

גָּרַשׁ put forth, cast forth. Niph. was cast, driven, out. Pi. גֵּרֵשׁ expel Pu. גֹּרַשׁ was expelled.

גֶּרֶשׁ m., produce, fruit, Deu. 33:14.

גְּרֻשָׁה expulsion.

מִגְרָשׁ m.—I. suburbs.—II. pastures, open places.—III. lands, surrounding the cities of the Levites; pl. מִגְרְשׁוֹת, מִגְרָשִׁים.

גֵּרְשֹׁם p. n. of the son of Moses.

גֵּרְשׁוֹן (Gershon), p. n. of a man; גֵּרְשֻׁנִּי a Gershonite.

גֶּשׁ, גְּשָׁה, גַּשׁ Kal imp., from נגש. גְּשׁוּ Kal imp. pl., from נגש.

גְּשׁוּר (bridge), p. n. of three places.—I. the country of the Canaanites to the east of Jordan.—II. of a district in South Palestine.—III. of a district in Syria. גְּשׁוּרִי a Geshurite.

גָּשַׁם Kal, root not used; (Arab. fatness). Hiph. part. pl. מַגְשִׁימִים cause to rain, Jer. 14:22.

גֶּשֶׁם m., heavy shower; pl. גְּשָׁמִים, גִּשְׁמֵי.

גֶּשֶׁם m., the same; with suff. גִּשְׁמָה.

גֶּשֶׁם m., body.

גֶּשֶׁם, גַּשְׁמוּ p. n. of a man.

גֹּשֶׁן (Goshen), p. n.—I. of the country bordering on Egypt, which was inhabited by the Israelites during the first captivity.—II. of a town in the tribe of Judah.

גִּשְׁפָּא‎ p. n. of a man.

גָּשַׁשׁ‎. Pi. fut. with ה‎ parag. נְגַשְׁשָׁה‎ we feel, grope about, Isa. 59:10.

גֶּשֶׁת‎ Kal inf. with suff. גִּשְׁתּוֹ‎, from נגשׁ‎.

גַּת‎ f.—I. the vat in which grapes were trodden; pl. גִּתּוֹת‎.—II. p. n. of a city of the Philistines in the country of Goliath. גַּת הַחֵפֶר‎ p. n. of a town in the tribe of Zebulun; גַּת רִמּוֹן‎ p. n. of cities of the Levites in Dan and Manasseh; גִּתִּי‎ a Gittite.

גִּתַּיִם‎ p. n. of a town in the tribe of Benjamin.

גִּתִּית‎ f., probably the name of a musical instrument; occurs in the titles of certain psalms.

גֶּתֶר‎ p. n. of a people of Syria, Gen 10:23.

ד

דָּא‎ pron. Ch. f. and neuter, this; דָּא לְדָא‎ together.

דָּאַב‎ same as דּוּב‎ was languid.

דְּאָבָה‎ f., pining away, Job 41:14.

דְּאָבוֹן‎ m., extreme languor, fainting; const. דַּאֲבוֹן‎, Deu. 28:65.

דָּאן‎ fish, same as דָּג‎; see דָּנָה‎.

דָּאַג‎ I. grieve, be anxious, with לְ‎.—II. fear, with מִן‎.

דֹּאֵג‎ (Syr. דּוֹאֵג‎), p. n. of a prince of the Edomites.

דְּאָנָה‎ f., anxiety, alarm.

דָּאָה‎ flew; fut. יִדְאֶה‎, וַיֵּרָא‎.

דָּאָה‎ f., name of a bird, kite, Lev. 11:14; LXX. γύψ; Vulg. milvus; corresponding passage, Deu. 14:13, רָאָה‎.

דֹּאר‎ p. n., same as דּוֹר‎.

דֹּב‎ bear; see דבב‎.

דָּבָא‎ root not used; (Arab. produced, multiplied).

דֹּבֶא‎ riches, power; LXX. ἰσχύς, Deu 33:25; with suff. דָּבְאֶךָ‎.

דָּבַב‎ crept, flowed softly (of wine) Cant. 7:10.

דֹּב, דּוֹב‎ m. (pl. דֻּבִּים‎) a bear.

דֹּב‎ m. Ch., the same.

דִּבָּה‎ f.—I. calumny.—II. calumniator, Pro. 25:10.

דְּבוֹרָה‎ bee; see דבר‎.

דְּבַח‎ Ch., sacrificed, Ezr. 6:3; see זבח‎.

דְּבַח‎ m. Ch., sacrifice, Ezr. 6:3.

מַדְבַּח‎ m. Ch., altar, Ezr. 7:17.

דִּבְיוֹנִים‎ m. pl., pigeons' dung, 2 Ki. 6:25.

דְּבִיר‎ oracle; see דבר‎.

דָּבַל‎ root not used; (Arab. pressed together).

דְּבֵלָה‎ f. (const. דְּבֶלֶת‎; pl. דְּבֵלִים‎) παλάθη, cake of dry figs.

דִּבְלָתַיִם, דִּבְלָה‎ בֵּית ד'‎ p. n. of a city of the Moabites.

דִּבְלַיִם‎ p. n. of a man.

דָּבַק‎ and דָּבְקָה‎ (fut. יִדְבַּק‎; inf. דָּבְקָה‎).—I. adhered, cleft to.—II. reached, attained, with בְּ, לְ, אֶל‎. Pu. fut. pl. יְדֻבָּקוּ‎ made to adhere. Hiph. (fut. יַדְבִּיק, וַיַּדְבֵּק‎) joined, caused to stick, attained. Hoph. part מֻדְבָּק‎ stuck to, Ps. 22:16.

דְּבַק‎ Ch., adhered, Dan. 2:43.

דָּבֵק‎ m., adhering; pl. דְּבֵקִים‎.

דֶּבֶק‎ m., solder, for joining metals; pl. דְּבָקִים‎ rivets (for armour).

דָּבַר not used in the pres. pret.; part. דֹּבֵר speaking; דָּבֻר spoken; inf. דָּבְּרֶךָ thy speaking. Piel דִּבֶּר, דִּבֵּר (fut. יְדַבֵּר) he spoke, uttered words to or with any one, with לְ, עַל, בְּ, אֶת, עִם, אֶל; concerning any one, with בְּ, אֶל, עַל; against any one, with עַל, בְּ; by any one, with בְּיַד, used idiomatically; דִּבֶּר לַעֲשׂוֹת he threatened; דִּבְּרִים 'ד he uttered words; שָׁלוֹם 'ד, with אֵת or עִם he spoke friendly with any one; with בְּ the same; 'ד לְאִשָּׁה he asked her in marriage. Pu. was spoken. Niph. became, i. e. set about speaking, with בְּ, עַל. Hiph. subdued (with his word); fut. וַיַּדְבֵּר. Hithp. part. מְדַבֵּר speaking.

דָּבָר m. (const. דְּבַר; pl. דְּבָרִים, דִּבְרֵי).—I. word; בַּעַל דְּבָרִים אִישׁ eloquent man.—II. thing.—III. thing, matter, subject in hand; דְּבַר יוֹם בְּיוֹמוֹ the thing (duty) of the day in its day; אַחַר הַדְּבָרִים הָאֵלֶּה after these things, μετὰ ταῦτα: לֹא דָבָר nothing; אֵין דָּבָר 'ד there is nothing; בַּעַל דְּ 'ד he who pleads a cause; עַל דִּבְרֵי 'ד and דְּבַר because; עַל דְּבַר אֲשֶׁר because of.

דֶּבֶר m., pestilence; pl. דְּבָרִים.

דְּבִיר m.—I. the oracle, i. e. the place in the temple whence responses were given.—II. p. n. of a city in the tribe of Judah.

דֹּבֶר m., fold, pasture, Mic. 2:12.

דִּבְרָה f., cause for adjudication; עַל דִּבְרַת because; with שֶׁ because that; עַל דִּבְרָתִי according to, after the order of, Ps. 110:4.

דִּבְרָה f. Ch., cause.

דְּבוֹרָה f.—I. a bee; pl. דְּבֹרִים.—II. p. n. of a woman who judged Israel.

דֹּבְרוֹת f. pl., floats, rafts, 1 Ki. 5:23.

דַּבְּרוֹת f. pl., sayings, Deu. 33:3.

מִדְבָּר m.—I. any large plain used for pasture.—II. a desert or wilderness; הַמִּדְבָּר the desert of Sinai.—III. speech, address, Cant. 4:3.

דְּבַשׁ m. (with suff. דִּבְשִׁי).—I. honey of bees.—II. honey dew, collected in large quantities in Palestine.

דַּבֶּשֶׁת f.—I. the hunch, or more probably, the pack-saddle of a camel.—II. p. n. of a place, Jos. 19:11.

דָּגָה multiplied, Gen. 48:16.

דָּג m., fish; pl. דָּגִים, דְּגֵי (דָּאג).

דָּגָה const. דְּגַת f., a fish, fish in general.

דָּגוֹן m., p. n. of an idol of the Philistines, probably in the form of a fish.

דָּגָן (const. דְּגַן) m.—I. bread.—II. corn.

דָּגַל part. דָּגוּל.—I. marked, signalised, Cant. 5:10.—II. fut. נִדְגֹּל we will set up our banner, Ps. 20:6. Niph. part. pl. נִדְגָּלוֹת having banners, i. e. an army, Cant. 6:4,10; see next word.

דֶּגֶל m. (with suff. דִּגְלוֹ; pl. דְּגָלִים, דְּגָלַי), standard, banner.

דָּגָן com.; see דָּגָה.

דָּגַר hatch, brood over eggs, Isa. 34:15; Jer. 17:11.

דַּד m., dual דַּדַּיִם דַּדֵּי the two breasts of a woman.

דָּדָה. Hith. fut. אֶדַּדֶּה *I will proceed gently, submissively, joyfully.*

דְּדָן (pl. דְּדָנִים), p. n. of the inhabitants of a district in the north of Arabia.

דֹּדָנִים m. pl., p. n. of a people.

דְּהַב m. Ch., *gold.*

מַדְהֵבָה f., an epithet of Babylon, lit. *place of gold,* Isa. 14:4.

דֶּהָיֵא p. n. of a people who were colonised in Samaria, Ezr. 4:9.

דָּהַם. Niph. part. נִדְהָם *reduced, impotent,* Jer. 14:9.

דָּהַר, part. דֹּהֵר *charging, attacking,* Nah. 3:2.

דַּהֲרָה f., *charge of cavalry;* pl. דַּהֲרוֹת, Jud. 5:22.

תִּדְהָר m., name of a tree; Vulg. ulnus; *the elm or box.*

דּוֹב same as דֹּב *bear;* see דבב.

דּוּב same as דָּאַב *wasting.* Hiph. part. pl. מְדִיבוֹת *things wasting,* Lev. 26:16.

דּוּג and דִּיג (from דָּן) *he shall fish,* Jer. 16:16.

דַּיָּג, דַּוָּג m., *a fisher.*

דּוּגָה f., *fishing,* Am. 4:2.

דּוּד I. root not used; Ch. *was agitated.*—II. same as יָדַד *he loved.*

דּוּד m.—I. *a pot or caldron;* pl. דְּוָדִים.—II. *basket;* pl. דּוּדִים.

דּוּדָאִים m. pl.—I. *baskets.*—II. *mandrakes,* plants used as philtres or love potions.

דּוֹד m. (pl. דּוֹדִים).—I. *love.*—II. *offices of love.*—III. *beloved.*—IV. *uncle.*

דּוֹדָה f., *aunt.*

דָּוִד, דָּוִיד p. n., *David* king of Israel.

דָּוָה I. *was sick.*—II. *was unclean, polluted;* inf. דְּוֹתָהּ *her uncleanness* (i. e. the menses), Lev. 12:2.

דָּוֶה m., דָּוָה f., *sick, unclean.*

דְּוַי m., *sickness, disease,* Ps. 40:4.

דַּי m., *habitual* (chronic) *disorder.*

דְּוַת inf. of דָּוָה, which see.

מַדְוֶה m., *consuming disease.*

דּוּחַ. Hiph. הֵדִיחַ I. *expel,* Jer. 51:34.—II. *dispel,* i. e. scour clean.

דָּוִיד p. n., same as דָּוִד; see דוד.

דּוּךְ same as דָּכַךְ *beat, pounded,* Nu. 11:8.

מְדֹכָה f., *mortar,* Nu. 11:8.

דּוּכִיפַת f., LXX. ἔποψ; Vulg. upupa; *the hoopoe,* Lev. 11:19; Deu. 14:18.

דּוּם root not used, same as דָּמַם *was silent.*

דּוּמָה f.—I. *silent.*—II. *death.*—III. *the grave.*—IV. p. n. of a people of Arabia.

דּוּמִיָּה f.—I. *remaining, abiding.*—II. *quietness, silence.*

דּוּמָם m., *very quiet, silent.*

דּוּמֶשֶׂק p. n., same as דַּמֶּשֶׂק.

דִּין; see דין.

דּוֹנַג, דּוֹנֵג m., *wax.*

דּוּץ (fut. יָדוּץ) *leaps, exults,* Job 41:14.

דּוּק Ch., *grind small,* Dan. 2:35.

דָּיֵק m., *entrenchment, foss, dyke,* used in sieges.

דּוּר I. *dwell, reside,* Ps. 84:11.—II. *encircle, place round,* Eze. 24:5.

דּוּר Ch., *dwell.*

דּוּר m.—I. a circle, Isa. 29:3.—II. a ball, Isa. 22:18.

דֹּר, דּוֹר m. (lit. circle of years).— I. age, generation.—II. race of men; עד דֹּר ,לְדֹר וָדֹר ,לְדֹר דֹּר ,דֹּר וָדֹר ,מִדֹּר דֹּר וָדֹר from generation to generation, for ever; pl. דּוֹר eternity; דֹּרוֹת generations of men, posterity.—III. habitation (see דּוּר); with אָבוֹת sepulchre, Ps. 49:20.

דָּר m. Ch., age, generation.

דֹּר ,דֹּאר דּוֹר נָפוֹת and דּ׳ p.n. of a city not far from Mount Carmel.

מְדוֹר m. Ch., habitation.

מְדָר m. Ch., the same.

מְדוּרָה f., pile of fire.

בִּתְדִירָא f. Ch., a revolution; continually, Dan. 6:17, 21.

דּוּרָא p. n. of a valley or plain in Babylonia.

דּוּשׁ and דִּישׁ (fut. יָדוּשׁ).—I. tread, trample on.—II. tread out corn.— III. metaphorically, conquer enemies. Niph. נָדוֹשׁ was trampled down; inf. abs. הִדּוֹשׁ. Hoph. fut. יוּדָשׁ is trodden, Isa. 28:27.

דּוּשׁ Ch., is trodden, Dan. 7:23.

דַּיִשׁ m., time of treading out corn, Lev. 26:5.

מְדוּשָׁה f., with suff. מְדֻשָׁתִי my treading out, Isa. 21:10.

דּוּת see דָּוָה.

דָּחָה drive, urge on to fall; inf. abs. דָּחֹה; part. f. דְּחוּיָה impelled. Niph. urged or impelled; part. pl. נִדְחִים. Pu. pl. דֹּחוּ are driven.

דְּחִי m. (with pause דֶּחִי), impulse, being driven on.

דַּחֲוָה Ch. f., pl. דַּחֲוָן Dan. 6:19 " instruments of music," Eng Ver.; meaning uncertain.

מַדְחֵה m., driving out, ruin, Prov 26:28.

דָּחַח Niph. fut. pl. יִדָּחוּ, same as דָּחָה Niph., is urged, impelled.

דְּחַל Ch., part. דָּחִיל fearful. Pa affright, Dan. 4:2.

דֹּחַן m., millet, Eze. 4:9.

דָּחַף, part. pl. דְּחוּפִים hurried, hastened. Niph. was hurried.

מַדְחֵפוֹת f. pl.; לְמַדְ׳ swiftly, hastily, Ps. 140:12.

דָּחַק press upon, Joel 2:8 ; part. דֹּחֵק oppressor, Ju. 2:18.

דַּי m. (const. דֵּי, with suff. דַּיִּי), a sufficiency, enough; דֵּי הָשִׁיב as much as shall restore, Lev. 25:28; דַּיָּם sufficient for them; דֵּי חֲלֵב enough of milk, Pro. 27:27; כְּדֵי same as כְּ; כְּדֵי as (it were) enough; מִדֵּי שָׁנָה בְשָׁנָה same as מִן ; מִדֵּי from year to year, yearly.

דִּי Ch.—I. the relative pron. who, which, what, like אֲשֶׁר.—II. of, like the de of the modern European languages. — III. conj. like אֲשֶׁר that.—IV. same as כִּי, ὅτι; כְּדֵי when, as; מִן דִּי from the time when; עַד דִּי until.

דִּי זָהָב (enough of gold); p.n. of a place in the desert near Sinai, Deut. 1:1.

דִּיבֹן p. n.—I. of a town of the Moabites.—II. of a place in the tribe of Judah; same as דִּימוֹנָה.

דַּיָּגִין, דַּיָּגִ fishermen; see דּוּג.

דִּיָה root not used; Ch. דְּהָא was black.

דַּיָּה f., *black vulture, turkey buzzard;* LXX. ἰκτινος, Vulg. milvus, Deut. 14:13, &c.

דְּיוֹ m., *ink,* Jer. 36:18.

דִּימֹן same as דִּיבוֹן p. n. of a town of Moab.

דִּימוֹנָה p. n. of a town in the tribe of Judah.

דִּין and דּוּן (pret. and part. דָּן; inf. and imper. דִּין; fut. יָדִין).—I. *judged.*—II. *pleaded, defended.*—III. *punished,* with בְּ.—IV. *contend with one,* with עִם.—V. *govern,* with בְּ. Niph. part. נָדוֹן *contend,* 2 Sa. 19:10.

דִּין and דּוּן Ch., the same.

דִּין (דּוּן Job 19:29.) m.—I. *judgment.*—II. *cause for judgment* (דָּן and דִּין עָשָׂה *he pleaded a cause*).—III. *litigation, strife.*

דִּין m. Ch.—I. *judgment.*—II. *court of judgment.*—III. *punishment.*

דִּינָה p. n. of the daughter of Jacob.

דִּינָיֵא Ch., p. n. of a people of Assyria.

דַּיָּן m., *a judge;* Ch. pl. דַּיָּנִין *judges.*

דָּן p. n., *Dan.*—I. a son of Jacob and his tribe.—II. a city in the north of Palestine.

דָּנִאֵל, דָּנִיֵּאל p. n., *Daniel.*

מָדוֹן m.—I. *dispute, contention;* pl. מְדָנִים, מִדְיָנִים.—II. מָדוֹן אִישׁ *man of height, stature* (see מִדָּה), 2 Sa. 21:20.—III. p. n. of a city of the Canaanites.

מָדָן m. (pl. מְדָנִים).—I. *strifes, disputes.*—II. p. n. of the son of Abraham and Keturah.

מָדְיָנִי (pl. מִדְיָנִים) *Midianite;* see מִדְיָנִים

מְדִינָה f., lit. *jurisdiction:* hence,—I *province.*—II. *region, country.*

מְדִינָה f. Ch., the same.

דִּיפַת p. n. of a son of Japhet, 1 Ch 1:6, a wrong reading for רִיפַת Gen. 10:3.

דָּיֵק *dyke;* see דּוּק.

דַּיִשׁ *tread;* see דּוּשׁ.

דִּישׁוֹן m.—I. a species of deer, Deut. 14:5.—II. p. n. of a son of Seir and of a district called after him.

דַּךְ *poor;* see דכך.

דֵּךְ Ch. pron., *this, he;* fem. דָּךְ *she.*

דָּכָא. Pi. דִּכָּא.—I. *beat small, break* —II. *trample on.*—Pu. *was broken, contrite.* Hith. fut. יִדַּכָּאוּ *shall be broken.* Niph. part., *beaten, oppressed,* Isa. 57:15.

דַּכָּא m.—I. *crushed.*—II. *humbled, dejected.*

דָּכָה *is broken,* Ps. 10:10. Niph. *broken, afflicted.* Pi. דִּכִּיתָ *thou hast broken.*

דְּכִי m., with suff. דָּכְיָם, *their beating, dashing,* Ps. 93:3.

דָּכַךְ root not used, same as דָּכָה and דּוּךְ.

דַּךְ (with pause דָּךְ m.), *poor, mean, afflicted,* Pro. 26:28; יִשְׁאָ דַּכָּיו *makes hateful those whom it has afflicted.*

דַּכָּה f., *bruising,* θλάσις, Deu. 33:2.

דְּכֵן Ch. pron., *this.*

דְּכַר Ch., same as זָכַר *male.*

דְּכַר m. Ch., *a ram;* pl. דִּכְרִין.

דָּכְרוֹנָה m. Ch. (emph. state *memorial, record,* Ezr. 6:2.

דָּכְרָן m. Ch. the same, Ezr. 4:15.

דַּל poor; see דַּלָּה and דָּלַל.

דָּלַג leaping, skipping. Pi. the same, with עַל.

דָּלָה I. draw (water from a well). Pi. draw up out of prison, Ps. 30:2. —II. totter, vacillate, be lame; דָּלְיוּ for דָּלוּ, Pro. 26:7.

דַּל m. for דֶּלֶת door, Ps. 141:3.

דֶּלֶת gate, door; dual דְּלָתַיִם folding, double doors or gates; דַּלְתֵי שָׁמַיִם the doors of heaven (clouds?); דַּ׳ פָּנִים doors of the face (jaws), Job 41:6; בֶּטֶן דַּ׳ doors of the womb. Pl. דְּלָתוֹת const. דַּלְתוֹת f. (m. Neh. 13:19). —I. doors.—II. leaves, valves of gates.—III. leaves of a book, Jer. 36:23.

דְּלִי m., bucket, Isa. 40:15.

דָּלִי m., dual דָּלָיִם (with suff. דָּלְיָו), his drawings up or forth, Nu. 24:7.

דָּלִית f., pl. דָּלִיּוֹת boughs, branches.

דְּלָיָה, דְּלָיָהוּ p. n. of a man.

דַּלָּה poverty; see דָּלַל.

דָּלַח disturb, render muddy (of water), Eze. 32:2, 13.

דְּלָיוּ for דָּלוּ Pi. imp. pl., from דָּלָה.

דָּלַל wasted, reduced, weakened. Niph. (fut. וַיִּדַּל) is wasted, reduced.

דַּל m. (pl. דַּלִּים, f. דַּלָּה, pl. דַּלּוֹת), poor, weak.

דַּלָּה f.—I. thin thread, Isa. 38:12.— II. smallness, poverty.—III. hair of the head, Cant. 7:6; pl. דַּלּוֹת.

דְּלִילָה p. n. of the concubine of Samson.

דִּלְעָן p. n. of a town in the tribe of Judah.

דָּלַף I. dropped.—II. shed tears.

דֶּלֶף m., rain drop.

דַּלְפוֹן p. n. of the son of Haman.

דָּלַק (fut. יִדְלַק).—I. burning, consuming.—II. applied metaphorically to strong mental affections, with אַחֲרֵי. Hiph. kindled, inflamed.

דְּלַק Ch., burnt, Dan. 7:9.

דַּלֶּקֶת f., burning fever, Deu. 28:22.

דְּלָתוֹת,דְּלָתַיִם,דֶּלֶת; see דֶּלֶת.

דָּם; see אדם.

I. דָּמָה was like to, resembled, with אֶל, לְ. Niph. was assimilated, with כְּ. Pi. דִּמָּה.—I. assimilated, compare, with אֶל, לְ.—II. imagined, thought, meditated. Hithp. fut. אֶדַּמֶּה same as Niph., Isa. 14:14.

II. דָּמָה same as דָּמַם.—I. silent, quiet.—II. ruined, destroyed. Niph. was silent, ruined. Pi. exterminate, destroy.

דְּמָה Ch., be similar, like.

דְּמוּת f., similitude, likeness; בִּדְמוּת (also without בְּ) as, like.

דֳּמִי m., silence, rest.

דֳּמִי m., the same.

דִּמְיוֹן m., same as דְּמוּת likeness, Ps. 17:12.

דָּמַם (pret. pl. דַּמּוּ; imp. and inf. דֹּם; fut. יִדֹּם; pl. יִדְּמוּ) was dumb, quiet, inactive, in consequence of some strong affection of the mind, with לְ; דֳּ׳ לַיחֹוָה to wait silently upon the Lord. Po. דּוֹמַמְתִּי made silent, Ps. 131:2. Hiph. הֵדַם reduced to silence, ruined, Jer. 8:14. Niph. נָדַם (fut. יִדַּמּוּ,תִּדְּמִי) became silent, destroyed.

דָּמָה f., cut off, ruined, Eze. 27:32.

דְּמָמָה f., *silence*, 1 Ki. 19:12.

דֹּמֶן m., *dung*.

דִּמְנָה p.n. of a town in the tribe of Zebulun.

מַדְמֵן p.n. of a town of Moab.

מַדְמֵנָה f.—I. *dung-hill*, Isa. 25:10.—II. p.n. of a town in the tribe of Benjamin.

מַדְמַנָּה p.n. of a town in the tribe of Judah, Jos. 15:31.

דֶּמַע m., lit. *tear* (with suff. דִּמְעֲךָ Ex. 22:29), *juice of the grape, olive, &c.*

דִּמְעָה f. (pl. דְּמָעוֹת) — I. *tear.*—II. *weeping.*

דּוּמֶשֶׂק, דַּרְמֶשֶׂק, דַּמֶּשֶׂק p.n. —I. *Damascus*, a city of Syria.—II. *a Damascene* (supp. אִישׁ), Gen. 15:2.

דְּמֶשֶׂק or דַּמֶּשֶׂק *damask*, silk cloth made at Damascus.

דָּן, see דִּין.

דֵּן Ch. pron., *this, that;* emph. דְּנָה; כִּדְנָה *thus;* עַל דְּנָה *thereupon;* אַחֲרֵי דְנָה *afterwards.*

דַּנָּה p.n. of a town in the tribe of Judah.

דִּנְהָבָה p.n. of a town in Edom.

דָּנִיֵּאל p.n.; see דִּין.

דְּנַנּוּ Kal pret. with suff. and נ epenth., from דִּין.

דֵּעַ, דֵּעָה *knowledge;* see ידע.

דְּעֵה Kal imp. with ה parag., from ידע.

דְּעוּאֵל p.n. of a man.

דָּעַךְ—I. *put out, extinguish.* — II. *made worse.* Niph. נִדְעֲכוּ *are extinguished*, Job 6:17. Pu. דֹּעֲכוּ *the same*, Ps. 118:12.

דַּעַת *knowledge;* see ידע.

דָּפָה root not used; (Arab. *slaying*). דְּפִי (with pause דֹּפִי m.) *stroke, destruction*, Ps. 50:20).

דָּפַק—I. *beat, drive* (as cattle), Gen. 33:13.—II. *knock at a door*, Cant. 5:2. Hith. *knocked*, Judg. 19:22.

דָּפְקָה p.n. of one of the stations of the Israelites in the desert.

דַּק, דַּקָּה; see דקק.

דִּקְלָה p.n. of a district of Joktan in Arabia, Gen. 10:27.

דָּקַק (fut. יָדֹק, with suff. יְדִקֶּנּוּ) *beat or grind small.* Hiph. הֵדַק (fut. with suff. אֲדִיקֵם for אֲדִקֵּם; inf. הָדֵק, also הָדֵק adv., *as fine as dust*, Ex. 30:36), *reduce to powder.* Hoph. fut. יוּדַק *is ground, powdered*, Isa. 28:28.

דְּקַק Ch., *pounded.* Aph. *made small;* see דּוּק.

דַּק m., דַּקָּה f., *small, thin, impalpable;* דַּק s., *small dust.*

דֹּק m., *thin, fine cloth*, Isa. 40:22.

דָּקַר (fut. יִדְקֹר) *pierce, run through.* Niph. fut. יִדָּקֵר *shall be thrust through*, Isa. 13:15. Pu. part. מְדֻקָּרִים—I. *they who are thrust through.*—II. *slain by want*, Lam 4:9.

דֶּקֶר p.n. of a man.

מַדְקָרוֹת f. pl., *piercings of the sword*, Pro. 12:18.

דָּר *marble;* see דרר.

דֹּר, דָּר *race;* see דּוּר.

דָּרָא root not used; (Arab. *excite evil*).

דְּרָאוֹן m., *abhorring, contempt*, Dan 12:2.

דֵּרָאוֹן m. *abomination*, Isa. 66 : 24.

דָּרַב root not used ; (Arab. *point*.)

דָּרְבָן m. *goad;* βούκεντρον, 1 Sa. 13 : 21.

דָּרְבוֹנוֹת f. pl. *goads*, Ecc. 12 : 11.

דָּרַג root not used ; (Arab. *step, stair*).

מַדְרֵגָה f. *steep place, precipice*.

דְּרוֹר דָּרְדַּר דָּרוֹם דְּרוֹר ; see דרר.

דָּרְיָוֶשׁ p. n. of the kings of Persia.—
—I. *Darius* the Median (Cyaxares II.).—II. *Darius* Hystaspes.—III. *Darius* Nothus.

דָּרַךְ I. *tread* (as grapes), with בְּ, עַל.
—II. *bend a bow*, by placing the left foot upon it; דּ׳ חִצִּים *he shot arrows from the bent bow.*—III. *tread down, destroy.*—IV. *enter, pass in*, with עַל, בְּ.—V. *walk in state.*—Hiph. I. *caused to proceed, led.*—II. *bent as a bow.*—III. *trod down.*—IV. *took possession of.*

דֶּרֶךְ com. (with suff. דַּרְכִּי ; pl. דְּרָכִים, דְּרָכַי ; dual דַּרְכַּיִם.)—I. *way, road;* דּ׳ עֵץ *way to the tree;* דּ׳ הַמֶּלֶךְ *king's highway.*—II. *journey;* דּ׳ הַיּוֹם *a day's journey.*—III. *mode, manner, custom;* דּ׳ יְהוָה *God's dealings.*—IV. *the fruits of one's ways*, Isa. 10 : 24, &c.

מִדְרָךְ m., *foot-prints*, Deu. 2 : 5.

דַּרְכְּמֹא *drachm*, same as אֲדַרְכֹּן.

דַּרְמֶשֶׂק *Damascus*, same as דַּמֶּשֶׂק.

דְּרָע com. Ch., *arm*, Dan. 2 : 32.

אֶדְרָע com. Ch., *arm*, Ezr. 4 : 23.

דַּרְקֹן p.n. of a man.

דָּרַר root not used ; (Arab. *flew, went, round*).

דְּרוֹר m.—I. *swallow* or *wild pigeon.*

—II. *spontaneously flowing myrrh*, Ex. 30 : 23, hence:—III. *liberty;* בְּ and לְ, קָרָא דּ׳ *he proclaimed liberty to any one, he manumitted his slave;* שְׁנַת הַדְּרוֹר *the year of Jubilee*, in which all Hebrew slaves were free, Lev. 25 : 10.

דַּר m., some unknown kind of *marble*, Ezr. 1 : 6 ; LXX. πίννινος λίθος.

דַּרְדַּע p. n. of a man.

דַּרְדַּר m., *brambles.*

דָּרוֹם m., the country south of Judea

דָּרַשׁ I. *he sought, enquired for, into,* &c., with בְּ, לְ, אֶל, אֶת.—II. *enquired about, concerning*, with עַל; used especially of asking super-natural counsel : with מֵעִם before the person asked; with בְּ, אֶל, before the being from whom the oracle is asked.—III. *demanded, asked, required:* with מִן before the person from whom the demand is made; דָּרַשׁ דָּם with מִן or מֵעִם or מִיַּד *required the blood of one slain*, i. e. avenge his death.—IV. *promoted, sought to accomplish ;* דּ׳ רָעַת פ׳ *sought to do him evil.*—V דּ׳ יְהוָֹה *sought the Lord*, in acts of worship.—VI. *cared for.* Niph. *was sought, enquired after.*

דְּרִיוֹשׁ m., *seeking*, Ezr. 10 : 16.

מִדְרָשׁ m., *book, commentary*, 2 Chron. 13 : 22.

דָּשָׁא *became grassy*, Joel 2 : 22. Hiph. *sent forth grass*, Gen. 1 : 11, 12.

דֶּשֶׁא m., *tender herb, first blades of grass.*

דָּשֵׁן *grew fat*, Deu. 31 : 20.—Pi. דִּשֵּׁן

I. *made, considered fat.*—II. *anointed.*—III. from דָּשֶׁן *removed ashes.*
Pu. *was made fat, satisfied.* **Hothpa.** pret. הֻדַּשְׁנָה *made fat* (of a sword), Isa. **34**:6.

דָּשֵׁן m., *fat, fruitful.*

דֶּשֶׁן m. (with suff. דִּשְׁנִי).—I. *fatness of meat.*—II. *fertility.*—III. *ashes,* specially those of burnt-offerings, &c. which were used for manure.

דָּת f. (pl. דָּתֵי, דָּתִים), *edict, mandate, law.*

דָּת f. Ch., *law, edict.*

דְּתָבָר m. Ch., *judges* or *lawyers,* Dan. **4**:12, 20.

דִּתְאָא emph. דִּתְאָה Ch. m., same as Heb. דֶּשֶׁא *grass.*

דֹּתַיִן p.n. of a place north of Samaria.

דָּתָן p.n. of one of the accomplices of Korah.

ה

הַ (הָ, הֶ).—I. def. art. ὁ, ἡ, τὸ *the.*—II. demon. pron. *this*; הַיּוֹם *this day.*—III. relat. pron. *who, which,* הֶחָלְכוּא *who went,* Jos. **10**:24; הָעֶלְיָה *that which is above her.*—IV. sign of the vocative; הַמֶּלֶךְ O *King!* הַבַּעַל O *Baal!* 1 Ki. **18**:26.

הֲ (הָ, הֶ) pref., sign of an interrogation; הֲשֹׁמֵר אָחִי אָנֹכִי *am I my brother's keeper,* Gen. **4**:9.

הָא (הָא Ch.) *behold!*

הֶאָח *aha!* exclamation of joy or scorn.

הָאֶנִיחוּ for הֶנִּיחוּ Hiph. pret. pl., from נוח.

הַב with ה parag. הָבָה; pl. הָבוּ Kal imper., from יהב.

הָבֵיא, הָבֵא Hiph. imper., from בוא.
הֵבָאת Hoph. pret. f., from בוא.
הֹבָאיש for הוֹבִישׁ Hiph., from באש.
הַבְהָבִים *gifts*; see יהב.
הֵבוּ Hos. **4**:18, pret. pl. for יָהֲבוּ, from יהב.
הָבוֹק Niph. inf., from בקק.
הָבִי Ruth **3**:15, Kal imp. f., from יהב, or Hiph. imp. f. for הָבֵיא, from בוא.

הָבַל (fut. יֶהְבַּל) *act vainly, sinfully.* Hiph. *cause to act vainly,* Jer. **23**:16

הֶבֶל m. (with suff. הֶבְלִי; pl. הֲבָלִים, הֲבְלֵי (הַבְלֵי).—I. *vanity, instability, deception.*—II. *idols.*—III. *abortions,* Ecc. **6**:4, and thence, *men in general.*—IV. adv., *vainly, in vain.*—V. p.n., *Abel,* the son of Adam.
הֲבֵל m., *vanity.*

הָבְנִים (הוֹבְנִים) *ebony,* Eze. **27**:15.

הֹבְרֵי (Arab. *that which cuts*); הֹבְרֵי שָׁמַיִם *they who cut, divide the heavens, astrologers,* Isa. **47**:13; Vulg. *augures cœli;* LXX. ἀστρολόγοι τοῦ οὐρανοῦ.

הָבֵר Hiph. inf. from בור.

הָגַג root not used; (Syr. *imagined).*
הָגִיג m., *deep, ardent meditation.*

הָגָה (fut. יֶהְגֶּה; inf. הָגֹה).—I. *murmur, coo, growl.* — II. *meditate.*—III. *declare one's meditations,* with בְּ—IV. *discern, separate.* Po. inf. הֹגוֹ *utter, speak.* Hiph. part. pl. מַהְגִּים *mutterers,* i. e. *enchanters,* Isa. **8**:19.

הֶגֶה m.—*murmur, whisper.*—II. *thunder.*

ההגו 65 יהו

הָנוּת f., *meditation*, Ps. 49:4.

הָנִין) m., *a musical stringed-instru-*
הָנִין) *ment* or *the sound of one.*

הֻנַּח 2 Sa. 20:13, for הוּנַח Hiph. from
יִנח *he removed*

הָנוֹ Kal inf. abs. from II. הנה.

הֻנּוֹ Po. inf. from הנה.

הָגִין m., הֲנִינָה f., *straight, commodi-*
ous, Eze. 42:12.

הֻנֵּלַת (Syr. for הֻגְלָתָה) Hoph. pret. f.,
from נגלה.

הָנָר p. n. of the mother of Ishmael.

הַנְרִיאִים הַנְרִים p. n. of a people eastward of Gilead.

הָד *shout*; see הדד.

הַדָּבְרִין m. pl. Ch., title of certain officers in the court of Babylon;
"counsellors," Eng. Ver.

הָדַד root not used; (Arab. *shouting*).

הֵידָד *shouting* (of bodies of men).

הָד m., *shouting*, Eze. 7:7.

הֲדַד p. n. of a king of Edom.

הֲדַדְעֶזֶר p.n. of a king of Syria.

הֲדַדְרִמּוֹן p. n. of a town not far
from Megiddo.

הָדָה *guided* (his hand), Isa. 11:8.

הֹדּוּ (for הֹנְדּוּ Hindu), p. n. *Hin-*
dustan, India.

הֲדוֹרָם p. n. of an Arab tribe, descended from Joktan, Gen. 10:27.

חוּרִי, הַדִּי p. n. of a man.

הָדַךְ *break down, overturn*, Job 40:12.

הָדַם root not used; (Arab. *destruc-*
tion).

הֲדֹם m., *footstool*.

הַדָּם m. Ch., *piece, fragment.*

הֲדַס m., *myrtle*; pl. הֲדַסִּים.

הֲדַסָּה p.n. the former name of Esther

הָדַף (fut. יֶהְדֹּף), *thrust out, drive*
back.

הָדַר (fut. יֶהְדַּר), *honoured, dignified*
(in dress), Isa. 63:1; with פְּ פְּנֵי
take the part of any one. Niph.
was honoured, Lam. 5:12. Hith.
was glorious, Pro. 25:5.

הֲדַר Ch. Pa. *honoured.*

הָדָר m., *glorious, honourable, dignified.*

הֶדֶר m., *honour*, Dan. 11:20.

הֲדָרָה f. (const. הֲדְרַת), *honourable* (in
apparel).

הָדַּשְׁנָה Hothp. pret. f., from דשׁן.

הָהּ *ah!* exclamation of grief.

הוֹ same as הוֹי *alas!*

הוּא pers. pron. m.—I *he, it.*—II.
this, the same.

הֲוָא Ch., *was*; same as הָוָה.

הֱוֵא for הֱוֵה imp., from הוה.

הוּבַד Hoph. pret., from אבד.

הוֹבָדָה Ch. Aph. inf., from אבד.

הוֹבִישׁ Hiph., from בּשׁ and יָבֵשׁ.

הוֹד *glory*; see with its comp. in
נהד.

הוֹדָה Hiph. pret. הוֹדוּ; imp. pi.
הוֹדוֹת; inf. from ידה.

הָוָה—I. *fell, descended.*—II. *existed,*
was; part. הֹוֶה; imper. הֱוֵא, הֱוֵה,
f. הֱוִי; fut. יְהֹוָא (for יִהְיֶה, יְהֹוֶה).

הֲוָא Ch., *was.*

הַוָּה f.—I. *intense desire, lust.*—II. *ac-*
cident, injury, ruin.

הֹוָה f., *accident, injury.*

הָיָה f., same as הַוָּה *calamity.*

יְהֹוָה *Jehovah*, the name whereby God
would be known to the Hebrews,
Ex. 3:14. Written with prefixes

מִיהוֹה, בִּיהוֹה, לִיהוֹה, אֲדֹנָי (like) with אֲדֹנָי it is written יָהֹוִה (like אֱלֹהִים).

יָהּ an abbreviated form of יְהוָֹה.

יֵהוּא p. n.—I. *Jehu, king of Israel.*— II. of a man.

יְהוֹאָחָז, יוֹאָחָז p. n.—I. a king of Israel, the son of Jehu.—II. a king of Judah, the son of Josiah.

יְהוֹאָשׁ, יוֹאָשׁ p. n.—I. a king of Judah, the son of Ahaziah.—II. a king of Israel, the son of Joash.

יְהוֹזָבָד p. n. of a man.

יְהוֹחָנָן, יוֹחָנָן (*the Lord is merciful*), Ἰωάννης, p. n. of a man.

יְהוֹיָדָע, יוֹיָדָע p. n. of a man.

יְהוֹיָכִין, יוֹיָכִין, יְכָנְיָהוּ p. n. of a king of Judah, the son of Jehoiakim.

יְהוֹיָקִים, יוֹיָקִים (*the Lord confirmeth*), p. n. of a king of Judah, the son of Josiah.

יְהוֹיָרִיב, יוֹיָרִיב p. n. of a man.

יְהוֹנָדָב, יוֹנָדָב (*the Lord's gift*), p. n. of a man.

יְהוֹנָתָן, יוֹנָתָן (*the Lord giveth*, Θεόδωρος), p. n. of a man.

יְהוֹעַדָּה (*the Lord adorneth*), p. n. of a man.

יְהוֹעַדָּן p. n. of a woman.

יְהוֹצָדָק, יוֹצָדָק (*the Lord is righteous*), p. n. of a man.

יְהוֹרָם, יוֹרָם (*the Lord is exalted*), p. n.—I. a king of Judah, the son of Jehosaphat. — II. a king of Israel, the son of Ahab.

יְהוֹשֶׁבַע (*the Lord hath sworn*), p. n. of a son of king Joram.

יְהוֹשֻׁעַ, יְהוֹשׁוּעַ (*the Lord saveth*), p. n. of a man, *Joshua*.

יְהוֹשָׁפָט (*the Lord judgeth*), p. n. — I.

of a king of Judah, the son of Asa. —II. of many men.

יוֹאָב p. n. of a man.

יוֹאָח p. n. of a man.

יוֹאֵל (*the Lord he is God*), p. n. of a man.

יוֹזָבָד p. n. of a man.

יוֹזָכָר p. n. of a man.

יוֹכֶבֶד p. n. of the mother of Moses.

יוֹעֵד (*the Lord is witness*), p. n. of a man.

יוֹעֶזֶר (*the Lord helpeth*), p. n. of a m.

יוֹעָשׁ p. n. of a man.

יוֹתָם p. n.—I. of a king of Judah, the son of Uzziah.—II. of a man.

הוֹהָם p. n. of a king.

הוֹי, הוֹ interj. of exhortation, threatening, grief, with עַל, אֶל and לְ.

הוּךְ Ch., *proceed, go;* fut. יְהָךְ; inf. מְהָךְ.

הוּכָּה for הֻכָּה Hoph., from נָכָה.

הוּלֶדֶת, הֻלֶּדֶת Hoph. inf., from יָלַד.

הוּלְלוּ for הֻלְּלוּ Pu. pret. pl., from הָלַל.

הוֹלֵלוֹת, הוֹלֵלוּת; see הָלַל.

הוּם pret. הָם *perturb, harass,* Deu. 7:23. Niph. *was moved, excited;* fut. f. וַתֵּהֹם. Hiph. *heave, swell, be tumultuous.*

מְהוּמָה f., *perturbation, tumult, vexation.*

תְּהוֹם com. (pl. תְּהוֹמוֹת), *the deep, the ocean;* from its *tossing and roaring.*

הוֹמָה, הוֹמִיָה part. f., from הָמָה.

הוֹמָם p. n. of a man.

הוּן Kal, root not used; (Arab. *was light*). Hiph. *made light of, despised,* with inf. and לְ.

הוֹן m.—I. *wealth, plenty.*— II. adv. *enough,* Pro. 30:15, 16.

הִין m., a liquid measure containing twelve logs (לֹג).

הוֹר, הֹ׳־עַד "thy progenitors," Eng. Ver., Gen. 49:26, from הרה.

הֻשְׁבּוֹתִים Zec. 10:6. Hiph. pret. 1. pers., with suff., for הֻשְׁבְּתִּים, from ישׁב.

הֹשָׁמֵע (*the Lord heareth*), p. n. of a m.

הוֹשֵׁעַ p. n., name of Joshua, afterwards changed to יְהוֹשֻׁעַ.

הֹשַׁעְיָה (*the Lord saveth*), p. n. of a m.

הוּת Po. fut. תְּהוֹתְתוּ *attack unjustly,* Ps. 62:4.

הֻנְחַל Pu. or Hoph., from חתל.

הָזָה *doze, sleep idly,* Isa. 56:10.

הַזְדָּה Ch. Aph. inf., from זוד.

הֻזְדַּמִּנְתּוּן Ch. Ithp., from זמן.

הֵילִי Hiph. pret. pl., from זלל.

הַזְתַּכּוּ for הִתְזַכּוּ Hithp. imper. pl., from זכה.

הִזְרוֹתֵיכֶם for הִזְרוֹתֵיכֶם Niph. inf., with suff., from זרה.

הֶחֱבָאַתָה Jos. 6:17. Hiph. pret. fem., with ה parag., for הֶחֱבִיאָה, from חבא.

הֶחֳדַלְתִּי Jud. 9:9, 11, 13, for Kal pret. 1.pers., with ה interrog., from חדל.

הֶחֱטִי Hiph. pret. for הֶחֱטִיא, הַחֲטִי inf. for הַחֲטִיא, from חטא.

הֶחֵל Hiph. pret., Eze. 20. Niph.inf, with suff. and pref., לְהֵחַלּוּ Lev. 21:4; see חלל.

הֵט Hiph. imp. apoc., from נטה.

הִטַּמָּא Hothp., from טמא.

הִטַּתּוּ Hiph.pret.3. pers. fem. with suff., from נטה.

הֻטָּתוּ Hiph. inf. with suff., from נטה.

הִי *lamentation;* see נחה.

הִיא pers. pron. f., *she, this;* see הוּא; with art. הַהִיא *the same, this very* (*woman, &c.*); Ch. the same.

הֲיָדוֹת f. pl., Neh. 12:8; wrong reading for הוֹדוֹת *dignities;* see in נחר.

הֵידָד *shouting;* see הדד.

הָיָה (inf. abs. הָיֹה; const. הֱיוֹת, הֱיוֹת, with pref. בְּהִיוֹת; imper. הֱיֵה f. הֱיִי, pl. הֱיוּ; fut. יִהְיֶה, apoc. יְהִי).—I. *came to pass* (יְהִי, with כְּ and וַ and *and it came to pass that.*—II. *was,* i.e. *existed;* never used as the logical copula, *is, was;* const. with לְ *there was to any one,* i.e. *he had;* with לְ and the inf. *was about to, intent upon;* with כְּ *was the same as;* with עִם *was, had communication with.* Niph. *came to be, took effect, had been,* Dan. 2:1; 8:27.

הָוָה *ruin;* see הוה.

הֵיךְ Ch., same as אֵיךְ *how?*

הֵיכָל m. (pl. הֵיכָלוֹת, הֵיכָלִים).—I. any great and splendid building, temple, palace, &c.—II. *the temple of Jehovah* built by Solomon.

הֵיכָל m. Ch.—I. *palace.*—II. *temple.*

הֵילִילִי Hiph. imp. f., from ילל, הלך. הֵילֵל *glorious;* see הלל.

הֵים *swell;* see הום.

הֵימָן p. n. of a man.

הֵימֵן Ch. Aph. pret., from אמן.

הֵימִיר for הֵמִיר Hiph., from מור.

הֵין *light;* see הון.

הַיְתִי Ch. Aph. pret.; הֵיתָיָה inf., הֵיתָיִת Hoph. pret. f. 3. pers.; הֵיתָיוּ pl., from אתה.

הַךְ Hiph. imp. apoc., from נכה.

הֻכַּם Hiph.pret. pl.,with suff.,from נכה.

הַכּוֹת Hiph. inf., from נכה.

חִבּוֹנֵן for הִתְכּוֹנֵן Hithpo., from כון.

הָכִיל Eze. 21:33, for הַאֲכִיל Hiph. inf., from אכל (others make it Hiph., from כול).

הַכֵּנִי Hiph imp., with suff. for הַכְּנִי, from נכה.

הִכְּךָ Hiph. pret. with suff., from נכה.

הִכְלַמְנוּ for הִכְלִמְנוּ Hiph. pret. pl. 1. pers., from כלם.

הִכָּם Hiph. pret. with suff., from נכה.

הֲכִנֻנוּ for הֲכִינֹנוּ Hiph. pret. pl. 1. pers., from כון.

הִכַּנִי Hiph. pret. with suff., from נכה.

הָכֵר, fut. תַּהְכִּרוּ ye contemn, Job 19:3.

הַכָּרָה astonishment; see נכר.

הַל, the הַ inter. and the pref. לְ written thus, for reverence sake, in the phrase הַל יְיָ Deu. 32:6.

הִלָּא Niph. part. f. נַהֲלָאָה removed, cast away, Mic. 4:7.

הָלְאָה removed; הָלְאָה pa., thence, farther, onward; denotes time and place.

הֶלְאָת for הֶלְאָתָה Hiph. pret. f., from לאה.

הִלּוֹ Kal inf. with suff., from הלל.

הַהִלּוּלִים great praise; see הלל.

הַלֵּזוּ, הַלָּזֶה, הַלָּז see זֶה.

הָלַךְ and יָלַךְ (part. הֹלֵךְ; pl. הֹלְכִים; f. הֹלְכָה, הֹלֶכֶת; inf. הָלוֹךְ; const. לֶכֶת, הֲלוֹךְ; with suff. לֶכְתְּךָ; imper. לֵךְ; with parag. לְכָה; fut. וַיֵּלֶךְ, יֵלֵךְ; poet. אֶהֱלָךְ, יַהֲלֹךְ; (תְּהֲלַךְ).—I. walked, went, proceeded; const. with many particles which modify the sense, e. g. with אַחֲרֵי followed; with אֵת, עִם,

accompanied; with בְּ walked with, i. e. brought, Hos. 5:6.—II. made way, progress; וַיֵּלֶךְ הָלֹךְ וְגָדֵל increased continually.—III. proceeded, went on.—IV. went off, disappeared, i. e. died, Gen. 15:2 ; Ps. 39:14. Niph. נֶהֱלַכְתִּי I set about departing, Ps. 109:23. Pi. הִלֵּךְ went, proceeded. Hiph. הוֹלִיךְ and הֵילִיךְ.—I. cause to go, lead, conduct.—II. let perish, Ps. 125:5. Hith. הִתְהַלֵּךְ become walking, proceed, go on, go about.

הֵלֶךְ m.—I. going, travel, 2 Sa.12:4. —II. a stream, 1 Sa. 14:26.

הֲלַךְ Ch., walked, proceeded. Aph. the same.

הֲלָךְ m. Ch., proceeds of the state, taxation.

הֲלִיךְ m.; הֲלִיכָה f.; pl. הֲלִיכוֹת.—I. step.—II. way.—III. procedure.

מַהֲלָךְ m.—I. walk.—II. journey.

תַּהֲלֻכָה f., procession, Neh. 12:31.

הֲלָכוֹא, הֶלָכוֹא who went, Jos.10:24. Kal pret. pl. with א parag. and ה relat., from הלך.

הָלַל shone. Pi. הִלֵּל.—I. praised. — II. gloried.—III. pronounced vain-glorious, foolish, mad; const. with לְ הַלְלוּ־יָהּ [without dag. forte] praise ye the Lord). Pu. הֻלַּל was praised; part. מְהֻלָּל praised, to be praised. Hiph. הֵלֵל shone. Hith. began to glory, boast. Po. fut. יְהוֹלֵל make a fool, shame. Poal part. מְהוֹלָל mad. Hithpo. became mad.

הֵילֵל m., Lucifer, i. e. the morning star, Isa. 14:12.

הוֹלֵלָה f. (pl. הוֹלֵלוֹת), glory, folly.

הוֹלֵלוּת f., *folly*, Ecc. 10:13.

הִלּוּלִים m. pl.—I. *great praise, subject of praise*, Lev. 19:24.—II. *songs of, feasts of, joy*, Ju. 9:27.

הִלֵּל p.n. of a man.

מַהֲלָל m., *praising*, Pro. 27:21.

מַהֲלַלְאֵל (*the praise of God*), p.n. of a m.

תְּהִלָּה f.—I. *praise*.—II. *hymn of praise*; pl. תְּהִלּוֹת *praises*; pl. m. תְּהִלִּים *the book of Psalms*.

תַּהֲלָה f., *folly, emptiness*, Job 4:18.

הָלַם *struck, beat*.

הֲלֹם adv., *hither*; עַד־הֲלֹם *thus far*.

הֶלֶם (*blow*), p.n. of a man.

הַלְמוּת f., *workman's hammer*, Jud. 5:26.

יַהֲלֹם m., *name of a gem, adamant*.

מַהֲלֻמּוֹת f. pl., *beatings, stripes*.

הָם or הֹם p.n. of an unknown place, Gen. 14:5.

הֵמָּה, הֵם pers. pron. m. pl., *these, they*; with the art. הָהֵמָּה, הָהֵם. הִמּוֹ Ch., *these, they*.

הַמְדָּתָא p.n. of a man.

הָמָה (inf. const. הָמוֹת; fut. יֶהֱמֶה; part. m. הֹמֶה, f. הוֹמָה).—I. *ferment* (as wine).—II. *moved* (as the bowels with mental emotions).— III. *roar, rage, murmur, moan*; part. f. pl. הוֹמִיּוֹת *noisy*, i.e. full of people, Pro. 1:21.

הָם or הֹם, pl. הָמִים; with suff. and pref. מֵהֶמְהֶם *their riches*, Ezr. 7:11.

הֶמְיָה f., *sound of the lute*, Isa. 14:11.

הָמוּ m. (f. Job 31:34).—I. *emotion*, lit. moving the bowels.—II. *musical sounds*.—III. *multitude of men, &c.*

הָמוֹן m., *abundance*; with suff. הֲמֹנְכֶם, Eze. 5:7.

הֲמוֹנָה *the mystical name of a city*, Eze. 39:16; see preceding verse.

הֵימִין for הֵימִן Hiph., from ימן.

הֲמִתִּיו 1 Sa. 17:35, for הַמִתִּיו, Hiph. pret. 1. pers. with suff., from מות.

הֻמְּכוּ for הוּמַכּוּ Hoph. pl., from מכך.

הָמַל root not used; (Arab. *rain continually*).

הֲמֻלָּה הָמֻלָּה f., *commotion, rushing of wings*.

הָמַם (fut. יָהֹם יָהֵם; inf. const. with suff. הֻמָּם).—I. *put in motion, agitated*.—II. *dispersed, put to the rout*.

הָמָן p.n. of a man.

הָמֹן *multitude*; see in הָמָה.

הַמְנִיךְ or הַמּוּנַךְ Ch., *collar, bracelet*, Dan. c. 5.

הֻמֵּס Niph. inf., from מסס

הֻמְסִיו Ch. for הֻמְסוּ Hiph. pl., from מסה

הֶמֶס m., pl. הַמָסִים *slight noises*, Isa. 64:1.

הָמַר root not used; (Arab. *poured water*).

מַהֲמֹרוֹת f. pl., *torrents, floods*, Ps. 140:11.

הַמְרוֹתָה Hiph. inf. with suff. and dag. euphon., from מרה.

הֵמַתָּה Hiph. 2. pers. with ה parag., הֱמִתִּי 1. pers., הֲמִיתִיה 1. pers. with suff., הֲמִתָּם 2. pers. pl., from מות.

הֵנָּה, הֵן pers. pron. f. pl., *they, them*; with art. הָהֵנָּה; adv., *here, hither*; הֵנָּה וָהֵנָּה *hither and thither*, מִמְּךָ וָהֵנָּה *from thee hitherwards*, עַד הֵנָּה *thus far*.

הַנּוּן pers. pron. m. pl. Ch., *he*; f. הַגִּין *she.*

הֵן, הֵן, הֶן, הִנֵּה, הִנֵּה interj., *behold! lo!* with suff. הִנֵּנִי, הִנְנִי, הִנְנִי *behold me! lo I am here!* הִנְּךָ *behold thou art,* &c.

הֵן Ch., *if, whether;* הֵן...הֵן *either... or.*

הַנַּח Hiph. imp., from יָנַח.

הַנִּיחַ Hiph., הַנִּיחַ Hoph., from יָנַח.

הֲנָחָה *rest;* see נוּחַ.

הִנֹּם p. n., גֵּי בֶן־הִנֹּם *the valley of the sons of Hinnom* (where Molech was worshipped).

הֲנַע p. n. of a city in Mesopotamia.

הַנְעָלָה Ch. Aph. pret., הַנְעָלָה inf., from עֲלַל.

הֲנָפָה Ch. for הָנִיף Hiph. inf., from נוּף.

הָסָה. Pi. imp. הַס; with pause הָס *hush! be silent!* pl. הַסּוּ. Hiph. (fut. apoc. וַיַּהַס), *made to be silent,* Nu. 13:30.

הֵסִית for הֵסִית Hiph., from סוּת.

הַעַל Hiph. imper. apoc., from עָלָה.

הֶעֱלָה for הֶעֱלָה Hiph., from עָלָה.

הָעֳלָה for הָעֳלָה Hoph., from עָלָה.

הֲפָנוֹת *remission;* see פוּג.

הַפְּדֶךְ part. with suff. and art., from פָּרָה.

הָפַךְ (fut. יַהֲפֹךְ; inf. הָפוֹךְ; const. הֲפֹךְ; with suff. הָפְכִי).—I. *turn over.* — II. *subvert, ruin.* — III. *change, pervert, convert.* Niph. נֶהְפַּךְ *was turned,* &c.; with לְ, עַל *to or into, was ruined.* Hoph. הָהְפַּךְ *turned upon, against,* Job 30:15. Hith. part. מִתְהַפֵּךְ *becomes turned about;* f. מִתְהַפֶּכֶת *the*

same; fut. f. תִּתְהַפֵּךְ *becomes changed,* Job 38:14.

הֶפֶךְ, הֵפֶךְ m., *perversion,* Eze. 16:34.

הֲפֵכָה f., *subversion,* Gen. 19:29.

הַפַכְפַּךְ m., *turning, tortuous,* Pro 21:8.

מַהְפֵּכָה f., *overthrow, subversion.*

מַהְפֶּכֶת f., *imprisonment, stocks* בֵּית הַמַּהְפֶּכֶת *prison-house.*

תַּהְפּוּכָה f. (pl. תַּהְפֻּכוֹת), *perversion, perverseness.*

הַפִרְכֶם Hiph. inf. with suff., from פָּרַר.

הִצְטַיֵּד Hith. denom., from צַיִד or צוּד.

הַצָּלָה *deliverance;* see נָצַל.

הַצֵּן m., *an armament, force,* Eze 23:24.

הַר m. (with art. הָהָר; pl. הָרִים with art. הֶהָרִים), aff. הַרְרֵי, הֲרָרִי; pl. הֲרָרֶיהָ; also const. הָרֵי, הֲרֵי.—I. *mountain.*—II. *mountainous district.* — III. *fastness, stronghold.*—IV. *strong men,* Isa. 41:15; with ה— affix (הָרָה), *towards the mountain.*

הֲרָרִי *a mountaineer,* 2 Sa. 23:33.

הֲרָרִי the same, v. 11, a title of Shammah.

הֹר p. n.—I. of the mountain in Edom where Aaron was buried.—II. of a mountain in Palestine.

הַר חֶרֶס p. n. of a mountain in the tribe of Dan, Jud. 1:35.

הָרֵא p. n. of a region in Syria.

הַרְאֵל p. n. of the altar of burnt-offering, Eze. 43:15; elsewhere אֲרִיאֵל which see in אָרָה.

הַרְבֵּ Hiph. imp. apoc., from רָבָה.

הָרַג (fut. יַהֲרֹג; inf. הֲרֹג; const. הֲרָג) with לְ, בְּ *kill, slay,* generally with

violence. Niph. *was slain.* Pu.
הֹרַג *slain.*

הֶרֶג m., } *slaughter, slaying.*
הֲרֵגָה f.,

הָרָה (inf. abs. הָרֹה, הָרוֹ; fut. f.
(וַתַּהַר, תֵּהַר).—I. *conceived, became pregnant,* with אֶת, לְ; part.
f. הוֹרָה; inf. הֲרוֹ *she that con-
ceiveth.*—II. *conceive in the mind,
devise.* Pu. הֹרָה *conceived,* Job
3:3.

הָרָה adj. f., *pregnant;* pl. הָרוֹת.
הָרִיָּה adj. f., pl. with suff. הָרִיּוֹתָיו *her
pregnant women.*

הֵרוֹן } m., *conception.*
הֵרָיוֹן

הַרְהֹר m. Ch., *imaginations,* Dan. 4:2,
from Pa. Ch. הַרְהֵר.

חֹרָם p. n. of a king of Canaan.
הָרָם p. n. of a man.
הָרְמוּ Niph. imp. pl., from רמם.
הַרְמוֹן m. (same as אַרְמוֹן) *palace,* Am.
4:3.

הָרָן p. n. of a man.
הוֹרֵנִי Hiph. pret. with suff., from ירה.

הָרַס (inf. הָרוֹס; fut. יֶהֱרֹם (יַהֲרֹם)
broke down.— 1. *houses,* &c.— 2.
men, i. e. *put down, reduced.*— 3.
teeth, Ps. 58:7. Niph. *was broken
down.* Pi. *destroyed;* as Kal

הֶרֶם m., עִיר הַהֶרֶם p. n. of an unknown city in Egypt, Isa. 19:18;
" city of destruction," Eng. Ver.;
some read חֶרֶם which see.

הֲרִיסָה f., *broken down,* Am. 9:11.
הֲרִיסוּת f., *ruin,* Isa. 49:19.
הֶרֶף Hiph. imp. apoc., from רפה.
הִרְצָתָה Ch. for הַרְצָתָה Hiph. pret. f.
3. pers., from רצה.
הָרָר, הֲרָרִי; see הַר.

הָשֵׁב with pause for הָשֵׁב, הָשֵׁב Hiph.
imp. from שׁוב.

הֻשַׁמָּה (in some editions הֳשַׁמָּה) Hoph.
inf. with suff., from שׁמם.

הַשֵּׁם p. n. of a man.
הַשְׁמָעוּת *hearing;* see שׁמע.
הָשַׁע Ps. 39:14, Hiph. imp., from שׁעה;
Isa. 6:10, Hiph. imp., from שׁעע.
הִשְׁתַּחֲוָה Hithp., from שׁחה.
הִשְׁתַּעֲשַׁע Hithpa., from שׁעע.
הִתְאשֵׁשׁוּ Hithp., from אׁשׁ.
הַתָּבֻתָךְ Ch. Aph. inf. with suff., from
תוב.
הִתְנַר Hithp. imp. apoc., from גרה.
הִתְוַדָּה Hithp., from ידה.
הִתְחַל Hithp. imp. apoc., from חלה.
הָאֱתָיו for הָאֱתָיו which is for
Hiph. imp. pl., from אתה.
הַתִמְךָ for הַתִמְךָ Hiph. inf. with suff..
from תמם.
melting; see נתך.
הָתָךְ p. n. of a Persian eunuch.
הָתַל Pi. הֵתֶל, הֵתֶל; (inf.;
fut. (תְּהָתֶל) יְהָתֵל, pl. יְהָתֵלּוּ *de-
luded, deceived.* Hoph. הוּתַל *deceived.*

הַתֻלִּים m. pl., *mockeries,* Job 17:2.
מַהֲתַלּוֹת f. pl., *delusions,* Isa. 30:10.
הָתֵל Pi.; see התל.
הִתְנַבֹּות Hithp. inf., from נבא.
הִתְנַבִּית Hithp. pret., from נבא.

ו

וְ, וּ, וָ conj., used to connect together
words, phrases, sentences, &c.; it
may be interpreted in modern languages by any of the particles
which are applied to the same use:
such as *and, but, if, moreover,* &c
according to the context.

וְדָן p.n. of a place in Arabia.

וָהֵב Num. 21:14, probably p. n. of a place or well.

וָו m., pl. וָוִים *hooks* or *pins* at the top of the pillars of the tabernacle.

וָזָר *loaded*; see וְזָר.

וַיְזָתָא p.n. of a son of Haman.

וָלָד see וֶלֶד, יֶלֶד.

וַנְיָה p.n. of a man.

וָפְסִי p.n. of a man.

וַשְׁנִי p.n. of a man.

וַשְׁתִּי p.n. of the wife of Ahasuerus.

ז

זְאֵב m.—I. *a wolf.*—II. p. n. of one of the princes of Midian.

זֹאת demonst. pron. f. of זֶה *this*, *that*.

זֹה for זֹאת *this*.

זוּ for זֶה relat. pron. *this*, Ps. 132:12.

זָבַב root not used; (Arab. *fly*).

זְבוּב m., *fly* or *bee*; בַּעַל זְבוּב (*fly-god*), p. n. Baalzebub, the idol of the Ekronites.

זָבַד *hath given, endowed*, Gen. 30:20.

זֶבֶד *a gift*, Gen. 30:20.

זָבָד p.n. of a man.

זַבְדִּי p.n. of a man.

זַבְדִּיאֵל (*gift of God*), p.n. of a man.

זְבַדְיָה (*given of the Lord*), p. n. of a man, Ζεβεδαῖος.

זְבַדְיָהוּ p.n. of a man.

זָבוּד p.n. of a man.

זַבּוּד p.n. of a man.

זְבִידָה, זְבוּדָה p.n. of a woman.

זְבוּב *fly*; see זבב.

זְבוּלוּן, זְבֻל, זְבוּל; see זבל.

זֶבַח (inf. const. זְבֹחַ; fut. יִזְבַּח), *slaughtered for sacrifice.* Pi. זִבַּח *sacrificed.*

זֶבַח m. (with suff. זִבְחִי; pl. זְבָחִים [זְבָחִים], זִבְחֵי, [זְבָחוֹת]).—I. *slaughter of men* or *animals*.—II. *the thing slaughtered.*—III. *sacrifice.*—IV. *that which is offered in sacrifice.*— V. p. n. of a king of Midian.

מִזְבֵּחַ m. (const. מִזְבַּח; with suff. מִזְבְּחִי, מִזְבַּחֲךָ, pl. מִזְבְּחוֹת), *altar*; הַמִּזְבֵּחָה *toward the altar.*

זַבַּי p.n. of a man.

זְבֻל fut. with suff. יִזְבְּלֵנִי *he will dwell with me*, Gen. 30:20.

זְבוּל, זְבֻל m.—I. *habitation, place of residence.*—II. p. n. of a man.

זְבוּלוּן, זְבוּלֻן, זְבֻלוּן (*residence*), p. n. of a son of Jacob; זְבוּלֹנִי *a Zebulonite.*

זְבַן Ch., *gaining* (time), Dan. 2:8.

זְבִינָא p.n. of a man.

זָג m., *the transparent skin of the grape*, Nu. 6:4.

זֵד; זָדוֹן see זוד.

זֶה demonst. pron., *he, it, this, that*; with art. הַזֶּה *this*; זֶה...זֶה *the one...the other*; זֶה אֶל־זֶה *the one to the other*; כָּזֶה וְכָזֶה *thus and thus*; sometimes same as אֲשֶׁר *that*; זֶה פַעֲמַיִם *these two times*; בָּזֶה *in this place, here, there*; מִזֶּה *hence*; מִזֶּה וּמִזֶּה *from this and that part*; מַה־זֶּה *what is this?* לָמָּה־זֶּה אֵי־זֶה *where? why?*

זוּ com., *this*; sometimes for אֲשֶׁר

הַלָּזֶה m.,
הַלֵּזוּ f.,   } *this.*
הַלָּז com.,

זָהָב m. (const. זְהַב, זַהַב).—I. gold; with a numeral preceding, supply שֶׁקֶל : עֲשָׂרָה זָהָב ten shekels of gold.—II. perhaps fair weather, Job 37:22.

זָהַר root not used; (Syr. splendour).
זִיו m. (beauty of flowers), the second month of the Hebrew year, which probably began on the thirty-first day after the sun had entered Aries.
זִיו m. Ch., majesty, splendour.

זָהַם. Pi. זִהַם abhorred, Job 33:20.
זָהַם p. n. of a man.

זָהַר. Hiph. הִזְהִיר I. enlighten, give light.—II. admonish, warn, with מִן of the thing to be avoided. Niph. נִזְהַר was admonished.
זְהַר Ch., part. זָהִירִין admonished, cautioned.
זֹהַר m., brilliancy.
זֶה this; see זֹאת.
זוּ the same; see זֶה.
זוּ see זהה.

זוּב.—I. issue, flow, as water, blood, &c.—II. abound, overflow.—III. waste away, expire; part. זָב; f. זָבָה; const. זָבַת.
זוֹב m., issue, discharge of blood, &c.

זוּד, זִיד.—I. boil, seethe, Gen. 25:29.—II. swell, behave or act insolently, with אֶל or עַל (fut. with נ parag. (יְזִידוּן), Deu. 17:13.
זוּד Ch. Aph., was proud, haughty, Dan. 5:20
זֵד m., proud, haughty.
זֵידוֹן m., overflowing, overwhelming, Ps. 124:5.

זָדוֹן const. זְדוֹן m., pride, haughtiness, insolence.
נָזִיד m. (part. Niph. for נָזוֹד), any viand prepared by boiling.

זָוָה root not used; (Arab. angle, corner).
זָוִית or זָוִיַת f. (pl. זָוִיוֹת), angle, corner of a building, &c.
מְזָוּ m. (pl. מְזָוִים), vault for corn, matadore, Ps. 144:13.

זִין, זוּן root not used; (Arab. abundance, riches).
זִיז m.—I. abundance, Isa. 66:11.—II. זִיז שָׂדַי wealth (i.e. cattle) of the fields, Ps. 50:11; 80:14.
זִיזָא p. n. of a man.
זִיזָה p. n. of a man.
מְזוּזָה f., doorpost, jamb.
זוּזִים p. n. of a race of giants.
זוֹחֵת p. n. of a man.

זוּל part. זוֹלִים removing, pouring forth, casting out, Isa. 46:6.
זוּלַת const. זוּלַת f. (lit. removal, rejection), prep. besides; with suff. זוּלָתִי besides me; זוּלָתְךָ besides thee, &c.; with י parag. זוּלָתִי besides.

זוּן. Hoph. part. מְזוּנִים fed, fattened, Jer. 5:8.
זוּן Ch. Hithp. nourished, fed, Dan. 4:9.
מָזוֹן m., food, meat.
מָזוֹן m. Ch., meat.
זוֹנָה; see זנה.
מְזֻנָּה, for זָנָה, Pu.; see זנה.

זוּעַ moved, was agitated. Pil. part. מְזַעֲזֵעַ vexing, Hab. 2:7.
זוּעַ Ch., part. pl. זָאֲעִין Dan. 5:19

(זְעִין) id. 6:27. *moving, in com-motion.*

זְוָעָה f., *agitation, commotion.*

זֵעָה f., *vexation.*

זֵעָה f., *sweat* (as the result of mo-tion), Gen. 3:19.

זַעַן p.n. of a man.

זִיעַ p.n. of a man.

זוּר (pret. זָר, זֹר; fut. יָזוּר, וַיָּזֶר).—I. *compressed, squeezed.*—II. (same as סוּר *departed*) *receded, was strange, abominable, adulte-rous;* part. זָר *a stranger, a bar-barian, an enemy;* f. זָרָה *strange woman, harlot.* Niph. נָזֹרוּ *been receding, falling off,* Isa. 1:4. Hoph. part. מוּזָר *made separate,* Ps.69:9.

זוּרָה m., *pressed together, broken,* Is. 59:5.

מָזוֹר m., *compression of a wound by bandages;* יָשִׂימוּ מ׳ *they make a binding* (wound), Obad. 7.

זָחַח Niph. *be removed, separated;* fut. יִזַּח.

זָחַל *withdrew, hesitated, delayed,* Job 32:6; part. pl. זֹחֲלֵי עָפָר *fearful things* (serpents of the dust).

זִיד זֵידוֹן *pride;* see זוד.

זִיו *splendour;* see זהה.

זִיז, זִיזָה, זִיזָא; see זוז.

זִיף p.n.—I. of a town and desert in the tribe of Judah; זִיפִי *a Ziphite.*—II. p.n. of a man.

זִיקוֹת *ornaments, &c.;* see זנק.

זַיִת const. זֵית m.—I. *olive tree.*—II. *olive;* הַר הַזֵּיתִים *Mount of Olives,* near Jerusalem.

זֵיתָן p.n. of a man.

זָכָה *same as* זָכַךְ *was pure.* Pi. זִכָּה

cleanse, purify. Hithp. imp. הִזַּכּוּ (for הִתְזַכּוּ) *be, become, clean,* Isa. 1:16.

זָכוּ f. Ch., *purity, innocence,* Dan. 6:23.

זָכַךְ *was pure, clean.* Hiph. הֲזֵךְ *have cleansed,* Job 9:30.

זַךְ m., זַכָּה f.—I. *pure, free from dregs.*—II. *innocent, upright.*

זְכוּכִית f., *glass* or *crystal,* Job 28:17

זַי p.n. of a man.

זָכַר (fut. יִזְכֹּר).—I. *remember.*—II. *me-ditate upon, call to mind,* with בְּ, לְ; part. זָכוּר *remembered.* Niph. נִזְכַּר.— I. *be remembered, recollec-ted.*—II. *be born a male,* from זָכָר, Ex. 34:19. — Hiph. הִזְכִּיר *record, commemorate, make mention of;* part. מַזְכִּיר לְבֹנָה *bringing a me-morial* or *praise-offering of frankin-cense,* Isa. 66:3; מַזְכִּיר s., *recorder,* ἱστοριογράφος.

זֵכֶר, זֶכֶר m. (with suff. זִכְרוֹ).—I. *me-mory.*—II. *memorial.*

זָכָר m., *male.*

זָכוּר m., *male.*

זַכּוּר p.n. of a man.

זִכָּרוֹן m. (const. זִכְרוֹן; pl. זִכְרֹנִים, ־ות) *memorial, record.*

זִכְרִי p.n. of a man.

זְכַרְיָהוּ, זְכַרְיָה (*whom the Lord re-members*), Ζαχαρίας, p.n. of a m.

אַזְכָּרָה f., *an offering for a memorial,* Lev. 2:2, &c.

זָלַג *root not used.*

מַזְלֵג m., *a fork with three teeth.* מִזְלָגָה f., pl. מִזְלָגוֹת *the same.*

זָלַל, part. זוֹלֵל *acting basely, profli-gately, obscenely.* Hiph. הֵזִיל *debase, defile.* Niph. נָזַל; pl. נָזֹלוּ נָזֹלוּ *were debased.*

זַלּוּת f., *baseness, lightness,* Ps. 12:9.

זַלְזַלִּים m. pl., *tender branches,* Isa. 18:5.

זַלְעָפָה, זִלְעָפָה f.—I. *poisonous wind,* Simoon.—II. *great excitement.*—III. *hunger, famine.*

זִלְפָּה p.n. of the hand-maid of Leah.

זַמָּה, זִמָּה, זְמַזִּים; see זמם.

זְמִיר, זָמִיר, זְמוֹרָה; see זמר.

זַמּוֹתִי Ps. 17:3, for זָמַמְתִּי; see זמה or זמם.

זָמַם (pret. זַמֹּתִי, זָמַמְתִּי; fut. pl. יָזֹמּוּ), *intended, determined;* part. זֹמֵם *determines, plots against.* Ps. 37:12.

זָמָם m., *determination, project,* Ps. 140:9.

זִמָּה f.—I. *intention, imagination.*—II. *sin,* specially *adultery.*—III. p.n. of a man.

זַמָּה f., pl. with suff. זַמּוֹתִי *my meditation* (Gesenius), Ps. 17:3.

זַמְזֻמִּים p.n. of a race of giants, same as זוּזִים, which see.

מְזִמָּה f., *thought, intention, purpose* (for good or evil).

זָמַן Kal, root not used; (Arab. *appointed time*). Pu. part. מְזֻמָּנִים עִתִּים *stated times.* עִתִּים מְזֻמָּנוֹת

זְמַן Ch. Pa. *appointed, concerted,* or Hith. הִזְדַּמִּן *according to* Ketib, Dan. 2:9.

זְמָן m., *appointed time;* pl. זְמַנִּים.

זְמָן זְמָן m. Ch. (pl. זִמְנִין), *appointed time;* זִמְנִין תְּלָתָה *thrice, three times.*

זָמַר (fut. יִזְמֹר), *cut, prune.* Niph. *was cut.* Pi. זִמֵּר *he sang,*

with בְּ; *celebrated the praises of,* with לְ.

זֶמֶר m., *mountain goat,* Deu. 14:5.

זָמִיר m., *pruning time,* Cant. 2:12.

זָמִיר m., *song, hymn;* pl. זְמִירוֹת.

זְמֹרָה f., *branch, bough;* pl. זְמֹרִים זִמְרַת, זְמֹרֶת, const. זִמְרָה f., *song, praise, music;* זִמְרַת הָאָרֶץ *the cropping, gathering of the earth,* Gen. 43:11.

זִמְרִי p.n. of a man.

זִמְרָן p.n. of a son of Abraham.

זְמָר m. Ch., *sound* (of musical instruments).

זַמָּר m. Ch., *singer,* Ezr. 7:24.

מִזְמוֹר m., *psalm or hymn.*

מְזַמֶּרֶת f., pl. מְזַמְּרוֹת *psalteries.*

מַזְמֵרָה f., pl. מַזְמֵרוֹת *pruning instruments.*

זַן, with pause זָן m. (pl. זְנִים), *kind species.*

זַן m. Ch., the same.

זָנָב m. (pl. זְנָבוֹת; const. זַנְבוֹת), *tail of an animal.*

זִנֵּב Pi., *cut off, smite the rear of an army,* lit. *tail it.*

זָנָה I. *play the whore.*—II. *become, be idolatrous,* with אֶל, בְּ, אַחֲרֵי; מֵעַל, תַּחַת, מִתַּחַת, מֵאַחֲרֵי, מִן; part. f. זוֹנָה *harlot.* Pu. זֻגָּה *committed fornication.* Hiph. הִזְנָה *caused to commit whoredom.*

זְנוּן m., pl. זְנוּנִים.—I. *whoredom.*—II. *idolatry.*

זְנוּת f., *idolatry;* pl. זְנֻתִים.

תַּזְנוּת f., the same; pl. תַּזְנוּתִים.

זָנַח I. *stank,* Hos. 8:5.—II. *rejected, loathed.* Hiph. הִזְנִיחַ.—I. *stank,* Isa. 19:6.—II. *rejected*

זָנוֹחַ p. n. of two towns in the tribe of Judah.

זָנַק. Pi. fut. יְזַנֵּק *strikes, restrains,* Deu. 33:22.

זִק f., pl. זִקִּים Pro. 26:18, " fire-brands," Eng. Ver.; *arrows tipped with fire;* see פקק.

זִיקָה f., pl. זִיקוֹת Isa. 50:11, "sparks," Eng. Ver.; *sparkling ornaments,* (Lee); meaning uncertain.

זַעֲוָה זְוָעָה זָעוֹן; see זוע.
זְעֵיר *little;* see זער.

זָעַךְ. Niph. נִזְעֲכוּ " are extinct," Eng. Ver.; *are swift* (Lee).

זָעַם (imp. זַעֲמָה; fut. אֶזְעַם), *was indignant, angry,* with עַל, אֶת. Niph. part. נִזְעָמִים *became indignant, angry,* Pro. 25:23.

זַעַם m. (with suff. זַעְמְךָ, זַעֲמִי), *indignation, anger.*

זָעַף I. *was indignant, enraged,* with עַל, עִם.—II. part. pl. זֹעֲפִים *mentally excited, wretched,* σκυθρωποί.
זָעֵף m., *indignant.*

זַעַף m. (with suff. זַעְפּוֹ).—I. *anger.*—II metaphorically, *the raging of the sea.*

זָעַק (fut. יִזְעַק; imp. זְעַק; inf. זְעֹק), *cry out, shout for help,* with אֶל, לְ of the person implored; with עַל, לְ of the cause of suffering. Niph. *was crying out.* Hiph. הִזְעִיק *summoned, proclaimed.*

זְעֵק Ch., *called to,* Dan. 6:21.

זַעַק m., } *a cry, shout for help.*
זְעָקָה f.,

זָעַר *root not used;* (Syr. *was little*).
זְעֵיר m., *a kittle.*

זְעֵירָה f. Ch., *the same,* Dan. 7:8.
מִזְעָר m., *a little* (of time or number).

זַפְרוֹן p. n. of a town in the north of Palestine, Nu. 34:9.

זֶפֶת f., *pitch.*

זֵק, זִקִּים; see זנק and פקק.

זָקָן com.—I. *the beard.*—II. *the chin.*
זָקֵן *was old;* fut. יִזְקַן. Hiph. *grew old.*

זָקֵן m. (const. זְקַן; pl. זְקֵנִים (זִקְנֵי, זְקֵנִים), *old, aged,* with מִן; pl. *heads of tribes* or *families;* f. pl. זְקֵנוֹת *old women,* Zec. 8:4.

זֹקֶן m., *age, old age,* Gen. 48:10.
זִקְנָה f., *old.*
זְקֻנִים m. pl., *the same.*

זָקַף *erected, lifted up.*

זְקַף Ch. part. זְקִיף *lift up, hang a criminal.*

זָקַק *pour out, melt, fuse.* Pi. זִקַּק *fuse as metals,* Mal. 3:3. Pu. *fused, purified.*

זֵק m., pl. זִקִּים *bonds, fetters;* see also in זנק.

אֵזֵק m., pl. אֲזִקִּים *fetters,* Jer. 40:1,4.
זָרָה זַר; see זור.
זֵר see זרר.

זָר part. from זור *strange, abominable,* Num. 11:20.

זָרַב. Pu. fut. יְזֹרְבוּ *they are bound, oppressed,* Job. 6:17.
זְרֻבָּבֶל p. n.; see זרה.
זֶרֶד p. n. of a valley in the land of Moab.

זָרָה *spread, disperse.* Niph. *was dispersed.* Pi. זֵרָה—I. *disperse.*—II. *discern, sift.* Pu. זֹרָה *was dispersed, spread out.*

זְרֻבָּבֶל p. n. of the leader of the Jews on their return from Babylon.

זֶרֶת f., *a span*, a measure of 10·944 inches.

מִזְרֶה m., *winnowing fan*.

מְזָרִים m., Job 37 : 9, probably the name of some northern constellation.

מַזָּרוֹת Job 38 : 32, probably the same; but see more under נזל.

זְרֹעַ, זְרוֹעַ *seed*; see זרע.

זַרְזִיף *shower*; see זרף.

זַרְזִיר *firm*; see זרר.

זָרַח (fut. יִזְרַח; inf. זְרֹחַ).—I. *rise as the sun*.—II. *give light, glory*.—III. *be white*; hence, *have leprosy*.

זֶרַח m.—I. *rising*.—II. p. n. of one of the sons of Judah, and others; זַרְחִי *a Zarchite*.

זְרַחְיָה, זְרַחְיָהוּ p. n. of a man.

אֶזְרָח m., *indigenous, home born*, a tree not transplanted, Ps. 37 : 35.

אֶזְרָחִי (יֶזְרָח) p. n., *an Ezrachite*.

מִזְרָח m., *the east*, the quarter of heaven whence the sun rises; מִזְרָחָה (and without ה affix) *towards the east*.

זָרַם *overwhelm*, Ps. 90 : 5. Po. זֹרֵם *made to pour down*, Ps. 77 : 18.

זֶרֶם m., *inundation*, of rain or otherwise.

זִרְמָה f., *effusion, emission*, Eze. 23 : 20.

זֹרֵם Pi. pret. with suff.; see זרה.

זָרַע (fut. יִזְרַע; inf. זְרֹעַ; imp. זְרַע). I. *sowing* (as seed, &c.).—II. *planting*.—III. metaphorically of righteousness, wickedness, &c. Niph. *was sown, was propagated, was dispersed*, Eze. 36 : 9. Pu. זֹרְעוּ *shall they be sown*, Isa. 40 : 24.

Hiph. part. מַזְרִיעַ *producing seed*; fut. תַּזְרִיעַ, Lev. 12 : 2.

זֶרַע m. (with suff. זַרְעִי, זַרְעֲךָ; pl. זְרָעִים, זְרָעִי).— I. *seed*.—II. *seed time*.—III. *semen* (of animals).—IV. *issue, progeny*.

זְרַע m. Ch., the same.

זְרוֹעַ f., sometimes m. (pl. זְרֹעִים, זְרֹעֹת, זְרֹעוֹת).— I. *arm*.—II. *fore-leg of an animal*.—III. *strength, power, violence*.

זֵרֹעַ m., *seed corn*; pl. זֵרֹעִים.

זֵרֹעִים and זֵרְעֹנִים m. pl., *legumes, vegetables*.

אֶזְרוֹעַ f., same as זְרוֹעַ *arm*.

יִזְרְעֶאל p. n.—I. of a town in the tribe of Issachar; m. יִזְרְעֵאלִי; f. יִזְרְעֵאלִית *a Jezreelite*.—II. of a town in the tribe of Judah.—III. of a man.

מִזְרָע const. מִזְרַע m., *sown field*, Isa. 19 : 7.

זרף root not used.

זַרְזִיף m., *copiously raining*, Ps. 72 : 6.

זָרַק (fut. יִזְרֹק) *scatter, sprinkle*; with עַל of grey hairs, Hos. 7 : 9. Pu. זֹרַק *was sprinkled*, Nu. 19 : 13, 20.

מִזְרָק m., *bowl* or *cup*; pl. מִזְרָקִים, מִזְרָקוֹת.

זֵר m., *border, moulding*.

זָרוּז m., *firm, compact*, Pro. 30 : 31.

זֶרֶשׁ p. n. of the wife of Haman.

זֶרֶת *span*; see זרה.

זַתּוּא p. n. of a man.

זֵתָם p. n. of a man.

זֵתַר p. n. of a eunuch of Ahasuerus.

ח

חָבָא Kal, root not used. Niph. נֶחְבָּא *became, was hidden*; with

בְּ, אֵל followed by inf. with לְ ἔλαθε, *in secret*; נַחְבֵּאתָ לִבְרֹחַ *thou fleddest secretly.* Pu. חֻבָּא *same as Niph.*, Job 24:4. Hiph. הֶחְבִּיא *hide, conceal.* Hoph. הָחְבָּא *same as Niph.*, Isa. 42:22. Hithp. הִתְחַבָּא *was, lay, hidden.*

מַחֲבֵא m., *hiding-place,* Isa. 32:2.

מַחֲבוֹא m., pl. מַחֲבֹאִים *the same,* 1 Sa. 23:23.

חָבַב part. חֹבֵב *loving, cherishing,* Deu. 33:3.

חֹב m., with suff. חֻבִּי *my bosom,* Job 31:33.

חֹבָב p. n. of *the father-in-law of Moses.*

חָבָה *same as* חָבָא *hide, be in concealment*; imp. f. חֲבִי. Niph. inf. הֵחָבֵה *lay hidden.*

חֲבָיָה p. n. of a man.

חֶבְיוֹן *covering, vail,* Hab. 3:4.

חוֹבָה p. n. of a place near Damascus, Gen. 14:15.

נַחְבִּי p. n. of a man.

חֲבֻרָה, חָבוֹר; see חבר.

חָבַט (fut. יַחְבֹּט) *beat off, threshed out.* Niph. *is beaten out,* Isa. 28:27.

I. חָבַל 1. *bind;* part. חֹבְלִים *binders, bands,* Zec. 11:7.—2. *bind by pledge, pledge;* inf. חָבֹל; imp. חֲבֹל; fut. יַחֲבֹל. Pi. חִבֵּל *brought forth with pain.*

ו. חָבַל *inflicting pain, oppressing.* Niph. *suffer pain, loss,* Pro. 13:13. Pi. *injure, corrupt.* Pu. חֻבַּל *injured, destroyed.*

חֲבַל Ch. Pa. *injure, destroy.* Ithp. *perish.*

חֵבֶל m.—I. *the throes of child-bearing,*

ὠδίς.—II. *pains generally,* Job 21:17; pl. חֶבְלֵי חֲבָלִים.

חֶבֶל m. (f. Zep. 2:6, with suff. חֶבְלוֹ; pl. חֲבָלִים, חַבְלֵי,)—I. *rope, cord.*— II. *measuring line.*— III. *tract of land, region, inheritance.*— IV. *snare, gin.*— V. *company, band of men,* 1 Sa. 10:5, 10.

חֲבֹל m., חֲבֹלָה f., } *pledge, deposit.*

חַבָּל m. Ch., חֲבָל m. Ch., } *injury, hurt*

חֲבוּלָא f. Ch., *corrupt thing,* Dan 6:23.

חֹבֵל m., *mast of a ship,* Pro. 23:34.

חֹבֵל m., *sailor.*

תַּחְבֻּלָה, תַּחְבֻּלוֹת f. pl.—I. *guidance, direction.*—II. *rule of action.*—III. *wisdom.*

חֲבַצֶּלֶת f., *bulbous-rooted flower, lily.*

חֲבַצִּנְיָה p. n. of a man.

חָבַק *embrace, fold together,* with לְ Pi. חִבֵּק *embraced.*

חִבֻּק m., *folding of the hands.*

חֲבַקּוּק p. n. of a prophet; LXX. Ἀμβακούμ.

חָבַר I. *joined, attached, assembled,* with אֶל.—II. *charm, bind with a spell.* Pi. חִבֵּר *bind, join,* with עִם. Pu. חֻבַּר *was joined,* with אֶל, לְ, Ps. 94:20. Hiph. fut. אַחְבִּירָה *I might compose, put together,* with עַל, Job 16:4. Hithp. *be joined.*

חָבֵר m., *companion;* pl. חֲבֵרִים חֲבֵרַי.

חֲבֶרֶת f., *associate.*

חַבָּר m. Ch., *companion.*

חַבְרָה f. Ch., *the same.*

חָבֵר m., pl. חֲבֵרִים *associates,* Job 40:30.

חֶבֶר m.—I. *association.*—II. *incantation,* Isa. 47:9,12; pl. חֲבָרִים.— III. p. n. of a man; חֶבְרִי *Heberite,* Nu. 26:45.

חֶבְרָה f., *association.*

חֹבֶרֶת f., *coupling,* Ex. 26:4, 10.

חָבוֹר p.n. of a river in Mesopotamia, *Chaboras.*

חַבּוּרָה,חַבֻּרָה f., *closing, seam, scar of a wound;* with suff. חַבֻּרָתִי; pl. חַבֻּרוֹת, with suff. חַבֻּרוֹתָי.

חֶבְרוֹן p. n.—I. of a town in the tribe of Judah.—II. of a man; חֶבְרֹנִי *a Hebronite.*

חֲבַרְבֻּרוֹת f. pl., *spots of the leopard,* Jer. 13:23.

מַחְבֶּרֶת f., *joining, seam;* with suff. מַחְבַּרְתּוֹ.

מְחַבְּרוֹת f. pl.—I. *binders, beams of timber,* 2 Chron. 34:11.—II. *iron cramps,* 1 Chron. 22:3.

הִתְחַבְּרוּת f., *league,* Dan. 11:23.

חָבַשׁ (inf. חֲבוֹשׁ; fut. יַחְבֹּשׁ). —I. *bind, gird,* with לְ, עַל.—II. *govern, restrain.* Pi. חִבֵּשׁ *restrain,* Job 28:11, with מִן. Pu. חֻבָּשׁ *was bound up.*

חָבִית m., pl. חֲבִתִּים *pancakes,* 1 Chron. 9:31.

מַחֲבַת f., *frying pan.*

חָגָב.—I. *locust.*—II. p. n. of a man.

חֲגָבָה p.n. of a man.

חָגַג (fut. יָחֹג), *feasting, revelling,* specially, *keeping the festivals prescribed by law.*

חַג m. (const. חַג; with art. הֶחָג;

with suff. חַגִּי); pl. חַגִּים (חֲגִים), *festival under the law.*

חָגָא f., *refuge,* Isa. 19:17.

חַגַּי p. n. of the prophet *Haggai;* LXX. Ἀγγαῖος.

חַגִּי p. n. of a son of Gad.

חַגִּיָה p. n. of a man.

חַגִּית p. n. of one of the wives of David.

חָגָה root not used; (Syr. *a rock*).

חֲגָוֵי חֲגָוִים m. pl., *fastnesses, clefts.*

חֲגוֹרָה,חֲגוֹר *girdle;* see חגר.

חָגְלָה p. n. of a woman.

חָגַר (fut. יַחְגֹּר).—I. *gird, attire;* with עַל of the part of the body attired; with בְּ of the object put on; part. חָגוּר *girt.*—II. *withhold, restrain.*

חֲגוֹר m.,
חָגוֹר m.,
חֲגוֹרָה f., } *girdle, belt;* pl. חֲגֹרוֹת.

מַחֲגֹרֶת f., *girding,* Isa. 3:24.

חַד Ch., *a, an, once;* see אֶחָד, also חדד.

חָדַד *are keen, fierce;* pret. חַדּוּ Hab. 1:8. Hiph.fut. יָחַד *sharpens,* Pro. 27:17. Hoph. הוּחַד *sharpened,* Eze. 21:14—16.

חַד m., חַדָּה f., *sharp.*

חִדּוּדֵי,חִדּוּדִים m. pl., *very sharp,* Job 41:22.

חֲדַד p.n. of a son of Ishmael.

חָדִיד p.n. of a town of the Benjamites.

חָדָה (fut. apoc. יַחְדְּ), *rejoice,* Ex. 18:9. Pi. fut. with suff. תְּחַדֵּהוּ *make glad,* Ps. 21:7. Hiph. יָחַד *delight, make glad,* Pro. 27:17.

חֶדְוָה f. Ch., *joy, gladness.*

חָדִין m. pl. Ch., Dan. 2:32, same as Heb. חָזֶה breast.

חָדֵל and חָדַל (inf. חֲדֹל; in p.l. חָדַל; fut. יֶחְדַּל) cease, desist, forbear, fail, with מִן.

חָדֵל m., ceasing, wanting, failing.

חָדֶל with pause חָדֵל m., leisure, Isa. 38:11.

חַדְלִי Jud. 5:7, with pause and with dag. euphon. for חֲדֵלוּ, חָדֵלוּ pret. pl., from חָדַל.

חַדְלִי p. n. of a man.

חֲדַלְתִּי; see הִתְחַדַּלְתִּי.

חֶדֶק root not used; (Arab. melongena spinosa, a thorny shrub).

חֵדֶק and חֶדֶק, with pause חָדֶק m., a species of thorn, Pro. 15:19.

חִדֶּקֶל a river of Mesopotamia, perhaps the Tigris.

חָדַר, part. f. חֹדֶרֶת enclosing, laying siege to, Eze. 21:19.

חֶדֶר m. (const. חֲדַר; with suff. חַדְרוֹ; pl. חֲדָרִים, חַדְרֵי), chamber, inner apartment; fig. חַדְרֵי־תֵמָן the chambers of the south, i. e. the south; חַדְרֵי בֶטֶן the inner parts of the body; מָוֶת h/ the tomb.

חַדְרָךְ p. n. of a part of Syria, near Damascus, Zec. 9:1.

חָדַשׁ. Pi. חִדֵּשׁ renew, restore. Hith. is renewed, Ps. 103:5.

חָדָשׁ m., new, recent, fresh; f. חֲדָשָׁה (pl. חֲדָשׁוֹת).

חֹדֶשׁ m. (with suff. חָדְשׁוֹ; pl. חֳדָשִׁים, חָדְשֵׁי)—I. new moon: hence,—II. certain feasts regulated by the moon.—III. month which began with the new moon; חֹדֶשׁ יָמִים a whole month. — IV. p. n. of a

woman; חָדָשׁ the son of Ho-dash.

חֲדַת m. Ch., new.

חוּב. Pi. חִיֵּב render due, forfeit, Dan 1:10.

חוֹב m., debt, Eze. 18:7.

חוֹבָה p. n.; see חָבָה.

חוּג circumscribe, Job 26:10.

חוּג m., sphere, globe.

מְחוּגָה f., compasses, Isa. 44:13.

חוּד propose a riddle, problem.

חִידָה f., parable, riddle.

אֲחִידָה f. Ch., the same, Dan. 5:12.

חָוָה. Pi. חִוָּה shew, declare.

חַגִּי, חַוָּה, חַוָּא. Pa. Ch., shew, declare. Aph. the same.

אַחֲוָה f., shewing, argument, Job 13:17.

אַחֲוָיָה f. Ch., the same, Dan. 5:12.

חַוָּה f., pl. חַוּוֹת villages of huts; see also under חוי.

חַיָּה f., crowd of men, 2 Sa. 23.11, 13; Ps. 68:11; see also under חוי.

חוּז root not used; (Arab. shore, coast)

מָחוֹז m., haven, harbour, Ps. 107:30

חוֹזַי p. n. of a man.

חוֹחַ m. (pl. חֲוָחִים, חוֹחִים).—I. thorn or bramble generally.—II. fish hook, Job 40:26.—III. a ring with spikes put round the necks of captives, 2 Ch. 33:11.

חָח m.—I. hook or ring put into the nose of animals, e.g. the camel. —II. a nose jewel, worn as an ornament.

חוּט Ch. Aph., join in one thread, Ezr. 4:12.

חוּט m., thread; מֵחוּט וְעַד שְׂרוֹךְ־נַעַל from a thread to a shoe-latchet, Gen. 14:23, i. e. nothing whatever.

חִוִּי p. n., the Hivites, a people of Canaan.

חֲוִילָה p. n. of an unknown district where there was gold.

חוּל and חִיל (fut. יָחִיל; apoc. וַתָּחֶל, וַיָּחֶל; imp. f. חוּלִי; pl. חִילוּ).—I. feel, be in pain.—II. tremble as a woman in labour.—III. bring forth, Isa. 54:1. — IV. precipitate, fall upon.—V. be strong, durable. — VI. waited; see יָחַל. Hiph. fut. יָחִיל.—I. shake, Ps. 29:8. —II. exult, Job 20:21. Hoph. fut. יוּחַל shall be brought forth, Isa. 66:8. Pil. חוֹלֵל.—I. dance in a circle, Jud. 21:23. — II. humble, Job 26:5.—III. bring forth.—IV. wait, Job 35:14. Pul. חוֹלָל was born. Hithpo. הִתְחוֹלֵל.—I. was tormented.—II. fell upon. — III. waited, Ps. 37:7. Hithpal. הִתְחַלְחָל was pained, Est. 4:4.

חוֹל m.—I. sand.—II. measure, number, Job 29:18.—III. weight.—IV. abundance.

חוּל p. n. of a son of Aram, Gen. 10:23.

חַיִל m. (const. חֵיל; with suff. חֵילוֹ; pl. חֵילִים).—I. strength, power; עֹשֵׂה חַיִל aid valiantly.—II. an army; אַנְשֵׁי ח' or בְּנֵי חַיִל soldiers; שַׂר הֶחָיִל general. — III. riches, wealth; עֹשֶׂה חַיִל acquired wealth. —IV. virtue, integrity.—V. חֵיל עֵץ strength (i. e. fruit) of the tree, Joel 2:22.

חַיִל m. Ch.—I. strength.—II. army.

חֵיל and חֵל m.—I. army.—II. outwork space before a fortification.

חִיל m. } חִילָה f. } —I. pain. —II. trembling, fear, Ex. 15:14.

חֵילָה Ps. 48:14, same as חֵיל fortification; others read חֵילָה.

חַלְחָלָה f., great, grievous pain.

מָחוֹל m.—I. dance, dancing.—II. p. n. of a man.

מְחֹלָה f., dance.

חוּם root not used; (Arab. was black).

חוּם m., black.

חוֹמָה f., a wall; const. חוֹמַת; pl. חוֹמוֹת; dual חֹמָתָיִם.

חוּס (fut. יָחוּס, יָחֹם; 1. pers. אָחוּם) spare, pity, grieve for; often with עַיִן the eye.

חוּף shore; see חפף.

חֻפָּם, חֻפִּים p. n. of a son of Benjamin; חוּפָמִי a Chuphamite.

חוּץ root not used; (Arab. surrounded).

חוּץ m. (pl. חֻצוֹת, חִצוֹת).—I. open place, court, garden.—II. out-fields, lands (without a city). — Adv. I. without, opposed to within; חוּצָה, הַחוּצָה without; בַּחוּץ the same; לַחוּצָה, לַחוּץ the same; מִחוּץ the same; with בְּ besides; מֵהַחוּץ without, Eze. 41:25; מִן הַחוּץ without; מֵחוּצָה the same, Eze. 40:40, 44; אֶל־הַחוּץ the same, Eze. 41:9; אֶל הַחוּצָה the same, Eze. 34:21; חוּץ מִן אֶל מֵחוּץ לְ the same; more than, Ecc. 2:25.

חַיִץ m., a wall, Eze. 13:10.

חִיצוֹן f., חִיצוֹן m., outer, exterior without; הַמְּלָאכָה הַחִיצוֹנָה לַחִיצוֹן outward business, i.e. civil, opposed to sacred, 1 Ch. 26:29.

חוּק, חוֹק same as חֵיק.

חָוַר, fut. pl. יֶחֱוָרוּ *shall be white, pale*, Isa. 29:22.

חֹר, חֻר, חוֹר, חָוֹר m.—I. *white linen.*——II. *nobles.*—III. *cavern, aperture, hole*; pl. חֹרִים, חוֹרִים, חֹרֵי; see also חרר.

חִוָּר m. Ch., *white*, Dan. 7:9.

חֹרִי m., *white bread*, Gen. 40:16.

חֹרִי (τρωγλοδύτης) p. n., *a Horite*, i.e. *dweller in a cave*, a Canaanitish nation.—II. p. n. of a man.

חֹרִי p. n. of a man.

הֹרִי same as הָרִי p. n. of a man.

חִירָם, חִירֹם p. n.—I. of a king of Tyre.—II. of a man.

חַוְרָן p. n. of a country beyond Jordan, Eze. 47:16, 18.

חֹרֹנַיִם p. n. of a city of the Moabites; חֹרֹנִי *a Horonite.*

חוֹרִים *white, &c.*; see חֹר in חרר.

חוּשׁ and **חִישׁ** (fut. יָחוּשׁ; apoc. וַתָּחַשׁ; imp. חוּשָׁה).—I. *hasten* (part. חָשִׁים *hasting*).—II. *felt, enjoyed*, Ecc. 2:25, with לְ. Hiph. הֵחִישׁ.—I. *hasten, accelerate.*—II. *stumble, fail.*

חוּשָׁה p.n. of a man; חֻשָׁתִי *a Cushathite.*

חוּשַׁי p. n. of one of David's companions.

חוּשִׁים p. n. of a man.

חִישׁ adv., *hastily*, Ps. 90:10.

חוֹתָם *seal*; see חתם.

חָזָה (inf. חֲזוֹת; imp. חֲזֵה; fut. יֶחֱזֶה; apoc. תֵּחַז, אֶחַז).—I. *saw visions.*—II. *saw with pleasure.*—III. *look at, regard*, with בְּ; *look for, search out, choose*, with מִן; part. חֹזֶה;

subst. const. חֹזֵה, חוֹזֶה; pl. חֹזִים —I. *prophet, seer.*—II. *agreement*, Isa. 28:15.

חֲזָא Ch., *he saw.*

חָזֶה m., *breast of an animal cut up* const. חֲזֵה; pl. חָזוֹת.

חֵזֶו m. Ch., *vision.*

חֵזוֹ p. n. of a man.

חִזָּיוֹן m., *vision, revelation.*

חָזוּת f.—I. *vision, revelation.*—II. *matter of vision.*—III. *agreement*, Isa. 28:18.

חֲזוֹת f., *vision*, 2 Ch. 9:29.

חֱזוֹת f. Ch., *appearance*, Dan. 4:8, 17; חִזָּיוֹן m. const. חֶזְוֵי; pl. חֶזְיֹנוֹת *dream, vision.*

חֶזְיוֹן p. n. of a man, 1 Ki. 15:18.

מַחֲזֶה m., *vision.*

מֶחֱזָה f., *window*, 1 Ki. 7:4, 5.

מַחֲזִיאוֹת p. n. of a man.

חֲזָאֵל p.n. of a king of Syria.

חֲזָיאֵל p. n. of a man.

חֲזָיָה p. n. of a man.

יַחֲזִיאֵל p. n. of a man.

יַחְזְיָה p. n. of a man.

חָזַז root not used; (Arab. *pierced*).

חָזִיז or **חֲזִיז** m., *thunder-bolt*, Zec. 10:1.

חֲזִיר m., *hog, swine.*

חֶזִיר p. n. of a man.

חָזַק (fut. יֶחֱזַק) *was strong, firm, powerful, unyielding*, applied to persons, mind, or things: const. with בְּ *in*; עַל, אֶל *on, to*; מִן *more than*; לְ *to, for.* Pi. חִזַּק *made strong, firm.*—I. with יָד 1. *strengthened the hand.*—2. *supported.*—II. with לֵב 1. *hardened the heart.*—2. *restored, healed* Hiph. הֶחֱזִיק I. *take fast* *hold of, obtain, retain,* with בְּ, לְ, עַל.—II. *applying strength to, repairing, confirming, prevailing.* Hith. הִתְחַזֵּק *became, waxed strong, received strength, &c.;* with לִפְנֵי *oppose, resist;* with בְּ or עִם *assist, aid.*

חָזֵק m., *becoming strong; waxing strong.* הוֹלֵךְ וְחָ'

חָזָק m., *strong, mighty, unyielding, prevailing,* used either in a good or bad sense.

חֹזֶק m., *strength;* with suff. חָזְקִי Ps. 18:2.

חֵזֶק m., the same; with suff. חֶזְקִי.

חָזְקָה f. (same as חֹזֶק חָזָק inf., see חָזָק), בְּחֶזְקָתוֹ *when he gained strength,* with בְּ; בְּחֶזְקַת־יַד *when the hand of God impelled.*

חׇזְקָה f.—I. *force, vehemence;* בְּחׇזְקָה *with power, vehemently.*—II. *repairing an edifice,* 2 Ki. 12:13.

חֶזְקִי p. n. of a man.

חִזְקִיָּהוּ, יְחִזְקִיָּהוּ, חִזְקִיָּה, חִזְקִיָּהוּ p. n., *Hezekiah,* king of Judah, and others; LXX. ʼΕζεκίας.

יְחֶזְקֵאל (*the Lord strengthens*), p. n., *Ezekiel* the prophet; LXX. ʼΙεζεκιήλ.

חָח, חַחִים *hook;* see חוֹחַ.

חָטָא (inf. חֲטוֹ חֲטוֹא; fut. יֶחֱטָא).—I. *err, wander from.*—II. *sin;* with בְּ, לְ, or עַל *by, against.*—III. *miss the mark, fall short of,* with מִן; part. m. חֹטֵא חוֹטֵא; pl. חֹטְאִים f. חֹטֵּאת. Pi. חִטֵּא *expiate, cleanse, free from sin.* Hiph. הֶחֱטִיא I. *miss the mark.*—II. *cause to sin.* Hith. I. *be, become erring,* Job 41: 17.—II. *be cleansed from sin.*

חֵטְא m. (with suff. חֶטְאִי; pl. חֲטָאִים (חֲטָאֵי), *sin, wickedness.*

חֵטְ or חֵטְא m. Ch., *sin,* Dan. 4:24.

חֲטָאָה f., *sin.*

חַטָּא m., *sinner;* חַטָּאָה f., Am. 9:8.

חֲטָאָה f., *sin,* Gen. 20:9.

חֲטָאָה f., *sin,* Ex. 34:7; Isa. 5:18.

חֲטָאָה f., *sin,* Nu. 15:28.

חַטָּאת f. (const. חַטַּאת; pl. חַטֹּאות; const. (חַטֹּאת).—I. *sin.*—II. *sin-offering.*— III. *idol.*— IV. *punishment of sin,* Zec. 14:19; Pro. 10:16.

חֲטָאָה Ch. (Kri), חַטָּיָא (Ketib), *sin-offering,* Ezr. 6:17.

חֲטֹא חֲטָא Kal inf. const., from חטא.

חָטַב (fut. יַחְטֹב) *cutting wood.* Pu. part. f. מְחֻטָּבוֹת *hewn stones,* Ps. 144:12.

חֲטֻבוֹת f. pl., *striped, variegated,* Pro. 7:16.

חִטָּה f., *wheat;* pl. חִטִּים; Ch. חִטִּין and חִנְטִין *grains of wheat.*

חֲטוּשׁ p. n. of a man.

חֲטִיטָא p. n. of a man.

חַטִּיל p. n. of a man.

חָטַם (lit. *ring a camel through the nose,* which is the mode of bitting that animal); fut. אֶחֱטָם־לָךְ *I will restrain my anger against thee,* Isa. 48:9.

חָטַף (fut. יַחְטֹף) *rob, take by violence.* חֲטִיפָא p. n. of a man.

חֹטֶר m., *stick, rod,* Pro. 14:3; Isa. 11:1. חִיאֵל, חַי; see חיי.

חִידָה *riddle;* see חוד.

חָיָה (inf. חָיֹה חָיוֹ; const. חֲיוֹת; imp. חֲיֵה; fut. יִחְיֶה; apoc. יְחִי) *he lived in health, safety, vigour, &c.;* with

מָן *recovered after sickness.* Pi.
חִיָּה—I. *giving, preserving, restor-*
ing life.—II. *strengthen, make ef-*
fectual; חִיָּה זֶרַע *preserve seed,*
Gen. 7:3. Hiph. הֶחֱיָה *give, pre-*
serve life.

חָיָה or חַיָא Ch., *he lived;* imp. חֱיִי.
Aph. part. מַחֵא *giving life.*

חָיָה m., not used; f. חָיָה; pl. חָיוֹת
lively, strong, Ex. 1:19.

יְחֱזְאֵל p. n. of a man.

מִחְיָה f.—I. *means of living, food.*—
II. *crude, raw, i.e. unsound, diseased,*
Lev. 13:10, 24; see also in חוה.

חָיַי *lived;* pret. m. חַי, וָחַי, i. וָחָיָה
Ex. 1:16.

חַי m. (const. חֵי; pl. חַיִּים; with
suff. חַיֶּיךָ), s. *living, alive;* חַי יְהוָֹה
וְחֵי נַפְשֶׁךָ *as the Lord liveth and*
thy soul liveth; adj. (f. חָיָה; pl.
חַיּוֹת) *living, alive, safe, reviving;*
כָּעֵת חַיָּה *according to the time of*
life; metaphorically, *living* (i. e.
springing) *water; living* (i.e. *fresh*)
meat.

חַי m. Ch., *living;* pl. חַיִּין, חַיֵּי, s. *life.*

חַיָּה f. (const. חַיַּת; with suff.
חַיָּתוֹ; pl. חַיּוֹת).—I. *life.*—II. *ani-*
mal, wild beast; see also in חוה.

חַוָּה (same as חַיָּה *life*), p. n. *Eve* the
first woman; LXX. Ἐυα, Vulg.
Heva; see also in חוה.

חֵיוָא f. Ch., *living creature.*

חַיּוּת f., *life.*

חַיָּתוֹ const. state with וּ parag. for חַיַּת
from חַיָּה; see in חַי.

יְחִיאֵל p. n. of a man; יְחִיאֵלִי *one of*
the family of Jehoel.

חִיאֵל p. n. of a man.

חִיל, חַיִל, חֵילָה; see חול.

חֵילָאם, חֵילָם p. n. of a city not far
from the Euphrates.

חֵילָן same as חֹלָן; see חנן.

חִין; see חנן.

חַיִן, חִיצוֹן, חִיצוֹנָה; see חוץ.

חֵיק and הֵק, חֵק m., *the bosom.*—I. in a
conjugal sense.—II. in a dishonest
sense, Pro. 5:20.—III. in a moral
sense, *the feelings, affections.*—IV.
bosom, lappet of a garment.—V.
hollow place in a chariot, 1 Ki. 22:
35; *in the altar,* Eze. 43:13, &c.

חִירָה p. n. of a man.

חִישׁ *hastily;* see חושׁ.

חֵךְ, חֶךְ *palate;* see חנך.

חָכָה *waiting,* with לְ, Isa. 30:18. Pi.
חִכָּה the same.

חִכֵּי for חִכָּה Pi. inf. of חָכָה.

חַכְלִילִי m., *brightened with wine* (of
the eyes), Gen. 49:12.

חַכְלִלוּת f., *fierceness of eyes,* Pro. 23:
29.

חֲכִילָה p. n. of a hill in the wilderness of Ziph.

חֲכַלְיָה p. n. of a man.

חָכַם (fut. יֶחְכַּם) *was wise, intelligent,*
taught. Pi. *made wise, taught.*
Pu. part. מְחֻכָּם *made wise.* Hiph.
part. f. מַחְכִּימָה *making wise,* Ps.
19:8. Hithp. *account oneself wise,*
cunning.

חָכָם m. (f. חֲכָמָה).—I. *wise.*—II.
teacher of wisdom.—III. *intelli-*
gent, clever; חֲכָמִים *wise men* (of
soothsayers, &c.); חֲכָמוֹת (i.e. קִינָה)
women skilled in lamenting at fu-
nerals, Jer. 9:16.

חַכִּים m. Ch., *wise man, magician.*

חָכְמָה f., *wisdom.*

חָכְמָה f. Ch., *wisdom.*

חַכְמוֹת חָכְמוֹת f., the same.

חַכְמוֹנִי p.n. of a man.

חֵל same as חַיִל *pain;* see חיל.

חֹל *profane;* see חלל.

חֵלְכָא same as חָלָה *sick, weak, afflicted.*

חֶלְאָה f.—I. *refuse, filth, scum,* Eze. 24:6.—II. p.n. of a woman.

חֶלְאִים *diseases;* see חֲלִי in חלה.

חָלָב m. (const. חֲלֵב; with suff. חֲלָבִי), *new milk* or *cream.*

חֵלֶב and חֶלֶב m. (with suff. חֶלְבּוֹ; pl. חֲלָבִים‎.)—I. *fat, fatness, the best of any thing;* ח' הָאָרֶץ *the fatness of the earth;* ח' חִטָּה *the best of the wheat.*—II. *hardness, impenitency,* Ps. 17:10, &c.—III. p.n. of a man.

חֶלְבָּה p.n. of a town in the tribe of Asher.

חֶלְבּוֹן p.n. of a city in Syria, Χαλυβών.

חֶלְבְּנָה f., *galbanum,* an odoriferous gum, Ex. 30:34.

חֶלֶד root not used; (Arab. *duration*).

חֶלֶד m. (with suff. חֶלְדִי), *time, duration;* מְתֵי מֶחְלָד *men of time,* i.e. of this world, Ps. 17:14.

חֹלֶד m., *a mole.*

חֻלְדָּה p.n. of a prophetess; LXX. Ὀλδά.

חֶלְדִּי p.n. of a man.

I. חָלָה (fut. apoc. וַיַּחַל), *was sick, weak, afflicted,* with עַל. Niph. נֶחְלָה *became sick, weak, afflicted;* part. נַחֲלָה (f. נַחְלָה), *diseased, infirm.* Pi. חִלָּה *afflicted;* with suff. חִלּוֹתִי *my sickness.* Pu. חֻלָּה

afflicted, infirm, Isa. 14:10. Hiph. הֶחֱלִי (for הֶחֱלָה) *afflicted, made sick, infirm.* Hoph. הָחֳלִי *wounded.* Hith. *feigned sickness;* imper. apoc. הִתְחָל, fut. apoc. וַיִּתְחַל.

חַלּוֹתִי Ps. 77:11. Pi. inf. with suff., from I. חלה.

חֲלִי with pause חֶלִי m. (with suff. חָלְיִי; pl. חֳלָיִים). *disease, sickness, evil, inconvenience.*

חֲלִי m., *ornament, necklace;* pl. חֶלְאִים.

חֶלְיָה f., the same.

אַחֲלַי m., *prayer;* אַחֲלֵי, אַחֲלַי *would that!*

מַחֲלֶה m., } *sickness, disease.*
מַחֲלָה f., }

מַחְלָה p.n. of a woman.

מַחְלוֹן p.n. of a man.

מַחְלִי p.n. of a man.

מַחֲלֻי m., pl. מַחֲלֻיִּים *circumstances of disease,* 2 Chron. 24:25.

מַחֲלַת m., a title of Ps. 53 and 88; meaning uncertain.

מַחֲלַת p.n. of a woman.

תַּחֲלֻאִים m., pl. תַּחֲלֻאִים *diseases.*

II. חָלָה Kal not used; (Arab. *was sweet*). Pi. חִלָּה, with פְּנֵי *make propitious, conciliate favour, satisfy;* imp. apoc. חַל, fut. apoc. וַיְחַל.

חַלּוֹן, חַלָּה; see חלל.

חֲלוֹם *dream;* see חלם.

חֹלוֹן p.n. of a town in the land of Moab.

חֲלוֹף *passing away;* see חלף.

חֲלוּשָׁה *defeat;* see חלש.

חֲלַח p.n. of a province in the kingdom of Assyria (Καλαχήνη).

תַּלְחָלָה *pain;* see חול.

חָלַט Hiph.fut. וַיַּחְלְטוּ 1 Ki. 20:33, "did hastily catch," Eng. Ver.; "hasted greatly" (Lee).

חֶלְיָה חֲלִי חֲלִי; see חלה.

חָלִיל pipe; see חלל.

חֲלִיפָה change; see חלף.

חֲלִיצָה spoil; see חלץ.

חָלַךְ root not used; (Arab. *intense blackness*).

חֵלְכָה with pause חֵלֶכָה m., *very miserable*, Ps.10:8,14; pl. חֵלְכָּאִים, v.10.

חָלַל *pierced, wounded*, Ps. 109:22. Niph. נָחַל *profaned, became common, prostituted*; inf. הֵחַל; fut. תֵּחַל יֵחַל. Pi. חִלֵּל—I. *wounded*, Eze. 28:9.—II. *profaned, made common, violated* (a covenant).—III. *played upon the flute*, 1 Ki. 1:40, from חָלִיל. Pu. part. מְחֻלָּל *profaned*. Po. חוֹלֵל *wounding*. Poal. part. מְחוֹלָל *wounded*. Hiph. הֵחַל.—I. *make profane, violate, loose, set free.*—II. *begin*; pret. 1. pers. הַחִלֹּתִי; inf. with suff. הַחִלָּם *their beginning*; fut. יָחֵל *shall begin*; יָחֵל *shall loose.* Hoph. הֻחַל *was begun*, Gen. 4:26.

חָלִילָה m., *pipe*; pl. חֲלִילִים; int. *profane! fie!* with לְ of the pers. and inf. with מִן: חָ לְךָ מֵעֲשׂוֹת *that be far from thee to do so.*

חָלָל (const. חֲלַל m.).—I. *pierced, wounded, slain.*—II. *profane, common*; f. חֲלָלָה *prostitute*, Lev. 21:7, 14.

חֹל m., *profane, common.*

חַלָּה const. חַלַּת f., *cake* (pierced with holes).

חַלּוֹן com., *window*, (i. e. opening); pl. חַלּוֹנִים.

מְחִלָּה f., pl. מְחִלּוֹת *caves, holes of the earth*, Isa. 2:19.

תְּחִלָּה f., *beginning*; בַּתְּחִלָּה *at first, formerly.*

חָלַם (fut. יַחְלֹם).—I. *dream.*—II. *be fat*, Job 39:4. Hiph.—I. *make stout, strong*, Isa. 38:16.—II. part. מַחְלִמִים *causing to see visions*, Jer. 29:8.

חֲלוֹם m., *a dream*; pl. חֲלֹמוֹת.

חֵלֶם m. Ch.—I. *dream.*—II. p. n. of a man.

חֲלֻמוּת f., Job 6:6, "egg," Eng. Ver., *cheese*, (Lee).

חַלָּמִישׁ m., *flint, stone striking fire.*

אַחְלָמָה f., *a precious stone*; LXX. ἀμέθυστος·

חֹלֹן p. n.—I. of a town in the tribe of Judah; same as חִילֵן.—II. חֹלוֹן in the land of Moab; same as חֹרוֹן.

חָלַף (יַחֲלֹף).—I. *pass by, away.*—II. *put away.* Pi. חִלֵּף *change* (as clothes). Hiph. הֶחֱלִיף—I. *change* (as clothes).—II. *renew.*

חֲלַף Ch., *pass by or away.*

חֵלֶף prep. *for, instead of*, Nu. 18:21, 31.

חֲלוֹף m.; בְּנֵי חֲ *children of those passed away, orphans*, Pro. 31:8.

חֲלִיפָה f., *change, renewal* (of clothes, troops, &c.).

מַחֲלָף m., *knife for sacrifice*, Ezr. 1:9.

מַחְלְפוֹת pl. f., *locks of hair*, Jud. 16:13, 19.

חָלַץ (fut. יַחֲלֹץ).—I. *deliver, free.*—II. *give the breast*, Lam. 4:3.—III. *gird, arm for battle*, with מִן; חֲלוּץ הַנַּעַל *without sandals.* Niph.—I. *was delivered.*—II. *was armed*

Pi. *deliver, set free* ; חָלוּץ *girt, armed, ready* ; חֲלוּץ צָבָא *host armed* ; חֲלֻצֵי־מוֹאָב *warriors of Moab.* Hiph. יַחֲלִיץ *make strong,* Isa. 58:11.

חֲלִיצָה f., *spoil,* Jud. 14:19 ; 2 Sa. 2:21.

חָלָץ m., dual חֲלָצַיִם *loins.*

חֵלֶץ p. n. of a man.

מַחֲלָצוֹת f. pl., *dress of honour, mantle.*

חָלַק (fut. יַחֲלֹק).—I. *apportioned, divided land, wealth, spoil.*—II. *was smooth, fallacious,* with עִם. Niph. *was divided, distributed.* Pi.—I. *divided, distributed,* with אֶת.—II. *dispersed,* with לְ. Pu. *was divided.* Hiph. הֶחֱלִיק—I. *make smooth, flattering.*—II. *taking portion,* Jer. 37:12. Hithp. *dividing, apportioning,* Jos. 18:5.

חָלָק m., *smooth, slippery, fallacious, flattering.*

חֵלֶק m. (with suff. חֶלְקִי ; pl. חֲלָקִים) —I. *part, portion, lot of land, field.* —II. *portion of the sacrifice.*—III. *prey*; חֶלְקֵי נַחַל Isa. 57:6, "smooth stones;" Eng. Ver. *river gods* (Lee) ; בְּ, עִם, אֶת with לִי חֵלֶק *my portion is with,* &c.—IV. *smoothness.*—V. p. n. of a son of Gilead ; חֶלְקִי *son of Chelek.*

חֲלָק m. Ch., *part, portion.*

חָלָק m., pl. חֲלָקִים *smooth stones,* 1 Sa. 17:40.

חֶלְקָה f.—I. *slipperiness.*—II. *flattery.* —III. *portion* ; pl. חֲלָקוֹת *slippery ways,* Ps. 73:18.

חֲלֻקָּה f., *division, divided part,* 2 Chron. 35:5.

חֲלַקָּוֹת f. pl. Ch., *blandishments,* Dan. 11:32.

חֶלְקֵי pl. const. with dag. euphon., from חֵלֶק.

חֶלְקַי p. n. of a man.

חִלְקִיָּהוּ, חִלְקִיָּה p. n.—I. of a man.— II. the high priest in Josiah's reign. —III. the father of Jeremiah the prophet.— IV. the father of Eliakim.

חֲלַקְלַקּוֹת *very slippery ways, devices.*

מַחֲלֹקֶת f. (with suff. מַחֲלֻקְתּוֹ ; pl. מַחֲלְקוֹת).—I. *appointment, distribution, order, course.*—II. p. n. of a place ; סֶלַע הַמַּחְלְקוֹת.

מַחְלְקָה f. Ch., *distribution, order,* Ezr 6:18.

חָלַשׁ (fut. יֶחֱלַשׁ) *grow feeble,* Job 14: 10 ; (fut. יַחֲלֹשׁ) *discomfit, reduce,* with עַל, Ex. 17:13.

חַלָּשׁ m., *weak person,* Joel 4:10.

חֲלוּשָׁה f., *discomfiture,* Ex. 32:18.

חָם m. (with suff. חֲמִיהָ, חָמִיךְ) *father-in-law*; see also in חמם.

חָמוֹת f., *mother-in-law.*

חֹם *hot*; see חמם.

חֶמְאָה root not used ; (Arab. *curdled,* of milk).

חֶמְאָה (Syr. חֵמָה) *cheese, curd.*

חֵמָה f., the same; see also in יחם.

מַחְמָאֹת f. pl., Ps. 55:22 ; read מֵחֵמ' *than butter.*

חָמַד (fut. יַחְמֹד) *desired, coveted* ; part. (חֲמוּדִים pl. m. חָמוּד, f. חֲמֻדוֹת) *desirable thing.* Niph. part. נֶחְמָד *desirable.* Pi. *greatly desired,* Cant. 2:3.

חֶמֶד m., חֶמְדָּה f., *desire, that which is desirable* ; חֶמְדַּת כָּל גּוֹיִם *the desire of all nations,* i. e. Messiah, Hag. 2:7.

חֲמֻדֹות, חֲמֻדֹות f. pl., desirable things.

חֶמְדָּן p.n. of a man.

מַחְמָד m. (pl. מַחֲמַדִּים) desirable, desirable things.

מַחֲמַדִּים m. pl., the same, Lam. 1:7, 11.

חַמּוֹן, חַמּוּאֵל, חַמָּה; see חמם.

חֶמְאָה same as חֶמְאָה butter; see also in יחם.

חֲמוּטַל p.n. of the wife of Josiah.

חָמוּץ sour; see חמץ.

חָמוּק surround; see חמק.

חֲמוֹר ass; see חמר.

חָמוֹת mother-in-law; see חם.

חֹמֶט m., kind of lizard, Lev. 11:30; LXX. σαύρα.

חֲמִישִׁי fifth; see חָמֵשׁ.

חָמַל (fut. יַחְמֹל; inf. חֶמְלָה) bear with, forbear with, with עַל; spare, with עַל, אֶל.

חֶמְלָה f., clemency.

מַחְמָל support, comfort, Eze. 24:21.

חָמַם (fut. יָחֹם יֵחַם; inf. חֹם, with suff. חֻמּוֹ).—I. be, grow hot; כְּחֹם הַיּוֹם in the heat of the day; חַם לוֹ he becomes warm.— II. hot with lust. Niph. became hot, inflamed; fut. יֵחַם יֵחַם; part. pl. נֶחָמִים Pi. warms, hatches, Job 39:14. Hithp. becomes warm, Job 31:20.

חָם m.—I. warm, growing hot; pl. חַמִּים—II. p.n. of a son of Noah. —III. perhaps Egypt (Copt. χημι), Ps. 78:51, &c.; see also חָם in its place.

חֹם m., heat; לֶחֶם חֹם hot bread, i.e. new.

חַמָּה f., const. חֲמַת heat; see in יחם.

חַמָּה f.—I. heat, glow, Ps. 19:7.—II. the sun.

חַמּוּאֵל p.n. of a man.

חַמּוֹן p.n.—I. of a town in the tribe of Asher.—II. of a town in the tribe of Naphtali.

חַמָּן m., pl. חַמָּנִים sun-images; probably the Amoun of Egypt; Greek ἄμουν.

חָמַס (fut. יַחְמֹס), doing violence, injury, wrong, with עַל. Niph. violated, Jer. 13:22.

חָמָס m. (const. חֲמַס; with suff. חֲמָסִי; pl. חֲמָסִים), violence, injury, that which is obtained by violence.

תַּחְמָס m., ostrich; LXX. γλαὺξ Vulg. noctua.

חָמֵץ (fut. יֶחְמָץ; with pause יֶחֱמָץ; inf. חִמְצָה), fermented, leavened; part. חָמוּץ scarlet; part. חֹמֶץ Hiph. part. f. מַחְמֶצֶת fermented Hith. was excited, perturbed, Ps. 73:21.

חָמֵץ m., leavened, fermented.

חֹמֶץ m., vinegar.

חָמוּץ m., injured, oppressed, Isa. 1:17.

חָמִיץ m., "clean provender," Isa. 30:24, Eng. Ver.; "a salt, sour plant of the desert, much relished by the camel" (Lee).

חָמַק withdrew, disappeared, Cant. 5·6. Hith. loiter, act undecidedly, Jer. 31:22.

חַמּוּק m., חֲ' יְרֵכַיִךְ Cant. 7:2; probably large beads, strung together and worn as a girdle; such girdles are often represented in the tombs of Egypt.

חָמַר (fut. pl. יֶחְמְרוּ), *fermented, was excited* Poal. חֳמַרְמְרוּ *excited, become inflamed.* (From חֵמָר) Hiph. fut. with suff. וַתַּחְמְרָה *she cemented it with pitch,* Ex. 2:3.

חֵמָר m., *mineral pitch,* ἄσφαλτος.

חֶמֶר m., *wine.*

חֲמַר m., *the same.*

חֹמֶר m. (pl. חֳמָרִים).—I. *clay, earth, mire.*—II. *heap, mound of earth.*—III. *measure of capacity,* containing ten baths.

חֲמוֹר, חֲמֹר m.—I. *an ass.*—II. *a heap,* Jud. 15:16, same as חֹמֶר; dual חֲמֹרָתַיִם.—III. p.n. of a man.

חָמְרָן, חַמְרָן p.n. of a man.

יַחְמוּר m., *goat* or *gazelle of a brown colour.*

חֹמֶשׁ m., *the abdomen;* see also in חָמֵשׁ.

חָמֵשׁ const. חֲמֵשׁ f., חֲמִשָּׁה m., *five;* pl. חֲמִשִּׁים *fifty;* with suff. חֲמִשָּׁיו, חֲמִשֵּׁיך; שַׂר חֲמִשִּׁים *captain of fifty.*

חִמֵּשׁ Pi. *divided into fifth part,* Gen. 41:34.

חֹמֶשׁ m., *fifth part,* Gen. 47:26.

חֲמִישִׁי, חֲמִשִּׁי m., *fifth;* f. חֲמִישִׁית, חֲמִשִּׁית; pl. with suff. חֲמִישִׁיתָיו *the fifth part of it.*

חֲמֻשִׁים m. pl., *compact in battle array;* Aquila ἐνωπλισμένοι; Vulg. armati.

חֵמֶת m., *bottle, skin for holding liquids;* const. חֵמַת, חֶמַת.

חֲמָת p.n., *Hamath in Syria, north of Palestine;* חֲמָתִי *a Hamathite.*

חַמֹּת דֹּאר p.n. of a town in the tribe of Naphtali.

חֲנַדְרָד, חֵן; see חנן.

חָנָה (fut. יֶחֱנֶה; apoc. יִחַן (וַיִּחַן).—I. *declined* (of the day), Jud. 19:9.—II. *pitch a tent, encamp;* with עַל *encamp against;* with לְ *defended.*—III. *dwell, reside,* Isa. 29:1.

חָנֻגוֹת f., pl. חֲנִיּוֹת *wells used as dungeons,* Jer. 37:16.

חֲנִית f., *spear, lance;* pl. חֲנִיתִים, חֲנִיתוֹת.

מַחֲנֶה m. (f. Gen. 32:9).—I. *camp.*—II. *army, body of people.*—III. *flock of cattle, locusts,* &c.; const. מַחֲנֵה; pl. מַחֲנִים (מַחֲנַיִם) מַחֲנוֹת. מַחֲנֵה־דָן (*camp of the Danites*), p.n. of a place in the tribe of Judah.

מַחֲנַיִם (*two troops*), p.n. of a town in the tribe of Gad.

תַּחֲנוֹת f. pl., *camp,* 2 Ki. 6:8.

תַּחַן p.n. of a man; תַּחֲנִי *son of Tachan.*

חֲנִינָה, חֲנִיאֵל, חָנָן, חַנּוּן, חֶנְרָה; see חנן.

חָנִיך, חֲנוֹך; see חנך.

חָנַט I. *ripened,* Cant. 2:13.—II. *embalmed, mummified,* Gen. 50:2, 2, 26.

חֲנֻטִים m. pl., *mummy, embalmed body.*

חֶנְטִין, חִטִּים *wheat;* see חִטָּה.

חָנַך *adapt, fit to certain ends.*—I. *teach a child,* Pro. 22:6.—II. *dedicate a temple.*

חֵך m. (with suff. חִכִּי).—I. *palate, taste.*—II. *moral perception,* Pro. 8:7.

חַכָּה f., *fish-hook.*

חָנִיך m., *trained men,* Gen. 14:14.

חֲנוֹך p.n. of a man; חֲנֹכִי *the son of Chanoch.*

חֲנֻכָּה f., *dedication*.

חֲנֻכָּה Ch., the same.

חִנָּם *in vain*; see חנן.

חֲנַמְאֵל p. n. of a man.

חֲנָמָל m., *frost*.

חָנַן (fut. נַיָּחָן יֶחֱנַן יָחֹן; with suff. תְּחָנֵּנִי יָחְנְךָ; with ל epenth. יְחֻנֶּךָ; inf. abs. חָנֹן; const. חֲנֹת; with suff. חֲנֻנְכֶם, חָנְנָה; imper. with suff. חָנֵּנִי, חָנְנֵנִי, הָחֻנֵּנִי; pl. חָנֵּנִי, חָנֻּנוּ), *being, acting favourably, graciously, kindly*. Niph. נֵחַן *was pitiable*, Jer. 22:23. Pi. fut. יְחֹן *be favourable, gracious to*. Po. חוֹנֵן the same, Pro. 14:21. Hoph. fut. יֻחַן *be favoured, find favour*. Hith. הִתְחַנֵּן *implore, supplicate favour*, with לִפְנֵי, אֶל, ל; inf. with suff. הִתְחַנֲנוֹ.

חֲנַן Ch., *show favour*. Hith. *implore favour*.

חֲנַנְאֵל p. n. of a fortress of Jerusalem.

חֲנָנִי p. n. of a man.

חֲנַנְיָה ('Aναvίας), p. n. of a man.

חֵן m. (with suff. חִנּוֹ).—I. *grace, favour*; מָצָא חֵן בְּעֵינֵי פ' *found favour in his sight*; נָתַן חֵן בְּעֵינֵי פ' *gave favour in the sight of him*.— II. *elegance, grace of deportment*.—III. *worth, value*.—IV. *prayer for grace*, Zec. 12:10.—V. p. n. of a man.

חֵנָדָד p. n. of a man.

חִין m., *destructiveness*, Job 41:4.

חַנָּה f. (pl. חַנּוֹת).—I. *entreaty for favour, showing favour*.—II. p. n. of a woman, *Άννα*.

חָנֻן p. n. of a man.

חַנּוּן m., *very gracious*.

חֲנִיאֵל p. n. of a man.

חֲנִינָה f., *grace, favour*, Jer. 16:13.

חִנָּם adv.—I. *freely, for nothing*.—II *in vain*.—III. *for nothing, undeservedly*.

תְּחִנָּה f.—I. *favour, mercy*.—II. *prayer for favour, prayer*.

תַּחֲנוּנִים m. pl., *prayers for mercy supplications*.

תַּחֲנוּנוֹת f. pl., the same.

חָנֵס p. n. of a city in Egypt ('Ηρα κλέους πόλις).

חָנֵף (fut. יֶחֱנַף), *was heathenish, profane, ungodly*. Hiph. הֶחֱנִיף the same.

חָנֵף m., *profane, ungodly*; חֲנֵפִים חֲנֵפֵי.

חֹנֶף m., *heathenism*, Isa. 32:6.

חֲנֻפָּה f., the same, Jer. 23:15.

חָנַק. Niph. fut. וַיֵּחָנַק *hanged himself*, 2 Sa. 17:23. Pi. part. מְחַנֵּק *suffocating*, Nah. 2:13.

מַחֲנַק m., *suffocation*, Job 7:15.

חָסַד. Pi. חִסֵּד *accuse of baseness, impiety*, Pro. 25:10. Hith. (fut. תִּתְחַסָּד) *show thyself merciful*, 2 Sa. 22:26; Ps. 18:26.

חֶסֶד m. (with suff. חַסְדּוֹ; pl. חֲסָדִים, חַסְדֵי).—I. *favour, kindness, mercy*; עָשָׂה חֶסֶד with אֵת, עַל, ל, עִם *he showed mercy to him*.—II. *goodness, benevolence*.—III. *shame, disgrace, incest*, Lev. 20:17.—IV. p. n. of a man.

חֲסַדְיָה p. n. of the son of Zerubbabel.

חָסִיד m., *gracious, confident*; חֲסִידֵי יְהוָֹה *they that trust in the Lord*.

חֲסִידָה f., *stork*, supposed by the ancients to be pious to its parents.

חָסָה (fut. אֶחֱסָה אָחֱסֶה), *trust, confide in*, with בְּ.

חֹסָה p. n. of a man.

חָסוּת f., *confidence*, Isa. 30:3.

חָסְיָה for חָסְתָה Kal pret. f.; pl. חָסָיוּ for חָסוּ, from חסה.

(מַחְסִי) מַחֲסֶה, מַחְסֶה m. (with suff. מַחְסִי), *refuge*.

מַחְסֵיָה p. n. of a man.

חָסַל *crop off, devour*, Deu. 28:38.

חָסִיל m., *kind of locust*, LXX. βροῦχος.

חָסַם (fut. יַחְסֹם), *bind, tie up, stop* (the mouth).

מַחְסֹם m., *bridle, curb*, Ps. 39:2.

חָסַן. Niph. fut. יֵחָסֵן *was strong, powerful*, Isa. 23:18.

חֲסַן Ch. Aph. *confirm, make strong.*

חֵסֶן m. Ch., *might, power.*

חֹסֶן m., *strength, power, wealth.*

חָסוֹן m., *strong, powerful.*

חָסִין m., *mighty*, Ps. 89:9.

חֶסֶף m., *potter's clay.*

מַחְסְפָּס m., *scaly, having scales*, Ex. 16:14.

חָסֵר (inf. חֲסוֹר; fut. יַחְסַר יֶחְסְרוּ) *want, lack, be in need.* Pi. *diminish, make to want.* Hiph. הֶחְסִיר *cause to fall short.*

חָסֵר m., *wanting, destitute of*, with מִן; חֲסַר־לֵב *without heart* (i. e. sense), *foolish.*

חֶסֶר m., *deficiency, want.*

חֹסֶר m., the same.

חֶסְרָה (תְּרְחַם) p. n. of a man.

חֶסְרוֹן m., *much want*, Ecc. 1:15.

חַסִּיר m. Ch., *deficient*, Dan. 5:27.

מַחְסוֹר m. (with suff. מַחְסֹרוֹ; pl. מַחְסֹרִים) *want, lack, need.*

חָפָא same as חָפַר. Pi. *acted secretly, clandestinely*, 2 Ki. 17:9.

חָפָה *covered, veiled.* Pi. חִפָּה *overlaid, cased* (with gold). Pu. חֻפָּה "defence;" Eng. Ver., Isa. 4:5 see חֻפַּף. Niph. נֶחְפָּה *covered, overlaid*, with בְּ, Ps. 68:14.

חָפַז (fut. יֶחְפַּז).—I. *affright, alarm.*—II. *hurry.* Niph. נֶחְפַּז *was hurried.*

חִפָּזוֹן m., *haste, hurry.*

חָפַן root not used; (Arab. a measure containing two hands full).

חֹפֶן m., dual חָפְנֵי חָפְנַיִם *both hands closed so as to contain something.*

חָפְנִי p. n. of the son of Eli.

חָפַף *cover, protect*, Deu. 33:12, with עַל.

חוֹף, חֹף m., *shore of the sea.*

חַף m., *pure, faultless*, Job 33:9 (lit. *protected*).

חֻפָּה f.—I. *defence;* see חָפַף.—II. *bridal chamber.*—III. p. n. of a man.

חֻפִּים p. n. of a man.

חָפֵץ (fut. יַחְפֹּץ יֶחְפַּץ).—I. *delight, be pleased with*, with לְ and בְּ.—II. *bend, move.*

חָפֵץ m., *willing, delighting, acquiescing;* אִם ח' אַתָּה *if thou wilt;* ח' רֶשַׁע *delighting in wickedness.*

חֵפֶץ m. (with suff. חֶפְצִי).—I. *pleasure, delight.*—II. *wish, desire, will.*—III. *costly, precious.*—IV. *business, concern, affair;* pl. חֲפָצִים *precious things.*

חֶפְצִי־בָהּ *my delight (is) in her.*—I. a mystic title of Christ's true church, Isa. 62:4.—II. p. n. of the mother of Manasseh, 2 Ki. 21:1.

חָפַר (fut. יַחְפֹּר).—I. dig (as a well, &c). —II. search out, investigate; חָפֵר (fut. יֶחְפָּר) blush, be ashamed, confounded. Hiph. הֶחְפִּיר.—I. blush. —II. cause to blush, put to shame.

חֵפֶר p. n.—I. of a city of Canaan.— II. of a man; חֶפְרִי a Hepherite.

חֲפָרַיִם p. n. of a town in the tribe of Issachar.

חֲפַרְפָּרוֹת (digger), a mole, Isa. 2: 20; probably wrong reading for חֲפַרְפָּרוֹת moles.

חָפְרַע p. n., Pharaoh Hophra king of Egypt; LXX. Οὐαφρή.

חָפַשׂ search, investigate. Niph. shall be sought out, Obad. v. 6. Pi. חִפֵּשׂ search diligently. Pu. חֻפַּשׂ is searched. Hithp. הִתְחַפֵּשׂ (from another root), was clothed, bound, equipped, accoutred.

חֵפֶשׂ m., search, enquiry, Ps. 64:7.

חָפַשׁ. Pu. חֻפְּשָׁה she was freed, Lev. 19:20.

חֹפֶשׁ m. בִּגְדֵי ח׳ clothes of liberation, i. e. spread out to exhibit for sale, Eze. 27:20.

חֻפְשָׁה f., freedom, Lev. 19:20.

חָפְשִׁי m. (pl. חָפְשִׁים), free from servitude, evil, &c.; בַּמֵּתִים ח׳ free from the dead, Ps. 88:6, i.e. free from the evils of life.

חָפְשִׁית חָפְשׁוּת f., freedom from business, servitude, &c. בֵּית ח׳ retreat, place of retirement, 2 Ki. 15:5.

חֵץ arrow; see חצץ.

חָצַב and חָצֵב (fut. יַחְצֹב) cut, hew out wood, stone, metal, &c.; part.

חֹצֵב s., hewer; applied to lightning, 1 Chron. 22:2, 15. Niph. was engraven, Job 19:24. Pu. hewn, Isa. 51:1. Hiph. cause to cut to pieces.

מַחְצֵב m., hewing (of stones).

חָצָה (fut. יֶחֱצֶה; apoc. וַיַּחַץ) divide, apportion, Ps. 55:24; לֹא־יֶחֱצוּ יְמֵיהֶם shall not live out half their days. Niph. was divided.

חֲצוֹת const. חֲצוֹת f., middle.

חֵצִי with pause חָצִי m. (with suff. חֶצְיוֹ) half, part, portion of any thing; see also in חצץ.

חֲצִי הַמְּנֻחוֹת p. n. of a man; patron. חֲצִי הַמְּנַחְתִּי

מֶחֱצָה f., half, Nu. 31:36, 43.

מַחֲצִית f., the same.

חָצִיר, חֲצֹצְרָה, חָצוֹר; see חצר.

חָצַן rootnot used; (Arab. bosom).

חֵצֶן m.—I. bosom, chest.—II. bosom of garment, perhaps, girdle, Neh. 5: 13; with suff. חֶצְנוֹ.

חֹצֶן m., the same; with suff. חָצְנִי.

חֲצַף Ch. Aph. was urgent, pressing, Dan. 2:15; 3:22.

חָצֵץ, part. חֹצֵץ rushing on, Pro. 30: 27. Pi. part. pl. מְחַצְצִים persons taking part (in conversation), Jud. 5:11. Pu. are cut, decided, Job 21:21.

חָצָץ m.—I. gravel.—II. arrow, i.e lightning, Ps. 77:18.

חֵץ m. (with suff. חִצִּי; pl. חִצִּים חֶצְיִי).—I. arrow; בַּעֲלֵי־חִצִּים bowmen.—II. metaph. lightning.

חַצְצֹן־תָּמָר and חַצְצֹן p. n. of a place in the tribe of Judah.

חֲצֹצְרָה trumpet; see חצר.

חָצֵר root not used.—I. (Arab. *surrounding*).—II. (Arab. *field*).

חָצֵר com. (pl. חֲצֵרִים, חֲצֵרוֹת).—I. *enclosure, area, court.*—II. *village;* חֲצַר־אַדָּר (*threshing-floor of Addar*), p. n. of a town in the tribe of Judah; סוּסִים ח׳, סוּסָה p. n. of a town in the tribe of Simeon; עֵינָן ח׳, עֵינָן ח׳ a town in the north of Palestine; שׁוּעָל ח׳ a town in the tribe of Simeon; חָצֵר הַתִּיכוֹן a town on the borders of Syria; חֲצֵרוֹת p. n. of a station in the desert.

חָצוֹר p. n.—I. of a town in the tribe of Naphtali.—II. of a town in the tribe of Benjamin.—III. of a region of Arabia.

חֶצְרוֹן p. n.—I. of a son of Reuben.—II. of a son of Perez; patron. חֶצְרוֹנִי.

חֶצְרַי p. n. of a man.

חֲצַרְמָוֶת (*court of death*), p. n. of a district in Arabia.

חָצִיר m.—I. *enclosure* (habitable place).—II. *grass;* see root II.

חֲצוֹצְרָה, חֲצֹצְרָה f., *trumpet;* from this word comes Pi. מְחַצְרִים or Hiph. מַחְצְרִים (ketib מַחֲצְצְרִים, מְחַצְרִים) *persons blowing with trumpets.*

חֵק *bosom;* see חֵיק.

חֹק־, חָק־, חָקָה; see חקק.

חָקָה. Pu. part. מְחֻקֶּה *engraven, carved.* Hith. with עַל *impressed, furrowed,* Job 13:27.

חֲקוּפָא p. n. of a man.

חָקַק *carve, engrave, inscribe;* part. חֹקֵק *legislator,* Jud. 5:9. Pu. part. מְחֻקָּק *statute,* Pro. 31:5. Po.

decide, decree, Pro. 8:15; part. מְחֹקֵק *lawgiver.* Hoph. fut. יֻחָקוּ *engraven, inscribed,* Job 19:23

חֵקֶק m., pl. const. חִקְקֵי—I. *impressions, imaginations,* Jud. 5:15.—II. *decrees,* Isa. 10:1.

חֹק, חָק־ m. (with suff. חֻקָּךְ); pl. חֻקִּים, חֻקֵּי, חֻקִּים).—I. *statute, law.*—II. *custom, privilege.*

חֻקָּה f.—I. *statute.*—II. *custom.*

חָקַר (fut. יַחְקֹר; inf. חֲקֹר), *search, investigate, try.* Niph. נֶחְקַר *that may be searched.* Pi. חִקֵּר *like Kal,* Ecc. 12:9.

חֵקֶר m., *investigation, search, enquiry.*

מֶחְקָר m., pl. const. מֶחְקְרֵי *depths* (of the earth), Ps. 95:4.

חֹר, חוֹר; see חָוַר חָרַר.

חָרָא root not used; (Arab. *dung*).

חֶרֶא or חֲרָא m., pl. חֲרָאִים *dung,* Isa. 36:12.

חַר or חֹר m., the same; pl. const. חֲרֵי.

מַחֲרָאָה f., *draught-house,* 2 Ki. 10:27.

חָרֵב (fut. יֶחֱרַב, יֶחְרַב).—I. *dry, be dry.*—II. *desolate, ruin.* Niph. נֶחֱרַב *was ruined.* Pu. חֹרַב *been dried.* Hiph. הֶחֱרִיב I. *dry up.*—II. *ruin.* Hoph. הָחֳרַב *was wasted, destroyed.*

חֲרַב Ch. Hoph. f., הָחָרְבַת *is wasted,* Ezr. 4:15.

חָרֵב m.—I. *dry.*—II. *desolate, devastated;* f. חֲרֵבָה; pl. חֲרָבוֹת.

חֶרֶב f. (with suff. חַרְבִּי; pl. חֲרָבוֹת).—I. *sword.*—II. *sharp weapon* or *cutting instrument.*—III. *drought,* Deut. 28:22.

חֹרֶב m.—I. *drought.*—II. *heat.*—III. *desolation.*

חֹלֶב, חֹרֵב (dry, desolate), p. n. of one of the summits of Sinai.

חָרְבָּה f., pl. חֲרָבוֹת (const. חָרְבוֹת) desolations.

חָרְבָה f., drought.

חֲרָבוֹן m., pl. const. חַרְבֹנֵי great droughts, Ps. 32:4.

חַרְבוֹנָא p. n. of a Persian eunuch.

חָרַג suffer pressure, trouble, Ps. 18:46.

חַרְגֹּל m., the larva of the locust, Lev. 11:22.

חָרֵד or חָרַד (fut. יֶחֱרַד), was timid, fearful, trembling, with אֶל, לְ, or מִן. Hiph. affrighted.

חָרֵד m.—I. fearful, anxious, with אֶל, בְּ.—II. trembling.

חֲרָדָה const. חֶרְדַּת f.—I. fear.—II. trembling.—III. p. n. of a station of the Israelites, Nu. 33:24.

חָרוֹד p. n. of a place in the mountain of Gilboa, Ju. 7:1; חֲרֹדִי a Harodite, 2 Sa. 23:25.

חָרָה (inf. abs. חָרֹה; fut. יֶחֱרֶה; apoc. וַיִּחַר), was, became hot, angry; חָרָה אַפּוֹ with בְּ, אֶל, עַל his anger was kindled against; חָרָה לוֹ he was angry; חָרָה בְּעֵינָיו it grieved him. Niph. נֶחֱרוּ were enraged, angry; part. נֶחֱרִים angry. Hiph. הֶחֱרָה.—I. made angry.—II. became warm, zealous, Neh. 3:20. Hithp. fut. apoc. תִּתְחַר be thou vexed.

חָרוֹן m.—I. אַף חֲרוֹן heat of anger.—II. angry person, Ps. 58:10.

חֳרִי m.; אַף חֳרִי heat, burning.

תַּחְרָא m., "habergeon," Eng. Ver., Ex. 28:32, &c.; meaning uncertain.

תַּחֲרָה contend with, emulate, Jer. 12:5; 22:15.

חָרוּז m., pl. חֲרוּזִים necklace of precious stones, Cant. 1:10.

חָרוּל m., a thorny shrub; pl. חֲרֻלִּים.

חָרוּץ fine gold; see חרץ.

חַרְחֻר heat; see חרר.

חָרַט (Arab. engraver).

חָרִיט m., pl. חֲרִיטִים pockets, purses.

חֶרֶט m.—I. graving tool, Ex. 32:4.—II. writing style, Isa. 8:1.

חַרְטֹם m., pl. חַרְטֻמִּים—I. the sacred scribes of Egypt who engraved hieroglyphics, ἱερογραμματείς.—II. the wise men of Babylon, Dan. 1:20; 2:2.

חַרְטֻמִּין m. pl. Ch., same as חַרְטֻמִּים wise men, magicians.

חֲרִי heat; see חָרָה.

חֹרִי bread; see חוּר.

חֲרִי pl. const. from חַר dung; see חרא

חָרִיץ cutting; see חרץ.

חֲרִישִׁי, חָרִישׁ; see חרש.

חָרַךְ (fut. יַחֲרֹךְ), roasts, Pro. 12:27.

חֲרַךְ Ch. Hith. was burnt, Dan. 3:27.

חֲרַכִּים m. pl., latticed windows, LXX. δίκτυα, Cant. 2:9.

חָרַם. Kal not used; (Arab. forbidden, sacred). Hiph. הֶחֱרִים—I. devote to destruction.—II. apply to sacred uses. Hoph. הָחֳרַם—I. was devoted to destruction, slain.—II. was consecrated.

חֵרֶם m. (with suff. חֶרְמִי).—I. devotion to destruction.—II. the thing so devoted.

חֳרֵם p. n. of a town in the tribe of Naphtali.

חֵרֶם m with suff. חֶרְמִי; (pl. חֲרָמִים).
I. *a net*.— II. *allurements*, Ecc. 7:
26.

חָרֻם m. (Arab. *cut off, tear*), *flat-
nosed*, Lev. 21:18.

חָרֻם p. n. of a man.

חָרְמָה p. n. of a town of the Canaanites.

חֶרְמוֹן p. n. of a range of hills in
Anti-Libanus; חֶרְמוֹנִים *Hermonites*.

חֶרְמֵשׁ m. (from חָרַם and חָרַשׁ),
sickle, reaping hook.

חָרָן p. n.—I. of a city of Mesopotamia,
Χαῤῥάν.—II. of a city of Arabia.
—III. of a man.

חֹרֹנַיִם p. n. of a place; see חוֹר.

חַרְנֶפֶר p. n. of a man.

חָרַשׂ, חֶרֶס root not used; (Arab.
scratching).

חֶרֶס m., *the itch*, Deu. 28:27.

חֶרֶס m. (with ה parag. חַרְסָה), *the
sun*, Ju. 8:13; 14:18; עִיר הַחֶרֶס
prophetic name of a city in Egypt,
Isa. 19:18; see הֶרֶס.

חֶרֶשׂ m., *earthenware, potsherd*; כְּלִי
חֶרֶשׂ *earthen vase*.

חַרְסוּת f., *pottery*; שַׁעַר הַחַרְסוּת *the
potter's gate*, one of the gates of
Jerusalem.

חָרַף (fut. יֶחֱרַף).— I. *pluck* (the fruit
of), *eat up*, Isa. 18:6.—II. *strip of
honour, value; reproach*. Pi. חֵרַף
I. *reproach, blaspheme*.—II. *expose
to reproach*, Ju. 5:18. Niph. part.
f. נֶחֱרֶפֶת *deprived of all right, espoused*, Lev. 19:20.

חֹרֶף m.—I. *autumn*.—II. *youth*, Job
29:4, (the year was supposed to
begin in autumn).

חֶרְפָּה f. (pl. חֲרָפוֹת; const. חֶרְפּוֹת)
—I. *reproach, contempt*.—II. *person or thing reproached*.

חָרִיף p. n. of a man; patron. חֲרִיפִי.

חָרֵף p. n. of a man.

חָרַץ (fut. יֶחֱרַץ).—I. *was sharp, active,
courageous*.—II. *was decided, determined*; part. חָרוּץ.—I. *maimed,
rent*, Lev. 22:22.—II. *decided, determined*.—III. *punishment*. Niph.
part. f. נֶחֱרָצָה *decided, determined, decreed*.

חָרוּץ m.—I. *ditch, foss*.—II. *the sharp
spikes of a thrashing dray*; pl.
const. חֲרֻצוֹת.—III. *sharpened, in-
structed*.—IV. *gold*.—V. *decree*;
pl. חֲרוּצִים; see חרץ.—VI. p. n. of
a man.

חָרִיץ m. (pl. const. חֲרִיצֵי).—I. *cut-
tings of cheese*, LXX. τρυφαλὶς,
1 Sa. 17:18.—II. same as חָרוּץ
spikes, sharp points.

חַרְצָן m., pl. חַרְצַנִּים *sour grapes*,
Nu. 6:4.

חֲרֵץ Ch., same as Heb. חָלָץ *loins*,
Dan. 5:6.

חַרְצֻבּוֹת f. pl.—I. *bonds, bandages*,
Ps. 73:4.—II. *grievous pains*, Isa.
58:6.

חָרַק (fut. יֶחֱרֹק), *ground, gnashed the
teeth*; (with שִׁנַּיִם, בְּשִׁנַּיִם and עַל
against).

חָרַר.—I. *was hot*.—II. *was dry*. Niph.
נָחַר (fut. יֵחַר), *was hot, dry*;
נָחַר *became dry*. Pilp. inf.
חַרְחַר *make hot, kindle*, as fire, Pro
26:21.

חֲרֵרִים m. pl., *dry, parched places*,
Jer. 17:6.

חֹר m., pl. חֹרִים, חוֹרִים nobles, great men; see also חוּר.

תַּחְרָא m.—I. inflammation, fever, Deu. 28:22.—II. p.n. of a man.

חֶרֶשׂ potsherd; see חרם.

חָרַשׁ (fut. יַחֲרֹשׁ).—I. cut, plough the land.—II. engrave, sculpture, with חֹרֵשׁ עַל ploughman).—III. (fut. יֶחֱרַשׁ) was dumb, silent, was deaf, with מִן. Niph. was ploughed. Hiph.—I. engrave, carve.—II. fabricate, devise evil, 1 Sa. 23:9.—III. be still, quiet. Hith. fut. pl. יִתְחָרְשׁוּ were silent, Ju. 16:2.

חָרִישׁ m., ploughing, tilling the land; חֲרִישׁוֹ his field.

חֲרִישִׁי m., חֲרִישִׁית f., very drying, Jon. 4:8.

חָרָשׁ m. (const. חָרַשׁ; pl. חָרָשִׁים, חָרָשֵׁי), worker, artificer, in wood, stone, metal, &c.; חָרָשֵׁי מַשְׁחִית forgers of destruction, Eze. 21:36.

חָרָשׁ m.—I. cunning work; גֵּי חֲרָשִׁים valley of the mechanics, near Jerusalem).—II. silence, silently.—III. p.n. of a man.

חֹרֶשׁ m. wood, forest; pl. חֳרָשִׁים; בַּחֹרְשָׁה into the wood; בַּחֹרְשָׁה in the wood.

חֹרֵשׁ m., artificer; cutting instrument (Gesen.), Gen. 4:22.

חֵרֵשׁ m., deaf; pl. חֵרְשִׁים.

חַרְשָׁא p.n. of a man.

חֲרֹשֶׁת f.—I. sculpture.—II. p.n. of a place in North Palestine.

מַחֲרֵשָׁה f., coulter, 1 Sa. 13:21; pl. מַחֲרֵשׁוֹת.

מַחֲרֶשֶׁת f. (with suff. מַחֲרֶשְׁתּוֹ), ploughshare, 1 Sa. 13:20.

חָרַת same as חָרַשׁ; part. חָרוּת cut, engraven, Ex. 32:16.

חֶרֶת (same as חֹרֶשׁ), p.n. of a wood in the tribe of Judah.

חָשׂוּף, חֲשַׁשְׂפָּא; see חשׂף.

חָשַׂךְ (fut. יַחְשֹׂךְ, תַּחְשֹׂךְ, אֶחְשֹׂךְ, וָאֶחְשֹׂךְ). I. withhold, keep back.—II. save, with מִן.—III. refuse.—IV. spare, sparing, Pro. 13:24. Niph. fut. יֵחָשֵׂךְ is restrained, Job 16:6; יֵחָשֵׂךְ id. 21:30.

חָשַׂף (fut. יַחְשֹׂף), make bare, denudate, expose.—II. draw (as water)

חֲשׂוּפָא p.n. of a man.

חָשִׂיף m., flock, 1 Ki. 20:27.

מַחְשׂף m., laying bare, Gen. 30:37.

חָשַׁב (fut. יַחְשֹׁב, יֶחְשָׁב).—I. think, devise, meditate.—II. consider, esteem, reckon, impute, with inf. and לְ; חֹשֵׁב artificer, deviser; with לֹא of no esteem. Niph. נֶחְשַׁב (fut. יֵחָשֵׁב) was thought, esteemed, computed, reckoned, with בְּ, עִם, כְּ, לְ. Pi. חִשֵּׁב think, compute, esteem, reckon, with אֶל. Hithp. עַל was accounted, Nu. 23:9.

חֲשַׁב Ch., considered, esteemed, Dan. 4:32.

חֵשֶׁב m., the belt, girdle of the ephod.

חֶשְׁבּוֹן m.—I. device, discovery.—II p.n. of a city of the Amorites, Ἐσσβοῦς.

חֶשְׁבֹּנוֹת m. pl., חִשְּׁבֹנוֹת warlike machines, 2 Chron. 26:15.

חֲשַׁבַּדָּנָה p.n. of a man.

חַשּׁוּב p.n. of a man.

חֲשֻׁבָה p.n. of a man.

חֲשַׁבְיָהוּ, חֲשַׁבְיָה p.n. of a man.

חֲשַׁבְנְיָה, חֲשַׁבְנָה p.n. of a man.

מַחֲשָׁבָה, מַחֲשֶׁבֶת f. (pl. מַחְשָׁבוֹת; const. מַחְשְׁבוֹת).—I. *thought, design, project.*—II. *work of art, ingenuity.*

חָשָׁה *was silent.* Hiph. הֶחֱשָׁה, part. מַחְשֶׁה *was* or *made silent.*

חֲשַׁח Ch., *persons, things wanting.*

חַשְׁחוּת f. Ch., *want, necessity,* Ezr. 7:20.

חֲשֵׁיכָה same as חֲשֵׁכָה *dark;* see חָשַׁךְ.

חָשַׁךְ (fut. יֶחְשַׁךְ) *be, become obscure, dark.* Hiph. הֶחְשִׁיךְ *made dark, obscure;* fut. יַחְשִׁיךְ.

חָשֹׁךְ m., pl. חֲשֻׁכִים *obscure persons,* Pro. 22:29.

חֹשֶׁךְ m. (with suff. חָשְׁכִּי).—I. *darkness.*—II. *ignorance.*—III. *calamity, misery, destruction.*

חֲשׁוֹךְ m. Ch., *darkness.*

חָשֻׁךְ m., pl. חֲשֻׁכִים *obscured, darkened.*

חֲשֵׁכָה, חֲשֵׁיכָה f., *obscurity, darkness.* חֶשְׁכָה, חָשְׁכָּה f., *the same.*

מַחְשָׁךְ m., I. *darkness.*—II. *adversity, trouble;* pl. מַחְשַׁכֵּי, מַחֲשַׁבִּים.

חָשַׁל. Niph. part. נֶחֱשָׁלִים *debilitated, infirm persons,* Deu. 25:18.

חֲשַׁל Ch., *pounded to powder,* Dan. 2:40.

חַשְׁמַל *some brilliant white or pale yellow metal;* LXX. ἤλεκτρον.

חָשֻׁם p.n. of a man.

חֶשְׁמוֹן p.n. of a town in the tribe of Judah.

חַשְׁמוֹנָה p.n. of a station of the Israelites in the desert.

חַשְׁמַן m., pl. חַשְׁמַנִּים *rich, powerful men,* Ps. 68:32.

חָשַׁן (Arab. *to adorn*).

חֹשֶׁן m., *breast-plate* of the high priest; called also חֹשֶׁן הַמִּשְׁפָּט.

חָשַׁק.—I. *desire, delight in,* with בְּ.—II. *it pleased, seemed good,* with לְ and inf. Pi. חִשֵּׁק *attached to,* Ex. 38:28. Pu. *was joined to,* Ex. 27:17.

חֵשֶׁק m. (with suff. חִשְׁקִי), *desire, delight.*

חֲשֻׁקִים, חֲשׁוּקִים m. pl.—the *tie-rods* or *poles* which passed through the upright pillars of the forecourt of the tabernacle.

חִשֻּׁקִים m. pl., *spokes of a wheel,* 1 Ki. 7:33.

חָשַׁר root not used; (Arab. *collected*)

חַשְׁרָה f., *collection of waters,* 2 Sam. 22:12.

חִשֻּׁרִים m. pl., *naves of wheels,* 1 Ki. 7:33.

חָשָׁשׁ m., *dry grass, hay.*

חֵת pl. חִתִּים p.n. of a people of Canaan.

חָתָה (fut. יַחְתֶּה), *take up* and *remove* (as fire, coals, &c.), *lay hold of;* fut. with suff. יַחְתְּךָ *he will lay hold on thee,* Ps. 52:7.

מַחְתָּה f.—I. *shovel* or *pan* for removing hot coals.—II. *censer.*—III. *dishes* for receiving the snuffs of the lamps; LXX. ὑπόθεμα.

חֲתִית, חֲתַחַת, חִתָּה, חַת; see חתת.

חָתַךְ. Niph. נֶחְתַּךְ *has been determined,* Dan. 9:24.

חָתַל. Pu. and Hoph. הָחְתֵּל לֹא חֻתַּלְתְּ, *thou wast not bandaged,* Eze. 16:4.

חִתּוּל m., *bandage for a wound,* Eze. 30:21.

חֲתֻלָּה f., *swaddling, bandage,* Job 38:9.

חִתֻּל p. n. of a place in Syria.

חָתַם (fut. יַחְתֹּם).—I. *seal, seal up.*—II. *conclude, finish,* with בְּ, בְּעַד. Niph. *was, became sealed.* Pi. *sealed, determined upon,* Job 24:16. Hiph. הֶחְתִּים *seal, shut up,* Lev. 15:3.

חֲתַם Ch., *sealed.*

חוֹתָם m. (with suff. חֹתְמֶךָ).—I. *seal-ring.*—II. *seal.*—III. p. n. of a man.

חֹתֶמֶת f., *seal,* Gen. 38:25.

חָתָן, part. m. חֹתֵן *father-in-law, wife's father;* f. חֹתֶנֶת *mother-in-law, wife's mother;* with suff. חֹתַנְתּוֹ. Hith. הִתְחַתֵּן *became related by marriage,* specially with a daughter, with בְּ, אֶת, לְ.

חָתָן m. (const. חֲתַן; with suff. חֲתָנוֹ; pl. חֲתָנִים).—I. *relative.*—II. *son-in-law.*—III. *bridegroom.*—IV. *relative by blood,* i. e. circumcision, חֲתַן־דָּמִים Ex. 4:25, 26.

חֲתֻנָּה f., *marriage,* Cant. 3:11.

חָתַף same as חָטַף; (Arab. *destruction;*) fut. יַחְתֹּף *snatch away,* Job 9:12.

חֶתֶף m., אִישׁ חִ׳ *man of rapine,* Pro. 23:28.

חָתַר (fut. יַחְתֹּר).—I. *dig, delve,* with בְּ *into.*—II. *row* (dig into water), Jon. 1:13.

מַחְתֶּרֶת f., *digging through,* i. e. breaking in.

חָתַת *be, become broken with shame, fear, &c.* Niph. נְחַת (fut. יֵחַת;

pl. יֵחַתּוּ), same as Kal, with מִן, מִפְּנֵי. Pi. חִתֵּת I. *broken to pieces, shivered.*—II. *affrighted,* Job 7:14. Hiph. הֵחַת (pret. הַחְתֹּתָּ, הַחְתִּתִּי), *break to pieces, ruin.*

חַת m.—I. *ruin,* Job 6:21.—II. p. n. of a man.

חַת m. (with suff. חִתְּכֶם; pl. חַתִּים) *broken, spoiled,* applied to persons or things.

חִתָּה f.—I. the same.—II. *fear,* Gen. 35:5.

חֲתִית f., *fear, terror, dread.*

חַתְחַת m., pl. חַתְחַתִּים *broken down with fear,* Ecc. 12:5.

מְחִתָּה f.—I. *stroke, injury, ruin.*—II. *fear, terror.*

ט

טְאֵב Ch., *was glad,* Dan. 6:24.

טָאמָא *debase;* see טוּא.

טָבְאֵל, טָב, see טוֹב.

טְבוּלִים m. pl. (Ethiop. טבלל *folded*) *turbans,* Eze. 23:15.

טַבּוּר m., *mountain, high place.*

טָבַח (inf. const. טְבֹחַ; imp. טְבָח) *slaughter,* specially animals for eating, also of men.

טַבָּח m.—I. *cook, butcher.*—II. *officer of state,* probably, *executioner;* שַׂר (רַב) טַבָּחִים *chief officer.*

טַבָּח m. Ch., *officer of state.*

טַבָּחָה f., *female cook.*

טֶבַח m. (with suff. טִבְחֹה).—I. *slaughter of animals.* — II. *animals slaughtered.*—III. p. n. of a man.

טִבְחָה f., the same.

אֲבַטִּיחִים (trans.) m. pl., *melons,* Nu. 11:5.

מַטְבֵּחַ m., *slaughter*, Isa. 14:21.

טִבְחָח (elsewhere טֶבַח), p. n. of a city of Syria.

טָבַל I. *dip, plunge.* — II. *stain, dye.* Niph. *were dipped,* Jos. 3:15.

טְבוּלִים ; see in its place.

טְבַלְיָהוּ p.n. of a man.

טָבַע *sank down* (as into mud). Pu. טֻבַּע *sank in, were immerged,* Ex. 15:4. Hoph. הָטְבַּע *were let in* (as pillars in their bases, &c.).

טַבַּעַת f. (pl. טַבָּעוֹת; const. טַבְּעוֹת). — I. *seal ring.* — II. *any ring.*

טַבָּעוֹת p.n. of a man.

טַבְרִמּוֹן ; see טוֹב.

טֶבֶת p.n. of a town in the tribe of Ephraim.

טֵבֵת m., the tenth month of the Hebrew year, Est. 2:16.

טָהַר (fut. יִטְהָר) *was, became, clean, pure,* from disease, from legal uncleanness, from moral impurity. Pi. טִהַר. — I. *cleanse, purify.* — II. *declare clean.* Pu. *was purified.* Hithp. הִטַּהֵר (pl. הִטַּהֲרוּ ; imp. pl. הִטַּהֲרוּ) *was, became clean, purified.*

טָהוֹר (const. טְהָר־, טְהוֹר; f. טְהֹרָה; pl. טְהֹרוֹת) *clean, pure.*

טֹהַר m. — I. *brightness, glory.* — II. *purification.*

טָהָר m., } the same.
טָהֳרָה f.,

טְמָא Ch., root not used; (Syr. *fasted*).
טְוָת f. Ch., *fasting,* Dan. 6:19.

טוּא or טָוָא Pil. מָאטְמָא *humble, debase;* part. מְטַאְטֵא *humbling, debasing,* Isa. 14:23.

טוֹב (pret. pl. טֹבוּ ; fut. יִיטַב from

טוֹב לִי (יָטַב) *was good, agreeable;* it *pleases me,* Nu. 24:1; with בְּעֵינַי the same. Hiph. הֵיטִיב *do well,* liberally, *make good,* Hos. 10:1; *make happy,* Ecc. 11:9.

טוֹב m. טוֹבָה f.—I. *good.*—II. *happy, prosperous.* — III. *valuable.* — IV. *handsome* (goodlike).—V. *kind.*— VI. used adverbially, *well, rightly;* s. m. and f. טוֹבָה.— I. *goodness* —II. *wealth.*—III. *prosperity, happiness;* לְטוֹב, לְטוֹבָה, with לְ *that it may be well with thee.*—IV. *beauty.* —V. p. n. of a country on the other side Jordan.

טָב m. Ch., *good, excellent.*

טָבְאֵל with pause טָבְאַל p. n. of a man, Syrian or Persian.

טַבְרִמּוֹן p. n., the father of Benhadad, king of Syria.

טוּב m.—I. *goodness.* — II. *wealth.*— III. *prosperity.* — IV. *beauty.* — V. *goodness* (of discernment).— VI. טוּב God, as the source of all good. טוּב אֶרֶץ *the best part of the land,* Gen. 45:18.

טוֹב אֲדֹנִיָּהוּ p.n. of a man.

טוֹבִיָּהוּ, טוֹבִיָּה p. n. of a man.

טָוָה *spin* (lit. *twine*), Ex. 35:25, 26.
מַטְוֶה m., *yarn,* Ex. 35:25.

טוּחַ I. *plaister, paint.* — II. *overlay.* Niph.inf. הִטּוֹחַ *was covered, plastered,* Lev. 14:43, 48.

טִיחַ m., *plastering,* Eze. 13:12.

טֻחוֹת f. pl.—I. *inward parts, viscera,* Ps. 51:8.—II. *the motive power of the heavenly bodies,* Job 38:36.

טוֹטָפוֹת *bandages;* see טוּף.

טוּל Hiph. הֵטִיל *cast forth, out, into,*

Hoph. הוּטַל *was, became cast out, forth, &c.* Pil. טִלְטֵל *cast out,* Isa. 22:17.

טַלְטֵלָה f., *entire casting out,* Isa. 22:17.

טוּף (Arab. *surrounded*).

טוֹטָפוֹת f. pl., φυλακτήρια, *frontlets; probably jewels worn on the fore-head.*

טוּר see דּוּר and תּוּר.

טוּר m. (pl. טוּרִים טֻרִים), *series, order, range.*

טִירָה f.—I. *any series of buildings.* —II. *palace.*—III. *certain chambers in the Temple.*

טוּר m. Ch., same as צוּר *mountain,* Dan. 2:35, 45.

טוּשׂ *fly swiftly,* Job 9:26.

טְוָת *fasting;* see צְוָא.

טָחָה (Arab. *expand*). Pil. part.— מְטַחֲוֵי־ קָשֶׁת *archers,* Gen. 21:16.

טְחוֹת *viscera;* see טוּחַ.

טְחוֹרִים *hæmorrhoids;* see טחר.

טָחַן (fut. יִטְחָן).—I. *grind with a hand-mill.*—II. *oppress.*

טַחוֹן m., *hand-mill,* Lam. 5:13.

טַחֲנָה f., *the same,* Ecc. 12:4.

טְחַר (Syr. *arms*).

טְחוֹרִים m. pl., *emerods (hæmorrhoids).*

טִיחַ *plaster;* see טוּחַ.

טִיט m., *mud, mire.*

טִין m. Ch., *clay, potter's clay.*

טִירָה *row;* see טוּר.

טַל *dew;* see טלל.

טָלָא, part. טָלוּא *patched, having patches of various colours;* pl. טְלֻאִים, טְלֻאוֹת. Pu. part. f. pl.

מְטֻלָּאוֹת *patched* (of shoes), Jos 9:5.

טָלָם; see טָלִי, טְלָאִים.

טָלֶה (Syr. *an infant*).

טָלֶה const. טְלֵה m., *young lamb.*

טְלִי m.—I. the same; pl. טְלָאִים.— II. p. n. of a town; see טָלָם.

טַלְטֵלָה, טִלְטֵל; see טוּל.

טָלַל. Pi. טִלֵּל *covered, roofed,* Neh. 3:15.

טְלַל Ch. Aph. אַטְלֵל *takes shade,* Dan. 4:9.

טַל m. (with pause טָל, with suff. טַלָּם), *dew.*

טַל m. Ch., *dew.*

טָלָם p. n. of a town in the tribe of Judah; also טְלָאִים.

טַלְמוֹן p. n. of a man.

טָמֵא (fut. יִטְמָא; inf. with ה parag. טָמְאָה), *was unclean, polluted,* with בְּ. Niph. נִטְמָא *was polluted,* with בְּ. Pi. טִמֵּא.—I. *polluted, defiled.*—II. *pronounced unclean.* Pu. part. f. מְטֻמָּאָה *polluted.* Hith. הִטַּמֵּא *polluted,* with לְ. Hothp. pret. f. הֻטַּמָּאָה the same, Deu. 24:4.

טָמֵא m., *unclean, polluted;* f. טְמֵאָה.

טֻמְאָה f. (pl. const. טֻמְאֹת), *polluted, defiled.*

טָמָה same as טָמֵא. Niph. pl. נִטְמִינוּ *we are unclean, despised.*

טָמַן *conceal, hide in the earth.* Niph. *was hidden.* Hiph. *hide,* 2 Ki. 7:8.

מַטְמוֹן m. (pl. מַטְמֹנִים), *treasure, that which is laid up, hidden.*

טֶנֶא (with suff. טַנְאֲךָ) m., *basket.*

מָנַף. Pi. *soil,* Cant. 5:3.

טָעָה same as תָּעָה. Hiph. הִטְעָה *made to err,* Eze. 13:10.

טָעַם (fut. יִטְעַם).—I. *taste.*—II. *discriminate, judge.*

טְעַם Ch. Pa. *make to eat.*

טַעַם m.—I. *reason, judgment.*—II. *taste.*

טַעַם m. Ch., *edict.*

טְעֵם m. Ch.—I. *taste.*—II. *judgment.*—III. *edict.*

מַטְעַמִּים m., מַטְעַמּוֹת f. pl., *dainty meats.*

טָעַן.—I. *load* (of beasts of burden), Gen. 45:17.—II. Pu. טֹעַן *pierced through,* Isa. 14:19.

טַעַת Kal. inf.; see נטע.

טַף *infant;* see טפף.

טָפַח. Pi. טִפַּח *spread out, extend* (from טֶפַח), spec. with the hand.

טֶפַח m.—I. *palm, hand-breadth,* a measure of about three and-a-half inches; pl. טְפָחוֹת Ps. 39:6.—II. *coping stones of a building.*

טֹפַח m., *hand-breadth, measure.*

טִפֻּחִים m. pl., Lam. 2:20, *that which is stroked with the hand.*

מִטְפַּחַת f. (pl. מִטְפָּחוֹת), *upper garment, mantle.*

טָפַל.—I. *lay on* or *over.*—II. *cover, conceal.*

טִפְסַר m., *prince, general.*

טַפְסָר m., the same; pl. טַפְסָרִים.

טָפַף *tripping, mincing,* Isa. 3:16.

טַף m. (with pause טָף; with suff. טַפֵּנוּ), *child, infant.*

טְפַר m. Ch., *nails, claws.*

טָפֵשׁ *fat, stupid,* Ps. 119:70.

טָפַת p. n. of a daughter of Solomon.

טָרַד *driving out;* part. טֹרֵד *perpetual, successive* (i. e. one driving out the other), Pro. 19:13; 27:15.

טְרַד Ch., *driving out, driven out.*

טָרָה root not used; (Arab. *was fresh*).

טָרִי m., טְרִיָּה f., *fresh, moist,* Jud 15:15; Isa. 1:6.

טְרוֹם ketib, same as טֶרֶם.

טָרַח. Hiph. *stretches out,* Job 37:11.

טֹרַח m. (with suff. טָרְחֲכֶם), *pressure, wearying.*

טָרַם root not used; (Arab. *cut off*).

טֶרֶם adv., *not yet;* בְּטֶרֶם and טֶרֶם *before that;* מִטֶּרֶם the same.

טָרַף (fut. יִטְרַף, יִטְרֹף), *tear in pieces, wound, injure.* Niph. *be torn in pieces.* Pu. טֹרַף the same. Hiph. *feed, provide for.*

טֶרֶף m., *prey, provision, food.*

טָרָף m., *leaf* (that which is plucked), Gen. 8:11.

טְרֵפָה f.—I. *any thing torn.*—II. *animal torn by a wild beast.*

טַרְפְּלָיֵא Ch., p. n., a people so called, Ezr. 4:9; LXX. Ταρφαλαῖοι.

י

יָאַב *desired, longed for,* with לְ.

יָאָה with לְ *it becometh,* Jer. 10:7.

יְאוֹר same as יָאֹר.

יָאֹתוּ Niph. fut. pl., from אות.

יַאֲזַנְיָה (*whom the Lord hears*), p. n. of a man.

יַאֲזַנְיָהוּ (contr. יְזַנְיָה, יְזַנְיָהוּ) p. n. of a man.

יָאִיר (the Lord enlightens, Ἰάειρος), p. n. of a man; patron. יָאִירִי.

יָאַל I. same as אַל Niph. נוֹאַל was foolish.—II. same as אול Hiph. הוֹאִיל (fut. וַיּוֹאֶל—1. undertook, began, with inf.—2. was willing, contented.

יֹאֶל ,וַיֹּאֶל Hiph. fut. apoc., from אלה.

יֹאֶל ,וְיֹאֶל Hiph. fut. apoc., from II. יאל.

יָאֹר Hiph. fut. apoc., יָאֹר Niph. fut., from אור.

יָאֹר Kal fut., from ארר.

יְאוֹר ,יְאֹר m., a river, specially the Nile; pl. יְאֹרִים rivers.

יָאַשׁ Niph. נוֹאַשׁ was hopeless, desperate, with מִן; part. נוֹאָשׁ desperate, in vain. Pi. inf. יָאֵשׁ rendered hopeless, Ecc. 2:20.

יֹאשִׁיָּה p. n. of a man.

יֹאשִׁיָּהוּ (Ἰωσίας) p. n. of a man.

יָאַת ,וַיֵּאָת Kal fut. apoc., יֶאֱתָיוּ fut. pl., יֶאֱתָיִי fut. with suff.; see אתה.

יִתְרִי p. n. of a man (same as אֶתְנִי).

יָבֵא Hiph. fut. apoc.; see בוא.

יְבָאֻנִי for יְבֹאוּנִי Kal fut. pl. with suff.; see בוא.

יָבַב Pi. יַבֵּב cried out, Jud. 5:28.

יוֹבָב p. n.—I. of a people in Arabia Felix.—II. of a king of Edom.—III. of a man.

יָבוֹ ,וַיָּבֹאוּ 2 Ki. 12:12, for וַיָּבֹא Kal fut.; see בוא.

יְבוּס p. n. of the Canaanitish inhabitants of Jerusalem; יְבוּסִי Jebusite.

יְבוּל produce; see יבל.

יָבֹשׁ Kal fut., from בוש.

יִבְחַר (chosen of the Lord), p. n. of a man.

יָבִין p. n. of two Canaanitish kings.

יֶבְךָ ,וַיֵּבְךְ Kal fut. apoc.; see בכה.

יָבַל Hiph. הוֹבִיל bare, carried, led Hoph. הוּבַל was borne, carried, led. Ch. Aph. הֵיבֵל bring, Ez. 5:14; 6:5.

יְבוּל m. (with suff. יְבוּלָה ,יְבֻלֹה).—I. produce (of the earth, &c.)—II. provision, wealth.

בּוּל m.—I. produce, increase.—II. name of a month 1 Ki. 6:38, the eighth of the calendar, answering to our October.

מַבּוּל m. flood of Noah, deluge.

יֻבַל m.—I. stream of water.—II. p. n. of a son of Lamech.

יוֹבֵל com. (lit. a protracted note or sound), the Jubilee, a feast of the Jews announced by the sounding of horns; שְׁנַת הַיּוֹבֵל and יֹבֵל the year of Jubilee.

יוּבַל m.—I. canal, Jer. 17:8.—II. p. n. of a son of Lamech.

אוּבָל ,אָבֵל m., a river, canal, Dan 8:2, 3, 6.

יַבֶּלֶת f., issue, running disease, Lev. 22:22; Vulg. papulas habens.

תֵּבֵל f., same as אֶרֶץ.—I. the world, the earth, specially the inhabited part of it.—II. the world's inhabitants, mankind.

יִבְלְעָם p. n. of a town in the tribe of Manasseh.

יָבָם m. husband's brother; יִבֵּם Pi. marry the brother's wife; see Deu. 25:5, 7.

יְבָמָה f. (with suff. יְבִמְתּוֹ) brother's wife; one married to her husband's brother.

יַבְנְאֵל p. n., two towns in the tribes of Judah and Naphtali.

יַבְנֶה p. n. of a town of the Philistines, Ἰαμνία, Ἰάμνεια.

יִבְנְיָה p. n. of a man.

יַבֹּק p.n. of a brook which runs into the river Jordan.

יֶבֶרֶכְיָהוּ (blessed of the Lord), p.n. of a man.

יָבְשָׁם p. n. of a man.

יָבֵשׁ (inf. const. יְבֹשׁ; fut. יִיבַשׁ; pl. יִיבְשׁוּ) was or became dry, arid. Pi. יִבֵּשׁ dry up. Hiph. הוֹבִישׁ. —I. dry up, make to wither.—II. was ashamed, confounded; see בּוֹשׁ.

יָבֵשׁ m., יְבֵשָׁה f.—I. dry.—II. p. n. of a town in Gilead; called also יָבֵישׁ —III. p. n. of a man.

יַבָּשָׁה יַבֶּשֶׁת f., dry land.
יַבֶּשֶׁת f. Ch., the same.
יַבֶּשֶׁת f., dried, Gen. 8:7.

וַיַּבְּשֻׁהוּ for וַיְיַבְּשֻׁהוּ Pi. fut. with suff.; see יבשׁ.

יְבֵשֶׁת Kal inf. const.; see יבשׁ.

יִגְאָל (the Lord redeemeth), p. n. of a man.

יָגֵב same as נוּב ploughed; part. יוֹגְבִים ploughmen.

יֶגֶב m. pl., יְגֵבִים ploughed lands, Jer. 39:10.

יָנְבָּה with ה parag. יָנְבָּהָה p. n. of a town in the tribe of Gad.

יִגְדַּלְיָהוּ (let the Lord be magnified), p.n. of a man.

יָגָה Niph. part. נוּגָה pained (perhaps cast out). Pi. יִגָּה afflict, pain, Lam. 3:33. Hiph. הוֹגָה.—I. afflicted.— II. removed, 2 Sa. 20:13.

יַגֶּה וַיַּגֶּה for וַיִּגֶּה Pi. fut., from יגה
יָגוֹן m., affliction, grief.
תּוּגָה f., sorrow, grief.

יָגוּר (the Lord dwelleth there), p.n. of a town in the tribe of Judah.

יִגְלִי p. n. of a man.

וַיָּגֶל יַגֵל Hiph. fut. apoc.; see נלה.

יָגַע (fut. יִיגַע; pl. יִיגְעוּ), labour to weariness; with ב and ל, be wearied. Pi. יִגַּע fatigue, cause to labour to weariness. Hiph. הוֹגִיעַ same as Pi. with בְּ.

יָגֵעַ m., wearying, wearied.
יְגִיעַ const. יְגִיעַ m.—I. wearied, fatigued.—II. labour.—III. the fruit of labour, wealth.

יֶגַע m., wealth, Job 20:18.
יְגִיעָה f., hard labour, exertion, Ecc. 12:12.

יְגָר m. Ch., heap of stones, Gen. 31:47.

יֻגַּר Niph. fut., from נגר.

יָגֹר (pret. יָגֹרְתִּי, יָגֹרְתָּ), fear, be afraid of, with מִפְּנֵי.

יָגֹר m., fearing, afraid of.

יָד com., generally f. (const. יַד; with suff. יָדִי; יֶדְכֶם; dual יָדַיִם, const. יְדֵי, with suff. יָדָיו (יְדֵיכֶם).—I. hand; with עִם, אֶת assist, aid; with אֶל, בְּ hand against, afflicting, troubling; with עַל upon him, inspiring, strengthening.—II. power, spirit or word of God, 1 Sa. 5:11, &c.—III. with prep. עַל יַד, לְיַד, בְּ same as בְּיַד; בְּעַד יַד, אֶל יַד, עַל יְדֵי at hand, near.—IV. space, place; אִישׁ עַל יָדֹו every man in his place.—V memorial, monument, 1 Sa. 15:12;

2 Sa. 18:18. — VI. *by means of.*
PI. יָדוֹת; const. יְדוֹת.—I. *tenons
of planks.*—II. *axletrees of wheels,*
1 Ki. 7:32, 33.—III. *arms of a
throne,* 1 Ki. 10:19. Used with
pref. בְּיַד with (בְּיָדוֹ *with him*), *by,
before, against;* מִיַּד, מִיָּדִי *from,
out of;* יָד לְיָד *hand in hand,* as
striking a bargain, Pro. 11:21.

יַד com. Ch., *hand.*

יָדָא *put forth;* see יָדָה.

וַיֵּרֶא יָרָא *fut. apoc.;* see רָאה.

יִרְאֲלָה p. n. of a place in the tribe of
Zebulun.

יָרְבֵּשׁ p. n. of a man.

יָדַד, same as דּוּד *loved.*

יָדִיד m., *beloved,* specially of God's
children; pl. f., יְדִידוֹת.

יִדּוֹ p. n. of a man.

יְדִידָה p. n. of the mother of king
Josiah.

יְדִידוּת f., *love,* Jer. 12:7.

יְדִידְיָה *beloved of the Lord,* a title of
Solomon.

יָדָה.—I. *put forth* (as casting stones).
—II. *uttering praise;* imp. pl. יְדוּ
they cast at her, Jer. 50:14. Pi. *cast
stones* or *lots;* fut. וַיַּדּוּ; inf. יַדּוֹת.
Hiph. הוֹדָה (fut. יוֹדֶה, יְהוֹדֶה;
with suff. אוֹדְךָ, אֲהוֹדֶךָ,) *recount,
commemorate* (God's mercies, with
עַל); *praise, celebrate,* with לְ. Hith.
הִתְוַדָּה *become known,* with עַל
and לְ.

יָדָא Ch. Aph. *praise, celebrate.*

תּוֹדָה f.—I. *confession.*—II. *praise,
thanksgiving.*—III. *company of persons giving thanks.*

וַיַּדּוּ יָדוּ for וַיָּיַדּוּ Pi. fut.; see יָדה.

יָדְכֶם יָדָן; see יָד *with suff.*

יָדֹם Kal fut.; pl. יָדְמוּ; see דמם.

יְהוּדָה p. n.—I. the patriarch *Judah.*
—II. Afterwards applied to the
kingdom of the house of David.
—III. Ultimately to the whole of
Palestine.—IV. p. n. of a man.

יְהוּד Ch., *the Jews,* the kingdom of
Judah.

יְהוּדִי (יְהוּדִים, יְהוּדִיִּים).—I. *a
Jew;* f. יְהוּדִיָּה *Jewess;* יְהוּדִית adv.
Hebrew, the Hebrew tongue —II.
p. n. of a man.

הִתְיַהֵד. Hith. *became a Jew.*

יְהוּדִי Ch., *a Jew.*

יְהוּדִית; see יְהוּדִי p. n. of a wife of
Esau.

יְהֻד p. n. of a town in the tribe of
Dan.

הוֹדַוְיָה p. n. of a man.

הוֹדַוְיָהוּ p. n. of a man.

יַדְלוֹן p. n. of a man.

יַדּוּעַ p. n. of a man.

יְדִיתוּן, יְדֻתוּן, יְדֻתּוּן p. n. of a Levite
skilled in music; probably also a
musical instrument invented by
him.

יַדַּי p. n. of a man.

יָדִיד, יְדִידָה, יְדִידוּת, יְדִידְיָה; see יָדד.

יְדָיָה p. n. of a man.

יִדְעֲאֵל p. n. of a son of Benjamin.

יַדְלָף p. n. of a son of Nahor.

יָדַע (fut. יֵדַע, יֵירַע; inf. abs. יָדֹעַ;
const. דַּעַת; with suff. דַּעְתָּהּ; imp.
דַּע, דְּעֶה; part. יוֹדֵעַ, יֹדֵעַ; f.
יֹדַעַת).—I. *perceive, become informed, aware of, feel.*—II. *know
carnally.*—III. *recognise, acknow-
ledge.*—IV. *regard;* part. יֹדֵעַ *wise,*
יָדֻעַ *noted, illustrious.* Niph. נוֹדַע
known, apparent, recognised. Pi

יָדַע made to know. Pu. part. מִידַע known, familiar. Po. יוֹדַע declared, indicated. Hiph. הוֹדִיעַ (imp. הוֹדַע; fut. יוֹדִיעַ; apoc. יוֹדַע), make known, show, confess, inform, teach. Hoph. הוֹדַע was, made known. Hith. הִתְוַדַּע made himself known; with אֶל.

יְדַע Ch., know, understand, perceive; fut. יִנְדַּע. Hoph. הוֹדַע made known, taught.

דֵּעַ m., pl. דֵּעִים } knowledge, science,
דֵּעָה f., pl. דֵּעוֹת } opinion.

דַּעַת f., knowledge, science, opinion.

יָדָע p.n. of a man.

יְדַעְיָה p.n. of a man.

יִדְּעֹנִי m. (pl. יִדְּעֹנִים), false prophet, soothsayer.

מַדָּע, מַדַּע m.—I. knowledge, experience.—II. mind.

מַדּוּעַ adv. interrog., why then? why indeed?

מַנְדַּע m. Ch.—I. knowledge.—II. intelligence.

מוֹדָע m., familiar, friend.

מוֹדַעַת f., the same.

יְדַשְׁנָה Pi. fut. with ה parag.; see דשן.

יָהּ one of the names of God; probably an abbreviation of יְהֹוָה.

יהַב I. give, allow.—II. appoint, place; imper. הַב; with ה parag. הָבָה; f. הָבִי; pl. הָבוּ.

יְהַב Ch., give, place. Ith. was given.

יְהָב m., burden; with suff. יְהָבְךָ Ps. 55:23.

הַבְהָבִים m. pl., gifts, Hos. 8:13.

יֶהְדָּי p.n. of a man.

יֶהוּ for יֶהֱו fut. apoc. pl., from הוה.

יֵהוּא p.n.; see הוה.

יְהוֹבֵד Ch. Aph. fut.; see אבד.

יְהוֹדֶה for יוֹדֶה Hiph. fut.; see ידה.

יְהוֹדִית, יְהוּדָה, יְהוֹדִי, יְהוֹד; see ידה.

יְהֹוָה the most sacred and unalienable name of God; see הוה.

יְהוֹשֵׁעַ for יוֹשִׁיעַ Hiph. fut.; see ישע.

יְהִי, וַיְהִי fut. apoc.; see היה.

יְהֵילִילוּ for יְיֵלִילוּ Hiph. fut.; see ילל.

יְהַךְ Ch. fut.; see הוך.

יָהֵל for יֶאֱהֵל Pi. fut.; see אהל.

יָהִיר m., haughty, vain.

יַהֲלֹם; see הלם.

יֶהֱמָיִן fut. pl. with נ parag.; see המה.

יַהְצָה, יַהַץ p.n. of a city of Moab.

יְהַתְלּוּ Pi. fut. pl. with dag. euphon. see התל.

יוֹב p.n. of a son of Issachar.

יוֹבֵב; see יבב.

יוּבַל, יוֹבֵל; see יבל.

יוּכְלוּ Eze. 42:5, for יָאָכְלוּ, Hoph. fut.; see אכל.

יוֹלַדְתְּ for יוֹלֶדֶת part. f.; see ילד.

יוֹם m.—I. day; הַיּוֹם this day, to-day, now; בַּיּוֹם this very day, immediately; בְּיוֹם with inf. on the day, when; כַּיּוֹם now, at present; כַּיּוֹם הַזֶּה as it is at this day; מִיּוֹם from the day since; יוֹם יוֹם, יוֹם בְּיוֹם, בְּיוֹם בְּיוֹם daily; dual יוֹמַיִם two days; pl. יָמִים, const. יְמֵי, sometimes יְמוֹת days, many days; מִקֵּץ יָמִים, מִיָּמִים after many days, some days, some time after; חֹדֶשׁ יָמִים i.e. יֶרַח an entire month; שְׁנָתַיִם יָ׳ two whole years.—II. duration, time; יָמֶיךָ so long as thou livest; כָּל־הַיָּמִים פ׳ all his days; בָּא בַיָּמִים advanced in years.—III. anniversary; מִיָּמִים

יְמָמָה annually; the same, Jud. 17:10; זֶבַח יָמִים annual sacrifice.

יוֹם m. Ch., day, period.

יוֹמָם adv., by day.

יָוָן p. n. Javan the founder of the Greeks, Ionians; בְּנֵי הַיְּוָנִים Ionians, Greeks.

יָוֵן mire, clay.

יַיִן m. (const. יֵין; with suff. יֵינִי).—I. wine.—II. intoxication.

יוֹנָה f. (pl. יוֹנִים).—I. dove.—II. p. n. of a prophet; see also in ינה.

יוֹנֶקֶת, יוֹנֵק; see ינק.

יוֹסֵף, יְהוֹסֵף (from אָסַף or יָסַף).—I. p. n. Joseph, the son of Israel, Ἰωσήφ.—II. given afterwards specially to the tribes of his sons, and generally to the kingdom of Israel.—III. p. n. of a man.

יוֹסִפְיָה p. n. of a man.

יוֹעֵאלָה p. n. of a man.

יוֹצֵאת for יוֹצֵאת part. f.; see יצא.

יוֹר, נִיוֹר Hiph. fut. apoc; see ירה.

יֹרֶא Pro. 11:25 (shall be watered), for יִרְוֶה Hoph. fut., see רוה; or for יוֹרֶה Hoph. fut., see ירה.

יוֹרֶה, יוֹרֵי teach; see ירה.

יוֹשָׁב חֶסֶד (confirming mercy), p. n. of a man.

יוֹשִׁבְיָה (the Lord confirmeth), p. n. of a man.

יוֹשָׁה p. n. of a man.

יוֹשַׁוְיָה p. n. of a man.

יוֹתֶרֶת, יוֹתֵר; see יתר.

יוֹשַׁבְתִּי Jer. 22:23, for יוֹשֶׁבֶת part. f. with ' parag.; see ישב.

יֵז, נִיֵז וַיֵּז Kal fut. apoc; see נזה.

יַז, וַיַּז Hiph. fut. apoc.; see נזה.

יְזִיאֵל p. n. of a man.

יִזַּח Niph. fut.; see זחח.

יִזְיָה p. n. of a man.

יִזְלִיאָה p. n. of a man.

יֵמוּ for יִמּוֹ Kal fut. pl.; see ימם.

יָזַן. (Arab. weighed, was heavy). Pu. part. מְיֻזָּנִים appointed, accoutred for war (of horses), Jer. 5:8, Kri.

יַאֲזַנְיָה, יְזַנְיָהוּ; see אֲזַנְיָה.

יְזְרַח, יִזְרַחְיָה; see זרה.

יֵזַע m., sweat, Eze. 44:18.

יַזֵּר, וַיָּזֶר Kal fut. apoc; see זור.

יִזְרְעֵאל p. n.; see זרע.

יָחַד (fut. יֵחַד) unite, be as one, with בְּ, אֵת. Pi. יִחַד unite, make as one, Ps. 86:11.

יָחִיד m., solitary one, only one; f. יְחִידָה.

יַחַד m., union, 1 Chron. 12:17; adv.—I. as one.—II. singly, at once.—III. wholly, entirely, together, יַחְדָּו the same; the pron. is a pleonasm.

וַיֵּחַד, יֵחַד Kal fut. apoc.; see חדה.

יַחַד for יֶחַד Hiph. fut.; see חדד.

יַחְדּוֹ (united), p. n. of a man.

יַחְדִּיאֵל (united with God), p. n. of a man.

יֶחְדְּיָהוּ (united to the Lord), p. n. of a man.

יַחֲזִיָה, יַחֲזִיאֵל p. n.; see חזה.

יְחִזְקִיָּהוּ, יְחִזְקִיָּה, יְחֶזְקֵאל p. n.; see חזק.

יַחֲזִין fut. pl. with נ parag.; see חזה.

יַחְזְרָה p. n. of a man.

יְחִיאֵל, יְחִיאֵל p. n.; see חיה, חיי.

וַיְחִי, יְחִי fut. apoc.; see חיה.

יַחְתִּים Hiph. fut. with suff. הֵן for הֶן because of the pause; see חתת.

יָחִיד ; see יחד.

יָחַל Pi.—יִחֵל.—I. *hope for, expect, wait.*—II. *cause to hope,* with לְ, אֶל. Hiph. הוֹחִיל same as Pi., with לְ, לִפְנֵי. Niph. נוֹחַל (fut. יָחֵל) same as Pi.

יָחֵם *he will begin;* יָחֵל *he will play,* Hiph. fut.; see חלל.

יָחִיל m., *one waiting,* Lam. 3 : 26.

יַחְלְאֵל p. n. of one of the sons of Zebulon ; patron. יַחְלְאֵלִי.

יֶחֱלוּ Pi. pret. pl. with dag. euphon., from יחל.

תּוֹחֶלֶת f., *expectation, hope.*

יָחַם (fut. יֵחַם, יֶחַם; יֶחֱמוּ ; pl. וַיֶּחֱמוּ; f. וַיֶּחֱמְנָה).—I. *be in heat* (for sexual intercourse): hence,—II. *conceive.* —III. *be hot with anger.* Niph. part. pl. m. נֶחָמִים *heated with idol worship,* Isa. 57:5. Pi. (inf. יַחֵם; pret. f. with suff. יְחֵמַתְנִי) *conceived.*

יֶחֱמוּ for יֶחֱמוּ Pi. pret. pl., from יחם.

יֶחֱמְנָה Gen. 30:38. for תֵּחַמְנָה Kal fut. pl. f., from יחם.

חֵמָה, const. חֲמַת f.—I. *heat.*—II. *anger, fury.*—III. *venom of noxious creatures,* Deut. 32:33.

חֲמָא חֱמָא f. Ch., *heat, anger.*

יַחְמִי p.n. of a man.

יַחְמוּר *gazelle;* see חמר.

יְחֵמַתְנִי for יְחֵמַתְנִי Pi. pret. f. with suff. ; see יחם.

וַיִּחַן, יִחַן Kal fut. apoc.; see חנה.

יָחְנְךָ for יְחָנְךָ Kal fut. with suff.; see חנן.

יֶחֱסָיוּן fut. pl. with ן parag.; see חסה.

יָחֵף m., *barefooted.*

יַחֲצִיאֵל יַחְצְאֵל p.n. of a man.

יָחַר same as אָחַר *tarrying,* 2 Sa. 20. 5 ; fut. וַיִּיחַר (וַיּוֹחַר) Kri Hiph fut. Ch.; see אָחַר).

יִחַר וַיִּחַר Kal fut. apoc.; see חרה.

יַחַשׂ m., *generation, family;* סֵפֶר הַיַּחַשׂ *register of descent,* Neh. 7:5. הִתְיַחֵשׂ. Hiph. *being, becoming registered* (as to pedigree); ἀπογράφεσθαι; inf. s., *registration.*

יַחַת Kal fut. pl. יֵחַתּוּ with dag. euphon.; see נחת. Niph. fut.; see חתת.

וַיֵּט, יֵט Kal fut. apoc.; see נטה.

וַיַּט יַט Hiph. fut. apoc.; see נטה.

יָטַב same as טוֹב (fut. יִיטַב, תִּיטְבִי) *be or seem, good, happy;* with לְ *it was well with him;* with לִפְנֵי, בְּעֵינֵי *it seemed good to him;* with לֵב *was glad* (did the heart good). Hiph. הֵיטִיב (fut. יֵיטִיב) (יֵיטִיב מֵיטִיב) *do good, well to;* הֵיטַבְתָּ לִרְאוֹת *thou hast rightly seen,* Jer. 2:12; מֵיטִיב לְנַגֵּן *skilled in music;* with אֶל, לְ, עִם; inf. הֵיטֵב adv. *well, rightly.*

יְטַב Ch., *was good, happy;* with עַל *it pleased him.*

מֵיטָב m., *good, choice, best.*

יָטְבָה p.n. of a place.

יָטְבָתָה p.n. of a station of the Israelites in the desert.

יוּטָה יָפָּה p.n. of a city in the tribe of Judah.

יְטוּר p.n. of a son of Ishmael and of the people descended from him. the Itureans.

יֵרַע for יֵדַע Kal fut.; see ירע.

יֵיטִיב for יֵיטִיב Hiph. fut ; see טב.

יֵילִיל for יֵילִיל Hiph. fut.; see ילל.

יַן ; see יין.

יִיף Kal fut. apoc.; see יפה.

יָד 1 Sa. 4:13. for יַד hand.

יַךְ וַיַּךְ Hiph. fut. apoc.; see נכה.

יְכַבְּדֻנִּי Pi. fut. with suff. and נ epenth; see כבד.

יְכוֹנְנֶנּוּ for יְכוֹנְנֶנּוּ Pil. fut. with suff.; see כון.

יָכַח. Hiph. הוֹכִיחַ—I. *show, evince.*—II. *convince, chastise, punish*, with אֶת, אֶל, עִם. Hoph. הוּכַח *was reproved*, Job 33:19. Niph. נוֹכַח *be contending*. Hith. הִתְוַכַּח same as Niph., with עִם Mic. 6:2.

תּוֹכֵחָה f., *reproof, punishment.*

תּוֹכַחַת f. (with suff. תּוֹכַחְתִּי; pl. תּוֹכָחוֹת).—I. *argument.*—II. *reproof, punishment.*

יָכִין p. n.; see כון.

יָכֹל (fut. יוּכַל; inf. abs. יָכוֹל; const. יְכֹלֶת) *capable of, equal to*, any action, so as to *succeed, prevail, overcome*, with ל.

יְכֵל יָכִיל Ch. (part. יָכִיל יָכֵל; fut. יוּכַל תֻּכַל) *was able, prevailed, overcame.*

יְכָלְיָהוּ יְכָלְיָה (*the Lord who prevaileth*), p. n., the mother of king Uzziah.

יְהֻבַּל p. n. of a man.

יְכַל Kal fut. apoc.; see כלה.

יִכַּל Ch. fut.; see יכל.

יְכֹלֶת inf. const.; see יָכֹל.

יָכָנְיָה p. n.; see יְהוֹיָכִין in יהוה.

יְכַסְיֻמוּ Ex. 15:5, for יְכַסְיֻמוּ, Pi. fut. with suff.; see כסה.

יֻכַּתּוּ יֻכַּת for יוּכַתּ יוּכַבְת Hoph. fut.; see כתת.

יֻכַּתּוּ for יֻכַּתּוּ יָכַתּוּ Hiph. fut. pl.; see כתת.

יָלַד יֵלֶד יָלַד (fut. יֵלֵד; inf. abs. יָלֹד, לָדָה; const. לֶדֶת, לָת; with suff. לְדְתָּה).—I. *bring forth.*—II. *beget* (part. יוֹלֶדֶת *mother*). Niph. נוֹלַד (fut. יִוָּלֵד), *was born.* Pi. יִלֵּד *aiding to bring forth*, Ex. 1:16; part. מְיַלֶּדֶת *midwife*; pl. מְיַלְּדוֹת Pu. יֻלַּד *was born.* Hiph. הוֹלִיד *cause to bring forth, produce, beget.* Hoph. inf. הֻלֶּדֶת, יוֹם הֻלֶּדֶת אֶת *be born*; פַּרְעֹה *Pharaoh's birthday*, Gen. 40:20. Hith. הִתְיַלֵּד *recorded in the genealogies as begotten*, Nu. 1:18.

וָלָד m., *son, progeny.*

וֶלֶד m., *the same.*

יֶלֶד m.—I. *lad, youth, child.*—II. *young of beasts*, Isa. 11:7.

יְלִיד m., *offspring, son*; יְלִיד בַּיִת *household slave.*

יִלּוֹד m., *offspring, son.*

יַלְדָּה f., *girl, female child.*

יַלְדוּת f.—I. *birth*, Ps. 110:3.—II. *youth*, Ecc. 11:9, 10.

מוֹלָדָה p. n. of a town in the tribe of Judah.

מוֹלֶדֶת f. (pl. מוֹלָדוֹת).—I. *nativity, birth.*—II. *birth-place.*—III. *person born.*—IV. *relatives, members of the same family.*

מוֹלִיד p. n. of a man.

תּוֹלָד p. n. of a town in the tribe of Simeon; same as אֶלְתּוֹלַד.

תּוֹלֵדוֹת f. pl.—I. *birth*, Ex. 28:10.—II. *posterity.*—III. *history*; סֵפֶר תּוֹלֵדוֹת *genealogy*, Gen. 2:4; 6:9.

יָלוֹן p. n. of a man.

יַלִּיז Rabbinical, for יָלִיז, Hiph. fut. pl.; see לוז.

יַלִּינוּ Hiph. fut. pl.; see II. לוּן.

יֵלֵךְ walk; see הָלַךְ.

יָלַל Hiph. הֵילִיל (fut. יְיֵלִיל, יֵילִיל, וְהֵילִיל), wail, howl, cry, mourn.

יְלֵל m., howling, Deu. 32:10.

יְלָלָה const., יְלֵלַת f., wailing, lamenting.

תּוֹלָלִים m. pl., those who cause to lament, Ps. 137:3.

יָלֶן Kal fut. apoc. in pause for יָלִן; see לוּן.

יָלַע retain, hold, Pro. 20:25.

יַלֶּפֶת f., itching scurvy, Lev. 21:20; 22:22.

יֶלֶק m., a hairy, winged locust.

יַלְקוּט bag; see לקט.

יָם, const. יָם, יַם m.—I. the sea.—II. any great lake.—III. any large river; pl. יַמִּים; הַיָּם הַגָּדוֹל or הָאַחֲרוֹן the Mediterranean, i.e. Western Sea: hence יָם the west; רוּחַ יָם the west wind; יָמָּה westward; מִיָּם from the west; לְיָם פְּאַת from the west of a district; יָם sea (that is western) quarter; יָם הַנְּחֹשֶׁת brazen sea, a large vessel for ablution in the temple of Solomon.

יְמוּאֵל p.n. of a son of Simeon.

יְמוֹת יָמִים days; see יוֹם.

וַיָּמַח, יְמַח Kal fut. apoc.; see מחה.

יָמִים m. pl., Gen. 36:24, perhaps hot springs; Vulg. aquæ calidæ.

יְמִימָה p.n. of one of Job's daughters.

יְמִין, יְמִינִי right hand; see ימן.

יִמְלָה, יִמְלָא p.n. of the father of Micaiah the prophet.

יִמָּלֵח for יִמָּלֵא Pi. fut.; see מלא.

יָמְלֵךְ p.n. of a prince of the Simeonites.

יָמַן Hiph. הֵימִין take the right hand or southward.

יָמִין m.—I. the right side, hand, leg, eye; יַד יְמִינוֹ his right hand; מִימִין, מִימִין עַל יָמִין with לְ and suff. יְמִין at the right hand; יְמִין, אֶל הַיָּמִין, לַיָּמִין to, towards the right.—II. south; מִימִין southward of any where.—III. p.n. of a man.

יִמְנָה p.n. of a son of Asher.

יְמָנִי m., יְמָנִית f., right hand, side, &c.; יְמִינִי a Benjamin; see בִּנְיָמִין in בָּנָה.

תֵּימָן lit. right (because a man facing the rising of the sun would have his hand to the south).—I. the south.—II. the south wind; תֵּימָנָה towards the south.—III. p.n. of a city and district of the Edomites; תֵּימָנִי a Temanite.

יִמְנָע p.n. of a man.

יִמָּצְאוּ for יִמָּצְאוּ Niph. fut. pl., see מצא.

יָמַר same as מור. Hiph. הֵימִיר change, exchange, Jer. 2:11. Hith. הִתְיַמָּר ye shall obtain rule, Isa. 61:6 (like Arab. word for commanded; whence "Emir"—Lee).

יֵמַר for יִמְרַר (was bitter) fut.; see מרר.

יִמְרָה p.n. of a man.

יִמְרוּךְ for יֶאְמְרוּךְ Kal fut. pl. with suff.; see אמר.

יָמַשׁ same as מָשַׁשׁ. Hiph. imp. הֲמִשֵׁנִי Kri, הַמְשֵׁנִי Ketib, let me grope, feel, Jud. 16:26.

יְנָאֵץ Syr. for יִנְאַץ Hiph. fut.; see נאץ.

יִנְדַּע for יָדַע Ch. Pe. fut.; see יָדַע.

יָנָה oppress, ruin; (part. f. יוֹנָה).
Hiph. הוֹנָה (fut. יוֹנֶה) same as
Kal; with מִן drove away.

יָנוֹחַ p. n., a town in the confines of
Ephraim and Manasseh.

יָנוּם p. n. of a place in the tribe of
Judah.

יָנַח, see נוּחַ. Hiph. הֵנִיחַ (fut. יָנִיחַ,
וַיָּנַח).—I. gave rest to.—II. gave
comfort to.—III. allowed to fall
down.—IV. caused to rest upon,
with לְ. Hoph. הֻנִּיחַ I. was placed,
Zec. 5 : 11.—II. left, remaining,
Eze. 41 : 9, 11.

יָנִי for יָנִיא Hiph. fut.; see נוּא.

יָנִיחַ Hiph. fut. וַיָּנַח fut. apoc.; see
יָנַח.

יָנַק (fut. יִינַק) suck in; trop. enjoy;
part: יוֹנֵק sucking infant. Hiph.
הֵנִיק suckle, give suck; part. f.
מֵנֶקֶת, מֵנִיקָת nurse; with suff.
מֵנִקְתָּהּ, m.—pl. מֵנִיקוֹת.

יוֹנֵק m.—I. suckling.—II. sucker
(young shoot).

יוֹנֶקֶת f., the same.

יְנִיקָה f., the same; pl. יְנִיקוֹת.

יִנָּשֵׂוא Niph. fut. with א parag.; see
נָשָׂא.

יַנְשׁוּף, יַנְשׁוֹף owl; see נָשַׁף.

יֹסֵב for יֹשֵׁב Kal fut.; see סָבַב.

יָסֵב for יָסֵב Hiph. fut.; see סָבַב.

יָסַד I. founded, established, placed.—
II fixed, laid up. Niph. נוֹסַד was
plotting, laying the ground-work
of, Ps. 2 : 2 ; was founded, Isa. 44 :
28. Pi. יִסֵּד cause to found, fix,
establish. Pu. יֻסַּד was founded,
Hoph. inf. הוּסַד was founded;

part. מוּסָד founded, secure, Isa
28 : 16, &c.

יְסוֹד m., foundation; pl. יְסֹדִים,
יְסֹדוֹת.

סוֹד m.—I. setting a fence about.—
II. decree, counsel.—III. delibera-
tion.—IV. consideration, prudence.
—V. assembly for deliberation.—
VI. secret.

סוֹדִי p. n. of a man.

יְסֹד m., beginning, i. e. foundation of
a building, Ezr. 7 : 9.

יְסוּדָה f., foundation, Ps. 87 : 1.

מוּסָד m., foundation, support, prop.

מוּסָדָה f., the same.

מוֹסָד m., foundation, support; pl
מוֹסָדוֹת and מוֹסָדִים.

מַסָּד m., foundation, 1 Ki. 7 : 9.

יֻסַּךְ was poured out, Ex. 30 : 32 ; see
נָסַךְ.

יִסְכָּה p. n. of Lot's sister.

יִסְמַכְיָהוּ p. n. of a man.

יָסַף (part. יֹסֵף; pl. יוֹסְפִים and Hiph
יֹאסִיף, וַיַּסֶף, יֹסֵף, יוֹסִיף; fut.
הוֹסִיף).—(מוֹסִיף); part. —I. added,
repeated, with עַל, אֶל, לְ.—II. used
as an auxiliary, with לְ, אֶל, עַל
before the inf. when it may mostly
be translated by again. Niph.
נוֹסַף was added, repeated; part.
f. pl. נוֹסָפוֹת additions of calamity
יְסַף Ch., Hoph. הוּסַף was added.

יָסַר (fut. with suff. אֶסָּרֵם; part. יֹסֵר).
Pi. יִסֵּר (fut. יְיַסֵּר; inf. יַסֵּר,
יַסְּרָה). chastised, corrected (as parents their
children), with מִן. Niph. נוֹסַר
was chastised; pl. נִוָּסְרוּ. Hiph.
fut. אֲיַסִּרֵם I will chastise them,
Hos. 7 : 12

יִסּוֹר will chastise, Job 40:2.

מוֹסֵר chains; see אָסַר.

מוּסָר m. — I. chastisement, discipline. —II. learning, doctrine.

מֹסֵר m., the same, Job 33:16.

יָע shovel; see יָעֶה.

יַעְבֵּץ p.n.—I. of a man.—II. of a town in the tribe of Judah.

יָעַד (fut. יִיעַד) appoint, determine. Niph. נוֹעַד.—I. brought together, assembled, met.— II. agreed, with עַל, אֶל, לְ. Hiph. הוֹעִיד appoint. Hoph. הוּעַד appointed, fixed, Jer. 24:1.

עֵדָה const. עֲדַת f.—I. an assembly.— II. party, persons united for a purpose.—III. a family.—IV. the congregation of Israel.—V. עֵ דְּבוֹרִים swarm of bees, Jud. 14:8.

מוֹעֵד m. (pl. מוֹעֲדִים, מוֹעֲדֵי). — I. coming together, congregation; אֹהֶל מוֹעֵד the tabernacle of the congregation.—II. time, season.—III. place appointed; see also מֹעֵד.

מוֹעֵד m., assembly, host, Isa. 14:31.

מוֹעָדָה f., pl. מוֹעָדוֹת solemn feasts, 2 Chron. 8:13.

מוּעָדָה f., appointment; עָרֵי הַמּוּעָדָה appointed cities of refuge

וַיֵּעַד Hiph. fut.; see עוּד.

יָעָה carry off, destroy, Isa. 28:17.

יָע m., pl. יָעִים shovels or fire-pans.

יְעִיאֵל, יְעוּאֵל p.n. of a man.

יְעוּץ p.n. of a man.

יְעוֹרִים m. pl., woods, Eze. 34:25; see יַעַר.

יְעוּשׁ p.n. of a man.

יָעֵז. Niph. part. נוֹעַז, Isa. 33:19; Vulg. impudens, powerful, formidable.

עֲזִיאֵל p.n. of a man.

יַעֲזִיָּה p.n. of a man.

יַעֲזֵר, יַעְזֵר (the Lord helpeth) p.n. of a town beyond Jordan of the tribe of Gad.

יָעַט clothe, cover, Isa. 61:10.

יְעַט Ch. same as Heb., יָעַץ advise, counsel. Ith. consulted together, Dan. 6:8.

יָעֲטִין m. pl., councillors.

עֵטָא f., counsel, wisdom, Dan. 2:14.

וַיַּעַט, יָעַט Kal fut.; see עוּט.

יָעוּר, יָעִיר p.n. of a man.

יַעְקָן p.n. of a man.

יָעַל. Hiph. הוֹעִיל be profitable, advantageous, with לְ.

יָעֵל m.—I. ibex, mountain goat; pl. יְעֵלִים.—II. p.n. of a judge of Israel.—III. p. n. of a woman.—IV. צוּרֵי הַיְעֵלִים p.n. of a rock in the desert of Engaddi.

יַעֲלָה f.—I. female ibex.—II. p.n. of a man.

יַעְלָם p.n. of the son of Esau.

יַעַמְדֻנָה Dan. 8:22. Kal fut. pl. f. for תַּעֲמֹדְנָה; see עָמַד.

יַעֲנֵי, יַעַן; see עָנָה.

יַעַן perhaps from עָנָה cried.

יְעֵנִים pl. יְעֵנִים f., ostriches, Lam. 4:3.

בְּנוֹת יַעֲנָה f. (pl. בַּת הַיַּעֲנָה) female ostriches.

יָעֵף (fut. יִיעַף) lit. ran swiftly, was fatigued, wearied. Hoph. part. מֻעָף swift, Dan. 9:21.

יָעֵף m., weary, fatigued, Isa. 40:29; 50:4.

יָעֵף m., flight, Dan. 9:21.

תּוֹעָפוֹת f. pl. — I. swiftness. — II

wealth, treasure (acquired by fatigue).

יָעַץ (fut. יִיעַץ) *advise, admonish, counsel self or others*, with עַל, אֶל; part. יוֹעֵץ *counsellor*. Niph. נוֹעַץ *be advised, counselling, consulting*, with עִם, אֶל, אֶת. Hithp. יִתְיָעֲצוּ same as Niph.

עֵצָה const. עֲצַת f., *counsel*; בְּעֵצָה *deliberately*; see also עצה

מוֹעֵצָה f., pl. מוֹעֵצוֹת *counsels, devices*.

יַעֲקֹב, יַעֲקֹבָה p. n.; see עקב·

בְּגִי־יַעֲקָן see יַעְקָן

יַעַר m.—I. *honey-comb* (const. יַעְרַת).
—II. *wood, forest*; יַעְרָה *to the wood*;
pl. יְעָרִים, יְעָרוֹת·—III. p. n.:
יַעַר אֶפְרַיִם *grove of Ephraim*;
קִרְיַת יְעָרִים *a city in the tribe of Judah*; יַעַר חָרֶת *the wood of Hereth in the tribe of Judah*.

וַיַּעַר Hiph. fut.; see עור·

יַעְרָה same as יְהוֹעַדָּה p. n. of a man.

יַעֲרֵי אֹרְגִים (*thickets*, perhaps abbreviated יְעָרִים) p. n. of a man.

יַעֲרֶשְׁיָה p. n. of a man.

יַעֲשַׂי p. n. of a man.

יַעֲשִׂיאֵל p. n. of a man.

יִפְדְּיָה (*the Lord redeemeth*), p. n. of a man.

יָפָה (fut. וַיִּיף, יִיפֶה) *was fair, beautiful*. Pi. *beautified*, Jer. 10:4. Pul. יֻפְּתָה *was very beautiful*. Hith. *beautify oneself*.

יָפֶה const. יְפֵה m.; יָפָה const. יְפַת f., *beautiful, excellent*.

יָפוֹא, יָפוֹ p. n., *Joppa*, a celebrated port on the Mediterranean, Ἰόππη.

יֳפִי m. (with pause יֳפִּי; with suff. יָפְיוֹ), *beauty, excellence*.

יְפֵה־פִיָּה f., *very beautiful*, Jer. 46:20

יְפֵיפִית Pul., Ps. 45:3, from יפה·

יָפַח same as פוח· Hith. *was panting in agony*, Jer. 4:31.

יָפֵחַ m.—I. *breathing out*.—II. *panting after, longing for*.

יַפְלֵט p. n. of a man; *patron*. יַפְלֵטִי·

יֻפֻּנֶּה p. n. of the father of Caleb and others.

יָפַע Hiph. הוֹפִיעַ *exhibit brilliancy, shine forth*.

יִפְעָה f., *beauty, brilliancy*, Eze. 28: 7, 17.

יָפִיעַ p. n.—I. of a town in the tribe of Zebulun.—II. of a man.

יָפֵר Hiph. fut. apoc.; see פרה·

יִפְתַּח Hiph. fut apoc.; see פתה·

יֶפֶת root not used.

מוֹפֵת m.—I. *sign, wonder*.—II. *intimation, portent* (τύπος).

יֶפֶת p. n., *Japheth*, son of Noah; LXX. Ἰάφεθ.

יִפְתָּח p. n.—I. a town in the tribe of Judah.—II. a judge of Israel (Ἰεφθά).

יִפְתַּח־אֵל p. n., a valley in the tribes of Zebulun and Asher.

יָצָא (fut. יֵצֵא; inf. abs. יָצֹא; const. צֵאת; imp. צֵא; with ה parag. צֵאָה; part. m. יוֹצֵא, f. יֹצֵא, יֹצֵאת, יֹצֵאת).—I. *go out, go forth*; with מִן of the place whence; with בְּ of the place whither.—II. *issue* (from the womb), *be born*.—III *descended*.—IV. *go forth* (from captivity or into captivity).—V *shooting of a tree*, Isa. 11:1, also *grew, came forth* (of plants and flowers).—VI. *arose* (of

and stars).—VII. *issue a decree.*
There are many similar usages, all
modifications of the primary meaning *go forth.* Hiph. הוֹצִיא *cause
to come out, bring out;* with דִּבָּה
brought up an evil report, Nu. 14:
36. Hoph. הוּצָא *was brought
forth, out.*

יְצָא **Ch.**, Shaph. שֵׁיצִיא *wrought out,
finished,* Ezr. 6:15.

יְצִיא m., *issue, child,* 2 Chron. 32:21.

מוֹצָא m.—I. *outgoing.*—II. *time of
outgoing.*—III. *place of outgoing.*
—IV. *the east.*—V. *that which
goeth out,* production, speech, &c.
—VI. p. n. of a man.

מוֹצָאָה f.—I. *going forth,* Mic. 5:1.—
II. *draught-house,* 2 Ki. 10:27.

תּוֹצָאוֹת f. pl.—I. *termination.*—II.
escape, Ps. 68:21.—III. *result,*
Pro. 4:23.

צֶאֱצָאִים m. pl.—I. *productions of the
earth.*—II. *offspring.*

יְצַב *same as* נָצַב. Hith. הִתְיַצֵּב I.
was set up, stood fast, with עַל,
לִפְנֵי.—II. *stood up against,* with
עַל.—III. *stood before, in presence
of,* with עִם, בִּפְנֵי, לִפְנֵי.

יְצַב **Ch.** Pa. *certify.*

יַצִּיב m. **Ch.**, *firm, fixed, settled;*
מִן יַצִּיב adv., *surely.*

יְצַג נָצַג, הַצִּיג see נצג.

יִצְהָר p.n.; see צהר.

יִצְחָק p. n.; see צחק.

יִצְטַבַּע **Ch.** Ithp. fut.; see צבע.

יִצְטַיָּרוּ Hith. fut. pl.; see ציר.

יְצַע, part. יָצוּעַ *laid, placed,* s. *bed.*
Hiph. הִצִּיעַ *place, strew.* Hoph.
הֻצַּע *spread* (as a couch), Isa. 14:11.

יָצִיעַ *same as* יָצוּעַ.

מַצָּע m., *bed or couch,* Isa. 28:20.

יָצַק (fut. יִצֹּק, וַיִּצֹק ; inf. const. צֶקֶת ;
imp. יְצֹק, צַק).—I. *pour out.*—II.
fuse (as metal), with בְּ, עַל ; part.
יָצוּק *hard* (like a cast of metal).
Hiph. הִצִּיק *put down, place, lay
out,* Jos. 7:23 ; 2 Sa. 15:24. Hoph.
הוּצַק *be, become poured out;* part.
מֻצָק *firm,* Job 11:15.

וַיִּצֶק, יִצֹק Kal fut., from יצק.

יִצֹק Kal fut., from יצק.

יְצֻקָה f., *casting, cast,* 1 Ki. 7:24.

מוּצָק, const. מְצַק m., *cast of brass,*
see also in צוק.

מוּצָקָה f., pl. מוּצָקוֹת *funnels* for
pouring the metal into moulds or
casts, Zec. 4:2.

מֻצַקְתּוֹ f., with suff. מֻצַקְתּוֹ *its being
fused,* 2 Chron. 4:3.

I. יָצַר (fut. יִצֹּר, וַיִּצֶר, וַיִּיצֶר), *form,
fashion, make;* part. יוֹצֵר *moulder,
potter ;* כְּלֵי יוֹצֵר *fictile vases ;
creator.* Niph. נוֹצַר and Hoph.
הוּצַר *was formed, made.* Pu. יֻצַּר
the same.

יֵצֶר m. (with suff. יִצְרֵנוּ).—I. *figment,
any thing formed.*—II. *thought,
imagination.*—III. p. n. of a son
of Naphtali; patron. יִצְרִי.

וַיִּצֶר, יִצֶר Kal fut., Gen. 2:19, from I. יצר.

יְצֻרִים m. pl., *things formed, members,*
Job 17:7.

II. יָצַר *same as* צור but intrans., *was
straitened, distressed, anxious :*
וַיֵּצֶר לוֹ *and he was in anxiety,*
Gen. 32:8.

יָצְרוּ, יֵצַר Kal fut. with suff., from
II. יצר.

וַיֵּצֶר, יֵצֶר Kal fut., from II. יצר.

וַיָּצַר, יָצַר Kal fut. apoc.; see צור.

יָצַת (fut. יָצַת, יִצַּתּוּ).—I. *burn*, Isa. 9:17, with בְּ—II. *was on fire*. Niph. נִצַּת I. *was on fire, burnt*.—II. *burnt with anger*, with בְּ, 2 Ki. 22:13,17. Hiph. הוֹצִית, הִצִּית *kindle, set fire to*.

יִצַּתּוּ Kal fut. pl. with dag. euphon., from יצת.

יָצַתִי for יָצָאתִי; see יצא.

יֶקֶב root not used; (Arab. *a tank*).

יֶקֶב m. (with suff. יִקְבְךָ).—I. *wine* or *oil vat*.—II. the *trough* in which grapes are trodden, Job 24:11.

יַקְבְצְאֵל p.n., same as קַבְצְאֵל.

יָקַד (fut. יֵקַד, יִיקַד) *burnt* (as fire). Hoph. הֻקַּד *became, was, burning*.

יְקַד Ch., *burning*, Dan. 3:6, &c.

יְקוֹד m., the same, *fire-brand*, Isa. 10:16.

יְקֵדָה f. Ch., the same. Dan. 7:11.

מוֹקֵד m.— I. *burning*, Isa. 33:14.—II. *fire-brand*, Ps. 102:4.

מוֹקְדָה f., *hearth* where the burnt-offerings were consumed, Lev. 6:2.

יָקְדְעָם p.n. of a city in the tribe of Judah.

יָקָה root not used; (Arab. *he obeyed*).

יִקְהָה or יְקָהָה, const. יִקְהַת f. *obedience*.

יָקֶה p.n. of a man.

יְקוּם *whatever has been called into existence*, Gen. 7:4, 23; Deut. 11:6; see קום.

יָקוֹשׁ יָקֻשׁ; see יקש.

יְקוּתִיאֵל p.n. of a man.

יִפַח Kal fut.; יִפַּח Hoph. fut.; see לקח.

יָקְטָן p.n., a descendant of Shem, the son of Eber, Gen. 10:25, 26.

יָקִים p.n. of a man.

יְקַמְיָה p.n. of a man.

יָקְמְעָם p.n. of a man.

יָקְמְעָם p.n., a city of the Levites in the tribe of Ephraim; see also קִבְצָיִם.

יָקְנְעָם p.n. of a city in the tribe of Zebulun.

יָקַע (fut. יֵקַע; pret. נָקַע which see).—I. *fell, became dislocated*, Gen. 32:26.—II. *fell away* (in mind, affection). Hiph. הוֹקִיעַ *suspend, hang*, ἀνασκολοπίζειν. Hoph. part. מוּקָעִים *hanged*, 2 Sa. 21:13.

יָקַץ (וַיִּיקַץ, יָקַץ יִיקַץ) *awake out of sleep*; see קוץ.

יִקַץ Kal fut.; see יקץ.

יָקַר (וַיִּיקַר, יֵיקַר, יָקַר) *became precious, prized, valued*, with בְּעֵינֵי, לְ. Hiph. הוֹקִיר (lit. *make precious*), *rare, scarce*.

יָקָר m. יְקָרָה f.— I. *precious, dear*.—II. *rare, scarce*. — III. *honorable, glorious*.

יְקָר m., *weight, value, honour, glory*.

יְקָר m. Ch.— I. *costly things*, Dan. 2:6.—II. *honor, glory*.

יַקִּיר m., *precious, honored*, Jer. 31:20.

יַקִּיר m. Ch., *honored, grave*.

יִקְרֶךָ Kal. fut. with suff. and dag. euphon.; see קרה.

יָקֹשׁ, יָקַשׁ (see נָקַשׁ קוֹשׁ) *snaring, taking by means of mares*; part. יוֹקֵשׁ *a fowler*. Niph. נוֹקֵשׁ *was ensnared as a bird*.

יָקֻשׁ יָקוֹשׁ m., *fowler*.

יֻקְשִׁים m., pl. *snared*, Ecc. 9:12

יָקְשָׁן p. n. of a son of Abraham.

מוֹקֵשׁ m. (pl. מוֹקְשִׁים, מוֹקְשׁוֹת) *snares* or *traps* for birds or beasts; mostly used metaphorically, as מוֹקְשֵׁי מָוֶת *snares of death*, &c.

וַיָּקֹשׁ, יָקֹשׁ Kal fut. apoc.; see קֹשֹׁה.

יָקֹשׁ Hiph. fut. apoc.; see קֹשֹׁה.

יָקְתְאֵל p. n.—I. a town in the tribe of Judah.—II. a city in Arabia.

יָרָא (fut. יִירָא, יָרָא; imp. יְרָא; inf. const. יְרֹא; with pref. לְרֹא; with ה parag. (יִרְאָה), *feared* God, man, anything; with מִן, עַל, לְ, בְּ, אֶת. Niph. fut. תִּוָּרֵא *thou art to be feared*, Ps. 130:4; part. נוֹרָא *fearful, terrible, marvellous thing*; pl. נוֹרָאוֹת. Pi. יֵרֵא *alarm, cause to fear*.

יָרֵא, const. יְרֵא m. (יִרְאָה, const. יִרְאַת f.), *fearing* God or man, with מִפְּנֵי.

יִרְאָה, const. יִרְאַת f., the same.

יִרְאוֹן p. n. of a city in the tribe of Naphtali.

מוֹרָא m.—I. *fear.*—II. *reverence*, Mal. 1:6.—III. *object of fear, reverence.*—IV. *fearful, stupendous act.*

מוֹרָה same as מוֹרָא; see also in מָרָה.

וַיִּרָא Kal fut. apoc.; see רָאה.

יִרְאוּ for יִירְאוּ Ps. 34:10, imp. pl.; see ירא.

יִרְאוּ Kal fut. pl., see ירא; יִרְאוּ Kal fut. pl., see רָאה.

וַיִּרְאוּ, יִרְאוּ 2 Sa. 11:24, for וַיֹּרוּ Hiph. fut. pl. apoc.; see ירה.

יִרְאִיָּה p. n. of a man.

יָרֵב; יְרֻבֶּשֶׁת see ריב.—וַיִּרֶב, יָרֶב, for יֶאֱרֹב, Hiph. fut.; see ארב.

יִרְבִּין Kal fut. pl. with נ parag.; see רבה.

יָרָבְעָם p. n., *Jeroboam*, the name of two of the kings of Israel.

יָרַד (fut. יֵרֵד, וַיֵּרֶד; imp. רֵד, רְדָה; inf. abs. יָרֹד, const. רֶדֶת). — *descended, went down*, κατέβη (used both of men and things in a great variety of acceptations). Hiph. הוֹרִיד *make descend, bring down, cast down* (of men and things); *subdued*, with תַּחַת. Hoph. הוּרַד *brought down, lowered.*

יֶרֶד p. n. of a man, 'Ιαρέδ.

יַרְדֵּן p. n. of the river *Jordan*.

מוֹרָד m., *descent, declivity*; מַעֲשֶׂה מוֹרָד *sloping*, perhaps *arched work*, 1 Ki. 7:29.

יְרַדֹּף Ps. 7:6, apparently a corruption, from יָרְדֹּף Kal fut. and יְרַדֵּף Pi. fut.; or possibly from two readings יָרְדֹף and יְרַדֵּף.

יָרָה (fut. יִירָה; inf. יָרֹה; const. יְרוֹת, יְרוֹא; imp. יְרֵה). — I. *cast out, shoot*, as arrows, &c.; part. יוֹרִים *archers*, Pro. 26:18.—II. *cast, lay a foundation*, see יְרָה. Niph. fut. יִירֶה *shall be shot*, Ex. 19:13. Hiph. (וַיּוֹר, יוֹרֶה הוֹרָה.—I. *cast forth, shoot*, as arrows, rain, &c.; מוֹרִים *archers*); see מוֹרָה.—II. *put forth*, as instruction, *teach*, with מִן, אֶל, לְ, בְּ.

יוֹרֶה m. (part. Kal).—I. *the former rain*, i. e. of the autumn.—II. p. n. of a man; same as חָרִיף.

יוֹרָי p. n. of a man.

מוֹרָה m. (part. Hiph.).—I. *teacher, doctor.*—II. *arrow, archer.*—III. *former rain.* — IV. p. n. אֵלוֹן or

אֵלוֹנֵי מוֹרֶה the oaks of Moreh, near Sichem; גִּבְעַת־הַמּוֹרֶה hill of Moreh in the valley of Jezreel.

תּוֹרָה f.—I. instruction, direction.—II. law, enactment.—III. the law, as revealed to Moses and recorded in the Pentateuch.

יָרַהּ (fut. תִּרְהוּ), was astounded with fear, Isa. 44:8.

וַיִּרְאוּ, יִירְאוּ Hiph. fut. pl.; see ירה.

יְראוּ, יֵרוֹא for יְרוּ Kal inf.; see ירה.

יְרוּאֵל p. n. of a desert.

יָרוֹחַ (same as יֶרַח), p. n. of a man.

יִרְיוֹן Kal fut. pl. with נ parag.; see רוה.

יָרוֹן Pro. 29:6, Kal fut.; see רנן. Others refer it to רון.

יָרוּץ for יְרוּץ Kal fut.; see רצץ.

יְרוּשָׁא p. n. of the mother of king Jotham.

יְרוּשָׁלַיִם, יְרוּשָׁלֵם for יְרוּשָׁלֵם (the habitation of peace), p. n. of the principal city of Palestine, Ἱερουσαλήμ, Ἱεροσόλυμα.

יְרוּשְׁלֵם Ch., the same.

יָרֵחַ m., the moon.

יֶרַח m., (pl. יְרָחִים).—I. month, one revolution of the moon round the earth.—II. p. n. of a people and country, Gen. 10:26.

יֶרַח m. Ch., month.

יְרִיחוֹ, יְרֵחוֹ, יְרִיחוֹ p. n., Jericho, a city in Palestine.

יַרְחָם p. n. of a man.

יְרַחְמְאֵל p. n. of a man; patron. ־י.

יְרַחַע p. n. of a woman

יָרַט cast down to ruin, ruin.

מוֹרָט m., "peeled" Eng. Ver.; "ruined" (Gesenius), Isa. 18:2, 7.

יְרִיאֵל p. n. of a man.

יְרִיבַי, יָרִיב; see ריב.

יְרִיָּה, יְרִיָּהוּ p. n. of a man.

יְרִיחָה, יְרִיחוֹ p. n.; see יְרִיחוֹ.

יְרִיעָה, יְרִיעוֹת shouting; see ירע.

יָרֵךְ m. (const. יֶרֶךְ; with suff. יְרֵכוֹ).—I. thigh; שׁוֹק עַל־יָרֵךְ hip and thigh, i. e. wholly, Ju. 15:8; יֹצְאֵי יָרֵךְ offspring, Ex. 1:5.—II. stem of the candlestick in the tabernacle; dual יְרֵכַיִם both thighs.

יַרְכָה f., side, part, quarter; dual יַרְכָתַיִם const. יַרְכְּתֵי the two sides.

יַרְכָּה f. Ch., thigh.

יֵרַךְ Niph. fut., from רכך.

יַרְמוּת p. n. — I. a town in the tribe of Judah.—II. a town of Israel.

יְרִימוֹת, יְרֵמוֹת p.n. of a man.

יְרֵמַי p. n. of a man.

יִרְמְיָה, יִרְמְיָהוּ (exalted of the Lord), p. n. Jeremiah, the prophet.

יָרַע same as רוֹע.—I. was in evil condition; fut. יֵרַע with לִי I am in affliction; with בְּעֵינֵי it was evil in the eyes of.—II. was grieved, pained.

I. יֵרַע Kal fut., from II. ירע Job 20:26; fut. apoc., from רעה.

יְרִיעָה f., veil, curtain of a tent.

יְרִיעוֹת (veiled), p. n. of a woman.

יַרְפְּאֵל p. n. of a place in the tribe of Benjamin.

יָרַק same as רָקַק spit.

יָרוֹק m., green herb, shoot, Job 39:8

יֶרֶק m., green herb.

יֶרֶק m., freshness, green herbage.

יֵרָקוֹן m.—1. *withering, wasting*; LXX. ὤχρα.—II. *the smut in corn.*

יְרַקְרַק m.—I. *gold colour,* Ps. 68:14.—II. *greenish* or *yellowish*; pl. f. יְרַקְרַקּוֹת

יָרַשׁ, יָרֵשׁ (fut. יִירַשׁ, יֵרַשׁ; inf. const. רֶשֶׁת; imp. רַשׁ, רֵשׁ, יְרַשׁ).—I. *possess, inherit.*—II. *dispossess others.*—III. *be, become poor;* יוֹרֵשׁ *heir.* Niph. *be, become poor.* Pi. יָרֵשׁ *take into possession,* Deu. 28:42. Hiph. הוֹרִישׁ.—I. *cause to possess.*—II. *dispossess.*—III. *make poor, desolate.*

יְרֵשָׁה f., *possession,* Nu. 24:18.

יְרֻשָּׁה f., *the same.*

רֶשֶׁת f. (inf. *to take;* with suff. רִשְׁתּוֹ).—I. *net.* — II. *snare.* — III. *network.*

מוֹרָשׁ m. } *possession.*
מוֹרָשָׁה f. }

מוֹרֶשֶׁת גַּת p.n. *of a district near Gath;* מוֹרַשְׁתִּי *a Moreshethite.*

תִּירוֹשׁ, תִּירֹשׁ m., *new wine, must.*

יִשְׂחָק *same as* יִצְחָק p.n.; see צחק.

יְשִׂימָאֵל p. n. *of a man.*

יָשֶׂם *same as* שׂוּם *intrans. was set, laid;* fut. וַיִּישֶׂם, וָאֲשִׂימָה.

יִשְׂרָאֵל (*a prince with God*), p.n., *Israel, the new name given by God to Jacob, afterwards applied to his descendants;* m. יִשְׂרְאֵלִי, f. יִשְׂרְאֵלִית *an Israelite.*

יִשָּׂשכָר p. n. *Issachar, the son of Jacob, and the tribe that descended from him.*

יֵשׁ, יֶשׁ־ (τὸ εἶναι), *is, are, was, were;* with suff. יֶשְׁךָ *thou art;* יֶשְׁנוֹ *he is;* יֶשְׁכֶם *ye are;* יֶשׁ לִי *I have;*

יֵשׁ אֲשֶׁר *it is, because that;* יֵשׁ וָיֵשׁ *it is, yea it is,* 2 Ki. 10:15.

יָשַׁב (fut. יֵשֵׁב; inf. יְשֹׁב; const. שֶׁבֶת; with suff. שִׁבְתִּי; imp. שֵׁב, שְׁבָה).—I. *sit, sit down,* with בְּ, עַל.—II. *lie in wait for.*—III. *have intercourse with,* with עִם.—IV. *remain.*—V. *dwell in.*—VI. *was inhabited,* with בְּ, עַל. Niph. נוֹשַׁב *was inhabited.* Pi. יִשֵּׁב *cause to remain,* Eze. 26:4. Hiph. הוֹשִׁיב *cause to sit, dwell, reside in or with, inhabit.* Hoph. הוּשַׁב *made, caused to dwell.*

יוֹשַׁבְתִּי; see יֹשַׁבְתִּי.

שִׁיבָה f., *residing,* 2 Sa. 19:33; see in שׁוּב.

יֹשֵׁב בַּשֶּׁבֶת p. n. *of one of David's generals.*

יִשְׁבְּאָב p. n. *of a man.*

יִשְׁבּוֹ בְנֹב p. n. *of a man.*

יִשְׁבְּקָשָׁה p. n. *of a man.*

מוֹשָׁב m. (pl. f. מוֹשָׁבוֹת; const. מוֹשְׁבֵי m.).—I. *residence.*—II. *seat.*—III. *time of residing,* Ex. 12:40.—IV. *act of sitting.*—V. *inhabitants.*

תּוֹשָׁב m., *settler, sojourner.*

יֻשַּׁבְחֶסֶד p. n. *of a man.*

יָשֻׁבִי לֶחֶם p. n. *of a man.*

יָשָׁבְעָם p. n. *of a man.*

יִשְׁבָּק p. n. *of a son of Abraham.*

יָשׁוּב p. n. *of a man;* patron. יָשֻׁבִי.

יָשׂוֹד *for* יָשׂר Kal fut.; see שׂדד.

יִשְׁוִי, יִשְׁוָה p. n. *of a man.*

יִשְׁוֹחָיָה p. n. *of a man.*

יְשׁוּעָה, יֵשַׁע *salvation;* see ישׁע.

יֶשַׁח m., *baseness, hypocrisy,* Mic. 6:14.

יִשָּׁחוּ Niph. fut.; see שׁחח.

יָשַׁט Hiph. הוֹשִׁיט extend, stretch out.

יִשַׁי p. n., *Jesse*, the father of David; LXX. Ἰεσσαί.

יִשָּׂיא for יַשִּׂיא Hiph. fut.; see נשׂא.

יְשִׁיָּה, יִשִׁיָּהוּ p. n. of a man.

יָשִׂים for יָשֵׂם Hiph. fut.; see שׂים.

יָשֶׁל Kal. fut. apoc., from III. שׁלה.

יָשֵׁם was desolate, laid waste; fut. תִּישַׁם, תֵּשַׁם; see שָׁמֵם.

יְשִׁימוֹן m.—I. any great desert.—II. specially, *the Desert of Sinai.*

יְשִׁימוֹת f., desolations, Ps. 55:16.

בֵּית־הַיְשִׁמוֹת p. n. of a place near the Dead Sea.

יָשֵׂם for יָשֵׂם Kal. fut.; see שׂים.

יִשְׁמֵם Hiph. fut.; see שׁמם.

יִשְׁמָא p. n. of a man.

יִשְׁמָעֵאל p. n.—I. *Ishmael,* the son of Abraham and Hagar.— II. of a man; יִשְׁמְעֵאלִים *Ishmaelites.*

יִשְׁמַעְיָהוּ, יִשְׁמַעְיָה p. n. of a man.

יִשְׁמְרַי p. n. of a man.

יָשֵׁן, יָשַׁן (fut. יִישַׁן) slept, slumbered, dozed. Niph. נוֹשַׁן grew old, dry. Pi. יִשֵּׁן made to sleep, Jud. 16:19.

יָשֵׁן m., old.

יְשֵׁנָה f.—I. the same.—II. p. n. of a town in the tribe of Judah.

יָשֵׁן m. יְשֵׁנָה f.—I. sleepy.—II. p. n. of a man.

יָשֵׁן f.—I. sleep.—II. dream, Ps. 90:5.

שֵׁנָא f., sleep, Ps. 127:2.

שֵׁנָא or שְׁנָה f. Ch., the same.

שְׁנָת f., sleep, Ps. 132:4.

יִשְׁנוּ compounded of יֵשׁ and suff. ו with נ epenth.

יָשַׁע Hiph. הוֹשִׁיעַ (fut. יוֹשִׁיעַ, יְהוֹשִׁיעַ; apoc. יֹשַׁע) deliver, set free, save, with מִן, ל, מִיַּד. Niph. נוֹשַׁע was delivered, with מִן; part. נוֹשַׁע one saved, Zec. 9:9.

יֵשַׁע, יֶשַׁע m. (with suff. יִשְׁעִי, יִשְׁעֲךָ), deliverance, freedom, safety, salvation.

יֵשַׁע, וַיֵּשַׁע Kal fut. apoc., from שׁעה.

יֵשַׁע Hiph. fut. apoc. יֹשַׁעֲכֶם fut. with suff., from יָשַׁע.

יֶשַׁעְי p. n. of a man.

יְשַׁעְיָהוּ p. n., *Isaiah* the prophet; LXX. Ἡσαΐας; Vulg. Isaias.

יְשַׁעְיָה p. n. of a man.

יֵשׁוּעַ (same as יְהוֹשֻׁעַ, Ἰησοῦς), p. n. of a man.

יְשׁוּעָה f., freedom, safety, salvation.

מוֹשָׁעוֹת f. pl., great salvation, Ps. 68:21.

יָשְׁפֵה, יָשְׁפֶה the jasper, a variegated gem.

יִשְׁפָּה p.n. of a man.

יִשְׁפָּן p. n. of a man.

יָשַׁר (fut. יִישַׁר, יִישָׁר).—I. proceed, go right, i. e. directly onwards; יָשַׁר בַּדֶּרֶךְ he went straight on his way. —II. with בְּעֵינֵי, בְּ he was right, upright, good. Pi. יִשַּׁר make right, direct. Pu. part. made direct, plain, laid smooth, 1 Ki. 6:35. Hiph. made direct, straight forward, Pro. 4:25.; (imp. הַיַּשֵּׁר make direct, Ps. 5:9.

יָשָׁר m., יְשָׁרָה f., right, upright, righteous, true; יָשָׁר s., the book of right, i. e. right things, Deu. 6:18.

יָשָׁר p. n. of a man.

יֹשֶׁר m., *rectitude, integrity.*

יִשְׁרָה f., *the same.*

יִשְׁרָאֵלָה p.n. of a man.

יְשֻׁרוּן m., *a periphrastic title of Israel, applied to the whole people generally, lit. entirely righteous.*

יִשַּׁרְנָה 1 Sa. 6:12, for תִּשַּׁרְנָה Kal fut. f. pl.3.pers., from יָשַׁר.

מִישׁוֹר m.—I. *a plain.*—II. *truth, righteousness;* adv. *righteously, truly.*

מֵישָׁרִים, מֵשָׁרִים m. pl.—I. *true men.* —II. *truth, righteousness.*—III. בְּמֵישָׁרִים, לְמֵישָׁרִים *truly, righteously.*

יָשֵׁשׁ m., 2 Chron.36:17, *aged, elderly person.*

יָשִׁישׁ m., *the same.*

יִשִּׁישַׁי p.n. of a man.

וַיִּשְׁתַּחוּ Hith. fut. apoc. sing. for יִשְׁתַּחֲוֶה; see שׁחה.

יִשְׁתָּיוּן Kal fut. pl. with נ parag., from שׁתה.

יִשְׁתַּקְשְׁקוּן Hith. fut. pl., from שׁקק.

יָת Ch., same as Heb. אֵת.

יֵתֵא, וַיֵּתֵא Kal fut. apoc. for יֶאֱתֶה; see אתה.

יִתְאָו Hith. fut. apoc., from אוה.

יְתֵב Ch., same as יָשַׁב *sit.* Aph. *reside,* Ezr. 4:17.

וַיִּתְגַּל, יִתְגַּל Hith. fut. apoc., from גלה.

יָתַד root not used; (Arab. *pin, nail*).

יָתֵד, const. יְתַד f. (pl. יְתֵדֹת).—I. *pin, peg.*—II. *tent-pin;* hence *wise* (i. e. firmly fixed) *rulers,* Isa. 22: 23, 25.—III. *dibble, to bore holes in the earth,* Deu. 23:14.

וַיִּתְוּ, יָתְוּ Pi. fut. apoc., from תוה.

יִתּוֹכָח Hith. fut., from יכח.

יָתַר *abundance;* see תגר.

יִתְּזִין Ch. Ithp. fut., from זון.

יָתַח root not used; (Arab. *smote with a club*).

תּוֹתָח m., *club;* LXX. σφύρα, Job 41:21.

יִתְכַּס Hith. fut. apoc., from כסה.

יִתְלָה p.n. of a city of the Danites.

יָתַם root not used; (Arab. *was an orphan*).

יָתוֹם m., *orphan.*

יִתַּם, יִתֹּמוּ, in pause יִתֹּמוּ Kal fut., from תמם.

יִתַּמּוּ Niph. fut. pl., from תמם.

יִתְמָה p.n. of a man.

יָתַן root not used; (Arab. *was enduring*).

אֵיתָן, אֵתָן m.—I. *mighty, irresistible, violent;* יֶרַח הָאֵיתָנִים *the month of the powerful,* i. e. Tisri, 1 Ki. 8:2.—II. *might, irresistibleness.*— III. p.n., perhaps the author of Ps. 89.

יַתְנִיאֵל p.n. of a man.

יִתְנָן p.n. of a city in the tribe of Judah.

יָתַר, part. יוֹתֵר *exceeding, redundant.* Hiph. הוֹתִיר I. *cause to remain, leave.*—II. *abound, be wealthy.* Niph. נוֹתַר *be left, remain;* part. m. נוֹתָר, f. נוֹתֶרֶת *that which is left.*

יֶתֶר m.—I. *excellence, abundance,* עַל־יֶתֶר *unto abundance,* Ps. 31: 24; adv. *abundantly, exceedingly.* — II. *residue, the rest of.* — III. *string* or *cord.*—IV. p.n. of a man: *patron.* יִתְרִי.

יִתְרָה f., *abundance, excess.*

יֶתֶר, יוֹתַר (part. Kal).—I. abundance, profit.—II. adv., more, further, moreover, excessively.

יוֹתֶרֶת f.—I. exceeding, redundant.—II. lobe, i.e. excess of the liver.

יַתִּיר m. Ch.—I. excellent, extraordinary; יַתִּירָה adv., very, exceedingly.—II. Heb. p. n., a town in the tribe of Judah.

יִתְרוֹ p. n., the father-in-law of Moses, who was also called יֶתֶר and חוֹבָב

יִתְרוֹן m., gain, profit, good.

יִתְרְעָם p. n. of a man.

מוֹתַר m.—I. increase.—II. excellence, Ecc. 3:19.

מֵיתָר m.—I. bow-string, Ps. 21:13.—II. tent-cord.

יִתְשָׁם Ch. Ithp. fut., from שׁוּם.

יְתֵת p. n. of a prince of Edom.

כ

כְּ, כָּ pa. pref. signifying comparison, resemblance.—I. as, as if, like; כְּ...כְּ, וּכְ...כֵּן as...so; with suff. כָּהֶם, כָּכֶם; see כְּמוֹ.—II. according to (κατά).—III. nearly, almost; כַּיּוֹם הַזֶּה as on this day; כַּחֲצֹת הַלַּיְלָה about midnight.—IV. with inf. (sometimes with part.) when, ὡς.

כָּאַב (fut. יִכְאַב) be pained. Hiph. I. cause pain, Eze. 13:22.—II. mar, ruin, 2 Ki. 3:19.

כְּאֵב m., pain.

מַכְאוֹב m. (pl. ־ים, ־וֹת).—I. pain.—II. cause of pain.—III. sorrow.

כָּאָה. Niph. pained, enfeebled, Dan. 11:30. Hiph. pain, enfeeble the heart, Eze. 13:22.

כֵּאֶה m., afflicted, helpless, Ps. 10:10

כָּאֹר Am. 8:8, for כַּיְאֹר.

כָּאֲרִי Ps. 22:17; see כּוּר.

כָּבֵד and כָּבַד (fut. יִכְבַּד)—I. be heavy, grievous.—II. be grave, respectable, honorable, with עַל, אֶל Niph. became honorable, glorious; part. נִכְבָּדִים nobles, נִכְבָּדוֹת made glorious, with בְּ. Pi. כִּבֵּד I. make heavy, sullen, unrelenting.—II. make honourable, honour, with לְ, לְשֵׁם Pu. כֻּבַּד was honoured. Hiph. I. made heavy, grievous, sullen.—II. made honorable, glorious.—Hith. מִתְכַּבֵּד fancying himself honorable, Pro. 12:9.

כָּבֵד const. כְּבַד, כָּבֵד m.—I. heavy.—II. rich.—III. numerous.—IV. stupid, sullen.—V. grievous.—VI. dense.—VII. slow of utterance.—VIII. hard to be understood.—IX. the liver.

כָּבוֹד m., lit. heaviness: hence,—I. glory, splendour, majesty.—II. abundance, wealth.—III. multitude.—IV. mind, soul.—V. honour, כְּבוֹד יְהוָֹה the glory of God, LXX. δόξα Κυρίου.

כָּבֹד, f. כְּבוּדָה glorious, precious.

כֹּבֶד m.—I. weight.—II. abundance.

כְּבֵדוּת f., heavily, Ex. 14:25.

כָּבָה was extinguished. Pi. extinguished.

כָּבוּל p. n.—I. a district of Galilee.—II. a town in the tribe of Asher

כַּבּוֹן p. n., a town in the tribe of Judah.

כַּבִּיר, כְּבִיר; see כבר.

כָּבַל root not used; (Arab. iron fetter)

כֶּבֶל m., *footlock of iron.*

כָּבַס part. כּוֹבֵס *fuller.* Pi. כִּבֵּס, כִּבֵּם *wash, cleanse* clothes and the like, not the body. Pu. כֻּבַּם *was washed.* Hothp. inf. הֻכַּבֵּם *to be washed,* Lev. 13:55, 56.

כָּבַע root not used; see נבע, קבע. כּוֹבַע, כּוֹבַע m., *helmet.*

כָּבַר Hiph. *multiplied,* Job 35:16; part. *abundance,* Job 36:31.

כְּבָר p. n. of a river in Mesopotamia, the *Chaboras.*

כְּבָר adv., *already, now.*

כַּבִּיר m., *mighty, powerful, great.*

כְּבִיר m., *cushion* or *pillow* cased with goat skin, 1 Sa. 19:13, 16.

כְּבָרָה f., *sieve,* Am. 9:9.

כִּבְרָה f., an unknown measure of length; LXX. ἱππόδρομος.

מַכְבֵּר m., *brazen lattice-work.*

מַכְבֵּר m., *carpet, coarse cloth,* 2 Ki. 8:15.

כָּבַשׁ root not used; same as כָּבַשׁ *subdue.*

כֶּבֶשׂ m., *a lamb.*

כַּבְשָׂה, כִּבְשָׂה f. (pl. כְּבָשֹׂת const. כִּבְשֹׂת) *a she-lamb.*

כָּבַשׁ I. *trample, tread under foot;* metaph. *shall trample on sling stones,* i.e. not be harmed by them, Zec. 9:15.—II. *subdue, humble.*—III. *force,* Est. 7:8. Niph. *be subdued, humbled.* Pi. *subdued,* 2 Sa. 8:11.

כֶּבֶשׁ m., *footstool,* 2 Chron. 9:18.

כִּבְשָׁן m., *smelting furnace.*

כַּד *jar;* see כדר.

כָּדָב m., כִּדְבָה f. Ch., *lying, false,* Dan. 2:9.

כָּדַד root not used; (perhaps from Arab. *straitness*).

כַּד f. (with suff. כַּדֵּךְ; pl. m. כַּדִּים) *earthen jar, water vessel.*

כִּידוֹד m., *spark of fire,* Job 41:11.

כַּדְכֹּד m., *a precious stone,* perhaps the *ruby.*

כְּדִי, see דַּי; כְּדִי, see דִּי; כִּדְנָה, see דֵּן.

כִּידוֹר m., *attack, onset,* Job 15:24.

כְּדָרְלָעֹמֶר p. n. of a king of Elam.

כֹּה pa.— I. *so, thus, in this form, manner, &c.;* כֹּה...בְּכֹה *on this manner and on that manner,* 1 Ki. 22:20.—II. *here, hither;* כֹּה...וְכֹה *hither and thither,* Ex. 2:12; עַד כֹּה *yonder,* Gen. 22:5.—III. *now;* עַד כֹּה *until now,* Ex. 7:16; עַד כֹּה וְעַד כֹּה *so and so long,* i.e. a very short time, 1 Ki. 18:45.

כָּה Ch., עַד כָּה *thus far,* Dan. 7:28.

כָּהָה (fut. יִכְהָה; apoc. וַתֵּכַהּ).— I. *become weak, languid* (of the eyes).—II. of the mind or person, Isa. 42:4. Pi. כֵּהָה, כִּהָה *made weak, disheartened.*

כֵּהֶה f. כֵּהָה—I. *expiring, fading* (of a lamp), Isa. 42:3.—II. of the eyes.— III. of a disease or eruption.— IV. כֵּהָה אֵין *not weak,* i.e. vigorous, Nah. 3:19.

כֵּהוֹת Pi. inf., from כהה.

כְּהַל Ch., *able, adequate.*

כָּהַן Pi. כִּהֵן *act, officiate as priest.*

כֹּהֵן m. (pl. כֹּהֲנִי, כֹּהֲנִים) *priest;* with הַגָּדוֹל or הָרֹאשׁ or הַמָּשִׁיחַ *the high priest.*

כָּהֵן m. Ch., *priest.*

כְּהֻנָּה f., priesthood, office of the priest.

כּוּב p.n., a country in the south, Eze. 30:5.

כּוֹבַע helmet; see כבע.

כָּוָה Niph. תִּכְוָה was, became burnt.

כַּו m. Ch., pl. כַּוִּין windows, casements, Dan. 6:11.

כְּוִיָּה f., burning, branding, Ex. 21:25.

כִּי m. (for כְּוִי) branding, Isa. 3:24.

כִּי pa.; see further.

מִכְוָה f., inflamed part (of body), Lev. 13:24, 25, 28.

כּוּחַ root not used; (Arab. conquer in battle).

כֹּחַ, כּוֹחַ m.—I. strength, vigour, power, ability.—II. wealth; כֹּחַ הָאָרֶץ fruit of the earth, Gen. 4:12.—III. a kind of lizard (from its strength), Lev. 11:30.

כּוֹכָב m., star, constellation.

כּוּל measured, Isa. 40:12. Hiph. הֵכִיל I. contain.—II. sustain. Pil. כִּלְכֵּל I. contain (as a vessel).—II. sustain (with food).—III. bear (with firmness). Pu. כָּלְכַּל were sustained.

כִּימָה the constellation of the pleiades.

כּוּמָז bracelet of gold beads.

כּוּן fashioned, set in order, Job 31:15. Pil. כּוֹנֵן dispose, prepare, fix, establish, with עַל, עַד, בְּ, אֶת. Pul. כּוֹנָן established, confirmed. Hiph. הֵכִין dispose, prepare, fix, establish. Hoph. הוּכַן was disposed, prepared. Niph. be, become disposed, set in order, fixed, established (of person or thing); part. נָכוֹן (f. נְכֹנָה) firm, established, sure;

שַׁחַר נָכוֹן the true dawn, as opposed to the false, or premature twilight in the East, Hos. 6:3; אֶל־נָכוֹן certainly, for certain. Hith. הִתְכּוֹנֵן same as Niph.

כֵּן adj.—I. substantial, true; pl. כֵּנִים.—II. part. really, truly: whence, אַחֲרֵי־כֵן, אַחַר כֵּן afterwards; בְּכֵן thus; לָכֵן therefore; עַל־כֵּן because; לָכֵן אֲשֶׁר because; עַד־כֵּן hitherto; see also in כנן.

כֵּן Ch., thus.

אָכֵן pa. (for הָכֵן inf. abs. Hiph. confirmed), surely, certainly, truly.

כּוּן p.n., a Phenician city, 1 Chron. 18:8, called in 2 Sa. 8:8, בֵּרֹתַי Berytus.

כַּוָּן m., small round cake, Jer. 7:18; 44:19.

כִּיּוּן p.n. of an idol, Am. 5:26, called Ρεμφαν, Acts 7:43, the planet Saturn.

יָכִין I. p. n. of a son of Simeon; patron. יָכִינִי.—II. one of the columns in the temple of Solomon.

מָכוֹן m.—I. place, establishment.—II. foundation.

מְכוֹנָה f.—I. basis.—II. p. n. of a town in the tribe of Judah.

מְכוּנָה f., place, Zec. 5:11.

תְּכוּנָה f.—I. presence.—II. arrangement.—III. furniture, stores.

כּוֹס f.—I. drinking cup; pl. כֹּסוֹת.—II. rough-billed pelican, Lev. 11: 17; Deu. 14:16; Ps. 102:7.

כּוּר root not used; (Arab. digging, piercing); כָּאֲרִי piercing, Ps 22:17.

כָּר m., *camel's pack-saddle*, Gen. 31: 34 ; see also כרר.

כָּרִי an officer of a certain rank, 2 Ki. 11:4,19; כָּרְתִי Kri, 2 Sa. 20:23.

כּוּר m., *furnace for melting metals*.

כּוּר עָשָׁן (*smoking furnace*), p. n. of a city in the tribe of Simeon.

כֹּר m., a measure of capacity, containing 10 baths.

כִּיּוֹר m. (pl. כִּיֹּרוֹת,כִּיֹּרִים).—I. *a pot* or *brazier* for fire, Zec. 12:6.— II. *laver of brass.*—III. *chafing dish*, 1 Sa. 2:14. — IV. *pulpit*, 2 Chron. 6:13.

כִּירַיִם m. dual, *pots or jars*, Lev. 11:35; LXX. χυτρόποδες.

כִּכָּר f. (for כִּרְכָּר).—I. *tract of country*. — II. כִּכַּר לֶחֶם *cake of bread*; pl. m. כִּכָּרוֹת *talent* (of gold or silver); dual כִּכָּרַיִם; const. כִּכְּרַיִם; pl. f. כִּכְּרֵי, כִּכָּרִים.

כִּכָּר f. Ch., pl. כִּכְּרִין the same.

מְכוֹרָה, מְכֻרָה f., *place of origin, birth*, lit. *digging*; see Isa. 51:1.

מְכֵרָה f., *sword*, Gen. 49:5.

כּוּשׁ p. n.—I. *Ethiopia.*—II. name of a man, Ps. 7:1.

כּוּשִׁי m. (pl. כּוּשִׁיִּים; f. כּוּשִׁית).—I. *an Ethiopian.* — II. p. n. of a man.

כּוּשָׁן f., Hab. 3:7, same as כּוּשׁ *Ethiopia*.

כּוּשַׁן רִשְׁעָתַיִם p. n. of a king of Mesopotamia.

כּוּשָׁרָה f., *wealth*; see כשׁר.

כּוּת, כּוּתָה p. n. of a region whence the kingdom of Israel was colonised after its depopulation.

כָּזַב, part. כֹּזֵב *deficient, falling short*, Ps. 116:11. Pi. כִּזֵּב.—I. *lie, deceive*.

—II. *fail*, with לְ or בְּ. Hiph. *convict of falsehood*, Job 24:25. Niph. *was fallacious, false.*

כָּזָב m., *falling short of truth, lying, falsehood.*

כֹּזְבָא p. n., same as כְּזִיב.

כָּזְבִּי p. n. of a Midianitish woman.

כְּזִיב p. n. of a town in the tribe of Judah.

אַכְזָב m., *deficient, deception, unstable*

אַכְזִיב p. n.—I. a town in the tribe of Judah.—II. a town in the tribe of Asher, on the Mediterranean. Ἔκδιππα.

כָּזַר root not used; (Arab. *muddy, turbid*).

אַכְזָר m., *untractable, cruel, fierce.*

אַכְזָרִי *very cruel.*

אַכְזְרִיּוּת f., *great cruelty*, Pro. 27:4 כֹּחַ *strength*; see כּוּחַ.

כָּחַד. Pi. כִּחֵד *keep back, conceal*, with מִן or לְ. Niph. I. *was concealed.*—II. *made useless, destroyed*. Hiph. I. *hold back.*—II. *bring to nought.*

כָּחַל *black* (the eyes) *with antimony*, Eze. 23:40.

כָּחַשׁ *fail, be deficient.* Pi. כִּחֵשׁ I. *withhold.* — II. *fail, deceive, deny, lie*, with בְּ and לְ. Niph. and Hith. *were, became liars*, with לְ.

כַּחַשׁ m.—I. *deficiency.*—II. *failure, falsehood.*

כֶּחָשׁ m., *lying*, Isa. 30:9.

כִּי pa.—I. *if, for*, at the beginning of a speech.—II. *because, therefore*, in the second member of a sentence: also,— III. *surely, without doubt*.

It connects the hypothesis and condition of an entire sentence, and may be translated by almost any particle that is so used; הֲכִי *whether? is not?* יַעַן כִּי עַל כִּי *because;* עַד כִּי *until;* כִּי עַל־כֵּן *therefore;* see also כֹּה.

כִּי אִם I. *that.*—II. *if not,* with oaths.—III. *except,* after a negative.—IV. *but, only.*

כִּיד m., *ruin, destruction,* Job 21:20.

כִּידֹן m.—I. *spear.*—II. גֶּרֶן כִּידֹן (*the plain of spears*), p. n. of a district; see נָכֹן.

כִּידֹד *sparks;* see כדד.

כִּידֹר *attack;* see כדר.

כִּיּוּן *an idol;* see כּוּן.

כִּיֹּר *pot;* see כּוּר.

כְּלִי, כֵּילַי *vessel;* see נבל.

כְּלַפּוֹת *axes;* see כלף.

כִּימָה *Pleiades;* see כּוּם.

כִּים *bag;* see נכם.

כִּיר *pot;* see כּוּר.

כִּיתְרוֹן Syr. for כִּיתְרוֹן.

כָּכָה *same as* כֹּה *thus;* אֵיכָכָה *how?* see אֵיךְ in אֵי.

כִּכָּר; see כּוּר.

כָּל־ כָּל *all;* see כלל.

כָּלָא *restrain, confine, withhold* (part. כָּלוּא, כָּלֵא *shut up*), with מִן; fut. יִכְלָה. Niph. *restrained, withholden.*

כֶּלֶא m. (with suff. כִּלְאוֹ), *prison;* בֵּית הַכֶּלֶא, בֵּית כֶּלֶא *the same;* pl. כְּלָאִים.

כֶּלֶא, כְּלֻא f., *all that,* from כֹּל; see כלל.

כִּלְאַיִם dual, *of two sorts or kinds,* ἑτερογενῆ.

כֶּלֶא (כְּלִיא) m., *prison.*

מִכְלָה f. (pl. מִכְלָאוֹת), *fold* or *pen for flocks.*

כִּלְאָב p. n. of a son of David.

כְּלוּב m.—I. *fruit-basket,* Am. 8:1,2.—II. *bird-cage,* Jer. 5:27.—III. p. n. of a man.

כֶּלֶב m.—I. *a dog.*—II. *bad, cruel man.*

כָּלֵב p. n. of a man, *Caleb;* patron. כָּלִבִּי.

כָּלָה (fut. תִּכְלֶה, יִכְלֶה; apoc. יֵכֶל (וַתֵּכֶל).—I. *was completed, finished*—II. *was wasted, ruined, decayed.* Pi. כִּלָּה I. *complete, determine.*—II. *waste, ruin, destroy,* with לְ. Pu. כֻּלָּה (fut. יְכֻלֶּה), *were completed.*

כָּלָה, f. כָּלָה *consuming,* Deu. 28:32.

כָּלָה f., *completion, destruction;* עָשָׂה כָּלָה *hath done even to destruction, altogether,* with בְּ, אֶת; adv. כָּלָה, לְכָלָה *completely, entirely.*

כְּלִי m. (with pause כֶּלִי; pl. כֵּלִים, כְּלִי).—I. *vessel.*—II. *boat,* Isa. 18:2.—III. *musical instrument.*—IV. *arms, weapon.*—V. *implement of husbandry.*—VI. *clothing.*

כְּלָיוֹת const., כִּלְיוֹת f. pl., *the reins, kidneys,* metaph. as the seat of sense, the feeling.

כִּלָּיוֹן const., כִּלְיוֹן m.—I. *consumption,* Isa. 10:22.—II. *wasting of the eyes,* Deu. 28:65.

כִּלְיוֹן p. n. of a man.

מִכְלוֹת f. pl., with זָהָב, 2 Chron. 4:21. *pure gold.*

תִּכְלָה f., *perfection;* LXX. συντέλεια.

תַּכְלִית f.—I. *extremity,* Neh. 3:21.—II. *boundary.* — III. *completeness, perfection.*

בְּלוּלוֹת, בַּלָּה; see בלל.

בִּלְגַּי p.n. of a man.

בִּלְהָם for בַּלָּם, from בַּל; see בלל.

בִּלְהָנָה for בַּלָּנָה, from בַּל; see בלל.

בְּלוּ 1 Sa. 6:10, Kal pret. pl., from בלא.

כֶּלַח m.—I. wealth.—II. insolence, Job 30:2.

כֶּלַח p.n. of a city, Gen. 10:11.

כִּלְיוֹן, כִּלְיוֹת, כְּלִי; see כלה.

כַּלְכֹּל p.n. of a man.

כָּלַל perfected, Eze. 27:4, 11.

כְּלַל Ch., finished, completed; Shaph. שַׁכְלֵל the same; passive אִשְׁתַּכְלַל was completed.

כָּלִיל m.—I. whole, entire; adv. wholly, entirely; כְּלִיל הָעִיר the whole city.—II. whole burnt-offering, i.e. offering entirely consumed, Deu. 33:10; Ps. 51:21.

כַּלָּה f.—I. daughter-in-law.—II. spouse.

כְּלוּלוֹת f. pl., espousals, Jer. 2:2.

כֹּל (בּוֹל Jer. 33:8)—כָּל.—I. the whole, all.—II. complete, entire.—III. all, every.—IV. many, most of; לֹא כֹל none: with suff. כֻּלָּנוּ all we; כֻּלְּכֶם all ye; כֻּלָּם all they; כֻּלְּהֶנָה, כֻּלָּנָה all they, f.; כֻּלֹּה all of it, m.; כֻּלָּהּ the same, f.; with adv. כָּל־עוֹד as long as, כָּל־עֻמַּת שֶׁ just as, Ecc. 5:15.

כֹּל, כָּל Ch., the same; כֹּלָּא adv., altogether, entirely.

מִכְלָל m., perfection, Ps. 50:2.

מִכְלוֹל m., the same (of clothing), Eze. 23:12, &c.

מִכְלָלִים m. pl., splendid garments, Eze. 27:24.

כָּלַם. Hiph. הִכְלִים, הַכְלִים put to

shame, make ashamed, injure. Hoph. was ashamed, confounded. Niph. was ashamed, confounded.

כְּלִמָּה f., shame, ignominy.

כְּלִמּוּת state of shame, Jer. 23:40.

כִּלְמָד p.n. of a region or city.

כַּלְנוֹ, כַּלְנֶה, כַּלְנֵה p.n. of a city on the river Tigris (Ctesiphon?).

כֶּלֶף root not used; (Arab. drove).

כֵּלַפּוֹת f. pl., axes or hammer, Ps. 74:6; LXX. λαξευτήρια.

כִּלַּתּוּ Pi. pret. 3. pers. f. with suff., from כלה.

כִּלְתַנִי 1 Sa. 25:33, Kal pret. 2. pers. f with suff., from כלא.

כָּמַהּ desired intensely even to fainting.

כִּמְהָם p.n. of a man.

מָה; see כַּמָּה, כַּמֶּה, כָּמֶה.

כְּמוֹ, כְּמוֹ pa., same as כְּ thus, as, whether; with suff. כָּמֹנִי as I am, כָּמֹךָ, כָּמֹכָה as thou art; כָּמֹהוּ as he is; כָּמֹהָ as she is; כָּמֹנוּ as we are, sometimes for כָּכֶם, כָּמֹהֶם, כָּמֹכֶם כָּהֶם as ye, they, are; כָּמוֹ...כְּמוֹ as...so.

כְּמוֹשׁ p.n., an idol of the children of Moab and Ammon; עַם כְּמוֹשׁ the Moabites.

כַּמֹּן m., the herb cummin, Isa. 28:25, 27.

מִכְמַנִּים m. pl., treasures, Dan. 11:43.

כָּמַס laid, treasured, up, Deu. 32:34.

כָּמַר. Niph. נִכְמַר I. was affected (warmed with intense feeling, love, compassion).—II. was black with burning, Lam. 5:10.

כֹּמֶר m., pl. כְּמָרִים idolatrous priests. כְּמָרִיר blackest, gloomiest thing, Job 3:5.

מַכְמֹר, מִכְמָר m., pl. מַכְמֹרִים *net used by fishermen.*

מִכְמֶרֶת,מִכְמֹרֶת f., *net used by fisher-men.*

כֵּן; see כּוּן and כָּנַן.

כָּנָה Kal not used; (Syr. *named*). Pi. כִּנָּה I. *call by name.*—II. *flatter.*

כָּנָת m. (man of the same name), *companion, associate;* pl. כְּנָוֹת (σύνδουλοι).

כְּנָת Ch., the same; pl. כְּנָוָן; with suff. כְּנָוָתְהוֹן, כְּנָוָתֵהּ.

כַּנֶּה; see כנן.

כַּבַּר p. n. of a city (perhaps for כַּלְנֶה).

כִּנּוֹר m. (with suff. כִּנֹּרִי; pl. כִּנֹּרִים, כִּנֹּרוֹת), *harp* (κινύρα).

כְּנָוֹת, כְּנָן from כָּנָת; see כנה.

כָּנְיָהוּ p. n. of a king of Judah; same as יְהוֹיָכִין.

כְּהַנְלֹתְךָ Hiph. inf. with pref. and suff. for כְּהַנְלוֹתְךָ; see נלה.

כִּנָּם; see כנן.

כְּנֵאמָא Ch., "as it is said" (for Lee).

כַּנָּה f., *stock, root,* Ps. 80:16.

כְּנַנִי p. n. of a man.

כְּנַנְיָה, כְּנַנְיָהוּ p.n. of a man.

כְּנַנְיָהוּ p. n. of a man.

כֵּן m. (with suff. כַּנֶּךָ, כַּנּוֹ.—I. *place, station.*—II. *base, foot of the laver;* see also כּוּן.

כֵּן m., *lice;* pl. כִּנִּים LXX. σκνίφες.

כִּנָּם for כִּנָּם same as כִּנִּים; see pre-ceding word, Ex. 8:12.

כָּנַס *collect, gather together.* Pi. like Kal. Hith. *being collecting, com-prehending,* Isa. 28:20.

מִכְנָס m., dual const. מִכְנְסֵי *drawers, breeches of linen* (for the priests).

כָּנַע. Hiph. הִכְנִיעַ *humble, debase, bring down.* Niph. נִכְנַע *was hum-bled, debased.*

כְּנָעָה f., *package, bale of merchan-dise,* Jer. 10:17.

כְּנַעַן I. p. n. of a son of Ham.—II. of the land inhabited by his pos-terity.—III. m., *a merchant.*

כְּנַעֲנִי (f. כְּנַעֲנִית; pl. כְּנַעֲנִים.)—I. *a Canaanite.*—II. *a merchant.*

כְּנַעֲנָה p. n. of a man.

כְּנַעֲנָיָה pl. with suff., from כְּנַעַן.

כָּנַף root not used; (Arab. *put away*). Niph. יִכָּנֵף *put away, remove,* Isa. 30:20.

כָּנָף f. (dual כְּנָפַיִם, כְּנָפֵי f.; pl. const. כַּנְפוֹת m. and f.).—I. *wing* (of a bird, &c.).—II. *wing* (of an army). —III. *skirt* (of a garment).—IV. *extreme part* (of the earth or land). —V. by meton. *person protected,* i. e. *wife* &c.

כִּנְּרֹת, כִּנְרוֹת, כִּנְרֶת p. n., *a city in the tribe of Naphtali, near the sea of Galilee* (Γεννησαρέτ); יָם כִּנֶּרֶת *the sea of Galilee.*

כְּנַשׁ Ch., *collect,* Dan. 3:2. Hith. *being assembled,* Dan. 3:3, 27.

כַּסְדָּי Ch., same as כַּשְׂדַּי *a Chaldean.*

כָּסָה, part. כֹּסֶה *covering, concealing,* Pro. 12:16, 23; כָּסוּי *covered,* Nu. 4:6, 14. Niph. נִכְסָה *being co-vered, concealed.* Pi. כִּסָּה *cover, conceal,* with אֶל, בְּ, לְ, עַל. Pu. כֻּסָּה *covered, was co-vered,* with בְּ. Hith. same as Niph. Pu. with בְּ.

כֵּס m., כֵּס יָהּ ב' the throne of Jehovah, Ex. 17:16.

בָּסֶה, כֶּסֶה m., the new moon, Ps. 81:4; Pro. 7:20.

כִּסֵּא, כִּסֶּה m. (with suff. כִּסְאִי; pl. כִּסְאוֹת), regal chair, throne.

כְּסוּת f.—I. covering.—II. clothing.

סוּת f., a false reading for כְּסוּת garments, Gen. 49:11.

כְּסָתוֹת f. pl., Eze. 13:18, 20, LXX. προσκεφάλαια, cushions, probably ornaments.

מִכְסֶה m., covering.

מְכַסֶּה m., covering, Isa. 14:11.

כָּסַח, part. כָּסוּחַ cut off.

כְּסוּחָה like filth, Isa. 5:25; see סוּח.

כָּסַל was a fool; fut. יִכְסְלוּ Jer. 10:8.

כְּסִיל m.—I. a fool.—II. the constellation Orion.—III. p. n. of a city in the tribe of Judah.

כְּסִילוּת f., foolish woman, Pro. 9:13.

כֶּסֶל m.—I. the loins.—II. the viscera; pl. כְּסָלִים.—III. expectation, confidence.—IV. foolishness.

כִּסְלָה f.—I. confidence.—II. folly.

כִּסְלֵו m., the ninth month of the Hebrew year, answering to our November and December.

כִּסְלוֹן p. n. of a town on the borders of the tribe of Judah.

כִּסְלוֹן p. n. of a man.

כִּסְלוֹת p. n. of a town in the tribe of Issachar.

כִּסְלוֹת־תָּבוֹר p. n. of a town at the foot of Mount Tabor.

כַּסְלֻחִים m. pl., p. n. a people so called.

כָּסַם adorn, Eze. 44:20.

כֻּסֶּמֶת f., a kind of corn, spelt, ζέα; pl. כֻּסְּמִים.

כָּסַם apportion, divide out, Ex. 12:4

מֶכֶס m., fractional part, number.

מִכְסָה f., number.

כָּסַף desired intensely (lit. grew pale with desire), with לְ. Niph. become desirous, earnestly longing for, with לְ.

כֶּסֶף m. (with suff. כַּסְפִּי; pl. כְּסָפִים).—I. silver.—II. money; with numerals, the shekel of silver; אֶלֶף כ' 1,000 shekels.

כְּסַף m. Ch., silver.

כַּסְפִּיָא p. n. of a country.

כְּסָתוֹת ornaments; see כסה.

כִּפַּתְנִי Pi. pret. 3 pers. f. with suff., from כסה.

כְּעַן adv. Ch.—I. so, therefore.—II. but.—III. now; כְּעֶנֶת so on; see עתת.

כָּעַס (fut. יִכְעַס).—I. was angry.—II irritated. Pi. כָּעַס irritate. Hiph הִכְעִיס.—I. was angry.—II. made angry, irritated.

כַּעַס m.—I. vexation, sadness.—II. anger; pl. כְּעָסִים excitements to anger.

כַּעַשׂ m., the same, in Job only.

כַּף f., כֵּפָה, כַּפּוֹת; see כפף.

כֵּף rock, Job 30:6; Jer. 4:29.

כָּפָה avert, appease, Pro. 21:14; see כבה.

כָּפִיר, כְּפִירָה, כְּפִיר see כפר.

כָּפַל doubled; part. כָּפוּל. Niph. be repeated, Eze. 21:19.

כֶּפֶל m., doubling, twofold; dual כִּפְלַיִם Job 11:6; Isa. 40:2.

כָּפַן became languid, Eze. 17:7.

כָּפָן m., hunger, Job 5:22; 30:3.

כָּפַס (Syr. *tie, join*).

כְּפִיס m., *tie-beam*; " *tenon* " (Lee); LXX. κάνθαρος.

כָּפַף *bend, bow down*, with distress. Niph. *bow myself down*, with לְ before, Mic. 6:6.

כַּף f.—I. *palm of the hand.*—II. *hand* (with suff. כַּפִּי; dual כַּפַּיִם *both hands*; pl. כַּפּוֹת).—III. *sole of the foot.*—IV. *foot of a beast.*—V. *bason or phial.*—VI. *receptacle for the stone in a sling*; כַּף־הַקֶּלַע *cup of the sling*, 1 Sa. 25:29.—VII. *bent palm branches*; כַּפּוֹת תְּמָרִים *bent palm branches*, Lev. 23:40.—VIII. כַּף־הַיָּרֵךְ *cup of the thigh joint*, Gen. 32:26, &c.

כִּפָּה f., *curved branch, branch.*

כָּפַר.—I. generally *cover.*—II. specially, *pitch, smear with pitch*, Gen. 6:14, with בְּ. Pi. כִּפֶּר (fut. יְכַפֵּר) I. *cover, expiate for sin*, used of the sinner and the sin.—II. *appease anger.*—III. *avert calamity*, with אֶת, בְּעַד, לְ, עַל. Pu. כֻּפַּר—I. *was expiated.*—II. *was abolished.* Hith. *was expiated*; נִתְכַּפֶּר for נִכַּפֵּר Deu. 21:8.

כְּפוֹר m.—I. *vessel, covered cup.*—II. *hoar frost*, Ex. 16:14; Ps. 147:16.

כְּפִיר m.—I. *a young lion.*—II. metaph. *fierce, bold man.*—III. *village*, Neh. 6:2.

כָּפָר m., *village.*

כְּפִירָה p. n. of a city of the Hivites.

כְּפַר הָעַמֹּנִי p. n., a town in the tribe of Benjamin.

כֹּפֶר m.—I. *pitch*, Gen. 6:14.—II. *a village*, 1 Sa. 6:18.—III. *expiation*,

lit. *covering for sin*, λύτρον.—IV *the cypress tree*, Cant. 1:14

כְּפֻרִים m. pl., *expiation.*

כַּפֹּרֶת f., *the covering of the ark; mercy-seat*; בֵּית הַכַּפֹּרֶת *the holy of holies.*

כָּפַשׁ Hiph. *overwhelmed, covered* Lam. 3:16.

כְּפַת Ch., *bound, tied.*

כַּפְתּוֹר p. n., a country of the Philistines; כַּפְתֹּרִים its inhabitants, Gen. 10:14.

כַּפְתֹּרִים m. pl.—I. *twisted capitals* or *columns.*—II. *ornamented bowls* of the golden candlestick, Ex. 25:36.

כַּר, see כּוּר; כֹּר, see כּוּר and כֹּר.

כְּרָה or כְּרָא Ch. Ithp. *was pained, afflicted.*

כִּרְבֵּל. Pu. part. מְכֻרְבָּל *equipped clothed*, 1 Chron. 15:27.

כַּרְבְּלָא Ch., *a cloak*, Dan. 3:21.

כָּרָה *dig* (as a well, pit); with אָזְנַיִם *mine ears hast thou digged*, opened, Ps. 40:7. Niph. I. *was dug.*—II. *buy, purchase*, Deu. 2:6; Hos. 3:2.—III. *feast*, 2 Ki. 6:23.

כֵּרָה f.—I. *digging*, Zep. 2:6; pl. const. כֵּרֹת.—II. *feast*, 2 Ki. 6:23.

מִכְרֶה m., *pit*, Zep. 2:9.

כְּרוּב m., pl. כְּרֻבִים, כְּרוּבִים.—I. *cherub*; a symbolical figure over the mercy-seat; described Eze. 4:6. —II. p. n. of a man, Ezr. c. 2; Neh. c. 7.

כְּרַז Ch. Aph. *proclaim*, κηρύσσειν, Dan. 5:29.

כָּרוֹז m. Ch., *herald*, Dan. 3:4.

כְּרִי ; see בֻּר.

כְּרִיתֻת, כְּרִית ; see כרת.

כַּרְכֹּב m. (with suff. כַּרְכֻּבּוֹ) *brazier* (on the grating of the altar for containing the fire).

תַּכְרִיךְ m., *robe*, Est. 8:15.

כַּרְכְּמִישׁ p. n. of a city on the Euphrates, *Carchemish* (Κιρκήσιον).

כַּרְכֹּם m., *saffron*, Cant. 4:14.

כַּרְכַּס p. n. a Persian eunuch.

כַּרְכֻּבֹּרֹת ; see כרב.

כֶּרֶם m. (f. Isa. 27:2, 3).—I. *vineyard*. —II. *olive yard*.—III. *orchard*.

כֹּרֵם m., *vine-dresser*.

כַּרְמִי p. n. of a man.

כַּרְמֶל m. (quasi כֶּרֶם־אֵל ; with suff. כַּרְמִלּוֹ).—I. *well-cultivated plain, orchard, field*.—II. *Carmel*, a very fruitful hill south of Asher, near the Mediterranean ; כַּרְמְלִי m.; כַּרְמְלִית f., a *Carmelite*.— III. נֶרֶשׁ כַּרְמֶל and כַּרְמֶל *first fruits* (of the most fertile land), Lev. 2:14 ; 23:14.

כַּרְמִיל m., *crimson*.

כְּרָן p. n. of a man.

כָּרְסֵא m. Ch., same as כִּסֵּא *throne*.

כִּרְסֵב quadrilit. *devoured*, Ps. 80:14.

כָּרַע —I. *bent his legs* (as an animal to lie down).—II. *bowed, lay down, crouched* (with לְ or לִפְנֵי before any one).—III. *was weak*. Hiph. *cause to bow down, depress, afflict.*

כְּרָעַיִם f. dual, *both the legs* or *leg bones*.

כַּרְפַּס m., *cotton cloth, calico*, Est. 1: 6 ; (Arab. the same).

כרר Pil. כִּרְכֵּר *leap about, dance*, 2 Sa. 6:14, 16.

כַּר m. (p. כָּרִים).—I. *fatted lamb*.— II. *the pasture where lambs feed.* —III. *battering ram.*

כִּרְכָּרֹות f. pl., *dromedaries*, Isa. 66:20.

כָּרֵשׂ m., *belly*, Jer. 51:34.

כֹּרֶשׁ p. n., *Cyrus* king of Persia.

כַּרְשְׁנָא p. n., a Persian prince.

כָּרַת (imp. כְּרֹת־ ; with ה parag כָּרְתָה, כְּרָתָה ; fut. יִכְרֹת).—I. *cut off, down* ; כָּרוּת and שָׁפְכָה כָּרוּת *eunuch*.— II. with or without בְּרִית *make a covenant* (ὅρκια τέμνειν), (lit. strike a bargain), with אֵת, עִם, לְ.—III. *kill men*, Jer. 11:19. Niph. *was cut down, cut off*. Pu. כֹּרַת, כָּרַת *cut off*. Hiph. הִכְרִית *cut off, destroy*. Hoph. הָכְרַת *was cut off*, Joel 1:9.

כְּרֻתֹות f. pl., *beams* (things cut).

כְּרִית p. n. of the brook *Cherith*, which falls into the Jordan not far from Samaria.

כְּרִיתֻת, כְּרִיתֻת f., *divorce* ; with סֵפֶר *bill of divorce.*

כְּרֵתִי p. n.—I. a tribe of the Philistines of the south west coast of Judea, derived from the Island of *Crete*.—II. title of certain brave soldiers in David's army.

כֶּשֶׂב m., same as כֶּבֶשׂ *lamb*.

כִּשְׂבָּה *female-lamb.*

כֶּשֶׂד p. n., a son of Nahor ; the progenitor of the Chaldees.

כַּשְׂדִּים pl.—I. *Chaldees*, inhabitants of Babylon.—II. *astrologer.*

כַּשְׂדָּי m. Ch., a *Chaldee.*

כָּשָׂה *covered with fat*, Deu. 32:15.

כָּשַׁל (fut. יִכְשׁוֹל).—I. *totter, stagger.*
—II. *stumble.*—III. *stumble to fall*
(part. כּוֹשֵׁל *weak, weary*), with בְּ.
Niph. נִכְשַׁל *be tottering from*
weakness. Pi. and Hiph. I. *cause*
to stumble.—II. *fail, become weak.*
Hoph. part. מֻכְשָׁלִים *made to*
stumble, Jer. 18:23.

כָּשִׁיל m., *an axe,* Ps. 74:6.

כִּשָּׁלוֹן m., *ruin,* Pro. 16:18.

מִכְשׁוֹל m.—I. *offence, delusion.*—II.
σκάνδαλον, *cause of offence, place,*
instrument or *cause of sin.*

מַכְשֵׁלָה f., *fall, ruin,* Isa. 3:6; Zep.
1:3.

כָּשַׁף. Pi. כִּשֵּׁף *used witchcraft,* 2 Ch.
33:6; part. מְכַשֵּׁף *magician, wi-*
zard; מְכַשֵּׁפָה *witch.*

כַּשָּׁף m., *magician,* Jer. 27:9.

כְּשָׁפִים m. pl., *magical rites, incan-*
tations.

כָּשֵׁר *do well, be acceptable,* Est. 8:5;
Ecc. 11:6. Hiph. *give prosperity,*
Ecc. 10:10.

כּוֹשָׁרָה f., pl. כּוֹשָׁרוֹת *great prosperity,*
wealth, Ps. 68:7.

כִּשְׁרוֹן *prosperity, profit,* Ecc. 5:10.

כִּישׁוֹר m., *distaff,* Pro. 31:19.

כָּתַב I. *write, engrave,* with בְּ, עַל,
אֶל before the material written
upon; with עַל, אֶל, לְ before the
person to whom the writing was
addressed. Niph. *was written.* Pi.
wrote, Isa. 10:1.

כְּתַב Ch., *he wrote.*

כְּתָב m.—I. *writing.*—II. *epistle.*—
III. *record.*—IV. *Scripture.*

כְּתָב m. Ch., *writing, edict.*

כְּתֹבֶת f., *writing,* Lev. 19:28.

מִכְתָּב m.—I. *writing.*—II. *epistle,*
ordinance (thing written).

כִּתִּיִּים, כִּתִּים p.n. the *Chittim,* probably the inhabitants of Cyprus
and of some part of Asia Minor.

כָּתִית *beaten small;* see כתה.

כֹּתֶל m., *wall,* Cant. 2:9.

כְּתַל m. Ch., *wall;* pl. emph. כֻּתְלַיָּא
Dan. 5:5.

כִּתְלִישׁ p.n. of a town in the tribe of
Judah.

כָּתַם Kal not used; (Arab. *treasure*
up). Niph. נִכְתָּם *treasured up,* or
as some interpret, *embroidered with*
gold; see the next word, Jer.
2:22.

כֶּתֶם m., *the purest gold.*

מִכְתָּם m., *Michtam,* a word of uncertain meaning, occurring in the
titles of Psalms 16, 56—60, probably the name of the tune or air
to which they were sung.

כְּתֹנֶת, כֻּתֹּנֶת (with suff. כֻּתָּנְתִּי;
pl. כֻּתֳּנוֹת; const. כָּתְנוֹת), *garment,*
shirt, χιτών.

כָּתֵף const. כֶּתֶף f.—I. *shoulder* (with
suff. כְּתֵפִי; pl. כְּתֵפִים).—II. *side*
(of a building, the sea, a town);
pl. כְּתֵפוֹת; const. כִּתְפוֹת; with
suff. כְּתֵפָיו *sides, jambs of doors,*
Eze. 41:2, 26.— III. *shoulders of*
axles, pivots, 1 Ki. 7:30, 34.

כָּתַר. Pi. כִּתֵּר *surround, encompass.*
Hiph. I. *surround, come about.*—
II. *comprehend.*

כֶּתֶר m., *diadem, crown.*

כּוֹתֶרֶת f. (pl. כֹּתָרוֹת), *cincture,*
capital of a column.

כָּתַשׁ break, bruise.

מַכְתֵּשׁ m.—I. mortar, Pro. 27:22.—
II. p. n. of a place, Jud. 15:19;
Zep. 1:11.

כָּתַת (fut. יְכֹת; imp. pl. כֹּתּוּ).—I.
break to pieces (as a vessel, &c.).
—II. beat out (as iron).—III. beat
down (as enemies); part. כְּתוּת
θλαδίας, eunuch. Pi. כִּתֵּת same
as Kal. Pu. was broken. Hiph.
(fut. יַכֵּתּוּ) defeat. Hoph. (fut.
יֻכַּתּוּ) pounded to dust.

כָּתִית m., fine, pure oil.

מְכִתָּה f., breaking, Isa. 30:14.

ל

ל insep. pa.—I. to, towards.—II. at,
in.—III. till, until.—IV. in order
to, for the purpose of.—V. for,
belonging to, with respect to:
לָהֵן therefore; לָכֵן so, thus, therefore; לָמָּה why? When joined
with subs. and adjs. it sometimes
admits of being translated adverbially: לְשֶׁקֶר falsely; לְצֶדֶק justly.
It is also used in a sense allied
to that of the Arab. ل, and very
foreign to the idiom of any European language: e. g. וַיִּקַּח לְיִרְמְיָהוּ
he took hold on Jeremiah, Jer. 40:
2, where it is equivalent to אֵת;
probably it corroborates the meaning like the Arabic. With suff. לִי;
לָנוּ; לָךְ, לוֹ, (לְכִי) לָךְ, (לָכָה) לָךְ,
מִן, see; לָמוֹ, לָהֶן, לָהֶם; לָכֶנָה, לָכֶם,
ל Ch., to, in order to, &c., like the
Hebrew.

לֹא sometimes לוֹא not, no; לֹא כָל

no one, none; לֹא אִישׁ no one; לֹא
דָבָר nothing, used for בְּלֹא without, and הֲלֹא is it? with pref. בְּלֹא
without, there is none; הֲלֹא is it
not? ἰδού; לְלֹא without; גַּם...לֹא
not even.

לָה, לָא Ch., not, nothing.

לָהֵן Ch., therefore, on that account
(see ל), for לָא הֵן unless.

לָכֵן therefore (see ל), for לָא כֵן but if.

לֹו דְבָר, לֹא דְבָר p. n., a town in Gilead.

לֹא עַמִּי (not my people) mystic name
given to the prophet Hosea, Hos.
1:9.

לָאַב (Arab. thirsted).

תַּלְאֻבוֹת, תַּלְאָבוֹת thirst, drought,
Hos. 13.5.

לְהַאֲדִיב for לְהַאְדִיב Hiph. inf. with
pref., from אדב.

לָאָה I. be weary, faint, Job 4:2, 5.—
II. be vexed, Gen. 19:11. Niph.
נִלְאָה I. become weary, faint.—II.
was vexed.—III. dislike. Hiph.
הֶלְאָה I. make weary.—II. vex.—
III. ruin.

לֵאָה p. n., Leah, one of Jacob's wives.

תְּלָאָה f., weariness, trouble, vexation.

לְהָאוֹר for לְהָאוֹר Niph. inf. with pref.,
from אור.

לָאַט same as לוּט vail, cover the
face, 2 Sa. 19:5; see also לָאַט,
לָאַט in אַט.

לָאַט same as לָט, בַּלְאָט secretly,
Jud. 4:21.

לָאַךְ root not used; (Ethiop. he sent
ministered).

מַלְאָךְ m.—I. messenger.—II. angel
(messenger of God).—III. the Word

of God, Jesus Christ, Ex. 23:20,
seq., &c.—IV. *prophet.*—V. *priest.*

מַלְאָךְ m. Ch., *angel.*

מְלָאכָה f. (const. מְלֶאכֶת; with suff.
מְלַאכְתּוֹ; pl. const. מְלַאכוֹת).—I.
ministry.—II. *work.*—III. *making,
acquisition, wealth.*—IV. *flocks.*

מַלְאֲכוּת f., *message, embassy,* Hag.
1:13.

מַלְאָכִי p.n., *Malachi,* the prophet,
Μαλαχίας.

לָאֵל p.n. of a man.

לְאֹם (Arab. *assemblage*).

לְאֹם m.(with suff. לְאֻמִּי; pl. לְאֻמִּים).
—I. *family, tribe, nation.*—II.
לְאֻמִּים p.n. of a people, Ἀλλου-
μαιῶται, Gen. 25:3.

לֵב, לֵב־, לִבִּי (with suff. לִבִּי; pl. לִבּוֹת).

לֵבָב (const. לְבַב; with suff. לְבָבִי,
לְבַבְכֶם; pl. לְבָבוֹת) m.—I. *the
heart of man* or *beast.*—II. *the seat
of thought, affection, &c.,* in man;
בְּלֵב וָלֵב *with a double heart,* i.e.
deceitful, Ps. 12:3.—III. *the middle
or interior of any thing.*

לֵב, לְבַב m. Ch., *heart, mind,* as Heb.

לֵבָב Niph. *take heart, be bold, daring,*
Job 11:12. Pi. לִבֵּב *give heart,
encourage,* Cant. 4:9; see also in
לְבִיבָה.

לִבָּה f., *heart, mind,* as לֵב.

לְבִיבָה f., pl. לְבִיבוֹת *pancakes* made
of fine wheaten flour. Pi. לִבֵּב
he made such pancakes, 2 Sa. 13:
6—10, only.

לַבָּה for לֶהָבָה *flame,* Ex. 3:2.

לָבִיא, לְבָאוֹת, לְבָאִים; see לָבִיא.

לְבַד *alone;* see בַּד, בָּדָד.

לָבַט Niph. נִלְבַּט *stumbled, fell,* Pro.
10:8, 10; Hos. 4:14.

לָבִיא *lioness;* perhaps also *lion.*

לְבִי m., pl. m. לְבָאִים.—I. *lions;* l
לְבָאוֹת *lionesses.*—II. p.n. of
town in the tribe of Simeon.

לְבִיָּא f., *lioness.*

לְבִיבוֹת; see in לֵב.

לָבַן (from לְבֵנָה) *make bricks,* Gen.
11:3. Hiph.—I. *was white, pure.*
—II. *made white, clean,* Dan. 11:
35. Hithp. *shall become white,
clean,* Dan. 12:10.

לָבָן m.—I. *white.*—II. p.n., *Laban,*
the father-in-law of Jacob.—III.
a place in the desert.

לְבָנָה f.—I. *the moon* (from her whiteness).—II. p.n. of a man.

לָבָן, לְבֵן m., *white.*

לִבְנֶה m., *the white poplar.*

לְבָנָה f.—I. *whiteness, clearness,* Ex.
24:10.—II. p.n., a city in the
tribe of Judah.—III. a station of
Israel in the desert.

לְבֵנָה f. (pl. לְבֵנִים) *brick* or *tile.*

לְבֹנָה, לְבוֹנָה f.—I. *pure frankincense,*
λίβανος.—II. p.n. of a town near
Shiloh.

הַלְּבָנוֹן, לְבָנוֹן p.n., *Mount Lebanon;*
so called from the whiteness of
the snow on its eastern peak.

לִבְנִי p.n. of a man.

מַלְבֵּן m., *brick kiln.*

לָבֵשׁ, לָבַשׁ (fut. יִלְבַּשׁ).—I. *put on
clothing, cloak;* part. לָבוּשׁ *clothed*
—II. used metaphorically for the
possession of certain qualities, as
clothed with, glory, justice, &c.,

covered with flocks (as a pasture); with many others. Pu. מְלֻבָּשִׁים *clothed.*—Hiph. I. *clothe, invest,* with עַל.—II. *cover* (as the sky with clouds).

לְבֵשׁ Ch., *clothe.* Aph. the same.

לְבֻשׁ ,לְבוּשׁ m., *upper or outer garment, cloak.*

מַלְבּוּשׁ m., the same.

תִּלְבֹּשֶׁת f., the same.

לַבַּת, Ex. 3:2, for לַהֲבַת const., from לֶהָבָה.

לֹג m., *the log,* a liquid measure containing 24·3 solid inches.

לֹד p. n., a town in the tribe of Benjamin, *Lydda.*

לֵדָה Kal inf., from יָלַד.

לֶדֶת Kal inf., from יָלַד.

לְמֶנָּה Kal inf. with suff. and ה parag., from יָלַד.

לָהַג root not used; (Arab. *tongue of fire, flame*).

לַהַב m.—I. *flame.*—II. *glitter* of a sword or other weapon.—III. the weapon itself.

לֶהָבָה f., *flame;* pl. לְהָבוֹת; const. לַהֲבוֹת; s. const. לַבַּת, Ex. 3:2.

לַהֶבֶת f., the same.

שַׁלְהֶבֶת *flame, destruction, fire.*

לְהָבִים same as לוּבִים *the Lybians,* Gen. 10:13.

לָהַג root not used; (Arab. *intense occupation*).

לַהַג m., *much study,* Ecc. 12:12.

לַהַד p. n. of a man.

לָהָה (fut. וַתֵּלַהּ) same as לָאָה *was faint, feeble,* Gen. 47:13.

לָהַהּ. Hithp. part. מִתְלַהְלֵהַּ *insane, mad person,* Pro. 26:18.

לָהַט *flaming,* Ps. 104:4; part. לֹהֲטִים *inflamed* (i.e. *furious*) men, Ps. 57: 5. Pi. לִהֵט *set on fire, inflame.*

לַהַט m., *flame,* Gen. 3:24.

לְהָטִים lit. *flames:* hence, *dazzlings, delusions,* Ex. 7:11.

לָהַם. Hith. part. מִתְלַהֲמִים *enchanting, fascinating things, dainties,* Pro. 18:8; 26:22.

לֶהֱוֵן f., לֶהֱוֵן (*that they may be*) Ch. fut., the preformant dropped with the pref. ל, from הֲוָה הוּא.

לְהֵן; see ל and לֹא.

מַהֲלָה לַהֲקָה (const. לַהֲקַת) trans. for *congregation,* 1 Sa. 19:20.

לוּא ,לוּ I. *if,* εἰ, ἐάν.—II. *would that* לוּלֵי ,לוּלֵא (compound of לֹא לוּ for לֹא) *unless.*

לוּבִים ,לֻבִּים p.n., *the Lybians,* inhabitants of the deserts west of Egypt.

לוּד p.n. of a people descended from Shem, Gen. 10:22; pl. לוּדִים; they inhabited some part of Africa, and probably Asia Minor.

לָוָה I. *borrow at usury.*—II. *get, obtain.* Niph. נִלְוָה *become turned, attached, joined,* with עַל ,אֶל ,עִם. Hiph. הִלְוָה.—I. *cause to borrow.*—II. *lend.*

לֵוִי p.n.—I. *Levi,* one of the sons of Jacob and Leah.—II. and לֵוִי *a Levite;* pl. לְוִיִם and בְּנֵי לֵוִי *Levites.*

לֵוִי Ch., *a Levite.*

לִוְיָה const. לִוְיַת *chaplet, garland,* Pro. 1:9, &c.

לִוְיָה f., pl. לֹוֹת for לָוָה ,לֹוֹה perhaps

architectural ornaments like *gar-lands*, 1 Ki. 7:29, 30, 36.

לִוְיָתָן m.—I. any *sea monster*.—II. *the sea serpent*, Isa. 27:1.—III. one of the carnivorous whales, Job 3:8, &c.

לְוָת Ch., *with*, Ezr. 4:12.

לוּז *escape, depart from*, Pro. 3:21. Niph. part. נָלוֹז *perverse, incorrigible*. Hiph. fut. יָלִיז *escape, flee from*.

לוּז m.—I. *almond tree*, Gen. 30:37.—II. p.n. of the town afterwards called בֵּית־אֵל, in the tribe of Benjamin.

לְזוּת f., *perverseness*, Pro. 4:24.

לוּחַ m.—I. *tablet of stone* or *wood*.—II. metaphorically, *of the heart*.—III. *leaf of a folding-door*, Cant. 8:9; לֻחֹת הָעֵדוּת, לֻחֹת הַבְּרִית *tables of the covenant, testimony*; dual לֻחַיִם *benches* for the rowers of a ship, Eze. 27:5.

לוּחִית p.n. of a town in Moab.

הַלּוֹחֵשׁ, לוֹחֵשׁ p.n. of a man.

לוּט *cover, conceal*; part. לוֹט *covering*; לוּטָה f., *concealed*. Hiph. hid.

לָט m., *covert*; בַּלָּט *secretly*; pl. לָטִים *secret parts*.

לוֹט m.—I. *veil, covering*, Isa. 25:7.—II. p.n., *Lot*, the nephew of Abraham.

לֹט m., *gum-ladanum*.

לוֹטָן p.n. of a man.

לֵוִי, לִוְיָה, לִוְיָתָן; see לֹוה.

לוּלִים m.pl., *winding-stairs*, 1 Ki. 6:8.

לֻלָאֹת, const. לֻלְאֹת f. pl., *loops* or *eyes* for hooks.

לוּלֵי, לוּלֵא; see לֹוּ.

I. לוּן and לִין (fut. יָלִין; apoc. יָלֶן; with pause יָלִין, יָלַן; imper. לִין).—I. *lodge, remain, pass the night*, with אֶת, בְּ. Hiph. הֵלִין *cause to remain*, Jer. 4:14. Hith. הִתְלוֹנֵן *lodge, remain*, Ps. 91:1; Job 39:28

מָלוֹן m.—I. *lodging-house, inn*.—II. *quarters* (as of soldiers).—III. *tent, cot, hut*; f. מְלוּנָה.

II. לוּן. Niph. נָלוֹן *complain, murmur*; with עַל *against*; fut. pl. יִלֹּנוּ Hiph. הֵלִין the same; fut. apoc. וַיָּלֶן; part. מַלִּינִים.

תְּלֻנּוֹת f. pl. (with suff. תְּלֻנֹּתֵיכֶם), *murmurings*.

לוּעַ *swallow*, Obad. v.16.

לֹעַ m., *throat*, Pro. 23:2.

לוּץ *deride, scorn*, Pro. 9:12; part. לֵץ *scorner*. Hiph. הֵלִיץ *derided*; part. מֵלִיץ *interpreter, orator, ambassador*. Hith. הִתְלוֹצֵץ *was mocking*, Isa. 28:22.

לָצוֹן m., *derision*, Pro. 1:22.

מְלִיצָה f.—I. *interpretation*.—II. *saying, parable, enigma*, Pro. 1:6; Hab. 2:6.

לוּשׁ *knead dough*.

לוּשׁ p.n. of a man, same as לַיִשׁ.

לְוָת; see לֹוה.

לְזוּת; see לוּז.

לָחָה root not used; (Arab. *cheek-bone*).

לְחִי, with pause לֶחִי f. (dual לְחָיַיִם; const. לְחָיֵי).—I. *cheek, jaw*.—II. לֶחִי and רָמַת לֶחִי p.n., a place on the borders of Philistia.

לָחַח root not used; (Arab *eyes wet with tears*).

לַח m., *moist, green, fresh, new.*

לֵחַ m. (with suff. לֵחֹה Deu. 34:7), *vigour of youth.*

לָחַךְ (inf. לְחֹךְ) and Pi. לִחֵךְ *licked,* Nu. 22:4, *lapped up (as a dog);* with עָפָר *lick the dust.*

לָחַם (fut. יִלְחַם; inf. לְחֹם; imp. לְחָם). —I. *eat, feast upon, devour;* with בְּ *of;* לַחְמֵי רֶשֶׁף *consumed of fever.* —II. *make, wage war,* with לְ, אֶת. Niph. נִלְחַם (inf. abs. נִלְחֹם; fut. pl. תִּלָּחֲמוּ).—I. *make war;* with בְּ, עִם, אֶל, *against;* with לְ *for.*—II. with בְּ, עַל *be-siege.*

לָחֻם m.—I. *eating, feasting* (with suff. לְחוּמוֹ).—II. *flesh* (with suff. לְחֻמָם Zep. 1:17).

לֶחֶם com.—I. *provision;* עֵץ בְּלַחְמוֹ *tree with its provision,* i. e. fruit, Jer. 11:19.—II. *feast.*—III. *bread.* — IV. *bread-corn,* Isa. 28:28; לֶחֶם הַפָּנִים (ἄρτος τοῦ προσώπου) *shew-bread,* lit. bread of the presence.

לְחֶם m. Ch., *a feast,* Dan. 5:1.

לֶחֶם m. (inf. Pi.), const. לְחֶם *war,* Jud. 5:8.

לַחְמִי p. n. of a man, 1 Chron. 20:5.

מִלְחָמָה f.—I. *battle, war.*—II. *in-struments of war,* Ps. 76:4; עָשָׂה מִלְחָמָה with אֶת, עִם *made war;* אִישׁ מ׳ *warrior, soldier;* עַם מ׳ the same.—III. *event of war, vic-tory,* Ecc. 9:11.

מִלְחֶמֶת f., the same; with suff. מִלְחַמְתּוֹ.

לַחְמָס p. n. of a place in the tribe of Judah.

לְחֵנָה f. Ch., *concubine,* Dan. 5:2, 3, 23.

לָחַץ (יִלְחַץ) *oppress, afflict;* part. לֹחֲצִים *oppressors.* Niph. *was pressed, injured,* Nu. 22:25.

לַחַץ m. *oppression, affliction.*

לָחַשׁ Pi. לִחֵשׁ; part. pl. מְלַחֲשִׁים *whisperers, pronouncers of charms* Hith. *muse of, secretly consider, discuss.*

לַחַשׁ m.—I. *whisper.*—II. *incantation, charm.*—III. pl. לְחָשִׁים *amulets,* Isa. 3:20.

לָט, לֵט ; see לוּט.

לָטָא (Arab. *cleave to the ground*).

לְטָאָה f., *a kind of lizard.*

לָטַשׁ *sharpen.* Pu. part. מְלֻטָּשׁ *sharp-ened,* Ps. 52:4.

לֵיוֹת ; see לוּט.

לַיְלָה (const. לֵיל) לַיְלָה (pl. לֵילוֹת) m. —I. *night.*—II. *time of adversity;* adv. בְּלֵילוֹת, בַּלַּיְלָה, לַיְלָה *by night;* יוֹמָם וָלַיְלָה *day and night*

לֵיל m., *night,* Isa. 21:11.

לֵילְיָא m. Ch., *night.*

לִילִית f., *screech owl,* Isa. 34:14.

לִין ; see לוּן.

לִיסוֹד Kal inf. with pref. and dag. eu-phon., from יָסַד.

לִיקְהַת for לִקְהַת ; see יָקַהּ.

לַיִשׁ m.—I. *strong lion.*—II. p. n. of a man.—III. of a town in the north of Palestine.

לֵךְ, לְכָה, לֵךְ imp., from הָלַךְ, יֵלֵךְ.

לָכַד I. *take,* (as a beast in toils, cap-tives in war, &c.)—II. *intercept*

Niph. *was taken.* Hith. was, became adhering, Job 41:9.

לֶכֶד m., *capture,* Pro. 3:26.

מַלְכֹּדֶת f., *snare, trap,* Job 18:10.

לְכָה imp. of יָלַךְ; לְכָה for לְךָ ; see לְ.

לָכֵחַ p. n. of a town in the tribe of Judah.

לָכִישׁ p. n. of a city in the tribe of Judah.

לְכֵן ; see לְ, בֵּן. לֹא

לֶכֶת Kal inf., from הָלַךְ, יָלַךְ.

לָלָאֹת ; see לוּל.

לָמַד (fut. יִלְמַד).—I. *accustom to,* with אֶל.—II. *learn,* with acc. inf. Pi. לִמַּד.—I. *accustom to.*—II. *teach,* with לְ of the person, and בְּ of the thing taught. Pu. לֻמַּד.—I. *was accustomed.*—II. *was taught.*

לִמֻּד, לָמוּד m.—I. *accustomed.*—II. *trained, taught.*—III. *disciple.*

מַלְמֵד m., *ox-goad,* Jud. 3:31.

תַּלְמִיד m., *learner,* 1 Ch. 25:8.

לָמָה, לָמֶה *why;* see מָה.

לְמוֹ ; see לְ.

לְמוּאֵל, לְמוֹאֵל p. n. or title of king Solomon, Pro. c. 31.

לֶמֶךְ p. n. of a man, *Lamech*

לְמַעַן ; see עָנָה.

לֶנָה Zec. 5:4, for לִינָה Kal pret. f., from לוּן.

לָנוּ for לַנֲנוּ Kal pret. pl., from לוּן.

לִנִים Kal part. pl., from לוּן.

לֹעַ *throat;* see לוּעַ.

לָעֵב Hiph. *ridiculing, deriding,* with בְּ, 2 Chron. 36:16.

לָעַג (fut. יִלְעַג) *mock, deride, scorn.* Niph. *stammer,* Isa. 33:19. Hiph. *mock,* with עַל, לְ, בְּ.

לַעַג m.—I. *derision, ridicule.*—II cause of derision.

לָעֵג m., *mocker,* Ps. 35:16.

לַעְדָּה p. n. of a man.

לַעְדָּן p. n. of a man.

לָעָה *was rash,* Job 6:3.

לָעַז *spoke barbarously,* Ps. 114:1.

לָעַט . Hiph. *feed, give to eat.*

לַעַן (Arab. *drove away*).

לַעֲנָה f.—I. *wormwood.*—II. metaph. *distress.*

לַפִּיד m., *lamp or torch.*

לַפִּידוֹת p. n., *Lapidoth* the husband of Deborah.

לִפְנֵי, לְפָנַי ; see פָּנִים or פָּנָה.

לָפַת *turned to, towards,* Jud. 16:29. Niph. *turned about.*

לְהַצְּבוֹת for לַצְּבוֹת Hiph. inf. with pref., from צָבָה.

לָצוֹן *scorn;* see לוּץ.

לֵצִים , part. לְצֵצִים *scorners,* Hos. 7:5.

לַקּוּם p. n., a town in the tribe of Naphtali.

לָקַח (fut. יִקַּח; inf. abs. לָקוֹחַ; const. קַחַת; imp. קַח, לְקַח; with pause קָח; with ה parag. קְחָה).—I. *take,* with בְּ.—II. idiom, like the English *take* and *do.*—III. *take away.*—IV. *take possession of.*—V. *receive.* Niph. נִלְקַח *was taken.* Pu. לֻקַּח same as Niph. Hoph. (fut. יֻקַּח the same). Hith. part. f. מִתְלַקַּחַת *being taken with,* i. e. mixed, mingled with (of fire), Ex. 9:24, Eze. 1:4.

לֶקַח m., *taking, receiving,* specially instruction in religion.

לְקָחִי p. n. of a man.

מַלְקוֹחַ m., *capture, spoil*; dual מַלְקְחַיִם *the jaws.*

מֶלְקָחַיִם m. dual.—I. *tongs.*—II. *snuffers.*

מַלְקָחַיִם m. dual, the same.

מִקָּח m., *accepting* (of gifts), 2 Chron. 19:7.

מַקָּחוֹת f. pl., *merchandise*, Neh. 10:32.

לָקַט and Pi. לִקֵּט *collect, gather, glean.* Pu. and Hith. *was gathered.*

לֶקֶט m., *collecting, gleaning.*

יַלְקוּט m., *bag* or *purse*, 1 Sa. 17:40.

לָקַק *lick* (as dogs); fut. יָלֹק; pl. יָלֹקּוּ. Pi. part. מְלַקְקִים *licking.*

לָקַשׁ (Syr. *late*). Pi. *cut, crop*, Job 24:6.

לֶקֶשׁ m., *latter grass, aftermath*, Am. 7:1.

מַלְקוֹשׁ m., *the latter rain* (in March and April).

לְרֹא for לִירֹא Kal inf. with pref., from ירא.

לָשַׁד (Arab. *sucking*).

לָשָׁד m. (with suff. לְשַׁדִּי) *moisture*, Ps. 32:4; לְשַׁד הַשָּׁמֶן perhaps *fluid oil*, Nu. 11:8.

לָשׁוֹן com.—I. *tongue*; אִישׁ לָשׁוֹן *calumniator.*—II. *language.*—III. *nation, community* (having one language).—IV. *tongue of flame*, Is. 5:24.—V. *tongue* (wedge) *of gold*, Jos. 7:21, 24.

לָשַׁן Po. part. with י parag. מְלֹשְׁנִי *calumniator*, Ps. 101:5. Hiph. the same, Pro. 30:10.

לִשָּׁן com. Ch., *tongue, language.*

לִשְׁכָּה f., *chamber*, specially those attached to the temple; with ה parag. לִשְׁכָּתָה *to the chamber*; pl. לְשָׁכוֹת.

לֶשֶׁם m.—I. *ligure*, a precious stone; LXX. λιγύριον.—II. p. n. of a city called also לַיִשׁ and דָּן.

לֶשַׁע p. n. of a city not far from Sodom.

לֶת for לֶדֶת with pref. לָרֶת Kal inf., from ילד.

לֶתֶךְ m., *measure* (of capacity), the *half-homer*, Hos. 3:2.

לָתַע (Arab. *he bites*).

מַלְתָּעוֹת f. pl., *teeth*, Ps. 58:7.

מְתַלְּעוֹת f. pl. (trans.), *teeth.*

מ

מ pref. prep.; see מִן.

מָא Ch., same as מה.

מַאֲבוּס m., *granary*, see אבס.

מְאָד; see אגד.

מֵאָה const. f.—I. *a hundred*; dual מָאתַיִם *two hundred*; pl. מֵאוֹת *hundreds*; שֵׁשׁ מֵאוֹת *six hundred*; שְׁמֹנֶה מֵאוֹת *eight hundred.*—II. a *hundred-fold.*—III. a *hundredth part*, Neh. 5:11.—IV. p. n. of one of the towers of Jerusalem, Neh. 3:1.

מְאָה f. Ch., *a hundred*; dual מָאתַיִן *two hundred.*

מַאֲוַיִּים *desires*; see אוה.

מְאוּם; see מום.

מְאוּמָה; see מה.

מָאֹר, מְאֵרָה *curse*; see אור.

מֹאזְנַיִן, מֹאזְנַיִם *balances*; see אזן.

מַאֲכֶלֶת, מַאֲכֹלֶת, מַאֲכָל; see אכל.

מָאן m. Ch., *vessel.*

מָאֵן or מָאֵן. Pi. מֵאֵן (inf. מָאֵן; fut. יְמָאֵן) refuse, be unwilling.

מָאֵן m., refusing.

מֵאֵן m., pl. מָאֲנִים recusants.

מָאַם (inf. מָאוֹם; const. with suff. מָאַסָם; fut. יִמְאַם).—I. despise, reject.—II. set at nought, lightly esteem, with בְּ. Niph. I. was despised, rejected. — II. same as מָסַם. Niph. dissolve, waste, Ps. 58:8; Job 7:5.

מַאֲפֶה baked; see אפה.

מַאֲפֵלְיָה, מַאֲפֵל; see אפל.

מָאַר (Arab. irritate a wound). Hiph. הַמְאִיר irritated, pained; צָרַעַת מַמְאֶרֶת the inflamed leprosy.

מַאֲרָב ambush; see ארב.

מְאֵרָה curse, see ארר.

מֵאֵת from the; see אֵת. בדל

מִבְדָּלוֹת separations; see בדל

מָבוֹא entry; see בוא.

מְבוּכָה confusion; see בוך.

מַבּוּל deluge; see יבל.

מְבוּסָה treading down; see בוס.

מְבוֹנִים understanding; see בון.

מַבּוּעַ spring; see נבע.

מְבוּקָה void; see בוק.

מְבָשִׁים, מְבֻשִׁים prudence; see בוש.

מִבְחָר, מִבְחוֹר choice; see בחר.

מֶבָּט, מַבָּט hope; see נבט.

מִבְטָא rashness; see בטא.

מִבְטָח confidence; see בטח.

מֵבִי for מֵבִיא Hiph. part., from בוא.

מַבְלִינִית exhilaration; see בלן.

מִבַּלְעֲדֵי besides; see בַּלְעֲדֵי in בלה.

מִבְנֶה building; see בנה.

מִבְנַי for סִבְכַי, 2 Sa. 23:27.

מִבְעָתְּךָ for מְבַעֲתָתְךָ Pi. part. f. with suff., from בעת.

מִבְצָר fortress; see בצר.

רֹאשָׁה מִפָּרֹאשָׁה comp. of בָּ, מָח and

מָג m., fire worshipper, magian, Jer 39:3.

מַגְבִּישׁ p. n. of a place or person.

מִגְבָּלוֹת devices; see נבל.

מִגְבָּעָה mitre; see נבע.

מָגַד (Arab. glory).

מֶגֶד m., excellence, glory.

מְגִדּוֹן, מְגִדּוֹ p.n., a city of the Manassites in the tribe of Issachar, LXX. Μαγεδδώ; בִּקְעַת־מְגִדּוֹ valley of Megiddo; מֵי מְגִדּוֹ brook Kishon.

מִגְדָּנוֹת f. pl., choice, precious things.

מַגְדִּיאֵל p. n. of a prince of the Edomites.

מִגְדָּל, מִגְדּוֹל p. n.; see גדל.

מָגוֹג p. n. of a people and country Magog.

מָנוֹר, מָנֵר, מְנוֹרָה, מְנוֹרָה; see גור.

מַגְזֵרָה axes; see גזר.

מַגָּל sickle; see נגל.

מַגְלֵדָה mound; see גלל.

מְנַמָּה desire; see נמם.

מָגַן. Pi. מִגֵּן give, give freely

מָגֵן, מִגְנָּה; see גנן.

מִגְעֶרֶת rebuke; see נער.

מַגֵּפָה plague; see נגף.

מַנְפִּיעַשׁ p. n. of a man.

מִגָּר, part. pl. const. מְגֹרֵי fallen, delivered up, Eze. 21:17. Pi. מִגֵּר cast down.

מְנַר Ch. Pa. מַגֵּר cast down, Ezr 6:12.

מִגְרוֹן p. n., a town in the tribe of Benjamin.

מְגֵרָה saw; see גרר.

מַעֲרָפָה *furrow*; see נרף.

מַנְרֵשׁ; see נרש.

מִדְבָּר *wilderness*; see דבר.

מָדַד (pret. מָדַדְתִּי, מָדֹדוּ, fut. יָמֹד).—I. *extend a line.*—II. *measure.*—III. *apportion,* Isa. 65:7. Niph. (fut. יִמַּד) *be, can be, measured.* Pi. מִדַּד *measure* (see also in נדד). Po. מוֹדֵד *the same,* Hab. 3:6; *"viewed"* (Lee); see מוד. Hith. הִתְמֹדֵד *extended, stretched out.*

מַד m.—I. *measure, extent*; with suff. מִדֹּה; pl. מַדִּים.—II. *upper garment, tunic,* with suff. מַדּוֹ; pl. מַדִּים, מַדִּין.—III. *hammer-cloth, covering for a throne,* Jud. 5:10.—IV. מָדִין p.n., a city in the desert of Judah.

מִדָּה f. (m. Neh. 3:30).—I. *extent, measure*; אִישׁ מִדָּה *tall man,* 1 Chron. 11:23; בֵּית מִדּוֹת *spacious house,* Jer. 22:14; מִדַּת יָמַי *measure of my days.*—II. *tribute.*—III. *vesture,* Ps. 133:2.

מִנְדָּה, מִדָּה f. Ch., *tribute.*

מְמַדִּים m. pl., *extents, measure,* Job 38:5.

מַד m. (pl. with suff. מַדְוֵיהֶם), *garment.*

מָדוֹן m., *height, tallness,* 2 Sa. 21:20; see also in דין.

מַדְוֶה *disease*; see דָּוָה.

מַדּוּחִים *drivings out*; see נדח.

מַדּוּעַ *why*; see ידע.

מַדְחֵפוֹת; see דחף.

מָדַי f., *Media, the Medes*; מָדִי Ch. *a Median,* const. emph. מָדָאָה *the same.*

מַדַּי; see מָה. מִדַּי; see דַּי.

מִדְיָן p.n., *the son of Abraham and*

מִדְיָנִית f., מִדְיָנִי m., מִדְיָנִי *Keturah; a Midianite.*

מָדִים pl. for מַד; see מַד in מדד.

מְדִינָה; see דִּין.

מַדְלֵכָה *mortar*; see דוך.

מַדְמֵנָה, מַדְמֵנָה, מַדְמֵן; see רמן.

מִדָּן, מְדָנִים; see דין.

מַדָּע, מַדָּע; see ידע.

מָדֹר Ch., *same as* מָדוֹר *habitation* see דור.

מַדְרֵגָה; see דרך.

הַמְּדָתָא with art. p.n. the father of Haman.

מָה, מֶה, מָה inter. pron.—I. *what?* מַה־לָּךְ *what wilt thou?* מַה־לִּי וָלָךְ *what have I to do with thee?*—II. *how? how much?*—III. *for what? why?*—IV. *what? what sort?*—V. *something, anything, anything whatever;* ...מַה שֶּׁ *that which, the thing which* (in the book of Ecclesiastes only); מַה־נּוֹרָא *how terrible*; מַה־זֶּה for מֶה *what is this?* מַה לָּכֶם *what mean ye?* Isa. 3:15; לְמַה־דִּי for לְמַדַּי *sufficiently,* 2 Chron. 30:3. Compounds: בַּמֶּה, בַּמָּה *why? how? wherefore?* כַּמֶּה, כַּמָּה *how many? how long? how much?* לָמֶה, לְמָה *why? wherefore?* לָמֶה זֶּה *why? wherefore?* לְמַבְּרִאשֹׁנָה (for לְמָה בְּ) *because at first,* 1 Chron. 15:13; עַד־מָה *how long?* עַל־מָה, עַל־מֶה *wherefore?*

מָה־שׁ (מָא) Ch., *why, wherefore?* לְמָה *that which,* Dan. 2:28, 29; כְּמָה *wherefore?* עַל־מָה *how? how much? so much?* Dan. 3:33; מָה דִי *that which.*

מָה אוֹ מָה וּמָה (comp. of מָה) or מָאוּמָה

מָה) any thing; with אֵין, לֹא nothing.

מָהַהּ. Hith. הִתְמַהְמָהּ *delay, tarry, wait.*

מְהוּמָה *tumult;* see הום.

מְהוּמָן p.n. of a Persian eunuch.

מְהֵיטַבְאֵל p.n.—I. of a man, Neh. 6:10.—II. of a woman, Gen. 36:39.

מְהֵימַן Ch., Aph. part. pass.; see אמן.

מְהַחְתִּין Ch. Aph. part.; see נחת.

מְהָךְ Ch. Pe. inf., from הוך.

מָהֻל, part. סָהוּל *debased, adulterated,* Isa. 1:22.

מְהֻמְהֶם Eze. 7:11, from הֵם; see המה.

מְהֻקְצָעוֹת for מְקֻצָעוֹת Hoph. part. f. pl., from קצע.

I. **מָהַר** *hasten, hurry,* Ps. 16:4. Pi. מִהַר *hasten, hurry;* used as an auxiliary, e.g. מִהֲרוּ שָׁכְחוּ *they soon forgot,* Ps. 106:13, &c. Niph. נִמְהַר *was hasty, hurried, rash.*

מָהִיר m., *ready, quick, skilful, hasty, speedy.*

מַהֵר m., מְהֵרָה f., *quick, ready, hasty, speedy, speed;* עַד־מְהֵרָה, בִּמְהֵרָה; מְהֵרָה adv., *quickly, readily, speedily.*

II. **מָהַר** *endow* (a wife with a dowry), Ex. 22:15; or *buy* (a wife with a dowry).

מֹהַר m., *gift* or *dower* (present made by a suitor to the parents of a damsel).

מַהֲרַי p.n., one of David's generals.

מוֹאָב p.n.—I. of a man, *Moab,* the descendant of Lot.—II. f., the land of *Moab,* situated between the Dead Sea and the river Arnon m. מוֹאָבִי, f. מוֹאָבִיָּה, מוֹאָבִית *Moabite.*

מוֹאֵל same as מול *over against,* Neh. 12:38.

מוֹבָא *entrance;* see בוא.

מוּג (fut. יָמוּג).—I. *flow.*—II. *dissolve, melt* (indicating weakness). Niph. נָמוֹג *were dissolved, undone.* Pil. מוֹגֵג I. *dissolve,* Ps. 65:11.—II. *waste away,* Job 30:22. Hith. *was dissolved, undone.*

מוּד Kal not used; see מוט. Po. מוֹדֵד *moved,* Hab. 3:6.

תָּמִיד m.—I. *perpetuity.*—II. *perpetual.*—III. *continually;* עוֹלַת הַתָּמִיד *the continual,* i.e. *daily offering;* לֶחֶם הַתָּמִיד *the bread constantly placed in the temple.*

מוֹדַעַת, מֹדַע, מוֹדָע; see ידע.

מוֹט (fut. יָמוֹט) *totter* (to a fall), *fail.* Niph. נָמוֹט *be moved, tottering.* Hiph. fut. יָמִיטוּ *cause to fall, come down.* Hithpo. *be moved,* Isa. 24:19.

מוֹט m.—I. *tottering, vacillating.*—II. *pole, staff.*—III. *yoke* (for burdens), Nah. 1:12.

מוֹטָה f., *pole or staff.*

מוּךְ same as מָכַךְ *become indigent.*

מוּל *circumcise.* Niph. I. *was circumcised.*—II. *circumcise one's self.* Pil. מוֹלֵל *cut off,* Ps. 90:6. Hiph. *cut off, down,* Ps. 118:10-12. Hithpo הִתְמוֹלֵל *is cut off, down,* Ps. 58:8.

מוּל מוֹל (מוֹאֵל Neh. 12:38).—I. *near, with.*—II. *opposite, over against,* ἀντικρύ: compounds

אֶל *before, over against;* אֶל מוּל פְּנֵי *in front of, before;* מִמּוּל *from before, opposite.*

מוּלָה f. (pl. מוּלֹת), *circumcisions,* Ex. 4:26.

מוֹלִיד, מוֹלֶדֶת, מוֹלָדָה; see ילד.

מוּם (מאום) m., *spot, blemish from disease.*

מוּמָת Hoph. part., from מות.

מוּן; see מין.

מוּסָב Hoph. part.; see סבב.

מוֹסָד, מוּסָדָה, מוֹסָדוֹת; see יסד.

מוּסָף *porch;* see סכך.

מוֹסֵר (from אסר), pl. מוֹסְרִים and מוֹסְרוֹת *chains.*

מוֹסֵר and ־וֹת — p. n. of a place in the wilderness.

מוּסָר *bonds;* see יסר.

מוֹעֵד, מוֹעָדָה, מוֹעֵד, מוֹעֵד; see יעד.

מוֹעֶדֶת, מוֹעֵד *assembly;* see יעד.

מוֹעָדֶת for מוֹעֶדֶת Kal part. f., from יעד.

מוּעָף *darkness;* see עוף.

מוֹעֵצָה *counsel;* see יעץ.

מוֹעָקָה *pain;* see עוק.

מוֹפֵת *sign;* see יפת.

מוּץ, part. מֵץ *oppressor,* Isa. 16:4. מוֹץ, מֹץ m., *chaff.*

מִיץ m., *pressing, squeezing* (cream to make butter), Pro. 30:33.

מוֹצָא, מוֹצָאָה; see יצא.

מוּצָא Hoph. part., from יצא.

מוּצָק, מוּצָקָה *fused, cast;* see יצק.

מוּצָק, מוּצָק; see צוק.

מוּק. Hiph. הֵמִיק *mock, insult,* Ps. 73:8.

מוֹקֵד, מוֹקְדָה *burning;* see יקד.

מוֹקֵשׁ *snare;* see יקשׁ.

מוּר Hiph. הֵמִיר — I. *change, alter,*

with בְּ. — II. *exchange.* Niph. נָמַר *was changed,* Jer. 48:11.

תְּמוּרָה f. — I. *equivalent, recompense.* — II. *restitution,* Job 20:18. — III. *exchange,* Ru. 4:7.

מוֹרָא; see ירא.

מוֹרִים for מוֹרָאִים Hiph. part. pl., from ירה.

(מוֹרִיגִים, מֹרִגִים) or מוֹרַג m. (pl. מוֹרִיגִים, מֹרִגִים) *threshing wain.*

מוֹרָד *descent, declivity;* see ירד.

מוֹרָה, Ps. 9:21, same as מוֹרָא *fear;* see also in מֹרָה; מוֹרֶה *teacher;* see ירה.

מוֹרָט *ruin;* see ירט.

מוֹרִיָּה p.n., same as מֹרִיָּה

מוֹרִינִים for מוֹרִגִים pl., from מֹרַג.

מוֹרָשָׁה, מוֹרָשׁ *possession, inheritance* see ירשׁ.

I. מוּשׁ I. *move.* — II. *remove,* Zec. 3:9. Hiph. הֵמִישׁ I. *move, depart.* — II. *remove, put away.* — III. *cease, desist,* Jer. 17:8, with מִן.

II. מוּשׁ same as מָשַׁשׁ *feel,* Gen. 27:21, &c. Hiph. the same, Ps. 115:7, &c.

מוּשִׁי, מֻשִׁי p. n. of a man.

מוֹשָׁב *dwelling,* &c.; see ישׁב.

מַשְׂכוֹת; see משׁך.

מוֹשָׁעוֹת *salvation;* see ישׁע.

מוּת (pret. מֵת; 1. pers. מַתִּי; pl. מֵתוּ; part. מֵת; f. מֵתָה; inf. abs. מוֹת; const. מוּת; imp. מֵת; fut. יָמוּת; apoc. יָמֹת, (וַיָּמָת) *die* (of man or beast). Pil. מוֹתֵת *put to death, caused to die.* Hiph. הֵמִית the same. Hoph. הוּמַת *was caused to die.*

מָוֶת m. (with ה parag. מָוְתָה; const

מוֹת; with suff. מוֹתוֹ; pl. (מוֹתִים) מוֹתָא.
—I. *death*; מִשְׁפַּט מָוֶת *sentence of death*, Deut. 19:6; בֶּן־מָוֶת or אִישׁ־מָוֶת *one guilty of a capital crime*.—II. *the grave*; שַׁעֲרֵי מָוֶת *gates of death*.—III. *person dead*, Isa. 38:18.— IV. *pestilence*.— V. *destruction, ruin*.

מוֹת m. Ch., *death*.

מָמוֹת m., pl. מְמוֹתִים *deaths*, Jer. 16:4; Eze. 28:8.

תְּמוּתָה f., *death*; בֶּן־תְּמוּתָה *condemned to death*.

מוֹתָר *abundance*; see יתר.

מֵזָא, with suff. מֵזְיֵהּ Ch. Pe. inf., from אזא.

מִזְבֵּחַ *altar*; see זבח.

מֶזֶג (Arab. *mixture*); see מסך.

מֶזֶג m., *mixed wine*, Cant. 7:3.

מָזֶה *exhausted, reduced* (by famine), Deut. 32:24.

מַזֶּה for מַהְזֶה, from מה.

מִזָּה p. n. of a man.

מְזָוִים *cellar*; see זוה.

מְזוּזָה *door-post*; see זוז.

מָזוֹן *food*; see זון.

מָזוֹר *bandage*; see זור.

מֵזַח, מְזִיחַ m.— I. *a girdle.* — II. *pride*, Job 12:21.

מֵזִין for מַאֲזִין Hiph. part., from אזן.

מַזָּלוֹת see נזל.

מִזְלָגָה, מַזְלֵג *fork*; see זלג.

מְזִמָּה *invention*; see זמם.

מַזְמוֹר, מִזְמֹרוֹת, see זמר.

מְזָרִים, מִזְרֶה, see זרה.

מְזֹרוֹת see נזל.

מִזְרָח *east*; see זרח.

מִזְרָק *cup*; see זרק.

מֵחַ, מֹחַ; see מחח.

מָחָא *smite, clap*; with כַּף יַד *hands*. Pi. the same, Eze. 25:6.

מְחָא Ch., *struck, smote.* Pa. *exult*, Dan. 4:32. Ithp. *was smitten*, Ezr. 6:11.

מְחָא Ch. Aph. part., from חיא; see חיה.

מַחֲבֵא, מַחֲבָאִים *hiding-place*; see חבא.

מַחֲבֶרֶת, מְחַבְּרוֹת; see חבר.

מַחֲבַת *frying-pan*; see חבת.

מָחָה I. *wipe away.*— II. *arrive at*, Nu. 34:11, with עַל. Niph. (fut. apoc. יִמַּח) *was blotted out.* Hiph. (fut. apoc. תֶּמַח) *blot out.*

מְחִי m., *striking*, Eze. 26:ד.

מְחֻנָּג *compasses*; see חגג.

מָחוֹן *harbour*; see חון.

מְחִיָּיאֵל, מְחוּיָאֵל p. n., *a descendant of Cain.*

מַחֲוִים p. n. of a place unknown.

מָחוֹל, מְחוֹלָה *dance*; see חגל.

מַחֲזֶה, מֶחֱזָה, מַחֲזִיאוֹת; see חזה.

מֹחַח (Arab. *marrow*).

מֵחַ m., *fat, rich.*

מֹחַ m., *marrow*, Job 21:24.

מְחִידָא p. n. of a man.

מְחִיָה; see חָיָה, חיה.

מְחִיר *price*; see מחר.

מַחְלִי, מַחְלוֹן, מַחְלָה, מַחֲלָה, מַחֲלָה, מַחֲלַיִים; see חלה.

מְחִלָּה *hole*; see חלל.

מַחֲלָף, מַחֲלָפוֹת; see חלף.

מַחֲלֹקֶת, מַחְלְקוֹת; see חלק.

מַחֲלַת, מָחֲלַת; see חלה.

מְחֹלָתִי *Meholathite*; see אבל.

מַחֲמָאוֹת; see חמא.

מַחֲמֶצֶת; see חמץ.

מְחַן Ch. Pe. inf., from חנן.

מַחֲנֶה ,מַחֲנַיִם camp; see חנה.

מַחְסֶה ,מַחֲסֶה ,מַחֲסְיָה; see חסה.

מַחְסוֹם curb; see חסם.

מְחֻסְפָּס part. of the quadriliteral verb חספס; see חסף.

מָחַץ (fut. יִמְחַץ).—I. dash violently (the head to pieces)—(the foot into blood), Ps. 68:22.—II. shoot arrows, Nu. 24:8.

מַחַץ m., contusion, bruise, Isa. 30:26.

מַחֲצָה ,מַחֲצִית; see חצה.

מחצצרים; see in חצר.

מָחַק destroyed, Jud. 5:26.

מָחְקָר; see חקר.

מָחַר same as מכר.

מְחִיר m.—I. price; בִּמְחִיר with a price.—II. p. n. of a man.

מָחָר m. — I. morrow, some future day; לְמָחָר to-morrow; בְּיוֹם מָחָר for the morrow; וּכְעֵת מָחָר and מָחָר כָּעֵת הַזֹּאת about this time to-morrow; כָּעֵת מָחָר הַשְּׁלִישִׁית this time the day after to-morrow. —II. adv. hereafter, henceforward.

מָחֳרָת f., to-morrow; מִמָּחֳרָת the day after; מִמָּחֳרַת הַשַּׁבָּת the day after the sabbath; עַד־מִמָּחֳרָת until the next day; לְמָחֳרָתָם adv. the day after.

מַחֲרֵשֶׁת ,מַחֲרֶשֶׁת; see חרש.

מַחְשֹׁף; see חשף.

מַחֲשֶׁבֶת ,מַחֲשָׁבָה; see חשב.

מַחְשָׁךְ darkness; see חשך.

מָחַח p. n. of a man.

מַחְתָּה shovel, &c.; see חתה.

מְחִתָּה breaking, &c.; see חתת.

מַחְתֶּרֶת digging; see חתר.

מְטָא Ch., come on, to, arrive at, with עַל.

מַטְאֲטֵא; see טוא.

מְטֹהָר for מִתְטַהֵר Hith. part.; see טהר.

מָטוֹת ,מַטֶּה ,מַטָּה ,מִטָּה ,מַטֶּה; see נטה.

מַטְוֶה yarn; see טוה.

מַטִּל (Arab. forged iron): hence, the English word metal.

מַטִּיל m., iron bar, Job 40:18.

מַטְמוֹן treasure; see טמן.

מַטָּע plant; see נטע.

מַטְעַמִּים dainties; see טעם.

מִטְפַּחַת mantle; see טפח.

מָטָר. Hiph. הִמְטִיר rain, cause, give rain; used also of lightning, hail, fire and brimstone, manna, bread. Niph. was rained on, Am. 4:7.

מָטָר m. (pl. מְטָרוֹת; const. מְטָרוֹת) rain, shower.

מַטְרִי p. n. of a man.

מַטְרֵד p. n. of a woman.

מַטָּרָה ,מַטָּרָא; see נטר.

מִי interrog. pron.—I. who? בַּר־מִי whose daughter? לְמִי to whom? בְּמִי whom? אֶת־מִי by whom? מִי מָנָה who can number? מִי יִתֵּן would that it were! וְהָיָה מִי יִתֵּן עֶרֶב would that it were evening! —II. without interrog., who, every one; מִי אֲשֶׁר whoever.

מֵידְבָא p. n. of a city in the tribe of Reuben.

מֵידָד p. n. of a man.

מֵיטָב good; see יטב.

מִיכָא p. n. of a man, same as מִיכָיָא

מִיכָאֵל (who is like unto God?) p. n.

—I. *Michael* the archangel.—II. of a man.

מִיכָה, מִיכָיְהוּ p. n.—I. *Micah* the prophet.—II. also of other men.

מִיכָיְהוּ p. n.—I. of a man.—II. of a woman.

מִיכָה, מִיכָיְהוּ p. n. of a man. מִיכָל p. n.; see מכל.

מַיִם m. pl. (const. מֵי, מֵימֵי; with suff. מֵימָיו; with ה loc. הַמַּיְמָה).—I. *water, waters,* used with pl. adj., with verb either pl. or sing.—II. *seed;* יָצְאָ מִמֵּי פ׳ *whose son, descendant he is,* Isa. 48:1.

מֵי־הַיַּרְקוֹן p. n., a city in the tribe of Dan.

מֵי־נִפְתּוֹחַ p.n., a fountain near Jerusalem.

מִין, מִן (Syr. *family*).

מִין m., *kind, species,* always with לְ pref.; פְּרִי לְמִינוֹ *fruit after his kind.*

תְּמוּנָה f., *resemblance, likeness.*

מֵינִיקוֹת, מֵינֶקֶת; see ינק.

מֵיפַעַת, מֵפַעַת p. n., a town of the Levites in the tribe of Reuben.

מִיץ *chaff;* see מוץ.

מֵישָׁא p. n. of a man.

מִישָׁאֵל p. n. of a man.

מִישׁוֹר; see ישׁר.

מֵישַׁךְ p. n., *Meshach,* one of the captivity, called also מִישָׁאֵל.

מֵישַׁע p. n., a king of Moab.

מֵישַׁע p.n., a son of Caleb.

מֵישָׁרִים; see ישׁר.

מֵיתָר *cord;* see יתר.

מַכְאוֹב *pain;* see כאב.

מְכְבְּנָא same as כִּבּוֹן.

מַכְבְּנַּי p.n. of a man.

מַכְבֵּר, מִכְבָּר *carpet;* see כבר.

מַכָּה *stroke;* see נכה.

מִבְוָה *burning;* see כוה.

מָכוֹן, מְכוֹנָה, מְכוּנָה, see כון.

מְכוּרָה; see כּר.

מָכִיר p. n., *Machir* the son of Manasseh, Gen. 50:23; perhaps for *a Manassite,* Jud. 5:14; patronymic מָכִירִי.

מָכַךְ. Niph. fut. יִמַּךְ *become weak,* Ecc. 10:18. Hoph. pl. הֻמְּכוּ for הֻמְּכוּ *they perish,* Job 24:24.

מְכָל root not used; (Arab. *empty of water*).

מִיכָל הַמַּיִם m.; *brooks of water,* 2 Sa. 17:20. — II. p. n., *Michal,* the daughter of Saul and wife of David.

מִכְלָאוֹת, מִכְלָה, see כלא; מִכְלוֹל, see כלה.

מַכְלִים, מִכְלָל, מִכְלוֹל, see כלל. מַאֲכֹלֶת for מַאֲכֹלֶת *food;* see אכל.

מִכְמָשׁ, מִכְמָשׁ, מִכְמָס (see כָּמַס), p.n. a town in the tribe of Benjamin, Μαχμάς.

מִכְמֶרֶת, מַכְמֹר, מִכְמָר *net;* see כמר.

מְכְמְתָת p.n., a town on the borders of Ephraim and Manasseh.

מַכְנַדְבַי p. n. of a man.

מִכְנָס *breeches;* see כנס.

מֶכֶס, מֶכֶס *price;* see כסס.

מְכַסֶּה, מִכְסָה; see כסה.

מַכְפֵּלָה p.n. of a district near Hebron.

מָכַר (fut. יִמְכֹּר; inf. with suff. מָכְרָהּ, מָכְרָם; imp. with ה parag. מָכְרָה).—I. *he sold,* with בְּ of the price.—II. *he gave a daughter in marriage* (in consideration of a gift).—III. *he gave up men* into the power of others. Niph. נִמְכַּר *was sold*. Hith. הִתְמַכֵּר I. *was sold*.— II. *was surrendered*.

מֶ֫כֶר m. (with suff. מִכְרָם).—I. *value, price*.—II. *valuable article*, Neh. 13:16.

מִכְרִי p. n. of a man.

מִמְכָּר m., מִמְכֶּרֶת f.—I. *sale*.—II. *thing sold*.

מַכָּר *relative*; see נכר.

מִכְרֶה *pit of salt*; see כרה.

מְכֵרָה *sword*; see כור.

מְכֵרָתִי *Macherathite*, patron. 1 Chron. 11:36.

מַכְשֵׁלָה, מִכְשׁוֹל; see כשל.

מִכְתָּב *writing*; see כתב.

מְכִתָּה *breaking*; see כתת.

מִכְתָּם; see כתם.

מַכְתֵּשׁ *mortar*; see כתש.

מָלֵא, מָלָא (fut. יִמְלָא; inf. מְלֹאת).—I. *fill*; מָלְאוּ הַשְּׁלָטִים *fill the shields*, i. e. *enlarge them so as to cover you*, Jer. 51:11; מָלֵא יָד *filled the hand*, i. e. *conferred an office*.—II. *fulfil, execute fully, thoroughly*; מָלְאָה צְבָאָהּ *her warfare is accomplished*; מָלְאָה נַפְשִׁי *my soul is full*, Ex. 15:9. Niph. נִמְלָא (fut. יִמָּלֵא) *is full, filled*, with מִן, לְ. Pi. מִלֵּא מָלָא (inf. מַלֵּא מַלֹּאת; fut. יְמַלֵּא).—I. *fulfil* (of time, promise, &c.).—II. *fill the hand*, i. e. *consecrate to the priest's office*.—III. *fill as a vessel* (with accus. מִן), *insert*, i. e. *fill in*, of the stones in the breast-plate, Ex. 28:17.—IV. used with other verbs, &c., implying the completion of their action; מִלֵּא יָדוֹ בַקֶּשֶׁת *he fully drew the bow*, lit. *filled his*

hand with, 2 Ki. 9:24; קָרְאוּ מָלֵא *cry out strongly*; מִלֵּא אַחֲרֵי *fulfilled the following*, i. e. *followed fully*. Pu. part. מְמֻלָּאִים *filled with gems*, Cant. 5:14. Hith. fut. יִתְמַלְּאוּן *they are fully set against me*, Job 16:10.

מְלָא Ch., *filled*, Dan. 2:35. Hith. *was filled*, Dan. 3:19.

מָלֵא m., מְלֵאָה f., *full* (used as מִלֹּא, see above Pi. IV.); בְּכֶסֶף מָלֵא *full (i. e. just), money*; מֵי מָלֵא *waters of fulness* (i. e. *ample*), *abundant*; מְלֵא יָמִים *full of days*, Jer. 6:11.

מְלֹא, מְלוֹא, מְלֹא m.—I. *filling, fulness*; מְלֹא כַף *the filling of the palm, palm full*; מְלֹא חָפְנֵיכֶם פִּיחַ *both your closed hands full of ashes*, Ex. 9:8; מְלֹא קוֹמָתוֹ *his full stature*, 1 Sam. 28:20.—II. *multitude*, Gen. 48:19.

מְלֵאָה f., *overplus, excess* of corn and wine which was to be offered to the Lord, Ex. 22:28; Nu 18:27.

מְלֹאת for מְלֵאת Kal inf., from מָלֵא. מֶלֶךְ for מְלָכִים pl., from כ' מַלְאָכִים.

מִלּוֹא m., p. n.—I. a certain part of the citadel of Jerusalem, called also בֵּית מִלּוֹא 2 Ki. 12:21.—II. a castle of the Sichemites, Jud. 9:6, 20.

מִלֻּאָה, מִלֻּאָה f., *insertion of gems* (see above מָלֵא Pi. III.).

מִלֻּאִים m. pl.—I. *inauguration, consecration* (of priests). — II. אַבְנֵי מִלֻּאִים *set* (inserted jewels); see מִלֻּאָה.

מִלֵּאת f., Cant. 5:12, *fulness*, perhaps *prominency*, some peculiar mode of setting jewels.

מַלְאָכִי, מְלָאכָה, מַלְאָכוּת; see מַלְאָךְ.

מַלְבֻּשׁ same as לְבוּשׁ clothing; see לבשׁ.

מַלְבֵּן brick kiln; see לבן.

מִלָּה saying, see מלל.

מָלוּ for מָלְאוּ Kal pret. pl., from מלא.

מְלוּכָה, מָלוּךְ rule; see מלך.

מְלוֹנָה, מָלוֹן inn; see לון.

I. מָלַח Niph. נִמְלַח pass away, vanish, Isa. 51:6.

מְלָחִים m. pl., rolling, passing away, Jer. 38:11, 12.

II. מָלַח (from מֶלַח), salted, Ex. 30:35. Pu. part. מְמֻלָּח. Hoph. salted, Eze. 16:4.

מֶלַח m., salt; יָם־הַמֶּלַח the salt sea, i.e. the Dead Sea; בְּרִית מֶלַח covenant of salt, i.e. perpetual, Nu. 18:19.

מְלַח m. Ch., salt.

מְלַח Ch., eat salt, Ezr. 4:14.

מַלּוּחַ m., ἅλιμος, salt plant, (halimus atriplex—Linn.).

מַלָּח m., pl. מַלָּחִים sailors.

מְלֵחָה f., salt land, waste.

מִלְחָמָה war; see לחם.

מָלַט Pi. מִלֵּט, מִלַּט—I. cause to escape, slip.—II. deliver, save.—III. hatch (of eggs), Isa. 34:15. Hiph. same as Pi. Niph. was delivered, set at liberty, saved. Hith. same as Niph.

מֶלֶט m., clay.

מְלַטְיָה p.n. of a man.

מְלִילוֹת ears of corn; see מלל.

מְלִינִים Hiph. part. pl., from לון.

מְלִיצָה saying; see לון.

מָלַךְ reigned; with בְּ, עַל was made a king. Hiph. make any one a king. with לְ. Hoph. was made a king. Dan. 9:1. Niph. took, sought, counsel.

מֶלֶךְ m. (with suff. מַלְכִּי; pl. מְלָכִים, מַלְכֵי) king, applied to God and also to idols; דֶּרֶךְ הַמֶּלֶךְ royal way.—II. p.n. of a man.—III. עֵמֶק הַמֶּלֶךְ p.n., a valley not far from the Dead Sea.

מֶלֶךְ m. Ch., king.

מְלַךְ m. Ch., counsel, Dan. 4:24.

מֹלֶךְ, with art. הַמֹּלֶךְ Μολόχ, Moloch, an idol of the Ammonites.

מַלְכָּה f., queen. Ch. the same.

מִלְכָּה p.n. of a daughter of Haran.

מְלֶכֶת f., מ' הַשָּׁמַיִם the queen of Heaven, Ashtoreth, Astarte, an idol of Canaan.

מֹלֶכֶת p.n. of a woman.

(מְלִיכוּ, מַלּוּבִי) מַלּוּךְ p.n. of a man.

מְלוּכָה f., rule, government, royalty.

מַלְכוּת f., rule, kingdom, royal dignity. מַלְכוּ f. Ch., the same.

מַלְכִּיאֵל p.n. of a man; — patron.

מַלְכִּיָּהוּ, מַלְכִּיָּה p.n. of a man.

מַלְכִּי־צֶדֶק p.n., Melchizedek, king of Salem.

מַלְכִּירָם p.n. of a man.

מַלְכִּי־שׁוּעַ p.n. of one of Saul's sons.

מַלְכָּם, מַלְכֹּם same as מֶלֶךְ.

מַה־לָּכֶם for מַלְּכֶם; see מָה.

מַמְלָכָה f. (const. מַמְלֶכֶת; with suff. מַמְלַכְתּוֹ; pl. מַמְלָכוֹת rule, regal government; בֵּית מ' seat of government; עִיר מ' capital city; זֶרַע מ' royal family;

מַמְלָכוּת const. מַמְלֶכֶת f., the same.

מַלְכֹּדֶת trap; see לכד.

מָלַל speaking. Pi. מִלֵּל announce, tell.

מְלַל Ch. Pa. מַלֵּל speak, announce.

מִלָּה f. (pl. מִלִּים, מִלִּין) — I. saying, argument. — II. thing spoken of.

מִלָּה f. Ch. (pl. מִלִּין) saying, decree.

מַלָּל p.n. of a man.

מַלֹּתִי p.n. of a man.

מְלִילָה f., pl. מְלִילוֹת ears of corn, Deu. 23:26.

מַלְמָד goad; see למד.

מָלַץ Niph. נִמְלְצוּ are become smooth, agreeable, Ps. 119:103.

מֶלְצַר a certain office in the king of Babylon's palace; nature of the office unknown, Dan. 1:11, 16.

מָלַק break, bruise, Lev. 1:15; 5:8; LXX. ἀποκνίζειν.

מַלְקָחַיִם, מֶלְקָחַיִם, מַלְקוֹחַ; see לקח.

מַלְקוֹשׁ latter rain; see לקש.

מֶלְתָּחָה f., wardrobe, 2 Ki. 10:22.

מַלְתָּעוֹת jaws; see לתע.

מַמְּגֻרוֹת granary; see גור.

מְמַדִּים measures; see מדד.

מְמוּכָן p.n. of a prince of Persia.

מְמוֹתִים, מְמוֹת; see מות.

מַמְזֵר m. — I. foreigner. — II. bastard.

מִמְכֶּרֶת, מִמְכָּר sale; see מכר.

מַמְלָכוֹת, מַמְלָכָה kingdom; see מלך.

מַמְרֹרִים, מְמֹר; see מרר.

מַמְרֵא p.n.; see מרא.

מֶמְשָׁלֶת, מֶמְשָׁלָה, מִמְשָׁל; see משל.

מָן manna; see מנן.

מָן, מֵן Ch. pron. — I. who? — II. what? מַן־דִּי whoever.

מִן, מְ, מֶ, מִנִּי, מֶנִי (with suff. מִמֶּנּוּ, מִמֶּנָּה, מִמֶּנִּי; מֶנִי, מֶנְהוּ, מֶנְהֶם or מִנְהֶם, מֶנְהֶם; see מִן in מֵן) prep. — I. from. — II. from out of. — III. of. — IV. by. — V. because of. — VI. besides. — VII. among; תִּשָּׁבֵל מִנָּשִׁים she shall be barren among women. — VIII. some of, part of. — IX. more than; used also with inf.; הִשְׁחִיתוּ מֵאֲבוֹתָם they are worse than the fathers; מָתוֹק מִדְּבַשׁ sweeter than honey; אֶגְדַּל מִמְּךָ I shall be greater than thee; מִן...וְעַד, מִן...עַד from ...unto; לְמִן from thence.

מִן Ch., the same.

מְנָאוֹת; see מְנָת in מנה.

מִנְדָּה same as מָדָּה; see מדד.

מַנְדַּע knowledge, &c.; see ידע.

מָנָה I. number. — II. appoint, constitute, with לְ. Niph. נִמְנָה was numbered, with אֶת. Pi. מִנָּה appoint, constitute, with עַל, לְ. Pu. part. מְמֻנִּים persons appointed, 1 Chron. 9:29.

מְנָה, מְנָא Ch., numbered, tried. Pa. constituted, appointed.

מָנֶה m., a certain weight, perhaps of one hundred shekels.

מָנָה f. (pl. מָנוֹת) part, portion.

מְנָת f. (pl. מְנָיוֹת, מְנָאוֹת) part, portion.

מֹנִים m. pl., times; עֲשֶׂרֶת מ׳ ten times, Gen. 31:7, 41.

מְנִי m., an idol, Isa. 65:11.

מִנְיָן m. Ch., number, Ezr. 6:17.

מְנָהָרוֹת; see נהר.

מָנוֹד refuge; see נוד.

מְנוּחָה, מָנוֹחַ; see נוח.

מָנַת; see נון.

מָנוֹס, מְנוּסָה; see נוס.

מָנוֹד; see נוד.

מְנוֹרָה; see נור.

מִנְחֹדָה; see נחר.

מְנָזְרִים same as נְזָרִים.

מָנָה (Arab. *he gave*).

מִנְחָה f. (pl. מְנָחוֹת; with suff. מִנְחֹתֵיכֶם).—I. *gift to men.*—II. *to God, meat-offering.*

מִנְחָה f. Ch., *gift.*

מְנַחֵם p. n. of a man.

מְנַחַת p. n.—I. of a man.—II. of a place.

מִנִּי p. n. of a place, perhaps *Armenia,* Jer. 51:27; see also in מֶן, מִן, מנן.

מִנְיָן, מָנְיוֹת, מְנִי; see מנה.

מִימִין, מִנְיָמִין p. n. of a man.

מָן m., *manna,* the food miraculously supplied to the Israelites in the wilderness.

מָן m. with suff. מָנֵהוּ *part of him,* with prep. מִן and suff.; מִמֶּנִּי *from me;* מִמְּךָ, מִמֵּךְ f. *from thee;* מִמֶּנּוּ *from him;* מִמֶּנָּה *from her;* see מִן.

מִנִּי, מִנַּיִם pl., *strings of an instrument,* Ps. 150:4; 45:9.

מִנִּית p. n., a place in Ammon.

מָנַע (fut. יִמְנַע) *keep back, withhold,* wit' מָן and לְ. Niph. נִמְנַע *was withholden, kept back.*

מִנְעָל, מַנְעוּל; see נעל.

מַנְעַמִּים *delicacies;* see נעם.

מְנַעֲנְעִים *cymbals;* see נוע.

מְנַקִּיּוֹת *bowls;* see מְנַקִּית in נקה.

מְנַקֶּת; see ינק.

מְנַשֶּׁה (*that which is forgotten*), p. n.

—I. *Manasseh the son of Joseph,* Μανασσῆς; patron. מְנַשִּׁי, הַמְנַשִּׁי.—II. given also to other men.

מְנָת *part;* see מנה.

מָם, מַם, מִסִּים; see מסס.

מְסַבּוֹת, מִסָבֵּי, מֵסַב; see סבב.

מִסְגֶּרֶת, מַסְגֵּר; see סגר.

מַסָּד *foundation;* see יסד.

מִסְדְּרוֹן *portico;* see סדר.

מָסָה same as מסס. Hiph. הִמְסָה I. *dissolved, melted.*—II. *fainted.*

מַסָּה, see מסס; מַסָּה, see נסה.

מַסְוֶה m., *veil of Moses,* Ex. 34:33-35.

מְסוּכָה same as מְשׂוּכָה *hedge;* see שׂוך.

מַסָּח; see נסח.

מִסְחָר *traffic;* see סחר.

מָסָךְ *mixed.*

מֶסֶךְ m., *mixture,* Ps. 75:9.

מִמְסָךְ *mixed wine.*

מְסֻכָה, מָסָךְ; see סכך.

מַסֶּכֶת, מַסֵּכָה; see נסך.

מִסְכְּנוֹת, מִסְכְּנֻת, מִסְכֵּן; see סכן.

מַסְלוּל, מְסִלָּה; see סלל.

מַסְמְרוֹת, מַסְמְרִים, מַסְמְרִים; see סמר.

מָסַס I. *dissolve, melt.*—II. *faint.* Niph. נָמֵס, with pause נָמַס (fut. יִמַּס; inf. הִמֵּס).—I. *was dissolved, melted.* — II. *enervated* by fear, grief, pain. Hiph. pl. הֵמַסּוּ *cause to faint,* Deu. 1:28; see מאס.

מָס m., *wasting, miserable,* Job 6:14.

מַס m., *tribute, tax;* הָיָה לָמַס and הָיָה לְמַס עֹבֵד *became tributary;* שׂוּם לָמַס or נָתַן *the same;* אֲשֶׁר עַל הַמַּס *who was over the tribute;* pl. שָׂרֵי מִסִּים *chief collectors* (of tribute), Ex. 1:11.

מַסָּה f., const. מַסַּת tribute, offering, Deu. 16:10.

מָסָס m., melting, wasting away, Ps. 58:9.

מַסַּע, מַסָּע ; see נסע.

מִסְעָד prop; see סעד.

מִסְפֵּד grief; see ספד.

מִסְפּוֹא provender; see ספא.

מִסְפָּחוֹת, מִסְפַּחַת ; see ספח.

מִסְפָּר, מִסְפֶּרֶת number; see ספר.

מָסַר, inf. לִמְסָר to stir up, wring out rebellion, Nu. 31:16. Niph. fut. וַיִּמָּסְרוּ were extracted, selected, Nu. 31:5.

מָסֹרֶת f., fetters, bonds, Eze. 20:37, from אסר.

מוּסָר discipline; see יסר.

מִסְתָּר, מִסְתּוֹר ; see סתר.

מַעֲבָד work, see עבד ; מַעֲבֶה deep, see עבה.

מַעְבָּרָה, מַעֲבָר passage; see עבר.

מַעְגָּל, מַעֲנָל, מַעֲנָלָה ; see ענל.

מָעַד vacillate. Hiph. cause to vacillate. Hoph. made to vacillate, Pro. 25:19.

מַעֲדָי p.n. of a man.

מוֹעַדְיָה, מַעֲדְיָה p.n. of a man.

מַעֲדַנּוֹת, מַעֲדַנִּים delicacies; see ערן.

מֵעָה (Arab. bowels)

מֵעִים const. מְעֵי m. pl. (with suff. מֵעַי, מֵעֶיךָ).—I. intestines.—II. belly.—III. womb.—IV. heart, mind.

מְעִין m. pl. Ch., belly.

מֵעָה f., מֵעוֹתֵי "its extent" (Lee), Isa. 48:19.

מָעוֹג cake; see עונ.

מָעוֹז, מָעֻזִּים ; see עזז.

מָעוֹךְ p.n. of a man, 1 Sa. 27:2.

מָעוֹן, מְעֹנָה, מְעוֹנִים, מְעוֹנֹתַי ; see עון.

מָעוּף ; see עוף.

מָעוֹר nakedness; see עור.

מַעֲזְיָהוּ, מַעַזְיָה p.n. of a man.

מָעַט was, became, few, small. Pi. מִעֵט the same, Ecc. 12:3. Hiph. הִמְעִיט I. make few.—II. give little.

מְעָט מַעַט (מְעָט) a little, few; pl. מְעַטִּים few; מְעַט מַיִם a little water, Gen. 18:4; מְתֵי מְעָט few men, Deu. 26:5; מְעַט מְעָט by little and little, Ex. 23:23; כִּמְעַט I. within a little.—II. shortly, soon.—III. as a few, as nothing.

מְעַט, f. מְעֻטָּה drawn, naked (lit. bald), of a sword, Eze. 21:20.

מַעֲטֶה garment; see עטה.

מַעֲטָפָה ; see עטף.

מְעִי ; see עוה.

מֵעָי p.n. of a man.

מְעִיל cloak; see מעל.

מֵעִים bowels, &c.; see מעה.

מַעְיָן well; see עין.

מָעוּךְ, part. מָעוּךְ I. pressed, 1 Sa. 26:7.—II. bruised, injured (θλαδίας), Lev. 22:24.with בְּ. Pu. מֹעַךְ pressed, Eze. 23:3.

מַעֲכָה, מַעֲכָת p.n.—I. of a region and city near Mount Hermon.—II. a name applied both to men and women; מַעֲכָתִי a Maachathite.

מָעַל (inf. מְעֹל; fut. יִמְעַל, וַיִּמְעַל), do perversely, wickedly, rebel, with בְּ.

מַעַל m., perverseness, sin, Job 21:34; see also in עלה.

מְעִיל m., long upper garment worn by persons of rank.

מַעֲלֶה, מַעֲלֶה, מֹעַל, מֵעַל; see עלה.

מֶעָלִין, מַעֲלָל, מַעֲלִיל; see עלל.

מֶעָמָד, מַעֲמֹו; see עמד.

מַעֲמָסָה; see עמס.

מַעֲמַקִּים depths; see עמק.

מַעֲנִית, מַעֲנֶה, מַעֲנֶה, (לְמַעַן) מַעַן; see ענה.

מְעוֹנָה same as מְעוֹנָה habitation; see עון.

מַעַץ p.n. of a man.

מַעֲצֵבָה labour; see עצב.

מַעֲצָד axe; see עצד.

מַעֲצוֹר, מַעֲצֹר; see עצר.

מַעֲקֶה; see עקה.

מַעֲשֵׂשִׂים; see עשׂשׂ.

מַעֲרַת, מְעָרֹות, מְעָרָה, מְעָרָה, מְעַר; see ערה.

מַעֲרָבָה, מְעָרָב; see ערב.

מַעֲרֶכֶת, מַעֲרָכָה, מַעֲרֶךְ; see ערך.

מַעֲרֻמִּים; see ערם.

מַעֲרָצָה terror; see ערץ.

מַעֲשֶׂה, מַעֲשֵׂי, מַעֲשֶׂה; see עשׂה.

מַעֲשֵׂר, מַעֲשְׂרֹות, מַעֲשֵׂר, מַעֲשֵׂר; see עשׂר.

מַעֲשַׂקּוֹת; see עשׁק.

מֹף and נֹף p. n., a city of Egypt.

מַפָּח, מַפֻּחַ; see נפח.

מְפִיבֹשֶׁת, מְפִבֹשֶׁת p. n.—I. a son of Saul.—II. a son of Jonathan.

מֵפִיץ; see פוץ.

מַפָּלֶת, מַפָּלָה, מַפָּל; see נפל.

מִפְלָאָה; see פלא.

מִפְלַגָּה classes; see פלג.

מִפְלָט escape; see פלט.

מִפְלֶצֶת idol; see פלץ.

מִפְלָשׂ poising; see פלשׂ.

מִפְעָל, מִפְעָלָה, מִפְעָל; see פעל.

מִפְעַת same as מֵיפַעַת.

מֵפֵץ, מַפָּץ; see נפץ.

מִפְקָד; see פקד.

מִפְרָץ; see פרץ.

מַפְרֶקֶת vertebra; see פרק.

מִפְרָשׂ; see פרשׂ.

מִפְשָׂעָה buttocks; see פשׂע.

מִפְתֵּחַ, מַפְתֵּחַ; see פתח.

מִפְתָּן threshold; see פתן.

מֹץ chaff, same as מוֹץ.

מָצָא (fut. יִמְצָא; imp. מְצָא; pl. f. מְצֶאןָ; inf. מְצֹא; with suff. מֹצַאֲכֶם; part. מוֹצֵא, מֹצֵא, f. מֹצֵאת, מֹצֵאת).—I. come to, arrive at.—II. obtain, acquire.—III. find, discover.—IV. find, i. e. meet with, discover.—V. be enough, with לְ, עַד. Niph. נִמְצָא (fut. יִמָּצֵא).—I. was obtained, acquired.—II. was found, arrived at.—III. was present, at hand, with לְ. Hiph. הִמְצִיא I. cause to come, deliver up, with בְּיַד into the power of any one.—II. recompense, repay.—III. present, offer up.

מַצָּבָה, מַצֵּבָה, מַצָּב, מַצָּב, מַצֶּבֶת; see נצב.

מִצְבָּיָה p. n. of an unknown place.

מְצוּדָה, מְצוּדָה, מָצוֹד, מָצֹד, מָצֹד; see צוד.

מָצָה suck, drain, wring out, with מִן. Niph. נִמְצָה become sucked, drained, wrung out.

מַצָּה see in מצץ and נצה.

מֹצָה p. n., a town in the tribe of Benjamin.

מִצְהָלָה neighing; see צהל.

מִצְוָה; see צוה.

מְצוֹלָה, מְצוּלָה depth; see צול.

מָצוֹק, מְצוּקָה, מָצוֹק restraint; see צוק.

מָצוֹר p. n., Egypt; יְאֹרֵי מ' the river of Egypt, the Nile; see also מָצוֹר, in צור מְצֻרָה.

מִצְרַיִם p. n.—I. a son of Ham.—II. Egypt.—III. an Egyptian.

מִצְרִי m.; pl. מִצְרִים; f. מִצְרִית; pl. מִצְרִיּוֹת an Egyptian.

מַצּוּת contention; see נצה.

מֵצַח m. (with suff. מִצְחוֹ; pl. const. מִצְחוֹת), forehead.

מִצְחָה f., greaves (guards for the legs), 1 Sa. 17:6.

מְצִלָּה, מְצִלּוֹת, מְצִלְתַּיִם ; see צלל.

מִצְנֶפֶת turban; see צנף.

מַצָּע bed; see יצע.

מִצְעָד ; see צעד.

מִצְעָר, מִצְעִירָה little; see צער.

מִצְפֶּה, מִצְפָּה ; see צפה.

מַצְפֻּנִים hidden places; see צפן.

מָצַץ suck (as an infant), Isa. 66:11.

מַצָּה f., ἄζυμον, pl. מַצּוֹת pure, unleavened bread, τὰ ἄζυμα; חַג הַמַּצּוֹת ἡ ἑορτὴ τῶν ἀζύμων, the feast of unleavened bread; see also in נצה.

מֵצַר, מְצָרִים trouble; see צרר.

מִצְרַיִם Egypt, &c.; see מָצוֹר.

מַק rottenness; see מקק.

מַקֶּבֶת, מַקָּבָה ; see נקב.

מַקֵּדָה p.n., a town in the tribe of Judah.

מִקְדָּשׁ ; see קדשׁ.

מַקְהֵלוֹת, מַקְהֵלִים assemblies; see קהל.

מִקְוֶה, מִקְנֶה hope; see קוה.

מָקוֹם place; see קום.

מָקוֹר fountain; see קור.

מַקְחוֹת, מִקְחֶה ; see לקח.

מִקְטָר, מְקַטֶּרֶת ; see קטר.

מַקֵּל m. (const. מַקֵּל, מַקַּל; with suff. מַקְלִי; pl. מַקְלוֹת), stick.

מְקֹלֹת p. n. of a man.

מִקְלָט safety; see קלט.

מִקְלַעַת sculpture; see קלע.

מִקְנֶה, מִקְנָה ,מִקְנֵיָהוּ ; see קנה.

מָקֵץ p. n. of a place.

מַקְצוֹעַ, מִקְצֹעוֹת, מַקְצֻעוֹת ; see קצע.

מָקַק. Niph. נָמַק waste away, consume, fail. Hiph. הֵמַק cause to waste, Zec. 14:12.

מָק m., rottenness, Isa. 3:24.

מִקְרָא ; see קרא.

מְקֵרָה, מִקְרֶה ; see קרה.

מְקֵרָה coolness; see קרר.

מְקַרְקֵר Pi. part., from קור.

מִקְשָׁה, מַקְשֶׁה ; see קשה.

מַר, מֹר ,מוֹר ,מֵר ; see מרר.

מָרָא, part. מוֹרָאָה rebellious, Zep. 3:1. Hiph. put forth courage, Job 39:19; see מָרָה.

מְרִיא m.—I. fattened.—II. specially a fatted calf.

מָרֵא m. Ch., Lord.

מֻרְאָה f., crop (of birds), Lev. 1:16.

מַמְרֵא p.n.—I. of a man, Mamre.—II. אֵלוֹנֵי מַמְרֵא (oaks of Mamre), and מַמְרֵא p. n. of a place near Hebron.

מְרָא p. n. of a woman.

בְּרֹאדַךְ בַּלְאֲדָן ,מְרֹאדַךְ ב' p. n., one of the kings of Babylon.

מַרְאֶה, מַרְאָה ; see ראה.

מְרַאֲשֹׁת, מַרְאֲשֶׁה, מַרְאָשׁוֹת ; see ראשׁ.

מֵרָב p. n., Merab, a daughter of Saul

מַרְבַדִּים coverlets; see רבד.

מַרְבִּית, מִרְבָּה ,מַרְבֶּה ; see רבה.

מִרְבָּץ ,מַרְבֵּץ ; see רבץ.

מַרְבֵּק stall; see רבק.

מַרְגֵּעָה ,מַרְגּוֹעַ ; see רגע.

מַרְגְּלוֹת *at the feet;* see רגל.

מַרְגֵּמָה *heap of stones;* see רגם.

מָרַד *rebelled,* with בְּ, עַל.

מְרַד Ch., *rebellion,* Ezr. 4:19.

מֶרֶד m.—I. *the same,* Jos. 22:22.—II. p. n. of a man.

מָרָד Ch., f. מָרָדָא *rebellious,* Ezr. 4:12,15.

מַרְדּוּת f., *rebellion,* 1 Sa. 20:30.

מְרֹדָךְ m., perhaps the name of an idol of Babylon, Jer. 50:2.

מָרְדְּכַי p. n., *Mordechai,* a Jew in Persia, Μαρδοχαῖος.

מָרָה *rebelled, rebelled against, disobeyed,* with בְּ; מ' אֶת־פִּי יְהוָה *they rebelled against the mouth* (i.e. words) *of the Lord.* Hiph. הִמְרָה *fought against, embittered, angered,* with בְּ, עִם.

מוֹרָה m., *razor.*

מְרִי m. (with pause מֶרִי; with suff. מֶרְיְךָ, מֶרְיָם).—I. *bitterness.*—II. *rebellion.*—III. *rebellious.*

מְרִיב בַּעַל מְרִי בַעַל p. n., the son of Jonathan, called also מְפִיבֹשֶׁת.

מְרָיָה p.n. of a man.

מְרָיוֹת p. n. of a man.

מִרְיָם p. n., *Miriam* the sister of Moses, Μαρία.

מָרָתַיִם dual f. (*double rebellion*), a prophetic title of Babylon, Jer. 50:21.

מֹרָה, מוֹרֶה, מֹרֶה, מָרוֹת; see מרד.

מֹרָד *persecuted;* see רגד.

מֵרֹם p. n., a town in the north of Palestine.

מָרוֹם; see מרח.

מָרוֹם, מְרוֹם; see רום.

מְרוּצָה מְרוּץ; see רוץ.

מִרְזֵחַ, מַרְזֵחַ; see רזח.

מָרַח *apply* (as a plaster). Isa. 38:21, with עַל.

מְרוֹחַ אֶשֶׁךְ m., מְרוֹחַ *with crushed testicles,* Lev. 21:20.

מֶרְחָב *wide;* see רחב.

מַרְחַקִּים, מֶרְחָק; see רחק.

מַרְחֶשֶׁת *pot;* see רחש.

מָרַט I. *pluck out hair:* hence,—II. *made smooth, polished.* Niph. *became bald.* Pu. *polished,* 1 Ki. 7:45.

מְרַט Ch., *plucked,* Dan. 7:4.

מִרְיָם, מְרָיָה, מְרִיּוֹת, מְרִי; see מרה.

מְרִיא *fat;* see מרא.

מְרִיבָה *strife;* see ריב.

מֹרִיָּה, מוֹרִיָּה f. p. n., *Moriah,* a hill in Jerusalem.

מְרִידֵי מְרִירוּת; see מרר.

מֹרֶךְ m., *softness, cowardice,* Lev. 26:36; LXX. δειλία.

מֶרְכָּבָה, מֶרְכָּבָת, מֶרְכָּב; see רכב.

מַרְבֹּלֶת *merchandise;* see רכל.

מִרְמָה *deceit;* see רמה.

מְרֵמוֹת p. n. of a man.

מֶרֶס p. n. of a Persian prince.

מַרְסְנָא p. n. of a Persian prince.

מַרְעִית, מִרְעֶה, מַרְעָה; see רעה.

מְרֹנֹתִי m., *a Maronothite.*

מַרְעֲלָה p. n., a town in the tribe of Zebulun.

מַרְפֵּה, מַרְפֵּא; see רפא.

מָרַץ Niph. *was, became, unsound, weak, diseased.* Hiph. *urge to folly,* Job 16:3.

מַרְצֵעַ *awl;* see רצע.

מַרְצֶפֶת; see רצף.

מָרַק *rubbed bright, polished.* Pu. *was polished,* Lev. 6:21.

מְרוּקִים m. pl., *purifications*, Est. 2:12.

מָרָק m., *broth*, Jud. 6:19, 20.

תַּמְרוּג m., *purification, cleansing*.

מִרְקַחַת, מֶרְקָחָה, מֶרְקָח; see רקח.

מָרַר ; מַר לִי *it is bitter to me*, with מִן. Niph. נָמַר *was offensive* (an odour), Jer. 48:11. Pi. מֵרַר (fut. יְמָרֵר) *makes bitter, grieves*; מֹ' בִּבְכִי *was bitter in weeping, wept bitter tears*. Hiph. הֵמַר (inf. הָמֵר) *make bitter*. Hithpalp. הִתְמַרְמַר *was angry*, Dan. 8:7; 11:11.

מַר m.— I. *a drop*, Isa. 40:15.— II. *bitterness*; adj. מַר (pl. מָרִים ; f. מָרָה) *bitter, bitterly*.

מֹר, מוֹר, מָר m., *myrrh*.

מָרָה f.— I. *bitterness, sorrow*, 2 Sa. 2:26.— II. p. n., *a well in the desert of Sinai*.— III. *title which Naomi gave herself*, Ru. 1:20.

מוֹרָה f., *sorrow*, Pro. 14:10.

מֹרָה f., *the same*, Gen. 26:35.

מָרוֹת p. n, *a town of Judah*.

מְרִירִי m., *bitter*, Deu. 32:24.

מְרִירוּת f., *bitter sorrow*, Eze. 21:11.

מְרֹרָה f.— I. *gall*.— II. *bitterness*.

מְרֵרָה f., *gall bladder*, Job 16:13.

מְרֹרִים m. pl., *bitter herbs*.

מְרָרִי p. n., *a son of Levi*.

מֶמֶר m., *bitterness*, Pro. 17:25.

מְמֹרָרָה f., *gall bladder*, Job 20:25.

מְמֹרִים m. pl., *bitter things*, Job 9:18.

תַּמְרוּרִים m. pl., *bitterness, bitter sorrow*; see also תמר.

מַשָּׂא, מַשֹּׂא, מַשְׂאָה, מַשֵּׂאת, מַשֹּׂאת; see נשא.

מִשֵּׁגָּב; see שׂגב

מֵשַׂךְ see מֹשֵׂךְ; מְשׁוּכָה, see שׂוך

מַשּׂוֹר *saw*; see נשׂר.

מַשֹּׂרָה; see משׂר.

מָשֹׂושׂ; see שׂושׂ.

מִשְׂחָק *object of laughter*; see שׂחק.

מַשְׂטֵמָה *hatred*; see שׂטם.

מַשְׂכִּית, מַשְׂכִּיּוֹת; see שׂכה.

מַשְׂכֹּרֶת *wages*; see שׂכר.

מַשְׂמְרוֹת *nails*; see סמר.

מִשְׂפָּח; see שׂפח.

מָשַׂר (Arab. *divided*).

מְשׂוּרָה f., *measure for liquids*.

מִשְׂרָה *government*; see שׂרה.

מַשְׂרְפוֹת *burning*; see שׂרף.

מַשְׂרֵקָה p. n., *a place in Edom*.

מַשְׂרֵת m., *frying-pan*, 2 Sa. 13:9.

מַשׁ p. n., *Mash*, Gen. 10:23, probably the district called Mount Masius, which separates Armenia from Mesopotamia.

מֵשָׁא p. n., *Mesha*, one of the boundaries of the district of the Joktanites, Gen. 10:30, not exactly known.

מַשָּׁא, מַשָּׁאָה, מַשָּׂא, see נשׁרה ; מַשָּׁאוֹן, see נשׁא.

מַשְׁאַבִּים *watering places*; see שׁאב.

מִשְׁאָלָה, מִשְׁאָל; see שׁאל.

מִשְׁאֶרֶת *kneading trough*; see שׁאר.

מִשְׁבְּצוֹת; see שׁבץ.

מִשְׁבָּר, מַשְׁבֵּר *pain*; see שׁבר.

מִשְׁבַּתִּים; see שׁבת.

מִשְׁגֶּה *mistake*; see שׁגה.

מָשָׁה *drew* (out of the water), Ex. 2:10. Hiph. the same.

מֹשֶׁה (*drawn out of water*, Ex. 2:10), p. n., *Moses*, the lawgiver, Μωϋσῆς (Josephus).

מֶשִׁי m. *figured silk*, Eze. 16:10,13.

מָשָׁה *debt*: see נשה.

מְשׁוֹאָה *desolation*; see שאה.

מַשְׁאוֹת, מַשֻׁאוֹת; see שאה.

מְשׁוּבָה, מְשֻׁבָה *apostasy*; see שוב.

מִשְׁגֶּה *error*; see שגג.

מָשׁוֹם, מָשׁוֹט *oar*; see שוט.

מָשַׁח (inf. מָשֹׁחַ, with ה parag. מָשְׁחָה; imp. מְשַׁח; fut. יִמְשַׁח).
—I. *anointed.*—II. *anointed to an office.*—III. *set apart to an office*, Isa. 61:1.—IV. *dedicate by anointing.*—V. *anoint oneself for a banquet*, Am. 6:6, const. with בְּ. Niph. נִמְשַׁח *was anointed.*

מָשִׁיחַ m.—I. *anointed.*—II. *the anointed One*, Christ.

מְשַׁח m. Ch., *oil.*

מִשְׁחָה f.—I. *unction.*—II. *portion*, Lev. 7:35.

מָשְׁחָה inf., see מָשַׁח, Nu. 18:8; לְמׇ׳ *for a dedication*, i.e. thing set apart for them.

מִמְשָׁח m., *extension, stretching out*, Eze. 28:14.

מִשְׁחָת, מָשְׁחָת, מַשְׁחִית; see שחת.

מִשְׁחָר *dawn*; see שחר.

מְשִׁי; see above משה.

מְשֵׁיזַבְאֵל p. n. of a man.

מָשַׁךְ I. *stretched out the hand*, Hos. 7:5.—II. *took hold of*, Ex. 12:21.—III. *seized as spoil.*—IV. *drew, a bow, yoke, net.* &c., with בְּ.—V. מָשַׁךְ הַיּוֹבֵל *lengthened the sound of the trumpet*, Ex. 19:13.—VI. *scattered seed*, Am. 9:13.—VII. *continued in a thing.*—VIII. *reckon with* (עִם), Ps. 28:3.—IX. *cheered,*

Ecc. 2:3. Niph. *was protracted, delayed.* Pu. I. *spoiled*, Isa. 18:2, 7.—II. *obtained*, Pro. 13:12.

מֶשֶׁךְ m.—I. *acquiring*, Job 28:18. —II. מֶשֶׁךְ הַזָּרַע *scattering of seed*, Ps. 126:6.

מַשְׁכּוֹת f. pl., *attractions, influences*, Job 38:31.

מֶשֶׁךְ p.n.—I. one of the sons of Japhet. —II. the people descended from him, Gen. 10:2. They were probably the Muscovites; LXX. Μοσόχ; Vulg. *Mosoch.*

מִשְׁכָּב, מָשְׁכָּב *bed*; see שכב.

מִשְׁכָּן *dwelling*; see שכן.

מָשַׁל I. *ruled.*—II. *had power over*, with בְּ.—III. *had power to do*, with לְ.—IV. *assimilated, compared to*, with בְּ, עַל. Niph. *became like*, with בְּ, עִם, אֶל. Pi. *speaking parables*, Eze. 21:5. Hiph. I. *give authority* (inf. הַמְשֵׁל)Dan. 11:39. —II. *made like*, Isa. 46:5. Hith. *become like*, Job 30:19.

מֹשֶׁל m.—I. *authority*, Zec. 9:10.— II. *anything like*, Job 41:25.

מָשָׁל m.—I. *solemn declaration.*—II. *decision, rule, proverb*, γνώμη.— III. *bye word, subject of taunt.*

מָשָׁל m., *taunting proverb*, Job 17:6.

מֶמְשָׁל m., *dominion*; pl. *rulers*, 1 Ch. 26:6.

מֶמְשָׁלָה f., *dominion, rule.*

מֶמְשֶׁלֶת f. (pl. מֶמְשָׁלוֹת), the same.

מִשְׁלַחַת, מִשְׁלוֹחַ, מִשְׁלָח; see שלח.

מִשְׁלָשׁ; see שלש.

מְשֻׁלָּם p. n. of a man.

שְׁלֶמְיָה, מְשֶׁלֶמְיָה p. n. of a man.

מְשֶׁלֶמוֹת, מְשֶׁלֵמִית p. n. of a man.

מְשֶׁלֶמֶת p. n., *Meshullemeth*, the wife of Manasseh.

מְשֻׁמָּה *desolation*, &c.; see שׁמם.

מִשְׁמָן, מַשְׁמַנִּים, מִשְׁמַנָּה; see שׁמן.

מִשְׁמָע, מִשְׁמַעַת; see שׁמע.

מִשְׁמָר, מִשְׁמֶרֶת, מִשְׁמָרוֹת; see שׁמר.

מִשְׁנֶה; see שׁנה.

מְשִׁסָּה *prey*; see שׁסס.

מִשְׁעוֹל *narrow way*; see שׁעל.

מָשָׁע (Arab. *take pains*).

לְמִי מִשְׁעִי *carefully*, Eze. 16:4.

מִשְׁעָם p. n. of a man.

מִשְׁעָן, מַשְׁעֵנָה, מַשְׁעֶנֶת, מִשְׁעֶנֶת; see שׁען.

מִשְׁפָּחָה, מִשְׁפַּחַת *family*; see שׁפה.

מִשְׁפָּט *judgment*; see שׁפט.

מִשְׁפְּתַיִם; see שׁפה.

מֶשֶׁק m., בֶּן־מֶשֶׁק, LXX. υἱὸς Μέσεκ, Gen. 15:2, probably the name of a tribe or district in Syria, whence דֻּרְמֶשֶׂק *Damascus*.

מִמְשָׁק m., *overspreading*, Zep. 2:9; but LXX. read Damascus.

מָשָׁק *running about*; see שׁקק.

מַשְׁקֶה *drink*; see שׁקה.

מִשְׁקָל, מִשְׁקֹלֶת, מִשְׁקֶלֶת, מִשְׁקוֹל; see שׁקל.

מַשְׁקוֹף see שׁקף.

מִשְׁרָה *juice*; see שׁרה.

מַשְׁרוֹקִיתָא *flute*; see שׁרק.

מִשְׁרָעִי p. n. of a man.

מָשַׁשׁ same as מוּשׁ *touch, feel*, Gen. 27:12. Pi. מִשֵּׁשׁ I. *examine by feeling*.—II. *felt his way, groped*. Hiph. (fut. יָמֵשׁ) *that may be felt*, Ex. 10:21; see in מוּשׁ.

מִשְׁתַּחֲוִיתֶם Eze. 8:16. Hith. part. pl with pers. pron., from שׁחה.

מֵת or מָת m., pl. מְתִים, מְתִם, const. מְתֵי *men*.

מֵתוּ, מַתִּי, מִתָּה, סַת, מְתָה, מֵת, מֵתִים, from מוּת Kal.

מֵתָא Ch. Pe. inf., from אתה.

מַתְבֵּן *heap of straw*; see תֶּבֶן.

מֶתֶג m. (with suff. מִתְגִּי), *bridle*.

מָתוֹק, מְתוּקָה; see מתק.

מְתוּשָׁאֵל p. n., *Methusael*, one of Cain's descendants.

מְתוּשֶׁלַח p. n., *Methuselah*, the patriarch, the son of Enoch.

מָתַח *stretched out* (as a curtain), Isa. 40:22.

אַמְתַּחַת f. (pl. const. אַמְתְּחוֹת), *sack* or *bag*.

מָתַי pa.—I. *when?*—II. *when*; אַחֲרֵי מָתַי *after how long?* Jer. 13:27; עַד מָתַי *how long?*

מַתְכֹּנֶת; see תכן.

מַתְלָאָה for מַה־תְּלָאָה *what trouble*. see לאה.

מִתְלַהְלֵהַּ Hith. part., from לָהַהּ.

מְתַלְּעוֹת *teeth*; see לתע.

מְתֹם *soundness*; see תמם.

מָתַן root not used; (Arab. *was firm*).

מָתְנַיִם m. dual, *loins*.

אֲמְתָנִי Ch. f., *powerful, mighty*, Dan. 7:7.

מַתָּנָה, מַתָּנָא, מַתְּנַי, מַתָּן, מַתַּנְיָה, מַתַּנְיָהוּ; see נתן.

מַתְנִי p. n. of a man.

מָתַק (fut. יִמְתַּק), *were, became sweet*. Hiph. הִמְתִּיק I. *was sweet*, Job 20:12.—II. *made sweet*, Ps. 55:15

מָתוֹק m. (pl. מְתוּקִים; f. מְתוּקָה).
—I. *sweet*.—II. *sweetness*.— III.
pleasant.

מֶתֶק m., *sweetness*.

מֹתֶק m., the same, Jud. 9:11.

מִתְקָה p. n., a station of the Israelites
in the desert.

מַמְתַּקִּים m., pl. מַמְתַּקִּים *sweetness*,
Neh. 8:10; Cant. 5:16.

מִתְרְדָת p. n., *Mithridates* the Persian
(Μιθριδάτης).

מַתְּתְיָהוּ, מַתָּה, מַתִּתְיָה, מַתַּתְיָהוּ; see
נתן.

מַתִּי Pil. pret. 1. pers., from מוּת.

נ

נָא interj., *I pray!* used,—I. in supplication.— II. in exhortation.—
III. in irony or blame; בָּא־נָא
go I pray! אָמְרִי־נָא *speak I pray!*
אֵלְכָה נָּא *let me go, I pray!*
אַל־נָא תַעֲבֹר *pass not over, I
pray!* יֵאָמֶר נָא *let it be told, I
pray!* אַל־נָּא *do not I pray!* with
particles: אִם־נָא *if indeed;* אַל־נָא
not so, I pray! הִנֵּה־נָא *behold!*
אוֹי־נָא *alas!* see also in נִיא.

נֹא, נֹא־אָמוֹן p. n.; Διόσπολις, με-
ρίς Ἀμμῶν, perhaps the city of
Thebes in Egypt.

נָאד root not used; (Arab. *poured out
water*).

נֹאד (נֹאוד) m. *skin bottle;* pl. נֹאדוֹת
bottles.

נָאוָה (pl. const. נָאווּ), *became, was
fair,* Ps. 93:5; see אָוָה.

נָאָה f., pl. const. נְאוֹת *the best, choice,
parts* of any thing; נְ' דֶשֶׁא *plea-*

sant herbage, Ps. 23:2; generally
translated *habitation,* Ps. 74:20,
and elsewhere; but the former
appears to give a better sense.

נָאוֶה m., נָאוָה—I. *becoming, seemly*
—II. *fair*.

נָאוּ for נָאווּ, from נאה.

נָאוֹת Niph. fut. pl. 1. pers., from אות.

נָאַם *make a solemn declaration,* Jer.
23:31; part. נֹאֵם; נְ' יְיָ *saith the
Lord,* passim: used of Agur, Pro.
30:1.

נָאַף (fut. יִנְאַף).—I. *committed adultery.*—II. *worshipped false gods,*
Jer. 3:9; part. נֹאֵף *adulterer,*
נֹאָפֶת *adulteress.* Pi. נִאֵף the
same.

נִאֻפִים m. pl.—I. *adulteries.*—II. *acts
of idolatry.*

נַאֲפוּפִים m. pl., *repeated acts of
adultery,* Hos. 2:4.

נָאַץ (fut. יִנְאַץ *turned away from,
despised, rejected.* Pi. נִאֵץ (fut.
יְנָאֵץ) the same. Hiph. fut. נָאַץ
it is despised, Ecc. 12:5. Hith.
part. מִנֹּאָץ *contemned,* Isa. 52:5.

נֶאָצָה f., *reproach, insult,* 2 Ki. 19:
3; Isa. 37:3.

נְאָצָה f., pl. נָאֲצוֹת (נֶאָצוֹתֶיךָ), the
same.

נָאַק same as אָנַק *cry out,* Job 24:12

נְאָקָה const. נַאֲקַת f., *cry of sorrow*

נָאַר. Pi. נִאֵר (pret. 2. pers. נֵאַרְתָּה)
rejected as worthless, Ps. 89:40;
Lam. 2:7.

נִאְשָׁאר Eze. 9:8, perhaps comp. of
נִשְׁאַר and אֶשָּׁאֵר; see שאר.

נֹב p. n., a city of the Levites in the

tribe of Benjamin; with ה, נֹבָה towards Nob.

נָבָא. Niph. נִבָּא *announced as the will of God, prophesied.* Hith. הִנַּבֵּא הִתְנַבֵּא (inf. וְהִתְנַבּוֹת).—I. *prophecy.*—II. *be mad.*

נְבָא Ch. Ithp. הִתְנַבִּי *prophesied*, Exr. 5:1.

נָבִיא m. (with suff. נְבִיאֲכֶם).—I. *a prophet*, one who declares future events.—II. probably one devoted to the study of the revealed will of God; whence בְּנֵי הַנְּבִיאִים *the sons*, i.e. *disciples of the prophets* who studied under them.

נָבִיא m. Ch., the same.

נְבִיאָה f.—I. *prophetess.*—II. *prophet's wife.*

נְבוּאָה f.—I. *prediction*, Neh. 6:12.—II. *prophetical book.*

נְבוּאָה f. Ch., the same.

נְבוֹ p. n., *Nebo.*—I. one of the idols of Babylon, Isa. 46:1.—II. a mountain and city in the land of Moab.—III. a town in the tribe of Judah.

נְבוּזַרְאֲדָן p. n., one of Nebuchadnezzar's generals.

נְבוּכַדְרֶאצַּר, נְבוּכַדְנֶצַּר, נְבוּכַדְנֶאצַּר p. n., *Nebuchadnezzar*, the king of Babylon; LXX. Ναβουχοδονόσορ.

נְבוּשַׁזְבָּן p. n., a prince of Assyria.

נָבוּב *proud;* see בּוּב.

נָבוֹחַ p.n. of a man.

נְבִזְבָּה, נְבִזְבָּה f. Ch., *gift, reward.*

נִבְזָה 1 Sa. 14:36, Kal fut. pl. 1. pers. with ה parag. and dag. f. dropped; see בזז.

נָבַח *bark* (as a dog), Isa. 56:10.

נֹבַח p. n. of a man; also of a town in Gilead, Nu. 32:42; Jud. 8:11.

נִבְחַז p.n., an idol of the Avites, 2 Ki 17:31.

נָבַט. Pi. נִבַּט and Hiph. הִבִּיט.—I. *looked.*—II. *look at, towards*, with אֶל, לְ; *looked after*, with אַחֲרֵי.—III. *looked favourably at*, with בְּ; same as רָאָה *perceived.*—IV. *attended to.*—V. *noticed*, Ps. 10:14.

נְבָט p. n., *Nebat*, the father of Jeroboam.

מַבָּט m., *expectation, hope*, Isa. 20:5:6.

מֶבָּט m., the same, Zec. 9:5.

נְבִיאָה, נָבִיא see נבא.

נְבָיוֹת p. n., *Nebaioth*, a people of the race of Ishmael, Gen. 25:13, &c.

נִבֵּאתָ, נִבֵּיתָ for נִבֵּאתָ, נִבֵּיתָ Niph. pret., from נבא.

נֵבֶךְ "*mazes of the sea*" (Lee), Job 38:16.

נָבֵל (fut. יִבֹּל).—I. *became shrivelled and fell* (as flowers, &c.).—II. *wasted away.*—III. *crumbled to dust.*—IV. *acted foolishly*, Pro. 30:32. Pi. נִבֵּל *treated as worthless, set at nought.*

נָבָל m., נְבָלָה f.—I. *foolish.*—II. *impious.*— III. p. n. of a man, 1 Sa. c. 25.

וַנְּבֶל, נָבֵל Isa. 64:5, Hiph. fut. pl. 1. pers. from בלל; or for וַנָּבֶל Kal fut., from נבל.

נִבְלָה for נָבְלָה Kal fut. pl. 1 pers, with ה parag.; see בלל.

נְבָלָה f.—I. *disgraceful action.*—II. *punishment of such an action*, Jos

7:15.— III. *impiety*, Isa. 32:6.—
IV. *folly*, 1 Sa. 25:25.

נְבֵלָה f. (const. נִבְלַת; with suff.
נִבְלָתִי, נִבְלָתוֹ).—I. *carcase of an
animal.*— II. *dead body of a man.*
—III. *idols*, Jer. 16:18; collect.
carcases.

נַבְלוּת f., *shame, nakedness*, Hos. 2:
12.

נֵבֶל, נֶבֶל m. (pl. נְבָלִים).—I. *bottle*
(of skin).— II. *earthen jar.*— III.
lute, νάβλιον.

נְבַלָּם p. n., a town in the tribe of Benjamin.

נֹבֵעַ, נָבַע *springing* (as a fountain),
Pro. 18:4.   Hiph. הִבִּיעַ.—I. *ut-
ters, declares* —II. *prepares.*

מַבּוּעַ m., *spring, fountain of water.*

נִבְקָה for נָבְקָה Niph. pret. f., from
בקק.

נָבַר Niph., from ברר.

נֶבְרַשְׁתָּא f. Ch., *lamp*, Dan. 5:5.

נִבְשָׁן p. n. of a town in the tribe of
Judah.

נִגְאֲלוּ for נִנְגְּאֲלוּ Niph. pret. pl., from
II. גאל.

נָגַב (Ch. נְגֵב *was dry*.)

נֶגֶב m. — I. *the arid desert to the
south of Judea.* — II. *the south;*
נֶגְבָּה *towards, on, the south;*
לַנֶּגְבָּה, בַּנֶּגְבָּה *towards the south;*
מִנֶּגֶב *from the south.*

נֶגֶד.   Hiph. הִגִּיד *brought before, told,
made known;* with ל of the per-
son to whom.   Hoph. הֻגַּד *was
told.*

נְגַד Ch., *proceeding, flowing*, Dan.
7:10.

נֶגֶד subst. *fore part of the body;* prep.
before, in front of, opposite to,
adv. *straight forwards;* נֶגֶד, כְּנֶגְדּוֹ
opposite to him; לְנֶגֶד *before, opposite to;* מִנֶּגֶד *in presence of, in
sight, out of sight, over against,
opposite to, against.*

נָגִיד m.—I. *leader.*—II. *prince.*—III.
chief.—IV. *one appointed to any
charge.*

נָגַהּ *shined.*   Hiph. הִגִּיהַּ *caused to
shine*, Isa. 13:10, *made light.*

נֹגַהּ f. (with suff. נֶגְהָם).—I. *the dawn.*
— II. *light.* — III. p. n. a son of
David.

נֹגַהּ f. Ch., *dawn*, Dan. 6:20.

נְגֹהָה f., *light*, Isa. 59:9.

נָגַח (fut. יִגַּח), *push with the horn.*
Pi. נִגַּח the same.   Hith. הִתְנַגַּח
entered into conflict, Dan. 11:40.

נַגָּח m., *addicted to pushing with the
horn*, Ex. 21:29, 36.

נָגַל root not used; (Arab. *sickle*).

מַגָּל m., *sickle*, Jer. 50:16; Joel 4:13

נָגַן and Pi. נִגֵּן *performed music.*

נְגִינָה f.—I. *music.*—II. *a song.*—III.
subject of a song.

מַנְגִּינָה f., *song of ridicule*, Lam.
3:63.

נָגַע (inf. נְגֹעַ, גַּעַת; with suff. נָגְעוֹ;
imp. גַּע; fut. יִגַּע; part. f. נֹגַעַת).
—I. *touched*, with בְּ, אֶל, עַל.—II
touched gently, awakened, with בְּ.
—III. *touched the heart*, with בְּ,
1 Sa. 10:26.—IV. *touched so as to
injure*, with בְּ.— V. *struck*, with
בְּ, Job 1:19. — VI. *arrived.* —
VII. *arrived at, reached*, with
בְּ, עַל, עַד, אֶל.—VIII. *reached the*

ear of, with אֶל, Jon. 3:6. Niph.
were beaten in battle, Jos. 8:15.
Pi. נִגַּע *struck with disease*. Pu. *are
afflicted*, Ps. 73:5. Hiph. הִגִּיעַ
I. *made to touch*, with עַד, ל, אֶל,
עַל.—II. *reached*, with עַד, ל, אֶל,
עַל.—III. *reached the ears of*, with
אֶל, Est. 9:26.—IV. *reached its
proper time*, with ל, Est. 9:1.—V.
came near, with ל, Ps. 88:4.—VI.
arrived (of time).—VII. *arrived
at*, with עַד, ל, אֶל.

נֶגַע m. (with suff. נִגְעִי; pl. נְגָעִים,
נִגְעֵי).—I. *stroke, blow.*—II. *infliction of evil.*—III. *affliction.*—IV.
mark of a blow, spot.

נָגַף (fut. יִגֹּף).—I. *struck.*—II. *wounded.*
—III. *killed.* — IV. *defeated.* — V.
struck with disease.—VI. *stumbled.*
Niph. נִגַּף (inf. abs. נָגוֹף), *was defeated, routed* (of an army), with
לִפְנֵי *of the enemy.* Hith. *stumble,*
Jer. 13:16.

נֶגֶף m.—I. *infliction of disease.*—II.
act of stumbling, Isa. 8:14.

מַגֵּפָה, const. מַגֵּפַת f.—I. *plague,
pestilence.*—II. *defeat.*

נָגַר. Niph. נִגַּר I. *was put forth* (the
hand), Ps. 77:3.—II. *overflowed,
was spilt.*—III. *was scattered, as
wealth*, Job 20:28. Hiph. הִגִּיר
I. *dragged away.*—II. *poured out*,
Ps. 75:9.—III. *scattered*, Mic.1:6.
Hoph. *poured out*, Mic. 1:4.

נָגַשׂ (fut. יִגֹּשׂ תִּנְגְּשׂוּ; *exacted a task,
debt or tax*; part. נוֹגֵשׂ *exactor,
taskmaster, slave-driver.* Niph.
נִגַּשׂ *was pressed, vexed, fatigued.*

נָגַשׁ (fut. יִגַּשׁ; inf. גֶּשֶׁת; with suff.

(נָשָׁה גַּשׁ, גְּשָׁה־ and נִגְּשָׁתוֹ;
imp. גַּשׁ, גְּשִׁי; גַּשׁ־נָה) and
Niph. נִגַּשׁ I. *came near to, up to,
touched*, with אֶל, ב, ל, עַד, עַל.—
II. perhaps *depart, go away*, Gen.
19:9. Hiph. הִגִּישׁ I. *brought near.*
—II. *offered*, i. e. *brought near* (an
offering). Hoph. הֻגַּשׁ *was brought,
placed.* Hith. *approach*, Isa. 45:20.

נֵד *heap*; see נדד.

נָדָא, fut. וַיַּדֵּא *drave away*, 2 Ki.
17:21.

נָדַב I. *rendered willing*, with לֵב and
רוּחַ.—II. *impelled.* Hith. הִתְנַדֵּב
offered or *performed willingly.*

נְדַב Ch. Hith. *was willing, gave
willingly.*

נָדָב p.n., *Nadab.* — I. the son of
Aaron.—II. given also to other men.

נְדָבָה, const. נִדְבַת f.—I. *voluntary
offering.* — II. *free-will* (בִּנְדָבָה,
נְדָבָה *of his own accord, willingly*),
—III. pl. *abundance*; גֶּשֶׁם נְדָבוֹת
plenteous rain, Ps. 68:10.

נְדַבְיָה p.n. of a man.

נָדִיב m.—I. *willing, liberal.*—II. *noble,
distinguished.* — III. Job 21:28;
perhaps " *a libertine* " (Lee).

נְדִיבָה f., *liberality.*

הִתְנַדָּבוּת (inf. Hith.) f. Ch., *free-
will offerings*, Exr. 7:16.

נִדְבָּךְ m. Ch., *layer, course of stones*
Exr. 6:4.

נָדַד (inf. נְדֹד; fut. יִדֹּד, וַיִּדַּד).—I. *fled*
—II. *wandered, walked to and fro.*
—III. *flapped the wings*, Isa. 10:
14; part. נוֹדֵד. Po. נוֹדַד *was
driven away*, Nah. 3:17. Hiph.
הִגַּר *cause to wander*, Job 18:18.
Hoph. הֻנַּד *made to wander*, Job

20:8; *driven about,* 2 Sa. 23:6. Hith. *was agitated.*

נְדַד Ch., *fled,* Dan. 6:19.

נְדֻדִים m. pl., *restlessness* (of body or mind), Job 7:4.

נֵד m.—I. *a heap,* Isa. 17:11.—II. *a mound.*

נִדָּה f.—I. *legal impurity.*—II. *a woman in that state.*—III. *moral impurity.*—IV. *that which is impure, worthless,* Eze. 7:19, 20; מֵי הַנִּדָּה *water of impurity,* i. e. for the cleansing of legal impurity

נִידָה f., *impurity,* Lam. 1:8.

מַדָּד m., *flight,* Job 7:4.

נָדָה same as נוד. Pi. נִדָּה *put aside, desired to avoid,* with לְ, Isa. 66:5; Am. 6:3.

נֵדֶה m., *present, gift,* Eze. 16:33.

נֵדָן m., the same; see also below.

נָדַח (fut. יִדַּח).—I. *drove an axe,* Deu. 20:19.—II. *drove away,* 2 Sa. 14:14. Hiph. הִדִּיחַ 1. *brought with violence,* with עַל.—II. *drove away.*—III. *induced to any thing,* Pro. 7:21. Niph. נִדַּח I. *was impelled.*—II. *was driven away.*—III. *was induced to an action;* part. נִדָּח (with suff. נִדְּחוֹ; נִדַּחֲךָ, f. נִדָּחָה). Pu. part. מְנֻדָּח *driven,* Isa. 8:22. Hoph. part. מֻדָּח *driven astray,* Isa. 13:14.

מַדּוּחִים m. pl., *expulsions, drivings out,* Lam. 2:14.

נָדִיב, נְדִיבָה; see נדב.

נִדְמָה for נִדַּמָּה Niph. fut. pl. 1. pers. with ה parag., from דמם.

נָדָן m., *sheath* (of a sword), 1 Chron. 21:27; see also in נָדָה.

נִדְנֶה m. Ch., "midst," Eng. Ver.; "sheath," Marg., Dan. 7:15.

נָדַף (fut. יִדֹּף, יִנְדֹּף).—I. *scattered, drove about.*—II. *routed, conquered* (an enemy), Job 32:13. Niph. נִדַּף (inf. הִנָּדֵף) *driven away.*

I. נָדַר (fut. יִדֹּר).—I. *made a vow.*

נֶדֶר m. (with suff. נִדְרִי; pl נְדָרִים, נִדְרֵי).—I. *vow.*—II. *thing vowed.*

II. נָדַר root not used; (Arab. *thresh corn*).

אַדַּר Ch., *threshing-floor,* Dan. 2:35; (Arab. the same).

נֹהַּ *lamentation,* Eze. 7:11; see נָהָה.

נָהַג (imp. נְהַג; fut. יִנְהַג).—I. *led, conducted.*—II. *drave cattle,* &c.—III. *guided.*—IV. *commanded an army.* Pi. נִהֵג (fut. יְנַהֵג) I. *brought on a wind:* hence—II. נֵהַג *breathed,* Nah. 2:8.—III. *led.*—IV. *drave.*

מִנְהָג m., *driving of horses,* 2 Ki. 9:20.

נָהַד root not used; (Arab. *swelled, grew vigorous*).

הוֹד m.—I. *vigour,* Pro. 5:9.—II. *glory, majesty.*—III. p.n. of a man

הוֹדַוְיָהוּ, הוֹדַוְיָה p.n.; see ידה.

הוֹדִיָה p.n. of a man.

הוֹדִיָה p. n. of a man.

נָהָה *lamented,* Mic. 2:4. Niph. fut. וַיִּנָּהוּ *mourn after the Lord,* 1 Sa. 7:2.

נְהִי, with pause נֶהִי m., *lamentation*

נְהִי, נֶהִי fut. apoc. pl.1. pers., from היה

נִהְיָה Mic. 2:4; see הוה.

נָהַל Pi. נִהֵל (fut. יְנַהֵל).—I. *led.*—

II. *tended, fed.*—III. *gave rest to,*
2 Chron. 32:22. Hith. *proceed
with a flock,* Gen. 33:14.

נַחֲלָל m.—I. *pasture,* Isa. 7:19.—II.
p. n., a town in the tribe of Zebulun, called also נַהֲלָל.

נָחַם (fut. יִנְהֹם).—I. *roared,* Isa. 5:
29, 30.—II. *groaned.*

נַהַם m., *roaring of a lion.*

נְהָמָה, const. נַהֲמַת f., *roaring of the
sea,* Isa. 5:30.—II. *groaning,* Ps.
38:9.

נָהַק (fut. יִנְהַק) *brayed* (as an ass),
Job 6:5; 30:7.

נָהַר I. *brighten* (of the face), Isa. 60:5;
Ps. 34:6.—II. (fut. יִנְהָר) *flow unto, assemble in.*

נָהָר m. (pl. נְהָרִים, נְהָרוֹת).
—I. *river, stream.*—II. *current of
the sea,* Jonah; הַנָּהָר הַגָּדוֹל
same as נְהַר פְּרָת *Euphrates;*
אֲרַם נַהֲרַיִם *Aram* (Syria) *of the
rivers,* Mesopotamia.

נְהַר m. Ch., *river.*

נְהוֹר (נְהִיר) m. Ch., *light,* Dan. 2:22.

נְהִירוּ f. Ch., *light, wisdom,* Dan.
5:11, 14.

נְהָרָה f., *light of day,* Job 3:4.

מִנְהָרוֹת f. pl., *clefts* in mountains,
serving as channels for the rain,
Jud. 6:2.

נוּא or נוּא. Hiph. הֵנִיא—I. *discouraged,* Nu. 32:7.—II. *prohibited.*
—III. *frustrated.*

תְּנוּאָה f.—I. *aversion,* Nu. 14:34.—
II. *heavy things,* Job 33:10.

נוּב (fut. יָנוּב).— I. *threw out shoots,*
Ps. 92:15.—II. *produced fruit,* Pro.

10:31.— III. *increased,* Ps. 62:
11. Pi. נוֹבֵב *makes fruitful,* Zec
9:17.

נִיב m., *produce, fruit.*

נִיבִי p. n. of a man.

תְּנוּבָה f., *produce, fruit.*

נֻגּוֹת Niph. part. pl. f. for נוּגוֹת, from
ינה.

נוּגֵי Niph. part. pl. for נוּגֵי, from ינה.
נוּגִים; see ינה.

נוּד (fut. יָנוּד).— I. *move to and fro.*
—II. *wandered as a fugitive;* part.
נָד *a fugitive.*— III. *departed.*—
IV. *shook the head,* expressing pity,
condoled. Hiph. הֵנִיד—I. *moved
to and fro.*— II. *drove out.*— III.
disturbed.— IV. *shake the head in
pity,* Jer. 18:16. Hoph. part. מֻנָּד
expelled, 2 Sa. 23:6. Hithpol
הִתְנוֹדֵד *bemoan himself,* Jer. 31:
18.

נוּד Ch., *departs,* Dan. 4:11.

נוֹד m.—I. *wandering,* Ps. 56:9.—II.
p. n. (*exile*), the country to which
Cain was banished.

נִיד m., *moving of the lips,* Job 16:5.

מָנוֹד m., *shaking the head,* Ps. 44:15.

נוֹדָב p. n., a son of Ishmael.

נָוָה (fut. יִנְוֶה) *dwelt,* Hab. 2:5. Hiph.
prepare a dwelling; fut. with suff.
אַנְוֵהוּ, Ex. 15:2.

נָוֶה m. (const. נְוֵה; with suff. נָוֵהוּ,
נְוֵהֶם, נָוֵהוּ).—I. *fold for cattle.*—
II. *dwelling of men.*—III. *habitation
of God.*

נָוָה f., *habitation,* Job 8:6; נְוַת בַּיִת
she that remaineth at home; οἰκου-
ρός, Ps. 68:13.

נָוָה *dwelt quietly,* Jer. 6:2.

נָיוֹת, Ketib נְיוֹת (*habitations*), p.n., a place near Ramah.

נוּחַ (fut. יָנוּחַ, וַיָּנַח).— I. *lay down, rested.* — II. *halted, ceased.* — III. *abode in,* with בְּ.—IV. *alighted on.* — V. *came down and possessed,* with עַל.— VI. *settled on* (as on a shoal, of the ark), Gen. 8:4. Hiph. I. הֵנִיחַ:— 1. *gave rest to.* — 2. *comforted.* — 3. *let fall,* Ex. 17:11.— 4. *caused to rest upon.*— II. הִפִּיחַ and הִנִּיחַ—1. *placed.*— 2. *left, forsook, quitted.*—3. *let rest, remain.* — 4. *permitted, gave into the power of.* — 5. *left untouched,* 2 Ki. 23:18, with לְ. Hoph. הוּנַח I. *rest was given,* Lam. 5:5.—II. *was placed, left, remaining.*

נֹחַ, נוֹחַ m. (with suff. נוּחֶךָ).—I. *rest,* Est. 9:16-18.— II. p. n., *Noah;* LXX. Νῶε.

נַחַת f., *being placed,* Job 36:16; see also נַחַת.

הֲנָחָה (verb. Hiph.) f., *rest, peace,* Est. 2:18.

מָנוֹחַ m. (pl. with suff. מְנֻחְכִּי).—I. *place of rest.*—II. p. n., *Manoah,* the father of Samson.

מְנוּחָה, מְנֻחָה f.—I. *rest, quiet.*— II. *place of rest.*—III. metaphorically, the land of Canaan.

נִיחֹחַ, נִיחוֹחַ m., *satisfaction, approbation;* רֵיחַ הַנִּיחֹחַ *a sweet* (pleasant) *savour.*

נִיחֹחַ m. Ch., *offerings to God or man.*

נוּט same as מוֹט *agitate, shake,* Ps. 99:1.

נָוַל root not used; Ch. Pa., *polluted.*

נְוָלִי, נְוָלוּ Ch. f., *dunghill.*

נוֹלְדוּ Niph. pret. pl. with dag. euphon. for נוֹלְדוּ, from יָלַד.

נוּם *slept.*

נוּמָה f., *sluggishness,* Pro. 23:21.

תְּנוּמָה f., *sleep, slumber.*

נוּן Niph. fut. יִנּוֹן (Ketib יָנִין Hiph. fut.) *drawn out, perpetuated,* Ps 72:17.

נוּן p. n., *Nun,* the father of Joshua.

נִין m., *posterity.*

מָנוֹן m., *despiser,* Pro. 29:21.

נוּס I. *fled.*—II. *escaped.*—III. *passed away.* Pol. נוֹסֵס *drive away,* Isa. 59:19. Hiph. הֵנִיס *caused to flee, put to flight;* see נֵסס.

נָיִס m., *fugitive,* Jer. 48:44; Kri. נָס.

מָנוֹס m. (with suff. מְנוּסִי).—I. *flight.* —II. *refuge.*

מְנוּסָה, const. מְנֻסַת f., *flight.*

נִתְפָּרוּ, Eze. 23:48 for נִתְוָּסְרוּ Nith., from יָסַר.

נוּעַ (fut. יָנוּעַ).—I. *was shaken.* — II. *was disturbed.* — III. *wandered about.*—IV. *varied,* Pro. 5:6.—V. *staggered* (as one drunken).—VI. *moved* (as the lips), 1 Sa. 1:13. Niph. *was shaken;* fut. יִנּוֹעַ. Hiph. הֵנִיעַ:— I. *shook.* — II. *caused to wander,* πλάζειν.— III. *dispersed* (as fugitives), Ps. 59:12.

מְנַעֲנְעִים m. pl., *a musical instrument,* allied to the tambourine; Vulg. " sistra."

נוֹעַדְיָה p. n. of men and women.

נוּף *have sprinkled,* Pro. 7:17. Hiph. הֵנִיף I. *cause to sprinkle,* Ps. 68: 10.—II. *shake to and fro.*—III.

lifted up the hand, over, and against,
with אֶל.—IV. *lifted up an instrument,* with עַל.—V. *presented an
offering.* Hoph. הוּנַף *was offered,*
Ex. 29:27. Pil. נוֹפֵף *beckons with
his hand,* Isa. 10:32.

נוֹף m., *elevated situation;* יְפֵה נ'
beautiful for situation, Ps. 48:3;
see also נֹף in מֹף.

נָפָה f.—I. *a sieve,* Isa. 30:28.—II.
נָפַת דּוֹר p. n. of a city.

נֶפֶת f., *elevated district,* Jos. 17:11.

נֹפֶת f., *dropping liquid, honey.*

תְּנוּפָה f.—I. *lifting up the hand,* Isa.
19:16.—II. *agitation, tumult,* Isa.
30:32.—III. *an offering.*

נוץ Hiph. הֵנֵץ *blossomed;* see נצץ.
נִיצוֹץ m., *a spark,* Isa. 1:31.

נוֹצָה *crest;* see נצה.

נוק *same as* יָנַק. Hiph. fut. with
suff. תְּנִיקֵהוּ *gave him suck,* Ex.
2:9.

נוּר f. Ch., *fire.*

נֵר m.—I. *a light.*—II. *prosperity.*—
III. p.n. of a man.

נֵיר *same as* נֵר.

נִיר m., *a light,* metaph. *prosperity,
rank;* see also in נִיר.

נֵרִיָּה p.n. of a man.

מְנוֹרָה f., *the candlestick used in the
Jewish ritual.*

נוֹשׁ *be diseased,* Ps. 69:21, same as
אָנַשׁ.

נָזָה (fut. יֵזֶּה, יֵז), *was sprinkled,*
with עַל and מִן. Hiph. הִזָּה (fut.
יֵז, יַזֶּה), *sprinkled,* specially with
blood, with עַל.

נָזִיד; see זוד.

נָזִיר; see נזר.

נָזַל (fut. יֵזַּל).—I. *sank down,* Jud. 5:
5.—II. *dropped, dropped down;*
part. נֹזְלִים *flowing streams.*
Hiph. הִזִּיל *caused to flow,* Isa.
48:21.

מַזָּלוֹת f. pl., *the planets,* 2 Ki. 23:5.

מַזָּרוֹת *a constellation;* according to
some from נָזַר *the northern crown.*
Others read מְאַזּוֹרֹת *a belt, the
belt of Orion.*

נֶזֶם m.—I. *a nose-jewel.*—II. *an earring,* Gen. 35:4.

נְזַק Ch., *suffered loss.* Aph. *caused
loss.*

נֶזֶק m., *injury, loss,* Est. 7:4.

נָזַר Niph. נִזַר I. *restricted himself.*—
II. *devoted him to,* with לְ.—III.
withdrew from. — IV. *abstained
from,* with מִן. Hiph. הִזִּיר I. *set
apart to,* with אֶל, אֶת.—II. *restrained from,* with אֶת, מִן.—III.
devoted himself to.

נָזִיר m.—I. *a Nazarite,* one precluded
by a vow from certain things lawful
to others.—II. Gen. 49:26, applied
to Joseph as separate from his brethren.—III. Lev. 25:5, 11, vines
not pruned.

נֵזֶר m. (with suff. נִזְרוֹ, נִזְרֶךָ).—I.
state of *separation* and *dedication.*
—II. mark of such *separation,* specially the plate of gold in the
high priest's mitre.—III. *diadem.*
—IV. *sovereignty,* Pro. 27:24.—V.
hair of the head, as shorn by the
Nazarites, Jer. 7:29.

נְזָרִים m. pl., *nobles, princes,* Nah.
3:17.

נָחְבִּי; see חבה.

נָחָה (pret. with suff. נָחָם; imp. נְחֵה; with suff. נְחֵנִי). Hiph. הִנְחָה (fut. with suff. יַנְחֵנִי), led, conducted, guided.

נָחוּם same as רָחוּם p. n. of a man.

נְחוּמִים, נָחֻם; see נחם·

נְחִירִים, נָחוֹר; see נחר.

נְחוּשָׁה, נָחוּשׁ; see נחש.

נָחַל (inf. נְחֹל; fut. יִנְחַל).—I. took possession of.—II. possessed.—III. took, received, as his portion.—IV. apportioned, Nu. 34:17. Pi. נָחַל gave settlement to. Hiph. הִנְחִיל I. caused to possess.—II. left as an inheritance to, 1 Chron. 28:8. —III. gave an inheritance, Eze. 46:18. Hoph. הָנְחַל was made to possess, Job 7:3. Hith. הִתְנַחֵל I. took for himself.—II. left as an inheritance, Lev. 25:46.

נַחֲלָה f.—I. settlement, dwelling.—II. possession.—III. assigned portion, share; נַחֲלַת יְהוָֹה the Lord's por- tion, i. e. Israel, his chosen people. —IV. inheritance.

נַחֲלָת f., portion, Ps. 16:6.

נְחִילוֹת f. pl. nom., Autes (root חָלַל), Ps. 5:1.

נָחַל Niph. pret., from חלל; also Pi. pret., from נחל.

נַחַל m. (dual נַחֲלַיִם; pl. נְחָלִים, נַחֲלֵי; with ה loc. נַחְלָה).—I. stream; נַחַל מִצְרַיִם the stream that di- vides Egypt and Palestine.—II. tor- rent.—III. valley.

נַחֲלָה same as נַחַל stream, Ps. 124:4.

נַחֲלִיאֵל p. n., one of the stations of Israel in the wilderness.

נְחֶלָמִי p. n., Nehelamite, a title.

נָחַם Niph. נִחַם I. was grieved, repented, with עַל.—II. pitied, felt pity, with מִן, לְ, אֶל, עַל.—III. pitied and withdrew an inflic- tion, with עַל.—IV. recovered from his grief, with עַל אַחֲרֵי.—V. avenged, freed himself from one displeasing, with מִן.—VI. mourned over, with אֶל, לְ or עַל.—VII. changed his purpose, with עַל. Pi. נִחַם sympathised with, comforted, with מִן, עַל. Pu. נֻחַם comforted, appeased. Hith. הִתְנַחֵם, הִנָּחֵם I. comforted himself.—II. changed his purpose, with עַל, Nu. 23:19. —III. gratified his anger, with לְ.

נַחַם p. n. of a man.

נֹחַם m., pity, change of purpose, Hos. 13:14.

נֻחָמִים, נְחוּמִים m. pl.—I. consola- tions.—II. pity, Hos. 11:8.

נַחוּם p. n., Nahum the prophet, Ναούμ.

נֶחָמָה f., consolation.

נְחֶמְיָה p. n. of a man, Nehemiah, Νεεμία.

נַחֲמָנִי p. n. of a man.

תַּנְחוּמִים m. pl., consolations, comforts.

תַּנְחוּמוֹת f. pl., the same, Job 15:11; 21:2.

תַּנְחֶמֶת p. n. of a man.

נֶחָם pret. Niph. and Pi., from חמם.

נֶחָמִים Niph. part. pl., from חמם.

נַחְנוּ we; see אֲנִי.

נַחֲנֹתִּי Niph. pret. f. 2. pers. with parag., from חנן.

נָחוּץ part. חוּץ urgent, 1 Sa. 21:9.

נָחַר (Arab. snorted).

נַחַר m., snorting, Job 39:20

נַחֲרָה f., the same, Jer. 8:16.

נַחֲרַי, נַחֲרִי p. n. of a man.

נָחוֹר p. n., *Nahor*, the brother of Abraham.

נְחִירִים m. pl., *nostrils*, Job 41:12.

נָחַר Niph. pret., from חרר.

נָחָשׁ m.—I. *serpent.*— II. p. n. of a man.— III. עִיר נָחָשׁ p. n., a city in the tribe of Judah.

נָחֵשׁ Pi. (denom. from ὀφιομαντεία, *divination by serpents*).— I. *used divination.*—II. *watched, observed.*

נַחַשׁ m., *divination.*

נַחְשׁוֹן p. n., *Naashon,* the son of Amminadab.

נְחָשׁ m. Ch., *brass* or *copper.*

נְחֹשֶׁת com. (with suff. נְחֻשְׁתֶּךָ).— I. *brass,* Lam 3:7; dual נְחֻשְׁתַּיִם *fetters, shackles.*— III. *money,* Eze. 16:36.

נְחֻשְׁתָּא p. n. of a woman.

נְחֻשְׁתָּן m., *the brazen serpent idolized,* 2 Ki. 18:4.

נָחוּשׁ m., *copper or brass,* Job 6:12.

נְחוּשָׁה f., the same.

נָחַת (fut. יֵחַת, יִנְחַת) same as יָרַד—I. *came down,* Job 17:16.—II. *came down violently,* with עַל.—III. *penetrated the mind,* with בְּ. Niph. נֵחַת *penetrated* (of arrows), with בְּ, Ps. 38:3. Pi. נִחַר *brought down,* levelled (the bow), Ps. 65:11. Hiph. imp. הַנַּחַת *depress,* Joel 4:11.

נְחַת Ch., *came down.* Aph. *placed.* Hoph. *made to descend,* Dan. 5:20.

נַחַת m.— I. *descent, lighting down,* Isa. 30:30.—II. *being placed,* Job 36:16; see also in נוּחַ.

נַחַת m., pl. נְחִתִּים *coming down* (of an army), 2 Ki. 6:9.

נַחַת p. n. of a man; same as תּוֹחַ.

נִחַת Niph. pret., from חתת.

נָטָה (inf. const. נְטוֹת; fut. יִטֶּה apoc. יֵט, וַיֵּט, (יֵט).— I. *stretch out, extend* (the hand, &c.).— II. *spread out, stretch, pitch a tent.*— III. *bowed, inclined.*—IV. *turn, lead to,* with אֶל, אַחֲרֵי, לְ; or *from,* with מִן.—V. *go, depart,* 1 Sa.14:7. Niph. נִטָּה *stretched out.* Hiph. הִטָּה (fut. יַטֶּה; apoc. יֵט, וַיֵּט; imp. הַטֵּה; apoc. הַט).— I. *stretch out.* — II. *spread out.*—III. *incline, bend down, lower.*—IV. *turn away, put away.* —V. *wrest, pervert.* Hoph. part. מֻטֶּה s., *wresting, perversion.*

מַטֶּה, const. מַטֵּה m. (f., Mic. 6:9).— I. *branch of a tree.*—II. *staff;* שָׁבַר מַטֵּה־לֶחֶם *he brake the staff of bread,* i.e. support, that on which life leans.—III. *rod.*—IV. *sceptre.* —V. *tribe, government,* of which the sceptre was a symbol; pl. מַטּוֹת.

מַטָּה *downwards;* לְמַטָּה, מִלְּמַטָּה the same.

מִטָּה f.— I. *couch, bed.*— II. *bier* (for the dead), 2 Sa. 3:31.

נְטִיפוֹת *earrings;* see נטף.

נָטַל (fut. יִטּוֹל).—I. *lifted up,* Isa. 40: 15.—II. *laid a burden on,* with עַל, Lam. 3:28. Hiph. *took up and removed.*

נְטַל Ch., *lifted up.*

נֵטֶל m., *burden,* Pro. 27:3.

נָטִיל m., *loaded,* Zep. 1:11.

נִטְמְתֶם for נִטְמָאתֶם Niph. pl., from טמא.

נָטַע (fut. יִטַּע; inf. נְטוֹעַ, מַטַּעַת).—I.
planted.—II. pitched a tent.—III.
set up an idol temple, Deut. 16:
21.—IV. drove a nail. Niph.
planted, Isa. 40:24.

נָטִיעַ m., pl. נְטָעִים planted, Ps. 144:
12.

נֶטַע m. (with suff. נִטְעֶךָ; pl. נְטָעִים,
נִטְעָי).—I. plant.—II. plantation.

נֶטַע const. נֵטַע m., plant, Isa. 5:7.

מַטָּע m., planting.

נָטַף (fut. יִטֹּף).—I. drop, Job 29:22.—
II. let drop. Hiph. הִטִּיף.—I. let drop
(water), Am. 9:13.—II. let fall (sen-
timents, prophetic declarations).

נָטָף m.—I. drop, Job 36:27.—II.
στακτή, myrrh, Ex. 30:34.

נְטֹפָה p.n., a town near Bethlehem;
נְטֹפָתִי a Netophathite.

נְטִיפוֹת f. pl., earrings or drops, Jud.
8:26; Isa. 3:19.

נָטַר (fut. יִטֹּר) (יִנְטוֹר) watched,—1. for
good.—2. for evil, with לְ, אֶת.
נְטַר Ch., kept, Dan. 7:28.

מַטָּרָה (מַטָּרָא), Lam. 3:12) f.—I. cus-
tody, prison.—II. mark, object, butt.

נָטַשׁ (fut. יִטֹּשׁ).—I. left.—II. forsook,
God, a law, &c.—III. left.—IV.
ceased to think of, 1 Sa. 10:2.—
V. spread, scattered.—VI. drew a
sword, Isa. 21:15.—VII. allowed.
Niph. I. was forsaken.—II. spread
itself.—III. became loose. Pu. was
forsaken, Isa. 32:14.

נְטִישׁוֹת f. pl.—I. shoots of the vine.
—II. small towns, shoots of the capital, Jer. 5:10.

בְּנֵיהֶם, נִי an error for נִיהֶם, Eze. 27:
32.

נִיא (Arab raw).
נָא m., raw (uncooked), Ex. 12:9
נִיב, גִּיבִי; see נוב.
נִיד, נִידָה; see נוד.
נִיוֹת; see נוה.
נִיחֹחַ; see נוח.
נִין posterity; see נון.
נִינְוֵה p.n., Nineveh, a city of Assyria
LXX. Νινευΐ.
נִינָם Kal fut. pl. 1. pers. with suff., from
ינה.
נִים; see נום.
נִיסָן m., the first month of the Hebrew year, called also אָבִיב, which
see.
נִיצֹץ sparks; see נוץ.
נִיר light; see נור.
נִיר I. clear ground for cultivation.—
II. cultivate ground.
נִיר m., field newly cultivated; see
also in נור.
מָנוֹר m., מְנוֹר אֹרְגִים weaver's beam,
1 Sa. 17:7; 2 Sa. 21:19.
נִירָם Kal fut. pl. 1. pers. with
suff., from ירה.
וַנַּךְ Hiph. fut. apoc. pl. 1. pers.,
from נכה.
נִכָא, נְכֵא, see נכה; נִכָאו, see באה.
נְכֹאת f., storax, Gen. 37:25; 43:11;
LXX. θυμίαμα; Aquila στύραξ.
נֶכֶד m. (with suff. נֶכְדִּי), posterity
always with נִין, which see.
נָכָה Hiph. הִכָּה (imp. הַךְ, הַכֵּה; fut.
יַךְ, וַיַּךְ; with ה parag. יַכֶּה, יִכְּבָה).—I.
struck.—II. wounded.—III. killed.
—IV. conquered.—V. taunted
(struck with the tongue).—VI.
struck the hands together.—VII

וַיַּךְ לֵב *his heart smote him*, 1 Sa. 24:6. Hoph. הֻכָּה, הֻכְּרָה *was smitten*, &c., pass. of Hiph. Niph. נִכָּה *was wounded*, 2 Sa. 11:15. Pi. inf. נַכֵּה—נַכֵּה *smiting*. Pu. נֻכָּה *smitten*.

נָכֶה m.—I. נְכֵה רַגְלַיִם *lame* (smitten in the feet), 2 Sa. 4:4; 9:3.—II. נ׳ רוּחַ *afflicted in spirit*, Isa. 66:2.

נָכֵה m., pl. נֵכִים *smiting* (with the tongue), *calumniators*, Ps. 35:15.

נָכֵא m., f. נְכֵאָה רוּחַ *afflicted, broken spirit*, Pro. 15:13, &c.

נָכֵא m., pl. נְכָאִים *smitten*, Isa. 16:7.

מַכָּה f (pl. מַבּוֹת, מַכִּים).—I. *stroke, blow*.—II. *wound*.—III. *slaughter*.—IV. *calamity*.

נְכֹה p. n., Pharaoh *Necho*, king of Egypt; LXX. Νεχαώ.

נָכוֹן (same as כִּידוֹן), p. n. of a place.

נֹכַח I. *straight forwards*.—II. *opposite, over against*.—III. *in sight of*; אֶל־נֹכַח *towards*; לְנֹכַח *in front of, in behalf of, straight forwards*; עַד־נֹכַח *as far as*.

נֶכַח (with suff. נִכְחוֹ) *opposite to, against*.

נָכֹחַ m. (f. נְכֹחָה; pl. נְכֹחוֹת).—I. *straight forward, upright*.—II. *uprightness*, Isa. 57:2.

נֹכַחַת Niph. part. f., from יכח.

נָכַל *withholding*, Mal. 1:14. Pi. *used artifice*, with לְ, Nu. 25:18. Hith. the same, with בְּ.

נֵכֶל m., pl. נְכָלִים *artifices*, Nu. 25:18.

כִּילַי m., *avaricious, oppressive*, Isa. 32:5, 7.

נְכָס root not used; same as כָּנַס.

נֶכֶס m., pl. נְכָסִים *treasures, wealth*.

נְכַס m. Ch., pl. נִכְסִין *treasures, wealth*.

פִּים m., *purse, bag*.

נִכְפָּר Nith., from כפר.

נָכַר Pi. נִכֵּר I. *recognised*.—II. *considered*.—III. *acknowledged*.—IV. *alienated*, Deu. 32:27.—V. *rejected*, with בְּ, 1 Sa. 23:7. Niph. נִכַּר I. *feigned himself unknown*, Pro. 26:24.—II. *was recognised*, Lam. 4:8. 11.—Hiph. הִכִּיר I. *recognised, knew, acknowledged*.—II. *was partial in judgment*, with פָּנִים.—III. *beheld*.—IV. *regarded*.—V. *esteemed, accounted*.—VI. *took judicial cognizance of*. Hith. הִתְנַכֵּר *make one's self strange*, Gen. 42:7.

נֵכָר, const. נֵכַר m., *strange, foreign, a foreigner*; בֶּן־נֵכָר *son of the stranger, foreigner*; אֱלֹהֵי נֵכָר *strange gods*.

נָכְרִי m. (pl. נָכְרִים; f. נָכְרִיָּה, pl. נָכְרִיּוֹת).—I. *foreign*.—II. *a stranger*.—III. *strange, singular*.

נֵכֶר m., *treating as a stranger, punishment*.

הַכָּרָה (verb Hiph.) f., *astonishment, consciousness of guilt*, Isa. 3:9.

מַכָּר m., *relative, neighbour*, 2 Ki. 12:6, 8.

נְלֹת, בֵּית נְלֹתֹה 2 Ki. 20:13; Isa. 39:2, *treasury*, γαζοφυλάκιον.

נָלָה root not used; (Arab. *succeeded*) Hiph. inf. with pref. and suff. כְּהַנָּלֹתְךָ for כַּנְּלֹתְךָ *when thou hast accomplished*, Isa. 33:1.

מִנְלָה possession, wealth, Job 15:29.

נִמְבְזֶה despised; see בזה.

נְמוּאֵל p. n. of a man.

נָמַל (fut. יִמַּל; pl. יִמֹּלוּ).—I. circumcise, Gen. 17:11.— II. withered, Ps. 37:2; Job 14:2. (some derive it from מָלַל same as מוּל). Niph. נָמוֹל was circumcised; part. נְמוֹלִים (some derive it from מוּל).

נְמָלָה f., ant, Pro. 6:6; pl. נְמָלִים, Pro. 30:25.

נָמֵר root not used; (Arab. was spotted).

נָמֵר m., a panther, Jer. 5:6; Hab. 1:8.

נְמַר m. Ch., the same, Dan. 7:6.

נָמֵר Niph. pret., from מרר.

נִמְרֹד p. n., Nimrod, the builder of Babylon, Νεβρώδης; אֶרֶץ נִמְרֹד Babylon.

בֵּית נִמְרָה, נִמְרִים p. n., same as בֵּית. see בֵּית.

נִמְשִׁי p.n., father of Jehu.

נְסִי נֵס; see נסס.

נָסֵבָּה for נָסַבָּה Niph. pret. fem., from סבב.

נְסַבָּה; see סבב.

נָסַג recoil, shrink back; inf. נָסוֹג, Isa. 59:13; fut. יִסַּג Mic. 2:6. Hiph. הִסִּיג I. remove a boundary.—II. carry away property, Mic. 6:14. Hoph. הֻסַּג was perverted, Isa. 59: 14.

נָסָה imp. נַסֵּה; (see נָשָׂא). Pi. נִסָּה I. tried.—II. proved, made a trial. —III. found on trial, experienced. מַסָּה f.—I. trial.—II. temptation by trial.

נַסָּה, Ps. 4:7, for נָשָׂא imp., from נשׁא.

נָסַח (fut. יִסַּח) dispersed, scattered. Niph. was dispersed.

נְסַח Ch. Ith. was pulled down, Ezr. 6:11.

מַסָּח m., disperser, driver away, 2 Ki. 11:6.

I. נָסַךְ I. poured out, Isa. 29:10.—II. melted.— III. anointed, Ps. 2:6.— IV. poured out a libation. Niph. נָסַךְ was anointed, Pro. 8:23. Pi. נִסֵּךְ and Hiph. הִסִּיךְ poured a libation.— Hoph. was poured out.

נְסַךְ Ch., Pa. made an offering, Dan. 2:46.

נָסִיךְ m.— I. libation. — II. molten image, Dan. 11:8.— III. anointed one, prince.

נֶסֶךְ, נָסֶךְ m. (with suff. נִסְכּוֹ, נִסְכֹּה pl. נְסָכִים).— I. drink-offering.— II. molten image.

נְסַךְ m. Ch., drink-offering, Ezr. 7:17.

מַסֵּכָה I. fusing; אֱלֹהֵי מ׳ molten images.—II. libation, Isa. 30:1.

II. נָסַךְ same as סָכַךְ covered, Isa. 25:7.

מַסֵּכָה covering, Isa. 25:7; 28:20.

מַסֶּכֶת f. (Arab. he wove), web, Jud 16:13, 14.

נָסַס raised, bore a standard, Isa. 10: 18; 59:19. Hithpo. הִתְנוֹסֵס I. rally round a standard, Ps. 60:6. —II. raise oneself as a standard, Zec. 9:16.

נֵס m. (with suff. נִסִּי).— I. banner.— II. flag-staff.—III. sail.— IV. example, warning.—V. the leader to whom the banner belongs, Isa. 11:10.

נָסַע (fut. יִסַּע; inf. נְסֹעַ; imp. pl. סְעוּ) —I. departed.— II. travelled.—III. arose (a wind), Nu. 11:31.— IV. removed.— V. pulled up or out.

Niph. נִפַּע *was pulled up.* Hiph.
הִסִּיעַ I. *caused to depart, &c.*—II.
made to blow, Ps. 78:26. — III.
quarried stone, 1 Ki. 5:31.

מַסָּע m.—I. *missile weapon,* Job 41:
18. — II. *march, journey;* pl.
מַסָּעִים.

נָסַק *go up,* Ps. 139:8.

נְסַק Ch., *go up.* Aph. *lifted up,*
Dan. 3:22. Hoph. *was lifted up,*
Dan. 6:24.

נִסְרֹךְ p. n., *Nisroch,* an idol of the
Ninevites.

נַעָה p.n., a town in the tribe of Zebulon.

נֹעָה p n. of a woman.

נָעוֹר for נָעוֹר Niph. pret., from עוּר.

נְעוּרִים *youth;* see נַעַר.

נְעִיאֵל p. n., a town in the tribe of
Naphtali.

נָעִים *pleasant;* see נעם.

נָעַל I. *put on sandals,* Eze. 16:10, lit.
latch them.—II. *bolted, latched the
door.* Hiph. fut. with suff. וַיַּנְעִלוּם
shod them, 2 Chron. 28:15.

נַעַל f., *shoe, sandal;* dual נַעֲלַיִם *pair
of sandals;* pl. נְעָלוֹת, נְעָלִים.

מַנְעוּל m., *bolt, lock of a gate.*

מִנְעָל m., *defence,* Deu. 33:25.

נָעֵם (fut. וַיִּנְעַם) *was pleasant, agreeable,* with לְ.

נָעִים m.—I. *pleasant.*—II. *sweet music.*—III. *amiable.*—IV. *becoming.*
—V. *prosperous;* pl. נְעִימִים.

נַעַם p. n. of a man.

נֹעַם m.—I. *pleasantness.*— II. *kindness, grace.*

נַעֲמָה p.n.—I. a town in the tribe of
Judah.—II. the daughter of La-

mech.—III. the mother of Rehoboam.

נָעֳמִי p. n., *Naomi,* the mother-in-
law of Ruth.

נַעֲמִי patron.; see נַעֲמָן.

נַעֲמָן m.—I. *pleasantness,* Isa. 17:10.
—II. p.n. of a man.

נַעֲמָתִי p. n., *Naamathite,* a title.

מַנְעַמִּים m. pl., *delicacies,* Ps. 141:4.

נַעַץ (Arab. a *thorny bush* in the Hed-
jaz).

נַעֲצוּץ m., a species of *thorn bush,* Isa.
7:19; 55:13.

נָעַר I. *roar as a lion,* Jer. 51:38.—II.
shook off, out. Niph. *was shaken
out.* Pi. נֵעַר *threw out.* Hithp.
Isa. 52:2, *shake thyself,* with מִן.

נַעַר m., *straying, strayed* (cattle), Zec.
11:16; see also below.

נְעֹרֶת f., *tow,* Jud. 16:9; Isa. 1:31.

נַעַר m. (with suff. נַעֲרְךָ; נַעֲרוֹ; pl.
נְעָרִים, נַעֲרֵי).—I. *infant.*—II. *boy.*
—III. *youth.*—IV. *servant.*

נַעֲרָה f.—I. *girl.*—II. *young woman.*
—III. *female servant.*—IV. p. n. of
a woman.—V. p. n., a town in the
tribe of Ephraim, also נַעֲרָן.

נֹעַר m., *childhood, youth.*

נְעוּרִים m. pl., *youth, early life.*

נְעֻרוֹת f. pl., the same.

נְעַרְיָה p. n. of a man.

נַעֲרָן p.n., same as נַעֲרָה.

נֹף same as מֹף.

נֶפֶג p. n. of a man.

נֻפָּה see נוּף.

נְפִישְׁסִים, נְפִיסִים, נְפוּסִים p.n. of a m.

נָפַח I. *blew, blew upon,* with בְּ.—II.
blew a fire.—III. with נֶפֶשׁ *ex-
pired;* דּוּד נָפוּחַ *seething pot* Jer.

15:9. Pu. נֻפַּח *was blown* (of a fire), Job 20:26. Hiph. *puffed at, despised.*

נֹפַח p. n., a town in Moab.

מַפֻּחַ m., *bellows*, Jer. 6:29.

מַפַּח m. מ׳ נָפֶשׁ, Job 11:20, *expiring*, "giving up the ghost," Eng. Ver.

נְפִילִים; see נפל.

נָפִישׁ p. n., *Naphish*, a son of Ishmael.

נֹפֶךְ m., an unknown precious stone; LXX. ἄνθραξ.

נָפַל (fut. יִפֹּל 'nf. נְפֹל; with suff. נָפְלוֹ, נִפְלוֹ).—I. *fell, fell down, was killed*, &c.; (נֹפֵל *one prostrate*).—II. *fell upon*, with עַל.—III. *fell to* (of an inheritance), with לְ.—IV. *fell on his face*, with or without עַל פָּנָיו, אֶל פָּנָיו.—V. *fell on* (was confined to) *his bed*, Ex. 21:18.—VI. *deserted to, joined*, with עַל or אֶל.—VII. *fell into the hand of*, with בְּיַד.—VIII. *perished*, Pro. 11:5, &c.—IX. *fell into a pit, mischief*, with בְּ, לְ.—X. נ׳ בְּעֵינָיו *sank in his own esteem*, Neh. 6:16.—XI. נ׳ בְּנַחֲלָה *obtained an inheritance*, Eze. 47:22.—XII. *sank* (of the heart), 1 Sa. 17:32.—XIII. נ׳ אַרְצָה *perished*. Hiph. הִפִּיל I. *caused to fall.*—II. *killed.* — III. *annihilated.* — IV. *threw down.*—V. *divide* (by lot), Jos. 23:4. with לְ.—VI. *knock out a tooth*, Ex. 21:27.—VII. *overcame.*—VIII. *cause to settle*, Ps. 78:55.—IX. *cast out, forsook.*—X. *threw into the fire*, with עַל or בְּ. Hith. I. *prostrate myself.* — II. *fell upon violently*, with עַל.

נְפַל Ch.—I. *fall, fell down.*—II. *prostrated.*—III. *was thrown down.*—IV. *descended*, Dan. 7:20.—V. *fell* (became needful) to one, Ezr 7:20.

נֵפֶל, נֶפֶל m., *abortion*.

נְפִילִים m. pl., a tribe of the first inhabitants of Canaan, who were of gigantic stature.

נִפְלָאתָה Niph. pret. f. with ה parag., from פלא.

נִפְלָל Eze. 28:23, probably an error for נָפַל.

מַפָּל m.—I. *that which falls out of the ear, the worst*, of the corn, Am. 8:6.—II. *pendulous, flaccid parts* (of the flesh), Job 41:15.

מַפֵּלָה, מַפָּלָה f., *ruins* of an edifice, Jeremiah only.

מַפֶּלֶת f.—I. *fall, ruin.*—II. *that which falls, leaf*, Eze. 31:13.—III. *carcase*, Jud. 14:8.

נָפַץ same as פוץ.—I. *broke, dashed down.*—II. *dispersed*, Isa. 11:12.—III. *dispersed itself.* Pi. same as Kal I., II. Pu. *was broken down*, Isa. 27:9.

נֶפֶץ m., *breaking forth, bursting.*

מַפֵּץ m., "battle axe," Eng. Ver., Jer. 51:20.

מַפָּץ m., *bruising*, Eze. 9:2.

נְפַק Ch., *came forth.* Aph. *brought out.*

נִפְקָא Ch. f., *outgoings, expence*, Ezr 6:4, 8.

נָפַשׁ. Niph. I. *had breathing time, rest*, Ex. 23:12.—II. *rested.*

נֶפֶשׁ f., seldom m. (with suff. נַפְשִׁי pl. נְפָשׁוֹת; const. נַפְשׁוֹת; נְפָשִׁים)

—I. *breath.*—II. *an animal* (that which breathes).—III. *a person;* שִׁבְעִים נֶפֶשׁ *seventy souls,* i. e. persons; כָּל נֶפֶשׁ *every one, who-soever.*—IV. *self;* נַפְשִׁי *myself;* נַפְשֶׁךָ *thyself.*— V. נֶפֶשׁ מֵת *dead body, carcase;* טָמֵא לָנֶפֶשׁ *polluted by a dead body.* —VI. *livelihood,* Deu. 24:6.—VII. *the feelings, desire, inclination.*

נֹפֶת, נֶפֶת; see נוּף.

נַפְתּוּלִים; see פתל.

נַפְתֻּחִים p.n. of a people.

נַפְתָּלִי (*my wrestlings,* Gen. 30:8), p.n., *Naphtali,* the son of Jacob and Bilhah.

נֵץ *hawk;* see נצץ.

נָצָה, נָצָא *flew away,* Jer. 48:9; Lam. 4:15.

נָצַב Niph. נִצַּב I. *stood.*—II. *was placed, appointed,* with עַל; part. נִצָּב *one set over, officer.* Hiph. הִצִּיב I. *placed.*—II. *set up.*—III. *fixed, appointed.*—IV. *set a trap,* Jer. 5:26.—V. *uphold,* Ps. 41:13. Hoph. הֻצַּב *set up,* Gen. 28:12.

נָצִיב m.—I. *pillar,* Gen. 19:26.—II. *garrison.*—III. *chief commander,* 1 Ki. 4:19.—IV. p. n., a *town* in the tribe of Judah.

נִצָּב m. (part. Niph.), *handle of a knife,* Jud. 3:22.

נִצְבָּא f. Ch., *firmness, strength,* Dan. 2:41.

מַצָּב, const. מַצַּב m.—I. *standing place.*—II. *station, dignity,* Isa. 22:19.—III. *station, column of soldiers.*

מֻצָּב m. (part. Hoph.), *the same.*

מַצָּבָה, מַצֵּבָה f., the same.

מַצֵּבָה, const. מַצֶּבֶת f.—I. *pillar set up as a memorial.*—II. *image, statue of an idol.*

מַצֶּבֶת f.—I. *pillar.*—II. *monument.*— III. *stem, root,* Isa. 6:13.

נָצַג Hiph. הִצִּיג *set up, make stand up.* Hoph. הֻצַּג *was stayed,* Ex. 10:24.

נָצָה. Kal *was laid waste;* fut. תִּצֶּינָה, Jer. 4:7. Niph. נִצָּה I. *excited to quarrel.*—II. *was st pped;* (part. pl. נִצִּים). Hiphil הִצָּה *was desolate;* see also נָצָא.

נֹצָה, f. affix נֹצָתָהּ *contents of a bird's crop, entrails,* Lev. 1:16.

נוֹצָה *a feather,* Eze. 17:3.

מַצָּה f., *quarrel, strife,* Pro. 13:10; 17:19; see also in מצץ.

מַצּוּת f., the same, Isa. 41:12.

נִצָּה *blossom;* see נצץ.

נָצַח Kal not used; (Arab. *was innocent).* Pi. נִצַּח *superintend, preside over;* part. מְנַצֵּחַ I. *leader, chief.* — II. *choragus, leader of music.*

נְצַח Ch. Ith. *superior,* with עַל.

נֵצַח, נֶצַח m.—I. *a title of God;* נ' יִשְׂרָאֵל *strength of Israel,* 1 Sa. 15:29.—II. *perpetuity.*—III. *success;* לָנֶצַח and נֶצַח I. *according to truth.* — II. *entirely, wholly;* נֶצַח, לָנֶצַח *continually, for ever.*

נֵצַח m., *juice of grapes,* Isa. 63:3,6; (Arab. *sprinkled).*

נָצַח (part. Niph.) f. נִצַּחַת *was perfected, finished.*

נִצְטַדָּק Hith. fut. pl. 1. pers., from צדק.

נָצִיב; see נצב.

נָצַל Pi. נִצֵּל I. *delivered*, Eze. 14:14.
—II. *plundered.*—III. *gained spoil*,
2 Chron. 20:25. Hiph. הִצִּיל I.
delivered, rescued.—II. *took away*,
with מִן.—III. *parted*, with בֵּין.—
IV. *deliver himself.* Hoph. part.
מֻצָּל *rescued.* Niph. נִצַּל I. *was
delivered, escaped.*—II. *ran away
to*, with אֶל. Hith. *strip themselves*, Ex. 33:6.

נְצַל Ch. Aph. *rescued.*

הַצָּלָה (verb Hiph.) f., *deliverance*,
Est. 4:14.

נָצַץ I. *glittering*, Eze. 1:7.—II. *fled.*

נֵץ m. (with suff. נִצּה).—I. *flower*,
Gen. 40:10.—II. *hawk.*

נִצָּה f., *blossom.*

נִצָּן m., pl. נִצָּנִים *flowers*, Cant. 2:12.

נָצַר (fut. יִנְצֹר, יִצֹּר; inf. abs. נָצוֹר;
const. נְצֹר; imp. נְצֹר; with ה
parag. נִצְרָה; with suff. מִן).—
I. *guarded.* — II. *preserved from
evil.*—III. *watched.*—IV. *besieged,
shut up.*— V. *observed*; נֹצְרִים
keepers.

נֵצֶר m., *shoot, branch*; (Arab. *shone*).

נָצִיד m., pl. const. נְצִירֵי (נְצוּרֵי) *preserved, liberated.*

נִצְרָה Kal imp. with ה parag. and dag.
euphon., from נצר.

נָקָא *white*; see נקה.

נָקַב (fut. יִקֹּב, יִנְקֹב).— I. *pierced.*—
II. *bored through.* — III. *bored a
hole.*— IV. *broke the head with a
staff*, Hab. 3:14.— V. *marked.*—
VI. *named.*—VII. *pronounced un-
fortunate.*— VIII. *cursed.* Niph.
were marked by name.

נֶקֶב m.— I. *holes bored in precious
stones*, Eze. 28:13.—II. הַנֶּקֶב p.n.,
a city in the tribe of Naphtali.

נְקֵבָה f., *female.*

מַקָּבָה f., *hammer*

מַקֶּבֶת f.—I. *hammer.*—II. *hole, shaft
of a well*, Isa. 51:1.

נָקֹד root not used; (Ch. נְקַד *mark
with spots*).

נָקֹד m. (pl. נְקֻדִּים; f. נְקֻדָּה) *spotted
sheep or goats*, Gen. 30:32, 33.

נְקֻדָּה f., *studs of silver*, Cant. 1:11.

נֹקֵד m., *shepherd*, 2 Ki. 3:4; Am.
1:1.

נִקֻּדִּים m. pl.—I. *bread*, Jos. 9:5, 12.
—II. *cakes* (probably pricked like
Passover cakes), 1 Ki. 14:3.

נְקוֹדָא p. n. of a man.

נָקָה inf. נָקֹה *was pure*, Jer. 49:12.
Niph. נִקָּה.—I. *was innocent, clear*
—II. *was made innocent, cleared*
with מִן.— III. *was swept away,
devastated.* Pi. נִקָּה I. *cleansed.*
— II. *treated as innocent, freed
from punishment*, with מִן.

נְקָא Ch., Pe. part. נְקֵא *pure, white*,
Dan. 7:9.

נָקִי m. (pl. נְקִיִּים).—I. *innocent.*—II.
clear from guilt, an oath, &c., with
מִן.—III. *exempt*, 1 Ki. 15:22.

נָקִיא the same, Joel 4:19; Jonah 1:
14.

נִקָּיוֹן m.—I. *innocency.*—II. *cleanness
of teeth*, i. e. hunger, Am. 4:6.

מְנַקִּיֹּת f., pl. מְנַקִּיּוֹת *bowls for drink-
offerings.*

נָקַט same as קוט *loathe*, Job 10:1.

נָקַל Niph. pret., from קלל.

נָקַם (fut. יִקֹּם).— I. *avenged, took re-*

מִיד, מֵאֵת, מִן, עַל, *venge on*, with
לְ — II. *punished.*—Niph. נִקַּם I.
revenged himself on.—II. *was punished,* with מִן, בְּ. Pi. נִקַּם I.
revenged, with מִן and בְּ. Hoph.
fut. יֻקַּם *shall be avenged.* Hith.
I. *revenged himself.* — II. part.
מִתְנַקֵּם *desired vengeance.*

נָקָם m., נְקָמָה f. (with suff. נִקְמָתִי;
pl. נְקָמוֹת).—I. *vengeance taken
or inflicted;* עָשָׂה, לָקַח, הֵשִׁיב'
took vengeance; נָתַן נְקָמוֹת *let
vengeance come upon any one.*—II.
punishment.—III. *thirst for revenge,* Lam. 3 : 60.

נָקַע (fut. יִקַּע; see יָקַע) *fell away,
was estranged from,* Eze. 23 : 18,
22, 28.

נָקַף; חַגִּים יִנְקֹפוּ "*let them kill sa-
crifices,*" Eng. Ver., Isa. 29 : 1.
Pi. נִקֵּף I. *cut down,* Isa. 10 : 34.—
II. *pierced,* Job 19 : 26. Hiph.
הִקִּיף I. *fixed, placed around,* with
עַל.—II. *surrounded.* — III. *went
round a place,* Isa. 15 : 8.—IV. *came
round* (of time), Job 1 : 5. — V.
shaved the head in a circle, Lev.
19 : 27; inf. הַקַּף הִקִּיף.

נֶקֶף m., *shaking* of an olive tree to
make the fruit fall, Isa. 17 : 6; 24 : 13.

נִקְפָּה f., "*a rent*" (in a garment),
Eng. Ver., Isa. 3 : 24.

נָקַק same as נָקַב.

נָקִיק m., *fissure in a rock.*

נָקַר (fut. יִקֹּר) and Pi. נִקֵּר.—I. *pierced
through.*—II. *pecked out* (as a bird).
—III. *put out an eye.* Pu. *dug out,*
Isa. 51 : 1.

נְקָרָה f., *cleft* (of a rock).

נָקַשׁ *snared* (as a fowler). Niph. *is
ensnared,* Deu. 12 : 30. Pi. *spread
a snare for,* with לְ. Hith. the
same, with בְּ.

נְקַשׁ Ch., *struck each other* (of knees),
Dan. 5 : 6.

נֵר, נֵר, גְּרִיָה; see נור.

נֵרְגַּל m., name of an idol, 2 Ki. 17 : 30

נֵרְגַּל שַׁרְאֶצֶר p. n. of an Assyrian
prince, Jer. 39 : 3, 13.

נִרְגָּן m., *babbler, calumniator.*

נֵרְדְּ m. (with suff. נִרְדִּי; pl. נְרָדִים).
spikenard, Cant. 1 : 12; 4 : 13, 14.

נָשָׂא (fut. יִשָּׂאוּ, יִשָּׂא, יִשָּׂא; inf. abs.
נָשׂוֹא, נָשׂא const. שְׂאֵת, שְׂאוֹ;
imp. שָׂא, נְשָׂא, שְׂאוּ).—I.
lifted up: (a) *his hand;* (b) with
בְּ *against;* (c) *beckoned;* (d) *lifted
up his voice;* (e) *lifted up his feet;*
(f) *lifted up his face, looked towards,*
with אֶל; (g) *lifted up his eyes;*
(h) *lifted up his soul* (set his
heart on, paid regard, with נֶפֶשׁ),
(i) *raised the head, elevated,* with
רֹאשׁ; (k) *took the sum of, examined
the case of,* with רֹאשׁ.—II. *took,
took up:* (a) *took into hand;* (b)
took into the mouth; (c) *uttered,
offered a prayer;* (d) *received a
precept;* (e) *took away, took hold
of, obtained.*—III. פָּנִים נ' *accepted
the person, acted with partiality.*
—IV. (a) עָוֺן נ' *took away iniquity;* (b) *forgave* (without עָוֺן,
with לְ of the person).—V. (a) *carried, brought;* (b) *carried away;*
(c) *endured;* (d) *bore punishment;*
(e) *supported dignity;* (f) *assisted;*

(g) *bore fruit*, &c.; (h) *supported*,
with בְּ; (i) *laid upon*, with עַל;
(k) *imposed an oath upon*, 1 Ki.
8:31; (l) *removed itself* (of the
earth), Nah. 1:5. Niph. נִשָּׂא I.
was lifted up; part. נָשָׂא *lifted
up*.—II. *raised himself*.—III. *was
carried*.—IV. *was carried away*.
Pi. נִשָּׂא, נִשֵּׂא I. *took away*.—II.
presented a gift.—III. *carried*.—
IV. *assisted*.—V. *raised in rank*,
Est. 3:1.—VI. נ' נֶפֶשׁ *set his heart*.
Hiph. הִשִּׂיא I. *caused to bear*.—
II. *brought*, 2 Sa. 17:13. Hith.
הִנַּשֵּׂא, הִתְנַשֵּׂא I. *arose*.—II. *exalted himself*.—III. *was exalted*.

נְשָׂא Ch.—I. *carried away*, Dan. 2:
35.—II. *took*, Ezr. 5:15. Ithpa.
exalted himself, Ezr. 4:19.

נָשִׂיא m.—I. *chief*.—II. *chief of a
tribe* among the Israelites.—III.
chief of a subdivision of a tribe.
—IV. *prince*.—V. pl. נְשִׂאִים
vapours.

נְשֻׂאָה f., *burden*, Isa. 46:1.

נִשֵּׂאת (Niph. part.) *a gift*, 2 Sa.
19:43.

שִׂיא m., *elevation, dignity*, Job 20:6.

שְׂאֵת inf.—I. *lifting up, elevation*,
Gen. 4:7. — II. *swelling in the
skin*.—III. *exaltation, dignity*.—
IV. *judgment, sentence*, Hab. 1:7.

שֵׂת same as שְׂאֵת *rising*, Job 41:
17.

מַשָּׂא m., מַשָּׂא פָנִים *preference of
persons*, 2 Chron. 19:7.

מַשָּׂא m.—I. *carrying*.—II. *a burden*.
—III. *a load*.—IV. *that which is
burdensome*.—V. *a tribute*.—VI.
calamity.—VII. *lifting up the*
voice to sing.—VIII. *solemn declaration*.—IX. *prophecy*.

מַשְׂאָה f., *rising of flame, burning*.
Isa. 30:27.

מַשְׂאֵת f. (const. מַשְׂאֵת; pl. מַשְׂאֹת).
—I. *the act of lifting up*.—II. *a
signal*.—III. *prophecy*.—IV. *gift*.
—V. *tribute*.

I. נָשַׂג. Hiph. הִשִּׂיג I. *reached*.—II.
was able to reach.—III. *attained,
obtained, overtook*.—IV. *befel*.

II. נָשַׂג same as סוּג. Hiph. הִשִּׂיג
removed (land marks), Job 24:2.

נָשַׂק. Hiph. הִשִּׂיק *kindled a fire*.
Niph. *was kindled*.

נָשַׂר root not used; (Arab. *saw*).

מַשּׂוֹר m., *a saw*, Isa. 10:15.

I. נָשָׁא. Hiph. הִשִּׁיא I. *caused to err,
led astray*.—II. *deceived*, with אֵת,
לְ, בְּ.—III. *laid a burden on*, with
בְּ. Niph. *was deceived*.

מַשָּׁאוֹן m., *deceit*, Pro. 26:26.

II. נָשָׁא same as נָשָׁה which see.

נָשַׁב *blew*, Isa. 40:7. Hiph. הִשִּׁיב
I. *caused to blow*.—II. *dispersed, as
dust*.

I. נָשָׁה I. *forgot*.—II. *neglected*, Jer.
23:39. Niph. the same, Isa. 44:
21. Pi. *cause to forget*. Gen. 41:
51. Hiph. הִשָּׁה I. *cause to forget*,
Job 11:6; 39:17.

II. נָשָׁא, נָשָׁה *lent money*, Jer. 15:
10, with בְּ; נֹשֶׁא *creditor*;
נֹשֶׂה *money lender*. Hiph. the
same, with בְּ; fut. יַשִּׁיא.

נָשֶׁה m., *the ischiatic nerve*, Gen. 32:
33; (Arab. the same).

נְשִׁי m., *a debt,* 2 Ki. 4:7.

נְשִׁיָּה f., *forgetfulness,* Ps. 88:13.

מַשֶּׁה m., *debt,* Deu. 15:2.

מַשָּׁא m., *interest,* Neh. 5:7.

מַשָּׁאָה const. מַשַּׁאת f., *debt.*

נָשׂוּ, נָשׁוּא for נָשׂאוּ, from נשׂא.

נְשׂוּא, Ps. 32:1. for נָשׂוּא Kal part. pass., from נשׂא.

נָשִׁים *woman;* see אשׁה in אנשׁ.

נַשִּׁים for נַשִּׁים or נָשֵׁם Hiph. fut. pl. 1. pers., from שׁמם.

נָשַׁךְ (fut. יִשֹּׁךְ, יִשַּׁךְ) I. *bit.* — II. *annoyed.* — III. *was lent on interest,* Deu. 23:20. Pi. *bit* (of a serpent). Hiph. *lent on interest,* with לְ, Deu. 23:20, 21.

נֶשֶׁךְ m., *interest.*

נִשְׁכָּה f., (pl. נְשָׁכוֹת for לִשְׁכָּה) *chamber of the temple* (book of Nehemiah only).

נָשַׁל (fut. יִשַּׁל; imp. שַׁל־). — I. *fell off.* — II. *pulled off a shoe.* — III. *drove out.* Pi. *drove out,* 2 Ki. 16:6.

נָשַׁם *snort;* fut. אֶשֹּׁם, Isa. 42:14; see שׁמם.

נְשָׁמָה f. — I. *breath.* — II. *life.* — III. *a human being.* — IV. *breath of God:* (a) *his anger;* (b) *the life he gives.* — V. *the wind.*

נִשְׁמָא f. Ch., *breath, life,* Dan. 5:23.

תַּנְשֶׁמֶת f. — I. *an unclean bird* (species uncertain), Lev. 11:18; Deu. 14:16. — II. *an unclean beast,* Lev. 11:30. (species unknown).

נָשַׁף I. *blew.* — II. *blew on,* with בְּ.

נֶשֶׁף m. (with suff. נִשְׁפּוֹ). — I. *dawn.* — II. *evening, twilight.* — III. *darkness.*

יַנְשׁוּף יַנְשׁוּף m., *bittern;* LXX. ἴβιϛ.

נָשַׁק (fut. יִשַּׁק; imp. שַׁק, שְׁקָה). — I. *kissed;* with לְ and אֶל *kissed each other.* — II. *adored,* with לְ. — III. *rule, order,* Gen. 41:40. — IV. *draw up in battle array,* with עַל. Pi. *kissed.* Hiph. *joined, touched,* Eze. 3:13.

נֶשֶׁק, נֵשֶׁק m. — I. *battle,* Ps. 140:8. — II. *battle array,* Job 39:21. — III. *arms.* — IV. *an armoury*

נְשִׁיקָה f., *kiss.*

נָשַׁר (Arab. *eagle*).

נֶשֶׁר m., *an eagle.*

נְשַׁר m. Ch., *an eagle.*

נָשַׁת I. *was parched,* Isa. 41:17. — II. *wasted away,* Jer. 51:30. Niph. *dried up,* Isa. 19:5.

נִשְׁתְּוָה Nith., from שׁוה.

נִשְׁתְּוָן m., *a letter.* Ch. the same (book of Ezra only).

נָתַב (Arab. *was lofty, raised up*).

נָתִיב m., נְתִיבָה f. — I. *path.* — II. *drift of a vein of metal,* Job 28:7. — III. *course of life.*

נָתַח. Pi. נִתַּח *divided, cut in pieces* (a slaughtered animal).

נֵתַח m., *joint, piece of flesh;* pl. נְתָחִים.

נָתַךְ (fut. יִתַּךְ) *poured out.* Niph. I. *was poured out.* — II. *was melted.* Hiph. הִתִּיךְ I. *poured out.* — II. *melted.* Hoph. הֻתַּךְ *be melted,* Eze. 22:22.

הִתּוּךְ (verb Hiph.) m., *melting* (metal), Eze. 22:22.

נָתַן (fut. יִתֵּן; יִתֵּן־, יִתָּן־; pl. נִתְּנוּ, נָתַן; inf. abs. נָתוֹן; const. תֵּת, נְתֹן; with uff. תִּתִּי; imp. תֵּן, (תְּנָה).—I. *gave* (as a present, in marriage, &c.).—II. *gave forth* (produced fruit, emitted odour, &c.).—III. *ascribed.*—IV. *sold.*—V. *offered*, Lev. 20:2, 3, with אֶת—VI. *placed*, with אֶל, בְּ, עַל, לְ—VII. *appointed.*—VIII. *imposed tribute*, with עַל—IX. *inflicted.*—X. *wrought miracles.*—XI. *rendered like, considered as*, with כְּ—XII. *made, rendered*, with לְ; מִי יִתֵּן; see מִי. Niph. נִתַּן *pass. of Kal.*—Hoph. fut. יֻתַּן *shall be given, &c.*

נְתַן Ch., *gave.*

נָתָן p. n.—I. *Nathan*, the prophet.—II. the name also of a son of David and of other men.

נְתַנְאֵל (*gift of God*), p. n. of a man, Ναθαναήλ.

נְתַנְיָהוּ, נְתַנְיָה (*gift of the Lord*), p. n. of a man.

נְתַן־מֶלֶךְ p. n. of king Josiah's chamberlain, 2 Ki. 23:11.

נְתִינִים m. pl., (*devoted*), *Nethinim*, servants of the Temple, waiting upon the Levites; Ch. נְתִינִין.

מַתָּן m.—I. *gift.*—II. p. n. of a man.

מַתָּנָה f.—I. the same.—II. p.n. of a place between Moab and the desert.

מַתְּנָא f. Ch., the same.

מַתְּנִי (for מַתַּנְיָה), p. n. of a man.

מַתַּנְיָהוּ, מַתַּנְיָה p.n. of a man.

מַתָּת f., *a gift.*

מַתִּתְיָהוּ, מַתִּתְיָה p. n. of a man, Ματθαθιας.

מַתַּתָּה p. n. of a man.

נָתַס *break down, cut off*, Job 30:13.

נָתַע Niph. *broken down, cut off*, Job 4:10, for נָתַץ.

נָתַץ (fut. יִתֹּץ).—I. *broke down, destroyed.*—II. *ruined a person.*—III. *struck out teeth*, Ps. 58:7. Pi. נִתֵּץ *destroyed.* Niph. נִתַּץ, Pu. נֻתַּץ and Hoph. הֻתַּץ *was destroyed.*

נָתַק I. *drew one away from* (a place), Jud. 20:32.—II. *drew off* (a ring), Jer. 22:24.—III. part. נָתוּק *castrated*, Lev. 22:24. Niph. נִתַּק I. *drawn away.*—II. *purged away*, Jer. 6:29.—III. *broken* (of a shoestring, cord). Pi. נִתֵּק I. *removed took off*, Isa. 58:6.—II. *pulled up, uprooted.* — III. *broke* a cord.—IV. *broke off, frustrated*, Job 17:11, &c. Hiph. הִתִּיק *drew away* Hoph. הָנְתַק pass. of Hiph., Jud 20:31.

נֶתֶק m., *scalled head;* lit. plucking off of hair, Lev. 13:30 — 37; 14:54.

נְתַקְנוּהוּ Jud. 20:32, Kal pl. 1. pers. with suff. and dag. euphon., from נתק.

נָתַר (fut. יִתֹּר), *beat violently* (the heart), Job 37:1. Pi. *leap* (as locusts), Lev. 11:21. Hiph. הִתִּיר I. *loosened*, Ps. 105:20, &c.—II. *stretched out the hand*, Job 6:9.—III. *straightened*, 2 Sa. 22:33.—IV. *made vibrate, caused to tremble*, Hab. 3:6.

נְתַר Ch., *fell off.* Aph. *shake off*, Dan. 4:11.

נֶתֶר m.—I. *nitre, natron*, Pro. 25:20.—II. *soap made of natron and oil* Jer. 2:22.

נָתַשׁ (fut. יִתַּשׁ), with אֵת.—I. expelled.—II. destroyed. Niph. I. was
expelled, destroyed.—II. failed (of
waters). Hoph. הֻתַּשׁ plucked up
(of trees), Eze. 19:12.

נְתַתָּ, נָתַתָּה, נָתַתִּי Kal pret.,
from נתן.

ס

סְאָה f., a dry measure, containing
one third of an ephah, σάτον;
dual סָאתַיִם; pl. סְאִים.

סַאסְאָה f., the same, Isa. 27:8.

סְאֹן part. סֹאן having greaves, Isa.
9:4.

סְאוֹן m., greaves (armour for the
legs), Isa. 9:4.

סָבָא drank wine, became drunk; part.
סֹבֵא drinker (pl. סוֹבְאִים Ketib,
סָבְאִים Kri, Eze. 23:42).

סֹבֶא m. (with suff. סׇבְאֵךְ).—I. wine.
—II. the act of drinking wine,
Nah. 1:10.

סְבָא p. n.—I. the son of Cush, Gen.
10:7.—II. the people descended
from him; סְבָאִים the Sabeans.

סָבַב (pret. סַבֹּתִי, סָבְבוּ; סַבּוּ; fut.
יָסֹב, יִסֹּב; pl. יָסֹבּוּ; inf. סְבֹב,
סֹב; imp. סֹב; סָב; part. סָבִיב, סוֹבֵב).
—I. turned about.—II. made a
circuit, with אֵת, בְּ.—III. reached
round.—IV. surrounded, with אֵת,
עַל.—V. ended a circuit at, with
אֶל or לְ.—VI. an act overtaken in
its consequences, with אֵת.—VII.
circumvented, entrapped. — VIII.
went round, examined in succes-
sion, Ecc. 7:25.—IX. arrived at a

conclusion (after going round), Ecc.
2:20. Niph. נָסַב (fut. יִסֹב; pl.
יִסַּבּוּ). — I. turn about, make a
circle, surround.—II. returned.—
III. came round in turn.—IV. was
changed, changed, changed his
conduct. Pi. סִבֵּב brought to pass,
2 Sa. 14:20. Poel סוֹבֵב I. made
a circuit, with עַל.—II. surrounded,
with עַל. Hiph. הֵסֵב (fut. יָסֵב;
יָסֵבּוּ).—I. caused to turn about,
make a circuit, surround. — II.
changed his name to. Hoph. הוּסַב
was turned round, enclosed.

סָבִיב m.—I. a circuit; adv. מִסָּבִיב,
סָבִיב סָבִיב around, from around,
סָבִיב לְ around.—II. pl. סְבִיבִים
around.—II. pl. סְבִיבוֹת
surrounding places, sub-
urbs, Jer. 17:26; 33:13; with suff.
סְבִיבוֹתַי around me.

סֹבֵב for סֹבֵב Kal part., from סבב.

סִבָּה f., change, turn in affairs, 1 Ki.
12:15.

נְסִבָּה f., the same, 2 Chron. 10:15.

מוּסַב m., the wall that surrounds a
house, Eze. 41:7.

מֵסַב m. (pl. const. מְסִבּוֹת, מְסִבֵּי).
I. sofas for reclining on (ranged
round), Cant. 1:12.—II. places
surrounding. — III. adv. round
about, 1 Ki. 6:29.

סָבַךְ wrapped, folded, coiled, entangled, Pu. סֻבַּךְ.

סֹבֶךְ m., thicket, tangled place.

סְבָךְ m., pl. const. סִבְכֵי; the same.

סֹבֶךְ m., the same; with suff. סׇבְכּוֹ.

סׇבְכּוֹ with dag. euphon. for סׇבְכוֹ,
from סֹבֶךְ.

סִבְּכַי p. n., Sibbechai, one of David's generals, 2 Sa. 21:18, &c.

שְׂבָכָא ,סַבְכָא f. Ch., a certain musical instrument, σαμβύκη, of what kind is unknown, Dan. 3:5, 7, 10.

סָבַל I. *carried* (a load), Isa. 46:4.—II. *carried* (as a child).—III. *bore consequences of.* Pu *laden*, Ps. 144:14. Hith. הִסְתַּבֵּל *become a burden.*

סְבַל Ch., the same. Po. *brought*, Ezr. 6:3.

סֵבֶל m., *burden, task.*

סַבָּל m., *porter.*

סֹבֶל m. (with suff. סֻבְּלוֹ), *burden*, Isaiah only.

סֻבְּלוֹ; see above.

סְבָלָה f., pl. const. סִבְלוֹת *burdens, labours, tasks*, Exodus only.

סֹבֶלֶת f. (in the dialect of the tribe of Ephraim, for שִׁבֹּלֶת), *ear of corn*, Jud. 12:6.

סְבַר Ch., *hope, propose*, Dan. 7:25.

סִבְרַיִם p.n., a city between Damascus and Hamath.

סַבְתָּה ,סַבְתָּא p.n., *Sabtah*, one of the sons of Cush, Gen. 10:7, and the people descended from him.

סַבְתְּכָא ,סַבְתְּכָה p.n., *Sabtechah*, one of the sons of Cush, Gen. 10:7.

סַגִּים same as סִיגִים; see סוג.

סָגַד *worshipped*, with לְ.

סְגַד Ch., the same.

סָגַל root not used; סָגַל *bought, acquired.*

סְגֻלָּה f.—I. *collection of valuables.*—II. *an object of special regard.*

סָגָן m., pl. סְגָנִים.—I. *chiefs* among the Babylonians and Persians.—

—II. *chiefs* among the Jews after the second captivity.

סְגַן m. Ch., pl. סִגְנִין the same.

סָגַר (fut. יִסְגֹּר).—I. *shut a door, shut in.*—II. *closed a breach*, 1 Ki. 11:27, with בְּעַד ,עַל; part. סָגוּר *shut up*; זָהָב סָגוּר *pure gold*, lit. such gold as is shut, hoarded up. Niph. נִסְגַּר *was shut.* Pi. סִגֵּר, with בְּיָד *delivered up, surrendered.* Pu. סֻגַּר *was shut up.* Hiph. הִסְגִּיר I. *shut up*, with בְּיָד ,אֶל ,לְ.—II. *delivered up*; part. מַסְגִּיר.

סְגַר Ch., *shut.* Dan. 6:23.

סָגוּר m.—I. *enclosure*, Hos. 13:8.—II. *refined gold*, Job 28:15.

סוּגַר m., *prison*, Eze. 19:9.

סַגְרִיר m., *rain*, Pro. 27:15.

מַסְגֵּר (part. Hiph.) m.—I. *confinement, prison.*—II. *joiner*, i.e. closer.

מִסְגֶּרֶת f. (pl. מִסְגְּרוֹת).—I. *inclosure.*—II. *border, moulding.*

סָדַד root not used; (Arab. *shut up*).

סַד m., *fetters.*

סְדֹם p.n., *Sodom*, one of the cities of the plain, Σόδομα.

סָדִן root not used; (Arab. *wool, covering*).

סָדִין m.—I. *fine cloth* of Syrian manufacture.—II. a dress made of it, Isa. 3:23.—III. a piece of it used as a sheet, Jud. 14:12, 13.

סָדַר root not used; (Syr. *set in order*).

סֵדֶר m., pl. סְדָרִים *ranks, orderly arrangement*, Job 10:22.

שְׂדֵרָה f., pl. שְׂדֵרוֹת the same.

מִסְדְּרוֹן m., *portico*, Jud. 3:23

סָהַר root not used (Samar. סהר), *encompassed about, was round.*

סַהַר m., *roundness* (like the full moon), Cant. 7:3.

סֹהַר m., בֵּית הַסֹּהַר *prison*, Gen. 39 & 40, only.

שַׂהֲרֹנִים m. pl., *small moons* (ornaments).

סוֹא p. n., *Sevechus* king of Egypt, 2 Ki. 17:4.

I. סוּג *slid back from God.* Niph. נָסוֹג (fut. יִסוֹג).—I. *driven back.*—II. *induced to go back.*

II. סוּג *fenced*, Cant. 7:3.

סִיג m. (pl. סִיגִים, סִינִים), *dross* (of metals).

סוֹדִי ; סוֹד see יסד.

סוּחָה root not used; same as סחה *cleanse.*

סוּחַ p. n. of a man.

סוּחָה f., *filth*, Isa. 5:25.

סוֹטַי (see שׂוּט) p. n. of a man.

סוּךְ same as נָסַךְ.—I. *anoint himself.*—II. *anoint another*, with בְּ. Hiph. *anointed himself*; fut. יָסֵךְ.

אָסוּךְ m., *vessel for anointing oil*, 2 Ki. 4:2.

סוּמְפֹנְיָה f. Ch., συμφωνία, a musical instrument, *the hautboy*, Ital. zampogna, Dan. 3:5, 15.

סְוֵנֵה p. n., *Syene*, a city of Egypt; (hierog. Soun).

סוּס m.—I. *a horse.*—II. *a swallow*, Isa. 38:14; Jer. 8:7.

סוּסָה f., *horses*, Cant. 1:9.

סוּסִי p. n. of a man.

סוּף *come to an end, perish.* Hiph. *cause to perish.*

סוּף Ch., *came to an end, was completed.* Aph. *destroyed.*

סוֹף m.—I *end, termination, comple-* tion, result.—II. *rear of an army*, Joel 2:20.

סוֹף m. Ch., *the same.*

סוּפָה f., *whirlwind, tornado*, with ה parag. סוּפָתָה.

סוּף m.—I. *sea weed*; יַם־סוּף *the Red Sea.*—II. p. n. of a man.

סוּר (fut. יָסוּר, וַיָּסַר).—I. *went, turned aside*, with מֵאַחֲרֵי, מֵעַל, מִן, אֶל—II. *went away*, with מִן.— III. *was removed.*—IV. *ceased.*—V. *rebelled against*, with בְּ. Pil. סוֹרֵר *turned away*, Lam. 3:11. Hiph. הֵסִיר (fut. יָסִיר וַיָּסַר).—I. *removed*, Lev. 1:16.—II. *laid aside, gave up.*—III. *drew off* (a ring). — IV. *set aside.*—V. *destroyed.* הֵסִיר רֹאשׁ 'וגו *cut off his head*; מֵאַחֲרֵי יְהוָֹה 'ב *estranged him from following the Lord.* Hoph. הוּסָר *was removed, taken away.*

סוּר m.—I. *degenerate branch*, Jer. 2:21.—II. p. n., one of the gates of the temple, 2 Ki. 11:6, called יְסוֹד in the parall. pass., 2 Chron. 23:5.

סִיר com.—I. *a thorn*; pl. סִירִים.—II. pl. סִירוֹת *hooks*, Am. 4:2.—III. *pot, vessel*; pl. סִירוֹת.

סָרָה f.—I. *turning from God, rebellion.*—II. ... *from the truth, falsehood*, Deu. 19:16; see סָרַר.

סֵרָה p. n. of a well or tank, 2 Sa. 3 26.

סוּת Hiph. הֵסִית הֵסִּית (fut. יָסִית, וַיָּסֶת יַסִּית; part. מֵסִית) *(urged, excited, induced*, with אֶת and בְּ.

סוּת, Gen. 49:11, wrong reading for כְּסוּת *covering*; see כסה.

סָחַב I. *drew along the ground*, 2 Sa. 17:13, &c.— II. *tore in pieces and devoured*, Jer. 49:20, &c.

סְחָבָה f., *tearing to pieces*; בְּלֹאֵי הַסְּחָבוֹת *"old cast clouts;"* Eng. Ver., Jer. 38:11, 12.

סָחָה. Pi. סָחָה *swept away*, Eze. 26:4.

סְחִי m., *offscouring*, Lam. 3:45.

שָׁחִיס, סָחִים m., *spontaneous produce*, that which comes without sowing, 2 Ki. 19:29; Isa. 37:30; LXX. αὐτόματα; Aquila αὐτοφυῆ.

סָחַף *beat down, crush*, Pro. 28:3. Niph. *beaten down*, Jer. 46:15.

סָחַר *travelled to a place*, with אֶל; *over a country*, with אֵת; part. סֹחֵר (pl. סֹחֲרִים, סֹחֲרֵי) *traveller, merchant*; f. סֹחֶרֶת. Pil. סְחַרְחַר *was agitated* (the heart), Ps. 38:11.

סַחַר m.— I. *commerce*.— II. *wealth acquired by commerce*.—III. *seat of commerce*, Isa. 23:3.

סָחַר m., *the same*.

סְחֹרָה f., *seat of commerce*, Eze. 27:15.

סֹחֵרָה f., *tower*, Ps. 91:4; (Syr. *tower*).

סֹחֶרֶת f., *black marble* or *tortoise-shell* (uncertain which), Est. 1:6; LXX. πάρινος λίθος.

מִסְחָר m., *traffic*, 1 Ki. 10:15.

סֵטִים *sinners*; same as שֵׂטִים; see שׂוּט.

סִיג *dross*; see סוּג.

סִיוָן m., name of the third month of the Jewish year, Est. 8:9.

סִיחוֹן p. n.—I. *Sihon*, king of the Amorites.—II. the district over which he ruled.

סִין p. n., a city of Egypt, "Pelusium," (Jerome); probably Syene; Eze. 30:15, 16; see סְוֵנֶה.

מִדְבַּר־סִין p. n., the wilderness of *Sin*.

סִינִי p. n.—I. a people of Canaan, Gen. 10:17; 1 Ch. 1:15.—II. אֶרֶץ סִינִים the land of *Sin*.

סִינַי p. n., a mountain on the promontory between Egypt and Canaan; its two summits are called *Sinai* and *Horeb*.

סִיס Jer. 8:7, same as סוּס *a swallow*.

סִיסְרָא p. n., *Sisera*, a Canaanitish leader, and other men.

סִיעָא, סִיעֲהָא p. n. of a man.

סִיר; see סוּג.

סָכַך I. *covered*.—II. *protected by covering*.—III. *placed as a covering*, with עַל.—IV. *compacted, put together*, Ps. 139:13; part. סוֹכֵךְ *defence*. Hiph. הֵסֵךְ I. *covered*, with עַל.—II. *protected*, with לְ.—III. *dressed himself*, 2 Sa. 12:20.—IV. *confined*, with בְּעַד. Hoph. הֻסַּךְ *was covered*, with בְּ. Pilp. סִכְסֵךְ *armed*, Isa. 9:10; 19:2.

סָךְ m., *multitude, crowd*, Ps. 42:5.

סֹךְ m. (with suff. סֻכּוֹ, סֻכֹּה), *thicket, hiding-place, dwelling*.

סֻכָּה f.—I. *thicket*, Job 38:40.—II. *hiding-place*, Ps. 31:21.—III. *hut* (of branches or wattles).— IV. *dwelling*; pl. סֻכּוֹת I. *tabernacles*; חַג הַסֻּכּוֹת *feast of tabernacles*.— II. סֻכּוֹת בְּנוֹת, 2 Ki. 17:30, probably a proper name.—III. p. n., a station of the Israelites.— IV. a town of the Gadites.

סִכּוּת f., shrine, Am. 5:26.

סֻכִּיִּים p. n., Sukkiims, 2 Ch. 12:3, some part of the invading army of Shishak; meaning unknown.

סְכָכָה p. n., a town in the tribe of Judah.

מָסָךְ const. מָסַךְ m.—I. covering (of tabernacle).— II. (with פָּרֹכֶת) a veil.—III. curtain of a fortress, Isa. 22:8.

מְסֻכָּה f., covering, Eze. 28:13.

מִיסָךְ (מוּסָךְ) m., covering, porch, 2 Ki. 16:18.

סָכַל Niph. became foolish, acted foolishly. Pi. made foolish. Hiph. acted the fool.

סָכָל m., a fool, foolish.

סֶכֶל m., folly, Ecc. 10:6.

שִׂכְלוּת, סִכְלוּת f., folly, book of Eccles. only.

סָכַן, with לְ, עַל.—I. was prosperous, Job 34:9.—II. was beneficial, Job 15:3.—III. part. סֹכֵן a companion, counsellor; f. סֹכֶנֶת. Hiph. was familiar with, accustomed to, with עִם. Pu. part. מְסֻכָּן poor, needy (Arab. was poor), Isa. 40:20. Niph. נִסְכַּן exposed himself to danger (Ch. סְכַן was in danger), Ecc. 10:9.

מִסְכֵּן m., poor.

מִסְכְּנֻת f., poverty, Deu. 8:9.

מִסְכְּנוֹת f. pl. (same as מִכְנְסוֹת; see כֵּנָם), magazines, treasuries.

I. סָכַר Niph. was shut. Pi. (see סָגַר), delivered up, Isa. 19:4.

II. סָכַר same as שָׂכַר hired, Ezr. 4:5.

סָכַת. Hiph. הִסְכִּית was silent, Deu 27:9.

סֵל, סַלִּים, סִלָּא; see סלל.

סָלָא. Pu. valued, Lam. 4:2

סָלַד. Pi. harden oneself, Job 6:10.

סֶלֶד p. n. of a man.

סָלָה trampled on, Ps. 119:118. Pi. the same, Lam. 1:15. Pu. valued, estimated, Job 28:16, 19.

סֶלָה a musical note, in the Psalms and the prayer of Habakkuk.

סָלַח (fut. יִסְלַח), forgave. Niph. was forgiven.

סַלָּח m., one who forgives, is placable, Ps. 86:5.

סְלִיחָה f., forgiveness.

סַלְכָה p. n., a town in the land of Bashan.

סָלַל threw up an embankment, levelled, made a road. Pilp. סִלְסֵל exalt, Pro. 4:8. Hithpo. הִסְתּוֹלֵל opposing, exalting himself, with בְּ, Ex. 9:17.

סַל m. (pl. סַלִּים) basket.

סִלָּא p. n. of a place.

סַלּוּ p. n. of a man.

סַלּוּא, סִלָּא p. n. of a man.

סָלּוּא p. n. of a man.

סַלַּי p. n. of a man.

סִלּוֹן a thorn, Eze. 28:24.

סַלּוֹן m., the same; metaph. wicked man, Eze. 2:6.

סֹלְלָה f., a mound.

סֻלָּם m., a ladder, Gen. 28:12.

סַלְסִלּוֹת f. pl., baskets, Jer. 6:9.

מְסִלָּה f.—I. raised highway.—II. road, path.—-III. terraces (Lee), "steps" (Gesenius), 2 Chron. 9: 11.

מְסִלּוֹל m., *highway*, Isa. 35:8.

סֶלַע m.—I. *cleft in a rock, cavern.* —II. *rock.*—III. p. n. of a city, perhaps *Petra* in Edom.

סָלְעָם m., a kind of *locust*, Lev. 11:22.

סָלַף Pi. סִלֵּף I. *perverts.*—II. *over- throws.*

סֶלֶף m., *capriciousness, perverseness.*

סְלִק Ch., *came up, grew up.*

סֹלֶת root not used; (Arab. *shelled grain*).

סֹלֶת com., *shelled grain, fine flour.*

סָמִים, סָם; see סמם.

סַמְגַּר־נְבוּ p. n., a prince of Babylon.

סְמָדַר m., *flower* (of the grape).

סָמַךְ I. (with אֶת יָדָיו עַל) *laid his hands on.*— II. *supported.* — III. *pressed, weighed upon,* with עַל, Ps. 88:8.—IV. *advanced towards,* with אֶל, Eze. 24:2. Niph. I. *leaned on.*— II. *trusted in.*— Pi. *support,* Cant. 2:5,

שְׂמִיכָה f., *coverlet,* Jud. 4:18.

סְמַכְיָהוּ p. n. of a man.

סֵמֶל, סֶמֶל m., *figure, form.*

סָמַם (Arab. *exhaled perfume*).

סָם m., pl. סַמִּים *perfumes.*

סָמַן Niph. part. נִסְמָן "appointed" Eng. Ver. (of barley), Isa. 28:25.

סָמַר *grew hard, rigid,* Ps. 119:120. Pi. the same, Job 4:15.

סָמָר m., *rough, bristly* (of a locust), ὀρθοθριξ, Jer. 51:27.

מַסְמְרִים.מַסְמְרוֹת m. pl., *nails.*

מַשְׂמְרוֹת, מַסְמְרוֹת, מַסְמְרוֹת f. pl., the same.

סְנָאָה p. n., a town of Judah.

סְנוּאָה p. n., probably of a woman, Neh. 11:9.

סַנְבַלָּט p. n. of a Persian governor of Samaria.

סְנֶה m., *the bush of Sinai,* Ex. 3: 2—4; Deu. 33:16.

סֶנֶה p. n., a rock near Michmash, 1 Sa. 14:4.

סַנְוֵרִים m. pl., *blindness,* Gen. 19:11; 2 Ki. 6:18.

סַנְחֵרִיב p. n., *Sennacherib,* king of Assyria.

סַנְסִנִּים m. pl., *the plume of the palm- tree,* Cant. 7:9.

סַנְסַנָּה p. n., a city of the tribe of Judah.

סְנַפִּיר m., *fin of a fish,* Lev. 11:9; Deu. 14:9.

סָס m., *clothes-moth,* Isa. 51:8.

סִסְמַי p. n. of a man.

סָעַד (fut. יִסְעַד; imp. סְעַד, סְעָד, סְעָד־; with ה parag. סְעָדָה).—I. *was prosperous,* Pro. 20:28.— II. *made prosperous,* Ps. 20:3. — III. *supported.*—IV. *cheered, refreshed,* with לֵב.

סְעַד Ch., *assisting,* Ezr. 5:2.

מִסְעָד m., *prop, support,* 1 Ki. 10:12.

סֹעָה; רוּחַ סֹעָה *rapid wind,* Ps. 55:9.

סָעַף Kal not used; (Arab. *palm branch*). Pi. סֵעֵף (perhaps from סְעִיף) *cut off branches,* Isa. 10:33.

סָעִיף m.—I. *cleft, cavern.*— II. *sect party,* 1 Ki. 18:21.—III. *a branch*

סְעַפּוֹת f. pl., *branches,* Eze. 31:6, 8.

סַרְעַפּוֹת f. pl., the same, Eze. 31:5.

סְעַף m., pl. סְעַפִּים *persons of divided minds*, Ps. 119:113.

שְׂעִפִּים *thoughts of the mind* (lit. *branches*).

שַׂרְעַפִּים m. pl., *thoughts*, Ps. 94:19; 139:23.

סָעַר I. *was tempestuous*, Jon. 1:11, 13, &c.—II. *tossed by calamity*, Isa. 54: 11. Niph. *was agitated* (the heart), 2 Ki. 6:11. Pi. סֵעַר *scattered*, Zec. 7:14. Po. *scattered*, Hos. 13:3; see שׂעֵר.

סַעַר m., *pestilential, violent wind, whirlwind*.

סְעָרָה const. סַעֲרַת f., the same.

סַף with pause סָף m. (pl. סִפִּים, סִפּוֹת).—I. *dish, bason, goblet, bowl*.—II. *threshold.*—III. p. n. of a man.

הִסְתּוֹפֵף Hith. inf., *remain at the threshold*, Ps. 84:11.

סָפָא (Arab. *filled*).

מִסְפּוֹא m., *provender, fodder.*

סָפַד *lamented, bewailed*, with לְ, עַל, לִפְנֵי‎. Niph. *was lamented.*

מִסְפֵּד const. מִסְפַּד m., *lamentation.*

סָפָה I. *came to an end, perished.*—II. *brought to an end, destroyed*; inf. סְפוֹת *increase*, Nu. 32:14. Niph. נִסְפָּה *was perished.* Hiph. הַסְפָּה *heap, accumulate* (trouble), Deu. 23:23.

סִפֻּן; see סָפַן.

סְפוֹרָה; see ספר.

סָפַח *admitted*, 1 Sa. 2:36. Niph. *was admitted*, Isa. 14:1. Pi. *poured out*, Hab. 2:15. Pu. *scattered*, Job

30:7. Hith. הִסְתַּפֵּחַ *obtained admission*, 1 Sa. 26:19.

סָפִיחַ m.—I. *pouring out of water* Job 14:19.— II. *spilt, self-sown grain*; pl. סְפִיחִים‎.

סַפַּחַת f., *a scar, scald*, Lev. 13:2; 14:56.

מִסְפַּחַת f., *scurf, scab*, Lev. 13:6—8.

מִסְפָּחוֹת f. pl., *cushions, pillows*, Eze 13:18, 21.

סְפִי p. n., same as סָף‎.

סַפִּיר m., *a sapphire.*

סֵפֶל m., *a bowl*, Jud. 5:25; 6:38.

סָפַן I. *covered.*—II. *secured*, Deu. 33: 21.

סִפֻּן m., *ceiling*, 1 Ki. 6:15.

סְפִינָה f., *ship*, Jon. 1:5.

סָפַף, הִסְתּוֹפֵף; see סָף‎.

סָפַק I. *clapped the hands together.*— II. *smote upon the thigh.*—III. *expressed contempt for.*

סֵפֶק m., *abundance, sufficiency*, with suff. סִפְקוֹ, Job 20:22.

סָפַר (fut. יִסְפֹּר) *numbered, reckoned*, part. סֹפֵר (pl. סֹפְרִים) *writer, scribe*, γραμματεύς. Niph. *was numbered.* Pi. סִפֵּר I. *counted.* — II. *recounted.*—III. *talked.* Pu. סֻפַּר *was related*, &c.

סָפַר m. Ch., *scribe.*

סֵפֶר m., *enumeration*, 2 Chron. 2:16.

סֵפֶר m. (with suff. סִפְרְךָ; pl. סְפָרִים, סִפְרֵי).—I. *enumeration*, Gen. 5:1. —II. *register.*—III. *book.*—IV. *letter.*—V. *writing.*

סְפַר m. Ch., *book.*

סִפְרָה f., *book*, Ps. 56:9.

סִפְרַת p. n. of a man.

מִסְפָּר f., *number*, Ps. 71:15

מִסְפָּר m.— I. *number;* אַנְשֵׁי מ' or מְתֵי מ' *few men.*—II. *narrative,* Jud. 7:15.—III. p. n. of a man; מִסְפֶּרֶת *the same.*

סְפֹר p. n. of a city, Gen. 10:30.

סְפָרַד p. n., a country into which the Jews were carried, Obad. *v.* 20.

סְפַרְוַיִם p. n., *Sepharvaim,* a city of Assyria; סְפַרְוִים *Sepharvites.*

סָקַל *stoned.* Pi.— I. *as Kal.*—II. *cleared of stones.* Niph. and Pu. *was stoned.*

סָרָב *rebellious,* Eze. 2:6.

סָרְבָּלִין m. pl. Ch., *drawers, trousers,* Dan. 3:21, 27.

סַרְגּוֹן p. n., *Sargon,* king of Assyria.

סֶרֶד p. n. of a man; patron. סַרְדִּי.

סֹרָה, סָרָה; see סרר, סור.

סָרַח I. *unconfined, loose,* Ex. 26:12, 13, &c.—II. *luxuriant* (of a vine), Eze. 17:6.—III. *loose, dissolute,* Am. 6:4, 7. Niph. *scattered, vanished* (of wisdom), Jer. 49:7.

סָרַח m., *portion of a thing left loose,* Ex. 26:12.

סִרְיוֹן *corslet,* same as שִׁרְיוֹן; see שׁרה.

סָרִיס m. (const. סָרִים; pl. סָרִיסִים, const. סָרִיסֵי).—I. *eunuch.*—II. *any chief officer.*

סָרְכִין m. pl. Ch., *superintendants of the whole empire,* Dan. 6:3.

סְרָנִים, const. סַרְנֵי m. pl.—I. *axles,* 1 Ki. 7:30.—II. the name of the five princes of the Philistines.

סַרְעַפּוֹת *branches;* see סעף.

שָׂרַף same as שָׂרַף Pi. part. מְסָרֵף *burning, he who burns,* Am. 6:10.

סַרְפָּד m., the name of an unknown shrub; LXX. κόννζα; Vulg. urtica.

סָרַר *was perverse, refractory,* Hos. 4:16; part. סֹרֵר (pl. סוֹרְרִים; f. סוֹרֶרֶת, סוֹרֵרָה) *perverse, rebellious;* סַר m., סָרָה f., *averse, disinclined, sad;* see also another סָרָה in סור.

סְתָה root not used; (Arab. *winter*). סְתָו (סִתָיו) m., *winter,* Cant. 2:11.

סָתַם I. *filled, blocked up.*—II. *repaired.*—III. *shut up, concealed* Niph. *was repaired,* Neh. 4:1. Pi. *blocked up,* Gen. 26:15, 18.

סָתַר *concealed,* Pro. 22:3. Niph. נִסְתַּר I. *concealed himself.*—II. *was concealed, unknown.*—III. *was sheltered.*—IV. *was distant.*—V. *was excluded;* part. נִסְתָּר *hidden, hidden thing;* pl. נִסְתָּרוֹת *hidden things.* Pi. *hide, shelter,* Isa. 16:3 Pu. *concealed,* Pro. 27:5. Hiph. הִסְתִּיר I. *concealed.*—II. *sheltered* —III. *placed for security,* Isa. 49:2.—IV. *turned his face from.* Hith. הִסְתַּתֵּר I. *concealed, lost.*—II. *hid himself.*

סְתַר Ch. Pa. סַתַּר *put out of sight, destroyed.*

סְתוּר p. n., a prince of Asher.

סֵתֶר m. (with suff. סִתְרִי).—I. *secrecy.*—II. *secret place.*—III. בַּסֵּתֶר *secretly.*—IV. *place of concealment.*—V. *place of security.*

סִתְרָה f., *shelter, protection,* Deu. 32:38.

סִתְרִי p. n. of a man.

מִסְתָּר m.—I. *ambush.*—II. *secret place.*

מִסְתּוֹר *hiding place,* Isa. 4:6.

ע

עַב m., *epistyle, frieze* (in architecture), 1 Ki. 7:6; Eze. 41:25, 26; pl. עָבִּים; see also עוּב.

עָבַד (inf. and imp. עֲבֹד; fut. יַעֲבֹד).
—I. *served* (God or man).—II. *worked, laboured.*—III. *tilled the ground.*—IV. *assented to,* 1 Ki. 12:7.—V. *performed a religious service.*—VI. *made to serve,* with בְּ of the person. Niph. נֶעֱבַד I. *became, was, served,* Ecc. 5:8.—II. *was tilled.* Pu. עֻבַּד *labour was imposed upon,* with בְּ. Hiph. הֶעֱבִיד I. *caused to labour.*—II. *caused to serve.*—III. *wearied,* Isa. 43:23, 24. Hoph. הָעֳבַד *was induced to worship.*

עֲבַד Ch.—I. *made.*—II. *performed, did,* with בְּ, עִם. Ith. *was made.*

עֶבֶד m. (with suff. עַבְדּוֹ; pl. עֲבָדִים).—I. *slave, servant.*—II. *vassal.*—III. עֶבֶד יְהֹוָה *servant of the Lord,* i. e. one who worships and serves him, or executes some special commission for him.—IV. *a submissive epithet.*—V. p. n. of a man.

עֲבַד m. Ch., the same.

עֹבֵד p. n. of a man.

עַבְדָּא p. n. of a man.

עַבְדְּאֵל p. n. of a man.

עַבְדּוֹן p. n., a city of the Levites in the tribe of Asher.

עַבְדִּי p. n. of a man.

עַבְדִּיאֵל p. n. of a man.

עֹבַדְיָה, עֹבַדְיָהוּ (*servant of the Lord,* Ἀβδίας), p. n., *Obadiah* the prophet and others.

עֶבֶד מֶלֶךְ p. n., an Ethiopian in the service of king Zedekiah, Jer. 38:7, &c.

עֲבֵד נְגוֹ (נְגוֹא) p. n., *Abednego,* one of the three holy children, Dan. chaps. I. II. III.

עֲבָד m., *work,* Ecc. 9:1.

עֲבֹדָה f.—I. *servitude.*—II. *employment.*—III. *tillage.*—IV. *religious service, worship.*—V. *service* required by the king.—VI. לַעֲבֹדַת הָאָדָם *for the service* (use) *of man,* Ps. 104:14.

עֲבֻדָּה f., *slaves, gang of slaves,* Gen 26:14; Job 1:3.

עֲבִידָא f. Ch.—I. *work, building.*—II. *worship, service,* Ezr. 6:18.—III. *business,* Dan. 2:49; 3:12.

עַבְדוּת f., *slavery,* Ezr. 9:8, 9; Neh. 9:17.

מַעֲבָד m. (Heb. and Ch.), pl. מַעֲבָדִים *works, doings,* Job 34:25; Dan. 4:34.

עָבָה *became large, thick, heavy.*

עֲבִי m., *thickness.*

עֳבִי m., the same.

מַעֲבֶה m., *thickness,* 1 Ki. 7:46.

עָבַט *gave a pledge;* fut. יַעֲבֹט. Pi. יְעַבֵּטוּן *break ranks,* Joel 2:7. Hiph. הַעֲבִיט *lent on security,* Deu. 15:6, 8.

עֲבוֹט m., *pledge,* Deu. 24:10-13.

עַבְטִיט m., *accumulation of pledges* in the hands of an unfeeling usurer; "thick clay," Eng. Ver., Hab. 2:6.

עָבַר (inf. and imp. עֲבֹר; fut. יַעֲבֹר).—I. *passed on.*—II. *passed away, ceased.*—III. *passed* a person, place, river, &c.—IV. *passed* a limit.—V. *trespassed, transgressed;* עָבַר

בְּרִית *transgressed a covenant.*—
VI. *exceeded, went beyond.*—VII.
overflowed, overwhelmed, with עַל.
—VIII. *passed through,* with עַל,
לִפְנֵי, עַל פְּנֵי, מֵעַל.—IX. *passed
away, disappeared.*—X. *passed
through,* with בְּ.—XI. *entered into,*
with בְּ; עָ' בִּבְרִית *made a covenant.*—XII. *dropped (as liquid).*—
XIII. כֶּסֶף עֹבֵר *current money,*
Gen. 23:16. Niph. *can be passed,*
Eze 47:5. Pi. עִבֵּר I. *conceived,*
Job 21:10.—II. *caused to pass,*
1 Ki. 6:21. Hiph. הֶעֱבִיר I. *caused,
allowed to pass.*—II. *removed, took,
or put away.*—III. *removed guilt,
&c.* — IV. *destroyed.* — V. *trans-
ferred.*—VI. *offered* presents to
God or idols; לַמֹּלֶךְ ה' *caused to
pass through fire to Moloch.*—VII.
שׁוֹפָר ה' *blew a trumpet,* lit. caused
the breath to pass through it.
Hith. הִתְעַבֵּר *allowed himself beyond proper limits, was angry,*
with עִם, בְּ, עַל.

עֲבוּר (only with pref.), בַּעֲבוּר I. prep.
because of, in return for; with suff.
בַּעֲבוּרִי *on my account;* בַּעֲבֻרְךָ
because of thee. — II. conj. 1. *for
the purpose that* (בַּ, אֲשֶׁר לְבַעֲבוּר
the same).—2. *because, while.*

עֲבוּר m., *produce of the ground,* Jos.
5:11, 12.

עֵבֶר m.—I. *ford.*—II. *mountain pass.*
—III. *passage over.*—IV. *banks of
a river.*—V. *side;* אֶל־עֵבֶר *towards,
on the other side;* אֶל־עֶבְרוֹ *separately, alone;* מֵעֵבֶר *beyond, opposite to, across;* מִכָּל־עֲבָרִים *from
every side;* עֵבֶר אֶחָד עֵבֶר אֶחָד

on this and on that side; עַל־עֵבֶר
פְּנֵי *in front of it,* Ex. 25:37; אֶל־
עֵבֶר פָּנָיו *forwards,* Eze. 1:9, 12.
—VI. p. n., *Eber,* the grandson of
Shem, Gen. 10:24, 25, and progenitor of Abraham, whose descendants were called from him;
עֵבֶר, בְּנֵי־עֵבֶר *Hebrews;* הָעִבְרִי or הַר
הָעֲבָרִים *a range of hills beyond
Jordan.*

עֲבַר Ch., *beyond.*

עִבְרִי m., *a Hebrew;* pl. עִבְרִים,
עִבְרִיּוֹת. f. עִבְרִיָּה; pl. עִבְרִיִּים.

עֲבָרָה f., *raft, passage boat,* 2 Sa. 19:
19.

עֶבְרָה f., *any unrestrained feeling,*
specially, *anger.*

מַעֲבָר m. — I. *ford.* — II. *mountain
pass.*

מַעֲבָרָה f., pl. מַעְבָּרוֹת *the same.*

עַבְרֹנָה p. n., a station of the Israelites.

עָבַשׁ *became shrivelled, worthless,* Joel
1:17.

עָבַת. Pi. *confirm, establish,* Mic. 7:3.
עָבֹת m., עֲבֹתָה f., *thick, entangled.*
עֲבוֹת m. (pl. עֲבֹתִים, עֲבֹתוֹת).—I.
thick branches, Eze. 31:3, 10, 14.
—II. *cord, rope.*—III. *twisted chain.*
—IV. *obligation, restraint.*

עָגַב (fut. יֶעְגַּב) *loved, fell in love with,*
with אֶל, עַל, Eze. c. 23.

עֲגָבָה f., *love;* with suff. עֲגָבָתָהּ, Eze
23:11.

עֲגָבִים m. pl., the same, Eze. 33:31, 32

עֻגָב, עוּגָב m., *a musical instrument
probably, the pipe,* Gen. 4:21, &c
עֲנֵה, עָנָה; see עוּג.

עָגוּר m., *crane.*

עָגַל (Syr. *turned round*).

עָגֹל m., עֲגֻלָּה f., *round, circular.*

עָגִיל m. *ear-ring.*

עֵגֶל m. (with suff. עֶגְלְךָ).—I. *calf.*— —II. *image of one.*— III. עֶגְלֵי עַמִּים *princes, leaders, of the people,* Ps. 68:31.

עֶגְלָה f.—I. *she-calf, heifer.*—II. p. n., one of the wives of David.

עֲגָלָה f. (with suff. עֶגְלָתוֹ; pl. עֲגָלוֹת עֲגָלֹת).—I. *waggon drawn by two bullocks.*—II. *war chariot,* Ps.46:10.

עֶגְלוֹן p. n.—I. a city in the tribe of Judah.—II. a king of Moab.

מַעְגָּל or מַעְגֵּל m. (pl. מַעְגָּלִים, מַעְגָּלוֹת).—I. *wheel.*—II. *track of a wheel.*— III. *way, path.*— IV. *way, manner.*—V. *waggon.*—VI. *barricade of waggons.*

מַעְגָּלָה f., the same.

עָגַם *despise.* Job 30:25.

עָגַן. Niph. *prevented from marrying,* Ru. 1:13.

עַד see עוּד, עֵד, עֵדָה, see עוּד.

עָדַד (Arab. *numbered, computed*).

עִדִּים *menstruous,* Isa. 64:5; (Arab. the same).

עִדָּן m. Ch.—I. *time.*—II. *a prophetic period of time.*

עֵדָה; see יָעַד, עוּד.

עָדָה (fut. יַעֲדֶה).—I. *passed through,* with עַל, Job 28:8.—II. *adorned.* — III. *put on as an ornament.* Hiph. *stripped off a garment,* Pro. 25: 20.

עֲדָה עֲדָא Ch.—I. *passed upon,* with בְּ.—II. *passed away,* with מִן.—III. *was altered.* Aph. *removed.*

עַד m.—I. *spoil,* Gen. 49:27; Isa. 33:23; Zep. 3:8.—II. *perpetuity, eternity.* — III. *antiquity ;* לָעַד. *for ever;* עַד (pl. עֲדֵי) pa. *unto, as far as, until, before, while, during, still;* עַד־אֲשֶׁר *while;* עַד־אַם (שֶׁ.) *while;* עַד־אֲשֶׁר אִם *until;* עַד־לֹא, עַד־אֲשֶׁר לֹא *before;* with suff. עָדַי *to me;* עָדֶיךָ, עָדָיו ; עֲדֵיכֶם, עֲדֵיהֶם ;

עַד Ch., *to, as far as, until ;* עַד־דִּי *while.*

עַד־הֵנָּה, Ecc. 4:3, same as הֲנָה *hitherto, as yet.*

עֲדֶנָה Ecc. 4:2, the same.

עָדָה p. n., *Adah.*—I. the wife of Lamech.—II. the wife of Esau.

עֲדִי m. (with pause עֶדִי; with suff. עֶדְיֵךְ, עֶדְיוֹ ; pl. עֲדָיִים).—I. *ornaments.*—II. *trappings of a horse.* —III. *lot, appointment,* Ps. 103:5.

עֲדִיאֵל p. n. of a man.

עֲדָיָה, עֲדָיָהוּ p. n. of a man.

עֲדִיתַיִם p. n., a town in the tribe of Judah.

עַדּוֹא, עִדּוֹ p. n. of a man.

עֲדִית ; see עוּד.

עַדְלַי p. n. of a man.

עֲדֻלָּם p. n., a cave and city of the tribe of Judah; עֲדֻלָּמִי *an Adullamite.*

עָדַן. Hith. *live luxuriously,* Neh. 9:25.

עֵדֶן, f. עֶדְנָה *luxurious, delicate,* Isa. 47:8; (s. *smiting,* perhaps), 2 Sa. 23:8; a very difficult place, see Ges. Thes.

עֲדִינָא p. n. of a man.

עֵדֶן m.—I. *pleasure.* — II. *Eden, the abode of our first parents.*

עֵדֶן p. n., a district of Mesopotamia; בֵּית עֵ see בֵּית.

עֶדְנָה f., *pleasure*, Gen. 18:12.

עַדְנָא p. n. of a man.

עַדְנָה p. n. of a man.

מַעֲדַנִּים, מַעֲדַנִּים, מַעֲדַנּוֹת pl., *delicacies, delights*; adv. *willingly*; מַעֲדַנּוֹת trans. for *bands*, i.e. *influences*, Job 38:31; see עָנַד.

עִדָּן *time*; see with עַד.

עֲדָעֲדָה p. n., a town in the tribe of Judah.

עָדַף I. *was superfluous.* — II. *exceeded*, with עַל. Hiph. הֶעְדִּיף *allowed to exceed.*

עָדַר *arranged, set in order.* Niph. נֶעְדַּר I. *was missing, left behind.* — II. *was dilatory, delayed*, Zep. 3:5. — III. *was cleared out.* Pi. עִדֵּר *omitted, neglected*, 1 Ki. 5:7.

עֵדֶר m. (with suff. עֶדְרוֹ; pl. עֲדָרִים, עֶדְרֵי). — I. *flock* or *herd.* — II. p. n., a town in the tribe of Judah. — III. p. n. of a man.

עֶדֶר p. n. of a man.

עַדְרִיאֵל p. n., *Adriel*, son-in-law of Saul, 1 Sa. 18:19, &c.

מַעְדֵּר m., *rake*, Isa. 7:25.

עֲדָשִׁים m. pl., *lentiles.*

עַוָּה, עַוָּא p. n. of an ancient unknown city; עַוִּים *the Avims*, either the inhabitants of this city, or the early settlers in Canaan.

עוּב Hiph. הֵעִיב *treated as worthless, rejected*, Lam. 2:1.

עָב com. (pl. עָבוֹת, עָבֵי, עָבִים). — I.

cloud. — II. *covering*, Ex. 19:9 see also עֵב in its place.

עֵיבָל, עוֹבָל p. n. of a people descended from Shem.

עוּג *bake cakes*, Eze. 4:12.

עֻגָּה, עֻגָּה f., *cakes*, ἐγκρυφίας.

מָעוֹג m., *round cake of bread.*

עוֹג p. n., *Og*, king of Bashan.

עוּד *testified*, Lam. 2:13, Ketib. Pi. עוֹדֵד *surrounded*, Ps. 119:61. Hiph. הֵעִיד I. *called witnesses, to, for, or against.* — II. *called as a witness* with אֶת and בְּ. — III. *made a declaration.* — IV. *enjoined, commanded, reproved*, with בְּ, עַל הֵעִיד עֵדוֹת בְּ *gave commandment to, &c.* Hoph. הוּעַד *information was given*, Ex. 21:29, with בְּ. Pil. עוֹדֵד *raised up, confirmed*, Ps. 146: 9; 147:6. Hithpo. הִתְעֹדֵד *stood upright*, Ps. 20:9, &c.

עֵד m. — I. *witness.* — II. *testimony.* — III. *proof*, עָנָה עֵד בְּ *gave testimony against.* — IV. *commander*, Isa. 55:4.

עֵדָה f. — I. *eye* or *ear witness.* — II *proof*; see also in יָעַד.

עֵדָה, עֵדוּת f. (pl. עֵדְוֹת). — I. *covenant* — II. *the law.* — III. *the book of the law.* — IV. *the decalogue.* — V. *religious ordinance*, Ps. 122:4 ; אֹהֶל הָעֵדוּת, אֲרוֹן הָעֵדוּת, לֻחֹת הָעֵדוּת *the tables, the ark, the tabernacle of the covenant.* — VI. Ps. 60:1; 80:1, the name of some unknown musical instrument.

עוֹד, עֹד I. *again.* — II. *besides.* — III *still.* — IV. *any longer*; with suff עוֹדֶנִּי I (am) *still*; עוֹדְךָ thou (art, still; עוֹדֶנּוּ, עוֹדֶנָּה he, she (is) still; עוֹדָם they (are) still, &c.; בְּעוֹד as yet, while, within; מֵעוֹד since; מֵעוֹדִי since I (am).

עוֹדֵד p.n., Oded.—I. the father of Azariah the prophet, 2 Chron. 15:1, 8.—II. another prophet, 2 Chron. 28:9.

תְּעוּדָה f.—I. institution, custom, Ru. 4:7.—II. law, oracle, Isa. 8:16, 20.

עַוִּים עֲוָה p.n.; see עַוָּא.

עוה was crooked, perverse, did wrong, Est. 1:16; Dan. 9:5. Niph. נַעֲוָה I. bent with pain, Isa. 21:3.—II. bowed with sorrow, Ps. 38:7.—III. perverse in mind, Pro. 12:8. Pi. עִוָּה I. made crooked, Lam. 3:9.—II. overturned, Isa. 24:1. Hiph. הֶעֱוָה I. made crooked, Jer. 3:21.—II. perverted, Job 33:27.—III. walked perversely.

עַוָּה f., being overturned, Eze. 21:32.

עָוָיָא f. Ch., iniquities, Dan. 4:24.

עֲוֹנֵה for עֲוֹנָה Kal imp. with ה parag., from עון.

עָוֹן, עָוֹן m. (const. עֲוֹן; with suff. עֲוֹנָה; pl. עֲוֹנוֹת, עֲוֹנִים).—I. sin, iniquity.—II. guilt.—III. punishment.

עֲוִית p.n., a town of Edom.

עִי m. (pl. עִיִּים).—I. ruin, heap of ruins, heap.—II. עִיִּים p.n.—1. a part of Mount Abarim.—2. a town in the tribe of Judah.

עַי, עַיָּה, עֲיָא p.n., a city of the Canaanites in the tribe of Benjamin.

עִיּוֹן p.n., a strong city in the tribe of Naphtali.

עִוְעִים m. pl., giddiness; Vulg. vertigo, Isa. 19:14.

מְעִי m., heap of ruins, Isa. 17:1.

עוז took refuge with, Isa. 30:2. Hiph. הֵעִיז I. took refuge, Isa. 10:31.—II. caused to take refuge, collected in a place of safety.

עוֹז; see עזז.

עוּט (Arab. dug into any thing).

עֵט m.—I. graver.—II. pen.

עוּל part. f. pl. עָלוֹת.—I. being with young.—II. suckling.

עוּל m., infant at the breast.

עֲוִיל m., suckling, Job 21:11; see also עוּל

עול. Pi. עִוֵּל acts unjustly.

עַוִּיל wicked.

עַוָּל m., one habitually unfair, unjust wicked.

עָוֶל, עֶוֶל m.—I. unfairness.—II. injustice.—III. iniquity.

עַוְלָה f., the same; with ה parag. עַוְלָתָה.

עוֹלָה f., the same; with ה parag. עֹלָתָה; pl. עוֹלוֹת; see also in עֹלָה.

עוֹלָל, עוֹלֵל, עוֹלְלוֹת; see עלל.

עוֹלָם; see עלם.

עון (Arab. to live with).

עוֹנָה f., conjugal rites, Ex. 21:10.

מָעוֹן m.—I. habitation.—II. refuge.—III. den of wild beasts.—IV. p.n.: (a) of a town in the tribe of Judah; (b) of a strange people, Jud 10:12, &c.; (c) of a man.

מְעוֹנָה, מְעֹנָה f., the same.

מְעוּנִים p.n., the inhabitants of the city of Meon.

מְעוּנֹתַי p. n. of a man

עוֹן עוֹנִים; see עוה.

I. עוּף (fut. יָעוּף).—I. flew.—II. flew

away.—III. *flew upon* (as a bird of prey). Pil. עוֹפֵף I. *flew.* — II. *brandished* (a sword), Eze. 32:10. Hiph. *turned the eyes on,* Pro. 23:5. Hithpo. same as Kal II., Hos. 9:11.

עוֹף m. collect., *birds.* Ch. the same.

II. עוּף (fut. יָעַף) *fainted.*

עֵיפָה f.—I. *darkness,* Am. 4:13. (with ה parag. עֵיפָתָה) *great darkness,* Job 10:22.—II. p. n.: (a) of a son of Midian and the people descended from him; (b) of a man; (c) of a woman.

עַפְעַפַּיִם, const. עַפְעַפֵּי m. dual.—I. *eyelids.*—II. synec. *eyes.*

מָעוּף m., *darkness,* Isa. 8:22.

מוּעָף m., the same, Isa. 8:23.

עוּץ (imp. pl. עֻצוּ) *consult ye,* Jud. 19:30; Isa. 8:10.

עוּץ p.n., a district of Arabia, Αὐσῖτις.

עוּק Hiph. הֵעִיק *presses, rushes,* Am. 2:13.

עָקָה f., *pressure, oppression,* Ps. 55:4.

מוּעָקָה f., *pressure, pain,* Ps. 66:11.

עוּר *aroused, awoke, arose* (imp. עוּרָה, עוּרִי *arise!*) Niph. נֵעוֹר I. *was awakened.* — II. *was raised to strike* (shoot), Hab. 3:9. Pil. עוֹרֵר —I. *roused.*—II. *excited, stirred up.* —III. *raised a spear, scourge, cry.* Hiph. הֵעִיר I. *roused, excited.*—II. *awoke,* Ps. 57:9; 108:3. Hith. הִתְעוֹרֵר *awoke.*

עִיר m. Ch., *watcher,* probably an angel, Dan. 4:10, 14, 20.

עוֹר m. (pl. עוֹרוֹת) *the skin of man or animals;* עוֹר שִׁנָּים *skin of his teeth,* Job 19:20, i.e. *gum.*

מְעָרָה f., *cave;* (Arab. *went under ground*).

מְעוֹרִים m. pl., *nakedness,* Hab. 2:15

עוּר Pi. עוֵּר *blinded.*

עוּר m. Ch., *chaff,* Dan. 2:35.

עוֵּר m., עוְרָה f.—I. *blind.*—II. *mentally blind.*

עִוָּרוֹן m., *blindness.*

עַוֶּרֶת f., the same, Lev. 22:22.

עוּשׁ *assemble yourselves,* Joel 4:11.

עוּת *aid, help,* Isa. 50:4.

עוּת Pi. עוֵּת I. *made crooked.* — II. *perverted.*— III. *treated unfairly, unjustly.* Pu. part. מְעֻוָּת *bowed down.* Hith. *bowed himself,* Ecc. 12:3.

עַוְתָה f., *oppression,* Lam. 3:59.

עֻוָתַי p.n. of a man.

עֵז f. (pl. עִזִּים).—I. *goat.*—II. *she goat* —III. pl. *goats' hair.*

עֵז f. Ch., the same, Ezr. 6:17.

עַז, עֵז, עָז; see עזז.

עֲזָאזֵל m. (lit. *goat of departure;* see אָזֵל) *the scape-goat,* Lev. 16:8, 10, 26; LXX. ἀποπομπαῖος.

עָזַב (fut. יַעֲזֹב). — I. *left behind.*—II. *allowed to remain.*—III. *went away from.*—IV. *forsook, neglected.*—V. *failed, allowed to fail.*— VI. *took away.*—VII. *gave loose to.*—VIII. with לְ, אֶל *entrusted to, left with;* also with עַל. Niph. נֶעֱזָב *was forsaken, entrusted,* &c., with לְ. Pu. עֻזַב *was forsaken.*

עֲזוּבָה f.—I *ruins,* Is. 17:9.—II. p.n. of a woman.

עִזְּבוֹנִים I. *merchandise.*—II. *a market,* Eze. c. 27.

עֲזְבּוּק p. n. of a man.

עֲזְגֵּד p. n. of a man.

עָזַז (fut. יָעֹז; inf. עֲזֹוז).—I. was strong.—II. prevailed.—III. considered himself strong, Ps. 52:9.—IV. showed himself strong, Ps. 68: 29. Hiph. הֵעֵז made bold; ה׳ פָּנָיו or בְּפָנָיו put on a bold face, Pro. 7:13; 21:29.

עַז with pause עָז m. (pl. עַזִּים; f. עַזָּה, pl. עַזּוֹת).—I. strong.—II. harsh.—III. strength.—IV. עַז־פָּנִים bold.

עַזָּה p. n., Gaza, a city of the Philistines; עַזָּתִי a Gazathite.

עֹז, עֹוז, עֹז m. (with suff. עֻזִּי, עֻזִּי, עֻזֵּנוּ).—I. strength, power, might.—II. ascription of power, praise, Ps. 8:3.—III. source of strength, refuge.—IV. עֹז פָּנִים impudence.

עַזָּא p. n. of a man.

עֻזִּי m.—I. might of God.—II. might in war, Isa. 42:25.

עִזּוּז m.—I. mighty, Ps. 24:8.—II. mighty men, Isa. 43:17.

עֻזָּא p. n. of a man.

עֻזִּיָּהוּ p. n. of a man.

עֻזִּי p. n. of a man.

עֻזִּיאֵל p. n. of a man.

עֲזַנְיָה same as יַעֲזַנְיָה.

עֻזִּיָּה, עֻזִּיָּהוּ (the strength of the Lord), p. n., Uzziah, king of Judah; LXX. Ὀζίας; elsewhere עֲזַרְיָה; applied also to other men.

עֲזִיזָא p. n. of a man.

עַזְמָוֶת p. n. of a man; בֵּית ע׳ a place in Judah or Benjamin.

מָעֹוז, מָעֹז m. (with suff. מְעֻזִּי, מְעֻזִּי, pl. מָעֻזִּים) place of strength, munition; often applied to persons.

עָזְנִיָּה f., the sea-eagle, Lev. 11:13 Deu. 14:12.

עָזַק. Pi. עִזֵּק digged, Isa. 5:2.

עִזְקָא f. Ch., engraved ring, seal, Dan. 6:18.

עֲזֵקָה p. n., Azekah, a city in the tribe of Judah.

עָזַר (fut. יַעֲזֹר; pl. יַעַזְרוּ; imp. with suff. עָזְרֵנִי; pl. עִזְרוּנִי) helped, assisted, with לְ, עִם, אַחֲרֵי; part. עֹזֵר helper, patron, companion Niph. נֶעֱזַר was holpen. Hiph. helped, 2 Ch. 28:23.

עֵזֶר m. (with suff. עֶזְרוֹ).—I. help.—II. helper.—III. p. n. of a man.

עָזֵר p. n. of a man.

עֶזְרָת, עֶזְרָה f. (with ה parag. עֶזְרָתָה).—I. help.—II. p. n. of a man; same as עָזֵר.

עֶזְרָא p. n., Ezra; LXX. Ἔσδρας.

עָזּוּר p. n. of a man.

עַזְרִאֵל p. n. of a man.

עֲזָרָה f.—I. court of the temple.—II. border, moulding.

עֶזְרִי p. n. of a man.

עַזְרִיאֵל p. n. of a man.

עֲזַרְיָה, עֲזַרְיָהוּ p. n., Azariah.—I. king of Judah; called also עֻזִּיָּה.—II used also for other men.

עַזְרִיקָם p. n. of a man.

עָט, see עוּט; עֲטָא, see יָעַט.

עָטָה I. put on, wore.—II. covered, with עַל.—III. invested.—IV. took possession of, invested with, Jer. 43: 12. with אֵת. Hiph. הֶעְטָה placed as a covering, Ps. 89:46, with עַל.

מַעֲטֶה m., garment (of praise), Isa. 61:3.

עֲטַלֵּף m., bat. Lev. 11:19; Isa.2:20.

עטן (Arab. *prepared skin*).

עָטִין m., pl. עֲטִינִים *water or milk skin*, Job 21:24.

עָטַף (fut. יַעֲטֹף).—I. *covered*, with לְ.—II. *covered himself.*—III. *covered his face, was exhausted*; part. עָטוּף *worn out, weak.* Niph. *was exhausted*, Lam. 2:11. Hiph. הֶעֱטִיף *the same*, Gen. 30:42. Hith. הִתְעַטֵּף *the same.*

מַעֲטָפָה f., *mantle*, Isa. 3:22.

עָטַר I. *surrounded.*—II. *covered*, Ps. 5:13. Pi. עִטֵּר I. *crowned*, Cant. 3:11.—II. *adorned, blessed*, with לְ. Hiph. part. f. מַעֲטִירָה *giving crowns*, Isa. 23:8.

עֲטָרָה (const. עֲטֶרֶת; pl. עֲטָרוֹת) f.—I. *crown, royal diadem.*—II. p.n. of a woman.

עֲטָרוֹת p.n., a city in the tribe of Gad; עֲטָרוֹת אַדָּר and עֲטָרוֹת a city in the tribe of Ephraim; ע׳ בֵּית יוֹאָב a place in Judah; ע׳ שׁוֹפָן a place in Gad.

עָטַשׁ (Arab. *sneezed*).

עֲטִישָׁה f., *sneezing*, Job 41:10.

עִיּוּת, עָיוֹן, עָיָא, עַיָּה, עַיִּים, עִי, עַי; see עוה.

עֵיבָל p.n.—I. same as עוֹבָל—II. a rock in the northern range of Mount Ephraim; LXX. Γαιβάλ.

עִיט I. *was angry with*, with בְּ.—II. *rushed on with anger, pounced on*, with אֶל; fut. וַיַּעַט.

עַיִט const. עֵיט m., *rapacious bird or beast.*

עֵיטָם p.n., a town and hill in the tribe of Judah.

עֵילוֹם same as עוֹלָם; see עלם.

עִילַי p.n., one of David's generals.

עֵילָם p.n., a people and district, situation uncertain; עֵלְמָיֵא pl. Ch., the Elamites.

עַיִם m., *drought*, Isa. 11:15.

עַיִן f. (const. עֵין; with suff. עֵינוֹ; dual עֵינַיִם, עֵינֵי).—I. *an eye.*—II. *the sight.*—III. *the judgment.*—IV. *appearance in the eye.*—V. עֵינַיִם *outward appearance*, 1 Sa. 16:7; לְעֵינֵי פ׳ *in the sight of*; בְּעֵינֵי *in the judgment of*; מֵעֵינֵי *without the knowledge of*; בֵּין עֵינַיִם *between the eyes, on the forehead*, עַיִן בְּעַיִן *eye to eye.*—VI. *fountain, spring*; with ה parag. עַיְנָה *to the fountain*; pl. עֲיָנוֹת, const. עֵינֹת; hence many p.n.:—I. עַיִן a town of the Levites in the tribe of Simeon.—II. a town in the north of Canaan.—III. עֵינַיִם a town of Judah.—IV. עֵין גֶּדִי a town of Judah.—V. עֵין גַּנִּים a town of Judah.—VI. a town of Issachar.—VII. עֵין דֹּאר a town of the Manassites.—VIII. עֵין חַדָּה a town of Issachar.—IX. עֵין חָצוֹר a town of Naphtali.—X. עֵין חֲרֹד a *well* near the town of *Charod.*—XI. עֵין מִשְׁפָּט a *well* in Kadesh.—XII. עֵין עֶגְלַיִם a town of Moab.—XIII. עֵין רֹגֵל a *well* on the confines of Judah and Benjamin.—XIV. עֵין רִמּוֹן a town in the tribe of Judah.—XV. עֵין שֶׁמֶשׁ a town on the confines of Judah and

Benjamin.—XVI. עֵין תַּנִּים a well near Jerusalem.—XVII. עֵין תַּפּוּחַ a town of Manasseh.

עַי com. Ch., *eye.*

עֵין m., *watching with an evil eye,* 1 Sa. 18:9.

עֵינָן p. n. of a man.

מַעְיָן m. (with ו parag.) מַעְיְנוֹ; with suff. מַעְיָנוֹ; pl. מַעְיָנִים, מַעְיְנֵי, (מַעְיָנוֹת מַעְיְנוֹת) *fountain, well of water.*

עָיֵף *is weary,* Jer. 4:31; וַיָּעַף, see עוּף.

עָיֵף m., עֲיֵפָה f. — I. *weary.* — II. *parched.*

עֵיפִי p. n. of a man.

עֵיפָה *darkness;* see עוּף.

עַיִר m. (with suff. עִירֹה; pl. עֲיָרִים).—I. *ass.*—II. *young ass.*

עִיר m.—I. *heat, anger, fear,* Ps. 73: 20; Jer. 15:8; Hos. 7:4; 11:9; Ges.)—II. *a city, town, settlement;* עִירָה *towards the city;* pl. עֲיָרִים see next word.

עָר m.— I. *an enemy.*— II. *city;* pl. עָרִים; עָר־מוֹאָב, *Ar of Moab,* otherwise *Rabbah,* the chief city of Moab.

עָר m. Ch., *an enemy.*

עִיר Ch.; see עוּר.

עִירָא p. n. of a man.

עִירוּ p. n. of a man.

עִירָם p. n., *a prince of Edom.*

עִירָד p. n. of a man.

עֵירֻמִּים, עֲרוּמִים; see ערם.

עַיִשׁ; see עָשׁ.

עַיִן *same as* עַי; see עוה.

עַכָּבִישׁ m., *a spider.*

עַכְבָּר *the jerboa;* "*dipus jaculus*" (Linn.)

עַכְבּוֹר p. n. of a man.

עַכּוּ p. n., a city in the tribe of Asher, Ἄκη, "Ptolemais."

עָכָן (עָכָר) p. n. of a man.

עֶכֶס m.—I. *fetter,* Pro. 7:22.—II. pl עֲכָסִים *anklets, rings for the feet,* Isa. 3:18.

עָכַס, Pi. *wear anklets,* Isa. 3:16.

עַכְסָה p. n., the daughter of Caleb.

עָכַר (fut. with suff. יַעְכָּרֶךָ) *caused sorrow, vexation, disgrace.* Niph. נֶעְכַּר *was irritated, excited.*

עָכוֹר p. n., a valley near Jericho.

עֶכְרָן p. n. of a man.

עַכְשׁוּב m., *an asp,* Ps. 140:4.

עֲלָא, עַל, עַל, עֲלָה see עלה.

עָלָא, עֲלָה, עַלָּא; see עלל

עִלֵּג m., *foreigner, stammerer,* Isa. 32:4.

עָלָה (fut. יַעֲלֶה; apoc. יַעַל) (const. with עַל, אֶל, לְ, בְּ.— I. *went up, came up.*—II. *arose* (ot the dawn).— III. *grew up, grew.*—IV. *increased.* — V. *produced,* Pro. 24:31.— VI. *was put upon.* Niph. נַעֲלָה I. *is exalted* (God).— II. *was lifted up,* Eze. 9:3.—III. *was led away,* 2 Sa. 2:27.—IV. *was taken up,* Eze. 36: 3. Hiph. הֶעֱלָה pret. הֶעֱלֵיתָ, הֶעֱלִיתִי; imp. apoc. הַעַל; fut. יַעֲלֶה; apoc. יַעַל).—I. *caused to go up.* — II. *offered a burnt-offering.*— III. *placed a thing on another.*— IV. *placed, set up,* Nu. 8:2. Hoph. הָעֳלָה I. *was offered,* Jud. 6:28.— II. *was brought up*

Nah. 2:8.— III. *was placed upon, inscribed*, 2 Chron. 20:34. Hith. fut apoc. יִתְעַל *lifts up himself*, Jer. 51:3.

עַל m., *the Lofty One, the Most High*; adv. *on high*, 2 Sa. 23:1; מֵעַל I. *from above*, Gen. 27:39; 49:25. —II. *above*, Ps. 50:4, &c.

עֲלֵי, עָלַי, עַל; (with suff. עָלֶיךָ, עָלַי; עֲלֵיהֶם, עֲלֵיכֶם, עָלָיו, עָלֵימוֹ) prep. (ὑπέρ, ἐπί).—I. *upon, on*.—II. *above, over*.—III. *beside, near, before*.— IV. *besides, over and above*. — V. *in reference to, towards, against*.— VI. *for, on account of, in behalf of*; עָלַי לָתֵת *it is mine to give* (the kingdom); ζῆν ἐπί, *live by* (bread), Deu. 8:3.

מֵעַל (with suff. מֵעָלָיו, מֵעָלֶיךָ, מֵעֲלֵיכֶם, &c.).—I. *from upon*.—II. *from above*.—III. *above*.

עַל Ch. same as Heb., *upon, above, besides, for*.

עֵלָּא Ch., with מִן *above*, Dan. 6:3.

עָלֶה, const. עֲלֵה m. (with suff. עָלֵהוּ; pl. const. עֲלֵי).— I. *leaf*.— II. *foliage*.

עוֹלָה, עֹלָה f.—I. *a step*.—II. *a burnt-offering*.

עֲלָתָא f. Ch., *burnt-offering*.

עִלִּי, f. עִלִּית *upper*, Jos. 15:19; Jud. 1:15; pl. עִלִּיּוֹת.

עִלָּי m. Ch. — I. *high, supreme* (of God).—II. *the Most High*.

עִלִּית f. Ch., *upper room, chamber*, Dan. 6:11.

עֵלִי p. n., *Eli*, 'Ηλί, the priest.

עֱלִי m., *pestle*, Pro. 27:22.

עֲלִיָּה f.— I. *upper room, chamber.*— II. *ascent, staircase*, 2 Chron. 9:4.

עֶלְיוֹן m., עֶלְיוֹנָה f.— I. *lofty*.— II. *higher, upper* (in place).—III. *high* (in rank).— IV. *the Supreme, the Most High* (of God).

עִלָּיוֹן m. Ch., *the Most High*.

מַעֲלֶה m.—I. *ascent*.—II. *mount*.

מַעַל m., with ה מַעְרָה — I. *over against, near*, Isa. 6:2, &c.— II. *above*; לְמַעְלָה *upwards, onwards, over, above*; מִלְמַעְלָה *from above, upward*; מִמַּעַל *from above*, with לְ *over, above*.

מֹעַל m., *elevating, lifting up of*, Neh. 8:6.

מַעֲלָה f.—I. *ascent*.—II. *step of stairs*. —III. *graduated face of a sun-dial*.—IV. *mental suggestions*, Ezr. 7:9.—V. an unknown title of some of the Psalms.

תְּעָלָה f.—I. *channel for water.*— II. *recovery from illness*, Jer. 30:13. 46:11.

עֲלָוָה f.—I. same as עוֹלָה.—II. p. n., *a tribe of the Edomites*.

עֲלוּמִים *youth*, see עלם.

עַלְיָן, עַלְוָן p. n. of an Edomite.

עֲלוּקָה f., *a leech*, Pro. 30:15.

עָלַז (fut. יַעֲלֹז; pl. יַעֲלְזוּ) *rejoiced, exulted*, with עַל or בְּ (of the subject of joy).

עַלֵּז m., *rejoicing*, Isa. 5:14.

עָלִיז m., *rejoicing, expressing joy*.

עָלַם (Arab. *was covered with clouds*).

עֲלָטָה f., *darkness*.

עֶלְיוֹן, עֲלִיָּה, עֲלִיַּת, עֲלִי; see עלה.

עֲלִיצוּת; see עלץ.

עֵלל (Syr. *entered*). Po. עוֹלֵל I. *made to enter*, Job 16:15.— II. *treated*,

עֲלַל 195 עָמַד

acted towards, with לְ. — III. af-
fected. — IV. gleaned. — V. part.
מְעוֹלֵל babyish boy, Isa. 3:12.
Poa. was done, caused, Lam.1:12.
Hith. I. exerted himself against.
—II. insulted. Hithpo. practised,
Ps. 141:4.

עֲלַל Ch., entered. Aph. הַנְעֵל brought
in. Hoph. הֻעַל was brought in.

עֹל עוֹל m. (with suff. עֻלּוֹ).—I. yoke,
—II. servitude.

עֻלָּא p. n. of a man.

עִלָּה f. Ch., pretext, ground for com-
plaint, Dan. 6:5, 6.

עֲלִיל m., crucible, Ps. 12:7.
עוֹלֵל עוֹלָל m. (pl. עוֹלָלִים, עוֹלְלִים)
infant, young child, child.

עוֹלֵלוֹת, עֹלְלוֹת f. pl., gleanings.

עֲלִילָה f.— I. action.— II. an action
(good- or bad).

עֲלִילִיָּה f., action, Jer. 32:19.

מֵעַל m. Ch., setting (of the sun), Dan.
6:15.

מַעֲלָל m., pl. מַעֲלָלִים habitual doings
(good or bad).

תַּעֲלוּל m., pl. תַּעֲלוּלִים.— I. children,
Isa. 3:4.—II. vexations, calamities,
Isa. 66:4.

עָלַם, part. עֹלְמִים hidden things, sins,
Ps. 90:8. Niph. נֶעְלַם was hidden; part. נַעֲלָמִים hidden (crafty)
men. Hiph. הֶעְלִים hide, conceal;
ה' עֵינָיִם מִן turned his eyes away
from, Pro. 28:27. Hith. הִתְעַלָּם
was hidden, with מִן.

עוֹלָם עֹלָם m.— I. antiquity.— II.
eternity.—III. duration of the earth.
— IV. whole life.— V. unlimited,
future time; מֵעוֹלָם from of old;

יְמוֹת עוֹלָם the ancient days,
עוֹלָם, עַד־עוֹלָם, לְעוֹלָם, עוֹלָמִים for
ever; future duration, unlimited,
but not endless.

עֵילוֹם m., eternity, 2 Chron. 33:7.

עָלַם m. Ch., eternity.

עֶלֶם m., a young man.

עַלְמָה f., damsel, virgin, ἡ παρθένος.

עֲלָמִים m. pl., youth.

עַלְמוֹן p. n. of a town in the tribe of
Benjamin; ע' דִּבְלָתַיְמָה p.n., a
station of Israel.

עֲלָמוֹת f. pl., an unknown title of
Psalm 46.

עַלְמוּת f., the same, Ps. 9:1; 48:15.

עֶלֶמֶת p. n. of a man.

עַזְמָוֶת p.n., same as עַלְמוֹן.

תַּעֲלֻמָה f., any thing hidden, secret;
pl. תַּעֲלֻמוֹת.

עֵלְמָיָא Elamites; see עֵילָם.

עָלַס exult, rejoice, Job 20:18. Niph.
is exulting, Job 39:13. Hith. be
exulting, Pro. 7:18.

עָלַע gulped, swallowed down, Job 39·
30.

עֲלַע com. Ch., rib, Dan. 7:5.

עָלַף. Pu. I. fainted, Isa. 51:20.—
II. covered, overlaid, Cant. 5:14.
Hith. was clothed, Gen. 38:14,
fainted.

עֻלְפֶּה m., languor, fainting, Eze. 31:
15.

עָלַץ (fut. יַעֲלֹץ) exult, rejoice; with בְּ
in, לְ against, לִפְנֵי before.

עֲלִיצוּת f., rejoicing, Hab. 3:14.

עַם, עָם; see עמם.

עָמַד (fut. יַעֲמֹד).—I. stood fast, still.
— II. stood over, overlooked, with

לִפְנֵי — III. *stood over, presided,* with עַל.—IV. *stood before,* with אֶת, עַל.—V *ceased,* with מִן—VI. *stood before,* with מִן, לִפְנֵי, בִּפְנֵי—VII. *persevere, remain in any occupation,* with בְּ.— VIII. *stood against, opposed,* with עַל. Hiph. הֶעֱמִיד I. *cause to stand.*—II. *set up, raise.*—III. *establish.*—IV. *appoint.* — V. *confirm, accomplish.* (הַעֲמַדְתָּ Eze. 29:7, a wrong reading for הַמְעַדְתָּ *thou madest to tremble.*) Hoph. הָעֳמַד *made to stand.*

עֹמֶד m., *standing-place, station.*

עַמּוּד m., *pillar.*

עֶמְדָּה f., *station, standing.* Mic. 1:11.

מַעֲמָד m. — I. *standing, order.* — II. *station.*

עֹמֶד, see עַם. עֻמָּה, עַמּוֹן, see עמם. עָמוֹס, see עמם; עָמוֹק, see עמק.

עָמִיר see עמר.

עָמִית *society, company.*

עָמֵל *wrought, laboured.*

עָמֵל m.—I. *working, labouring;* pl. עֲמֵלִים *labourers.* — II. *weary, wretched.*

עָמָל m.—I. *labour.*—II. *sorrow, vexation.*— III. *sorrow brought on by sin.* — IV. *weariness.*—V. *fruit of labour.*—VI. p. n. of a man.

עֲמָלֵק p.n., *Amalek,* a people inhabiting the south of Palestine and the borders of the desert of Sinai; עֲמָלֵקִי *Amalekite;* הַר הָעֲמָלֵקִי *hill of the Amalekites* in the tribe of Ephraim.

עָמַם *concealed,* Eze 28:3; ?1:6.

Hoph. הֻעַם *was obscured,* Lam. 4:1.

עַם, עָם com. (with suff. עַמִּי), *people, nation;* בְּנֵי עַמִּי *the children of my people;* pl. עַמִּים, עֲמָמִים.

עַם m. Ch., *people;* pl. עַמְמִין.

עִם prep. (with suff. עִמִּי, עִמְּךָ; עִמָּדִי, עִמְּךָ; עִמָּם, עִמָּכֶם; עִמָּנוּ, עִמּוֹ; עִמָּהֶם (עִמָּהֶם) *with, along with;* מֵעִם *from with,* (like the French *de par*).

עִם Ch., *the same.*

עֻמָּה f.—I. .. שֶׁ כָּל-עֻמַּת *in the same way as;* לְעֻמַּת *near, towards, like, opposite to;* pl. לְעֻמּוֹת *like;* מִלְעֻמַּת *near.*—II. p. n., a town of Asher.

עַמּוֹן p.n., *Ammon,* the son of Lot's daughter, and his descendants, בְּנֵי עַמּוֹן pl. עַמֹּנִים, עַמֹּנִי f.; pl. עַמֹּנִיּוֹת *Ammonites.*

עַמִּיאֵל p. n. of a man.

עַמִּיהוּד p. n. of a man.

עַמִּינָדָב p. n. of a man.

עַמִּיחוּר p. n. of a man.

עַמִּינָדָב p. n. of a man.

עַמִּישַׁדַּי p. n. of a man.

עַמְעָד p. n., a town in the tribe of Asher.

עַמְרָם p. n. of a man; patron. עַמְרָמִי.

עִמָּנוּאֵל (*God with us*), *Immanuel,* one of our Lord's prophetic titles, Ἐμμανουήλ, Isa. 7:14.

עָמַס, עָמַשׂ (fut. יַעְמֹס) *load, lay a burden upon.* Hiph. הֶעֱמִיס *caused to be laden,* 1 Ki. 12:11; 2 Chron. 10:11.

עָמוֹס p.n., *Amos,* the prophet.

עֲמַסְיָה p.n. of a man.

מַעֲמָסָה f., *burden,* Zec. 12:3.

עָמַק was very deep, Ps. 92:6. Hiph. הֶעֱמִיק make deep, Isa. 30:33.

עָמֹק m., עֲמֻקָה f.—I. deep.—II. subtle, unsearchable.

עֵמֶק or עֹמֶק m., the same; pl. const. עִמְקֵי

עָמוֹס p. n. of a man.

עֵמֶק m. (with suff. עֶמְקֵךְ; pl. עֲמָקִים).—I. deep place.—II. unintelligible.

עֹמֶק m., depth, Pro. 25:3.

עַמִּיק m. Ch., deep, profound thing, Dan. 2:22.

מַעֲמַקִּים m. pl., depths.

עָמַר. Pi. עִמֵּר binding-sheaves, Ps. 129:7. Hith. הִתְעַמֵּר treat as a slave, with בְּ.

עָמִיר m., sheaf of corn.

עֹמֶר m.—I. sheaf; pl. עֳמָרִים.—II. omer, a dry measure, the tenth part of an ephah.

עֲמֹרָה p. n., Gomorrah, one of the cities of the plain; LXX. Γομόρρα.

עָמְרִי p. n.—I. Omri, king of Israel.—II. of other men.

עֲמַר m. Ch., wool, Dan. 7:9.

עַמְרָם p. n.; see עמם.

עָמַשׂ same as מָשַׂ carried.

עֲמָשָׂא p. n. of a man.

עֲמָשַׂי p. n. of a man.

עֲמָשְׂסַי p. n. of a man.

עֵנָב (Arab. grapes).

עֵנָב p. n., a town in the tribe of Judah.

עֵנָב m. (pl. עֲנָבִים, עִנְּבֵי), grapes.

עָנוּב p. n. of a man.

עִנְּבֵי pl. const. with dag. euphon., from עֵנָב.

עָנַג Pu. delicately brought up, Jer.

6.2. Hith. delighted himself in, with עַל, מִן.

עָנֹג m., עֲנֻגָּה f., delicate, tender.

עֹנֶג m., delight, pleasure.

תַּעֲנוּג m., delight, pleasure, enjoyment, luxury.

עָנַד bound, Job 31:36; Pro. 6:21.

I. עָנָה (fut. יַעֲנֶה, וַיַּעַן).—I. spoke—II. celebrated.—III. shout.— V. bellow, bleat.—V. answer. Niph. נַעֲנָה was answering, answered. Pi. עִנָּה answered, sang in response. Hiph. answer favorably, Ecc. 5:19.

עֲנָה Ch.—I. answered, spoke, began to speak.—II. was afflicted; see below.

II. עָנָה I. was humbled.—II. was afflicted. Niph. was humbled, afflicted, with מִפְּנֵי. Pi. I. humbled, subdued.—II. afflicted; with אִשָּׁה had connexion with a woman with נֶפֶשׁ fasted. Pu. was afflicted, humbled; inf. עֻנֹּתוֹ his suffering affliction, Ps. 132:1. Hiph. oppressed. Hith. הִתְעַנָּה I. was afflicted, 1 Ki. 2:26.—II. was humbled, with לִפְנֵי.

עֲנָה p. n.—I. the son of Seir, and his descendants.—II. the son of Zibeon.

עָנָו m. (pl. עֲנָוִים, עֲנָוֵי), humble, meek, poor, afflicted.

עֲנָוָה f., meekness, humility.

עֲנָוָה f., the same.

עֱנוּת f., affliction of the humble (Lee). Ps. 22:25.

עָנִי adj. m. (pl. עֲנִיִּים; f. עֲנִיָּה), afflicted, miserable, poor.

עֹנִי, with pause עֹנִי m., misery

עֻנִּי p. n. of a man.

עֲנָיָה p. n. of a man

עִנְיָן m., *thing, matter.*

עֲנָת p. n. of a man; see בֵּית.

עֲנָתוֹת p.n.—I. a city of the Levites in Benjamin; עֲנְתֹתִי *inhabitant of Anathoth.*—II. of a man.

עֲנְתֹתִיָה p. n. of a man.

יַעַן pa., *because;* יַעַן כִּי אֲשֶׁר *because, because of;* יַעַן וּבְיַעַן *because* יַעַן בְּיַעַן *the same.*

יַעֲנַי p. n. of a man.

מַעֲנֶה m.—I. *answer.*—II. *answer to prayer,* Pro. 16:1.

לְמַעַן, מַעַן *intent, purpose.* — I. *because.*—II. *thence, so, accordingly;* לְמַעַן אֲשֶׁר *in order that, because that.*

מַעֲנָה f., *furrow,* Ps. 129:3.

מַעֲנִית Kri, the same.

תַּעֲנִית f., *self-humiliation,* Ezr. 9:5.

עֵנִים p.n., a town of Judah.

עֵנִם p.n., a town of Issachar; elsewhere עֵין-גַּנִּים.

עֲנָמִים p.n., a foreign people unknown.

עֲנַמֶּלֶךְ p.n., an idol of the Sepharvites.

עָנַן (part. עֹנֵן; f. עֹנְנָה) and Po. עוֹנֵן (fut. יְעוֹנֵן; part. מְעוֹנֵן) *divined, used auguries,* Isa. 2:6, &c. Pi. (inf. with suff. עַנְנִי) *my bringing on a cloud,* Gen. 9:14; see עָנָן.

עָנָן, const. עֲנַן עָן m.—I. *a cloud.*—II. p. n. of a man.

עֲנָנָה f., *cloud,* Job 3:5.

עֲנַן m. Ch., *cloud,* Dan. 7:13.

עֲנָנִי p.n. of a man.

עֲנַנְיָה ('Ανανίας) p.n.—I. of a man. —II. of a place in Benjamin.

עָנָף, const. עֲנַף m. (pl. with suff. עֲנָפַיִם, עֲנַפֵּכֶם) *a branch.*

עֲנַף m. Ch., *a branch.*

עֲנֵפָה f. עֲנֵפָה *branching out,* Eze. 19 10.

עֲנָק m. (pl. עֲנָקִים, עֲנָקוֹת).—I. *a chain* (collar for the neck).—II. p.n., הָעֲנָק, יְלִידֵי עֲנָק (הָעֲנָק), עֲנָקִים בְּנֵי עֲנָקִים *the Anakims,* the first inhabitants of Canaan, who were giants.

עֲנַק *put on a collar,* i.e. exalted, lifted up, Ps. 73:6. Hiph. הֶעֱנִיק *place on the neck like a collar,* Deu 15:14.

עָנֵר p.n.—I. a man of Canaan, Gen. 14: 13, 24.—II. p. n., 1 Chron. 6:55, probably a wrong reading for תַּעְנָךְ.

עָנַשׁ (fut. יַעֲנֹשׁ).—I. *taxed.*—II. *fined in money,* with לְ. Niph. *was fined, mulcted.*

עֹנֶשׁ m., *mulct, fine, tax*

עֲנַשׁ m. Ch., *tax.*

עֲנָת, עֲנָתֹת, עֲנָתֹתִיָה; see עָנָה.

עָתָת, כָּעְנַת; see עַתְּ.

עָסַס *tread* (as grapes), Mal. 3:21.

עָסִיס m.—I. *new wine-juice.*—II. *juice of the pomegranate,* Cant. 8:2.

יַעֲרוּ עֹעֵר for יַעֲרְעֲרוּ *raised a cry,* Isa. 15:5; see עוּר Pil.

עֲפָתָה, עֵפָה; see עֵיפָה in עוּף.

עָפָה root not used ; (Syr. *flourished.*)

עֲפִי m., pl. עֳפָאִים *leaves,* Ps. 104:12.

עֳפִי m. Ch., *leaves.*

עָפַל. Pu. *swollen, inflated,* Hab. 2: 4. Hiph. *raised themselves,* Nu 14:44.

עֹפֶל m. — I. *swelling tumour.* — II *mount, hill.*

הָעֹפֶל p.n. of a peak of Mount Zion, to the east.

עֳפָלִים pl. const. עָפְלֵי *hæmorrhoids, emerods*; see also מְחֹרִים.

עׇפְנִי p. n., a city of Benjamin, Jos. 18:24.

עֲפָעֵי עַפְעַפַּיִם; see עוּף.

עָפַר Pi. עִפַּר *dashed with dust,* 2 Sa. 16:13. with בֶּעָפָר.

עֹפֶרֶת f., *lead.*

עָפָר, const. עֲפַר m.—I. *earth, mould, clay.*— II. *dust.*—III. *the earth.*—IV. *depth of the earth ;* pl. const. עַפְרֹת *dusts,* i. e. small dust, molecules.

עֹפֶר m., *kid, young goat.*

עׇפְרִי p. n. of a man.

עׇפְרָה p. n.—I. a city of Benjamin. —II. a city of Manasseh.—III. of a man.

עֶפְרוֹן (עֶפְרַיִן) p.n.—I. a town on the borders of Ephraim.—II. a mountain between Judah and Benjamin. —III. the name of a Hittite, Gen. 23:8, &c.

עֵץ, עֲצֵי, עֵצִים; see עֵצָה.

עָצַב *pained, grieved, thwarted.* Niph. *was pained, grieved,* with בְּ, עַל, אֶל. Pi. I. *bound together,* Job 10: 8.—II. *pained, thwarted.* Hiph. I. *grieved, thwarted,* Ps. 78:40.—II. *worship,* Jer. 44:19; (see Lee). Hith. *was grieved.*

עֲצַב Ch., *grieved.*

עֶצֶב m., pl. עֲצַבִּים *idols.*

עֶצֶב, עֹצֶב m.— I. *tendon, sinew,* Jer. 22:28.—II. *labour.*—III. *pain.*

עֹצֶב m.—I. *idol.*—II. *pain, grief.*

עֶצֶב m. (pl. with suff. עַצְבֵיכֶם) *your labours,* Isa. 58:3.

עֲצֶבֶת עֲצֵבֶת f. (const. עִצְבַת ; pl. with suff. עִצְּבוֹתָם).—I. *pain, grief.* —II. "*sorrows,*" Eng. Ver.; perhaps *idols,* Ps. 16:4.

עִצָּבוֹן m., *painful, great, labour,* Gen 3:16, 17.

מַעֲצֵבָה f., *labour, affliction,* Isa. 50: 11.

עָצַד (Arab. *axe*).

מַעֲצָד m., *axe.*

עָצָה *close the eyes,* Pro. 16:30.

עֵץ m. (pl. עֵצִים).—I. *a tree* עֵץ פְּרִי *fruit-tree.*—II. *wood.*—III *gallows.*

עֵצָה f., *wood,* Jer. 6:6; see also in יָעַץ.

עָצֶה m., *spine of the back,* Lev. 3:9.

עֶצְיוֹן גֶּבֶר p.n., a sea-port, probably on the eastern coast of the Red Sea.

עָצֵל Niph. *be sluggish,* Jud. 18:9.

עָצֵל m., *sluggard;* book of Proverbs only.

עַצְלָה *sloth,* Pro. 19:15, עַצְלוּת f., Pro. 31:27; dual עַצְלָתַיִם *great sloth,* Ecc. 10:18.

עֹצֶם, עָצַם I. *was numerous.*—II. *was strong.*—III. *was great.* Pi. עִצֵּם I. *bind the eyes,* Isa. 29:10.—II. *break the bones,* Jer. 50:17, from עֶצֶם. Hiph. *strengthens,* Ps 105:24.

עָצוּם m.—I. *numerous.*— II. *strong.* — III. *great;* pl. עֲצוּמִים *great ones,* Ps. 10:10.

עֶצֶם f. (pl. עֲצָמוֹת, עֲצָמִים).—I. *bone* —II. *body.*—III. *self-same (never of persons);* בְּעֶצֶם הַיּוֹם הַזֶּה *or this very day* —IV. p.n., a city of Judah.

עֹצֶם m., עָצְמָה f.—I. *strength.*—II.
  power.—III. *multitude,* Nah. 3:9.

עַצְמוֹן p. n., a town in the southern
  borders of Canaan.

עֲצֻמוֹת f. pl., *defence in argument,*
  Isa. 41:21.

תַּעֲצֻמוֹת f. pl., *strength,* Ps. 68:36.

עֵצֶן m., p. n. of a place, 2 Sa. 23:8.

עָצַר (fut. יַעֲצֹר).—I. *shut up, restrain,*
  detain, with לְ.— II. with כֹּחַ *re-*
  tain power, reign. Niph. נֶעֱצַר
  was shut up, detained.— II. *was*
  assembled.

עֶצֶר m., *rule, supreme power,* Jud.
  18:7.

עֹצֶר m.— I. *shutting up the womb*
  from child-bearing, Pro. 30:16.—
  II. *in prison,* Isa. 53:8

עֲצָרָה, עֲצֶרֶת f.—I. *day of assembly.*
  —II. *restraint.*

מַעְצָר m., *restraint, hindrance,* Pro.
  25:28.

מַעְצוֹר m., the same, 1 Sa. 14:6.

עָקַב (fut. יַעְקֹב).—I. *take by the heel,*
  Hos. 12:4; see עָקֵב.—II. *circum-*
  vent, defraud; part. עֲקֻבָּה *traced,*
  marked, Hos. 6:8. Pi. *trace,* Job
  37:4.

עָקֵב m.— I. *heel.*— II. *impression of*
  the heel, track; pl. עֲקֵבִים *heels;*
  עִקְּבוֹת *footsteps.*—III. *rear of an*
  army, Gen. 49:19, &c.— IV. עֲוֹן
  עֲקֵבַי *iniquity of my tracks,* i. e.
  ways, Ps. 49:6.

עָקֹב m., *steep place,* Isa. 40:4; see
  above.

עֵקֶב m.—I. *in consequence that, for*
  the sake of.—II. *consequence, fruit;*
  עֵ רַב, Ps. 19:12, "great reward,"

Eng. Ver.; עֵקֶב, עַל עֵקֶב *in con-*
  sequence, because, for that reason,
  with כִּי, אֲשֶׁר the same.

עָקְבָה f., *fraud, deceit,* 2 Ki. 10:19.

עָקוּב p. n. of men.

יַעֲקֹב (*took by the heel*), p. n., *Jacob,*
  the son of Isaac, afterwards Israel; קְהִלַּת יְ‎, בֵּית יְ‎, בְּנֵי יַעֲקֹב,
  זֶרַע יְ‎ I. his descendants, the Israelites.—II. the name also of their
  land and national polity.

יַעֲקֹבָה p. n. of a man.

עָקַד (fut. יַעֲקֹד) *he binds, ties,* Gen.
  22:9.

עָקֹד m. (pl. עֲקֻדִּים) *stripe, streak on*
  cattle.

עָקָה s., *oppression;* see עוק.

מַעֲקֶה m., *parapet, battlement;* LXX
  στεφάνη, Deut. 22:8.

עָקַל. Pu. part. מְעֻקָּל *became per-*
  verted, Hab. 1:4.

עֲקַלָּתוֹן m., *very crooked,* Isa. 27:1.

עֲקַלְקַל m., עֲקַלְקַלּוֹת f. pl., *very crooked,*
  perverted.

עָקַר *eradicate,* Ecc. 3:2. Niph. *was*
  rooted up, destroyed, Zep. 2:4. Pi.
  עִקֵּר *hough, cut the hamstring.*

עֲקַר Ch. Ith. *was rooted,* Dan. 7:8.

עָקָר m., עֲקָרָה f., *barren,*
  sterile.

עֵקֶר m.—I. *root,* i. e. head of a strange
  family, Lev. 25:47.—II. p. n. of a
  man.

עִקַּר m. Ch., *nerve, stump,* Dan. 4:12

עֶקְרוֹן p. n., one of the five principal
  cities of the Philistines, Ἀκαρών;
  עֶקְרֹנִי an Ekronite.

עַקְרָב m.—I. *a scorpion.*—II. *some*
  implement of torture.—III. *a war-*

like engine.—IV. מַעֲלֵה עַקְרַבִּים p. n., a place in the south of Palestine, 'Ακραβίν.

עָקַשׁ *convict of perverseness*, Job 9:20. Niph. *is perverse*, Pro. 28:18. Pi. *made crooked.*

עִקֵּשׁ m.—I. *perverse, tortuous.*—II. p. n. of a man.

עַקְשׁוּת m., *perverseness.*

מַעֲקָשׁ m., pl. מַעֲקַשִּׁים *unlevel, abrupt places,* Isa. 42:16.

עָרִים; see עִיר.

עֵר p. n., *Er,* the son of Judah, and other men.

עָרַב I. *was agreeable, sweet.*—II. *agreed, made compact.*—III. *became surety, pledged,* with לְ.— IV. *became dark;* imp. עֲרֹב; fut. יֶעֱרַב. Hith. הִתְעָרֵב I. *intermixed with,* with בְּ, לְ, עִם.—II. *agreed, made compact with,* with אֶת. Hiph. inf. הַעֲרֵב *growing late* (of the day), 1 Sa. 17:16.

עֲרַב Ch., *mixed.* Ith. *was mixed, associated.*

עֲרָב *Arabia;* עַרְבִי, עֲרָבִי *an Arab;* pl. עֲרָבִים עַרְבִיאִים *Arabs.*

עֹרֵב m.—I *a raven.*—II. p. n., a prince of Midian.—III. *Oreb,* a rock beyond Jordan.

עָרֵב m., *agreeable, sweet,* Pro. 20: 17, &c.

עָרֹב m., *gad-fly;* LXX. κυνόμυια.

עֶרֶב m. (with art. הָעֵרֶב).—I.*foreigner, stranger, mixed multitude.* — II. *woof in weaving.*

עֶרֶב m. (f. 1 Sa. 20:5).—I. *evening,* לָעֶרֶב, עֶרֶב, בָּעֶרֶב *in the evening;* pl. עֲרָבוֹת; dual בֵּין הָעַרְבַּיִם *from*

evening to evening, i.e. a whole day.—II. pl. עֲרָבִים, עַרְבֵי *oziers, willows.*—III. נַחַל ע' *a stream in Moab,* Isa. 15:7.

עֲרָבָה f.—I. *plain, open country.*— II.*desert.*—III. הָעֲרָבָה the country between Jericho and the gulf of Akabah, called by the Arabs *El Arabah;* יָם הָע' *Sea of Arabah,* Dead Sea; נַחַל הָע' *brook Kedron.* —IV. p. n., a town in Benjamin; עַרְבָתִי *an Arbite.*

עֲרֻבָּה f., *pledge, surety.*

עֵרָבוֹן m. (ἀρραβών), *security, pledge,* Gen. 38:17, &c.

מַעֲרָב m.—I. *the west.*—II. *merchandise,* Eze. c. 27; מַעֲרָבָה *towards the west.*

מַעֲרָבָה f., *the west.*

תַּעֲרוּבָה f., *security, hostages.*

עָרַג *bleat, cry as an animal from desire,* with אֶל, עַל; fut. יַעֲרֹג.

עֲרוּגָה f., *raised bed in a garden, parterre.*

עָרַד root not used; (Arab. *fled away*)

עָרוֹד m., *wild ass,* Job 39:5.

עֲרָד m. Ch.—I. *wild ass,* Dan. 5:21. —II. p. n., a place in the wilderness of Judah.—III. p.n. of a man.

עָרָה Pi. עָרָה (inf. עָרוֹת; fut. apoc. תְּעַר).—I. *make naked.*—II. *empty, pour out.* Hiph. הֶעֱרָה I. *make bare, expose,* Lev. 20:18,19.—II. *pour out,* Isa. 53:12. Niph. נֶעֱרָה *was poured out,* Isa. 32:15. Hith. הִתְעָרָה I. *was stripped, exposed.* Lam. 4:21.—II.*was spread abroad,* Ps. 37:35.

ערה 202 ערי

עָדָה f., pl. עָרוֹת *bare places, pastures,* Isa. 19:7.

עֶרְוָה f.— I. *unfortified country,* Gen. 42:9, 12.—II. *nudity.*—III. *shame, disgrace.*

עֶרְוָה f. Ch., *loss,* Ezr. 4:14.

עֶרְיָה f., *nakedness.*

מַעֲרֶה m., *bare place, moor,* Jud. 20: 33.

מַעַר m., *nudity.*

מַעֲרוֹת f. pl., *plains, suburbs,* 1 Sa. 17:23.

מַעֲרָת p. n., a town in Judah.

תַּעַר m. (with suff. תַּעְרָה).— I. *razor.* — II. *penknife,* Jer. 36:23.—III. *scabbard of a sword.*

עָרוֹם, עֲרוּמִים, עָרוֹם; see עֲרֹם.

שְׁרוֹעֵר p. n.; see עֲרֹר.

עֵרִי p. n., one of the sons of Gad.

עֲרִיסוֹת *dough;* see עֲרֹס.

עֲרִיפִים *nobles;* see עֲרֹף.

עָרִיץ; see עֲרֹץ.

עֲרִירִי, עֲרִירִים; see עֲרֹר.

עָרַךְ (fut. יַעֲרֹךְ).— I. *set in order, arrange, dispose;* with or without מִלְחָמָה *set in battle array;* with or without מִלִּים *prepared an address, speech;* with לְ *to any one;* with אֶל *against any one;* with or without מִשְׁפָּט *prepared a cause for judgment;* בְּרִית עֲ *prepare a covenant.* — II. *compared together, valued, estimated,* with לְ. Hiph. הֶעֱרִיךְ *valued, set a tax on.*

עֵרֶךְ m.—I. *order, arrangement, system.*—II. *value, estimation.*

מַעֲרָךְ m., *disposings* (of the heart), Pro. 16:1.

מַעֲרָכָה f., *disposition, arrangement.*

מַעֲרֶכֶת f., the same.

עָרֵל *esteem profane,* Lev. 19.23. Niph. *appeared uncircumcised,* Hab. 2:16.

עָרֵל, const. עֲרַל m., *uncircumcised person;* שְׂפָתַיִם עֲ *hesitating of speech;* עֲרַל לֵב *uncircumcised of heart;* לִבָּם הֶעָרֵל *their heart uncircumcised;* עֲרֵלָה אֹזֶן *uncircumcised of ears.*

עָרְלָה f., *foreskin;* לֵב עֲ *uncircumcised of heart;* עָרְלָתוֹ פִּרְיוֹ *uncircumcision of its fruits,* i.e. *first fruits of a tree,* Lev. 19:23; pl. עֲרָלוֹת, const. עָרְלוֹת I. *foreskins.* — II. p. n., a hill not far from Gilgal.

עָרַם *was cunning, subtle.* Hiph הֶעְרִים I. *act cunningly.*—II. *act prudently, wisely.* Niph. נֶעֶרְמוּ *became swollen, heaped,* Ex. 15:8.

עָרוּם m.— I. *cunning.*— II. *prudent, cautious.*

עָרֹם, עָרוֹם m. (pl. עֲרוּמִּים; f. עֲרֻמָּה), —I. *naked.*—II. *exposed, spoiled.*

עֵרֹם, עֵירֹם m.— I. *nakedness.* — II. *naked;* adj. pl. עֵירֻמִּים.

עֹרֶם m., *craftiness, cunning,* Job 5: 13.

עָרְמָה f.—I. *cunning.*—II. *prudence.*

עֲרֵמָה f., pl. ־וֹת — ־ים *heap* (of ruins of corn, &c.).

עַרְמוֹן m., *the plane tree.*

מַעֲרֹם m., pl. מַעֲרֻמִּים *nudities* 2 Chron. 28:15.

עֵרָן p. n. of a man.; patron. עֵרָנִי.

עָרַס root not used; (Ch. עֲרַס *mixed*).

עֲרִיסָה f., pl. עֲרִיסוֹת *dough;* LXX φύραμα.

עשׂו 203 ערע

ערֹעֵר ,עַרעָר ,עַרעִי; see ערר.

עָרַף (fut. יַעֲרֹף).—I. *behead*, Ex. 13:13, &c.—II. *destroy, ruin*, Hos. 10:2. —III. *drop* (as blood from a decapitated bird); applied to speaking.

עֹרֶף m., *neck*; פָּנָה ע׳ or נָתַן עֹרֶף *he turned the back, turned from any one*, with אֶל; הָפַךְ ע׳ ,פָּנָה ע׳ *turned the back, fled*; נָתַן אֹויְבִים עֹרֶף *gave him the back of his enemies*, i.e. made them flee before him, Ps. 18:41, with לְ or אֶל.

עָרְפָּה p.n., *Orpah*, a woman of Moab.

עֲרִיפִים m.pl., *clouds*; metaph. nobles, Gen. 37:9.

עֲרָפֶל m., *thick darkness*.

עָרַץ (fut. יַעֲרֹץ).—I. *feared, trembled.* —II. *affrighted, alarmed.*—III. *shook*, with acc. מִפְּנֵי. Niph. part. נַעֲרָץ *terrible*, Ps. 89:8. Hiph. הֶעֱרִיץ *causing to fear*, Isa. 8:13.

עָרוּץ m., *abrupt, fearful place*, Job 30:6.

עָרִיץ m.—I. *strong, mighty.*—II. *violent, cruel.*

מַעֲרִיץ m., *terrible, fearful one*, Isa. 8:13.

מַעֲרָצָה f., *fearfulness, terror*, Isa. 10:33.

עָרַק *fled, escaped*, Job 30:3.

עֹרְקַי *my nerves*, Job 30:17.

עַרְקִי p.n., *the Arkites*, a people of Canaan.

עָרַר (imp. עֹרָה) *was naked*, Isa. 32:11. Po. עֹורֵר I. *stir up.*—II. *make*

naked. Pil. עִרְעֵר and Hithpa. הִתְעַרְעֵר *was, became, exposed.*

עֲרִירִי m. (pl. עֲרִירִים) *childless.*

עַרְעָר m., *naked, destitute, poor.*

עַרְעָר ,עֲרֹועֵר I. perhaps *stump, dead tree*, Jer. 48:6.—II. p.n., *Aroer*, a town on the river Arnon, called also עֲרֹועֹור.—III. a town near Rabbath Ammon.—IV. p.n., a town in Judah; עֲרֹעֵרִי *an inhabitant of Aroer.*

עֶרֶשׂ f. (pl. עֲרָשֹׂות) *couch, bed.*

עֵשֶׂב m. (with suff. עֶשְׂבָּם; pl. const. עִשְׂבֹות) *green herb* (considered as food).

עֲשַׂב m. Ch., the same.

עָשָׂה (fut. יַעֲשֶׂה; וַיַּעַשׂ; inf. abs. עָשֹׂה, עָשֹׂו; const. עֲשֹׂות ,עֲשֹׂות).—I. *wrought, laboured in*, with בְּ.—II. *made, fabricated, produced, constituted, appointed*, with לְ.—III. *did, performed, made, exercised.*—IV. *passed time*, Ecc. 6:12. Niph. נַעֲשָׂה (pret. f. נֶעֶשְׂתָה; fut. f. תֵּעָשֶׂה; apoc. תֵּעַשׂ).—I. *was made.* —II. *was done*; יֵעָשֶׂה *to be done.* Pu. עֻשֵּׂיתִי *I was made*, Ps. 139:15. Pi. עִשָּׂה *pressed, injured*, Eze. 23:3, 8.

עֲשָׂהאֵל p.n. of a man.

עֲשִׂיאֵל p.n. of a man.

עֲשָׂיָה p.n. of a man.

מַעֲשֶׂה m. (pl. מַעֲשִׂים).—I. *work* (of an artificer).—II. *labour, business, occupation.*

מַעֲשַׂי p.n. of a man.

מַעֲשִׂיָהוּ ,מַעֲשִׂיָה p.n. of a man.

עֵשָׂו (*hairy*), p.n., *Esau*, the son of Isaac; בֵּית ע׳ ,בְּנֵי עֵשָׂו *the* sons of Esau, Edomites; see אֱדֹם; הַר עֵשָׂו mountains of Edom.

עֲשִׂירִי, עָשׂוֹר, see עֶשֶׂר.

עָשַׁק Hithp. contend with, Gen. 26:20.

עֵשֶׂק (strife), p.n. of a fountain.

עֶשֶׂר f., עֲשָׂרָה m., ten; pl. עֲשָׂרוֹת tithes.

עָשָׂר m., עֶשְׂרֵה f. (used only in composition with the other numbers), ten; אַחַד עָשָׂר eleven, the eleventh; f. אַחַת עֶשְׂרֵה; שִׁשָּׁה עָשָׂר m., שֵׁשׁ עֶשְׂרֵה f., sixteen; pl. עֶשְׂרִים twenty.

עָשַׂר v. (fut. יַעֲשֹׂר) decimate, tithe, 1 Sa. 8:15, 17. Pi. עִשֵּׂר take or pay tithe. Hiph. inf. with pref. לַעְשֵׂר to pay tithe.

עָשׂוֹר m., ten; בְּעָשׂוֹר לַחֹדֶשׁ the tenth (day) of the month; נֶבֶל עָשׂוֹר a lute of ten strings.

עֲשַׂר f., עֲשְׂרָה m. Ch., ten; עֶשְׂרִין twenty.

עֲשִׂירִי m., tenth; f. עֲשִׂירִיָה.

עִשָּׂרוֹן m. (pl. עֶשְׂרֹנִים) a dry measure, the tenth part of an ephah.

מַעֲשֵׂר m. (const. מַעֲשַׂר; with suff. מַעֲשְׂרוֹ; pl. מַעֲשְׂרוֹת) tithe.

עָשׁ for עָשְׁתָה Kal pret. f., from עשׂה.

עַשׁ m., name of a constellation, probably the great bear, Job 9:9; (38:32;) see also עָישׁ.

עַיִשׁ m.; בְּנֵי עַיִשׁ the three stars in the tail of the bear, Job. 38:32.

עֲשׁוּ p.n. of a man.

עָשַׁן (fut. יֶעְשַׁן).—I. smoked.—II. metaphorically, of the divine wrath.

עָשֵׁן m., smoking, Ex. 20:18.

עָשָׁן m. (const. עֲשַׁן; with suff. עֲשָׁנוֹ).

—I. smoke.—II. fierce anger.—III. cloud.—IV. p.n. of a town, same as כּוֹר עָשָׁן.

עָשָׁן m., the same, Ex. 19:18.

עָשַׁק (fut. יַעֲשֹׁק).—I. oppressed, injured, wronged, defrauded.—II. press upon. Pu. part. f. מְעֻשָּׁקָה one oppressed, Isa. 23:12.

עָשׁוֹק m., fraudulent, oppressive person, Jer. 22:3.

עֲשׁוּקִים m. pl., frauds, oppressions.

עֵשֶׁק p.n. of a man.

עֹשֶׁק m.—I. oppression, injury.—II. that which is obtained thereby.

עָשְׁקָה f., oppresses, ruins me, Isa. 38:14.

מַעֲשַׁקּוֹת f. pl., oppressions.

עָשַׁר (fut. יֶעְשַׁר) was rich. Hiph. הֶעֱשִׁיר I. made rich.—II. was, became, rich. Hith. part. מִתְעַשֵּׁר becomes rich, Pro. 13:7.

עָשִׁיר m.—I. rich.—II. proud.—III. rich (in grace), Ecc. 10:6.

עֹשֶׁר m., riches.

עָשֵׁשׁ became old, wasted.

עָשׁ m., moth (that which wastes, eats).

עָשַׁת was made smooth, shone, Jer. 5:28. Hith. remember, Jon. 1:6.

עֲשִׁית, עֲשַׁת Ch., thought, designed, Dan. 6:4.

עֶשֶׁת m.—I. net-work of ivory, Cant. 5:14.—II. עֶשְׂרֵה, עָשָׂר with עַשְׁתֵּי (perhaps excess beyond ten) eleven.

עַשְׁתוּת f., taunting, Job 12:5.

עֶשְׁתֹּנוֹת f. pl., devices, machinations, Ps. 146:4.

עַשְׁתֹּרֶת f., Ἀστάρτη, perhaps the deified planet Venus. It is probably the feminine of אֲשֵׁרָה;

pl. עַשְׁתָּרוֹת *statues of Ashtoreth.*
—II. p. n. of a city of Bashan,
called also עַשְׁתָּרוֹת קַרְנַיִם *Ashtoreth with horns;* עַשְׁתְּרָתִי *an
inhabitant of Ashtoreth;* עֶשְׁתְּרוֹת
צֹאן *produce of the flock;* LXX.
ποίμνια τῶν προβάτων, Deu. 7:
13, &c.

עֵת, עֶת־ com. (with suff. עִתִּי), *time,
season,* ὁ καιρός; בְּעֵת הַזֹּאת *about
this time;* בְּעֵת מָחָר *about this
time to-morrow;* כָּעֵת חַיָּה *this
time next year,* or, *as in the times
of a vigorous woman* (Lee), Gen.
18:10, 14; בְּעֵת *as at this
time;* בָּעֵת הַהוּא *in that time;*
בְּעִתּוֹ *in his time;* לְעֵת עֶרֶב *in
the evening;* מֵעֵת עַד עֵת *from
time to time, always;* עֵת adv.
now, sometimes; pl. עִתִּים *times,
vicissitudes;* עִתּוֹת *times,
vicissitudes;* רַבּוֹת עִתִּים
many times, on many occasions,
Neh. 9:28.

עַתָּה (with pause עָתָּה adv. νῦν, νύν).
—I. *now, shortly, speedily.*—II.
then; מֵעַתָּה *from this time;* עַד
עַתָּה *until this time.*

עִתִּי m., *seasonable,* Lev. 16:21.

עִתַּי p. n. of a man.

עֵת קָצִין p. n. of a man; with ה loc.
עִתָּה קָצִין p. n., *a city of Zebulon.*

עָתַד Pi. *prepare,* Pro. 24:27. Hith.
have become prepared, Job 15:28.

עָתִיד m., *prepared, ready.* Pl. עֲתִידוֹת
I. *things ready to take place.*—II.
wealth.

עֲתִיד m. Ch., *ready,* Dan. 3:15.

עַתּוּד m.—I. *he-goat.*—II. *leader,
governor.*

עֲתָיָה p. n. of a man.

עָתָךְ p. n., *a town of Judah.*

עַתְלַי p. n. of a man.

עֲתַלְיָהוּ, עֲתַלְיָה p. n.—I. *Athaliah, the
wife of Joram.*—II. *used also for
men.*

עָתַם. Niph. נֶעְתַּם *is burnt, consumed,* Isa. 9:18.

עָתְנִי p. n. of a man.

עָתְנִיאֵל p. n., *Othniel, a judge of Israel;*
LXX. Γοθονιήλ.

עָתַק (fut. יֶעְתַּק).—I. *remove quickly,
hurry from,* with מִן.—II. *grow
old.* Hiph. הֶעְתִּיק I. *cause to remove.*—II. *transcribe,* Pro. 25:1.—
III. *put away, silenced,* Job 32:15.

עָתָק m., *insolent, biting word.*

עֹתֶק m., *freedom, liberty,* Pro. 8:18.

עָתִיק m., *freely,* Isa. 23:18.

עַתִּיק m.—I. *ancient,* 1 Chron. 4:22.
—II. *removed,* with מִן, Isa. 28:9.

עַתִּיק m. Ch., *ancient,* Dan. 7:9, 13, 22.

עָתַר (fut. יֶעְתַּר), *prayed, supplicated,*
with אֶל, לְ. Niph. נֶעְתַּר (inf.
הֵעָתוֹר) I. *was prevailed upon by
prayer, was made propitious.*—II.
נַעְתָּרוֹת *seemingly propitious* (false),
Pro. 27:6, with לְ. Hiph. הֶעְתִּיר
I. *prayed,* with לְ, בְּעַד.—II. *multiplied,* Eze. 35:13.

עָתָר m.—I. *suppliant,* Zep. 3:10.—
II. *abundance,* Eze. 8:1.

עֶתֶר p. n., *a town of Simeon.*

עֲתֶרֶת f., *riches, abundance,* Jer. 33:6.

פ

פֹּא *here,* Job 38:11, for פֹּה.

פָּאָה. Hiph. fut. with suff. אַפְאֵיהֶם
I will scatter them far and wide
Deu. 32:26.

פֵאָה, const. פְאַת f.—I. *corner, angle*
(of a field, table, &c.).—II.
קְצוּצֵי פֵאָה *having the hair clipped or
shaven in angles; a Canaanitish
custom forbidden to the Israelites;*
פַאֲתֵי מוֹאָב, Nu. 24:17, *the clipped cornered ones of Moab,* i.e. who
trim their hair thus.

פֶּה m. (const. פִּי; with suff. פִּיךָ,
פִּיהוּ, פִּיהָ, פִּיו; pl. פִּים, פִּיפִיֹּת.)
—I. *mouth;* פֶּה אֶל פֶּה *mouth to
mouth, without intervention,* Nu.
12:8; פֶּה אֶחָד *unanimously.*—
II. *mouth of a sack, aperture in
anything.*— III. *edge of a sword,
&c.*— IV. *border of the sea,* Pro.
8:29.—V. פֶּה לָפֶה *from end to
end.*—VI. *share, portion;* פִּי שְׁנַיִם
two parts.— VII. *word, command.*
— VIII. *expression, tenor;* with
pref. כְּפִי *as, according to;* כְּפִיךָ
as thou (art); כְּפִי אֲשֶׁר *so as;*
according to; עַל פִּי *according to.*

פֵּיָה f., *edge of a sword;* pl. פִּיּוֹת,
Jud. 3:16.

פִּיפִיֹּות f. pl., *edges, two-edged,* Ps.
149:6; Isa. 41:15.

פִּי-בֶסֶת p.n., *a city of Egypt, Bu-
bastis.*

פִּי-הַחִירֹות הַחִירֹות p.n., *a place on
the Red Sea.*

פִיכֹל p.n. of a man.

פִּינְחָס p.n. of a man.

פָּאַר. Pi. פֵּאֵר I. *adorned, made beautiful.*— II. *went over the branches
accurately,* Deu. 24:20. Hith.
הִתְפָּאֵר I. *felt complacency,* with
בְּ—II. *boasted himself,* with עַל.

פְּאֵר m. (pl. פְּאֵרִים, פְּאֵרֵי) *ornamental
head-dress.*

פֹּארָה, פֻּארָה f., *a branch.*

פָּארוּר m., *blackness, paleness* (of face)
Joel 2:6; Nah. 2:11.

תִּפְאֶרֶת, תִּפְאָרָה f.—I. *beauty, ornament.*—II. *glory.*—III. *boast, subject of glorying.*

פָּארָן p. n., *Paran,* the wilderness between Egypt and Palestine.

פַּג (Arab. *unripe fig*).

פַּג m., pl. פַּגִּים *unripe figs,* Cant. 2:
13.

פִּגּוּל m., pl. פִּגֻּלִים *impure, disgusting*
(thing).

פָּגַע I. *came to a place, reached,* with
בְּ.—II. *met, fell in with,* with אֶל,
בְּ.— III. *met hostilely, fell upon,*
with בְּ.—IV. *waited on in prayer,
entreated.*— V. *admitted favourably.* Hiph. הִפְגִּיעַ I. *cause to
come, fall in with, wait upon.*—II.
fell upon.—III. *entreated.*

פֶּגַע m., *occurrence, accident.*

פַּגְעִיאֵל p. n., *a prince of Asher.*

מִפְגָּע m., *object of attack, butt,* Job
7:20.

פָּגַר. Pi. פִּגַּר *became languid, unable
to proceed,* 1 Sa. 30:10, 21, with
מִן.

פֶּגֶר m. (pl. פְּגָרִים, פִּגְרֵי) *dead body of
man or beast.*

פָּגַשׁ I. *met,* with בְּ.—II. *met hostilely,*
Hos. 13:8, &c. Niph. נִפְגַּשׁ *met
each other.* Pi. *stumble against,*
Job 5:14.

פָּדָה I. *redeemed,* with בְּ (of the price).
—II. *delivered.* Niph. נִפְדָּה *was
redeemed, delivered.* Hiph. הִפְדָּה
allowed to be redeemed, Ex. 21:8

Hoph. inf. הָפְדֵּה same as Niph., Lev. 19:20.

פְּדַהְאֵל p. n. of a man.

פְּדָהְצוּר p.n. of a man.

פְּדוּיִים m. pl., λύτρον.—I. redemption price, ransom. — II. redeemed, delivered persons.

פָּדוֹן p. n. of a man.

פְּדוּת f.— I. redemption. — II. separation, Ex. 8:19.

פְּדָיָה, פְּדָיָהוּ p. n. of a man.

פִּדְיוֹם, פִּדְיוֹן m., ransom.

פַּדָּן m., plain, Gen. 48:7; פַּדַּן אֲרָם Padan-Aram; with ה, פַּדֶּנָה אֲרָם towards Padan-Aram.

אַפֶּדֶן Ch., palace, camp, Dan. 11:45.

פָּדַע redeem, deliver, Job 33:24.

פֶּדֶר m. (with suff. פִּדְרוֹ) fat.

פֶּה; see פאה.

פֹּה (פֹּא).—I. here. — II. hither; מִפֹּה hence; עַד פֹּה thus far; אֵיפֹה where?

פּוּאָה (פֻּוָּה) p. n. of a man.

פּוּג (fut. יָפֻג, וַיָּפָג) became chilled, languid, ceased to act. Niph. the same, Ps. 38:9.

פוּגָה f., intermission, Lam. 2:18.

הֲפוּגָה f., intermission, Lam. 3:49.

פּוּחַ I. blew.— II. became cool by a breeze. Hiph. הֵפִיחַ I. inflamed, Pro. 29:8.— II. blew, blew a fire, with בְּ.—III. puffed at (scornfully), with בְּ.—IV. uttered.— V. (from פַּח) ensnared, Ps. 12:6.

פִּיחַ m., ashes, Ex. 9:8, 10.

פּוּט p. n., one of the sons of Ham, and his descendants.

פּוּטִיאֵל p.n. of a man.

פּוֹטִיפַר p.n. (πετεφρη, he who is devoted to the sun), an officer in Pharaoh's household.

פּוֹטִי פֶרַע (the same); p. n., Joseph's father-in-law.

פּוּךְ m.—I. stibium, powdered antimony.—II. אַבְנֵי פוּךְ; LXX. λίθοι πολυτελεῖς, a precious stone; קֶרֶן הַפּוּךְ p. n. of a woman.

פּוֹל m., beans.

פּוּל p.n.—I. a people and nation of Africa.—II. a king of Assyria.

פֻּם, פּוּם m. Ch., mouth, aperture.

פּוּן, fut. אָפוּנָה; LXX. ἐξηπορήθην; Vulg. conturbatus sum, I pine away, Ps. 88:16.

פּוּנָה p.n., a gate of Jerusalem.

פּוּנִי p.n. of a man.

פּוּנֹן p.n., a town on the borders of the desert.

פּוּעָה p.n. of a woman.

פּוּץ I. dispersed themselves, were scattered.—II. overflowed. Niph. were scattered. Pil. פֹּצֵץ and Pilp. פִּצְפֵּץ shatter, shake to pieces. Hiph. הֵפִיץ I. scattered, confused. —II. poured out.— III. was scattered. Hithpo. are shattered, Hab. 3:6. Tiphel תְּפוֹצוֹתִיכֶם I will scatter you, Jer. 25:34.

מֵפִיץ m.—I. disperser.—II. club, Pro. 25:18.

I. פּוּק stagger, stumble, Isa. 28:7. Hiph. stagger, stumble, Jer. 10:4.

II. פּוּק Hiph. הֵפִיק 1. supplied, Isa. 58:10.—2 obtained.—3. prospered, Ps. 140:9.

פוּקָה f., *cause of stumbling*, 1 Sa. 25:31.

פִּיק m., *staggering*, Nah. 2:11

I. פּוּר (Arab. *bubbled*); see פָּרַר.

פּוּרָה f., *wine-press*.

פָּרוּר m., *pot for boiling*.

II. פּוּר m., a Persian word.—I. *lot*; pl. פּוּרִים.—II. *the feast of Purim*.

פּוֹרָתָא p.n., a son of Haman.

פּוּשׁ (pret. פָּשׁתֶּם).—I. *became numerous, flourished.* — II. *spread themselves*, Hab. 1:8. Niph. *were scattered*, Nah. 3:18.

פָּשׁ m., *extent*, Job 35:15.

פִּישׁוֹן p.n., one of the rivers of Paradise.

פּוּת (Arab. *interstice*).

פֹּת m., Isa. 3:17; pl. פֹּתוֹת *hinges*, 1 Ki. 7:50.

פּוּתִי p. n. of a man.

פָּז (fut. pl. יָעֹזּוּ) *are strong and active*, Gen. 49:24. Pi. פִּזֵּז *dancing*, 2 Sa. 6:16. Hoph. part. מוּפָז *purified*, 1 Ki. 10:18.

פָּז m.—I. *refined gold.* — II. *refined*, Cant. 5:11.

פָּזַר *dispersed*, Jer. 50:17. Pi. פִּזֵּר I. *dispersed.*—II. *distributed liberally.* Niph. and Pu. *was scattered*.

פַּח m. (pl. פַּחִים).—I. *snare, gin.*—II. *any concealed danger.*—III. *plate of metal*, Ex. 39:3; Nu. 17:3.

פָּחַד (fut. יִפְחַד).—I. *feared*, with מִן —II. *was agitated.*—III מִפְּנֵי *hastened.* Pi. *feared greatly, continually.* Hiph. *caused to shake, tremble*, Job 4:14.

פַּחַד m. (with suff. פַּחְדְּכֶם; pl. פְּחָדִים).—I. *fear, dread, reverence* —II. *object of fear.*— III. *thigh*, Job 40:17; פ' אֱלֹהִים *fear of God*.

פַּחְדָּה f., *fear*, Jer. 2:19.

פֶּחָה m. (const. פַּחַת; with suff. פֶּחָתֶךָ, פֶּחָם; pl. פַּחוֹת; const. פַּחֲווֹת).—I. *governor of a province.* — II. *captain.* — Ch. the same; hence the modern word *Pacha*.

פָּחַז (*swelling like boiling water*).—I. *was dissolute*, Jud. 9:4.— II. *was proud*, Zep. 3:4.

פַּחַז m., *wantonness, pride*, Gen. 49:4.

פַּחֲזוּת f., *pride*, Jer. 23:32.

פָּחָם root not used; (Arab. *charcoal*).

פֶּחָם m., *charcoal*.

פָּחַר root not used; (Syr. *he founded*).

פֶּחָר m. Ch., *potter*, Dan. 2:41.

פַּחַת m. (pl. פְּחָתִים).—I. *a pit, well.*—II. *destruction.*

פַּחֶתֶת f., *corrosion, fretting into a garment*, Lev. 13:55.

פַּחַת־מוֹאָב p.n. of a man.

פַּחַת Kal inf., from נפח.

פִּטְדָה f., *a precious stone, topaz or emerald*.

פָּטַר (fut. יִפְטַר).—I. *slipped out, or away.*—II. *let out* (of water).—III. *expand* (of flowers), 1 Ki. c. 6.—IV. *exempt from duty*, 1 Chron. 9:33. Hiph. *open wide* (the mouth), Ps. 22:8.

פָּטִיר Ketib, same as פָּטוּר (part. see פָּטַר), *exempt from duty*, 1 Chron 9:33.

פֶּטֶר m., *opening, beginning*; פֶּטֶר רֶחֶם *first-born.*

פִּטְרָה f., the same, Nu. 8:16.

פָּטַשׁ root not used; (Arab. *beat out iron with a hammer, spread out*).

פַּטִּישׁ m., *a hammer.*

פְּטִישׁ m. Ch., *a tunic*, Dan. 3:21.

פִּי with comp. פִּיהָ; see פֶּה in פָּאָה.

פִּיד root not used; (Arab. *disappeared, died*).

פִּיד m., *destruction.*

פִיחַ; see פּוּחַ.

פִּילֶגֶשׁ; see פִּלֶגֶשׁ.

פִּים root not used; (Arab. *was fat*).

פִּימָה f., *fatness, food, strength*, Job 15:27.

פִּינֹן p. n., *a prince of Edom.*

פִּיפִיּוֹת; see פָּאָה.

פִּיק; see פּוּק.

פִּישׁוֹן; see פּוּשׁ.

פִּיתֹן p. n., *a man.*

פָּכָה. Pi. *flowing out*, Eze. 47:2

פַּךְ m., *flask, cruse.*

פֹּכֶרֶת הַצְּבָיִים p. n., *a man.*

פָּלָא. Niph. נִפְלָא I. *was marvellous.* —II. *appeared marvellous*, with בְּעֵינֵי.—III. *was concealed*, with מִן.—IV. *was struck with wonder*; part. pl. נִפְלָאוֹת, נִפְלָאִים *wonderful things, wonderfully.* Pi. פִּלֵּא *set apart*; פִלֵּא נֶדֶר *set apart by vow, devoted.* Hiph. הִפְלִיא, הִפְלָא I. *set apart.*—II. *made wonderful.* —III. *acted wonderfully.* Hith. *show one's self wonderful*, with בְּ, Job 10:16.

פֶּלֶא m. (with suff. פִּלְאֲךָ).—I. *sepa-*

ration, peculiarity.—II. *marvellous-ness.*—III. *a miracle*; pl. פְּלָאִים adv. *wonderfully*; פְּלָאוֹת *wonderful things.*

פִּלְאִי or פִּלְיִ m., *wonderful*, Jud. 13:18; Ps. 139:6.

פִּלְאָה f., or פְּלָאִיָּה the same.

פְּלָאיָה p. n. of a man.

פְּלָיָה p. n. of a man.

פַּלּוּא p. n., *a son of Reuben*; patron. פַּלֻּאִי.

מִפְלָאָה f., *miracle*, Job 37:16.

פָּלַג. Niph. *was divided.* Pi. I. *cut out, formed*, Job 38:25.—II. *divided*, Ps. 55:10.

פְּלַג Ch., *divided*, Dan. 2:41.

פְּלַג m. Ch., *half*, Dan. 7:25.

פֶּלֶג m.—I. *channel, stream.*—II. p. n., *a son of Eber.*

פְּלַגּוֹת f. pl., *brooks.*

פְּלֻגָּה f., pl. פְּלֻגּוֹת *divisions*, 2 Chron. 35:5.

מִפְלַגָּה f., pl. מִפְלַגּוֹת the same, 2 Chron. 35:12.

פִּילֶגֶשׁ, פִּלֶגֶשׁ f. (pl. פִּילַגְשִׁים, פִּלַגְשִׁי), *concubine*, παλλακή.

פְּלָדָה f., pl. פְּלָדוֹת *iron of chariots*, perhaps *scythes*, Nah. 2:4.

פִּלְדָּשׁ p. n. of a man.

פָּלָה same as פָּלָא. Niph. *are sepa-rated*, Ex. 33:16. Hiph. הִפְלָה I. *separated.*—II. *set apart*, Ps. 4:4.

פְּלֹנִי m.—I. with אַלְמֹנִי ὁ δεῖνα, *a certain one.*—II. p. n. of a man.

פַּלְמֹנִי m., *this particular one*, Dan 8:13.

פָּלַח *cut*, Ps. 141:7. Pi. פִּלַּח I. *cut to*

pieces, 2 Ki. 4:39.—II. *disentangle*, Job 39:3. - III. *pierce through*, Pro. 7:23.—IV. *harrow*, Job 16:13.

פֶּלַח m.—I. *piece, part.*—II. *mill-stone*; פֶּלַח רֶכֶב *upper mill-stone*; פֶּ' תַּחְתִּית *nether mill-stone.*

פִּלְחָא p. n. of a man.

פְּלַח Ch., *served, worshipped.*

פָּלְחָן m. Ch., *service, worship,* Ezr. 7:19.

פָּלַט *escaped,* Eze. 7:16. Pi. 1. *delivered.*—II. *bring forth safely,* Job 21:10. Hiph. *delivered.*

פָּלִיט m., *fugitive, one escaped.*

פְּלֵטָה, פְּלֵיטָה f., *the escaped, remnant.*

פֶּלֶט m., *deliverance.*

פֶּלֶט p. n. of a man.

פַּלְטִי p. n. of a man.

פַּלְטִי p. n. of a man.

פְּלַטְיָה p. n. of a man.

פְּלַטְיָהוּ p. n. of a man.

מִפְלָט m., *escape, safety,* Ps. 55:9.

פֶּלִיָּה, פְּלִיאָה, פֶּלִיא, פְּלִי ; see פלא.
פְּלִילִי, פְּלִילָה, פָּלִיל ; see פלל.

פָּלֵךְ *root not used;* (Arab. *was round*).

פֶּלֶךְ m.—I. *spinning distaff.*—II. *circuit, district.*

פָּלַל. Pi. פִּלֵּל I. *judged,* 1 Sa. 2:25.—II. *adjudged punishment,* with לְ, Eze. 16:52.—III. *inflicted punishment,* Ps. 106:30.—IV. *expected,* Gen. 48:11. Hith. *prayed* (lit. *appealed to a judge*), with בְּעַד, לִפְנֵי, אֶל, לְ, עַל.

פָּלִיל m., *a judge;* pl. פְּלִילִים.

פְּלִילָה f., *justice,* Isa. 16:3.

פְּלִילִי m., *judicial,* Job 31:28.

פְּלִילִיָּה f., *judgment,* Isa. 28:7.

פָּלָל p. n. of a man.

פְּלַלְיָה p. n. of a man.

תְּפִלָּה f.—I. *prayer.*—II. *intercession.*—III. *hymn,* Ps. 72:20.

פְּלֹנִי, פַּלְמֹנִי; see פלה.

פָּלַס. Pi.—I. *pondered,* Isa. 26:7.—II. *approved.*—III. *planned.*

פֶּלֶס m., *balance, steel-yard.*

מִפְלָשׂ m., *poising, balancing,* Job 37:16.

פָּלַץ. Hith. *shook, trembled,* Job 9:6.

פַּלָּצוּת f., *trembling, fear.*

מִפְלֶצֶת f., *idol, image.*

תִּפְלֶצֶת f., *terror,* Jer. 49:16.

פָּלַשׁ. Hith. *rolled themselves in dust.*

פְּלֶשֶׁת p. n., *Philistia,* the sea-coast of the south of Palestine; it was divided into five provinces. פְּלִשְׁתִּי *a Philistine,* pl. פְּלִשְׁתִּים, פְּלִשְׁתִּיִּים *Philistines* ; LXX. Ἀλλόφυλοι.

פֶּלֶת p. n. of a man.

פְּלֵתִי m., *mercenary soldier, Pelethite.*

פֵּן, פֶּנָּה, פָּנָה, see פנן; פֵּן, see פנה.

פַּנַּג, perhaps *millet,* in English, *panic,* Eze. 27:17.

פָּנָה (fut. יִפְנֶה, תֵּפֶן, וַיִּפֶן, עֹרֶף).—I. *turn himself to go away.*—II. *turned towards.* — III. *changed, declined, began;* לִפְנוֹת בֹּקֶר *at the turn of the morning,* i.e. in the morning; לִפְנוֹת עֶרֶב *in the evening.* Pi. פִּנָּה I. *removed.* — II. *cleared a road or house.* Hiph. הִפְנָה (fut. apoc. וַיִּפֶן).—I. *turned.*—II. *turned himself.* Hoph. *were made to turn themselves,* Jer. 49:8.

פָּנֶה m., pl. פָּנִים; const. פְּנֵי I. *face*

פָּנִים בְּפָנִים ,פָּנִים אֶל־פָּנִים *face to face.*—II. *person, presence;* שׂוּם פָּנִים, with אֶל or עַל נָתַן פָּ׳ ,*he set his face toward;* נָתַן פָּ׳, with לְ and inf. *he designed to do;* פָּנַי *my person, i.e. I;* פָּנֶיךָ *thy person,* i.e. thou, &c.— III. *surface.*—IV. *front;* פָּנִים בַּ *in front;* לְפָנִים *before, formerly;* מִפָּנִים *in, from the presence of;* מִלְּפָנִים *from ancient time;* with prefixes אֶל־פְּנֵי *before, in presence of;* אֶת־פְּנֵי *before;* מֵאֵת פְּנֵי *from before;* בִּפְנֵי *before;* לִפְנֵי *in the sight of, before, preceding, against, in time;* with suff. לְפָנַי, לְפָנֶיךָ, לְפָנָיו, מִלְּפְנֵי, לִפְנֵיהֶם, לִפְנֵיכֶם *from, because of;* מִבְּנֵי אֲשֶׁר *because of;* עַל־פְּנֵי *in presence of, in preference to, towards;* מֵעַל־פְּנֵי *from before.*

פֶּן, part. μή, *lest.*

פְּנִיאֵל, פְּנוּאֵל p.n.—I. *a place beyond Jordan.*—II. *of a man.*

פְּנִים m., *within;* פְּנִימָה *to, on, the inside;* לִפְנִימָה *within, on the inside;* מִפְּנִימָה *within.*

פְּנִימִי m., פְּנִימִית f., *inner.*

פְּנִינִים m. pl., *pearls.*

פֵּן m. (with suff. פִּנָּה; pl. פִּנִּים) *corner.*

פִּנָּה f.—I. *corner;* אֶבֶן פִּ׳ ,רֹאשׁ פִּ׳ *chief corner-stone.*—II. *battlement, parapet.*—III. *dignitary, prince.*

פְּנֻנָּה p.n. of a woman.

פָּנַק. Pi. *brought up delicately,* Pro. 29:21.

פָּנָג. Pi. *count, observe,* Ps. 48:14.

פַּס, פַּסִּים, פִּסָּה; see פסס.

פְּסַג. Pi. *count, observe,* Ps. 48:14.

פִּסְגָּה p.n., *a peak on the mountains of Moab.*

פָּסַח *passed over for defence, defended, protected.* Niph. *was lamed,* 2 Sa. 4:4. Pi. *leaped about,* 1 Ki. 18:26.

פֶּסַח p.n. of a man.

פֶּסַח m.—I. *feast of the Passover.*—II. *the paschal lamb;* עָשָׂה פֶּ׳ *keep the Passover.*

פִּסֵּחַ m. (pl. פִּסְחִים) *lame.*

תִּפְסַח p.n., *a city on the Euphrates, Thapsacus.*

פָּסַךְ p. n. of a man.

פָּסַל *hewed, carved.*

פָּסִיל m., pl. פְּסִילִים *carved images, idols.*

פֶּסֶל m. (with suff. פִּסְלִי) *an idol.*

פְּסַנְתְּרִין, פְּסַנְטֵרִין m. Ch., ψαλτήριον, *a musical instrument.*

פָּסַס *ceased to exist, disappeared,* Ps. 12:2.

פַּס m. כְּתֹנֶת פַּסִּים *coat of many colours,* Gen. 37:3; *long cloak, covering the hands and feet* (Ges. and Lee); *but Jacob knew Joseph's coat when torn and dipped in blood; it was the quality or colour of the cloth, therefore, not the shape that distinguished it;* LXX. χιτὼν ποικίλος.

פַּס m., *palm of the hand.*

פִּסָּה f., *abundance,* Ps. 72:16

אֶפֶס דַּמִּים פַּס דַּמִּים p. n., same as.

פָּסָה p.n. of a man.

פָּעָה *cry out,* Isa. 42:14.

אֶפְעֶה com., *adder, viper.*

אֶפַע the same.

פְּעִי, פָּעַי p. n., a city of Edom.

פְּעוֹר; see פְּעוֹר.

פָּעַל v. (fut. יִפְעַל, יִפְעָל).—I worked.
—II. made, formed.—III. did, performed.— IV. practised, with לְ or
בְּ of the person for whom the action is performed.

פֹּעַל m. (with suff. פָּעֳלִי, פָּעֳלוֹ, פָּעֳלְךָ;
pl. פָּעֳלִים).—I. work, action, prac-
tice.— II. wages.— III. acquisition,
Pro. 21:6.

פְּעֻלָּה f.—I. work, employment.— II.
wages, Lev. 19:13.—III. reward or
punishment.

פֹּעֳלוֹ for פָּעֳלוֹ, from פֹּעַל.

פְּעֻלְּתַי p. n. of a man.

מִפְעָל m., } work, doings.
מִפְעָלָה f., }

פָּעַם moved, excited to action, Jud. 13:
25. Niph. was moved, disturbed.
Hith. same as Niph., Dan. 2:1.

פַּעַם f. (m. Jud. 16:28).—I. pl. פְּעָמִים
footsteps, feet.— II. progress.—III.
an anvil, Isa. 41:7. — IV. pl.
פְּעָמוֹת feet of the ark (Lee).—V.
an act, and the time of its perform-
ance, a time, once; dual פַּעֲמַיִם
twice; שֶׁבַע פְּעָמִים seven times;
פַּעַם וּשְׁתַּיִם once or twice, Neh.
13:20; בְּפַעַם הַזֹּאת, הַפַּעַם,
בַּפַּעַם הַהִיא now, at the present
time; כְּפַעַם בְּפַעַם even so as before; פַּעַם...פַּעַם sometimes.

פַּעֲמֹן m., bell, Ex. chapters 38 and
39 only.

פַּעֲנֵחַ; see פ' צָפְנַת.

פָּעַר open the mouth, gape, with פֶּה,
בְּפֶה.

פְּעוֹר p. n. of a mountain of Moab;

בַּעַל־פְּעוֹר and פְּעוֹר an idol of
Moab.

פַּעְרִי p. n., one of David's generals;
elsewhere נַעֲרִי.

פָּצָה I. opened the mouth.—II. rescued.

פָּצַח broke forth into singing, with
רִנָּה. Pi. broke to pieces, Mic. 3:3.

פְּצִירָה; see פצר.

פָּצַל. Pi. פִּצֵּל peeled, Gen. 30:37, 38.
פְּצָלוֹת f. pl., the parts peeled,
stripped of bark, Gen. 30:37.

פָּצַם broke the earth, Ps. 60:4.

פָּצַע wounded; פְּצוּעַ דַּכָּה eunuch.

פֶּצַע m. (with suff. פִּצְעִי; pl. פְּצָעִים),
a wound.

פָּצַץ Hithpo.; see פוץ.

פֶּצֶץ p. n. of a man.

פָּצַר (fut. יִפְצַר).—I. pressed upon to
injure, Gen. 19:9.— II. urged to
consent, with בְּ. Hiph. inf. הַפְצֵר
was too urgent, obstinate, 1 Sam.
15:23.

פְּצִירָה f., a file, 1 Sam. 13:21.

פָּקַד I. visited, enquired for.—II. enquired for without finding, missed.
—III. enquired into or after, cared
for.—IV. punished, with אֶל of
the crime, or עַל of the person,
and בְּ of the punishment.—V.
examined and arranged—VI. numbered, took account of.—VII. placed,
appointed, set over, with עַל, אֶת,
(פְּקֻדִים) officers).—VIII. laid a
charge upon any one, with עַל.
Niph. I. was missed. — II. was
punished.— III. was numbered.—
IV. punishment was inflicted.—V.
was visited with evil. Pi. ex-

amined, numbered. Pu. I. was taken account of, Ex. 38:21.—II. was deprived of, Isa. 38:10. Hiph. I. placed, appointed, with עַל or לְ.—II. committed to some one, with עַל־יְדֵי, בְּיַד, אֶת. Hoph. I. was punished, Jer. 6:6.—II. placed, appointed; part. מֻפְקָדִים officers. Hith. was examined, numbered. Hoth. pl. הָתְפָּקְדוּ the same.

פְּקֻדָּה f.—I. providence, Job 10:12.—II. office.—III. government.—IV. class, 1 Chron. 23:11.—V. treasure, Isa. 15:7.—VI. punishment; בֵּית הַפְּקֻדּוֹת prison.

פִּקָּדוֹן m., deposit.

פְּקִדֻת f., captain of the guard, Jer. 37:13.

פָּקוּד m.—I. punishment, an allegorical name of Babylon, Jer. 50:21.—II. dominion, Eze. 23:23.

פִּקּוּדִים m. pl., precepts of God.

פָּקִיד m., officer, chief, superintendent.

מִפְקָד m.—I. arrangement, 2 Chron. 31:13.—II. census publicly appointed, 2 Sa. 24:9.—III. שַׁעַר הַמִּפְקָד one of the gates of Jerusalem, Neh. 3:31.

פָּקַח (fut. יִפְקַח) opened the eyes or ears. Niph. was opened.

פֶּקַח p.n., Pekah, king of Israel.

פְּקַחְיָה p.n., Pekahiah, king of Israel.

פִּקֵּחַ m., having the eyes opened, able to see.

פְּקַח־קוֹחַ m., complete opening, opening of the prison, Isa. 61:1.

פָּקִיד officer; see פקד.

פַּקֻּעוֹת f. pl., the fox-grape, 2 Ki. 4:39.

פְּקָעִים m. pl., architectural ornaments of a globular form, 1 Ki. 6:18; 7:24.

פַּר, פָּר m., young bull.

פָּרָה f.—I. young cow, heifer.—II. הַפָּרָה p.n., a town in the tribe of Benjamin.

פָּרָא same as פָּרָה Hiph., propagate, Hos. 13:15.

פֶּרֶא com. (pl. פְּרָאִים), wild ass

פִּרְאָם p.n., a king of Canaan.

פֵּארֹת same as פֹּארֹת; see פֵּארָה.

פַּרְוָר, פַּרְבָּר m., suburb.

פָּרַד separated, spread (of wings). Niph. separated himself, with מֵעַל. Pi. go aside, Hos. 4:14. Pu. part. מְפֹרָד separate, Est. 3:8. Hiph. same as Kal. Hith. same as Niph.

פֶּרֶד m. (with suff. פִּרְדּוֹ; pl. פְּרָדִים), a mule.

פִּרְדָּה f., she-mule.

פְּרֻדוֹת f. pl., seeds scattered, corn sown, Joel 1:17.

פַּרְדֵּס m., παράδεισος, enclosure, park, Neh. 2:8; Cant. 4:13; Ecc. 2:5.

פָּרָה heifer; see פַּר; פֶּרֶא same as פֶּרֶא wild ass.

פָּרָה bore fruit, was fruitful (of trees, plants, men, animals, &c.); part. f. פֹּרִיָּה, פֹּרָת fruit tree. Hiph. הִפְרָה (fut. apoc. וַיֶּפֶר) made fruitful.

פְּרִי m. (with pause פֶּרִי; with suff. פִּרְיוֹ, פֶּרְיְךָ, פִּרְיָם, פִּרְיֵהֶם). I. fruit of a tree; עֵץ פְּרִי fruit tree.—II. produce of the ground; אֶרֶץ פְּרִי a fruitful land.—III. fruit of the womb, offspring.—IV *result of actions, reward* or *punishment.*

פָּרֻדָה p. n. of a man.

פְּרִידָא, פְּרוּדָא p. n. of a man.

פַּרְוָיִם p. n. of a country, same as סְפַרְוַיִם, which see.

פַּרְוָר *suburb;* see פַּרְבָּר.

פָּרוּר *pot;* see פּוּר.

פָּרַז (Arab. *separated*). see פָּרָז.

פְּרָז m., *ruler*, Hab. 3 : 14.

פְּרָזוֹן m., *justice;* with suff. פְּרָזוֹנוֹ, Jud. 5 : 7, 11.

פְּרָזוֹת f. pl., *unwalled towns, villages.*

פְּרָזִי m., *one living in a village;* pl. פְּרָזִים; Ketib פְּרוֹזִים.

פְּרִזִּי p. n., *the Perizzite,* a people of Canaan.

פַּרְזֶל m. Ch., *iron;* Heb. בַּרְזֶל.

פָּרַח (fut. יִפְרַח).—I. *budded.*—II. *shot up, flourished.*—III. *spread, extended itself.* Hiph. *caused to bud, budded.*

פֶּרַח m. (with suff. פִּרְחָם; pl. פְּרָחִים). —I. *young shoot.* — II. *bud.* — III. *the artificial representation of a bud.*

פַּרְחַח p. n. of a man.

פִּרְחָח m., *insolent, with insult,* Job 30 : 12.

אֶפְרֹחַ m., pl. אֶפְרֹחִים *young of birds.*

פָּרַט *abounded* or *sang;* LXX. ἐπικροτοῦντες, Am. 6 : 5.

פֶּרֶט m., *omission, what is omitted,* Lev. 19 : 10.

פְּרִי *fruit;* see פרה.

פָּרִיץ *wild beast;* see פרץ.

פֶּרֶךְ m., *harshness, oppression.*

פָּרֹכֶת f., *the veil which separates the holy place from the holy of holies.*

פָּרַם (fut. יִפְרֹם) *rent, torn* (of garments), Leviticus only.

פַּרְמַשְׁתָּא p.n., a son of Haman.

פַּרְנָךְ p.n. of a man.

פָּרַס *broke, distributed, bread.* Hiph. *dividing the hoof;* see פַּרְסָה.

פְּרַס Ch., *divide.*

פֶּרֶס m., *the osprey,* Lev. 11 : 13; Deu 14 : 12.

פַּרְסָה f., *a hoof;* pl. const. פַּרְסוֹת פַּרְסֵי.

פָּרַס *Persia;* פָּרְסִי *a Persian, Parsee*

פָּרַע I. *uncovered the head.*—II. *placed in a state of disorder,* Ex. 32 : 25. III. *was disregarded.*— IV. *left a road,* Pro. 4 : 15. — V. *exempted,* Eze. 24 : 14.—VI. *avenged,* Jud. 5 : 2. Niph. *became lawless,* Pro. 29 : 18. Hiph. I. *made idle,* Ex. 5 : 4.— II. *brought vengeance on,* 2 Chron. 28 : 19.

פֶּרַע m., *head of hair;* pl. פְּרָעוֹת, פְּרָעוֹת, *vengeance,* Deu. 32 : 42; Jud. 5 : 2.

פִּרְעָתוֹן p.n., a town of Ephraim; פִּרְעָתֹנִי a Pirathonite.

פַּרְעֹה title of all monarchs of Egypt (lit. φρη *the sun*); Φαραώ.

פַּרְעֹשׁ m.—I. *a flea.*—II. p. n. of a man.

פַּרְפַּר p. n., a small river which joins the Amana near Damascus, 2 Ki. 5 : 12.

פָּרַץ (fut. יִפְרֹץ).—I. *broke down, made a breach in, a wall.*— II. *burst forth, overflowed* (of water).— III. *broke in pieces, afflicted.*—IV. *urged* (a person).—V. *dispersed an enemy*

VI. *distributed* persons, 2 Chron. 11:23. Niph. part. נִפְרָץ *much, frequent* (Lee), 1 Sa. 3:1. Pu. *broken down*, Neh. 1:3. Hith. *breaking loose*, 1 Sa. 25:10.

פָּרִיץ m.—I. *violent, lawless, person.* —II. *wild beast*, Isa. 35:9.

פֶּרֶץ m. (pl. פְּרָצוֹת, פְּרָצִים).—I. *breach in a wall.*—II. *overflowing of water.*—III. *sudden calamity.*— IV. p. n. of a man; patron. פַּרְצִי.

מִפְרָץ m., probably, *creek*, marg. (*breach*, Eng. Ver.), Jud. 5:17.

פָּרַק I. *pulled off*, with מֵעַל, Gen. 27:40.—II. *tore in pieces*, Ps. 7:3.— III. *rescued.* Pi. פֵּרֵק I. *tore in pieces.* — II. *pulled off*, Ex. 32:2. Hith. הִתְפָּרֵק I. *was broken off*, Eze. 19:12.—II. *pulled off from himself.*

פְּרַק Ch., *break off*, Dan. 4:24.

פֶּרֶק m. (Kri מָרֶק *without authority*), *fragments*, Isa. 65:4.

פֶּרֶק m.—I. *tearing in pieces, prey*, Nah. 3:1.—II. *cross way*, Obad. v. 14.

מַפְרֶקֶת f., *vertebræ of the neck*, 1 Sa. 4:18.

פָּרַר *cleft, divided*; inf. abs. פּוֹר. Pil. פּוֹרֵר *cleft*, Ps. 74:13. Hithpo. *was cloven*, Isa. 24:19. Pilp. פַּרְפַּר *shattered, agitated, the mind*, Job 16:12. Hiph. הֵפִיר; הָפֵר with pause הָפֵר I. *broke a covenant or command.*—II. *frustrated.* — III. *annulled.* — IV. *withdrew, broke off.* Hoph. הֻפַּר *was disannulled.*

פָּרַשׂ (fut. יִפְרֹשׂ).— I. *spread.* — II. *stretched out the hands.*—III. *gave, assisted*, Pro. 31:19.— IV. *seized*, Lam. 1:10.— V. *broke*, like פָּרַס. Niph. *was scattered*, Eze. 17:21. Pi. פֵּרַשׂ, with pause פֵּרָשׂ I. *spread out the hands.*—II. *scattered.*

מִפְרָשׂ m.—I. *expansions of*, Job 36:29.—II. *sail of a ship*, Eze. 27:7.

פָּרַשׁ *mark distinctly*, Lev. 24:12. Niph. *scattered*, Eze. 34:12; see פָּרַשׂ. Pu. פֹּרַשׁ I. *was marked out distinctly*, Num. 15:34.—II. *made clear*, Neh. 8:8. Hiph. *stung*, Pro. 23:32.

פְּרַשׁ Ch., the same. Pa. part. מְפָרַשׁ *made clear.*

פֶּרֶשׁ m. (with suff. פִּרְשׁוֹ) *dung.*

פָּרָשָׁה f., *distinct account*, Est. 4:7, 10:2.

פָּרָשׁ m., pl. פָּרָשִׁים *horses*; בַּעֲלֵי הַפָּרָשִׁים *horsemen.*

פָּרָשׁ, const. פָּרַשׁ m., *horseman*; pl. פָּרָשִׁים.

(פַּתְשֶׁגֶן), פַּרְשֶׁגֶן m. Heb. and Ch., *copy of a writing*, Ezra only.

פַּרְשְׁדֹנָה or פַּרְשְׁדֹן *dung*, as some render, *podex* as others, Jud. 3:22.

פַּרְשֵׁז *spreading*, Job 26:9

פַּרְשַׁנְדָּתָא p.n., *a son of Haman.*

פְּרָת p. n., the river *Euphrates*, Εὐφράτης.

פְּרָת; see פָּרָה.

פַּרְתְּמִים m. pl., *chiefs, nobles.*

פָּשָׂה *spread itself* (an eruption), Leviticus only.

פָּשַׂע *stepped, trod*, with בְּ, Isa. 27:4

פֶּשַׂע m., a step, 1 Sa. 20:3.

מִפְשָׂעָה f., buttocks, 1 Chron. 19:4

פָּשַׂק opened, expanded, Pro. 13:3.
Pi. the same, Eze. 16:25.

פֻּשׁ spreading; see פּוּשׁ.

פָּשַׁח Pi. tore to pieces, Lam. 3:11.

פַּשְׁחוּר p.n. of a man.

פָּשַׁט (fut. יִפְשֹׁט).—I. stripped off his
dress.— II. spread, extended itself,
with אֶל, בְּ, עַל. Pi. stripped another. Hiph. I. stripped another.
II. skinned, with מֵעַל. Hith. stripped himself, 1 Sa. 18:4.

פָּשַׁע I. rebelled, rebelled against, with
מִתַּחַת and בְּ.— II. transgressed.
Niph. transgressed against, Pro.
18: 19.

פֶּשַׁע m. (with suff. פִּשְׁעִי; pl. פְּשָׁעִים).
—I. rebellion.— II. transgression,
sin.— III. injury (by loss), Ex.
22:8.

פְּשַׁר Ch., interpreted, explained. Pa.
the same.

פְּשַׁר m. Ch., interpretation.

פֵּשֶׁר m. Heb., the same, Ecc. 8:1.

פִּשְׁתָּה m.—I. flax.—II. linen.

פִּשְׁתָּה f., a lamp-wick of flax, Isa.
42 : 3; 43 : 17 ; (pl. פִּשְׁתִּים) linen,
Ex. 9 : 31.

פַּת, פִּתִּים, see פָּתַת, פַּת, see פּוּת.

פְּתָאִים; see פֶּתִי.

פִּתְאֹם suddenly; see פֶּתַע.

פַּתְבַּג m. Heb. and Ch., portion of
food, mess.

פִּתְגָּם m. Ch.—I. decree.— II. royal
letter.— III. epistle ; Heb. decree,
sentence.

פָּתָה was silly, Deu. 11:16, Job 31:
27. Niph. was persuaded, enticed
Pi. I. led to folly, persuaded, enticed.—II. deceived.—III. used fair
words to. Pu. pass. of Pi. Hiph.
(fut. apoc. יַפְתְּ) declared foolish,
idolatrous, with לְ, Gen. 9:27.

פְּתוּאֵל p.n. of a man.

פֶּתִי, with pause פֶּתִי m. (pl. פְּתָיִים,
פְּתָאִים).—I. ignorant.—II. foolish
—III. folly, Pro. 1:22.

פְּתַי m. Ch., breadth.

פְּתַיּוּת f., folly, Pro. 9:13.

פָּתוֹר, see פתר ; פְּתוֹת, see פתת.

פָּתַח (fut. יִפְתַּח).— I. opened.—II.
uttered, opened his mouth.—III.
opened the ears, Isa. 50:5.—IV.
cleft a rock, Ps. 105:41.— V.
loosened, untied, Isa. 14:17.—VI.
brought out for sale.—VII. drew
a sword, Ps. 37:14. Niph. was
opened, unloosed. Pi. I. opened, &c.,
as Kal.— II. carved, engraved.
Pu. engraven. Hith. loose thyself, Isa. 52:2.

פְּתַח Ch., opened.

פֶּתַח m. (with suff. פִּתְחוֹ; pl. פְּתָחִים,
פִּתְחֵי).— I. opening, gateway,
entrance.—II. door or gate ; בְּפֶתַח,
הַפֶּתְחָה, פֶּתַח to the gate.

פֵּתַח m., opening, laying open, Ps.
119:130.

פְּתִיחוֹת f. pl., drawn swords, Ps.
55:22.

פִּתּוּחַ m., engraving, carving.

פִּתְחוֹן, const. פִּתְחוֹן m., opening of
the mouth.

פְּתַחְיָה p.n. of a man.

מַפְתֵּחַ m., key.

מִפְתָּה m., *opening the lips*, Pro. 8:6.

פָּתִיגִיל m., "stomacher," Eng. Ver., Isa. 3:24, meaning uncertain.

פָּתַל. Niph. *was twisted with, struggled together*, Gen. 30:8. Hith. *struggled against*, Ps. 18:27; תִּתְפַּל for תִּתְפַּתָּל the same, 2 Sa. 22:27.

פָּתִיל m.—I. *lace, thread, cord.*—II. *string* for a signet-ring.—III. *plate of gold.*—IV. *cloth for a cover*, Nu. 19:15.

פְּתַלְתֹּל m., *perverse*, Deu. 32:5.

נַפְתּוּל m., *struggles*, Gen. 30:8.

פִּתֹם p.n., a city of Egypt in the vicinity of Goshen, probably Damietta.

פֶּתֶן m., *an asp*.

מִפְתָּן m., *threshold of a door, gate, &c.*

פֶּתַע m.—I. *suddenness.*—II. adv. *suddenly;* בְּפֶתַע the same.

פִּתְאֹם adv., *suddenly, immediately;* בְּפֶתַע פִּתְאֹם the same; פ׳ לְפֶתַע and פ׳ לְפֶתַע the same; פַּחַד פ׳ *sudden fear*.

פָּתַר (fut. יִפְתֹּר) *interpreted, explained*, Gen. chaps. 40 and 41 only.

פִּתְרֹון m., *interpretation*, Gen. chaps. 40 and 41 only.

פְּתוֹר p.n., the country of the prophet Balaam, probably *Petra*.

פַּתְרֹוס p.n., some nation bordering upon Egypt; פַּתְרֻסִים its inhabitants.

פַּרְשֶׁגֶן same as פַּתְשֶׁגֶן.

פָּתַת *broke to pieces*, Lev. 2:6.

פַּת f. (with suff. פִּתִּי; pl. פִּתִּים), a *piece, piece of bread*.

פְּתוֹת m., the same, Eze. 13:19.

צ

צֵא, with ה parag. צֵאָה Kal imp, from יָצָא.

צֵאָה *excrement;* see צוֹא.

צֶאֱלִים m., pl., *trees in dry places, shady bushes*, Job 40:21, 22.

צֹאן (צאון) com.—I. coll. *sheep or goats.*—II. *a flock of sheep* or goats.—III. *a people* (the flock of God).

צָאֲנָן p.n., a city in the tribe of Judah; called also צְנָן.

צֶאֱצָאִים; see יָצָא.

צֵאת Kal inf., from יָצָא.

צָבִים, צֹב; see צבב.

צָבָא I. *assembled for war, fought.*—II *assembled for a service, performed it.* Hiph. *marshalled an army*.

צָבָא m. (pl. צְבָאִים, צְבָאוֹת Ps. 103: 21).—I. *an army.*—II. *any multitude;* אַנְשֵׁי הַצָּבָא *soldiers;* שַׂר הַצָּבָא *commander in chief.*—III *warfare, military service.*—IV. *any appointed service or trial,* צְבָא הַשָּׁמַיִם *the host of heaven,* i. e.—1. *the stars.*—2. *the angels;* יְהוָה צ׳, אֱלֹהֵי צְבָאוֹת *the Lord of Hosts*, one of the titles of God; see also צְבָאוֹת in צְבִי under צְבָה.

צְבוֹיִם, צְבֹאִים p. n., one of the cities of the plain destroyed with Sodom.

צְבָא Ch., *wished, was willing*.

צְבוּ f. Ch., *determination, resolution*, Dan. 6:18.

צָבַב (Arab. *hid, concealed*).

צָב m.—I. *a covered waggon;* pl. צַבִּים.—II. *a kind of lizard,* Lev. 11:29.

צֹבֶבָה p. n. of a woman.

צָבָה same as צָבָא; part. צֹבָה I. *waging war.*—II. *burst,* Nu. 5:27. Hiph. *caused to burst,* Nu. 5:22.

צָבֶה m., צָבָה f., *swelling,* Nu. 5:21.

צְבִי m.—I. *beauty, ornament, honour.* — II. *an antelope;* pl. צְבָיִים, צְבָאִים; f. צְבָאוֹת.

צְבִיָה f., *she antelope.*

צִבְיָה p. n. of a woman.

צִבְיָא p. n. of a man.

צָבַט *took up in his hand,* Ru. 2:14.

צָבַע (Arab. *dyed*).

צְבַע Ch. Pa. *dyed, made wet.* Hith. *was dyed.*

צֶבַע m., *a dyed dress,* Jud. 5:30.

צָבוּעַ m., *hyæna,* Jer. 12:9 (Arab. *hyæna*).

צְבֹעִים p. n., *a valley and town of Benjamin.*

צִבְעוֹן p. n., *a son of Seir.*

אֶצְבַּע f. (with suff. אֶצְבָּעוֹ; pl. אֶצְבָּעוֹת).—I. *a finger.*—II. *a toe.* —III. *the hand.*—IV. *a digit.* Ch. the same.

צָבַר (fut. יִצְבֹּר).—I. *heaped up.*—II. *laid up, treasured up.*

צְבָרִים m. pl., *heaps,* 2 Ki. 10:8.

צָבַת (Arab. *took in his hand*).

צֶבֶת m., pl. צְבָתִים *handfuls,* Ru. 2:16.

צָדַד (Arab. *turned the face away*).

צַד m. (with suff. צִדֹּה; pl. צִדִּים). —I. *side,* with parag. ה צִדָּה *to the side;* עַל צַד *at the side;* מִצַּד the same.—II. *adversary,* Jud. 2:3.

צַד m. Ch. *side;* מִצַּד *at the side;* לְצַד *against.*

צָדָד p. n., *a town in the north of Palestine.*

צִדִּים p. n., *a town of Naphtali.*

צָדָה *laid wait for,* Ex. 21:13. Niph *was destroyed,* Zep. 3:6.

צְדָא m. Ch., *perverseness,* Dan. 3:14.

צְדִיָה f., *lying in wait,* Nu. 35:20, 22.

צָדַק (fut. יִצְדַּק).—I. *was righteous, equitable.*—II. *acted justly.*—III. *was in the right.*—IV. *was acknowledged to be just, in the right.* Niph. *was purified, exculpated,* Dan. 8:14. Pi. *justified, cleared, himself* or *another.* Hiph.—I. *did justice.*—II. *gave judgment in favour of, acquitted.*—III *justified before God,* Ex. 23:7. Hith. fut. pl. נִצְטַדָּק *cleared himself,* Gen 44:16.

צֶדֶק m. (with suff. צִדְקוֹ).—I. *truth.* —II. *fairness, equity.*—III. *a just cause.*—IV. *acquittal, justification.* V. *righteousness.*

צְדָקָה f.—I. *truth, equity.*—II. *a just cause* or *claim.* — III. *righteousness.*—IV. *favor, approbation.*

צִדְקָה f. Ch., *equity, righteousness.*

צַדִּיק m.—I. *righteous.*—II. *having a just cause.*—III. *innocent.*—IV *true,* Isa. 41:26.

צָדוֹק p. n. of a man.

צִדְקִיָּה, צִדְקִיָּהוּ p. n.—I. *Zedekiah king of Judah.*—II. also of other men.

צַדְקָתֶךְ Eze. 16:52. Pi. inf., with suff. and f. termination, from צָדַק.

צָהַב. Hoph. part. מֻצְהָב *of a gold colour,* Ezr. 8:27.

צָהֹב m., *red.*

I. צָהַל 1. neighed. — 2. shouted for joy. Pi. shouted for joy or sorrow, with קוֹל.—II. same as זָהַר. Hiph. הִצְהִיל caused to shine, Ps. 104: 15.

מִצְהָלָה f., neighing.

צָהַר same as זָהַר. Hiph. made the fine oil called יִצְהָר, Job 24:11.

צֹהַר m.—I. a light, window, &c.—II. noon.

יִצְהָר m.—I. fine olive oil.—II. p.n. of a man; patron. יִצְהָרִי.

צַו, צָו; see צָוָה.

צוֹא m., filthy, Zec. 3:3, 4.

צוֹאָה f., filth, dung.

צֵאָה f., excrement.

צַוָּר, צַוָּאר, const. צַוַּאר m. (pl. צַוְּארֵי, צַוָּארִים; צַוְּארוֹת) neck, shoulder, back; Ch. the same.

צַוְּרֹנִים m. pl., the neck, Cant. 4:9.

אֲרָם צ׳ or צוֹבָה p.n., a city and district of Syria.

צוּד hunted, pursued, watched for, men or animals. Pil. צוֹדֵד ensnare, beguile. Hith. הִצְטַיָּד (see צַיִד) furnished with provisions, Jos. 9: 12.

צַיִד, const. צֵיד m.—I. hunting.—II. game, prey. — III. provisions (of any kind).

צֵידָה f., provisions.

צַיָּד m., hunter, Jer. 16:16.

צִידוֹן p.n., Zidon, a city of Phenicia; צִידֹנִי m., צִידֹנִית f., a Zidonian.

מְצָד m. (pl. מְצָדוֹת) fortress, strong place.

מְצוֹד m. } —I. prey.—II. net.—III.
מְצוֹדָה f. } fortress.

מָצוֹד m., hunter's net, Job 19:6.

מְצָדָה, מְצוּדָה f.—I. prey.—II. net —III. fortress.

צָוָה. Pi. צִוָּה (fut. יְצַוֶּה; apoc. יְצַו; imp. צַוֵּה; apoc. צַו).—I. commanded, gave orders, with אֶל, עַל—II. appointed.—III. caused, i.e appointed a thing; צִוָּה אֶל בֵּיתוֹ he gave his last orders to his house, 2 Sa. 17:23. Pu. צֻוָּה was commanded.

צַו, צָו m., precept, command.

צִיּוּן m.—I. sepulchral monument.— II. waymark, Jer. 31:21.

מִצְוָה f. (pl. מִצְוֹת) command, precept.

צָוַח shouted for joy, Isa. 42:11.

צְוָחָה f., cry of sorrow.

צוּל (Arab. lay hid); see צָלַל sank.

צוּלָה f., the deep, Isa. 44:27.

מְצוֹלָה, מְצוּלָה f., depth (of the sea, &c.)

צוּם fasted.

צוֹם m. (pl. צוֹמוֹת) fasting.

צוּע (Arab. formed, designed).

מַעֲשֵׂה צ׳, צַעֲצֻעִים m. pl., carvings, 2 Chron. 3:10.

צוֹעֵר, צֹעֵר; see צָעַר.

צוּף flowed, Lam. 3:54. Hiph. הֵצִיף I. caused to flow. — II. caused to float.

צוּף m.—I. honey-comb. — II. צוּף, צוֹפַי, צִיף p.n., the son of Elkanah.

צָפָה f., overflowing, Eze. 32:6.

צַפְצָפָה f., a willow, Eze. 17:5.

צִיץ see צוּץ.

I. צוּק same as יָצַק pour, Job 28:2; 29:6.

II. צוּק *was in difficulty*, Dan. 9:25.
Hiph. הֵצִיק I. *urged, constrained.*
—II. *distressed.*

צוּקָה f., *distress.*

מָצוֹק m., *restraint, difficulty, trouble.*

מָצוּק m.— I. *pillars, supports.* — II.
peaks, projections of rocks, 1 Sa. 14:5.

מוּצָק with pause מֻצָּק m., *constraint*;
see also in יָצַק.

מְצוּקָה f., *restraint, difficulty, trouble.*

צוּר I. *formed, fashioned.*—II. *tied up
money.* — III. *surrounded.* — IV.
overlaid.—V. *acted hostilely.*—VI.
besieged, with עַל אֶל.

צוּר m. (pl. צוּרִים, צוּרוֹת).—I. *a rock.*
—II. *a refuge* (applied to God).—
III. *a stone,* Isa. 8:14. — IV. *a
sharp stone used as a knife,* Jos.
5:2, 3.—V. *edge of a sword,* Ps.
89:44.— VI. *form, figure,* Ps. 49:
15.—VII. p. n. of a man.

צֻר m.— I. *a rock,* Eze. 3:9. — II. *a
knife,* Ex. 4:25.

צוֹר, צֹר p. n., *Tyre,* the capital of
Phenicia, Τύρος; צֹרִי *a Tyrian.*

צוּרָה f., *form, figure,* Eze. 43:11.

צוּרִיאֵל p.n. of a man.

צוּרִישַׁדַּי (*my rock is the Almighty*),
p. n. of a man.

צִיר m.—I. *figure, image,* Isa. 45:16.
—II. *hinge,* Pro. 26:14. — III.
pangs of a woman in labour; see
also in loc.

צַר m., צָרָה f., *narrow, small, close;*
see also in צרר.

צֵר p.n., a town in the tribe of Naphtali.

מָצוֹר m.—I. *restraint.*—II. *siege.*—
III. *mound of besiegers.*—IV. *munition, citadel.* — V. p. n., *Egypt,*
same as מִצְרַיִם, which see.

מְצוּרָה f., *fortress, citadel, mound.*

צִנּוֹר; see צַוָּאר, צַוְרוֹנִים.

צוּת. Hiph. הֵצִית *set on fire,* Isa. 27:
4; same as יָצַת.

צָחָה root not used; Ch. *thirsted.*
צָחֶה m., *parched,* Isa. 5:13.
צָחָא p. n. of a man.

צָחַח *was white,* Lam. 4:7.
צַח m., צְחֶה f.— I. *hot, burning.*—
II. *bright, white.* — III. *distinctly,
plainly,* Isa. 32:4.

צְחִיחַ m.—I. *dry, bare.*—II. *open, exposed,* Neh. 4:7.

צְחִיחִי m., pl. צְחִחִים *dry places,*
Neh. 4:7.

צְחִיחָה f., *a parched land,* Ps. 68:7.

צְחִיחוֹת f. pl., *dry places,* Isa. 58:
11.

צָחַן (Arab. *was hot*).
צַחֲנָה f., *the heat of putrefaction,
stench,* Joel 2:20.

צָחַק *laughed,* with לְ. Pi. צִחֵק I.
made laughter, joked.—II. *laughed
at, insulted,* with בְּ.

צְחֹק m., *laughter, ridicule.*

יִצְחָק, יִשְׂחָק p. n., *Isaac,* the son of
Abraham and Sarah; LXX
Ισαάκ.

צָחַר m., *whiteness,* Eze. 27:18.

צָחֹר m., *white,* Jud. 10:5.

צֹחַר p. n. of a man.

צִיבָא p. n. of a man.

צֵידָה, צַיִד, צֵידָה, צִידוֹן; see צוּד.

צִיָּה root not used; (Arab. *drought*).
צִי m. (see צִיָּה), *a ship;* pl. צִיִּים,
צִים.

צִיָּה f.—I. *drought,* Job 24:19.— II
parched land, wilderness.

צִיִּים m. pl., *inhabitants of the desert, men or beasts.*

צִיּוֹן m., *parched land.*

צִיָּה; see צָוָה.

צִיּוֹן f. (*citadel*), p. n., *Zion,* the well known hill on and around which Jerusalem was built.

צִין, צִן p.n., the desert between Canaan and the land of Edom.

צִינֹק *fetters;* see צָנַק.

צִיעֹר p. n., a town of Judah.

צִיץ (pret. צָץ; fut. יָצִיץ).—I. *flowered.* — II. *flourished.* Hiph. *looked cheerfully,* Cant. 2:9.

צִיץ m.—I. *a flower;* pl. צִצִּים.—II. *anything shining, plate of metal.*—III. *plumage, wings.*—IV. p. n. of a place.

צִיצָה f., *flower,* Isa. 28:4.

צִיצִת f.—I. *lock of hair,* Eze. 8:3.— II. *fringe,* Nu. 15:38,39.

צִקְלַג, צִיקְלַג, צִיקְלָן p. n., a city of the Philistines in the land of Simeon.

צִיר Kal not used; (Arab. *went*). Hith. הִצְטַיֵּר *prepared for a journey,* Jos. 9:4.

צִיר m., *person sent on a journey, messenger;* see also in צוּר.

צֵל, צָלָה, צָלוּל; see צָלַל.

צְלָא Ch. Pa. *prayed.*

צָלָה *roasted,* Isa. 44:16,19.

צָלִי m., *roasted.*

צָלַח, צָלֵחַ (fut. יִצְלַח).—I. *crossed a river.*—II. *fell upon, descended,* with עַל, אֶל.—III. *advanced, flourished.*—IV. *was useful, fit,* with לְ. Hiph. הִצְלִיחַ I. *made to pros-*

per, with לְ.—II. *accomplished.*—III. *was prosperous.*

צְלַח Ch. Aph. הַצְלַח I. *made prosperous.*—II. *was prosperous.*

צְלֵחוֹת f. pl., *dishes.*

צְלֹחִית f., *a dish,* 2 Ki. 2:20.

צְלַחַת f., the same.

I. צָלַל I. *sank in the water,* Ex. 15:10.—II. *became shaded,* Neh.13:19. Hiph. part. מֵצֵל *giving shade,* Eze. 31:3.

צָלוּל (צָלִיל) m., *a barley cake,* Jud. 7:13.

צֵלֶל m. (with suff. צִלְלוֹ; pl. צְלָלִים, צְלָלֵי), *a shadow,*

צֵל m. (with suff. צִלָּה).—I. *a shadow.* —II. *dusk.*—III. *shelter, protection*

צִלָּה p.n., *Zillah,* the wife of Lamech.

צַלְמָוֶת m., *shadow of death,* applied to any thick darkness.

צַלְמֻנָּע p.n., a king of the Midianites.

צַלְלְפּוֹנִי (with art.), p. n. of a man.

מְצִלָּה f., *shady place.*

II. צָלַל I. *tingled (of the ears).*—II. *quivered (of the lips),* Hab. 3:16.

צְלָצַל, const. צִלְצַל m.—I. *a cymbal.*— II. *a species of locust,* Deu. 28:42. — III. *tumult of an army or shadowing;* see I. צָלַל Isa. 18:1. —IV. *harpoon,* Job 40:31.

צֶלְצְלִים, pl. const. צִלְצְלֵי *cymbals.*

מְצִלָּה f., pl. מְצִלּוֹת.—I. *cymbals.*— II. *bells.*

מְצֶלֶת f., dual מְצִלְתַּיִם *pair of cymbals.*

צָלַם root not used; (Arab. *was dark*).

צֶלֶם m.—I. *a shadow,* Ps. 39:7.—II. *an imagination,* Ps. 73:20.—III

representation, picture, image.—
IV. resemblance.

צֶלֶם‎, צְלֵם‎ m. Ch., an image.

צַלְמוֹן‎ (shady ?) p. n., a mountain of
Ephraim.

צַלְמֹנָה‎ p. n., one of the stations in
the wilderness.

צַלְמָוֶת‎; see in I. צלל‎.

צָלַע‎ part. צֹלֵעַ‎; f. צֹלֵעָה‎ halting,
lame.

צֶלַע‎ m., limping, falling.

צֵלָע‎ f. (const. צֶלַע‎, צֵלַע‎; with suff.
צַלְעוֹ‎).—I. a rib.—II. a plank
for wainscoting. —III. a side.—IV.
side chamber; pl. צְלָעוֹת‎; const.
צַלְעוֹת‎ side planks, side chambers;
צְלָעִים‎ folding doors.— V. p. n.,
the town of Benjamin where Saul
was buried.

צֶלַף‎ p. n. of a man.

צְלָפְחָד‎ p. n. of a man.

צֵלְצַח‎ p. n., a piace in Benjamin.

צְלָצַל‎, צִלְצֵל‎, צְלָצְלִים‎; see II. צלל‎.

צֶלֶק‎ p. n., one of David's captains.

צִלְּתַי‎ p. n. of a man.

צָמֵא‎, fut. יִצְמָא‎.—I. thirsted.—II.
earnestly desired.

צָמֵא‎ m., צְמֵאָה‎ f., thirsty.
צָמָא‎ m., thirst.

צִמְאָה‎ f., thirst, Jer. 2:25.
צִמָּאוֹן‎ m., thirsty land.

צָמַד‎. Niph. was bound, yoked (to
idolatry). Pu. tied, fastened, 2 Sa.
20:8. Hiph. contrived, Ps. 50:19

צָמִיד‎ m.—I. tied, fastened, Nu. 19:15.
—II. a band, bracelet.

צֶמֶד‎ m. (with suff. צִמְדּוֹ‎; pl. צְמָדִים‎,

צִמְדֵּי‎).—I. a pair, yoke (of oxen,
&c.).—II. the quantity of land
ploughed in a day by a yoke of
oxen.

צָמוּק‎; see צמק‎.

צָמַח‎ (fut. יִצְמַח‎).—I. shot, grew up.
—II. flourished.—III. sprang up,
arose, began.—IV. produced. Pi.
grew (of hair). Hiph. (fut. יַצְמִיחַ‎
וַיַּצְמַח‎) caused to grow, produced.

צֶמַח‎ m. (with suff. צִמְחֹה‎).—I. shooting.—II. a shoot.—III. plants.—
IV. the Branch (a title. of Christ).

צְמִיתַת‎; see צמת‎.

צָמַם‎ root not used; (Arab. tied); Ch.
covered.

צַמָּה‎ f., a woman's veil.

צַמִּים‎ m.—I. noose, snare.—II. destruction.

צָמַק‎ dry (of the breasts), Hos. 9:14

צִמּוּק‎ m., dry grapes; Ital. simmuki.

צֶמֶר‎ m. (with suff. צַמְרִי‎), wool.

צַמֶּרֶת‎ f., foliage.

צְמָרִי‎ p. n., an unknown people, Gen.
10:18.

צְמָרַיִם‎ p. n., a town of Benjamin.

צָמַת‎ silenced, destroyed, Lam. 3:53.
Niph. was put to silence. Pi. and
Hiph. put to silence, destroyed.
Pilp. צִמְתַת‎ the same.

צְמִיתַת‎ f., perfect silence; לִצְמִתַת‎,
לִצְמִיתֻת‎ completely (without power
of redemption), Lev. 25:23, 30.

צִמְּתֻתֻנִי‎ Ps. 88:17. Pil. pret. pl,
with suff., from צמת‎.

צֵן‎; see צִין‎.

צֹנֶה‎, צֹנָא‎; see צֹאן‎.

צַנֵּף, צְנִים, צְנִינִים; see **צנן**.

צַנּוֹר m., *watercourse, cataract.*

צָנַח I. *dismounted.*—II. *went down,* Jud. 4:21.

צָנַם part., f. pl. **צְנֻמוֹת** "withered," Eng. Ver.; Gen. 41:23 (meaning not very certain).

צִנִּים m. pl., *fence of thorns, thorns.* **צְנִינִים** m. pl., *thorns.*

צִנָּה f.—I. *barb of hook,* Am. 4:2.—II. *a shield.*—III. *a shield-shaped vessel* used for snow, Pro. 25:13.

צִנְצֶנֶת f., *a basket,* Ex. 16:33.

צֵן same as **צְאֹן**.

צָנַע *ready, prepared,* Pro. 11:2. Hiph. *being ready,* Mic. 6:8.

צָנַף I. *bound, wrapped round,* Isa. 22:18. — II. *wrapped round the head,* Lev. 16:4.

צָנִיף (צָנוֹף) m., *turban.*

צְנֵפָה f., *wrapping,* Isa. 22:18.

מִצְנֶפֶת f., *turban* worn by the high priest.

צָנַק root not used; (Arab. *fetters*). **צִינֹק** m., *fetters,* Jer. 29:26.

צַנְתָּרוֹת f. pl., *pipes, tubes,* Zec. 4:12.

צָעַד (fut. **יִצְעַד**; inf., with suff. **צְעַדְּךָ**). —I. *walked, advanced.*—II. *went over a country.*—III. *shot up,* Gen. 49:22. Hiph. *caused to walk, brought over,* Job 18:14.

צַעַד m.—I. *stepping,* Pro. 30:29.—II. *a step,* 2 Sa. 6:13.—III. *progress, action, conduct.*

צְעָדָה f., *marching;* pl. **צְעָדוֹת** *anklets,* Isa. 3:20.

אֶצְעָדָה f., *bracelet.*

מִצְעָד m., *step, proceeding.*

צָעָה *wandering for plunder, losing one's way, perishing.* Pi. **צָעָה** *plundered,* Jer. 48:12.

צָעִיף m., *woman's veil.*

צְעִירָה, צָעִיר *little;* see **צער**.

צָעַן *removed,* Isa. 33:20.

צַעֲנַנִּים p. n., *a city of the Kenites* in Naphtali.

צֹעַן p. n., *Zoan,* a city of Lower Egypt; possibly *Tanis.*

צַעֲצֻעִים; see **צוע**.

צָעַק (fut. **יִצְעַק**) *cried out for help,* with **אֶל, לְ**. Pi. *cried vehemently,* 2 Ki. 2:12. Hiph. *cause to be summoned,* 1 Sa. 10:17. Niph. I. *were called, summoned.*—II. *assembled themselves.*

צְעָקָה const. **צַעֲקַת** f., *a cry for help.*

צָעַר *was small, of little importance* **צֹעַר, צֹעַר** p. n., *one of the cities of* the plain, formerly **בֶּלַע**.

צָעִיר m., **צְעִירָה** f.—I. *small.*—II. *young.*—III. p. n. of a place, 2 Ki. 8:21.

צָעוֹר Ketib, same as **צָעִיר**, Jer. 14:3; 48:4.

צְעִירָה f., *smallness, inferiority in age.* **מִצְעָר** m., *little, small;* **לְמִצְעָר** *for a little time.*

מִצְעִירָה f., *of a small kind,* Dan. 8:9.

צָפַד *adhered, cleaved to,* Lam. 4:8.

I. **צָפָה** I. *kept watch.*—II. *looked for, expected;* **צוֹפֶה** *observer, watchman.*—III. *watched, observed,* with **בְּ**.—IV. *plotted against,* with

לְ. **Pi.** צִפָּה I. *kept watch.*—II. *looked, expected help.*

צְפִיחַ f., *watch-tower*, Lam. 4:17.

צָפִית f., *watch-tower*, Isa. 21:5.

צְפַת p. n., *a town of Canaan, afterwards called* חָרְמָה.

צְפָתָה p. n., *a valley near Maresha in Judah.*

מִצְפֶּה m.—I. *watch-tower.*—II. p. n., *a town in Judah.*—III. *in Moab.* —IV. *in Gad.*—V. *in Benjamin.*— VI. *a valley in the north of Palestine.*

מִצְפָּה p. n.—I. *a town in Gilead, same as* מִצְפֵּה־גִלְעָד.—II. *a town in Benjamin, same as* מִצְפָּה.

II. צָפָה *covered, overlaid with wood or metal,* with בְּ, אֶל. **Pu.** *was overlaid.*

צִפָּה s. f.; see צוּף.

צְפִי, צְפוֹ p. n., *a son of Eliphaz.*

צִפּוּי m., *covering, coat.*

צָפוֹן, צְפִין p. n. of a man; *patron.* צְפוֹנִי.

צָפוֹן, צְפוֹנִי; see צפן.
צַבֹּר, צַבָּרִים; see צפר.

צָפַח (Arab. *made broad*).

צוֹפַח, צֹפַח p. n. of a man.

צַלַּחַת f., *a dish, vessel.*

צַפִּיחִית f., *flat cake, cake.*

צִפְעוֹת, צָפִיעַ; see צפע.
צְפִירָה, צָפִיר; see צפר.
צָפִית; see צפה.

צָפַן I. *hid, concealed.* — II. *excluded,* Job 17:4.—III. *laid up, treasured up.*—IV. *lay hid, lay in wait,* with לְ: part. צָפוּן *a secret, treasure, one hidden* (of God). **Niph.** I. *was*

hidden, with מִן.—II. *was laid up, destined for,* with לְ. **Hiph.** *hid.*

צָפוֹן com. (*hidden, dark quarter*).—I. *the north.* — II. *the north wind;* מִצָּפוֹן לְ, צָפוֹן לְ *northward of any where;* צָפוֹנָה *towards the north;* לַצָּפוֹנָה *the same;* מִצָּפוֹנָה *from the north;* with לְ *from the north of any where.*—II. p. n., *a town of Gad; see also* צָפוֹן *same as* צָפִיּוֹן *in* II. צָפָה; *see also in* בַּעַל.

צְפוֹנִי m., *northern,* Joel 2:20.

צָפִין (צָפוּן) m., *treasure.*

צְפַנְיָה, צְפַנְיָהוּ (*whom the Lord hath hidden*), p. n.—I. *Zephaniah,* the prophet; LXX. Σοφονίας. — II. *other men.*

מַצְפּוּן m., *hidden place,* Obad. v. 6.

צָפְנַת פַּעְנֵחַ *the Egyptian title of Joseph; its meaning altogether unknown,* Gen. 41:45.

צֶפַע m., *basilisk,* Isa. 14:29.

צִפְעוֹנִי m. (pl. צִפְעֹנִים) *the same.*

צָפִיעַ m., pl. צְפִיעִים *dung,* Eze. 4:15 צְפִיעָה f., pl. צְפִיעוֹת, "*issue,*" Eng. Ver., Isa. 22:24.

צָפַף. **Pil.** צִפְצֵף I. *chirped* (as a bird), Isa. 10:14, &c.—II. *spoke in a low voice.*

צַפְצָפָה; see צוף.

צָפַר *hastened* (fut. יִצְפֹּר), Jud. 7:3.

צָפִיר m., *goat, he-goat.*

צְפִיר m. Ch., *the same.*

צְפִירָה f.—I. *a crown,* Isa. 28:5.—II. "*morning,*" Eng. Ver., Eze. 7:7, 10; *sense uncertain.*

צִפּוֹר com. (pl. צִפֳּרִים).—I. *a bird.*— II. *specially, a sparrow.*—III. p. n. *the father of Balaam the prophet*

צִפֹּר com. Ch., *a bird.*

צִפֹּרָה p. n., *the wife of Moses.*

צְפַרְדֵּעַ com., *a frog.*

צִפֹּרֶן m.—I. *nail of the finger.*—II. *point of the graver.*

צְפָתָה ,צִפַּח; **see** צפה.

צֶפֶת f., *capital of a pillar,* 2 Chron. 3:15.

צִצִּים; see צִיץ.

צֵק Kal. imp., from יצק.

צִקְלָג same as צִיקְלַג.

צִקָּלֹן m., *husk,* 2 Ki. 4:42

צֶקֶת Kal inf., from יצק.

צֹר ,צֵר ,צַר, see צור; צָרִי ,צְרִי, see צרר.

צָרַב. Niph. *was scorched,* Eze. 21:3.

צָרֶבֶת f.—I. *burning,* Pro. 16:27.—II. *inflammation,* Lev. 13:23, 28.

צְרֵדָה p. n., *a town of Manasseh;* צְרֵדָתָן ,צָרְתָן the same.

צָרָה s. f.; see צרר.

צְרִי ,צֳרִי, with pause צֳרִי m., *mastich,* the gum from the pistachia lentiscus.

צְרִי p. n., same as יִצְרִי; see יֵצֶר.

צְרוּיָה ,צְרוּיָה ,צְרוּדָה p. n., *the mother of Joab.*

צָרוֹד same as צָרֹד.

צָרַח *shouted,* Zep. 1:14. Hiph. the same, Isa. 42:13.

צָרִיחַ m., *a high tower.*

צֹרֶךְ m., *need, necessity,* 2 Chron. 2:15.

צָרַע, part. צָרוּעַ and Pu. part. מְצֹרָע m., מְצֹרַעַת f., *struck with leprosy.*

צְרוּעָה p. n., *the mother of Jeroboam.*

צָרְעָה p. n., *a town of the Danites in Judah;* צָרְעָתִי ,צָרְעִי *a Zarathite.*

צִרְעָה f., coll. *wasps, hornets.*

צָרַעַת f. (with suff. צָרַעְתּוֹ) *the leprosy.*

צָרַף (fut. יִצְרֹף).—I. *refined metals.*—II. *purified a person's character.*—III. *tried a person's character;* part. צֹרֵף *refiner, goldsmith, silversmith;* צָרוּף *purified, pure.* Niph. *shall be purified,* Dan. 12:10. Pi. part. מְצָרֵף *goldsmith,* Mal. 3:2, 3.

צָרְפִי (with art.), p. n. of a man.

צָרְפַת p.n., *a town between Tyre and Zidon,* Σάρεπτα, with ה loc. צָרְפַתָה.

מַצְרֵף m., *crucible.*

צָרַר I. *tied* or *bound up.*—II. *acted hostilely to.*—III. *was straitened;* part. צֹרֵר *an adversary;* impers. צַר לִי *I am distressed, grieved, concerned for some one,* with עַל. Niph. הֵצַר (inf. הָצֵר) *distressed.* Pu. part. מְצֹרָר.

צַר, with pause צָר m.—I. *difficulty, adversity, distress;* f. צָרָה; בַּצַּר לִי *when I am in distress.*—II. *enemy, besieger.*—III. *rival;* with art. הַצַּר; with suff. צָרִי; pl. צָרִים.—IV. *rock;* see צור.

צָרָה f., *enemy, adversary;* with ה parag. בַּצָּרָתָה לִי *when I am in trouble.*

צְרוֹר m. (pl. צְרֹרוֹת).—I. *a bundle.*—II. *a bag of money.*—III. *a small stone, a particle, grain.*—IV. p. n. of a man.

מֵצַר m., *restraint, trouble.*

צְרֵדָה; see צְרָרָה.

צָרֶת p. n. of a man.

צֶרֶת הַשַּׁחַר p. n., a town of Reuben.

צְרָפָם ; see צְרֵדָה.

ק

קָא vomit; see קוּא.

קָאם for קָם Kal pret., from קום.

קָאֵם Ch. Pe. part., from קום.

קָאַת (with art. הַקָּאַת ; const. קְאַת f.), a pelican or heron, not certain which.

קָבַר cursed; imp. with suff. and נ epenth. קָבְנוּ ; with ה parag. קָבָה.

קַב m., a measure, the sixth part of סְאָה, 2 Ki. 6:25.

קֻבָּה f., alcove, tent, Nu. 25:8, again in the same verse אֶל קֻבָּתָהּ "in her alcove" (Lee), generally interpreted of the person of the woman.

קֻבָּתָה, קֻבָה ; see נקב.

קָבָה root not used; (Arab. stomach).

קֵבָה f., the stomach, Deut. 18:3.

קָבָה (pronounced kŏbāh), Kal imp. with ה parag., from קבב.

קָבַל Pi. קִבֵּל I. accepted.—II. took. —III. undertook, Est. 9:23, 27. Hiph. taking hold of.

קַבֵּל Ch. Pa., received, took.

קֵבֶל prep., before, the front, 2 Ki. 15:10.

לָקֳבֵל m. (with suff. קָבְלוֹ or קֳבְלוֹ), opposing, Eze. 26:9.

קֳבֵל, לָקֳבֵל m. Ch., the front; 1. in front of.—2. in consideration of; with דִּי in consequence of; כָּל קֳבֵל דְּנָה all before that, i. e. for this reason, therefore; כָּל קֳבֵל דִּי because.

קָבְנוּ Kal imp. with suff. and נ epenth., from קבב.

קָבַע forsook, neglected.

קוֹבַע m., a helmet.

קֻבַּעַת f., a drinking cup, Isa. 51: 17, 22.

קָבַץ collected, gathered together. Niph. were assembled, assembled themselves. Pi. I. collected.—II. acquired. Pu. was gathered together, Eze. 38:8. Hith. assembled themselves.

קְבֻצָה f., collection, heap, Eze. 22:20.

קִבּוּץ m., company, troop, Isa. 57:13.

קִבְצַיִם (two heaps), p. n., a town in Ephraim.

יָקַבְצְאֵל, קַבְצְאֵל p. n., a town of Judah.

קָבַר (fut. יִקְבֹּר) and Pi. קִבֵּר buried. Niph. and Pu. was buried.

קֶבֶר m., burial place, sepulchre, with suff. קִבְרוֹ; pl. קְבָרִים, קִבְרֵי, קִבְרוֹת קְבָרוֹת.

קִבְרוֹת הַתַּאֲוָה (the graves of lust), p. n., a place in the wilderness of Sinai, Nu. 11:34.

קְבֻרָה f.—I. קְבֻרַת const. קְבוּרַת burial.—II. burial place.

קָדַד bowed his head; fut. יִקֹּד.

קִדָּה f., cassia.

קָדְקֹד m. (with suff. קָדְקֳדוֹ), crown of the head.

קָדוֹשׁ ; see קדש.

קָדַח I. struck, kindled a fire.—II. a fire was kindled.

קַדַּחַת f., a fever.

אֶקְדָּח m., a precious stone, the carbuncle, Isa. 54:12.

קָדַם. Pi. קִדֵּם I. *preceded, came before.* — II. *came upon, against.* — III. *hastened, was early,* Ps. 119: 147. Hiph. I. *anticipate,* Job 41:3. — II. *come upon any one of misfortune,* Am. 9:10.

קֶדֶם m. (*that which precedes*) — I. adv., *before, in place.* — II. s., *the east;* אֶרֶץ קֶדֶם and קֶדֶם *the east,* i. e. *eastern country;* קֵדְמָה *towards the east;* מִקֶּדֶם *from the east;* with לְ *from the eastward of any place;* בְּנֵי קֶדֶם *those to the east of Palestine.* — III. *antiquity;* מִקֶּדֶם *from of old;* adv. *formerly;* קַדְמֵי אֶרֶץ *the ancient ones of the earth.*

קָדִים m. — I. *the east.* — II. *the east wind;* קָדִימָה *eastward.*

קַדְמֹנִים m. pl., *the ancients,* Jud. 5:21.

קָדָם, קֳדָם Ch. — I. *before.* — II. מִן קֳדָם *from the presence, power of, by order of.*

קַדְמָה f. — I. *former condition.* — II. *origin,* Isa. 23:7. — III. const. קַדְמַת *before* (in time), Ps. 129:6.

קַדְמָה f. Ch., *former state or time;* מִן קַדְמַת דְּנָה *before.*

קֵדְמָה f., const. קִדְמַת *eastward of any place.*

קֵדְמָה p. n., *a son of Ishmael.*

קְדֵמוֹת p. n., *a town of the Reubenites.*

קַדְמַי m. Ch., *first, former.*

קַדְמִיאֵל p. n. of a man.

קַדְמֹן m., קַדְמֹנָה f., *eastern,* Eze. 47:8.

קַדְמֹנִי m. — I. *eastern.* — II. *former, ancient;* pl. קַדְמֹנִים *ancestors;* f.

קַדְמֹנִיּוֹת *former things.* — III. p. n. of a man.

קָדְקֹד *crown of head;* see קדד.

קָדַר I. *was dark, black, darkened.* — II. *was gloomy, distressed;* קֹדֵר *darkening, mourning.* Hiph. *made dark,* Eze. 31:15; 32:7, 8. Hith. *became dark,* 1 Ki. 18:45.

קֵדָר (*blackness*), p. n., *Kedar,* the son of Ishmael and his descendants; בְּנֵי קֵדָר *the sons of Kedar.*

קִדְרוֹן p. n., *Kedron,* a brook which flows by Jerusalem.

קַדְרוּת f., *darkness,* Isa. 50:3.

קְדֹרַנִּית adv., *mournfully,* Mal. 3:14.

קָדַשׁ, קָדֵשׁ (fut. יִקְדַּשׁ). — I. *hallowed, consecrated.* — II. *rendered sacred, set apart from,* Isa. 65:5. Niph. I. *was made holy,* Ex. 29:43. — II. *was reverenced,* with בְּ. Pi. קִדֵּשׁ I. *hallowed, set apart.* — II. *reverenced,* Deu. 32:51. — III. *kept holy.* — IV. *rendered sacred by contact,* Eze. 44:19. — V. *purified by rites.* — VI. *appointed a religious service.* — VII. *prepared,* Mic. 3:5. Pu. *was consecrated, &c.* pass. of Pi. Hiph. I. *hallowed.* — II. *reverenced.* — III. *purified.* — IV. *prepared.* Hith. I. *made himself to be reverenced.* — II. *was celebrated* (a festival). — III. *purified himself.* — IV. *kept himself pure.*

קָדֹשׁ, קָדוֹשׁ m. — I. *holy, pure* (of God, angels, and men). — II. *sacred, set apart to God;* pl. קְדֹשִׁים.

קַדִּישׁ m. Ch., *holy.*

קֹדֶשׁ, קֹדֶשׁ m. (with suff. קָדְשִׁי; pl. קֳדָשִׁים or קָדָשִׁים, const. קָדְשֵׁי). — I. *holiness.* — II. *that which is*

consecrated to God, holy; קֹדֶשׁ קָדָשִׁים Holy of Holies (the place within the vail of the tabernacle and temple).

קָדֵשׁ m. (one devoted to an idol).—I. Sodomite or, perhaps, priest of Baal-peor.—II. f. קְדֵשָׁה a harlot. III. קָדֵשׁ בַּרְנֵעַ p. n., a city of the wilderness, between Edom and Egypt.

קֶדֶשׁ p. n.—I. a town of Judah.—II. of Naphtali.—III. of Issachar, called also קִשְׁיוֹן.

מִקְדָּשׁ (מִקְדָּשׁ) m.—I. sanctuary (the tabernacle or temple).—II. sacred thing, part, Nu. 18:29.—III. asylum (place of safety).

קָהָה were set on edge (of teeth). Pi. קֵהָה became blunt (of an instrument), Ecc. 10:10.

קְהָת p. n., Kohath, the son of Levi; patron. קְהָתִי.

קָהַל. Hiph. הִקְהִיל called together, summoned. Niph. assembled themselves.

קָהָל m.—I. a meeting.—II. assemblage, multitude.—III. הַקְּ the congregation of Israel.

קְהֵלָה p. n., a station of Israel in the wilderness.

קְהִלָּה f., assembly.

קֹהֶלֶת m. (f., Ecc. 7:27), p. n. (preacher), applied to Solomon in the book of Ecclesiastes; LXX. ἐκκλησιαστής.

מַקְהֵלִים m. pl., congregations, assemblies.

מַקְהֵלוֹת f. pl.—I. the same.—II. p. n., a station in the wilderness.

קָם קוּם; see קוה.

קוא I. vomited.—II. expelled with disgust. Hiph. הֵקִיא the same.

קֵא m., a vomit, Pro. 26:11

קִיא m., the same.

קִיקָלוֹן m., "shameful spewing," Eng Ver.; Hab. 2:16.

קוֹבַע; see קבע.

קָוָה hoped in, waited for; part. קֹוֶה. Pi. קִוָּה (inf. קַוֵּה קַוֹּה; fut. יְקַוֶּה יְקַו).—I. trusted in, expected, with אֶל, לְ. — II. watched for evil, plotted against. Niph. assembled themselves.

קַו קָו m.—I. a measuring line.—II. a boundary line.—III. a limit, rule, direction, Ps. 19:5; with suff. קַוָּם.

קֶוֵה m., 1 Ki. 7:23, Ketib for קָו.

מִקְוֶה m.—I. expectation, confidence, hope.—II. one confided in.—III. collection, assemblage.

מִקְוָה f., collection, repository, Isa. 22:11.

תִּקְוָה f.—I. hope, expectation.—II. a cord, thread.—III. p. n. of a man.

קוֹחַ; see פקח.

I. קוּט (fut. יָקוּט), was wearied, loathed, scorned, with בְּ. Niph. were loathed. Hith. הִתְקוֹטֵט same as Kal, with בְּ.

II. קוּט (Arab. was broken); fut. יָקוּט will be broken, Job 8:14.

קוּל (Arab. he said).

קוֹל m. (with suff. קוֹלִי, קֹלְךָ; pl. קֹלוֹת).—I. voice.—II. cry of animals.—III. any sound; קוֹל יְהוָה the voice of the Lord, thunder.

קוֹלָיָה p. n. of a man.

קָל m. Ch., *voice, sound.*

קוּם (fut. וַיָּקָם, יָקֻם, יָקוּם).—I. *rose up.*—II. *arose from bed.*—III. *arose from an ambush.*—IV. with עַל, אֶל, בְּ *arose against in anger* (abs. קָמַי *they that rise up against me*).—V. *stood up.*—VI. *began anything.*—VII. *came into being, appeared.*—VIII. *took place.*—IX. *stood, stood firm.*—X. *was permanent* (an office).—XI. *was fixed* (of the eyes). Pi. קִיֵּם I. *strengthened, supported.*—II. *kept a resolution.*—III. *fixed a time.* Pil. קוֹמֵם I. *set up, restore.*—II. *set himself up*, Mic. 2:8. Hiph. הֵקִים (fut. וַיָּקֶם, יָקֵם, יָקִים).—I. *caused to rise up.*—II. *raised up.*—III. *strengthened.*—IV. *set up, fixed.*—V. *raised up, appointed.*—VI. *made or confirmed a covenant, or other engagement.*—VII. *put in force.* Hoph. הוּקַם I. *was set up.*—II. *was appointed.*—III. *was confirmed.* Hith. הִתְקוֹמֵם *arose against,* with לְ.

קוּם Ch. I. *arise.*—II. *stand up.*—III. *stand.* Pa. קַיֵּם *confirmed an engagement.* Aph. הֲקֵים אֲקִים (fut. יְהָקֵים, יְקִים).—I. *set up.*—II. *established.*—III. *appointed.*—IV. *confirmed.* Hoph. הֳקִים *was set up,* Dan. 7:4.

קוֹמָה f., *height, stature.*

קִים *an adversary,* Job 22:20.

קִימָה f., *the act of rising up,* Lam. 3:63.

קְיָם m. Ch., *a decree,* Dan. 6:8, 16.

קַיָּם m., קַיָּמָה f. Ch., *enduring, steadfast.*

קָמָה f. (pl. קָמוֹת), *standing corn,* specially *in the ear.*

קָמוֹן p. n., *a town of Gilead.*

קוֹמְמִיּוּת adv., *at full height, erect,* Lev. 26:13.

יְקוּם m., *all that lives,* i.e. *has been raised up,* Gen. 7:4, 23; Deu. 11:6.

מָקוֹם com. (pl. מְקוֹמוֹת).—I. *place.*—II. *habitation, residence.*—III. *room, space.*—IV. *place, country, neighbourhood;* בִּמְקוֹם אֲשֶׁר *in the place where.*

תְּקוּמָה f., *power of resisting,* Lev. 26:37.

תְּקוֹמֵם m., *an adversary,* Ps. 139:21.

קָנַן Pil. קוֹנֵן *uttered a lamentation, lamented,* with עַל, אֶל.

קִינָה f.—I. *lamentation;* pl. קִינִים קִינוֹת.—II. p. n., *a city of Judah.*

קוּם or קָסַם Pil. קוֹסֵם *cut off,* Eze. 17:9, same as קָצַץ.

קוֹץ m., *prince,* Eze. 23:23; etymon unknown.

קוֹף *ape,* 1 Ki. 10:22; 2 Chron. 9:21.

קוּף *go round,* like נָקַף; not used.

תְּקוּפָה f.—I. *orbit of the sun,* Ps. 19:7.—II. *circle of the year.*

קוּץ I. *loathed,* with בְּ.—II. *feared,* with מִפְּנֵי.—I. Hiph. הֵקִיץ *besieged,* Isa. 7:6.—II. Hiph.—1. *awoke.*—2. *arose from the dead, came to life.*—3. *was vigilant, active;* קָץ from קַיִץ *pass the summer,* Isa. 18:6.

קוֹץ m.—I. *a thorn bush;* pl. קוֹצִים, קוֹצֵי.—II. p. n. of a man.

קַיִץ m.—I. *summer.*—II. *summer fruits.*

קְוֻצּוֹת f. pl., *locks of hair*, Cant. 5:2.

קוּר *dig a well.* Pil. קִרְקֵר I. *dug down*, Num. 24:17.—II. *destroyed a people*, Isa. 22:5. Hiph. הֵקִיר *threw up water* (a well), Jer. 6:7.

קוּר m., *thread*, Isa. 59:5, 6.

קוֹרֵת; see קרה.

מָקוֹר I. *spring.*—II. *origin.*—III. *wife.*

קוֹשׁ (fut. pl. יְקוֹשׁוּן) *ensnared*, Isa. 29:21.

קִישׁ p. n. of a man.

קוּשָׁיָהוּ קִישִׁי p. n. of a man.

קִישׁוֹן p. n., *Kishon.* — I. a river of Palestine.—II. a town in Issachar.

קֶשֶׁת com. (pl. קְשָׁתוֹת).—I. *a bow.*—II. *the rainbow.*

קַשָּׁת m., *an archer*, Gen. 21:20.

קַח, in pause קָח, with ה parag. קְחָה Kal imp., from לקח.

קַח for לְקַח, Eze. 17:5; with suff. קָחָם for לְקָחָם, Hos. 11:3.

קַחַת קְחַת Kal inf., from לקח.

קֶטֶב, קֶקֶב m. (with suff. קָטְבְךָ) *cutting down, destruction.*

קָטַט same as קוט.

קָטַל *slew.*

קְטַל Ch., *slew.* Pa. קַטֵּל the same. Ithpe. and Ithpa. *was slain.*

קֶטֶל m., *slaughter*, Obad. v. 9.

קָטֹן (fut. יִקְטַן) *was small, of little importance.* Hiph. *made small*, Am. 8:5.

קָטֹן m. (pl. קְטַנִּים; f. קְטַנָּה).— I. *small, in size, quantity* or *importance.*— II. *young.*— III. s. *the little finger*; with suff. קָטְנִי or קָטְנִי.—IV. הַקָּטָן p. n. of a man.

קָטַף *plucked off.* Niph. *was cut off, withered*, Job 8:12.

קָטַר. Pi. קִטֵּר I. *burnt incense.*—II. *fumigated.*—III. *burnt fat*; part. f. pl. מְקַטְּרוֹת *altars of incense* Pu. part. f. מְקֻטֶּרֶת *was perfumed*, Cant. 3:6. Hiph. הֶקְטִיר I. *burnt incense.*—II. *burnt sacrifice.* Hoph הָקְטַר *was burnt in sacrifice*; part מֻקְטָר *offering of incense*, Mal. 1: 11.

קְטוֹרָה f., *incense*, Deu. 33:10.

קְטוּרָה p. n., *Keturah*, one of Abraham's wives.

קָטָר, pl. חַצְרוֹת קְטֻרוֹת "courts joined," Eng. Ver.; "with chimneys," marg.; *covered* (Ges.), Eze. 46:22.

קְטֹרֶת f., *incense.*

קִיטוֹר m.—I. *smoke.*—II. *vapour*, Ps. 148:8.

מִקְטָר m., *incense*, Ex. 30:1.

מִקְטֶרֶת f., *a censer.*

קְטַר (Syr. *bound*).

קְטַר m. Ch., pl. קִטְרִין.—I. *joints, ligatures.*—II. *difficulties.*

קִטְרוֹן p. n. of a place in Zebulun, called also קַטָּת.

קִיא; see קוא.

קָיָה *vomited*; imp. pl. קִיא, Jer. 25: 27.

קַיִט m. Ch., *summer*, Dan. 2:35.

קִיטוֹר; see קטר.

קִימָה, קַיִם, קָים, קִים; see קום. קִימוֹשׁ same as קִמּוֹשׁ; see קמשׁ.

קִין root not used; (Arab. *cane, a spear*).

קַיִן m.—I. *a spear made of cane*, 2 Sa 21:16.—II. p. n., *Cain*, the son of Adam.—III. p. n., the *Kenites*, a tribe of Canaan.—IV. הַקַּיִן a town of Judah.

קִינִי קֵנִי קֵינִי the *Kenites*, one of the tribes inhabiting Canaan.

קִינָה; see קון.

קֵינָן p. n. of a man.

קַיִץ *summer, &c.;* see קוץ.

קִיצוֹנָה קִיצוֹן; see קצץ.

קִיקָיוֹן m., the shrub *palma Christi*, *ricinus comm.*, κίκι.

קִיקָלוֹן; see קוא.

קִיר ,קִר com. (pl. קִירוֹת).—I. *a wall.*—II. *side of the altar.*—III. *sides of the heart*, Jer. 4:19.—IV. *city*, Isa. 15:1; 16:7.—V. קִיר מוֹאָב, קִיר חֶרֶשׂ קִיר חֲרֶשֶׂת p. n., a city of Moab.—VI. p. n., a part of Assyria.

קָרֵס קֵירֹס p. n. of a man.

קִישׁוֹן קִישׁ; see קושׁ.

קִיתָרֹם m. Ch., κίθαρις, *a harp.*

קַל קֻלָּה; see קלל.

קָל Ch. קֹל *voice;* see קול.

I. קָלָה I. *roasted.* — II. *burnt alive*, Jer. 29:22. Niph. part. נִקְלֶה *burning disease*, Ps. 38:8.

קָלִי קָלִיא m., *corn roasted in the ear.*

II. קָלָה same as קָלַל. Niph. *was despised;* part. *despised, mean.* Hiph. *despised*, Deu. 27:16.

קָלוֹן m.—I. *worthlessness.*—II. *shame.*—III. *contempt.*—IV. *pudenda.*

קַלַּחַת f., *a caldron.*

קָלַט (Arab. *deformity*); part. קָלוּט *dwarfish.*

מִקְלָט *asylum, place of refuge.*

קְלָיָה קְלָיָה p. n. of a Levite.

קָלַל (fut. יֵקַל, יֵקַלּוּ).—I. *was diminished, became shallow.*—II. *was swift.*—III. *was worthless, unworthy.* Niph. נָקַל, נָקֵל (fut. יֵקַל, יֵקַלּוּ).—I. *was thought a small, easy thing;* impers. מִן נָקַל *it is a small thing that;* עַל־נְקַלָּה *lightly, easily.*—III. *lowered himself*, 2 Sa. 6:22.—IV. *became easy*, Pro. 14:6. Pi. קִלֵּל *revile, wished ill to*, with בְּ. Pil. קִלְקֵל I. *shook arrow in divination*, Eze. 21:26 (like the Arab. *removed, shook*). Hiph. הֵקַל I. *slighted.*—II. *lightened, removed a load*, with מֵעַל, מִן. Hithpal *was shaken*, Jer. 4:24.

קַל m. (pl. קַלִּים; f. קַלָּה).—I. *swift.*—II. *swiftly.*—III. *swift-footed.*

קֵלָי p. n. of a man.

קָלָל m., *polished, shining.*

קְלָלָה, const. קִלְלַת f.—I *reviling.*—II. *a curse.*—III. *object of reviling.*

קִלְקֵל m., *worthless food*, Nu. 21:5.

קָלַס Pi. and Hith. *mocked, scorned.*

קֶלֶס m., *scorn, contempt.*

קַלָּסָה f., *the same*, Eze. 22:4.

קָלַע I. *cut out, carved.*—II. *slung*, Jud. 20:16.—III. *expelled*, Jer. 10:18; קֹלֵעַ *a slinger.* Pi. *slung a stone.*

קֶלַע m. (with suff. קַלְעוֹ; pl. קְלָעִים)—I. *a sling.*—II. *a curtain*, from its tremulous motion.

קַלָּע m., pl. קַלָּעִים *slingers*, 2 Ki. 3:25

מִקְלַעַת f., *carving, sculpture*, 1 Ki only.

קַלְקֵל; see קלל.

קַלְּשׁוֹן m., 'שְׁלֹשׁ ק three pronged pitch-fork, 1 Sa. 13:21.

קְמוּאֵל p.n. of a man.

קֹמֵץ, see קום; קְמֹשׁ, see קמשׁ.

קֶמַח m., flour.

קָמַט (Arab. bound with a rope), bound as a captive, Job 16:8. Pu. was seized and carried off, Job 22:16.

קָמַל, קָמֵל withered.

קָמַץ grasped, took up in the hand.

קֹמֶץ m. (with suff. קֻמְצוֹ).— I. the hand, fist.— II. abundance.— III. pl. קְמָצִים handfuls.

קָמַשׁ root not used.

הֶמֶשׁ קִימֹשׁ, pl. קִמְּשׂוֹנִים m., net-tles.

קֵן, קֵנִים; see קנן.

קָנָא. Pi. קִנֵּא I. was jealous for, with לְ (ζηλοῦν).— II. emulated, with בְּ; envied, with בְּ, לְ.— III. was jealous of, with בְּ. Hiph. הִקְנִיא made jealous, angry.

קַנָּא m., jealous (of God against idols only).

קַנּוֹא m., the same.

קִנְאָה f.— I. jealousy.— II. envy.— III. anger.— IV. zeal.

קָנָה (fut. apoc. וַיִּקֶן).— I. make.— II. acquire, appropriate to one-self. Niph. was acquired, pur-chased, Jer. 32:15, 43. Hiph. I. appropriated as a slave, Zec. 13: 5.— II. provoked to jealousy, Eze. 8:3.

קְנָא Ch., acquired, procured, Ezr. 7: 17.

קָנַת p.n., a town of Manasseh.

קִנְיָן m., possession, wealth.

מִקְנֶה m. (with suff. מִקְנֵהוּ; pl. מִקְנִים) possession, wealth of land, flocks, cattle; אַנְשֵׁי מ׳ possession of cattle; אֶרֶץ מ׳ land full of cattle.

מִקְנָה f., acquirement, purchase, pos-session.

מִקְנֵיָהוּ p.n. of a man.

קָנֶה m. (const. קְנֵה; with suff. קָנֶה; pl. קָנִים קְנוֹת).— I. reed, cane.— II. sweet cane.— III. measuring reed of six cubits.— IV. beam of the balance.— V. stalk of wheat.— VI. branch of candlestick.— VII. arm-bone above the elbow, Job 31: 22.— VIII. a staff to lean upon.

קָנָה p.n.— I. a place on the borders of Ephraim and Manasseh.— II. a town in Asher.

קַנּוֹא same as קַנָּא; see קנא.

קְנַז p.n.— I. of a man; קְנִזִּי patron — II. of a people of Canaan.

קֵנִי same as קֵינִי.

קִנָּמוֹן, const. קִנְּמָן m., cinnamon.

קָנַן Pi. קִנֵּן built a nest. Pu. part. מְקֻנַּנְתִּי(ב)was built (of a nest).

קֵן, const. קַן m. (with suff. קִנִּי; pl. קִנִּים).— I. a nest.— II. a dwelling —III. a family.— IV. cells, cham-bers.

קִנְצֵי for קַצֵּי, Job 18:2; see קץ in קצץ.

קָסַם divine with arrows, &c.; part. קֹסֵם diviner.

קֶסֶם m.— I. divination, enchant-ment.— II. the reward of divina-tion.

233 קצם קסם קצף

מִקְסָם m., *divination*, Eze. 12:24; 13:7.

קֶסֶם; see קום.

קֶסֶת; see קשׂה.

קְעִילָה p.n., a city of Judah.

קַעֲקַע m., *mark, impression*, Lev. 19:28.

קָעַר root not used; (Arab. *being deep*).

קְעָרָה f. (const. קַעֲרַת; pl. קְעָרוֹת, קַעֲרֹת; with suff. קְעָרֹתָיו) *deep saucer, dish.*

קָפָא I. *congealed* (of waters).— II. *hardened* (of men), Zep. 1:12. Hiph. *condense*, Job 10:10.

קִפָּאוֹן m., *congealing, denseness*, Zec. 14:6.

קָפַד (Arab. *finished his work*). Pi. *finished, cut short*, Isa. 38:12.

קֶפֶד, with ה parag. קְפָדָה m., *destruction*, Eze. 7:25.

קִפֹּד m., *a hedge-hog*; (Arab. the same).

קָפַז (Arab. *springing serpent*). קִפּוֹז m., *one of the springing snakes*, Isa. 34:15.

קָפַץ *shut up, close, constrict* (the hand, &c.)— Niph. *are shut up*, Job 24:24. Pi. *leaping*, Cant. 2:8.

קֵץ *end*; see קצץ.

קָצַב I. *cut wood*, 2 Ki. 6:6.—II. *shear sheep*, Cant. 4:2.

קֶצֶב m., *clefts of the mountains*.—II. *form, character*, Jon. 2:7.

קָצָה I. *cut off, destroy*.—II. *cut down*. Pi. *cutting off, down*, 2 Ki. 10:32; Pro. 26:6. Hiph. *cut, scraped, off*; inf. הַקְצוֹת.

קָצֶה m. (const. קְצֵה; with suff. קָצֵהוּ; pl. קְצָוִים, (קְצֵי) *end, extremity, limit*; הָעָם מִקָּצֶה *men from all parts*; מִקְצֵה שְׁלֹשֶׁת יָמִים *at the end of three days*.

קֵצֶה m., the same.

קָצָה f., *extremity, border, limit*; מִקָּצֶה *from the extreme parts*; pl. קָצוֹת, with הָעָם *the extremities of the people*, i.e. any of them.

קְצָה f. Ch., *end*.

קָצְו m., pl. const. קַצְוֵי *extremities, borders.*

קְצָווֹת f. pl., the same.

מִקְצָת f.—I. *end, limit*; מִקְצָת יָמִים *at the end of ten days*.— II. Ch. *a part*.

קָצִין m.—I. *judge*.— II. *governor*.— III. *prince*.

מִקְצָת f., *part, limit*.

קֶצַח m., *black pepper*, Isa. 28:25, 27.

קָצִיר *harvest*; see קצר.

קָצַע. Hiph. הִקְצִיעַ *scrapes off*, Lev. 14:41. Pu. part. מְקֻצְעוֹת and Hoph. part. מְהֻקְצָעוֹת *small courts*, Eze. 46:22.

קְצִיעָה f., κασσία.—I. *cassia*, Ps. 45:9.—II. p.n., a daughter of Job, *Keziah*.

מִקְצוֹעַ m., *corner, angle*; pl. מִקְצֹעִים, מִקְצֹעוֹת.

מַקְצֻעָה f., "planes," Eng. Ver., Isa. 44:13.

קָצַף *was angry, wroth, enraged*, with אֶל, עַל. Hiph. *made angry*, with אֶת. Hithp. *became wroth*, Isa. 8:21.

קְצַף Ch., *was angry*.

קֶצֶף m.— I. *a broken branch, stick*,

Hos. 10:7. — II. *anger, wrath of God*, with suff. קִצְפִּי ,קִצְפְּךָ.

קְצַף m. Ch., *anger.*

קְצָפָה f., *fracture, wasting*, Joel 1:7.

קָצַץ *cut off.* Pi. קִצֵּץ ,קִצַּץ *cut off.* Pu. part. מְקֻצָּצִים, Jud. 1:7.

קְצַץ Ch. Pa. *cut off.*

קֵץ m. (with suff. קִצּוֹ; pl. קִצִּים ,קְצֵי).
—I. *end, limit.*—II. *end, cessation.*—III. *end, ruin;* מִקֵּץ *from the end* (of the earth), *at the end* (of a time); לְקֵץ *the same;* עֵת קֵץ, קֵץ הַיָּמִים ,מוֹעֵד קֵץ *the time of the end,* i.e. of our Lord's first and second advent.

קִיצוֹן m., קִיצוֹנָה f., *the last*, Exodus only.

I. קָצַר (fut. יִקְצֹר), *cut down, reap;* part. *reaper.* Hiph. *reaped*, Job. 24:6.

קָצִיר I. *crop.* — II. *harvest.* — III. *branches.*

II. קָצַר (fut. יִקְצַר).—1. *short, deficient, unable for.*—2. with רוּחַ or נֶפֶשׁ *unable to bear up, discouraged.* Pi. קִצֵּר *made short*, Ps. 102:24. Hiph. *made short*, Ps. 89:46.

קָצֵר m., *short, cut off;* קְצַר אַפַּיִם, קְצַר רוּחַ *angry.*

קֹצֶר m., with רוּחַ *impatience*, Ex. 6:9.

קָר קָרִים ,קֹר; see קָרַר.
קַר *same as* קִיר.

I. קָרָא (inf. קְרֹא קְרֹאות with suff. קָרְאִי; imp. קְרָא; fut. יִקְרָא).—
1. *cried, called, shouted.*—2. *called to* or *for*, with אֶל.—3. *called after*, with אַחֲרֵי.—4. *call upon in prayer.*—5. *celebrate.*—6. *call*

by name, name, with לְ.—7. *call together, assemble, invite*, with אֵת ,אֶל.—8. *called into question litigation.*—9. *appointed to an office.*—10. *called forth soldiers*, Isa. 13:3.—11. *proclaim, publish, preach.*—12. *read from a book, read aloud*, Deu. Niph. נִקְרָא 1. *called for, summoned.*—2. *called together, assembled*, with בְּ or בְּשֵׁם פ' *in the name of some one.*—3. *named*, with שֵׁם פ' עַל *the name of some one is upon thee*, with שֵׁם יְהֹוָה עַל *the name of the Lord is named upon thee*, Deu. 28:10. Pu. קֹרָא *called, named*, with לְ.

קְרָא Ch., *read, recited, proclaimed.* Ithp. *was called*, Dan. 5:12.

קֹרֵא m.—I. *partridge.*—II. p. n. of a man.

קָרִיא m., *called, sent*, Numbers only.

קְרִיאָה f., *cry, proclamation*, Jon. 3:2.

מִקְרָא m.—I. *act of assembly.*—II. *convocation.*—III. *reading, reciting*, Neh. 8:8.

II. קָרָא *same as* קָרָה 1. *approached, met hostilely.*—2. *met.*—3. *happened;* inf. לִקְרַאת ,קִרְאָה *to meet, meeting with;* with suff. לִקְרָאתְךָ *over, against thee;* לִקְרָאתְכֶם *over against you.* Niph. 1. *met, happened to meet*, with עַל.—2. *happened;* fut. יִקָּרֵא; inf. נִקְרֹא. Hiph. *cause to happen to*, Jer. 32:23.

קָרֶאןָ for קְרֶאנָה Kal imp. pl. f., Ex 2:20, from I. קָרָא

קְרֹאות Kal inf., with וּ quiescent, Jud 8:1, from I. קָרָא

קָרֵב ,קָרַב (fut. יִקְרַב; inf. קְרֹב; imp. קְרַב; קָרְבָה).—I. *approached*

drew near, with לִפְנֵי, בְּ, לְ, אֶל.
—II. *attacked*, with עַל, אֶל.—III.
keep by thyself, with אֶל. Isa. 65:5.
Niph. *should, ought to draw near.*
Pi. קֵרַב *made, caused to draw near.*
Hiph. I. *made approach.*— II. *pre-
sented.*—III. *removed*, with בְּ, מִן.

קְרֵב Ch., *came to.* Pa. *offered.* Aph.
brought to, offered.

קָרֵב m., *approaching, drawing near.*

קָרוֹב m., קְרוֹבָה f., *near, at hand*,
with אֶל, לְ (*of time, place, things,
&c.*); מִקָּרוֹב adv., *short, shortly,
soon.*

קְרָב m., *contest, battle, war;* pl.
קְרָבוֹת.

קְרָב m. Ch., the same.

קֶרֶב m. (with suff. קִרְבִּי; pl. with
suff. קְרָבַי).—I. *inward part, entrails.*—II. *amidst, among,* often
בְּקֶרֶב, מִקֶּרֶב the same.

קִרְבָה const. קִרְבַת f., *approach, access.*

קָרְבָּן const. קָרְבַּן m., *offering.*
קֻרְבָּן m., the same.

קָרְבָתָם Kal inf., with ה parag. and
suff., from קרב.

קַרְדֹּם (with suff. קַרְדֻּמּוֹ; pl. קַרְדֻּמִּים,
קַרְדֻּמּוֹת), *an axe.*

קֹרָה s. f.; see קרר.

קָרָה; see קָרָא II. (fut. יִקְרֶה, וַיִּקֶר),
met, happened, with לְ. Niph. *met
with persons only,* with אֶל, לִפְנֵי,
עַל *met accidentally, dropped in
with.* Pi. קֵרָה *framed together,
made to join.* Hiph. I. *made,
caused to meet with him*, Gen.
27:20.—II. הִקְרָה לוֹ *made convenient for him*, Nu. 35:11.

קְרֵה m., קְרֵה־לַיְלָה *accidental pollution during sleep,* Deu. 23:11.

קוֹרָה f.—I. *a beam.*—II. *a roof*, Gen.
19:8.

קְרִי in pause קֶרִי m., *meeting, opposing*; בְּקֶרִי or הָלַךְ קְרִי עִם *he
opposed, resisted.*

קִרְיָה f., *a town* or *city,* combined in
the names of many cities.—I. קִרְיַת
in the tribe of Benjamin.—II.
קִרְיַת אַרְבַּע in the tribe of Judah,
afterwards Hebron.—III. ק׳ בַּעַל
same as ק׳ יְעָרִים.—IV. ק׳ חֻצּוֹת
in Moab.—V. ק׳ יְעָרִים, ק׳ עָרִים
in Judah.—VI. ק׳ סַנָּה, ק׳ סֵפֶר in
Judah, called also דְּבִיר.— VII.
קִרְיָתַיִם 1.in Reuben.—2. in Naphtali, called also קַרְתָּן.—VIII. קִרְיוֹת
in Moab. קִרְיָא, קִרְיָה Ch.

קֶרֶת f.—I. *a city.*—II. *a pulpit*, Job
29:7.

קַרְתָּה p. n., a town of Zebulun.

מִקְרֶה m.—I. *accident.*—II. *event,
result.*

מְקָרֶה m., *building, edifice,*Ecc.10:18.

קָרַח and Hiph. הִקְרִיחַ *shaved, made
bald.* Niph. and Hoph. *have made
themselves, become, bald.*

קֹרַח p. n. of a man.

קֵרֵחַ m., *bald* (on the crown of the
head).

קֶרַח m.—I. *cold.*—II. *frost, ice.*—III.
crystal, Eze. 1:22.

קֹרַח m.—I. *frost, ice,* Ps. 147:17.—
II. p. n., *Korah*, a son of Esau.—
III. a son of Eliphaz.—IV. the
Levite who conspired against Moses,
patron. קָרְחִי.—V. applied to other
men.

קָרְחָא, קָרְחָה f., *baldness.*

קָרַחַת f., *thread bare* (of cloth), Lev.
c. 13 only

קְרִיוֹת ,קְרִיַת ,קְרִיָה ,קְרִי; see קרה.
קְרִיאָה ,קָרִיא; see קרא.

קָרַם *overlaid, cased,* with עַל; fut. יִקְרְם Eze. 37:6, 8.

קֶרֶן f. (dual. קַרְנַיִם ,קַרְנַיִם, pl. קְרָנוֹת, (קְרָנוֹת).—I. *the horn of an animal.*—II. *used as a vessel for oil.*—III. *used as a trumpet,* Jos. 6:5.—IV. Isa. 5:1, " a very fruitful hill," Eng. Ver.; " a horn, the son of oil ;" marg. perhaps Mount Tabor.—V. metaphorically, *power, strength,* in men or states.—VI. probably the name of a weapon, 2 Sa. 22:3.—VII. *the ornaments at each corner of the altar.*—VIII. *rays of light,* Hab. 3:4.

קְרֵן com. Ch., *horn.*
קָרַן *v.* denom., *emitted rays, shone* (the face of Moses), Exodus c. 34 only. Hiph. *produced horns,* Ps. 69:32.

קָרַס *became bent, bowed down,* Isa. 46:2.
קֶרֶס m., *hook, link, loop.*
קֶרֶס same as קֵירַם.

קַרְסֻלַּיִם m. dual, *ankles.*

קָרַע *tore, rent* (as a garment, &c.); once, of the eyes, Jer. 4:30, "*thou rendest* thine eyes with stibium," i. e. givest them an enlarged appearance as if they were torn open; this is the effect of it. Niph. *was torn, rent.*

קְרָעִים m. pl., *rendings, pieces, rags.*

קָרַץ *closed, pressed together* (the lips or eyes, denoting fraud or cunning). Pu. *was cut, hewn out,* Job 33:6.

קֶרֶץ m., *destruction,* Jer. 46:20.
קְרַץ m. Ch., *rending.*

קַרְקַע m.—I. *basis, foundation of the Tabernacle.*— II. p.n., a town of Judah.
קַרְקֹר p.n. of a place.

קָרַר (Arab. *was cold, quiet*).
קַר or קָר m., *cold water*; pl. קָרִים *cool, quiet,* Pro. 17:27.
קֹר m., *cold* (season), Gen. 8:22.
קָרָה f., *cold, chilliness.*
מְקֵרָה f., *coolness, refreshing,* Jud. 3:20.

קָרַשׁ (Arab. *he cut*).
קֶרֶשׁ m.—I. *plank or board.*—II. *bench of a ship,* Eze. 27:6.

קָרַת ,קַרְתָּה ,קַרְתָּן; see קרה.

קָשָׂה (Arab. *wicker basket*).
קְשָׂוֹת ,קְשָׂוֹת f. pl., *small vessel, patten, phial,* or the like.
קֶסֶת f., *inkhorn carried in the girdle,* Eze. 9:2, 3, 11.
קַשְׂקֶשֶׂת m., pl. קַשְׂקַשִּׂים.—I. *scales of a fish.*— II. *scale armour,* 1 Sa. 17:5.
קַשְׂקֶשֶׂת f., the same.

קָשַׂט (Arab. *pair of scales*).
קְשִׂיטָה f., *a piece of silver, weighed out to pass for a given value as money.*
קַשׁ; see קָשַׁשׁ.
קִשֻּׁאִים; see קשה.

קָשַׁב (fut. יִקְשַׁב) *attend, listen,* Isa. 32:3. Hiph. *attended to, regarded* with בְּ, לְ, עַל, אֶל.
קֶשֶׁב m., *attention, hearkening.*
קַשָּׁב f. קַשֻּׁבָה *attentive,* Neh. 1:6, 11.

קָשׁוּב, f. pl. קַשֻׁבוֹת attentive.

קָשָׁה I. was hard, grievous.—II. was difficult, Deu. 1:17. Niph. part. נִקְשָׁה subject to difficulty, Isa. 8: 21. Pi. hardened (fut. apoc. וַתְּקַשׁ). Hiph. הִקְשָׁה (fut. apoc. וַיַּקְשׁ).— I. hardened. — II. made grievous, difficult. — III. made refractory, Pro. 28:14; Job 9:4.

קָשֶׁה m., קָשָׁה f.—I. obdurate, unyielding, cruel. — II. with עֹרֶף stiff-necked, obstinate.—III. with פָּנִים impudent, Eze. 2:4. — IV. hard, grievous (of servitude).—V. with רוּחַ overwhelmed, depressed, 1 Sa. 1:15.

קְשִׁי m., obstinacy, Deu. 9:27.

קִשְׁיוֹן p.n., a place in Issachar; קֶדֶשׁ the same.

קִשֻּׁאִים m. pl., cucumbers, Nu. 11:5.

מִקְשֶׁה m., wreathed work.

מִקְשָׁה f.—I. wreathed work. — II. place, garden, of cucumbers, Isa. 1:8.

קָשַׁח. Hiph.—I. made obdurate, Isa. 63:17.—II. treated hardly, Job 39:16.

קֹשְׁט, קֶשֶׁט m., religious truth.

קְשׁוֹט m. Ch., truth.

קָשַׁר (fut. יִקְשֹׁר).—I. tied, bound; part. קָשׁוּר bound, firm.—II. conspired against. Niph. bound, made firm, sure, Neh. 3:38; metaph., 1 Sa. 18:1. Pi. I. bind on (as ornaments), Isa. 49:18. — II. secure to thyself, Job 38:31. Pu. part. f. מְקֻשָּׁרוֹת compact, Gen. 30:41. Hith. conspired.

קֶשֶׁר m. (with suff. קִשְׁרוֹ) conspiracy treason.

קִשֻּׁרִים m. pl., bandages, belts.

קָשַׁשׁ collect, assemble together, Zep. 2:1. Po. קֹשֵׁשׁ collect, gather. Hithpo. assemble yourselves, Zep. 2:1.

קַשׁ m.—I. stubble.—II. chaff.

קֶשֶׂת מֶשֶׁת; see קוּשׁ.

קִיתָרֹם same as קַתְרֹם.

ר

רָאָה (inf. abs. רָאֹה, רָאוֹ; const. רְאוֹת, רְאֹה; imp. רְאֵה; fut. יִרְאֶה; apoc. יֵרֶא, וַיַּרְא, וַתֵּרֶא).— I. saw, viewed, observed, with לְ.— II. looked out, provided, chose, cared for, with עַל, בְּ, אֶל.— III. visited (a sick person, &c.).— IV. saw the sun, lived, Ecc. 7:11.—V. perceived, found, felt, with בְּ.— VI. discern, discriminate (as a soothsayer). Niph. נִרְאָה (inf. הֵרָאֶה, הֵרָאוֹת; imp. הֵרָאֵה; fut. יֵרָאֶה; apoc. וַיֵּרָא).—I. was seen, apparent, appearing, with אֶת-פְּנֵי, לְ, אֶל. — II. was provided. Pu. רֹאוּ were seen, Job 33:21. Hiph. הִרְאָה (fut. יַרְאֶה, וַיַּרְא).—I. showed.—II. see, experience, evil, with בְּ. Hoph. הָרְאָה.—I. was seen.—II. was shown. Hith. הִתְרָאָה looked at each other.

רָאָה, Deu. 14:13, an incorrect reading for דָּאָה, a vulture or kite.

רֹאֶה m., seer, prophet.

רַאֲוָה, Eze. 28:17, Kal inf., from ראה.

רְאוּת, רְאִית seeing, viewing, Ecc. 5:10.

רְאוּבֵן (*behold a son!*), p.n., Reuben, Jacob's eldest son; patron. רְאוּבֵנִי *a Reubenite.*

רְאִי m., *mirror*, Job 37:18

רְאִי with pause רֹאִי m.—I. *vision, revelation.*—II. *appearance, sight.*—III. *monstrosity*, Nah. 3:6.

רְאָיָה p.n. of a man.

רֵו m. Ch., *aspect, appearance.*

מַרְאֶה m.—I. *vision, appearance.*—II. *view, sight.*

מַרְאָה f.—I. *vision* (seen by a seer).—II. *mirror*, Ex. 38:8.

רָאַם *was raised, elevated*, Zec. 14:10.

רְאֵם m.(pl. רֵמִים, רְאֵמִים, רְאָמִים) *buffalo, wild ox*; LXX. *unicorn*, μονόκερως.

רָאמוֹת f. pl.—I. *things high, sublime*, Pro. 24:7.—II. *most precious.*—III. p.n.: (a) a town of Issachar; (b) of Gilead.

רְאוּמָה p.n. of a woman.

רָאמֹת נֶגֶב p.n., same as רָמֹת נֶגֶב; see רֹאשׁ רֹאשׁ.

רֹאשׁ m. (pl. רָאשִׁים; with suff. רָאשֵׁיהֶם, רֹאשָׁיו).—I. *head of man or beast.*—II. *chief, leader.*—III. *metropolis, chief city.*—IV. *top of a mountain*, &c.—V. *first, chief, principal of any thing*; רֹאשׁ שִׂמְחָה *chief joy.*—VI. *capital, amount, sum* (of numbers, money, &c.).—VII. *source, commencement* (of a river).—VIII. *an unknown poisonous plant, poison.* Phrases: נָשָׂה רֹאשׁ מֵרֹאשׁ *appointed a chief; from the beginning*; רֹאשׁ חֳדָשִׁים *the first month* (of the year);

רֹ' פִּנָּה *head stone of the corner*; רֹ' דֶּרֶךְ *a cross way*, Eze. 16:25; רֹאשׁ חוּצוֹת *the head of the streets*, רֹאשִׁים *sources of rivers*, Gen. 2:10

רֹאשׁ m. Ch. (pl. רֵאשִׁין, רָאשִׁין).—I. *head.*—II. *chapter, summary*, Dan. 7:1.

אֶבֶן הָרֹאשָׁה f., *head stone*, Zec. 4:7.

רֵאשָׁה f., *beginning*, Eze. 36:11.

רַאֲשׁוֹת pl. const. מְרַאֲשֹׁתָי *the part about the head* (of Saul), 1 Sa. 26:12.

רִאשׁוֹן (for רֵאשׁוֹן, רִאישׁוֹן) m.—I. *first, former, foremost* (in time, place, dignity, &c.); pl. רִאשֹׁנִים *ancestors*; מֵרֵאשׁוֹן *from the beginning*; f. רִאשֹׁנָה *the same.*—II. adv. *formerly*; בָּרִאשֹׁנָה *in front*; כְּבָרִאשֹׁנָה *as formerly*, Isa. 1:26; לָרִאשֹׁנָה *formerly*; pl. רִאשֹׁנוֹת *former things.*

רִאשֹׁנִי, f. רִאשֹׁנִית *first*, Jer. 25:1.

רֵאשִׁית, רֵשִׁית f.—I. *first, former, in state or time.*—II. *firstfruits, firstborn.*—III. *first of way, beginning.*

מַרְאָשׁוֹת f. pl., *places or things where the head is.*

מְרַאֲשׁוֹת f. pl., the same; with suff. מְרַאֲשׁוֹתָיו *at his head.*

מָרֵשָׁה, מַרְאֵשָׁה p.n.: (a) a fortress of Judah, Μαρισά; (b) of a man.

רֹאשׁ, רוֹשׁ m., *poison*; see רֹאשׁ.

רֹאשׁ p.n., a northern nation: probably the Ῥῶς of the Byzantine authors; now Russia.

רֵב same as רִיב.

רָבַב (pret. רָב, inf. רֹב).—I. *became many, numerous.* Pu. see רְבָבָה

רַב m. (in pause רָב, pl. רַבִּים; f. רַבָּה, pl. רַבּוֹת).—I. *much, many.* — II. *abundant, enough.* — III. *great, vast,* in extent, station, dignity, &c.

רַבָּה (*metropolis*) p.n.—I. the chief city of Ammon.—II. a city of Judah.

רַב m. Ch. (pl. רַבְרְבִין).—I. *great, large.*—II. s., *great men, nobles.*

רֹב, רוֹב, רֻבְּכֶם m. (with suff. רֻבְּכֶם) *multitude, abundance.* לָרֹב *abundantly.*

רְבָבָה f., *ten thousand, myriad;* pl. רְבָבוֹת *myriads.* Pu. denom. part. מְרֻבָּבוֹת *increased to myriads,* Ps. 144:13.

רִבּוֹ, רְבוֹא f., the same; dual רִבּוֹתַיִם *two myriads;* pl. רִבְּאוֹת, רִבֹּאוֹת *myriads.*

רִבּוֹ Ch., the same; pl. רִבְּבָן (רִבְוָן).

רְבִיבִים m. pl., *showers.*

רַבִּית p.n., a city of Issachar.

רַבְרְבָן m. Ch., *a prince.*

רַבְשָׁקֵה p.n., *Rabshakeh,* leader of the Assyrians.

II. רָבַב *shot,* as arrows, &c. Pret. pl. רַבּוּ.

רָבַד *spread, strewed, made up,* Pro. 7:16; (Arab. *tied, bound*).

רָבִיד m., *collar, neck-chain;* (Arab. the same).

מַרְבַדִּים m. pl., *coverlets.*

רָבָה (fut. יִרְבֶּה, apoc. יֵרֶב, יִרֶב).—I. *became many, multiplied.*—II. *grew.*—III. *was great, powerful.* Pi. רִבָּה *made much,* Ps. 44:13. Hiph. הִרְבָּה (fut. יַרְבֶּה; apoc. יֶרֶב; imp. הֶרֶב; inf. abs. הַרְבֵּה, הַרְבָּה;

const. הַרְבּוֹת).—I. *multiplied, increased.*—II. *extended, made large.* — III. *made great.* Inf. הַרְבֵּה, sometimes הַרְבּוֹת adv. *much, very much;* לְהַרְבֵּה *plentifully.*

רְבָה Ch., *grew great,* Dan. 4:8, 19. Pa. *became great,* Dan. 2:48.

רַבָּה, רִבּוֹא, רִבּוֹא, רְבוֹת, רְבִיבִים; see רבב.

רְבוּ, רִבְבוּת f. Ch., *greatness.*

אַרְבֶּה m., a species of *locust,* so called from the multitudes of them.

מַרְבֶּה m., *greatness, abundance.*

מִרְבָּה f., *much, too much,* Eze. 23:32.

מַרְבִּית, f.—I. *abundance.*—II. *increase, interest.*—III. *offspring.*

תַּרְבּוּת f., *progeny,* Nu. 32:14.

תַּרְבִּית f., *usury.*

רָבִיד; see רבד.

רְבִיעִי, רְבִיעִית; see רבע.

רָבַךְ (Arab. *mixed*). Hoph. part. מֻרְבֶּכֶת *mixed, saturated.*

רִבְלָה p.n., *Riblah,* a city to the north of Palestine.

I. רָבַע *lying with* (carnally). Hiph. *cause to lie with.*

רֶבַע m., *lying down,* with suff. רִבְעִי Ps. 139:3; see also below.

II. רָבַע from רֶבַע; אַרְבַּע, אַרְבָּע part. רָבוּעַ *four-sided;* pl. רְבֻעִים. Pu. part. מְרֻבָּע m., מְרֻבַּעַת f., *made four-sided.*

רֶבַע I. *fourth part of anything, side* of anything square.—II. p.n., a king of Midian.

רֹבַע m., *fourth part.*

רְבִיעִי m., *the fourth,* רְבִיעִית f., *fourth part;* בְּנֵי רִבֵּעִים *children of the fourth generation.*

רְבִיעַ m. Ch., *fourth*.

רִבֻּעִים m. pl., *posterity in the fourth degree*.

אַרְבַּע f., אַרְבָּעָה, אַרְבַּעַת m. — I. *four*; with suff. אַרְבַּעְתָּם *they four*; dual אַרְבַּעְתַּיִם *fourfold*; pl. אַרְבָּעִים *forty.*—II. p. n. of a giant.

אַרְבַּע f., אַרְבָּעָה m. Ch., *the same*.

רָבַץ (fut. יִרְבַּץ).— I. *lie down* (of beasts, &c.)—II. *lie upon the conscience, soul*, of sin, Gen. 4:7, &c. Hiph. I. *cause to lie down.*—II. *set* (of precious stones), Isa. 54:11.

רֶבֶץ m.—I. *crib, lying place of cattle.*—II. *resting place* (for man), Pro. 24:15.

מַרְבֵּץ m., *a resting place, for cattle or wild beasts*, Zep. 2:15.

מִרְבָּץ m., *the same*, Eze. 25:5.

רָבַק (Arab. *tied up to fatten*.)

רִבְקָה p. n., *Rebecca*, the wife of Isaac, Ῥεβέκκα.

מַרְבֵּק m., *stall for feeding cattle*.

רַבְשָׁקֵה, רַבְרְבִן, רַבְרְבִין; see I. רבב.

רֶגֶב m., pl. רְגָבִים—I. *clods of earth*, Job 38:38.—II. *stones set up as monuments*, Job 21:33.

רָגַז (imper. רְגַז, רְגָזָה pl. רִגְזוּ; fut. יִרְגַּז).—I. *shook, trembled.*—II. *became disturbed, agitated*. Hiph. I. *move.*—II. *agitate, disturb*, with לְ. Hith. *thy commotion, excitement*, with אֶל.

רְגַז Ch. Aph., *provoked, excited to anger*.

רֹגֶז m. — I. *vexation, trouble*. — II. *neighing*, Job 39:24. — III. *fury*,

anger, Hab. 3:2. — IV. *roar of thunder*, Job 37:2.

רְגַז m. Ch., *anger*, Dan. 3:13.

רַגָּז m., *trembling*, Deu. 28:65.

רָגְזָה f., *perturbation*, Eze. 12:18

אַרְגָּז m., "*coffer*," Eng. Ver., 1 Sa 6:8, 11, 15; (Arab. *a panier*, on one side of a camel's pack saddle: also, the sack of stones hung on the other side when but one panier is used.)

רָגַל *go about speaking evil, backbite*, Ps. 15:3. Pi. I. *goes about calumniating*, with בְּ, 2 Sa. 19:28. — II. *explore as a spy*; part מְרַגְּלִים *spies*, Gen. 42:9. Tiphel תִּרְגַּל *was near* (at foot, i. e., at hand), Hos. 11:3.

רֶגֶל com. (dual רַגְלֵי, רַגְלַיִם) *the foot*, בְּרַגְלֵי פּ׳ *at the feet of any one*; לְרַגְלֵי פּ׳ *on account of any one*. (For many other idiomatic usages of רֶגֶל see Fürst's Concordance.) Pl. רְגָלִים *strokes of the feet, times, repetitions*.

רְגַל com. Ch., *foot*.

רַגְלִי m., *foot soldier*; pl. רַגְלִים *infantry*, Jer. 12:5.

דֹּגְלִים p.n.—I. see עֵין.—II. pl. a place in Gilead.

מַרְגְּלוֹת f. pl., *at the feet, anything at the feet*.

רָגַם *stone to death*, with בְּ, עַל.

רִגְמָה f., *stone of defence*, Ps. 68:28

מַרְגֵּמָה f., *heap of stones*, Pro. 26:8

רֶגֶם p. n. of a man.

רֶגֶם מֶלֶךְ p. n. of a man.

רָגַן and Niph. נִרְגָּן *murmuring*; with בְּ *against*.

רָגַע I. *hastens to decay* (the skin), Job 7:5.—II. *calms* (the sea), Job 26:12. Niph. *rested*, Jer. 47:6. Hiph. I. *rested, found rest.* — II. *give, restore to, make to, rest.*

רָגֵעַ m., *quiet, peaceable*, Ps. 35:20.

רֶגַע m., *instant, moment of time*; רֶגַע כְּרֶגַע בְּרֶגַע adv. *in a moment, suddenly*; לִרְגָעִים *moment after moment, incessantly.*

מַרְגּוֹעַ m., *rest, quiet*, Jer. 6:16.

מַרְגֵּעָה f., the same, Isa. 28:12.

רָגַשׁ *are tumultuous, in uproar*, Ps. 2:1.

רְגַשׁ Ch., the same. Aph. *assembled tumultuously.*

רֶגֶשׁ m., *tumult, multitude shouting*, Ps. 55:15.

רִגְשָׁה f., the same, Ps. 64:3.

רֵד, Isa. 45:1, Kal inf., from רדד; Jud. 19:11, for יָרַד.

רֵד Kal imp., from ירד.

רָדַד *brings down, subdues*, Ps. 144:2; Isa. 45:1. Hiph. *lays down on*, 1 Ki. 6:32.

רַדַּי p.n. of a man.

רָדִיד m., *loose mantle, veil*, Cant. 5:7; Isa. 3:23.

רָדָה (fut. apoc. יֵרְדְּ; pl. יִרְדּוּ).—I. *subdue, rule, govern*, with בְּ; of fire, Lam. 1:13.—II. *took down*, Jud. 14:9. Hiph. *cause to rule, govern*; fut. apoc. יַרְדְּ, Isa. 41:2.

רְדָה I. in pause רָדָה Kal imp. with ה parag., Gen. 46:3, inf. with ה parag., from ירד.

רָדַם. Niph. נִרְדָּם *be insensible, as in deep sleep, fast asleep.*

תַּרְדֵּמָה f., *deep sleep, stupor, trance.*

רֹדֵם Kal part. with suff., from רדה.

רוֹדָנִים p.n., 1 Chron. 1:7, an unknown people to the west of Canaan.

רָדַף I. *followed after.*—II. *pursued as an enemy*, with אֶל, לְ, אַחֲרֵי. Pi *followed, pursued.* Hiph. *chased*, Jud. 20:43. Niph. and Pu. I. *was pursued.* — II. *succeeded*, Ecc. 3:15.

מֻרְדָּף m. (Hoph. part.) *pursued, chased*, Isa. 14:6.

רֶדֶת Kal inf., from ירד.

רָהַב I. *deal with as fearing*, Pro. 6:3.—II. *insult*, with בְּ. Hiph. *embolden*, Cant. 6:5.

רַהַב m.—I. *insolence*, Job 9:13; 26:12.—II. a prophetic name for Egypt.

רְהָב m., *insolent*, Ps. 40:5.

רֹהַב m., *pride, insolence*, Ps. 90:10.

רְהָבָה p. n. of a man.

תִּרְהוּ, רָהָה; see יָרֵא.

רָהַט (Syr. *stream*; Arab. *strap, thong, household goods*).

רַהַט m., pl. רְהָטִים—I. *watering trough.* — II. *thongs*, Cant. 7:6; " *like a king bound in thongs*" (Lee).

רָהִיט m., pl. רָהִיטִים *furniture, furnishing* (of a house), φατνώματα, Cant. 1:17.

רוּ *aspect*; see ראה.

רוּב *strife*; see ריב.

רוֹב same as רֹב *many*; see רבב.

רוּד *walked with* (God), Hos. 12:1. Hiph. I. *wander* (mentally), Ps. 55:3.—II. *wander, be a nomade people*, Gen. 27:40.

שָׂרוּד m., *one persecuted*, Lam. 3:19; מָרוּדִים *persecuted ones*, Lam. 1:7.

רָוָה *was satiated* (with anything), with מִן. Pi. רִוָּה I. *was satiated, filled.* — II. *fill, delight, satisfy.* Hiph. הִרְוָה *satiate, fill.*

רָוֶה m., רָוָה f.—I. *soaked, satiated.* — II. *drunken*, Deu. 29:18.

רִי m., *irrigation*, Job 37:11.

רְוָה f., *abundance, plenty of water.*

רָז m. Ch., *a secret.*

רִיחַ, רוּחַ Hiph. הֵרִיחַ I. *smell* (sweet odour).—II. *was satisfied, appeased.* —III. *was inspired with*, with בְּ, Isa. 11:3.—IV. *feel the fire*, Jud. 16:9. —V. *perceive*, Job 39:25.

רוּחַ com. (pl. רוּחוֹת, רֻחוֹת).—I. *air, breeze, cool breeze.* — II. *breath.*— III. *spirit, soul of man.*—IV. *mind, spirit, disposition.* — V. *spirit of God.*—VI. *the wind.*—VII. *anger, wrath.*— VIII. *vanity, folly* (used idiomatically in many ways; see Concordance).

רוּחַ com. Ch.—I. *the wind.*—II. *spirit, mind.*

רַחַת f., *winnowing fan*, Isa. 30:24.

רֵיחַ m., *odour, smell*; Ch. the same.

רָוַח (fut. יִרְוַח) *there was relief*, with לְ 1 Sa. 16:23; Job 32:20. Pu. part. מְרֻוָּחִים *spacious, ample*, Jer. 22:14.

רֶוַח m.—I. *space, distance.*—II. *deliverance, quiet.*

רְוָחָה, רַוְחָה f., the same.

רוּם (fut. יָרוּם, יָרֻם).— I. *was high, lofty.* — II. *raised himself, was raised.*—III. *was high in rank or power.* — IV. *was lifted up, haughty* (fut. וַיָּרָם); part. רָם m.,

רָמָה f. — I. *high.*—II. *loud*, Deu 27:14.— III. *high in rank.* — IV. *haughty*; pl. רָמִים *the heights of heaven.*—V. p.n. of a man.. Pil. רוֹמֵם I. *lifted up, raised.*—II. *made to grow.* —III. *brought up* (children).—IV. *exalted with praise.*— V. *raised a building.* Pul. רוֹמַם *was lifted up, raised, high.* Hiph. הֵרִים I. *lifted up.*—II. *took up.*— III. *took out for an offering.*—IV. *offered.*—V. *removed.*—VI. *set up.* Hoph. הֻרַם I. *was offered.* — II. *was removed.* Hithpal. *raised, exalted himself*, Dan. 11:36.

רוּם Ch., *was lifted up*, Dan. 5:20. Pil. *exalting with praise*, Dan. 4: 34. Aph. *exalting in power*, Dan. 5:19. Ithpal. *exaltest thyself*, Dan. 5:23.

רָמָה f.—I. *high place for idolatry*, Eze. c. 16.—II. p.n., *Ramah*: (a) a town of Benjamin; (b) a town of Ephraim, called also רָמָתַיִם צֹפִים; (c) a town of Naphtali; (d) רָמַת הַמִּצְפֶּה a town in Gilead, called also רָאמוֹת, רָמוֹת *Ramoth Gilead*; (e) רָמַת לֶחִי same as לֶחִי; רָמָתִי *a Ramathite.*

רָמֻת f., *pile, heap of dead bodies*, Eze. 32:5.

רוּם m. — I. *height*, Pro. 25:3.— II. *haughtiness.*

רוּם m. Ch., *height.*

רוֹם m., רוֹמָה f.—I. *height*, Hab. 3: 10.— II. *on high, haughtily*, Mic 2:3.

רוּמָה p.n. of a place.

רוֹמֵם m., *extolling praise*; pl. const. רוֹמְמוֹת, Ps. 149:6.

רוֹמֵמֻת f, *exaltation, majesty*, with suff. רֹמְמֻתְךָ, Isa. 33:3.

רְמַמְתִּי־עֶזֶר p. n. of a man.

רֶמֶת p. n., *a town of Issachar.*

מָרוֹם m.—I. *high, on high, height.*— II. *a high place.*—III. *haughtiness; adv. haughtily.*

מֵי מָרוֹם p. n., *a lake in the north of Canaan,* Σαμοχωνίτις.

תְּרוּמָה f.—I. *contribution, gift.*— II. *offering to God.* — III. *sacrificial gift, heave-offering.*

תְּרוּמִיָה f., *offering*, Eze. 48:12.

רן (Arab. *conquer*). Hithpa. part. מִתְרוֹנֵן *overcome* (of wine), Ps. 78: 65.

I. רוֹעַ (pret. רַע; inf. רֹעַ) *was evil*, with בְּעֵינֵי *displeased.* Niph. (fut. יֵרוֹעַ).—I. *got worse*, Pro. 13:20.— II. *suffer evil, injury*, Pro. 11:15. Hiph. הֵרַע, הֵרֵעַ I. *did evil.* — II. *did evil to, afflicted;* part. מֵרַע, מֵרֵעַ *evil doer*, with בְּ, עַל, עִם, לְ. Hith. הִתְרוֹעֵעַ *suffered injury*, Pro. 18:24.

רַע in pause רָע m., רָעָה f.—I. *wicked.* II. *fatal, deadly.*—III. *calamitous.* IV. *sad.*—V. *ill-favoured.*—VI. s.: (a) *wickedness;* (b) *harm, injury, calamity.*

רוֹעַ, רֹעַ m.—I. *badness, evil condition.* —II. *sadness of countenance*, Ecc. 7:3.

II. רוּעַ *shout, call together*, רֵעוּ, Isa. 8:9. Hiph. הֵרִיעַ (pl. הֵרֵעוּ).—I. *shouted.*—II. *sounded a trumpet.* Pil. fut. יְרֹעָע *there shall be shouting*, Isa. 16:10. Hithpal. *shouted.*

רֵעַ m., *shouting, crying out* see also רֵעָה.

תְּרוּעָה f.—I. *shout of joy.* — II. *shout of battle.*—III. *sound of a trumpet.*

רוּץ I. *ran, ran to, after.* — II. *rushed upon*, with עַל, אֶל.—III. *ran into for a refuge*, with בְּ.—IV. *hastened.* —V. *did a thing readily*, Hab. 2: 2. Part. pl. רָצִים *runners, couriers.* Pil. רוֹצֵץ *ran swiftly*, Nah. 2:5. Hiph. I. *caused to run.*—II. *brought quickly.*—III. *stretched out his hands quickly*, Ps. 68:32.

מֵרוֹץ m., *a race*, Ecc. 9:11.

מְרוּצָה f.—I. *mode of running.*—II. *course of life.* See also רָצַץ.

רוק; see רִיק.

רוּר *spat*, Lev. 15:3.

רִיר m.—I. *spittle*, 1 Sa. 21:14.—II. *whey*, Job 6:6.

רוֹש; see רֹאש.

רוּש *was poor, in want*, Ps. 34:11; part. רָש, רָאש *poor, a poor man.* Hith. הִתְרוֹשֵׁשׁ *feigned himself poor*, Pro. 13:7.

רָאש, רֵיש, רֵיש m., *poverty.*

רוּת p. n. of a woman, *Ruth.*

רָזָה *diminished, brought low*, Zep. 2: 11. Niph. *was wasted away*, Isa 17:4.

רָזֶה m.—I. *lean* (of cattle), Eze. 34 20.—II. *barren* (of land), Nu. 13 20.

רָזִי m., *destruction;* רָזִי לִי *woe is me* רָזוֹן m., *wasting, destruction.* See also in רָזַן.

רזח root not used; Arab. *cried out*) מַרְזֵחַ m., *lamentation*, Jer. 16:5. מִרְזַח *cry of merriment*, Am. 6:7.

רָזַם *laid hold on*, Job 15:12.

רָזַן (Arab. *weighty*); part. רוֹזְנִים *chiefs, princes*.

רָזוֹן m., *prince*; see also רָזֶה.

רְזוֹן p.n., *Rezon*, king of Damascus.

רָחַב *was widened, enlarged, opened.* Niph. part. *enlarged, extended,* Isa. 30:23. Hiph. הִרְחִיב I. *made broad.*—II. with נֶפֶשׁ *extended his desires, enlarged itself.*—III. *opened the heart, mouth, &c.*—IV. with לְ, *liberated, made room for, gave way.*

I. רָחָב m., רְחָבָה f., *broad, large, extensive, capacious*; with יָדַיִם *broad on both hands, very broad*; with לֵב *of unlimited desires.*

II. רָחָב p.n., *Rahab*, the woman of Jericho.

רַחַב m., *plenty*, Job 36:16; 38:18.

רֹחַב m. (with suff. רָחְבָּהּ).—I. *breadth, width.*—II. *extent, expanse*, Job 37:10.—III. with לֵב *extent of understanding*, 1 K. 5:9.

רְחוֹב רְחֹב f. (pl. רְחֹבוֹת).—I. *broad, open place in a town, square, street, market-place.*—II. בֵּית רְחֹב and רְחֹב p.n., a town in the north of the tribe of Asher; a Syrian city near it was called אֲרַם בֵּית רְחוֹב and אֲרַם רְחֹב.—III. רְחֹבוֹת p.n., (a) the name of a well; (b) ר' עִיר a town in Assyria; (c) ר' הַנָּהָר a town on the Euphrates.

רְחַבְיָהוּ p.n. of a man.

רְחַבְעָם p.n., *Rehoboam*, the son of Solomon, king of Judah. LXX. Ῥοβοάμ.

מֶרְחָב m.—I. *wide places.*—II *prosperity*, considered as freedom.

רָחִיק רָחוֹק; see רחק.

רָהִיטִים Ketib for רְחִיטִים; see רהט.

רֵחַיִם m. dual, *pair of millstones.*

רָחֵל f.—I. *a ewe.*—II. *any sheep*—III. p.n., *Rachel*, the wife of Jacob; LXX. Ῥαχήλ.

רָחַם or רָחֵם *loved*, Ps. 18:2. Pi. רִחַם *loved, pitied, had mercy on*, with accus. עַל. Pu. רֻחַם *obtained mercy.*

רָחָם, רָחָמָה m., *the aquiline vulture;* vultur percnopterus (Linn.), Lev. 11:18; Deu. 14:17.

רַחוּם m., *merciful* (of God only).

רָחוּם p.n. of a man.

רֶחֶם רַחַם m. (f. Jer. 20:17).—I. *the womb.*—II. *a girl;* dual רַחֲמָתַיִם.—III. רֶחֶם p.n. of a man.

רַחֲמִים m. pl.—I. *the viscera.*—II. *pity, mercy.*

רַחֲמִין m. pl. Ch., *mercy.*

רַחֲמָנִי m., f. pl. רַחֲמָנִיּוֹת *tender, merciful*, Lam. 4:10.

רָחַף *shook, trembled*, Jer. 23:9. Pi. רִחֵף *fluttered, hovered*, Deu. 32:11; part. מְרַחֶפֶת *hovering, brooding* (of the Spirit of God), Gen. 1:2.

רָחַץ (fut. יִרְחַץ; imp. רְחַץ, pl. רַחֲצוּ; inf. רְחַץ (רָחְצָה) *washed himself or another; washed away.* Pu. *was washed.* Hith. *washed himself*, Job 9:30.

רַחַץ m., *washing*, Ps. 60:10.

רַחְצָה f., *washing-place for sheep*, Cant. 4:2; 6:6.

רְחַץ Ch. Ith. *depend on, trust to,* Dan. 3:28.

רָחַק (fut. יִרְחַק; inf. רָחֳקָה) I. *was distant.*—II. *kept at a distance, withdrew himself.* Pi. רִחַק *placed at a distance, forsook.* Hiph. הִרְחִיק I. *caused to be distant.*—II. *went to a distance;* inf. הַרְחֵק adv., *afar off.*

רָחֵק m., *one who forsakes,* Ps. 73:27.

רָחוֹק m., רְחוֹקָה f.—I. *a distance, interval.*—II. *distant.*—III. *out of reach.* — IV. *difficult,* Pro. 31:10 (i. e., *brought from afar, precious*); בְּרָחוֹק *afar off;* מֵרָחוֹק *from, at a distance* (of time or space); לְמֵרָחוֹק *at a distance* (time or space); עַד־רָחוֹק *to a distance.*

רָחִיק m. Ch., *distant,* Ezr. 6:6.

מֶרְחָק m. (pl. מֶרְחַקִּים), *distance, distant part.*

מַרְחָק m., *the same;* pl. מַרְחַקִּים.

רָחַשׁ *threw up, bubbled up* (as a spring), Ps. 45:2.

מַרְחֶשֶׁת f., *pot for boiling.*

רַחַח; see רגח.

רָטֹב (fut. יִרְטֹב) *was wet* (with rain), Job 24:8.

רָטֹב m., *moist, fresh,* Job 8:16. (Arab. the same).

רָטָה, יִרְטְנוּ; see יָרט.

רָטַט root not used; Ch. *trembled;* Syr. the same.

רֶטֶט m., *trembling,* Jer. 49:24.

רֻטֲפַשׁ *grew fresh, moist,* Job 33:25.

רָטַשׁ Pi. רִטֵּשׁ *smote, killed.* Pu. *were killed.*

רִי; see רָוָה.

רִיב (pret. רָב, רַבְתָּ, רִיבוֹת; inf. abs רֹב; inf. const. and imp. רִיב; fut. יָרִיב).—I. *disputed, quarrelled with,* with עִם, אֵת, אֶל, בְּ.—II. *defended,* with לְ.—III. *opposed,* with עַל.—IV. *decided a cause favourably.* Hith. part. מֵרִיב *opposed, contended with.*

רִיב, רִב m. (pl. רִיבִים, רִיבוֹת).— I. *controversy, suit.* — II. *quarrel, strife.*

רִיבַי p. n. of a man.

יָרֵב m., *an adversary,* Hos. 5:13, 10:6.

יָרִיב m.—I. the same.—II. p. n. of a man.

יְרִיבַי p. n. of a man.

יְרֻבֶּשֶׁת, יְרֻבַּעַל p. n., titles of Gideon.

מְרִיבָה f.—I. *strife, contention.* — II. p. n., a spring in the desert of Sinai.

רִיחַ, הָרִיחַ, רֵיחַ; see רוח.

רֵים same as רְאֵם.

רִיעַ, הָרִיעַ, רֵעַ, see רוע; רֵעָ, see רָעָה.

רִיפוֹת f. pl., *grain.*

רִיפַת p. n., one of Japhet's sons, and his descendants.

רִיק Hiph. הֵרִיק — I. *emptied.* — II. *made empty, poured out.*—III. *drew a sword, made ready for war,* Gen. 14:14. Hoph. הוּרַק *was poured out.*

רִיק m.—I. *empty.*—II. *an empty, vain thing.*—III. *in vain.*—IV. adv. רִיק, לָרִיק *in vain.*

רֵיק, רֵק m., רֵקָה f.—I. *empty.* — II. *hungry, poor.* — III. *unimportant,* Deu. 32:47. — IV. *worthless in character.*

רֵיקָם adv. — I. *emptily.* — II. *empty*

handed.—III. *without cause.*—IV. *without effect.*

רִיו רָן; see רגר.

רֵישׁ רֵישׁ *poverty;* see רושׁ.
רֵישׁוֹן Job 8:8; same as רִאשׁוֹן *first.*
רַךְ רֹךְ; see רכך.

רָכַב (fut. יִרְכַּב; inf. רְכֹב).—I. *rode on a horse, ass,* or *camel.*—II. metaph. of God on the clouds or wind, with בְּ, עַל, accus.; part. רֹכֵב *a horseman.* Hiph. I. *caused to ride.*—II. *carried in a chariot.*—III. *placed upon.* — IV. *caused to be ridden,* Hos. 10:11.

רֶכֶב m. (f. Nah. 2:5).—I. *riding, a rider.* — II. *the upper millstone* (that which rides).—III. *a chariot, chariots.*

רֵכָב p.n.—I. *Rechab,* the father of Jonadab, from whom the Rechabites (רֵכָבִים) were descended.—II. used also of other men.

רְכוּב m., *vehicle, chariot,* Ps. 104:3.
רַכָּב m.—I. *horseman.*—II. *charioteer.*
מֶרְכָּב m.—I. *any carriage to ride in,* Lev. 15:9.—II. *chariots,* 1 K. 5:6.
מֶרְכָּבָה f. (with suff. מֶרְכַּבְתּוֹ; pl. מֶרְכְּבוֹת, מַרְכְּבוֹת), *a chariot.*
מִרְכֶּבֶת f., the same.
רֵכָה p.n. of a place unknown.
רְכוּשׁ *wealth;* see רכשׁ.
רָכִיל *slander;* see רכל.

רָכַךְ *was timid, gentle.* Niph. *was timid;* fut. יֵרַךְ. Pu. *was softened,* Isa. 1:6. Hiph. הֵרַךְ *rendered timid,* Job 23:16.

רַךְ m., רַכָּה f.— I. *tender, young.*— II. *object of care.*—III. *effeminate.* — IV. *weak, timid, gentle.* — V.

tender-eyed, i. e. having sore eyes. Gen. 29:17.

רֹךְ f., *effeminacy,* Deu. 28:56.

רָכַל *went to and fro, travelled as a merchant;* part. רֹכֵל, f. רֹכֶלֶת *a merchant, dealer.*

רָכָל p. n., a town of Judah.

רָכִיל m.—I. *a busy body.*— II. *slander;* הָלַךְ רָכִיל *he went about tale bearing.*

רְכֻלָּה f., *merchandise* (Ezekiel only).
מַרְכֹּלֶת f., *merchandise,* Eze. 27:24.

רָכַס *tied, fastened.* Ex. 28:28; 39:21.

רְכָסִים אִישׁ רֹכֶס m., *combinations, artifices,* Ps. 31:21.

רֶכֶס m., pl. רְכָסִים *rugged places,* Isa. 40:4.

רָכַשׁ *acquired, gained* (Genesis only).
רְכֻשׁ, רְכוּשׁ m., *property, wealth.*
רֶכֶשׁ m., *swift species of horse.*

רָמָה רָם, see רום; רֵם same as רְאֵם.

רָמָה I. *threw.*—II. *shot with a bow* Pi. רִמָּה *deceived,* lit. *threw down.*
רְמָא Ch.—I. *threw.*—II. *imposed tribute.* Ithpe. *were thrown placed.*

רִמּוֹן, רָמָה; see רמם.
רָמוֹת, רָמוּת; see רום.

רְמִיָּה f.—I. *deceit.*—II. *negligence.*
רְמִיָּה p.n. of a man.
מִרְמָה f.—I. *deceit, artifice.*—II. p.n. of a man.

תַּרְמָה f., *deceit, craft,* Jud. 9:31.
תַּרְמִית (תַּרְמוֹת) f., the same.

רֹמַח m. (pl. רְמָחִים; with suff. רָמְחֵיהֶם) *a spear.*
רַמִּי pl. הָרַמִּים same as הָאֲרַמִּים *the Syrians.*

רִמָּךְ f., *a mare*, Est. 8:10.

רְמַלְיָה p. n., *Remaliah*, the father of Pekah, king of Israel.

רָמַם (pret. pl. רֹמּוּ רַמּוּ) *was high, lofty*; part. f. רוֹמְמָה *high*. Niph. (imp. pl. הֵרֹמּוּ; fut. pl. יֵרֹמּוּ) *was raised*, Eze. 10:15, 17, 19.

רִמָּה f., *a worm, worms*

רִמּוֹן m.—I. *a pomegranate fruit* or *tree*.—II. *an artificial imitation of the fruit.*—III. p. n.: (a) a city of Simeon; (b) a city near Gibeah; (c) an idol of the Syrians; (d) רִמּוֹן הַמֵּתֹאָר a town of Zebulun; (e) רִמּוֹן פֶּרֶץ one of the stations of the Israelites.

רָמַס I. *trampled on, trod on.* — II. *walked in*; part. רֹמֵס *an oppressor*, Isa. 16:4. Niph. *was trodden down*, Isa. 28:3.

מִרְמָס m., *that which is trampled under foot.*

רָמַשׂ I. *move* (as a quadruped).—II. *creep* (as a reptile).

רֶמֶשׂ m. collec.—I. *reptiles.*—II. *small land animals.*— III. *sea creatures*, perhaps *seals*, Ps. 104:25.

רָמַת; see רום.

רָנָה *rang, rattled*, Job 39:23.

רָנַן (fut. יָרֹן).—I. *sung.*—II. *shouted.*—III. *invited.* — IV. *called for help.* Pi. רִנֵּן I. *sung, rejoiced*, with בְּ, עַל.—II. *sung of, celebrated*, with לְ, אֶל. Pu. fut. יְרֻנַּן *there shall be singing*, Isa. 16:10. Hiph. הִרְנִין I. *caused to sing.* — II. *rejoiced.* Hith. see in רון.

רְנַן m., pl. רְנָנִים *ostriches* Job 39:13.

רְנָנָה f., *singing, rejoicing.*

רֹן m., pl. רַגִּים *songs*, Ps. 32:7.

רִנָּה f.—I. *singing, shout of joy.*—II. *a shout or cry of any kind.*—III. *a cry for help.*—IV. p. n. of a man.

רֶסֶן m.—I. *bridle, halter.*— II. p. n. *a city of Assyria.*

רָסַס *sprinkled*, Eze. 46:14.

רִסָּה p.n., one of the stations in the wilderness.

רְסִיסִים m. pl. — I. *sprinkling, drop*, Cant. 5:2.—II. *fractures*, Am. 6:11.

רָעָה, רוּעַ, רֵעַ, see רוּעַ; רַע, רֵעַ, see רֹעַ, רָעַע.

רָעֵב (fut. יִרְעַב).—I. *was hungry.*—II. *hungered for, was famished.*—III. *suffered from famine*, with לְ. Hiph. הִרְעִיב *allowed, caused to suffer hunger.*

רָעֵב m., רְעֵבָה f., *hungry, famishing.*

רָעָב m.—I. *hunger.*—II. *famine.*

רָעָבוֹן, const. רַעֲבוֹן m., the same.

רָעַד (fut. יִרְעַד) *trembled*, Ps. 104:32. Hiph. the same.

רַעַד m., רְעָדָה f., } *trembling, awe.*

רָעָה (fut. יִרְעֶה; apoc. יִרַע).— I. *fed.* —II. *consumed.*—III. *devastated.* —IV. *fed on, delighted in.* — V. *associated with.*—VI. *fed cattle.*— VII. *governed a people.* — VIII. *nourished.* — IX. for רָעַע *injured, oppressed*; part. רֹעֶה *a shepherd.* Pi. רֵעָה *became a companion*, Jud. 14:20. Hiph. pres. aff. יַרְעֵם *ruled them*, Ps. 78:72. Hith. הִתְרָעָה *was intimate with, became a companion*, with אֶת.

רֵעֶה m. (pl. with suff. רֵעֵהוּ רֵיעַ, רֵעֶה, רֵעַ,

רֵעַ (רֵעֵיהוּ)—I. *a friend, neighbour, companion, lover*; רֵעַ אִישׁ *one... the other.*—II. *thought, will*, Ps. 139:2, 17; see also רוּעַ.

רֵעָה f., pl. רֵעוֹת *female friend, companion.*

רֹעַ f., *evil, &c.*; see רַע in רוּעַ.

רֵעָה *breaking*; see רֵעַ.

רְעוּת f.—I. *friend, neighbour.*—II. with רוּחַ *feeding on the wind.*

רְעוּת f. Ch., *wish, will.*

רְעוּ p. n. of a man.

רְעוּאֵל p. n. of a man.

רֶעִי m., *pasture*, 1 Ki. 5:3.

רֹעִי m., *a shepherd.*

רֵעִי m. of a man.

רַעְיָה f., *female companion, friend.*

רַעְיוֹן m., *desire, pursuit.*

רַעְיוֹן m. Ch., *desire, purpose, thought.*

מֵרַע m. (with suff. מֵרֵעֵהוּ; pl. מֵרֵעִים) *desire, purpose, thought.*

מִרְעֶה m., *pasture.*

מַרְעִית f.—I. *pasturing, feeding cattle.*—II. *a flock.*

רָעַל. Hoph. הָרְעַל *were thrown* (of javelins), Nah. 2:4.

רַעַל m.—I. *trembling, giddiness*, Zec. 12:2.—II. pl. רְעָלוֹת *veils*, Isa. 3:19.

רְעֶלְיָה p. n. of a man.

תַּרְעֵלָה f., *trembling, staggering.*

רָעַם (יִרְעַם).—I. *resounded, roared* (of the sea).—II. *was excited*, Eze. 27:35. Hiph. הִרְעִים I. *thundered.*—II. *caused anger, vexation.*

רַעַם m.—I. *thunder.*—II. *tumult, rage*, Job 39:25.

רַעְמָה f.—I. *rage*, Job 39:19.—II. p. n. of a city of Cush.

רַעְמְסֵס, רַעַמְסֵס (*born of the sun*),

p. n.—I. the district which forms the eastern boundary of Egypt, called also Goshen.—II. a city built there by the Israelites.

רַעֲנַן. Pil. רַעֲנַן *was green.*

רַעֲנָן m.—I. *green, flourishing.*—II. *prosperous.*—III. *surrounded with foliage*, Cant. 1:16.—IV. *anointed*, Ps. 92:11.

רַעֲנַן m. Ch., *green, flourishing.*

רָעַע (רֹעַ).—I. *broke, broke to pieces.*—II. *crushed.* Niph. fut. יֵרוֹעַ and Hiph. הֵרַע; see in רוּעַ. Hith. הִתְרֹעֵעַ *was broken to pieces, ruined.*

רְעַע Ch. (fut. f. תֵּרֹעַ), *broke.* Pa. the same.

רֹעָה f., *breaking*; שֵׁן רֹעָה *a broken tooth.*

רָעַף and Hiph. הִרְעִיף *flowed, let drop.*

רָעַץ *crushed, overpowered, oppressed.*

רָעַשׁ (יִרְעַשׁ), *was shaken, trembled.* Niph. *quaked* (of the earth), Jer. 50:46. Hiph. I. *shook.*—II. *filled with eagerness* (of a horse), Job 39:20.

רַעַשׁ m.—I. *shaking.*—II. *an earthquake.*—III. *rumbling of wheels.*—IV. *rattling of a horse's hoofs*, Job 39:24.—V. *any tumult*, Job 41:21.—VI. *the rattling of a spear.*

רָפָא (imp. רְפָא, רְפָה; fut. יִרְפָּא; pl. f. תִּרְפֶּינָה).—I. *healed.*—II. *restored to prosperity, delivered from calamity.*—III. *healed*, i. e., *removed transgressions*; part. רֹפֵא *a physician.* Niph. נִרְפָּא (pret. f. נִרְפְּתָה; inf. הֵרָפֵה, הֵרָפֵא; fut.

pl. (יֻרְפּוּ).—I. *was repaired* (a vessel). — II. *was healed* (a person or wound).—III. *was rendered wholesome* (water), Eze. c. 47.—IV. *was restored to prosperity*, Isa. 53:5. Pi. רִפָּא (fut. pl. יְרַפְּאוּ).— I. *repaired*, 1 Ki. 18:30.—II. *healed*.—III. *caused to be cured*, Ex. 21:19.—IV. *made wholesome*, 2 Ki. 2:21. Hith. *get himself cured*.

רְפָאֵל p. n. of a man.

רְפָיָה p. n. of a man.

רְפָאִים p. n., the name of a people inhabiting the country on the east of the Dead Sea, supposed to have been giants; called also יְלִידֵי הָרָפָה. עֵמֶק רְפָאִים *the valley of the Rephaims*, close to mount Moriah.

רִפְאוּת f., *health*, Pro. 3:8.

רְפֻאוֹת f. pl., *bandages, remedies*.

רָפוּא p. n. of a man.

מַרְפֵּא, מַרְפֶּה m.—I. *remedy.*—II. *healing*.—III. *soundness*. See also in רָפָה.

תְּרוּפָה f., *healing*, Eze. 47:12.

רָפַד *supported himself*, Job 41:22; fut. יִרְפָּד. Pi. I. *constructed a couch*, Job 17:13. — II. *refreshed*, Cant. 2:5.

רְפִידָה f., *a throne*; Vulg. reclinatorium, Cant. 3:10.

רְפִידִים p.n., *Rephidim*, a station in the wilderness.

רָפָה (fut. יִרְפֶּה, יִרְפָּה).—I. *hung down* (the hands).—II. *declined* (the day).—III. *sank down* (fuel in the fire), Isa.5:24.—IV. *gave way* (to anger), Jud. 8:3; with מִן. — V. *became weak*, Jer. 49:24. — VI. *desisted*.

Niph. part. נִרְפִּים *became, were idle*, Ex. 5:8, 17, &c. Pi. רִפָּה I. *allowed to hang down*, Eze. 1:24, 25. — II. *weakened* (part. מְרַפֵּא). Hiph. הִרְפָּה (imp. apoc. הֶרֶף ; fut. apoc. יַרְף) I. *ceased from*, with מִן.—II. *withheld.*—III. *gave up.*—IV. *let go.*—V. *ceased*. Hith. *relaxed himself, was slothful*.

רָפֶה m. (pl. f. רָפוֹת), *weak*.

רָפֶה p.n.; see in רָפָא.

רִפָּיוֹן m., *weakness*, Jer. 47:3.

מַרְפֵּא m., *yielding*, Ecc. 10:4; see also in רָפָא.

רֶפַח p. n. of a man.

רָפַשׂ, רָפַס, *trampled down*. Niph. part. נִרְפָּשׂ *disturbed by trampling*. Hith. הִתְרַפֵּס *submitted, humbled himself*.

רְפַס Ch., the same.

מִרְפָּשׂ *water made muddy by trampling*, Eze. 34:19.

רַפְסֹדוֹת f.pl., *floats, rafts*, 2 Ch. 2:15.

רָפַף Po. רוֹפֵף *trembled*.

רָפַק. Hith. *trembled*, Cant. 8:5.

רָפַשׂ; see רפס.

רֶפֶשׂ m., *mud*, Isa. 57:20.

רְפָתִים m. pl., *stalls for oxen*, Hab. 3:17.

רָצֵי, רַץ, see רצץ; רָצִים, see רוּץ.

רָצָא, Eze. 1:14; same as רוּץ *he ran*.

רָצַד. Pi. *he laid wait for*, Ps. 68:17.

רָצָה (וַתִּרֶץ, יִרְצֶה).—I. *approved of, took pleasure in*, with בְּ.—II. *received favourably.*—III. *loved.*—IV. *fulfilled.*—V. *associated with*,

with עִם.—VI. *was received favourably*; (part. רָצוּי *accepted*). Niph. נִרְצָה I. *was received favourably.*—II. *was fulfilled*, Isa. 40:2. Pi. *satisfied by restitution*, Job 20:10. Hiph. *fulfilled*, Lev. 26:34. Hith. *made himself acceptable*, 1 Sa. 29:4.

רָצוֹן m. — I. *approbation, favour* (עַל רְ׳, לִרְצוֹן *acceptable, well-pleasing*).—II. *object of approbation.*—III. *will, pleasure, choice.*—IV. *uncontrolled will, violence*, Gen. 49:6.—V. *enjoyment.*

רָצַח (fut. יִרְצַח) *struck fatally, killed*; with or without נֶפֶשׁ; part. רֹצֵחַ *homicide.* Niph. *was killed.* Pi. *killed habitually, was a murderer by profession.* Pu. *be killed*, Ps. 62:4. תְּרָצְחוּ, תְּרָצָחוּ for תְּרְצְחוּ.

רֶצַח m. — I. *crushing*, Ps. 42:11.— II. *slaughter*, Eze. 21:27.

רִצְיָא p. n. of a man.

רְצִין p.n., *Rezin, king of Syria.*

רָצַע *pierced, bored*, Ex. 21:6.

מַרְצֵעַ m., *an awl.*

רָצַף *covered, overlaid*, Cant. 3:10.

רֶצֶף m.—I. *burning coals*, 1 Ki. 19:6. —II. p. n., a city of some country subdued by the Assyrians.

רִצְפָה f.—I. *burning coal*, Isa. 6:6. — II. *an inlaid pavement.* — III. p. n., *Rizpah*, the concubine of Saul.

מַרְצֶפֶת f., *the pavement on which the brasen sea stood*, 2 Ki. 16:17.

רָצַץ (fut. יָרוּץ, תֵּרָץ).—I. *bruised, broke, crushed.*—II. *oppressed.*—III. *became broken, burst.*—IV. *relaxed*

himself, Isa. 42:3. Niph. נָרֹץ *was bruised.* Pi. רִצֵּץ I. *bruised.* — II. *oppressed.* Po. רוֹצֵץ the same; see also in רוּץ. Hiph. *bruised*; fut. וַתָּרָץ. Hithpo. *struggled together*, Gen. 25:22.

רַץ m. (pl. const. רַצֵּי), *small piece of silver*, Ps. 68:31.

מְרוּצָה f., *oppression*, Jer. 22:17; see also in רוּץ.

רַק, רֹק, רְקִי; see רקק.

רִיק; see רוק.

רָקַב (fut. יִרְקַב) *became rotten, decayed*

רָקָב m, *decay, rottenness.*

רִקָּבוֹן m., the same, Job 41:19.

רָקַד *leaped, danced.* Pi. the same. Hiph. *made to leap*, Ps. 29:6.

רַקָּה, רִקּוֹן; see רקק.

רָקַח (fut. יִרְקַח) *compounded, prepared*, Ex. 30:33; part. רֹקֵחַ *a compounder of drugs and aromatics.* Pu. part. מְרֻקָּחִים *compound, ointment*, 2 Chron. 16:14. Hiph. *threw in spices*, Eze. 24:10.

רֶקַח m., *perfuming, the preparing of perfumes*, Cant. 8:2.

רֹקַח m., *ointment*, Ex. 30:25, 35.

רַקָּח m., *apothecary, perfumer*; f. pl. רַקָּחוֹת.

רִקֻּחִים m. pl., *perfumes*, Isa. 57:9.

מֶרְקַח m., pl. מֶרְקָחִים *perfumes*, Cant. 5:13.

מֶרְקָחָה f.—I. *a pot of ointment*, Job 41:23.—II. *spices eaten as condiments*, Eze. 24:10.

מִרְקַחַת f., *perfumery.*

רָקִיק, see רקק; רָקִיעַ, see רקע.

רָקַם *streaked*; part. רֹקֵם s. *an embroid*

erer. Pu. *wrought with art* (met. of Christ's mystical body), Ps. 139:15.

רִקְמָה f.—I. *embroidery.*—II. *variety of colours,* Eze. 17:3; dual רִקְמָתַיִם *embroidered on both sides,* Jud. 5: 30.

רֶקֶם p. n.—I. *a town of Benjamin.*— II. *of a man.*

רָקַע I. *stretched out* (of God in creation). — II. *stamped on,* 2 Sa. 22: 43. — III. *stamped with the feet,* Eze. 6:11. Pi. I. *beat into thin plates.* — II. *covered with a thin plate of gold,* Isa. 40:19. Pu. part. *overlaid,* Jer. 10:9. Hiph. *stretched out,* Job 37:18.

רָקִיעַ m.—I. *the expanse of heaven, atmosphere, sky,* Vulg. *firmamentum.*—II. *a canopy* (Ezekiel only).

רִקֻּעִים m. pl., *plates of metal,* Nu. 17:3.

רָקַק same as יָרַק *spit,* with בְּ; fut. יָרֹק, Lev. 15:8.

רָקִיק m., *a thin cake.*

רֹק m. (with suff. רֻקִּי) *spittle.*

רַק m., רַקָּה f. (Arab. *was thin*) *thin, lean,* Gen. c. 41.

רַק adv. — I. *only.*—II. *certainly,* i. e. this only. — III. *except,* with a negative.

רַקָּה f.— I. *the temple* (of the head), Jud. 4:21, 22; 5:26.—II. *the cheek,* Cant. 4:3; 6:7.

רַקּוֹן p. n., a town of Dan.

רַקַּת p. n., a town of Naphtali.

רֹשׁ; see רוּשׁ.

רֵשׁ רָשׁ Kal imp., from יָרַשׁ.

רָשָׁה root not used; (Syr. *he gave*).

רִשְׁיוֹן m., *grant, permission,* Ezr. 3:7.

רֵשִׁית *beginning;* see רֵאשִׁית in רֹאשׁ.

רָשַׁם *wrote, decreed,* Dan. 10:21.

רְשַׁם Ch., the same.

רָשַׁע *was, acted, wickedly, unjustly impiously.* Hiph. הִרְשִׁיעַ I. *condemned.* — II. *declared, proved guilty.*—III. *acted wickedly.*

רָשָׁע m., רְשָׁעָה f.— I. *wicked.*—II. *guilty, faulty.*

רֶשַׁע m. (with suff. רִשְׁעוֹ) *wickedness, impiety, injustice;* pl. רְשָׁעִים.

רִשְׁעָה f.— I. *wickedness.* — II. *fault,* Deu. 25:2.

רִשְׁעָתַיִם p. n.; see כּוּשָׁן.

מִרְשַׁעַת f., *wickedness,* 2 Chron. 24:7.

רֶשֶׁף m. (pl. const. רִשְׁפֵי).—I. *a burning coal,* Cant. 8:6.—II. *lightning.* III. בְּנֵי ר' *burning arrows,* Job 5:7; רִשְׁפֵי קֶשֶׁת the same, Ps. 76:4.—IV. *burning disease,* Deu. 32:24.—V. *lust,* Cant. 8:6.—VI. p. n. of a man.

רָשַׁשׁ. Po. רֹשֵׁשׁ *reduced, subdued,* Jer. 5:17. Pu. רֻשַׁשׁ *was subdued,* Mal. 1:4.

תַּרְשִׁישׁ I. p.n., *Tarshish,* some country far distant from Canaan; אֳנִיּוֹת 'תּ probably *merchant ships.* — II. *a precious stone,* probably *the topaz.*—III. p. n. of a man.

רֶשֶׁת Kal inf., from יָרַשׁ.

רָתַח. Pi. and Hiph. *boil, caused to boil.* Pu. *was boiled, agitated,* Job 30:27.

רֶתַח m., *boiling,* Eze. 24:5.

רָתַם *bind, yoke,* Mic. 1:13.

רֹתֶם m. (pl. רְתָמִים), the broom; in Spanish, retama.

רִתְמָה p. n., one of the stations in the wilderness.

רָתַק (Arab. joined). Niph. was bound, Ecc. 12:6, Kri. Pu. the same, Nah. 3:10.

רַתּוֹק m., a chain, Eze. 7:23.

(רַתִּיקוֹת) רַתּוּקוֹת f. pl., chains, 1 Ki. 6:21.

רְתֻקוֹת f. pl., the same, Isa. 40:19.

רָתַת (Syr. he trembled); see רטט.

רְתֵת m., trembling, Hos. 13:1.

שׂ

שָׂא Kal imp. and inf. from נשא.

שְׂאֹר m., leaven.

שְׂאֵת from נשא.

שָׂבַךְ same as סָבַךְ, twist.

שׂוֹבֶךְ m., entangled branch, 2 Sa. 18:9.

שְׂבָךְ m., pl. שְׂבָכִים ornaments of wreathing, 1 Ki. 7:17.

שְׂבָכָה f.—I. network on the capitals of pillars.—II. lattice, 2 Ki. 1:2.—III. a net, Job 18:8.

שְׂבְכָא same as סַבְכָא.

שְׂבָם, שְׂבָמָה p. n., a city of the Reubenites.

שָׂבַע, שָׂבֵעַ was full, satisfied, surfeited, with בְּ, מִן. Pi. satisfied. Hiph. filled, with לְ of the person; with בְּ, מִן of the thing.

שָׂבֵעַ m., שְׂבֵעָה f., full, satisfied, surfeited.

שֹׂבַע m., abundance.

שָׂבָע m., the same; לָשֹׂבַע to the full.

שָׂבְעָה, שִׂבְעָה f., the same, Eze. 16:49.

שָׂבַר looked at, examined, Neh. 2:13, 15; with בְּ. Pi. looked to, hoped for or in, with אֶל, לְ.

שֵׂבֶר m. (with suff. שִׂבְרִי), hope.

שָׂנָא same as שָׂנָה. Hiph. I. increased, Job 12:23. — II. magnified, Joh 36:24.

שְׂנָא Ch., increased, became great.

שַׂגִּיא m., the Great One (of God), Job 36:26; 37:23.

שַׂגִּיא m., שַׂגִּיאָה f. Ch.—I. great.—II. much, many.—III. greatly.

שָׂגַב was exalted. Niph. I. was lofty, exalted.— II. was secure, Pro. 18:10. Pi. I. raised, placed in security.—II. made powerful, Isa. 9:10. Pu. pass. of Pih., Pro. 29:25. Hiph. was lofty, Job 36:22.

שָׂגִיב, שָׂגוּב p. n. of a man.

מִשְׂגָּב m. (with suff. מִשְׂגַּבִּי).—I. a hill, strong place.—II. refuge (of God).

שָׂגָא same as שָׂנָא. Pil. שִׂנְשֵׂן cause to grow; according to others, from סוג he fences, Isa. 17:11.

שָׂגָה increased, became great. Hiph increased, Ps. 73:12.

שָׂדַד. Pi. harrowed.

שִׂדִּים p. n., the valley of the Dead Sea, Siddim.

שָׂדֶה m. (with suff. שָׂדֵהוּ; pl. שָׂדוֹת; const. שְׂדֵי, שְׂדוֹת).—I. a field.—II. the country.—III. any country; אִישׁ שָׂדֶה husbandman; חַיַּת הַשָּׂדֶה the beasts of the field; שְׂדֵה מוֹאָב the land of Moab; שְׂדֵה אֲרָם Mesopotamia.

שָׂדַי sing., the same.

שְׁדֵרוֹת ; see סדר.

שָׁח same as שָׁחָה.

שָׂהֵד (Syr and Ch. סָהַד *bare witness*).

שָׂהֵד m., *eye witness*, Job 16:19.

שָׂהֲדוּת f. Ch., *testimony*, Gen. 31:47.

שַׂהֲרֹנִים *crescents*; see סהר.

שׂוֹא Kal inf., from נשא.

שׁוּב ; see שׁיב.

שׁוֹבֵךְ ; see שׂבך.

שׁוּג same as סוג *drove back*, 2 Sa. 1:22.

שׂוּחַ same as שׂיח *to meditate*, Gen. 24:63.

שׂוּם *turn aside*, Ps. 40:5.

שֵׂטִים ,שָׂטִים m. pl., *they who turn aside to*, Ps. 101:3; Hos. 5:2.

שׂוּךְ *hedged with thorns*. Pil. שׂוֹכֵךְ the same, Job 10:11.

שׂוֹךְ m., } *a bough*, Jud. 9:48, 49.
שׂוֹכָה f., }

שׂוֹכֹה p.n., *a town of Judah*.

שׂוּכָתִי *a Succothite*.

מְסוּכָה ,מְשׂוּכָה f., *a thorn hedge*.

שׂוֹם ,שִׂים (fut. יָשׂוּם ,יָשִׂים : apoc. יָשֵׂם ,וַיָּשֶׂם ; inf. aos. שׂוֹם ; const. שִׂים ,שׂוֹם ; imp. שִׂים, (שִׂימָה).—I. *placed, set.*—II. *set up.*— III. *set in array.*—IV. *placed aside.*—V. with עַל, *set over.*—VI. with עַל *place upon.*—VII. with עַל ,בְּ, לְ, *impute to any one.*—VIII. with שֵׁם לְ *named.*—IX. with שְׁמוֹ *placed His name* (of the Lord), i.e. the true worship.—X. with or without לִבּוֹ *set his heart, considered, regarded,* with עַל לֵב, עַל ,אֶל ,לְ,—XI. with אֶל לֵב or בְּלֵב or *considered* mid

to heart. — XII. שׂוּם עַל לֵב *he considered.*—XIII. with לְנֶגְדּוֹ *considered, set before him.*—XIV. with בְּאָזְנֵי פ׳ *he told.* — XV. שׂוּם אַף *heaped up wrath.* (For other idiomatic usages of שׂוּם see concordance.) Hiph. (imp. הָשִׂימִי ; part. מֵשִׂים (*place, set.* Hoph. *was placed* ; fut. יוּשַׂם.

שׂוּם Ch.—I. *appointed.*—II. with טְעֵם *made a decree.*—III. with טְעֵם עַל ,ל *regarded.* — IV. with בָּל ל *endeavoured.* — V. שֵׁם דִּי פ׳ *named.* Ithpe. אִתְּשֶׂם I. *was made, placed.* —II. with טְעֵם *was decreed.*

תְּשׂוּמֶת f., with יָד *a deposit*, Lev. 5:21; [6:2.]

שׂוּר I. *governed*; fut. וַיָּשַׂר, Jud. 9:22. Hiph. הֵשִׂיר *appointed princes*, Hos. 8:4.—II. same as שָׂרָה *strove, contended*, Hos. 12:5.— III. same as סוּר *departed.* — IV. same as Ch. נְסַר *he sawed*, 1 Chron. 20:3; fut. וַיָּשַׂר.

שׂוּרָה f., *a row, in rows*, Isa. 28:25; (Arab. the same).

שׂישׂ ,שׂושׂ (fut. יָשׂישׂ ,יָשׂושׂ ; inf. abs. שׂושׂ ; const. שׂושׂ ; imp. שׂישׂ) *rejoiced, exulted in,* with בְּ, עַל.

שָׂשׂוֹן m., *joy, rejoicing*.

מָשׂושׂ m., *joy*.

שָׂח ; see שׂיח.

שָׂחָה *swam*, Isa. 25:11. Hiph. *overflowed*, Ps. 6:7.

שָׂחוּ m., *swimming*, Eze. 47:5.

שָׂחַט *squeezed, crushed*, Gen. 40:11.

שָׂחַק I. *laughed.*—II. with אֶל *approved.*—III. with עַל *laughed at.*—IV

with לְ *despised.* — V. *caused laughter.* Pi. שִׂחֵק (inf. שַׂחֵק; fut. יְשַׂחֵק).
—I. *rejoiced, sported.*—II. *played on an instrument,* 2 Sa. 6:21. — III. *made sport,* Jud. 16:25.—IV. *skirmished,* 2 Sa. 2:14. Hiph. *derided,* with עַל, 2 Chron. 30:10.

שְׂחוֹק, שְׂחֹק m.—I. *laughter.*—II. *subject or object of laughter.*

מִשְׂחָק m., *object of laughter,* Hab. 1:10.

שָׂטָה (fut. יִשְׂטֶה; apoc. יֵשְׂטְ).— I. *went aside,* Pro. 7:25. — II. *went astray,* Nu. c. 5.

שֵׂטִים; see שׂוּט.

שָׂטַם *acted fiercely, hardly towards, was hated.*

מַשְׂטֵמָה f., *hatred,* Hos. 9:7, 8.

שָׂטַן *was an adversary to, opposed;* part. שֹׂטֵן *an adversary,* Ps.71:13.

שָׂטָן m.—I. *an adversary.*—II. הַשָּׂטָן *the devil, the great adversary.*

שִׂטְנָה f.—I. *accusation,* Ezr. 4:6.— II. p. n. of a well.

שִׂיא; see נשׂא.

שִׂיאוֹן p. n., *one of the peaks of Hermon.*

שִׂיב *was grey-headed.* Part. שָׂב, Job 15:10; Ch. the same.

שֵׂיב m., *grey hairs, old age,* 1 K. 14:4.
שֵׂיבָה f., *the same.*

שִׂיג m., *retirement,* 1 K. 18:27.

שִׂיד *plastered,* Deu. 27:2, 4.
שִׂיד m., *plaster.*

שֶׂה, שָׂיָה com. (const. שֵׂה, with suff. שֵׂיוֹ, שֵׂיֵהוּ), *a sheep or goat.*

שִׂיחַ I. *meditated,* with בְּ.—II. *spoke,*

with לְ *with,* or בְּ *of.* — III. *composed a psalm, sung,* with בְּ. Pil. I. *uttered,* Isa. 55:8.—II. *meditated,* Ps. 143:5.

שֵׂחַ m., *purpose, design,* Am. 4:13.

שִׂיחַ m.—I. *a plant, bush.*—II. *speech, message.*—III. *a complaint.*—IV. *sorrow,* Job 7:13.

שִׂיחָה f., *complaint, prayer, meditation.*

שִׂים; see שׂוּם.

שֵׂךְ, שֹׂךְ, שִׂכִּים, שְׂכוֹת; see שׂכך.

שָׂכָה *root not used;* (Syr. *expected*)
שׂכוּ p. n., *a place near Ramah.*

שֶׂכְוִי m., *"a thunderstorm"* (Lee), Job 38:36.

שְׂכִיָּה f., *objects* (of sight or thought), Isa. 2:16.

מַשְׂכִּית f. (pl. מַשְׂכִּיוֹת).— I. *figure, external image.*—II. *imagination internal image.*

שַׂכִּין m., *a knife,* Pro. 23:2; (Arab. the same).

שְׂכִירָה, שָׂכִיר; see שׂכר.

שָׂכַךְ *placed as a covering,* Ex. 33:22.

שֵׂךְ m., pl. שִׂכִּים *thorns,* Nu. 33:55.
שֹׂךְ m. (with suff. שֻׂכּוֹ), *a fence,* Lam. 2:6.

שֻׂכָּה f., pl. שֻׂכּוֹת *spears,* Job 40:31.
מְשׂוּכָה f., *a fence,* Pro. 15:19; Isa. 5:5; see שׂוּךְ.

שָׂכַל *was wise, careful, skilful,* 1 Sa. 18:30. Pi. *acted wisely, designedly,* Gen. 48:14. Hiph. I. *looked at.*—II. *reflected.*—III. *cared for.*—IV. *acted wisely, was wise.*—V *prospered.*—VI. *made wise, taught,* with בְּ, עַל, אֶל; part. מַשְׂכִּיל 1 *thoughtful, prudent.*—II. *a didactic*

poem (title of Psalms); inf. הַשְׂכֵּל,
הַשְׂכִּיל understanding, wisdom,
with accus. לְ. Ch. Ith. part. מִשְׂתַּכַּל considered,
looked at, with בְּ.

שֶׂכֶל, שֵׂכֶל m. (with suff. שִׂכְלוֹ).—I.
understanding, skill. — II. estimation, esteem, Pro. 3:4. — III. sig-
nification, Neh. 8:8.

שִׂכְלוּת ; see סכל.

שָׂכְלְתָנוּ f. Ch., understanding, skill,
Dan. 5:11, 12, 14.

שָׂכַר I. hired. — II. bribed. Niph.
hired himself, 1 Sa. 2:5. Hith.
הִשְׂתַּכֵּר the same, Hag. 1:6.

שָׂכָר m.—I. reward, hire.—II. p. n.
of a man.

שֶׂכֶר m., hire.

שָׂכִיר m., hired person or thing.

שְׂכִירָה f., the act of hiring, τὸ μι-
σθοῦν, Isa. 7:20.

מַשְׂכֹּרֶת f. (with suff. מַשְׂכֻּרְתִּי).—I.
wages.—II. reward, Ru. 2:12.

שְׂלָו f. (pl. שַׂלְוִים), a quail.

שַׂלְמָה trans. for שִׂמְלָה f.(pl. שְׂלָמוֹת).
—I. a garment.—II. any cloth.—
III. clothing.—IV. p.n., the father
of Boaz, who was called also
שַׂלְמוֹן.—V. p. n. of a man.

שַׂלְמַי p. n. of a man.

שְׂמֹאל, שְׂמֹאול m., the left hand
or side; מִשְּׂמֹאל on the left or
north; עַל שְׂמֹאל or שֶׂל שְׂ on or to
the left or north. הִשְׂמִיל, הִשְׂמְאִיל, הַשְׂמְאִיל Hiph.—
I. went to the left. — II. used the
left hand.

שְׂמֹאלִי, שְׂמָלִי m., שְׂמָאלִית f., belonging to the left, on the left.

שָׂמַח, שָׂמֵחַ I. was glad. — II. expressed joy.—III. burned brightly,
with בְּ, עַל, לְ. Pi. שִׂמַּח made to
rejoice, with עַל, לְ, מִן. Hiph. the
same.

שָׂמֵחַ m. (pl. const. שִׂמְחֵי; f.
שְׂמֵחָה).—I. joyful.—II. expressing
joy.—III. rejoicing in or at, with
לְ.

שִׂמְחָה f. (pl. שְׂמָחוֹת).—I. joy.—II.
a festival.—III. merriment.

שְׂמִיכָה ; see סמך.

הַשְׂמִיל ; see in שׂמאל.

שִׂמְלָה f. (pl. שְׂמָלוֹת), garment; see
שַׂלְמָה I.

שַׂמְלָה p.n., a king of Edom.

שְׂמָמִית f., a species of lizard, Pro.
30:28.

שָׂנֵא (fut. יִשְׂנָא; inf. abs. שָׂנֹא, const.
שְׂנֹא, שְׂנֹאת, שִׂנְאָה) hated, with
לְ; part. שֹׂנֵא hater, enemy. Niph.
was hated. Pi. part. מְשַׂנֵּא an
enemy.

שָׂנֵא Ch. part. שָׂנְאִין, haters.

שִׂנְאָה f., hatred.

שָׂנִיא m., שְׂנִיאָה f., hated, Deu. 21:15.

שְׂנִיר p.n., the name of mount Hermon
among the Amorites.

שְׂעִפִּים ; see סעף.

שָׂעַר I. shuddered. — II. feared, Deu.
32:17, with עַל.—III. swept, tore
away as a tempest, Ps. 58:10.
Niph. a tempest raged, Ps. 50:3.
Pi. swept away with a tempest, Job
27:21. Hith. raged like a tempest, Dan. 11:40.

שָׂעִיר m., שְׂעִירָה f.—I. hairy, Gen. 27:
11, 23. — II. a goat (always with
עִזִּים). Pl. שְׂעִירִים I. probably

wild goats, Isa. 13:21; 34:14.—II. showers, Deu. 32:2.

שֵׂעִיר p.n., *Seir.*—I. the district between the Dead Sea and the gulf of Akabah.—II. a mountain of Judah.

שְׂעִירָה p.n., a district unknown.

שֵׂעָר const. שְׂעַר m., *the hair.*

שְׂעַר m. Ch., *the hair.*

שַׂעַר m.—I. *a storm, tempest.*—II. *shuddering, horror;* same as סַעַר.

שְׂעָרָה f., *a tempest.*

שַׂעֲרָה f.—I. *a hair.*—II. *the hair.*

שְׂעֹרָה f., *barley* (the plant); pl. שְׂעֹרִים *barley* (the grain).

שְׂעָרִים p.n. of a man.

שָׂפָה f. (dual שְׂפָתַיִם, שִׂפְתֵי; with suff. שְׂפָתָיו; pl. const. שִׂפְתוֹת).—I. *a lip.*—II. *a language.*—III. *words.*—IV. *brim of a vessel.*—V. *shore of the sea, bank of a river.*—VI. *edge, edging.*—VII. *border of a country,* Jud. 7:22.

שָׂפַח Pi. *struck with baldness,* Isa. 3:17.

מִשְׂפָּח *"oppression,"* Eng. Ver., Isa. 5:7.

שָׂפָם m., *the chin, the beard.*

שָׂפַן *hid, concealed,* Deu. 33:19.

שָׂפַק I. *clapped the hands,* Job 27:23—II. *sufficed,* 1 Ki. 20:10. Hiph. *bargained with,* Isa. 2:6; with בְּ.

שֶׂפֶק m., *contempt,* Job 36:18.

שַׂק m. (with suff. שַׂקּוֹ; pl. שַׂקִּים).—I. *sack-cloth.*—II. *a sack.*

שָׂקַד Niph. *was bound, tied,* Lam. 1:14.

שָׂקַר Pi. *painted the eyes with stibium* (a black powder), Isa. 3:16.

שֵׂר; see שַׂר.

שָׂרַג Pu. *was interwoven,* Job 40:17. Hith. the same, Lam. 1:14.

שְׂרוּג p.n. of a man.

שָׂרִיגִים m. pl., *branches of a vine.*

שָׂרַד *fled, escaped,* Jos. 10:20; (Arab. the same.)

שָׂרִיד m., *one that escapes.*—II. *a remnant,* Isa. 1:9.

שְׂרָד m., *colour;* בִּגְדֵי שְׂ *coloured garments* (Exodus only).

שְׂרָד m., *only.*

שָׂרָה *was a prince, prevailed,* with אֶת, עִם; see שָׂרַר.

שָׂרָה s. f.; see שַׂר.

שָׂרַי p.n., *Sarai* (afterwards *Sarah*), the wife of Abraham..

שְׂרָיָה, שְׂרָיָהוּ p.n. of a man.

מִשְׂרָה f., *government,* Isa. 9:5, 6.

שֶׂרַח p.n. of a man.

שָׂרַט *cut, made incisions.* Niph. *was crushed,* Zec. 12:3.

שֶׂרֶט m., *an incision,* Lev. 19:28.

שָׂרֶטֶת f., *the same,* Lev. 21:5.

שָׂרִיגִים, see שׂרג; שָׂרִיד, see שׂרד.

שָׂרַךְ Pi. part. f. מְשָׂרֶכֶת *twisting its course, wandering in all directions,* Jer. 2:23.

שְׂרוֹךְ m., *shoe latchet.*

שַׂרְסְכִים p.n. of an Assyrian eunuch.

שָׂרַע, part. שָׂרוּעַ *stretched out, monstrously prolonged* (of a limb). Hith. *stretched himself out,* Isa. 28:20.

שַׂרְעַפִּים *thoughts;* see סעף.

שָׂרַף I. *burned, consumed.*—II. *burned spices at a funeral.* — III. *baked bricks*, Gen. 11:3.   Niph. and Pu. *was burnt.*

שָׂרָף m.—I. *a venomous serpent*, probably the coluber cerastes — II. p. n. of a man.

שְׂרָפִים m. pl., *seraphim, six-winged spirits*, Isa. 6:2, 6.

שְׂרֵפָה f.—I. *burning fire.*—II. *a funeral burning.*

מִשְׂרָפוֹת f. pl. — I. *burning.* — II. מִשְׂרְפוֹת מַיִם p. n., a place near Sidon.

שָׂרַק *combed, hackled flax*, Isa. 19:9.

שׂרֵק m., שְׂרֵקָה f. — I. *a vine of a choice quality.*—II. שֹׂרֵק p. n., a valley between Askelon and Gaza.

שָׂרֻקִים m. pl., *shoots of the vine*, Isa. 16:8.

שָׂרֹק m., pl. שְׂרֻקִּים *bay* (colour of a horse), Zec. 1:8.

שָׂרַר *acted as a prince.* Hith. הִשְׂתָּרֵר *made himself a prince.*

שַׂר m. (pl. שָׂרִים), *prince, ruler, chief, captain.*

שָׂרָה f. — I. *a princess, a woman of rank.* — II. p. n., *Sarah*, the wife of Abraham ; see שָׂרַי.

שָׂשׂוֹן ; see שׂוֹשׂ.

שֵׂת for שְׂאֵת ; see נשׂא.

שִׂתַם *shut out*, Lam. 3:8.

שָׂתַר . Niph. *were concealed*, 1 Sa. 5:9.

שׁ

...שֶׁ...שְׁ an abbreviation of אֲשֶׁר, prefixed to every part of speech.

שָׁאַב (fut. יִשְׁאַב) *drew water.*

מַשְׁאָב m., pl. מַשְׁאַבִּים *watering places*, Jud. 5:11.

שָׁאַג (fut. יִשְׁאַג).—I. *roared as a lion.* —II. *shrieked for anguish*, Ps. 38:9.

שְׁאָנָה const. שַׁאֲנַת f. — I. *roar of a lion.* — II. *groan, shriek of anguish.*

שָׁאָה *was desolate* (a city), Isa. 6:11. Niph. I. *was desolate* (a city), Isa. 6:11. — II. *were dashed together*, Isa. 17:12, 13.   Hiph. *lay waste*, Isa. 37:26.   Hith. הִשְׁתָּאָה *wondered, was in astonishment*, with לְ.

שׁאָה f., Pro. 1:27, Ketib *a storm* ; same as שׁוֹאָה.

שְׁאֵיהֶם ; see שׁוֹא.

שֵׁאיָה f., *crash, destruction*, Isa. 24:12.

שְׁאֵת f., *desolation*, Lam. 3:47.

שֵׁת f., *noise, tumult of war*, Num. 24:17.

שָׁאוֹן m. — I. *shouting, the noise of waves.*— II. *desolation, ruin.*

מַשּׁאוֹת, מַשּׁוּאוֹת f. pl., *desolation, a desolate place.*

שְׁאָט, שָׁאט *contempt* ; see שׁוּט.

שָׁאט part. from II. שׁוּט.

שָׁאַל, שָׁאֵל (fut. יִשְׁאַל). — I. *questioned, enquired.* — II. *requested, prayed for.* — III. *borrowed*, with מֵעִם, מֵאֵת, מִן, or לְ ; שָׁאַל לְשָׁלוֹם *enquired of his welfare, saluted* ; שָׁאַל בֵּאלֹהִים *enquired of God.*   Niph. *requested for himself.*   Pi. שִׁאֵל *asked earnestly*, with בְּ.   Hiph. *gave in answer to a request, gave.*

שְׁאֵל Ch., *asked, enquired.*

שָׁאָל p. n. of a man.

שָׁאוּל p. n. of a man, *Saul.* Patron שְׁאוּלִי.

שְׁאוֹל, שְׁאֹל com., *the abode of the*

soul after death (see אֲבַדּוֹן), with
ה loc. שְׁאֵלָה.

שְׁאֵלָה f. (with suff. שְׁאֶלְתִּי, שְׁאֵלְתֶךָ,
שְׁאֵלָתָם), *asking, a request.*

שֵׁלָה I. same as שְׁאֵלָה. — II. p.n.,
one of the sons of Judah ; patron.
שֵׁלָנִי.

שְׁאֵלָא f. Ch., *demand,* Dan. 4:14.

שַׁלְתִּיאֵל, שְׁאַלְתִּיאֵל p.n. of a man.

מִשְׁאָל p. n., a town of the Levites in
the tribe of Asher.

מִשְׁאָלָה f., *prayers.*

שָׁאַן. Pil. שַׁאֲנַן *was quiet, secure,
wanton.*

שַׁאֲנָן m., שַׁאֲנַנָּה f.— I. *quiet.* — II.
wanton, luxurious. — III. *wantonness, pride.*

שָׁאסִיךָ, שַׁאֲסֶיךָ ; see שסס.

שָׁאַף I. *panted, gasped,* Ps. 119:131.
— II. *panted for, desired eagerly.*
—III. *swallowed up, destroyed.*

שָׁאַר *was left,* 1 Sa. 16:11. Niph. the
same. Hiph. *left, had left.*

שְׁאָר m., *the remainder, remnant.*

שְׁאָר m. Ch., the same.

שְׁאָר יָשׁוּב (*a remnant shall return*).
Prophetic name of the son of
Isaiah, Isa. 7:3.

שְׁאֵר m. — I. *flesh.* — II. *any near
relation.*—III. *a right arising from
marriage,* Ex. 21:10.

שַׁאֲרָה f., *near, relation, relationship,*
Lev. 18:17.

שְׁאֵרָה p. n. of a woman.

שְׁאֵרִית f., *remainder, remnant.*

מִשְׁאֶרֶת f., *kneading trough.*

שֵׁאת ; see שאה.

שֵׁב, with ה parag. שְׁבָה Kal imp.
from ישׁב.

שְׁבָא p. n. of a country, probably
Arabia Felix.

שָׁבַב (Arab. *kindled*).

שָׁבִיב m., *flame,* Job 18:5.

שָׁבִיב m. Ch., the same.

שְׁבָבִים m. pl., *fragments,* Hos. 8:6.

שָׁבָה (imp. וּשֲׁבֵה ; fut. apoc. וַיִּשְׁבְּ)
*carried captive, took prisoners, car-
ried off;* part. שֹׁבִים m., שֹׁבִיוֹת f.,
captives. Niph. *was led captive.*

שְׁבוּאֵל p. n. of a man ; written also
שׁוּבָאֵל.

שְׁבִי, with pause שֶׁבִי m. (with suff.
שֶׁבְיְךָ, שֶׁבְיְכֶם); f. שִׁבְיָה I.
captive. — II. *troop of captives.* —
III. *captivity.*

שִׁבְיָה f.— I. *troop of captives, spoil.*
—II. *captivity.*

שְׁבִית, שְׁבוּת f.— I. *captivity.* — II.
captives. שׁוּב שׁ I. *turned from
captivity.* — II. *restored to prosperity.*

שְׁבוֹ m., *an agate* ; LXX. ἀχάτης.

שָׁבַח. Pi. שִׁבַּח I. *praised, commended*
—II. *quieted, restrained, kept back.*
Hiph. *quieted,* Ps. 65:8. Hith.
boast of, glory in, with בְ.

שְׁבַח Ch. Pa. *praised.*

שֵׁבֶט, שֶׁבֶט com. (with suff. שִׁבְטִי).
— I. *staff.*—II. *rod* (for punishment).— III. *sceptre.* — IV. *dart,
short spear.*—V. *tribe.*

שְׁבַט com. Ch., *a tribe,* Ezr. 6:17.

שְׁבָט m., *the eleventh month of the
Jewish year, corresponding to our
February and March.*

שַׁרְבִיט m., *a sceptre* (Esther only).

שִׁבְיָה, שְׁבִי *captive, &c.;* see שבה.

שֶׁבִי and שְׁבִי p. n. of a man.

שְׁבִיסִים m. pl., " *sun-like ornaments of the neck*," (Schrœder); "*cauls,*" Eng. Ver., Isa. 3:18; sense uncertain.

שְׁבִיעִי, שְׁבִיעִית; see שׁבע.

שְׁבִירָה; see שׁבה.

שְׁבִיל m., *a path, mode of conduct;* (Arab. the same).

שׂבֶל m., "locks" (of hair), Eng.Ver., Isa. 47:2.

שׁבֶל or שׁבֶל f., pl. const. שִׁבְלֵי a *branch*, Zec. 4:12.

שִׁבֹּלֶת f. (pl. שִׁבֹּלִים).—I. *a stream of water.*—II. *an ear of corn.*

שַׁבְלוּל m., *a snail.* Ps. 58:9.

שֶׁבְנָא, שֶׁבְנָה p. n., *Shebna*, the scribe.

שְׁבַנְיָה p. n. of a man.

שֶׁבַע, const. שְׁבַע, f. שִׁבְעָה, const. שִׁבְעַת m., *seven, the seventh;* adv. *seventh, sevenfold;* שִׁבְעָה שִׁבְעָה *by sevens;* שִׁבְעָה עָשָׂר m., שְׁבַע עֶשְׂרֵה f., *seventeen;* dual שִׁבְעָתַיִם I. *sevenfold.* — II. *seventimes.* Pl. שִׁבְעִים *seventy.*

שִׁבְעָנָה m., *seven*, Job 42:13.

שָׁבֻעַ m. (dual שְׁבֻעַיִם; pl. שָׁבֻעִים; חַג שָׁבֻעוֹת).—I. *a week;* שָׁבֻעוֹת *the feast of weeks.*—II. *a week of years*, Dan. c. 9 & 10.

שְׁבִיעִי m., שְׁבִיעִית f., *seventh.*

II. שֶׁבַע p. n., (a) *a town of Simeon;* (b) *of a man;* (c) שִׁבְעָה *name of a well.*

שׁבע *bound by oaths*, Eze. 21:28. Niph. נִשְׁבַּע *swore*, with לְ; *swore to*, with בְּ; *swore by.* Hiph. I. *caused to swear.*—II. *adjured.*

שְׁבֻעָה, שְׁבוּעָה f., *an oath.*

שָׁבַץ Pi. " embroider," Eng. Ver., Ex. 28:39; sense doubtful. Pu. *set* (of a precious stone), Ex. 28:20.

שָׁבָץ m., *perplexity,* 2 Sa. 1:9.

מִשְׁבְּצוֹת f. pl.—I. *gold settings* (for stones).—II. *cloth of gold,* Ps. 45:14.

תַּשְׁבֵּץ m., *embroidery,* Ex. 28:4.

שְׁבַק Ch. *left.* Ith. *was left.*

שָׁבַר fut. יִשְׁבֹּר).—I. *broke to pieces.*—II. *tore* (as a wild beast).—III. *broke the heart.* — IV. *broke the power of, destroyed.*—V. *quenched thirst.*—VI. *assigned,* with חֵק.—VII. from שֶׁבֶר *sold corn,* Gen. 41:56. — VIII. *bought corn.* Niph. I. *was broken.*—II. *was torn.*—III. *was broken* (the heart).— IV. *was destroyed.* Pi. שִׁבֵּר, *broke with violence.* Hiph. I. *caused to suffer labour pains,* Isa. 66:9. — II. *sold corn.* Hoph. *was broken-hearted,* Jer. 8:21.

שֶׁבֶר, שֵׁבֶר (with suff. שִׁבְרוֹ) I. *breaking, fracture.* — II. *vexation, sorrow.* — III. *calamity, ruin.* — IV. *provision, corn.*—V. *interpretation,* Jud. 7:15.—VI. p. n., *a place near Ai.*

שִׁבָּרוֹן m.—I. *breaking,* i.e. *pain, sorrow,* Eze. 21:11. — II. *calamity, ruin,* Jer. 17:18.

מַשְׁבֵּר m. — I. *pains of childbirth.* —II. *violent pains* (of any kind), 2 Sa. 22:5.—III. *breakers* (of the sea).

מִשְׁבָּר m., the same.

שְׁבַשׁ Ch. Ith., *perplexed,* Dan. 5:9.

שָׁבַת (יִשְׁבֹּת, יִשְׁבַּת, fut.).—I. ceased.—
II. rested; with מִן from.—III. was
interrupted, Neh. 6:3.—IV. ceased
to exist, came to an end.—V. with
שַׁבָּת kept the sabbath. Niph.
came to an end. Hiph. I. caused
to cease. — II. interrupted. — III.
brought to an end.

שֶׁבֶת m.—I. ceasing. — II. intermission; see also in יָשַׁב.

שַׁבָּת com. (with suff. שַׁבַּתּוֹ; pl.
שַׁבָּתוֹת; const. שַׁבְּתוֹת) cessation, time of rest, sabbath; שַׁבַּת
שָׁנִים a sabbath of years.

שַׁבָּתוֹן m., rest, a time of rest.

שַׁבְּתִי p. n. of a man.

מִשְׁבָּת m., pl. מִשְׁבַּתִּים cessations,
Lam. 1:7.

שֶׁבֶת Kal inf., from יָשַׁב.

שְׁבַת Ch. Kal pret. f., from שׁוּב.

שְׁנָא same as שָׁנָה.

שָׁגַג erred, committed an error, Lev.
5:18; inf. בְּשַׁגָּם because of their
sin.

שְׁגָגָה f., error, unintentional fault.

שָׁגָה erred, went astray, with מִן.
Hiph. I. allowed to err, Ps. 119:
10.—II. caused to go astray.

שָׁגֵא p. n. of a man.

שְׁגִיאָה f., error, Ps. 19:13.

שִׁגָּיוֹן m. (pl. שִׁגְיֹנוֹת) a doleful song,
lament, Ps. 7:1; Hab. 3:1.

מִשְׁגֶּה m., mistake, inadvertency, Gen.
43:12.

שָׁגַח Hiph. looked to.

שָׁגַל lay with a woman; fut. יִשְׁגָּל.
Niph. and Pu. pass. of Kal.

שֵׁגָל f., a queen.

שֵׁגָל f. Ch., the same.

שַׁגֵּן Kal inf. with suff., from שָׁגַן

שָׁגַע. Pu. part. מְשֻׁגָּע maddened, mad
Hith. acted like a madman.

שִׁגָּעוֹן m., madness, impetuosity.

שֶׁגֶר, שְׁגַר m., offspring, progeny
Exod. 13:12.

שַׁד, see שָׁדֶה; שֵׁד, see שׁוּד; שׁד
see שָׁדֶה, שָׁדַד.

שָׁדַד (יְשָׁדֵּם, יְשָׁדְּדֵם, fut. with suff.).—
I. attacked, invaded.—II. plundered,
laid waste, ruined; part. שֹׁדֵד in-
vader, plunderer; שָׁדוּד destroyed.
Niph. was laid waste. Pi. laid waste,
ruined utterly. Pu. שֻׁדַּד, שֻׁדָּד
was laid waste. Po. laid waste.
Hoph. הֻשַּׁד was laid waste.

שֹׁד, שׁוֹד m.—I. destruction, ruin.—
II. violence, oppression.— III. ex-
torted property, Am. 3:10.

שַׁדַּי m., the Almighty (the name of
God as revealed to the Patriarchs); LXX. παντοκράτωρ.

שָׁדָה root not used; (Arab. was well
watered).

שַׁד m.—I. teats of an animal. — II.
breast of a woman; dual שָׁדַיִם
שְׁדֵי the breasts.

שֹׁד m., the same.

שִׁדָּה f., שִׁי וְשִׁדּוֹת, Ecc. 2:8, "musical instruments and that of all
sorts," Eng. Ver.—pleasures of
every kind (Ges. and Lee).

שַׁדְרִאוּר p. n. of a man.

שְׁדֵמָה f., blighted corn; pl. שַׁדְמוֹת,
שְׁדֵמוֹת—I. fields.—II. corn fields
Hab. 3:17.—III. vineyards.

שָׁדַף blighted.

שְׁדֵפָה I., *blight in corn*, 2 Ki. 19: 26.

שִׁדָּפוֹן m., the same.

שְׁדַר Ch. Ithp. *exerting himself*, Dan. 6:15.

שַׁדְרַךְ p.n., *Shadrach*, one of the three holy children.

שֹׁהַם m.—I. *onyx* or *sardonyx*.—II. p. n. of a man.

שׁוֹא m. (pl. with suff. שְׁאִיהֶם) *ragings*, Ps. 35:17.

שָׁוְא m.—I. *guilt*.-II. *calamity*.-III. *worthlessness, vanity.*— IV. *falsehood.*

שָׁו same as שָׁוְא.

שׁוֹאָה f.—I. *a storm*.—II. *destruction*. —III. *a desolate place.*

מְשׁוֹאָה f., *desolation, a desolate place.*

תְּשֻׁאָה f., pl. תְּשֻׁאוֹת *tumult, shouting.*

שׁוֹב, Jer. 42:10, for שׁוּב Kal inf., from יָשַׁב.

שׁוּב (fut. וַיָּשָׁב ,יָשֹׁב ,יָשׁוּב).—I. *went or came back*; with מִן *from*; *turned to, returned*, with אֶל ,לְ ,עַל, עַד *to.* — II. *turned himself about*, 1 Chron. 21:20. — III. *changed his course of life.* (For many uses with other words which slightly modify these primary meanings, see Concordance.) Pil. שׁוֹבֵב I. *led back.*—II. *restored.*—III. *led astray*, Isa. 47:10. — IV. *refreshed*, Ps. 23:3. Pul. שׁוֹבַב *was brought back.* Hiph. הֵשִׁיב (fut. וַיָּשֶׁב ,יָשֵׁב ,יָשִׁיב).—I. *brought back.*—II. *restored.*—III. *requited.* —IV. *brought upon a person.*—V. *sent as a tribute* or *atonement.*—

VI. *distributed, assigned.* — VII. *moved away, put aside.*—VIII. *repelled, hindered.* —IX. *recalled, revoked a declaration.*—X. *caused to turn from sin.* — XI. *withheld, withdrew.*—XII. *brought down, reduced.*—XIII. *caused to answer*, Job 20:2. With דָּבָר *answered*; with פָּנָיו *turned away his anger;* with (עַל) אֶל־לֵב *laid to heart, considered;* with פָּנִי *turned away, refused.* Hoph. הוּשַׁב *was returned, brought back.*

שׁוּבָה f., *returning*, Isa. 30:15.

שִׁיבָה f., *returning*, Ps. 126:1 ; see another meaning in יָשַׁב.

שׁוֹבָב m.—I. *a rebellious person*.—II. p.n. of a man.

שׁוֹבֵב m., שׁוֹבֵבָה f., *a rebel.*

שׁוּבָאֵל p. n., same as שְׁבוּאֵל.

מְשׁוֹבָב p.n. of a man.

מְשׁוּבָה ,מְשֻׁבָה f.—I. *turning away* (from God).—II. *rebellious, back sliding.*

תְּשׁוּבָה f.—I. *return.*—II. *an answer.*

שׁוֹבָךְ p.n. of a man.

שׁוֹבָל p.n. of a man.

שׁוֹבֵק p.n. of a man.

שׁוּג same as שָׁנָה ,שָׁנַג.

מְשׁוּגָה f., *error*, Job 19:4.

שׁוֹד same as שָׁדַד *laid waste*; fut. יָשׁוּד, Ps. 91:6.

שׁוֹד same as שֹׁד; see שָׁדַד.

שֵׁד m., pl. שֵׁדִים *idols*, Deu. 32:17 ; Ps. 106:37; LXX. δαιμόνια.

שָׁוָה I. *was equal to, resembled.* — II. *was of equal value* or *importance.* —III. *was fitting, proper*, Est. 3:8. —IV. *was sufficient*, Est. 7:4. With

שָׁוָה‎ Pi. שִׁוָּה‎ I. *made level,
smoothed,* Isa. 28:25. — II. *made
similar,* Ps. 131:2. — III. *made
himself like,* Isa. 38:13. — IV.
placed, proposed. — V. *produced
fruit,* Hos. 10:1. Hiph. *made
like, compared.* Nithpa. נִשְׁתָּוָה‎
being made like, Pro. 27:15.

שְׁוָא‎ Ch. Pa., *placed, made equal,* Dan.
5:21, with עִם‎. Ithpa. *was made
into,* Dan. 3:29.

שָׁוָה‎ f., *equity,* Job 33:27.

שָׁוֵה‎ p.n., *a plain to the north of Jerusalem;* שָׁוֵה קִרְיָתַיִם‎ *a city of
Moab.*

שׁוּחַ‎ *went down, sank.*

שׁוּחַ‎ p. n. of one of Abraham's sons;
patron. שׁוּחִי‎.

שׁוּחָה‎ f.—I. *a pit, pitfall.*—II. p.n.
of a man.

שִׁיחָה‎ f., *a pit,* Ps. 119:85.

שׁוּחָם‎ p.n. of a man.

שַׁחַת‎ f.—I. *a pit.*—II. *a dungeon.*—
III. *a grave;* see also in שָׁחַת‎.

I. שׁוּט‎ 1. *spread like water, went to
and fro.*—2. *struck, struck into the
water,* i.e. *rowed.* Pil. שׁוֹטֵט‎ *ran
far and wide.* Hithpal. הִתְשׁוֹטֵט‎
same as Pil.

שׁוֹט‎ m.—I. *a whip, scourge.*—II.
calamity.

שַׁיִט‎ m., *an oar, oars,* Isa. 33:21.

שֵׁטֶם‎ m., *a whip, scourge,* Jos. 23:13.

מָשׁוֹט‎ m., *an oar, rudder,* Eze. 27:29.

מִשּׁוֹט‎ m., *the same,* Eze. 27:6.

II. שׁוּט‎ (Syr. *despised*); part. שָׁאט‎
despised (Ezekiel only).

שְׁאָט‎ m. (with suff. שְׁאָטְךָ‎), *contempt*
(of another), Ezekiel only.

שׁוּל‎ m., *skirt* (of a garment), *train.*

שׁוֹלָל‎ *spoil;* see שָׁלָל‎.

שׁוּלַמִּית‎; see שָׁלֵם‎.

שׁוּם‎ m., *garlick,* Nu. 11:5.

שׁוּנִי‎ p n., *a son of Gad.*

שׁוּנֵם‎ p.n., *a town of Issachar;* שׁוּנַמִּי‎
m., שׁוּנַמִּית‎ f., *a Shunemite.*

שׁוּעַ‎, שָׁוַע‎ Pi. שִׁוַּע‎ *cried out for help,
implored,* with אֶל‎. Pil. and Hiph.
see in שָׁעַע‎.

שֶׁוַע‎ m. (with suff. שַׁוְעִי‎), *a cry for
help,* Ps. 5:3.

שׁוֹעַ‎ m.—I. *affluent,* Job 34:19.—II.
liberal, Isa. 32:5.

שֶׁוַע‎ m.—I. *safety,* Job 30:24. — II.
affluence, Job 36:19 —III. p.n. of
a man.

שַׁוְעָה‎ f., *cry for help.*

שׁוּעָא‎ p. n. of a man.

תְּשׁוּעָה‎, תְּשֻׁעָה‎ f., *freedom, safety,
salvation, deliverance.*

שׁוּעָל‎; see שָׁעַל‎.

שׁוֹעֵר‎; see שָׁעַר‎.

שׁוּף‎ (fut. יָשׁוּף‎).—I. *bruised, shattered,*
Gen. 3:15; Job 9:17. — II. *con-
cealed,* Ps. 139:11.

שׁוּפָךְ‎ p.n., *same as* שׁוֹבָךְ‎.

שׁוּפָמִי‎ p. n. of a man.

שׁוֹפָר‎ *trumpet;* see שָׁפַר‎.

שׁוּק‎ *same as* שָׁקַק‎. Hiph. הֵשִׁיק‎ I.
caused to run over, Joel 2:24. —
II. *overflowed,* Joel 4:13. Pil.
שׁוֹקֵק‎ *cause to overflow,* Ps. 65:10.

שׁוּק‎ m. (pl. שְׁוָקִים‎), *a street.*

שׁוֹק‎ com. (dual שֹׁקַיִם‎), *leg* (of a man
or animal); trop. שׁוֹקֵי הָאִישׁ‎ perhaps *infantry,* Ps. 147:10

שָׁק‎ m. Ch., *leg.*

תְּשׁוּקָה‎ f., *desire.*

שׁוּר (fut. יָשׁוּר).— I. *viewed, beheld, perceived.* — II. *watched* (for good or evil). — III. *went,* Is. 57:9; part. f. pl. שָׁרוֹת *travellers,* Eze. 27:25. See also in שִׁיר.

שׁוּר m. — I. *an enemy* (one who watches for evil), Ps. 92:12.— II. *a wall;* pl. שׁוּרוֹת.— III. p. n., a place in the wilderness; מִדְבַּר שׁוּר *the wilderness of Shur,* between Egypt and Palestine.

שׁוּר m. Ch., *a wall.*

שָׁרוֹת f. pl., *walls,* Jer. 5:10.

שׁוֹר m. (pl. שְׁוָרִים).— I. *an ox.*— II. *a herd of oxen.*

תְּשׁוּרָה f., *a present,* 1 Sa. 9:7.

שׁוּשׁ root not used; (Syr. *alabaster*).

שַׁיִשׁ m., *white marble,* 1 Ch. 29:2.

שֵׁשׁ m.— I. *white marble,* Est. 1:6.— II. *very fine linen.* (See also in its place.)

שׁוּשָׁן m.— I. *a lily.*— II. *an artificial lily.*— III. שׁוּשַׁן עֵדוּת probably the name of a musical instrument.— IV. שׁוּשָׁן p. n.: (a) the city of *Susa* in Persia; (b) a place unknown.

שׁוֹשָׁן m., *a lily;* pl. שׁוֹשַׁנִּים.— I. *lilies.*— II. *musical instruments.*

שׁוֹשַׁנָּה f., the same.

שׁוּשַׁנְכְוָא Ch., *an inhabitant of Susa.*

שׁוֹשַׁתִּי Po. pret. from שׁוּשׁ; same as שָׁשָׂה.

שׁוּת; see שִׁית.

שׁוּתֶלַח p. n. of a man. Patron. שׁוּתַלְחִי.

שֵׁזַב Ch. Pe. שֵׁיזִיב, שֵׁיזִב *delivered, rescued.*

שֵׁזַף *beheld, saw.* (See also in שָׂרַף.)

שָׁזַר Hoph. part. שֵׁשׁ מָשְׁזָר *fine twined*

linen (probably wrung out for the purpose of bleaching it).

שֵׁח; see שָׁחַח.

שָׁחַד *bribed.*

שֹׁחַד m.— I. *a present.*— II. *a bribe.* —III. *bribery,* Job 15:34.

שָׁחָה *bowed himself,* Isa. 51:23. Hiph. הִשְׁחָה *bowed down,* Pro. 12:25. Hith. הִשְׁתַּחֲוָה (inf. הִשְׁתַּחֲוֹת Ch. הִשְׁתַּחֲוָיָה; imp. f. הִשְׁתַּחֲוִי; fut. יִשְׁתַּחֲוָה; apoc. יִשְׁתַּחוּ) I. *prostrated himself;* with לְפָנֵי, לְ *before.*—II. *worshipped.*

שַׁחֲגָת f., *a pit,* Pro. 28:10.

שְׁחִית f., the same.

שָׁחוֹר same as שִׁיחוֹר; see שָׁחַר

שָׁחַח (pret. שָׁחֲחוּ, שַׁחוּ; fut. יִשַּׁח). — I. *bowed himself, stooped.* — II. *was brought low, humbled.* Niph. the same. Hiph. הֵשַׁח *brought low, humbled.* Hithp. הִשְׁתּוֹחֵחַ *brought low, broke.*

שַׁח m., *having downcast eyes, meek,* Job 22:29.

שָׁחַט (fut. יִשְׁחַט; inf. שְׁחָטָה). — I. *slaughtered* (an animal).—II. *slew* (a person).—III. זָהָב שָׁחוּט "*alloyed gold*" (Lee). Niph. *was slaughtered.*

שְׁחִיטָה f., *slaughtering, sacrifice,* 2 Ch. 30:17.

שְׁחִין; see שָׁחַן.

שָׁחִים *spontaneous;* see סָחִישׁ.

שָׁחִית, see שָׁחַת; שְׁחִיתָה, see שָׁחַת.

שָׁחַל m., *a lion.*

שְׁחֵלֶת f., *some kind of perfume,* or *pastil;* LXX. ὄνυξ, Ex. 30:34.

שָׁחַן (Arab. *fever*).

שָׁחִן m., *inflammation, any burning disease*; שְׁ מִצְרַיִם *the ulcer of Egypt*.

שָׁחַף root not used ; (Arab. *was thin*).

שָׁחִיף m., *thin covering of wood*, Eze. 41:16.

שַׁחַף m. LXX. λάρος ; *a sea gull*, Lev. 11:16; Deu. 14:15.

שַׁחֶפֶת f., *consumption*.

שָׁחַן (Arab. *was lifted up*).

שַׁחַץ m., *mightiness, fierceness*.

שַׁחֲצִים p. n., a place in the tribe of Issachar.

שָׁחַק *reduced to dust, crushed, wasted away*.

שַׁחַק m.—I. *dust*, Isa. 40:15.—II. *a cloud*; pl. שְׁחָקִים *clouds*.—III. *the sky*.

שָׁחַר I. *was black*, Job 30:30.—II. *did a thing early, sought early.* Pi. שִׁחַר *sought early*, with אֶל.

שָׁחֹר, שָׁחוֹר m., שְׁחֹרָה f., *black*.

שְׁחוֹר m., *blackness*, Lam. 4:8.

שַׁחַר m.—I. *the dawn*; בֶּן־שַׁחַר *lucifer*, "the morning star." — II. adv. *in the morning.* — III. *rise, origin*, Isa. 47:11.

שַׁחֲרוּת f., *dawn of life, youth*, Ecc. 11:10.

שְׁחַרְחֹרֶת f., *very black*, Cant. 1:6.

שְׁחַרְיָה p. n. of a man.

שְׁחַרַיִם p. n. of a man.

מִשְׁחָר m., *the dawn*, Ps. 110:3.

שִׁחֹר, שָׁחוֹר, שִׁיחוֹר m.—I. the name of a river of Egypt, probably the *Nile.* —II. שִׁיחוֹר לִבְנָת a river in Asher.

שָׁחַת Niph. I. *was spoilt.*—II. *was corrupted*, Gen. 6:11, 12. — III. *was destroyed*, Ex. 8:20. Pi. שִׁחֵת

I. *acted corruptly.*—II. *destroyed* — III. *broke a covenant*, Mal 2:8. — IV. *laid aside* (of pity), Am. 1:11. Hiph. הִשְׁחִית *same as Pi.*; with or without דַּרְכּוֹ *corrupted his way.* Hoph. הָשְׁחַת ; part. מָשְׁחָת I. *injured*, Mal. 1:14. —II. *polluted*, Pro. 25:26.

שְׁחַת Ch., part. שְׁחִיתָה *a fault.*

שַׁחַת m.—I. *corruption.*—II. *destruction*; see also שׁוּחַ.

מַשְׁחִית m. (Hiph. part.).—I. *destroyer*, Ex. 12:23—II. *plunderer*,

מָשְׁחָת m., *defilement*, Lev. 22:25.

מַשְׁחֵת m., *destruction*, Eze. 9:1.

מִשְׁחָת m., *disfigured*, Isa. 52:14.

שִׁטָּה f.—I. *the pea-thorn*; (Arab. שנט ; Egypt. *shont*); pl. שִׁטִּים *shittim wood, the wood of the pea-thorn.*—II. p. n., a valley of Moab.

שָׁטַח *spread abroad, strewed.* Pi. שִׁטַּח *spread abroad* (the hands in prayer), Ps. 88:10.

מִשְׁטָח, מִשְׁטוֹחַ m., *place for spreading nets*, Eze. 26:5, 14; 47:10.

שָׁטַט ; see שׁוּט.

שָׁטַף I. *washed off* or *away.*—II. *cleansed by washing.* —III. *swept away* (of a torrent). Niph. I. *was cleansed*, Lev. 15:12. — II. *was swept away*, Dan. 11:22. Pu. *was cleansed*, Lev. 6:21.

שֶׁטֶף, שָׁטֶף m., *washing away, overflowing, inundation.*

שָׁטַר ; part. שֹׁטֵר *magistrate, ruler*, Ex. 5:10, 14 ; Deu. 1:15

שִׁטְרַי p. n. of a man.

מִשְׁטָר m., *authority, influence*, Job 38:33.

שְׂמַר m. Ch., *sovereignty* (if the reading be correct; some suppose an error for שְׂטַר *side*), Dan. 7:5.

שַׁי m., *offering, present* (always with יוֹבִילוּ *bring ye*).

שִׂיאוֹן p. n., a name of Hermon.

שִׂיבָה; see שׁוּב ,יָשַׁב.

שָׁיָה ,fut. apoc. תֶּשִׁי *thou forgettest;* LXX. ἐγκατέλιπες, Deu. 32:18; see נָשָׁה.

שִׁיזָא p. n. of a man

שֵׁיזִיב; see שׁוּב.

שַׁיִט; see שׁוּט.

שִׁיחָה; see שׁוּחַ.

שִׁילֹה ,שִׁילֹנִי; see שָׁלָה.

שִׁין ,שׁוּן (Syr. *minxit*).

שָׁיִן or שֵׁיִן m., pl. שֵׁינִים *urine.*

שֵׁיצָא Ch.; see יָצָא.

שִׁיר ,שׁוּר (fut. יָשִׁיר ,וַיָּשַׁר).— I. *sung;* with לְ *to.*—II. *sung of;* part. שָׁרִים ,שָׁרוֹת *singers.* Pil. שֹׁרֵר *sounded*, Zep. 2:14; part. a *singer.* Hoph. הוּשַׁר *was sung.*

שִׁיר m.—I. *singing.*—II. *a song.*— III. *instrumental music;* כְּלֵי שִׁיר *musical instruments.*

שִׁירָה f., *a song.*

שַׁיִשׁ; see שֵׁשׁ.

שִׁישַׁק p. n., *Shishak*, king of Egypt; LXX. Σεσωγχις.

שִׁית ,שׁוּת (fut. יָשֵׁת ,יָשִׁית ,וַיָּשֶׁת inf. abs. שֹׁת; inf. const. and imp. שִׁית) same as שׂוּם.—I. *placed, laid;* with עַל ,לְ *upon;* with עָלָיו *decorated himself:*—also II. *set over, appointed.*—III. *set together, compared,* with עִם.—IV. שָׁ פָּנָיו אֶל *looked towards.*—V. שָׁ עֵינָיו

looked out after, Ps. 17:11.— VI. שִׁי לֵב *set his heart upon, regarded,* with לְ ,אֶל.— VII. שִׁי יָד עִם *assisted.*—VIII. שִׁי לְנֶגְדּוֹ *looked at, examined,* Ps. 90:8.—IX. *laid up treasure.*—X. *rendered.* Hoph. הוּשַׁת *was required,* with עַל, Ex. 21:30.

שַׁיִת m. (with suff. שִׁיתוֹ) *thorn* (Isaiah only).

שִׁית m., *putting on a dress.*

שָׁתוֹת m. pl., *foundations.*

שֵׁת p. n.—I. *Seth,* the son of Adam. —II. an epithet of the Moabites, Nu. 24:17.

שַׁךְ ,שֹׁךְ Kal inf., from שָׁכַךְ.

שָׁכַב (fut. יִשְׁכַּב; inf. שְׁכַב ,שְׁכֹב; imp. שְׁכָבָה ,שְׁכַב).— I. *lay down.* —II. *slept.*—III. *kept his bed.*—IV. *slept with his fathers, died.*—V *rested* (of the head).—VI. *lay with* (carnally). Pu. *to be laid, to lie.* Niph. I. *placed.*—II. *caused to rest, stoppea.* Hoph. *was placed, laid.*

שְׁכָבָה, const. שִׁכְבַת f.—I. *the act of lying with.*— II. *covering of dew,* Ex. 16:13, 14.

שְׁכֹבֶת f., *act of lying with.*

מִשְׁכָּב m. (pl. מִשְׁכָּבִים ,מִשְׁכָּבוֹת).— I. *a bed.*—II. *a bier,* 2 Chron. 16: 14.—III. *lying in bed.*—IV. *lying with.*

מִשְׁכַּב m. Ch., *a bed.*

שָׁכָה. Hiph. part. מַשְׁכִּים *wandering about lasciviously,* Jer. 5:8.

שְׁכוֹל ,שַׁכּוּל; see שָׁכַל.

שִׁכּוֹר; see שָׁכַר.

שָׁכַח ,שָׁכֵחַ (fut. יִשְׁכַּח) *forgot, disregarded, neglected,* with מִן. Niph. *was forgotten, neglected.* Pi. and

Hiph. *cause to forget.* Hithpa. same as Niph., Ecc. 8:10.

שָׁכֵחַ m. (pl. const. שִׁכְחֵי) *forgetting, neglecting.*

שׁכח Ch. Ithp. הִשְׁתְּכַח *was found, was.* Aph. הַשְׁכַּח *found, discovered.*

שְׁכַנְיָה p.n. of a man.

שָׁכַךְ (inf. שֹׁךְ, שֵׁךְ; fut. pl. וַיָּשֻׁכּוּ). I. *stooped.* — II. *abated.* Hiph. הֵשֵׁךְ I. *placed.* — II. *emptied.*

שָׁכַל (fut. יִשְׁכַּל) *lost children, became childless.* Pi. I. *made childless.* — II. *stripped of inhabitants.* — III. *destroyed* (of a sword), Deu. 32:25. — IV. *produced an abortion.* — V. *lost fruit, &c., was barren;* part. מְשַׁכֵּלָה *an abortion.* Hiph. *lost its inhabitants* (a land).

שִׁכּוֹל m. — I. *privation of children.* — II. *destitution.*

שַׁכּוּל m., שַׁכֻּלָה f. — I. *childless.* — II. *deprived of, without young.*

שִׁכֻּלִים m. pl., *loss of children,* Isa. 49:20.

אֶשְׁכֹּל m. (pl. const. אֶשְׁכְּלוֹת, אַשְׁכְּלוֹת). I. *a cluster, bunch of grapes or flowers;* (Arab. *bound).* — II. p. n.: (a) of a valley in the south of Palestine; (b) of a man.

שְׁכַלָל; see בְּלַל.

שָׁכַם Hiph. הִשְׁכִּים I. *arose in the morning.* — II. *as soon as he arose.* — III. *came in the morning.*

שְׁכֶם with pause שָׁכֶם m. (with suff. שִׁכְמוֹ). — I. *shoulder, shoulders.* — II. *a load, portion,* Gen. 48:22. — III. p. n., *Shechem,* a city of the Levites in Ephraim; with ה loc.

IV שִׁכְמָה, with pause שְׁכָמָה p.n. of a man.

שְׁכֶם p.n. of a man; patron. שִׁכְמִי

שִׁכְמָה f., *the shoulder-blade,* Job 31:22.

שָׁכַן, שָׁכֵן (fut. יִשְׁכֹּן). — I. *lay down to rest, rested.* — II. *continued* — III. *dwelt.* — IV. *inhabited, was inhabited;* part. שֹׁכֵן *inhabiting.* Pi. I. *caused to dwell.* — II. *placed;* שָׁכֵּן שְׁמוֹ *placed his name.* Hiph. I. *caused to dwell.* — II. *fixed.*

שְׁכֵן Ch. Pa., same as Pi. Heb.

שָׁכֵן, const. שְׁכֵן m., שְׁכֵנָה, שְׁכֶנֶת f. — I. *inhabitant.* — II. *neighbour, neighbouring people.*

שֶׁכֶן m., *a dwelling;* with suff. שְׁכָנוֹ, Deu. 12:5.

שְׁכַנְיָה p.n. of a man.

שְׁכַנְיָהוּ p.n. of a man.

מִשְׁכָּן m. — I. *habitation, dwelling.* — II. *the Tabernacle and Temple.* — III. *lair of beasts.*

מִשְׁכַּן m. Ch., *habitation.*

שָׁכַר (fut. יִשְׁכַּר). — I. *drank wine or strong drink.* — II. *was exhilarated, intoxicated.* — III. *became giddy.* Pi. and Hiph. *made drunken.* Hith. *made himself drunken,* 1 Sa 1:14.

שִׁכּוֹר, שִׁכֹּר m., שִׁכֹּרָה f., *drunken, a drunkard.*

שֵׁכָר m. — I. *strong drink (not wine)* — II. *wine,* Nu. 28:7.

שִׁכָּרוֹן m., *drunkenness* (Ezekiel only)

שִׁכְרוֹן p.n., a place of Judah.

אֶשְׁכָּר m., *rich gift, present.*

שֶׁל; see אֲשֶׁר.

שִׁלְאָנָן, שַׁל; see שָׁלָה.

שָׁלָב. Pu. part. מְשֻׁלָּבוֹת joined together (Ex. 26 : 17 ; 36 : 22).

שְׁלַבִּים m. pl., edges, borders, 1 Ki. 7:
28, 29.

שֶׁלֶג m., snow.

הִשְׁלִיג Hiph. "was white as snow,"
Eng. Ver., Ps. 68 : 15.

שָׁלָו, שָׁלָה (pret. שָׁלוּתִי, שָׁלוּ; fut.
יִשְׁלָיוּ; fut. apoc. יֵשֶׁל).— I. was
prosperous, at ease.—II. made prosperous, gave ease to. Niph. became negligent, 2 Ch. 29 : 11. Hiph.
flattered, deceived, 2 K. 4 : 28.

שְׁלָה Ch., was at rest, Dan. 4 : 1.

שָׁל m., fault, error, 2 Sa. 6 : 7.

שָׁלוּ f. Ch., error; same as שָׁלוּת,
Dan. 3 : 29. Ketib.

שֵׁלָה, 1 Sa. 1 : 17, same as שְׁאֵלָה; see
שָׁאַל.

שְׁלֵו m. (pl. const. שְׁלֵוָה (שַׁלְוֵי f.—
I. prosperous, at ease.—II. un-
mindful of God, Eze. 23 : 42.

שָׁלֵיו, שָׁלֵו m.—I. prosperous. — II.
prosperity.

שַׁלְוָ m. (with suff. שַׁלְוִי), prosperity,
Ps. 30 : 7.

שַׁלְוָה f.—I. prosperity, ease.—II. negligence of God.

שַׁלְוָה f. Ch., prosperity, Dan. 4 : 24.

שָׁלוּ, שָׁלוּת f. Ch., error, fault, trespass.

שֶׁלִי m. בַּשֶּׁלִי quietly, privately, 2 Sa.
3 : 27.

שִׁלְיָה f., the after-birth, Deu. 28 : 57.

שַׁלְאֲנָן (from שַׁאֲנָן and שָׁלָה) m.,
wholly at rest, Job 21 : 23.

שִׁילֹה, שִׁלֹה, שִׁלֹ, Gen. 49 : 10 ; quasi
אֲשֶׁר לוֹ, i. e., he whose it is ; "Shiloh,"
Eng. Ver.

שִׁלוֹ, שָׁלוּ, שִׁילוֹ, שִׁילֹה, שִׁילָה p. n., a
city of Ephraim, where the taber-
nacle stood ; שִׁילֹנִי a native of
Shiloh.

שַׁלְהֶבֶת flame ; see לַהַב.

שִׁלוּם, שִׁלֻּם, שִׁלוֹם, שַׁלּוֹם ; see שלם.

שִׁלּוֹן p. n. of a man.

שִׁלְשׁוֹן ; same as שָׁלִישׁ.

שָׁלַח (fut. יִשְׁלַח ; inf. שְׁלֹחַ, שְׁלַח
שַׁלֵּחַ ; imp. שְׁלַח, שִׁלְחָה (שִׁלְחָה).—I. sent
(a person or thing), with לְ, or אֶל,
sometimes עַל — II. sent word,
charge ; with לְ to ; and בְּיַד by,
by the hand of.—III. sent a message
to, with or without דָּבָר.—IV. יַד
or בְּ put forth his hand (to injure),
laid his hand on, with אֶל. It has
the same meaning without יַד
2 Sa. 6 : 6.— V. shoot out arrows
(For other modifications of the
primary senses, see Concordance.)
Niph. inf. נִשְׁלוֹחַ to be sent, Est.
3 : 13. Pi. שִׁלַּח I. sent.—II. sent
away.—III. allowed to depart, dismissed. — IV. set at liberty. — V.
gave in marriage.—VI. sent away,
divorced (a wife). — VII. put in a
place.—VIII. put forth (his hand).
—IX. with בָּאֵשׁ set on fire. — X.
inflicted a calamity.—XI. caused,
Pro. 16 : 28.—XII. threw, threw off.
—XIII. cast out, shoot forth. (See
also Concordance.) Pu. שֻׁלַּח was
sent, dismissed, set at liberty, divorced, thrown. Hiph. with בְּ I.
sent.—II. inflicted a calamity.

שְׁלַח Ch.—I. sent word, orders. — II.
put forth (his hand).

שִׁלּוּחִים m. pl., divorce (of a wife),
Ex. 18 : 2. — II. renunciation (of a

claim), Mic. 1:14. — III. *presents,
dowry*, 1 Ki. 9:16.

שֶׁלַח m. (with suff. שִׁלְחוֹ).—I. *missile.*
—II. *rejection, contempt.*—III. pl.,
shoots, produce.—IV. p. n. of a man.
—V. p. n., *Siloah*, a stream which
ran through Jerusalem; called
also שִׁלֹחַ.

שְׁלֻחוֹת f. pl., *shoots*, Isa. 16:8.

שִׁלְחִי p. n. of a man.

שְׁלָחִים p. n., a town of Judah.

שֻׁלְחָן m. (pl. שֻׁלְחָנוֹת), *table*; עָרַךְ
שֻׁלְחָן *spread, provided, a table*;
שֻׁלְחַן הַפָּנִים שׁ׳ הַמַּעֲרֶכֶת *the table
of shew-bread.*

מִשְׁלָה m.—I. *the sending forth of
cattle* (to graze).—II. (with יָד) *the
putting out the hand.*

מִשְׁלוֹחַ, מִשְׁלָח m., the same; I.
and II.

מִשְׁלַחַת f., the same as II.

שָׁלַט (fut. יִשְׁלָם) *ruled, had power
over,* with עַל, בְּ. Hiph. I. *allowed
to rule.*—II. *gave authority to, permitted,* with בְּ and לְ.

שְׁלֵט Ch., with בְּ.—I. *ruled.*—II. *had
power over.* — III. *seized.* Aph.
caused to rule.

שֶׁלֶט m., pl. שְׁלָטִים, שְׁלָטֵי *shields.*

שַׁלִּיט m., שַׁלֶּטֶת f.—I. *ruler, prince.*—
II. *violent,* Eze. 16:30.

שַׁלִּיט m. Ch.—I. *a ruler.*—II. *that
which is permitted, lawful;* לֹא
שַׁלִּיט *it is not lawful,* Ezr. 7:24.

שִׁלְטוֹן m., *power, authority,* Ecc. 8:
4, 8.

שָׁלְטָן m. Ch., *authority, ruler,* Dan.
3:2, 3.

שָׁלְטָן m. Ch., *authority, empire.*

שֶׁלִי שָׁלָיו, שִׁלְיָה; see שָׁלָה.

שָׁלַךְ Hiph. הִשְׁלִיךְ I. *threw into,* אֶל;
on, בְּ, עַל; *to,* לְ; *from,* מִן. — II.
threw down, out, away.—III. *cast
off* (as a plant its leaves).—IV. *expelled* (a people).—V. with אַחֲרָיו
נַוּ אַחֲרֵי *cast behind him, despised.* — VI. with עַל יְהֹוָה *committed to the Lord.* Hoph.
הֻשְׁלַךְ, הָשְׁלַךְ I. *was thrown down,
out.*—II. *was thrown upon the Lord*
(for help), with עַל

שָׁלָךְ m., *the gannet*; LXX. κατα-
ράκτης, Lev. 11:17; Deu. 14:16

שַׁלֶּכֶת f.—I. *felling a tree,* Isa. 6:13.
II. p. n., *a gate of the temple.*

שָׁלַל (pret. שָׁלֹּלוּ,שָׁלֹתִי; inf. שָׁלֹל, שָׁלֹל
fut. תָּשֹׁלָּ, with suff. יִשְׁלֹּוּךָ).—I.
plundered, spoiled.—II. *carried off
spoil.*—III. *scattered,* Ru. 2:16.
Hith. הִשְׁתּוֹלֵל אֶשְׁתּוֹלָל (Ch. for
spoiled.

שָׁלָל m.—I. *spoil, plunder.*—II. *gain,*
Pro. 31:11.

שׁוֹלָל m., (spoiled) *a captive, captives.*

שָׁלֵם (fut. יִשְׁלָם). — I. *was at peace,*
Job 9:4.—II. *was completed.* Part.
שֹׁלְמִי *one at peace with me,* Ps.
7:5; שָׁלוֹם *peaceable,* 2 Sa. 20:19.
Pi. שִׁלֵּם, שִׁלַּם I. *completed.* — II.
restored.—III. *gave in return, requited.*—IV. *performed a vow.* Pu.
I. *was requited.*—II. *was performed*
(a vow). Part. *made perfect,* Isa.
42:19. Hiph. I. *made peace with*
— II. *made at peace with,* with
אֶת, עִם, אֶל. — III. *completed.* —
IV. *brought to an end.* Hoph
was made at peace, Job 5:23.

שְׁלַם Ch., *completed.* Aph. I. *terminated,* Dan. 5:26.—II. *restored,* Ezr. 7:19.

שָׁלֵם m., שְׁלֵמָה f.—I. *perfect, complete, full.* — II. אֲבָנִים שְׁלֵמוֹת *rough, unhewn stones.* — III. אֶבֶן שְׁלֵמָה *hewn, prepared stone,* 1 Ki. 6:7.—IV. *peaceable, at peace,* with עִם.—V. *at peace with God,* with עִם יְהֹוָה.—VI. p.n. of a place, Gen. 33:18.—VII. p.n., *Jerusalem,* Σόλυμα.

שָׁלוֹם m.—I. *peace.*—II. *public quiet.* —III. *prosperity.*—IV. *safety.*—V. *soundness of body.*—VI. *friendship.* Phrases: הֲשָׁלוֹם לְ *is he well?* שָׁאַל לְשָׁלוֹם לְ *enquired after their welfare;* שָׁלוֹם עֲשֵׂה *farewell!* שִׂי *made peace with them;* קָרָא לְשָׁלוֹם אֶת *named peaceable proposals;* עָנָה שָׁלוֹם אֶת *gave a peaceable answer.*

שְׁלָם m. Ch., *peace, safety.*

שֶׁלֶם and pl. שְׁלָמִים m. — I. *peace offering.*—II. *thank offering.*—III. *offering in completion of a vow.*

שִׁלֵּם m. — I. *retribution,* Deu. 32:35. —II. p.n., *a son of Naphtali;* patron. שִׁלֵּמִי.

שִׁלּוּם m., *retribution.*

שִׁלֻּמָה f., *the same,* Ps. 91:8.

שַׁלּוּם, שַׁלֻּם p.n.—I. *Shallum, king of Israel.*—II. *used for other men.*

שְׁלֹמֹה p.n., *Solomon, king of Israel;* LXX. Σαλωμών.

שִׁלְמִי p.n. of a man.

שַׁלְמִיאֵל p.n. of a man.

שֶׁלֶמְיָהוּ p.n., *same as* מְשֶׁלֶמְיָה.

שְׁלֹמִית p.n. of a man.

שְׁלֹמִית p.n. of a woman.

שַׁלְמוֹן m., pl. שִׁלְמֹנִים *bribes, penalties,* Isa. 1:23.

שַׁלְמַנְאֶסֶר, שַׁלְמֶן p.n., *a king of Assyria.*

שָׁלַף I. *drew a sword.*—II. *took off a shoe,* Ru. 4:7, 8. — III. *plucked up grass,* Ps. 129:6; אִישׁ שֹׁלֵף חֶרֶב *a man drawing the sword;* i.e., *armed.*

שֶׁלֶף p.n. of some foreign nation, perhaps Σαλαπηνοί.

שָׁלֹשׁ, שָׁלוֹשׁ; שְׁלָשׁ־, שְׁלֹשׁ const. f. שְׁלֹשָׁה, const. שְׁלֹשֶׁת m., *the numeral three;* with suff. שְׁלָשְׁתְּכֶם *ye three;* שְׁלָשְׁתָּם *they three,* שְׁלֹשׁ עֶשְׂרֵה *thirteen;* pl. שְׁלֹשִׁים *thirty, thirtieth.*

שִׁלֵּשׁ Pi. I. *divided into three parts.*— II. *did a thing the third time.*— III. *did a thing on the third day.* Pu. part. I. *threefold.* — II. *three years old,* Gen. 15:9.

שֶׁלֶשׁ p.n. of a man.

שְׁלִישִׁי m., שְׁלִישִׁית, שְׁלִישִׁיָּה f., pl. שְׁלִישִׁים I. *third parts.*—II. *chambers third in order, third stories;* f. *a third part;* בַּשְּׁלִישִׁית, שְׁלִישִׁיתָה *the third, on the third;* see מָחָר.

שָׁלִישׁ m.—I. *a measure,* probably *the third part of an Ephah.* —II. *abundantly;* pl. שָׁלִישִׁים.— III. *a musical instrument, a trichord* (either harp or lute). — IV. *officers of high rank.* — V. *a peculiar class of soldiers,* LXX. ἀναβάται ριστάται; *their commander was called* רֹאשׁ הַשָּׁלִישִׁים *and* רֹאשׁ הַשָּׁלִישִׁי.

שִׁלֵּשִׁים m. pl., *descendants of the*

third generation, great grandchildren.

שְׁלִשָׁה p.n., a region of Palestine.

שִׁלְשָׁה p.n. of a man.

שִׁלְשׁוֹם, שִׁלְשׁם adv. three days ago; תְּמוֹל שִׁלְשׁוֹם yesterday and the day before, i.e. formerly; כִּתְמוֹל שִׁ as before; מִתְּמוֹל שִׁ heretofore, previously.

כְּמִשְׁלֹשׁ חֳדָשִׁים m., a triad; a triplicity of, i.e. three months, Gen. 38:24.

שְׁלֻתֵךְ 1 Sa. 1:17, for שְׁאֵלָתֵךְ; see שָׁאַל in שְׁאֵלָה.

שָׁם adv., there, thither; אֲשֶׁר...שָׁם where; שָׁם...שָׁם here...there; שָׁמָּה thither, there; אֲשֶׁר..שָׁמָּה whither...where; מִשָּׁם thence; אֲשֶׁר...מִשָּׁם whence.

שֵׁם, שֶׁם־ m. (with suff. שְׁמִי, שִׁמְךָ; pl. שֵׁמוֹת).—I. a name; בְּשֵׁם פְּ in the name of any one.—II. fame, reputation (good or bad).—III. memory.—IV. p. n., Shem the son of Noah.

שֵׁם m. Ch. (with suff. שְׁמֵהּ; pl. שְׁמָהָן), a name.

שְׁמֵאֵבֶר p.n., a king of Zeboim.

שְׁמוּאֵל (perhaps for שְׁמוּעַאֵל heard of God), p. n.—I. Samuel, the judge of Israel.—II. used also of other men.

שְׁמִידָע p.n., a son of Gilead; patron. שְׁמִידָעִי.

שַׁמָּא p. n. of a man.

שַׁמָּה p. n. of a man; שַׁמְאָם the same.

שַׁמְגֵּר p. n., Shamgar, a judge of Israel.

שָׁמַד Hiph. destroyed; inf. destruction. Niph. was destroyed.

שְׁמַד Ch. Aph. to destroy.

שָׁמָה root not used; (Arab. heaven).

שָׁמַיִם, const. שְׁמֵי m. pl.—I. heaven, the sky.—II. toward heaven, the sky.

שְׁמַיִן emph. state, שְׁמַיָּא m. pl. Ch., heaven.

שְׁמָהוֹת, שָׁמָה; see שמם.

שָׁמוּעַ p n., same as שִׁמְעָא.

שְׁמוּעָה; see שמע.

שַׁמּוֹת Eze. 36:3, Kal inf., from שמם.

שָׁמַט I. gave up a debt.—II. left the land to itself.—III. threw down.—IV. stuck fast. Niph. was thrown down, Ps. 141:6. Hiph. gave up, forgave, Deu. 15:3.

שְׁמִטָּה f., release, acquittal; שְׁנַת הַשְּׁמִטָּה year of release.

שָׁמַיִם heavens; see שָׁמָה.

שְׁמִינִית, שְׁמִינִי; see שְׁמֹנֶה.

שָׁמִיר; see שָׁמַר.

שְׁמִרָמוֹת p. n. of a man.

שַׁמְלַי p. n. of a man.

שָׁמֵם (fut. יִשֹּׁם; pl. יֵשַׁמּוּ; imp. שֹׁם). I. was desolate, laid waste.—II. was astonished; part. שׁוֹמֵם desolate, solitary; שׁוֹמֵמוֹת desolate places. Niph. נָשַׁם was desolate, astonished. Po. part. מְשׁוֹמֵם I. a desolator.—II. astonished, Ezr. 9:3, 4. Hiph. הֵשַׁם (fut. יָשִׁים; inf. הַשֵּׁם; part. מְשִׁמִּים) I. made desolate, laid waste.—II. astonished —III. was astonished. Hoph. הֻשַּׁם or הָשַּׁם (pl. הֻשַּׁמּוּ) was made desolate. Hith. הִשְׁתּוֹמֵם (fut. תִּשׁוֹמֵם, יִשְׁתּוֹמֵם) I. was disconsolate (of the heart).—II. wondered.—III. destroyed himself, Ecc. 7:16.

שְׁמֵם Ch. Ith., was astonished, Dan. 4:16.

שָׁמֵם m., שְׁמֵמָה f., desolate.

שְׁמָמָה f.—I. desolation.—II. astonishment.—III. a desolate place.

שְׁמָמָה f.—I. desolation, Eze. 35:7, 9.

שַׁמָּה f.—I. desolation (pl. שַׁמּוֹת).—II. astonishment.—III. p.n.: (a) a brother of David, called also שִׁמְאָא; (b) used also for other men.

שַׁמְהוּת, שַׁמּוֹת p.n.; same as שַׁמָּה.

שִׁמָּמוֹן m., astonishment, terrors, Eze. 4:16; 12:19.

מְשַׁמָּה f.—I. astonishment, Eze. 5:15. —II. desolation.

שָׁמֵן or שָׁמַן (fut. יִשְׁמַן) was fat, prosperous. Hiph. I. became fat, Neh. 9:25. — II. made fat, Isa. 6:10.

שָׁמֵן m., שְׁמֵנָה f.—I. plump (of an animal). — II. robust, stout (of a man).—III. nourishing (of food).—IV. rich, fertile, abundant.

שֶׁמֶן m.—I. oil.—II. ointment.— III. richness, delicacy of food, I 25:6. — IV. fertility.—V. prosperity, Isa. 10:27. (עֵץ שֶׁמֶן any resinous tree.

שְׁמָנִים m. pl., fatness, Gen. 27:28, 39.

אַשְׁמַנִּים m. pl., "desolate places," Eng. Ver., Isa. 59:10.

מִשְׁמָן m., fatness; pl. מִשְׁמַנִּים fertile places.

מַשְׁמַנִּים m. pl., rich food, Neh. 8:10.

מִשְׁמַנָּה p.n. of a man.

שְׁמֹנֶה f., שְׁמֹנָה const. שְׁמֹנַת m., eight; pl. שְׁמֹנִים eighty.

שְׁמִינִי m., eighth; שְׁמִינִית a musical instrument, probably with eight strings.

שָׁמַע, שָׁמֵעַ (fut. יִשְׁמַע; inf. שְׁמֹעַ; const. שְׁמֹעַ, with ה parag. שָׁמְעָה, with suff. שָׁמְעוֹ; imp. שְׁמַע, with ה parag. שִׁמְעָה).—I. heard.—II. hearkened, with בְּ, אֶל, לְ.—III. understood. Niph. I. was heard.—II. was hearkened to. Pi. I. caused to hear, summoned. Hiph. I. הִשְׁמִיעַ (fut. apoc. תַּשְׁמַע).— I. caused to hear, be heard.—II. proclaimed.—III. summoned.

שְׁמַע Ch., he heard. Ith. he obeyed.

שֶׁמַע p.n. of a man.

שֵׁמַע, שֶׁמַע m. (with suff. שִׁמְעִי, שִׁמְעֲךָ).—I. the act of hearing.—II. report, fame.—III. sound.

שָׁמָע p.n. of a man.

שְׁמָע p.n., a town of Judah.

שֵׁמַע m. (with suff. שִׁמְעוֹ), fame.

שִׁמְעָא p.n. of a man; see שַׁמָּה.

שִׁמְעָה p.n., same as שַׁמָּה; patron. שִׁמְעָתִי.

שַׁמָּה (with art.) p.n. of a man.

שִׁמְעוֹן p.n.—I. Simeon, the son of Jacob and Leah (LXX. Συμεών). —II. used also of his descendants, שִׁמְעֹנִי a Simeonite.

שִׁמְעִי p.n. of a man, Shimei.

שְׁמַעְיָה, שְׁמַעְיָהוּ p.n. of a man.

שִׁמְעוֹן Kal imp. pl. f. for שְׁמַעְנָה from שׁמע.

שִׁמְעַת p.n. of a woman.

שְׁמוּעָה, שְׁמֻעָה f.—I. a report.—II. a message.

הַשְׁמָעוּת f., a hearing, Eze. 24:26.

מִשְׁמָע m.—I. act of hearing, Isa. 11:3 —II. p.n. of a man.

מִשְׁמַעַת f. — I. *court of hearing, council.*—II. *subjects,* Isa. 11:14.

שָׁמֵן root not used; (Arab. *hastened*).

שֶׁמֶץ m., *a small portion, a hint,* Job 4:12; 26:14.

שִׁמְצָה f., *defeat,* Ex. 32:25.

שָׁמַר (fut. יִשְׁמֹר).—I. *kept watch over, watched.*—II. *guarded, preserved.* —III. *kept in mind.*—IV. *attended to an office.*—V. *took heed.*—VI. *observed, remembered.* — VII. *regarded, reverenced.*—VIII. *guarded against, avoided.* Niph. I. *noticed, was aware of, perceived.*—II. *was preserved, delivered.* — III. *took heed.* — IV. *guarded himself, abstained,* with מִן and מִפְּנֵי; imp. הִשָּׁמֶר, הִשָּׁמֶר. Pi. *regarded,* Jon. 2:9. Hith. הִשְׁתַּמֵּר *kept, guarded himself.*—II. *was observed.*

שָׁמִיר m.—I. *a thorny shrub, "spina Egyptiaca."*—II. *a diamond.*—III. p.n.: (a) *a town of Judah;* (b) *a town or Ephraim;* (c) *of a man.*

שְׁמָרִים m., pl. שְׁמָרִים.—I. *sediment, lees, dregs.*—II. מְזֻקָּקִים שֵׁי *clear wine.*—III. p.n. of a man.

שֹׁמֵר p.n. of a man, and of a woman.

שִׁמְרָה f., *a watch,* Ps. 141:3.

שְׁמֻרוֹת f. pl., *the same,* Ps. 77:5.

שִׁמֻּרִים m.pl., *observance of a festival,* Ex. 12:42.

שִׁמְרוֹן p.n. — I. *a town of Zebulun.* —II. *a son of Issachar.* Patron. שִׁמְרֹנִי.

שֹׁמְרוֹן p.n.—I. *Samaria* (Σεβάστη). —II. *the land of Israel;* שֹׁמְרֹנִי *a Samaritan.*

שָׁמְרַיִן Ch., p. n., *Samaria.*

שִׁמְרִי p. n. of a man.

שְׁמַרְיָה p. n. of a man

שְׁמַרְיָהוּ p. n. of a man.

שְׁמָרִית p. n. of a woman; same as שֶׁמֶר.

שֶׁמֶר p. n. of a man.

אַשְׁמוּרָה f., *night-watch;* const. אַשְׁמֹרֶת; pl. אַשְׁמֻרוֹת.

מִשְׁמָר m. — I. *the act of guarding, watching.* — II. *keeping guard.* III. *imprisonment.*— IV. *a prison.* —V. *an appointed duty.*

מִשְׁמֶרֶת f. (pl. מִשְׁמָרוֹת).—I. *guarding, watching.*—II. *imprisonment.*

שְׁמַשׁ Ch. Pa., *attended, served,* Dan. 7:10.

שֶׁמֶשׁ com. (with suff. שִׁמְשֵׁךְ), *the sun,* pl. שְׁמָשׁוֹת *thy pinnacles,* Isa. 54:12; עִיר שֶׁמֶשׁ *a city or* Dan.

שִׁמְשׁוֹן p.n., *Samson.* (LXX. Σαμψών.)

שִׁמְשִׁי p. n. of a man.

שַׁמְשְׁרַי p. n. of a man.

שִׁמְשָׁתִי p. n. of a man.

שְׁנָאָב, שְׁנֹו, שֵׁן; see שׁן.

שִׁנְאָן, שְׁנָא; see שׁנה.

שְׁנָא *sleep,* Ps. 127:2; see יָשֵׁן.

שִׁנְאַצַּר p.n.

שָׁנָב (Arab. *had a cool mouth*).

אֶשְׁנָב m., *a latticed window.*

שָׁנָה (fut. יִשְׁנָא, יִשְׁנֶה).—I. *repeated an action.*—II. *was different,* with מִן.—III. *was changed.*—IV. *was disobedient* (part. שֹׁנִים *rebellious*). Niph. *being repeated,* Gen. 41:32. Pi. שִׁנָּה, שָׁנָא I. *changed.* — II. *violated a promise.*— III. *removed a person to another place,* Est. 2:9:

with אֶת־טַעְמוֹ *changed his mind,
feigned himself mad.* Pu. fut.
יְשֻׁנֶּא *was changed*, Ecc. 8 : 1. Hith.
changed, disguised himself, 1 Ki.
14 : 2.

שְׁנָא Ch.—I. *was changed.* — II. *was
different from,* with מִן. Pa. I.
changed. — II. *made different*; part.
pass. *different.* Ith. *was changed.*
Aph. *changed.*

שָׁנָה f. (pl. שָׁנִים, שְׁנֵי, שְׁנוֹת).
—I. *a year.* — II. *the produce of a
year*; מִדֵּי שָׁנָה בְּשָׁנָה, שָׁנָה שָׁנָה *year;* בִּשְׁנַת שְׁתַּיִם *yearly*; שָׁנָה בְּשָׁנָה
לְיוֹאָשׁ *in the second year of Joash;*
בִּשְׁנַת שֵׁשׁ מֵאוֹת שָׁנָה *in the six
hundredth year.* Dual שְׁנָתַיִם *two
years;* שְׁנָתַיִם יָמִים *for two years.*

שְׁנָא, שְׁנָה f. Ch., *year;* pl. שְׁנִין.

שֵׁנָה, שְׁנָת *sleep;* see יָשֵׁן.

שֶׁנְהַבִּים *ivory;* see שֵׁן.

שָׁנִי m., *bright, scarlet colour;* pl.
שָׁנִים.

שְׁנַיִם const. שְׁנֵי m., שְׁתַּיִם const.
שְׁתֵּי f. dual, *the numeral two*;
שְׁנַיִם שְׁנַיִם *apiece;* with suff.
שְׁנֵיהֶם *both of them;* f., *twice,
again*; בִּשְׁתַּיִם *again.* שְׁנֵים עָשָׂר
m., שְׁתֵּים עֶשְׂרֵה f., *twelve.*
שֵׁנִי m., שֵׁנִית f., *second;* f., *again.*
Pl. שְׁנִיִם.

שִׁנְאָן m., "*angels,*" Eng. Ver.;
אַלְפֵי שִׁנְאָן *thousands repeated* (Ges.),
Ps. 68 : 18.

מִשְׁנֶה const. מִשְׁנֵה m.—I. *second.*—
II. *the second rank, second in rank.*
III. *double.*—IV. *a copy.*—V. *of an
inferior kind,* 1 Sa. 15 : 9.—VI. *a
division of Jerusalem.*

שָׁנַן (pret. שָׁנַנְתִּי, שִׁנַּנּוּ).—I. *sharpened*

a sword, &c.— II. *sharpened the
tongue* (of slanderers), Ps. 64 : 4
140:4. Pi. *taught assiduously,* with
לְ, Deu. 6 : 7. Hithpo. אֶשְׁתּוֹנָן *was
pained acutely,* Ps. 73 : 21.

שֵׁן, שֵׁן com. (with suff. שִׁנִּי; dual
שְׁנַיִם, שִׁנֵּי).—I. *a tooth.*—II. *ivory*
—III. *the ridge of a rock;* שֵׁן סֶלַע
— IV. *the prong of a fork.* — V.
p. n. of a place.

שֶׁנְהַבִּים m. pl., *elephant's tooth, ivory.*
(The word is probably a compound
of שֵׁן *a tooth,* and הָב *an elephant;*
from the Sanscrit *ibha.*)

שְׁנִינָה f., *pointed saying; taunt:*
הָיָה לִשְׁנִינָה *he was for a taunt.*

שִׁנְאָב p. n. of a king.

שָׁנַס. Pi. שִׁנַּס *girded his loins,* 1 Ki.
18:46.

שִׁנְעָר p. n., one of the names of Babylon and its vicinity.

שָׁסָה *plundered;* part. שֹׁסִים *spoilers.*
Po. שׁוֹשֵׂה *the same,* Isa. 10 : 13.

שָׁסַס (fut. יָשֹׁס) *the same;* part. שֹׁאֵס,
with suff. שֹׁאֲסָיִךְ. Niph. נָשַׁס *was
plundered.*

מְשִׁסָּה f., *prey.*

שָׁסַע *having a division;* שֶׁסַע
פַּרְסָה or שֹׁסַעַת *having divided
hoofs;* פַּרְסָה הַשֹּׁסַעַת *having a
divided hoof.* Pi. I. *clove,* Lev. 1 :
17. — II. *tore asunder,* Jud. 14 : 6,
&c.—III. *withheld,* 1 Sa. 24 : 8.
שֶׁסַע m., *division in a hoof.*

שָׁסַף. Pi. שִׁסַּף *cut down,* 1 Sa. 15 : 33.

I. שָׁעָה (fut. apoc. וַיִּשַׁע) *looked at favourably, approved,* with אֶל.—II.
looked at with attention, with בְּ

- III. *looked to for help*, with אֶל, עַל. — IV. *looked away from, respited*, with מִן, Job 7:19. Hiph. imp. הִשָּׁע I. *looked away from*, with מִן, Ps.39:14.—II. *turn away the eyes*, Isa. 6:10. See also in שָׁעַ. Hith. fut. apoc. תִּשְׁתָּע *look about with alarm*, Isa. 41:10; pl. with ה parag. נִשְׁתָּעָה *we may look with alarm, be dismayed*, Isa.41:23.

II. שָׁעָה same as שָׁעַע; imp. שׁעוּ *be blinded* (Ges.); "*cry*," from שׁוּעַ, Eng. Ver., Is. 29:9.

שָׁעָה f. Ch., *an hour*; בַּהּ שַׁעְתָּא *immediately*.

שַׁעֲטָה f., *stamping of hoofs*, Jer. 47:3. (Arab. *pounded*.)

שַׁעַטְנֵז m., *cloth of a mixture of wool and flax*, Lev. 19:19; Deu. 22:11.

שֹׁעַל, שַׁעַל (with suff. שָׁעֳלוֹ; pl. שְׁעָלִים, שָׁעֳלֵי).—I. *palm of the hand*, Isa. 40:12.—II. *a handful*.

שׁוּעָל m.—I. *a fox*. — II. p. n. of a man.

שַׁעֲלִים p. n. of a district.

שַׁעַלְבִּים, שַׁעֲלַבִּין p. n., *a town of the Danites*; שַׁעַלְבֹנִי *a Shaalbonite*.

מִשְׁעוֹל m., *a narrow way*, Nu. 22:24.

שָׁעַן. Niph. נִשְׁעַן I. *leaned on*, with עַל.—II. *reclined*.—III. *touched a boundary* with לְ, Nu. 21:15.—IV. *depended on*, with בְּ, אֶל, עַל.

מִשְׁעָן m., *a support*.

מַשְׁעֵן m., מַשְׁעֵנָה f., *the same*, Isa. 3:1.

מִשְׁעֶנֶת f. (pl. מִשְׁעֲנוֹת), *walking stick, staff*.

שָׁעַע Pil. שִׁעֲשַׁע I. *delighted*. — II.

played, Isa. 11:8. Pul. שֻׁעֲשַׁע *was fondled*, Isa. 66:12. Hiph. imp. הָשַׁע *cover the eyes, make blind*, Isa. 6:10; see in שָׁעָה. Hithpal. הִשְׁתַּעֲשַׁע *delighted himself*, with בְּ.

שַׁעֲשֻׁעִים m. pl., *delights, source of delight*.

שָׁעַף p. n. of a man.

שָׁעַר Pro. 23:7, "*thinketh*," Eng Ver.; meaning uncertain.

שַׁעַר m.—I. *value, measure*, Gen. 26:12. — II. m. (f. Isa. 14:31). — 1. *opening, gate of a city*. — 2. *the people assembled at the gate*, Ru. 3:11. — 3. *the city itself*; with ה loc. שַׁעְרָה; pl. שְׁעָרִים, שַׁעֲרֵי.

שְׁעָרִים p. n., *a town of Judah*.

שׁוֹעֵר m., *a porter*.

שׁוֹעָר m., pl. שֹׁעֲרִים *blighted figs*, Jer 29:17.

שַׁעֲרוּר m., f. שַׁעֲרוּרָה *causing to shudder, horrible*.

שַׁעֲרוּרִי m., f. שַׁעֲרוּרִיָּה, שַׁעֲרוּרִית *horrible*, Jer. 18:13.

שְׁעַרְיָה p. n. of a man.

שַׁעֲשְׁגַּז p. n. of a man.

שַׁעֲשֻׁעִים, שִׁעֲשֻׁעִים; see שעע.

שָׂפָה (Arab. *became visible*). Niph. נִשְׂפָּה הַר *a lofty, conspicuous mountain*, Isa. 13:2. Pu. שֻׁפּוּ *became prominent* (the bones), Job 33:21.

שְׂפָה or שָׂפָה f., *cheese*; pl. const. שְׂפוֹת, 2 Sa. 17:29.

שְׁפִי in pause שֶׁפִי m. (pl. שְׁפָיִים, שְׁפָיִם) *elevated, conspicuous place*

שְׁפִי, שְׁפוֹ p. n. of a man.

שִׁפְחָה f. (pl. שְׁפָחוֹת) *female servant or slave.*

מִשְׁפָּחָה const. מִשְׁפַּחַת f. (with suff. מִשְׁפַּחְתִּי; pl. מִשְׁפָּחוֹת). — I. *a household.* — II. *a family or clan.* — III. *a race or kind*

שָׁפַט I. *judged.* — II. *decided a cause.* — III. *defended the right of.* — IV. *decided between,* with בֵּין־וּבֵין, ל...בֵּין. — V. *punished.* — VI. *ruled;* part. שֹׁפֵט *a judge, ruler.* Niph. נִשְׁפַּט 1. *was judged,* Ps. 9:20. — II. *reasoned with another, disputed,* with עַל, ל, עִם, אֵת, אֶת. Po. part. מְשֹׁפְטִי *my judge.*

שְׁפַט Ch. part. שָׁפֵט *judge,* Ezr. 7:25.

שְׁפוֹט m. (pl. שְׁפוּטִים) *judgments.*

שְׁפָט p. n. of a man.

שֶׁפֶט m., pl. שְׁפָטִים *judgments, punishments.*

שְׁפַטְיָה p. n. of a man.

שְׁפַטְיָהוּ p. n. of a man

שִׁפְטָן p. n. of a man.

מִשְׁפָּט m. — I. *deciding, decision, sentence.* — II. *punishment.* — III. *a court of justice.* — IV. *a cause for trial.* — V. *justice, equity.* — VI. *any positive institution; the right claimed upon such institution.* — VII. *custom.* — VIII. *manner, appearance.*

שְׁפִי, שֶׁפִי, שְׁפָיִים; see שׁפה.

שָׁפִים, שִׁיפוֹן; see שׁפף.

שָׁפִיר, שַׁפִּיר; see שׁפר.

שָׁפַךְ I. *poured out.* — II. *shed blood.* — III. *threw up a mound.* — IV. *uttered a prayer.* — V. metaph. *poured out his soul, his heart, his*

anger. — VI. *gave abundantly* Niph. trop. *was poured out, was shed.* Pu. 1. *was poured out.* — II. *slipped.* Hith. הִשְׁתַּפֵּךְ *was shed.*

שֶׁפֶךְ m., *the place of pouring out,* Lev. 4:12.

שָׁפְכָה f., *membrum virile,* Deu. 23:2.

שָׁפֵל (fut. יִשְׁפַּל; inf. שְׁפַל). — I. *was low, was lowered.* — II. *was humbled.* Hiph. I. *brought low.* — II. *sent down,* Isa. 57:9. — III. *cast down, humbled;* ש' רוּחַ *humble in spirit.*

שְׁפַל Ch. Aph. *humbled, brought low.*

שָׁפָל m., שְׁפָלָה f. — I. *low.* — II. *low in rank or importance.* — III. *humble.*

שְׁפַל m. Ch., *low in rank,* Dan. 4:14.

שֵׁפֶל m. (with suff. שִׁפְלֵנוּ), *lowly place, condition.*

שִׁפְלָה f., *the same,* Isa. 32:19.

שְׁפֵלָה f., *low country;* הַשְּׁפֵלָה *the low country,* i. e. the plain between Joppa and Egypt.

שִׁפְלוּת f., *lowness of the hands, inactivity,* Ecc. 10:18.

שָׁפָם p. n. of a man.

שִׁפְמוֹת, שְׁפָם p. n., *a town of Judah;* שִׁפְמִי *a Shiphmite.*

שָׁפָן m. — I. *the jerboa;* LXX. χοιρογρύλλιος, Lev. 11:5; Deu. 14:7. — II. p. n. of a man.

שָׁפַע (Syr. *inundated*).

שֶׁפַע m., *overflowing, abundance,* Deu. 33:19.

שִׁפְעָה f. — I. *inundation.* — II. *multitude.*

שִׁפְעִי p. n. of a man.

שָׁפַף (Syr. *he crept;* Arab. *a speckled snake*).

שְׁפִיפֹן m., *a species of serpent*, Gen. 49:17.

שְׁפוּפָם p.n., *a son of Benjamin*.

שְׁפוּפָן p.n. *of a man*.

שֻׁפִּים p.n. *of a man*.

שָׁפַר *was pleasing*, with עַל, Ps. 16:6.

שִׁפְרָה f., *beauty*, Job 26:13.

שְׁפַר Ch., *was fair, pleasing*, with עַל קֳדָם.

שׁוֹפָר m. (pl. שׁוֹפָרוֹת), *trumpet, curved horn*.

שֶׁפֶר m. — I. *pleasantness, beauty*, Gen. 49:21. — II. p.n., *a mountain in the wilderness*.

שִׁפְרָה p.n. *of a woman*.

שָׁפִיר p.n., *an unknown place*.

שַׁפִּיר m. Ch., *pleasing, fine*.

שַׁפְרִיר (שַׁפְרוּר) m., *royal canopy*, Jer. 43:10.

שְׁפַרְפָּרָא m. Ch., *the dawn*, Dan. 6:20.

שָׁפַת *fixed, placed*.

שְׁפַתַּיִם m. dual, *cooking vessels*.

מִשְׁפְּתַיִם dual, *the same*.

שֶׁצֶף m., *overflowing*, Isa. 54:8.

שָׁק Ch., *leg*, same as שׁוֹק.

שָׁקַד I. *was sleepless, awake.* — II. *watched, kept watch for*, with עַל. Pu. see next word.

שָׁקֵד I. *almond tree.* — II. *almond.* Hence denom. Pu. part. מְשֻׁקָּדִים *formed like almonds*.

שָׁקָה Niph. *was overflown* (see שֶׁקַע), Am. 8:8. Hiph. הִשְׁקָה (fut. apoc. יַשְׁקְ) I. *gave drink to any one.* — II. *watered the ground*; part. מַשְׁקֶה *giving water*, Ps. 104:13. Pu. *watered, refreshed*, Job 21:24.

שֹׁקֶת f., *drinking-trough;* pl. const שִׁקֲתוֹת.

שִׁקּוּי m. (pl. with suff. שִׁקֻּוָי). — I. *refreshment.* — II. *drink.*

שֵׁקֶן or שִׁקּוּי m. (pl. with suff. שִׁקֻּוָי), *drink.*

מַשְׁקֶה m. — I. *cup-bearer.* — II. *drink.* — III. *a watered country.*

שָׁקָה Kal imp. with ה parag., from נשק שִׁקּוּן; see שקק.

שָׁקַט I. *was quiet, undisturbed.* — II. *ceased.* — III. *remained inactive.* — IV. *was silent.* Hiph. I. *caused to cease.* — II. *was quiet, ceased*, with לְ and מִן; inf. הַשְׁקֵט *rest, tranquillity.*

שֶׁקֶט m., *rest, quiet*, 1 Chron. 22:9.

שָׁקַל I. *weighed.* — II. *weighed in payment, paid.* — III. *estimated, judged.* — Niph. 1. *was paid.* — II. *was judged.*

שֶׁקֶל m. (pl. שְׁקָלִים, שִׁקְלֵי). — I. *a certain standard weight, the shekel.* — II. *a silver coin of that weight.*

מִשְׁקָל m., *act of weighing, weight.*

מִשְׁקוֹל m., *weight*, Eze. 4:10.

מִשְׁקֶלֶת f., *balance*, Isa. 28:17.

מִשְׁקֹלֶת f., *the same*, 2 Ki. 21:13

שִׁקְמָה f., pl. שִׁקְמִים, שִׁקְמוֹת *sycamore tree, a species of fig.*

שָׁקַע I. *sank.* — II. *was overflown.* — III. *abated (of fire).* Niph. *was overflown*, Am. 8:8 (Ketib נִשְׁקָה) which see in שָׁקָה.

מַשְׁקָע m., *a pond*, Eze. 34:18.

שְׁקַעֲרוּרֹת f. pl., *hollows, parts corroded*, κοιλάδες, Lev. 14:37.

שָׁקַף. Niph. and Hiph. I. *looked.* —

II. *looked down, through, towards.* —III. *threatened.*

שְׁקֶף m., *covering, coping,* 1 Ki. 7:5.

שְׁקֻפִים m. pl., *coped, having copings,* 1 Ki. 6:4.

מַשְׁקוֹף m., *lintel, beam over a doorway.*

שָׁקַץ. Pi. I. *regarded with disgust.* —II. *loathed,* Ps. 22:25.—III. *polluted.*

שֶׁקֶץ m., *abominable thing.*

שִׁקּוּץ m., *an abomination.*

שָׁקַק (fut. יָשֹׁק).—I. *ran to and fro.*— II. *was eager.* Hithpal. *ran to and fro;* fut. pl. יִשְׁתַּקְשְׁקוּן, Nah. 2:5.

מַשָּׁק m., *running to and fro,* Isa. 33:4.

שָׁקַר (fut. יִשְׁקֹר) *acted falsely towards,* with לְ. Pi. שִׁקֵּר with בְּ.—I. *uttered a falsehood.*—II. *acted falsely.*

שֶׁקֶר m. — I. *falsehood.* — II. *a deceitful thing.* — III. עֵד שֶׁ *false witness;* לַשֶּׁקֶר *in vain, falsely;* בַּשֶּׁקֶר, בְּשֶׁקֶר *falsely;* שֶׁקֶר adv. *in vain.*

שְׁקָתוֹת, שֹׁקֶת; see שקה.

שֹׁרֶד, שֹׁר; see שרר.

שְׂרָא; see שרה.

שַׁרְאֶצֶר p. n. of an Assyrian prince; see נֵרְגַּל שַׁ.

שָׁרָב m.—I. *drought,* Isa. 49:10.—II. *the mirage,* Isa. 35:7 (Arab. the same).

שְׁרֵבְיָה p. n. of a man.

שַׁרְבִיט same as שֵׁבֶט *a sceptre* (Esther only).

שָׁרָ *set at liberty,* Job 37:3. Pi. שֵׁרָה *the same,* Jer. 15:11.

שְׂרָא Ch.—I. *untied.*—II. *solved.*—III. *halted, dwelt.* Pa. I. *untied.*—II. *began.* Ithpa. *was loose.*

שָׁרוֹת, שֵׁרוֹת *walls;* see שׁוּר.

שָׁרִי p. n. of a man.

שִׁרְיָה f., *coat of mail,* Job 41:18.

שִׁרְיָן m., *the same.*

סִרְיֹן, שִׁרְיֹן m. (pl. שִׁרְיֹנִים, שִׁרְיֹנוֹת, (סִרְיֹנוֹת).—I. *a coat of mail.*—II.

שִׂרְיֹן p.n., a part of Mount Hermon.

מִשְׁרָה f., מִשְׁרַת־עֲנָבִים *juice of grapes,* Nu. 6:3.

שֵׁרוֹת, שָׁרָה; see שרר.

שָׁרוּחֶן p. n., a city of the tribe of Simeon.

שָׁרוֹן p. n., the plain between Joppa and Cesarea.

שְׁרִיקוֹת; see שרק.

שְׁרִירוּת, שָׁרִיר; see שרר.

שְׁאֵרִית same as שְׁאֵרִית; see שאר.

שָׁרַץ (fut. יִשְׁרֹץ). — I. *became numerous.* — II. *produce in great numbers, swarm.*—III. *creep, crawl,* Eze. 47:9.

שֶׁרֶץ m. col., *small creatures,* whether insects, reptiles, or fishes.

שָׁרַק (fut. יִשְׁרֹק).—I. *whistle, or hiss for, call by whistling,* with לְ.—II. *hiss at in contempt,* with עַל.

שְׁרֵקָה f., *derision, scorn.*

שְׁרִיקוֹת f., *hissing, derision,* Jer. 18:16.—II. *whistling, piping,* Jud. 5:16.

מַשְׁרֹקִית m. Ch., "*flute,*" Eng. Ver.; LXX. σύριγγος, Dan. 3:5—15.

I. שָׁרַר (Arab. *made wicked*); part. שֹׁרֵר *adversary.*

שָׁרָר p. n. of a man.

II. שָׁרַר (Syr. *was firm*).

שֳׁרִי m. (with suff. שָׁרְרֵךְ), the navel, Cant. 7:3.

שֹׁר m. (with suff. שָׁרְךָ), the same.

שָׁרִיר m., pl. שְׁרִירִים firm, solid parts, Job 40:16.

שְׁרִירוּת f. with לֵב, firmness, obstinacy of heart.

שֵׁרָה f., pl. שֵׁרוֹת chains, bracelets, Isa. 3:19.

שַׁרְשָׁרָה f., a chain.

שַׁרְשְׁרָה f., pl. const. שַׁרְשְׁרוֹת chains, small bracelets, Ex. 28:22.

שֹׁרֶשׁ m. (with suff. שָׁרְשָׁם; pl. שָׁרָשִׁים, שָׁרָשִׁים).— I. a root.— II. shoot, suckers, Isa. 11:10; 53:2. — III. lowest part of any thing; e. g., sole of the foot, bottom of the sea, &c.—IV. foundation, ground-work; שֹׁ דָּבָר ground of com-plaint, Job 19:28.

שֵׁרֵשׁ Pi. denom. rooted up. Pu. שֹׁרַשׁ was rooted up. Poel שֹׁרֵשׁ and Poal שֹׁרָשׁ took root. Hiph. הִשְׁרִישׁ the same.

שֹׁרֶשׁ m. Ch., a root.

שֶׁרֶשׁ p. n. of a man.

שְׁרֹשׁוּ (שְׁרֹשִׁי) f. Ch., rooting up, banishment, Ezr. 7:26.

שַׁרְשׁרֹת, שַׁרְשׁרוֹת; see שרר.

שֵׁרֵת Pi. שֵׁרֵת.— I. waited on, with אֶת.—II. attended to, with accus., לְ — III. שׁ or שֵׁ בְּשֵׁם יְהֹוָה אֶת־יְהֹוָה performed the service of the sanctuary.— IV. worshipped, Eze. 20:32. Part. מְשָׁרֵת m., מְשָׁרֵת f., minister.

שֵׁשָׁה Po. שׁוֹשֵׁה; see שָׂסָה.

שֵׁשׁ שֵׁשׁ f., שִׁשָּׁה const., שֵׁשֶׁת m., six; pl. שִׁשִּׁים sixty; see also in שׁוּשׁ.

שִׁשָּׁה Pi. gave a sixth part of, Eze. 45:13.

שִׁשִּׁי m., שִׁשִּׁית f., the sixth; in f. a sixth part.

שֵׁשָׁא. Pi. שִׁשָּׁא caused to walk, led, Eze. 39:2.

שֵׁשְׁבַּצַּר p. n., the Persian name of Zerubbabel.

שֵׁשִׁי p. n. of a man.

שׁישִׁי p. n. of a man.

שֵׁשַׁךְ p. n., a prophetic title of Babylon

שֵׁשָׁן p. n. of a man.

שֶׁשֶׁק p. n. of a man.

שֵׁשֵׁר with pause שֵׁשֵׁר m., red ochre or red lead; LXX. μίλτος.

שֵׁת, שָׁתָּה, שַׁתִּי pret. from שׁוּת.

שֵׁת tumult, see שׁאה.

שֵׁת p. n., שֵׁתוֹת, see שִׁית.

שֵׁת, שְׁתוֹת, see שׁתת.

שֵׁת Ch., six; pl. שָׁתִּין sixty.

שָׁתָה (inf. שָׁתֹה, שְׁתוֹ, שְׁתוֹת; fut יִשְׁתֶּה; apoc. יֵשְׁתְּ).— I. he drank —II. sat at table, banqueted, Est. 7:1.—III. met., experienced.—IV. consumed. Niph. fut. יִשָּׁתֶה, was drunk, Lev. 11:34.

שְׁתָא, שְׁתָה Ch., he drank; pret. with א pros., אִשְׁתִּיו.

שְׁתִי m.—I. drinking.—II. the warp of a well.

שְׁתִיָּה f., drinking, Est. 1:8.

מִשְׁתֶּה m.—I. the act of drinking.—II. a banquet.—III. the drink itself.

מִשְׁתֶּה emph. מִשְׁתְּיָא m. Ch., the same.

שַׁתּוּ Ps. 73:9, pret. pl., from שׁתת; שְׁנָתַיִם; see שְׁנַיִם.

שָׁתַל planted a tree.

שְׁתִיל m., pl. שְׁתִלֵי זֵיתִים olive shoots, branches, Ps. 128:3.

שָׁתַם (Copt. to close); שְׁתֻם הָעָיִן "whose eyes were opened," Eng. Ver., Nu. 24:3, 15.

שָׁתַן. Hiph. made water; מַשְׁתִּין בְּקִיר that ... against the wall; i.e., a very mean man.

שָׁתַק I. became still, was at rest.—II. ceased (of strife), Pro. 26:20.

שְׁתָר p. n., a prince of Persia.

שְׁתַר בּוֹזְנַי p. n. of a Persian.

שָׁתַת same as שִׁית placed.

שֵׁת m. (pl. with suff. שְׁתוֹתֵיהֶם), the buttocks.

ת

תָּא m., a room or chamber; pl. תָּאִים תָּאוֹת; (Arab. habitation).

תָּא; see תָּוָה.

ı. תָּאַב desired, longed for, with לְ, Ps. 119, 40, 174.

תַּאֲבָה f., desire, Ps. 119:20.

ıı. תָּאַב same as תָּעַב. Pi. part. מְתָאֵב abhorring, Am. 6:8.

תָּאָה. Pi. mark, mark out; fut. pl. תְּתָאוּ Nu. 34:7, 8.

תֵּאָהֲבוּ for תֶּאֱהָבוּ Kal fut. pl., from אהב.

תּוֹא, תּאוֹ m., the Egyptian antelope; antelope oryx (Linn.).

תַּאֲוָה desire; see אוה.

תּאכְלֻהוּ Pi. fut. with suff. for תָּאכְלֻהוּ or Kal fut. with suff. for תָּאכְלֻהוּ, from אכל.

תַּאֲלָה cursing; see אלה.

תָּאַם was double, part. תּאֲמִים twins. Hiph. produced twins.

תְּאוֹם m., pl. תְּאוֹמִים תּוֹמִים twins, pl. const. תֹּאֲמֵי.

תַּאֲנִיָּה, תֹּאֲנָה, תְּאֵנָה; see אנה.

תְּאֵנִים, תְּאֵנָה; see אנן.

תַּאֲנַת שִׁלֹה p. n., a town of Ephraim.

תָּאַר I. turned, made a circuit.—II. was formed, drawn, used in both senses of a boundary only. Pi. delineated, marked the form of.

מְתֹאָר p. n. of a place, Jos. 19:13.

תֹּאַר m. (with suff. תָּאֲרוֹ).—I. form, personal appearance.—II beauty.

תַּאְרֵעַ p. n. of a man.

תְּאַשּׁוּר; see אשר.

תָּאבָה for תָּבֹה Kal fut. 2. pers., from אבה.

תְּבֹאֶינָה Kal fut. pl. f., from בוא.

תֵּבָה const. תֵּבַת f. (Coptic an ark, chest; Hierog. the same).—I. Noah's ark.—II. the basket in which Moses was exposed.

תְּבוּאָה; see בוא.

תְּבֹאתִי, תְּבֹאתָה for תְּבוֹא; תְּבֹאָה for תָּבֹא Kal fut. with ה parag., and with suff. תְּבֹאֶתְךָ for תְּבוֹאֶךָ, from בוא.

תְּבוּנָה, תְּבוּן; see בין.

תְּבוּסָה; see בוס.

תָּבוֹר p. n.—I. a mountain of Galilee on the borders of Zebulun and Naphtali.—II. a city of the Levites in Zebulun.—III. a grove of oaks in Benjamin.

וַתֵּבְךְ, תֵּבְךְ Kal fut. apoc., from בכה.

תֵּבֵל, see ובל; תָּבֶל, see בלל.

תֻּבָל same as תּוּבָל.

תַּבְלִית; see בלה.

תְּבַלֻּל ; see בלל.

תֶּבֶן m., *straw*.

תִּבְנִי p.n. of a man.

מַתְבֵּן m., *heap of straw*, Isa. 25:10.

תַּבְנִית ; see בנה.

תִּבְעָיוּן Kal fut. pl. with נ parag. from בעה.

תַּבְעֵרָה ; see בער.

תֵּבֵץ p.n., a place not far from Sichem.

תְּבַר Ch. part., f. תְּבִירָה *brittle*, Dan. 2:42.

תִּנְבְּהֵינָה for תִּנְבַּהְנָה Kal fut. pl. f. from נבה.

תִּנְיוּן Hiph. fut. pl. with נ parag. from ינה.

תֵּגַל Niph. fut. apoc. from נלה.

תִּ׳ פִּלְנְאֶסֶר, תִּלְנַת פִּלְסֶר, תִּלְנַת פִּלְאֶסֶר תִּ׳ פִּלְנֶסֶר p.n., a king of Assyria.

תַּנְמוּל ; see נמל.

תִּגְרָה ; see נרה.

תּוֹנַרְמָה, תּוֹגַרְמָה p.n., some country to the north of Palestine.

תִּדְהָר ; see דהר.

תִּדְיָרָא ; see דור.

תִּדְמִיֵנִי Pi. fut. pl. with suff. from דמה.

תַּדְמֹר p.n., a city in the Syrian desert, *Palmyra*.

תִּדְעָל p.n. of a king, Gen. c. 14.

תֹּהָה (Arab. *a desert*).

תֹּהוּ m. — I. *emptiness*. — II. *a vain thing, nothing*. — III. *desolation*. — IV. *a desert, wilderness*. — V. adv. *in vain*.

תְּהוֹם *the deep*; see הום.

תְּהִי, וַתְּהִי, in pause תֶּהִי, fut. apoc. from היה.

תְּהִימֵנוּ for תְּהִימֶינָה Hiph. fut., from הום.

תְּהִלָּה, תְּהִלָּה ; see הלל.

תְּהִלָּתֶךָ for תְּהִלָּתְךָ ; see תְּהִלָּתִיד in הלל.

תַּהֲלוּכָה *procession* ; see הלך.

תַּהְפֻּכוֹת, תַּהְפּוּכָה ; see הפך.

תְּהִתְלוּ Pi. fut. pl. with dag. euphon., from התל.

תָּו ; see תָּוָה.

תֹּא same as תָּאו.

תּוּב Ch., *returned*. Aph. I. הֵתִיב *returned, carried back*. — II. *answered*, with פִּתְגָּם.

תֻּבַל, תֻּבָל p.n. of some northern nation, perhaps *the Tibarenes*.

תּוּבַל קַיִן p.n., a son of Lamech, the first artificer in iron.

תּוּנָה ; see ינה.

תּוֹדָה ; see ידה.

תְּוַהּ Ch., *was amazed*, Dan. 3:24.

תָּוָה Pi. תָּוָה *made marks, scrabbled*, 1 Sa. 21:14. Hiph. I. with תָּו *made a mark*, Eze. 9:4. — II. metaph. *provoked*, i.e. made a painful mark, scratch, wound, Ps. 78:41; Vulg *exacerbaverunt*.

תָּו m., *a mark* or *sign*, Eze. 9:4; (Arab. *a mark in the form of a cross*, put upon the necks of camels; hence the Phœnician and Greek letters τ *tau*).

תּוֹחַ p.n. of a man.

תּוֹחֶלֶת ; see יחל.

תָּוֶךְ, const. תּוֹךְ m., *the middle*; בְּתוֹךְ *in the middle, among, within, through*; מִתּוֹךְ *from the midst of*; אֶל-תּוֹךְ *into the midst of*; תּוֹךְ *oppression*; see in תָּכַךְ.

תִּיכוֹן m., תִּיכוֹנָה f., *middle*.

תּוֹכַחַת ,תּוֹכֵחָה; see יכח.

תּוֹלָד ,תּוֹלֵדֹת; see ילד.

תּוֹלֵל; see ילל.

תּוֹלָע ,תּוֹלֵעָה ,תּוֹלַעַת; see תלע.

תּוֹמִים same as תְּאוֹמִים; see תאם.

תּוֹמִיךְ for תֹּמֵךְ Kal part., from תמך.

תּוֹעֵבָה ,תּוֹעֵבֹת; see תעב.

תּוֹעָה; see תעה.

תּוֹעָפוֹר; see יעף.

תּוּף (Arab. *spit through detestation*).
תֹּפֶת f.—I. לְפָנִים ת' *object of detestation* (one in whose face they spit), Job 17:6.—II. תֹּפֶת, with ה parag. תָּפְתֶּה p.n., *a place in the valley of Hinnom, near Jerusalem.*

תּוֹצָאוֹת; see יצא.

תּוּר I. *go about as a spy, spy out.*—II. *search out, explore.*—III. *travel about,* 1 Ki. 10:15.—IV. *seek after the heart, go astray,* Nu. 15:39, with אַחֲרֵי. Hiph. I. *send spies,* Jud. 1:23.—II. *direct aright,* Pro. 12:26.

תּוֹר m.—I. *turn, order,* Est. 2:12, 15.—II. *row, string of beads,* Cant. 1:10, 11.—III. *a turtle dove.*—IV. same as תּוֹרָה *way, manner,* 1 Chron. 17:17.

תּוֹר m., "*that which one discovers*" (Ges.); "*abundance,*" see יֶתֶר (Lee); "*range,*" Eng. Ver., Job 39:8.

תּוֹרָה; see ירה.

תּוֹר m. Ch., *an ox.*

תּוֹשָׁב; see ישב.

תּוּשִׁיָּה f.—I. *abundance, wealth.*—II. *abundantly, entirely,* Job 30:22.—III. *security.*—IV. *wisdom.*

תּוֹתָח; see יתח.

תָּזַז ,הֵתַז; see תזז.

תָּאֳזְלִי ,תּוּזְלִי for תָּאֹזְלִי ,תּוּזְלִי Kal fut. 2. pers. from אזל.

תַּזְנֻת; see זנה.

תַּאָזְרֵנִי for תַּזְרֵנִי Pi. fut. with suff. from אזר.

תַּחְבֻּלוֹת ,תַּחְבּוּלוֹת; see חבל.

תֹּחוּ p.n., same as תּוֹחַ.

תַּחַז Kal fut. apoc. from חזה.

תֹּאחֵז for תֹּאחֵז Kal fut. from אחז.

תְּחִי fut. apoc. from חיה.

תַּחְכְּמֹנִי p.n. of a man.

תָּחֵל for תָּחֵל Niph. fut. from חלל.

תְּחִלָּה; see חלל.

תַּחֲלֻאִים; see חלה.

תַּחְמָס; see חמס.

תַּחֲנוֹת ,תַּחַן; see חנה.

תַּחֲנוּנוֹת ,תַּחֲנוּנִים ,תְּחִנָּה; see חנן.

תַּחְפַּנְחֵס ,תַּחְפְּנֵס (תַּחְפַּנְחֵם), p.n.—I. a city of Egypt.—II. תַּחְפְּנֵיס a queen of Egypt.

תַּחֲרָה ,תַּחְרָא; see חרה.

תַּחְרֵעַ p.n. of a man.

תַּחַשׁ עוֹר ,תְּחָשִׁים m. עֹרֹת תְּחָשִׁים.—I. *a colour of which skins were dyed, probably* blue; "badgers' skins," Eng. Ver.—II. p.n. of a man.

וַתֵּחַשׁ ,תֶּחֱשׁ, Job 31:5; Kal fut. apoc. (חָשָׁה); see חוש.

תָּחַת root not used; (Ethiop. "cast down").

תַּחַת m., *that which is under, below.* Adv. *below;* prep. ὑπό.—I. *under.*—II. *instead of.*—III. *in return for;* תַּחַת אֲשֶׁר *whereas, because that;* ת' כִּי *because;* (also without כִּי). With suff. תַּחְתֶּיךָ ,(תַּחְתֵּנִי); תַּחְתֵּינוּ (תַּחְתֵּנָה) ,תַּחְתֶּיהָ ,תַּחְתָּיו;

תַּחְתֵּיהֶם, תַּחְתֵּיכֶם, תַּחְתָּם. Comp. מִתַּחַת *from under, under;* אֶל־תַּחַת *under;* לְ *under, beyond.*

תַּחַת p. n.—I. one of the stations of Israel in the wilderness.—II. name of a man.

תַּחַת Ch., תְּחוֹת Ch., } *under.*

תַּחְתִּי m., תַּחְתִּיָּה תַּחְתִּית f., *lower, lowest;* pl. m. תַּחְתִּיִּים, f. תַּחְתִּיּוֹת *lowest parts* or *places.*

תַּחְתּוֹן m., תַּחְתּוֹנָה f., *lower, lowest.*

תַּחַת Ch. Aph. fut. from נחת.

תַּחַת Kal fut. f. from נחת.

תֵּט Kal fut. apoc. from נטה.

תִּיז Hiph. הֵתַז, with pause הֵתַז *cut off.*

תִּיכוֹן; see תּוֹךְ.

תִּילוֹן p. n. of a man.

תֵּימָא תֵּמָא p. n. of a people of Arabia, and of their country.

תֵּימָן; see ימן.

תִּימָרוֹת; see תמר.

תֵּעָשֶׂה, Ex. 25:31, for Niph. fut. from עשׂה.

תִּירוֹשׁ תִּירֹשׁ; see ירשׁ.

תִּירְיָא p. n. of a man.

תִּירָס p. n., one of the sons of Japhet.

תַּיִשׁ m. (pl. תְּיָשִׁים), *he-goat* or *ram.*

תָּכָה Pu. תֻּכּוּ *were seated, sat down,* Deu. 33:3.

וַתֵּכֶה, תֵּכֶא Kal fut. apoc. from כהה.

תְּכוּנָה; see כון. תכן.

תּוּכִּיִּים, תּוּכִּים m. pl., probably *peacocks,* 1 Ki. 10:22; 2 Ch. 9:21.

תְּכַךְ Ch., *injured, hurt.*

תֹּךְ תּוֹךְ m., *craft, oppression;* see also תּוֹךְ in תָּוֶךְ.

תְּכָכִים m. pl., *oppressions, injuries,* Pro. 29:13.

תִּכְלָה, תַּכְלִית; see כלה.

תְּכֵלֶת f., *violet blue.*

תָּכַן I. *weighed.* — II. *pondered, examined.* Niph. I. *was measured, examined.*—II. *was of just measure, fair, equal.* Pi. תִּכֵּן I. *measured.* —II. *fixed,* Ps. 75:4.—III. *directed,* Isa. 40:13. Pu. *measured, reckoned,* 2 Ki. 12:12.

תֹּכֶן m.—I. *fixed quantity,* Ex. 5:18. —II. *measure, standard,* Eze.45:11. —III. p. n., a town of the Simeonites.

תְּכוּנָה f. — I. *arrangement, order, structure.* — II. *costly thing,* Nah. 2:10; see also in כון.

תָּכְנִית f., *measure, standard.*

מַתְכֹּנֶת f. (with suff. מַתְכֻּנְתּוֹ), *measure, proportion.*

תְּכַס Pi. fut. apoc. from כסה.

תְּכַסֶּה Hith. fut. from כסה.

תַּכְרִיךְ; see כרך.

תָּלָה; see תלל.

תְּלָאִים, תְּלָא; see תלה.

תְּלָאָה; see לאה.

תְּלָאֹבוֹת תְּלָאוּבָה; see לאב.

תְּלַאשָּׂר p. n., a city of **Syria** or Mesopotamia.

תִּלְבֹּשֶׁת; see לבשׁ.

תְּלַג m. Ch., *snow.*

תִּלְנַת; see תְּנָלַת.

תָּלָה (part. תָּלוּי) pl. תְּלוּיִם, תְּלוּאִים (תְּלָאִים).—I. *hung,* with בְּ עַל *upon* (a tree). — II. *"made dependent,"* Job 26:7 (Lee).—III. *placed in sus*

pense. Niph. *was hanged.* Pi.
hung. Eze. 27:10, 11.

לָחָה Kal fut. apoc., from תְּלָה, וַתֵּלָה.

תְּלִי m. (with suff. תֶּלְיֶךָ) *quiver* (that
which is suspended), Gen. 27:3.

תְּלֻנּוֹת; see לון.

תֶּלַח p. n. of a man.

תָּלַל *raised a mound;* part. תְּלַלִל
elevated, thrown up, Eze. 17:22;
(הַתֵּל, see הָתַל).

תֵּל m. (with suff. תִּלָּהּ, תֶּלָם).—I. *heap
of ruins.*—II. *hill, mound.*—III. תֵּל
אָבִיב p. n. of a town of Babylonia.
—IV. תֵּל חַרְשָׁא p.n.; see חָרַשׁ.
—V. תֵּל מֶלַח (*hill of salt*), p.n., a
place in Babylonia.

תֶּלֶם m., *furrow.*

תַּלְמַי p. n. of a man.

תַּלְמִיד; see למד.

תֵּלֶן Kal fut. apoc., from לון.

תָּלַע Pu. part. מְתֻלָּעִים *clothed in
scarlet,* Nah. 2:4.

תּוֹלָע m. (pl. תּוֹלָעִים) — I. *worm of
any kind.*—II. *the worm used in
dying scarlet.* — III. *scarlet cloth.*
—IV. p.n., *Tolah:* (a) a son of
Issachar; patron. תּוֹלָעִי.—(b) a
judge of Israel.

תּוֹלֵעָה f., *a worm.*

תּוֹלַעַת f. (with suff. תּוֹלַעְתָּם) *a worm;*
שָׁנִי ת׳, ת׳ שָׁנִי I. *scarlet or crimson.*—II. *the kermes insect whence
it was dyed.*

תַּלְפִּיּוֹת f. pl., "an armoury," Eng.
Ver.,Cant.4:4; meaning uncertain.

תִּלְשָׁר same as תְּלַאשַׁר.

תְּלַת f., תְּלָתָא תְּלָתָה m. Ch., *three;*
pl. תְּלָתִין *thirty.*

תְּלַת m. Ch., the same; שַׁלִּיט תַּלְתָּא
and תַּלְתָּא *prince third in rank.*

תַּלְתִּי m. Ch., *third.*

תְּלִיתָאָה Ch., f. תְּלִיתָי the same.

תַּלְתַּלִּים m. pl., *hanging, flowing of
hair;* LXX. ἐλάται, Cant. 5:11.

תָּם Ch., with ה parag. תַּמָּה *there.*

תֹּם, תַּמָּה תֶּם, תֻּמָּה תֵּם; see תמם.

תֵּימָא same as תֵּימָה.

תָּמַהּ *wondered, was amazed.* Hith.
imp. הִתַּמְהוּ *be astonished,* Hab.
1:5.

תְּמַהּ m. Ch., *wonder, miracle.*

תִּמָּהוֹן m., *astonishment, terror.*

תַּמּוּז p. n. a Syrian idol, perhaps
Adoni

תְּמוֹל adv., *yesterday;* אֶתְמוֹל,
אִתְמוֹל, אֶתְמוּל the same.

תְּמוּנָה; see מין.

תְּמוּרָה; see מור.

תְּמוּתָה; see מות.

תֶּמַח p. n. of a man.

תֶּמַח Hiph. fut. apoc., with י parag.
תֶּמְחִי, from מחה.

תָּמִיד; see מוד.

תָּמִים; see תמם.

תָּמַךְ I. *took hold of,* with בְּ.—II. *held,
held up, supported.*—III. *obtained.*
—IV. *apprehended.*—V. *arrived at,
reached.* Niph. *was holden,* Pro.
5:22.

תָּמַם (fut. תָּמַם, יָתֹּם יִתּוֹם; pl.
יִתַּמּוּ, with pause יִתַּמּוּ).—I. *was
completed, ended.*—II. *was perfec.
in character, upright.*—III. *ceased,
came to an end, finished.* — IV.
wasted away, consumed, destroyed;
עַד תֹּם *until they were destroyed*

Niph. (fut. pl. יַתֹּמּוּ).— I. was finished.—II. was consumed. Hiph. הֵתַם (fut. יָתֵם; inf. with suff. הֲתִימֹךָ).—I. finished, consumed.—II. declared perfect.—III. took the sum of, counted, 2 Ki. 22:4.—IV. cause to cease, remove, with כָּן, Eze. 22:15. Hithpa. showed himself perfect; fut. תִּתַּמָּם, 2 Sa. 22:26; Ps. 18:26.

תָּם m., תְּמִימָה f.—I. complete.—II. whole, entire.—III. free from fault, defect.—IV. integrity.

תֹּם m., תֻּמָּה f., blameless, honest, virtuous, pious.

תֹּם, תֹּום, תֹם m. (with suff. תֻּמּוֹ).—I. completeness.—II. security, peace, prosperity.—III. innocence, integrity; pl. תֻּמִּים probably truth; see אוּרִים.

תֻּמָּה f., innocence, integrity.

תֹּאֲמִים double, contr. for תְּאֹמִים.

מְתֹם m., unhurt, sound, soundness.

תִּמְנָה p.n., a city of Judah.

תִּמְנָתָה p.n., a town of the Philistines; תִּמְנִי a Timnite.

תִּמְנַת חֶרֶס 'ת, סֶרַח p.n., a town in Mount Ephraim.

תִּמְנַע p.n.—I. of a woman.—II. of one of the tribes of Edom.

תָּמֵס; see מסס.

וַתָּמָס, תָּמָס Hiph. fut. apoc., from מסה.

תָּמָר m.—I. a palm tree; pl. תְּמָרִים.—II. p.n. of a woman.—III. p.n. of a town in south Palestine.—IV. p.n., same as תַּדְמֹר.—V. עִיר הַתְּמָרִים (city of palms), a name of Jericho.

תֹּמֶר m. palm-tree, Jer. 10:5.

תִּמֹרָה f. (pl. תֹּמָרִים, תֹּמָרוֹת), artificial palm tree.

תַּמְרוּרִים m. pl., columns, Jer. 31:21; see also in מָרַר.

תִּימָרָה f., pl. const. תִּמְרוֹת pillars of smoke.

תָּמֹר Ex. 23:21, for תָּמָר Hiph. fut. from מרר (same as מרה).

תָּמְרוּ for תֹּאמְרוּ Kal fut. pl., from אמר.

תַּמְרוּק; see מרק.

תֹּן, תַּנִּים; see תנן.

תֶּן Kal imp., from נתן.

תֻּנַּע Ch. Pe. fut., from ידע.

תָּנָה hired, Hos. 8:10. Pi. I. ascribed praise to, Jud. 5:11.—II. celebrated an action, Jud. 11:40. Hiph. same as Kal, Hos. 8:9.

תַּנּוֹת f. pl., habitations, Mal. 1:3; see also in תַּנִּים.

אֶתְנָה f., gift, wages of prostitution, Hos. 2:14.

אֶתְנִי p.n. of a man.

אֶתְנַן m. (with suff. אֶתְנַנָּה).—I. fee, gift, wages of prostitution.—II. p.n. of a man.

תִּנְיָן m. Ch., the second: f. תִּנְיָנָה, Dan. 7:5.

תִּנְיָנוּת Ch. adv., a second time, again, Dan. 2:7.

תְּנוּאָה; see נוא.

תְּנוּבָה; see נוב.

תְּנוּךְ; see תנך.

תְּנוּמָה; see נום.

תְּנוּפָה; see נוף.

תַּנּוּר m., a furnace, oven.

תַּנְחֻמָת, תַּנְחוּמוֹת, תַּנְחוּמִים; see נחם.

תְּנוּךְ m., with אֹזֶן the lower part of the ear.

תַּן or תָּן m., pl. תַּנִּים, תַּנִּין jackals, or

other wild animals of the desert; the precise meaning unknown.

תַּנִּים m. sing., for תַּנִּין Eze. 29:3; 32:2.

תַּנִּין m. (pl. תַּנִּינִים).— I. *a serpent.*— II. *any large marine animal.*—III. *a crocodile.*

תִּנְשֶׁמֶת; see נשם.

תֹּאסֵף for תֹּאסַף Kal fut., from אסף.

תָּעַב Pi. תִּעַב I. *abhorred.* — II. *rendered loathsome.* — III. *was abominable.* Hiph. הִתְעִיב I. *acted abominably.*—II. adv. *abominably.* Niph. נִתְעַב *was abhorred.*

תּוֹעֵבָה const. תּוֹעֲבַת f.—I. *abomination.*—II. *impure detestable action.* —III. *anything polluting.*—IV. *an idol.*

תַּעֲנֶה for תַּעֲנֶּה Niph. fut. pl., from ענן.

תָּעָה (fut. apoc. תֵּתַע).— I. *wandered, went astray.*—II. *staggered through drunkenness.* — III. *was in confusion, disorder.*—IV. with מַעַל, מִן, מֵאַחֲרֵי *departed from the true worship.* Niph. נִתְעָה I. *was led astray.*—II. *was made to stagger.* Hiph. הִתְעָה (fut. apoc. יֵתַע) I. *caused to wander, go astray.*— II. *deceived, led astray.*—III. *acted deceitfully.*

תּוֹעָה f.—I. *apostacy,* Isa. 32:6; II. *hurt, injury,* Neh. 4:2,8.

תֹּעוּ, תֹּעִי p. n. of a man.

תְּעוּדָה; see עוד.

תְּעָלֶת, תְּעָלָה; see עלה.

תַּעֲלוּלִים; see עלל.

תַּעֲלֻמָה; see עלם.

תַּעֲנֻג; see ענג.

תַּעֲנִית; see ענה.

תַּעְנָךְ, תַּעֲנָךְ p. n., a city of the Manassites in the tribe of Issachar.

תָּעַע. Pil. part. מְתַעְתֵּעַ *mocking,* Gen. 27:12. Hith. part. pl. מִתַּעְתְּעִים *mocked,* 2 Chron. 36:16.

תַּעְתֻּעִים m. pl., *mockeries, deceptions,* Jer. 10:15; 51:18.

תַּעֲצֻמוֹת; see עצם.

תַּעַר; see ערה.

תַּעֲרוּבָה; see ערב.

תֻּפִּים, תֹּף; see תפף.

תִּפְאֶרֶת, תִּפְאָרָה; see פאר.

תַּפּוּחַ m.—I. *apple-tree.*—II. *apple.*— III. p. n.: (a) a town of Judah; (b) a town of Ephraim; (c) a town between Ephraim and Manasseh; (d) the name of a man.

תְּפוֹצוֹתֵיכֶם Thiphel 1. pers. with suff., from פּוּץ.

וַתִּפְהוּ, תֹּפֵהוּ for תֹּאפֵהוּ Kal fut. with suff., from אפה.

תְּפִינִים; see אפן.

תָּפֵל (Arab. *was unseasoned*).

תָּפֵל m.—I. *that which is insipid, unsavoury,* Job 6:6. — II. *insipid, foolish,* Lam. 2:14. — III. *lime, lime-wash for walls* (Eze. only).

תֹּפֶל p. n., a place in the wilderness

תִּפְלָה f., *insipidity, folly.*

תְּפִלָּה; see פלל.

תִּפְלֶצֶת; see פלץ.

תִּפְסַח; see פסח.

תָּפַף, part. f. pl. תֹּפֵפוֹת *beat the tambourine* or *drum,* Ps. 68:26. Pi *smite the bosom,* Nah. 2:8.

תֹּף m. (pl. תֻּפִּים), *tambourine, drum*

תָּפַר *sew, join together.* Pi. the same, Eze. 13:18.

תָּפַשׂ I. *laid hold of, seized,* with בְּ

—II. *took in war.*—III. *handle, manage the bow,* &c.—IV. *carry on war.*—V. *set, enchase,* Hab. 2:19.— VI. *administer the law,* Jer. 2:8.—VII. *used the name of God irreverently, perjured himself,* Pro. 30:9. Niph. *was taken, caught.* Pi. *took hold,* Pro. 30:28.

תָּפַת, תָּפְתָּה; see תּוּף.

תִּפְתָּיֵא Ch. m. pl. emph. *lawyers* or *judges,* Dan. 3:2, 3.

תִּצְלֶנָה for תְּצַלֶּינָה Kal fut. pl., from צלל.

תִּקְוָה; see קוה.

תְּקוֹמֵם, תְּקוּמָה; see קום.

תְּקוֹעַ; see תקע.

תְּקוּפָה, see קוף; תַּקִּיף, see תקף.

תְּקַל Ch., *weighed;* part. pass. תְּקִל; *weighed;* pret. תְּקַלְתְּ *thou art weighed.*

תָּקַן *was arranged, straight.* Pi. I. *set in order.* — II. *made straight* (Ecclesiastes only).

תְּקַן Ch., the same. Hoph. הָתְקַן *was set in order, established.*

תָּקַע I. *smote the hands together* (for joy, &c.).— II. *thrust in, stabbed* (of a weapon).—III. *fixed, fastened.*—IV. *pitched a tent.*—V. *threw into the sea,* Ex.10:19.—VI. with שׁוֹפָר, בַּשּׁוֹפָר *blew a trumpet;* with תְּרוּעָה *blew a horn.* Niph. I. with לְיָד *strikes hands, becomes a surety,* Job 17:3.—II. with שׁוֹפָר *a trumpet is blown.*

תֶּקַע m., *blast with a trumpet,* Eze. 7:14.

תָּקַע m., *the same,* Ps. 150·3.

תְּקוֹעַ p.n., *Tekoa,* a town of Judah, whence the name מִדְבַּר תְּקוֹעַ *the wilderness of Tekoa;* m. תְּקֹעִי, f תְּקֹעִית *a Tekoite.*

תָּקַף *overpower, prevail over.*

תְּקַף Ch.—I. *was strong.*—II. *was violent.* Pa. *made strong.*

תֹּקֶף m., *might, power.*

תְּקָף m. Ch., the same.

תְּקוּפָה *circuit;* see קוף.

תַּקִּיף m., *strong, powerful,* Ecc. 6:10.

תַּקִּיף m.Ch., *strong, powerful.*

תְּרָאֵלָה p.n., a town of Benjamin.

וַתֵּרֶב, תֶּרֶב Kal fut. apoc., from רבה.

תַּרְבִּית, תַּרְבּוּת; see רבה.

תְּרַגֵּל see רֶגֶל.

תַּרְגֵּם Ch. quadrilitt., *interpreted, translated;* part. pass. מְתַרְגְּנַם, Ezr. 4:7.

תִּרְדְּמָה see רדם.

תִּרְהָקָה p.n., *Tirhakah,* king of Egypt and Ethiopia.

תְּרוּמִיָּה, תְּרוּגְמָה; see רום.

תְּרוּעָה; see רוע.

תְּרוּפָה; see רפא.

תֵּרוֹץ Niph. fut., from רצץ.

תִּרְזָה f., name of a tree, *the holly.*

תֶּרַח p.n.—I. a station of Israel in the wilderness.— II. the father of Abraham.

תִּרְחֲנָה p.n. of a man.

תְּרֵין const. תְּרֵי m., תַּרְתֵּין f. Ch., *two.*

תַּרְמִית, תַּרְמָה; see רמה.

תֹּרֶן I. *mast of a ship.*—II. *flag* or *banner.*

תְּרַע m. Ch.—I. *entrance, door.* — II *palace* (the porte).

תָּרָע m. Ch., *door keeper.*

תַּרְעֵלָה; see רעל.

תַּרְעָתִי p.n. of a man.

תְּרָפִים m. pl., *Teraphim*; idols of some kind.

תַּרְפֵּינָה, Job 5:18, Kal fut. pl., from רפה.

תִּרְצָה p.n.—I. one of the royal cities of Israel.—II. the name of a woman.

תֶּרֶשׁ p.n. of a Persian.

תַּרְשִׁישׁ; see רשש.

תִּרְשָׁתָא, with art., a title of Nehemiah.

תַּרְתָּן p.n., a chief of the Assyrians.

תַּרְתָּק p.n., an idol of the Arvadites.

תִּשָּׂנָה, תִּשֶּׂאנָה for תִּשֶּׂאנָה Kal fut. pl., from נשא.

תִּשּׂוֹמֵחַ see שׂים.

תִּשָּׂאוֹת see שׁוא.

תִּשְׁבִּי p.n. of a man.

תְּשֻׁבָּה; see שׁוב.

תְּשׁוּעָה; see שׁוע.

תְּשׁוּאָה; see שׁוג.

תְּשׁוּרָה; see שׁור.

תֻּשִׁי, Deu. 32:18, fut. apoc., from שׁיח.

תֻּשֵׂם fut., from ישׂם.

תֵּשַׁע const. תְּשַׁע, f. תִּשְׁעָה const. תִּשְׁעַת m., *nine, the ninth*; pl. תִּשְׁעִים *ninety*.

תְּשִׁיעִי m., תְּשִׁיעִית f., *the ninth*.

תֵּשְׁתְּ Kal fut. apoc., from שׁתה.

תִּשְׁתַּחוּ Hith. fut. apoc. sing. for תִּשְׁתַּחֲוֶה, from שׁחה.

תִּשְׁתָּעֶה Hith. fut. apoc. for תִּשְׁתָּעֶה, from שׁעה.

תֵּת, with suff. תִּתִּי Kal inf., from נתן.

תִּתְבָּרַר for תִּתְבָּרַר Hith. fut., from ברר.

תַּתָּה for נָתַתָּה Kal pret., from נתן.

תִּתְחַר Hith. fut. apoc., from חרר.

תִּתֹּם, תִּתַּם Kal fut., from תמם.

תַּתְנַי p.n., a Persian noble.

וַתֵּתַע, תֵּתַע Kal fut. apoc., from תעה.

תִּתְפַּל, 2 Sa. 22:27, transpos for תִּתְפַּתָּל Hith. fut., from פתל.

תִּתְעַצַּב, Ex. 2:4, for תִּתְיַצֵּב Hith. fut., from יצב.

וַתֹּתַר, אֹתֵר Hiph. fut. in pause from יתר.